CO-ATU-008

The Sociology of Youth:
Evolution and Revolution

Harry Silverstein
City College of the City University
of New York

Macmillan Publishing Co., Inc.
NEW YORK

For my daughters, Elizabeth, Jennifer, and Vanessa

Macmillan Publishing Co., Inc.
866 Third Avenue, New York, New York 10022

Collier-Macmillan Canada, Ltd., Toronto, Ontario

Library of Congress catalog card number: 77-190672

Printing: 4 5 6 7 8 9   Year: 7 8 9

PREFACE

In organizing an anthology on the sociology of youth, there are several preliminary problems and issues with which one must ultimately deal. Among these is the sheer quantity of sociologically oriented works on the subject of youth that have been written during the past decade or so. It may surprise the younger student that the enormous interest in and attention paid to contemporary youth has not been a central or critical component of every era's regular stock-taking. In fact, most works on the subject of youth, although uneven in quality and varying in materials, methodologies, and perspectives, are essentially products of the 1960s. This should not suggest that prior to this time youth was entirely overlooked or ignored either historically or within the social sciences, but rather that our present view of youth as a dramatic and compelling presence and force in society is only just beginning to bridge previous deficiencies in knowledge and understanding.

The purpose of this book is to bring together both historical and contemporary works in the field of youth studies and to afford the student an opportunity to explore those areas that can now be said to constitute the main elements of a sociology of youth. Included in these selections are materials that may be deemed somewhat outside the boundaries of "pure" sociology, among them conceptions that are more appropriately defined as belonging to psychology and social psychology, but that nonetheless have a strategic bearing upon sociological perspectives of youth.

The guiding principle in organizing this book has been to approach the subject of youth as a cumulative effort by a number of observers and commentators during a period of approximately thirty-five years and to present in a single volume many of those works that have shaped our conceptions and theories of the so-called youth phenomenon. Although the selections are heavily weighted with more recent contributions to the field, the reader will also find several works that reflect both historical and comparative formulations on the subject. Indeed, reintroducing the historical dimension of youth studies has been a primary objective of this work.

The book has been organized into six major areas, each of which has been arranged to permit an examination of both the development of descriptive materials and theoretical analyses as they have emerged from earlier periods to the present time. Each section includes works that *primarily focus* upon a given topic area, although any given work may be found to extend itself somewhat beyond its essential focus. In this sense, the reader may discover that several articles have an overlapping concern with other aspects of youth studies.

Finally, the six major sections have excluded at least one major area of youth studies: juvenile delinquency. This subject is discussed within several of the included articles; however, it was felt that to treat adequately the range of issues and materials on delinquency would require the sacrifice of many of the works that are found herein. In any event, there are a number of excellent anthologies on juvenile delinquency, criminology, and deviance already available to the student of youth.

I wish to express my appreciation to those authors and publishers who have given me permission to reprint their works. I also wish to thank my students in the several courses that I have taught on this subject over the years at Hunter College, The New School for Social Research, and City College of New York. Their astute comments and observations have provided a significant impetus to this work. Finally, I wish to express my deepest gratitude to my wife, Olga, for her critical appraisal of this effort and for shouldering the most difficult and arduous tasks, thus enabling the entire volume to come to fruition.

H. S.

New York

CONTENTS

Contents

GENERAL INTRODUCTION

In the concluding years of World War II, and for approximately a decade thereafter, a simple demographic fact, the "baby boom," introduced to modern industrial society the essential ingredients of that now highly visible and complex process of coming of age, often referred to as the "contemporary youth phenomenon." In the early days of this boom, it was at once evident that sound social planning and social policy necessitated the initiation of rational and programatic efforts toward making room for the forthcoming chronological underclass. For the most part, strategies in this direction were primarily calibrated by economic guidelines and considerations. Solutions to potential youth problems were based on expansionary projections, i.e., the construction of more physical plants and facilities designed to ease such apparently inevitable problems as overcrowding in schools and recreational structures. All that seemed necessary and clear was the appropriate and efficient deployment of material resources; the blueprint for social progress through successive and, in this case, unduly oversized youth generations simply involved alterations and enlargements of the physical landscape.

Yet, the obvious and reasonable, when implemented, often come to naught. For as we may have since learned, economic and material solutions to human problems, although necessary, are not in themselves sufficient. This is perhaps particularly true in American society, where affluent growth in the last two decades, however unevenly distributed, brought with it a sociological and humanistic complacency concerning youth and its formative experiences.

Indeed, only few suspected that the post-second-war-to-end-all-wars-children upon reaching their adolescence would emerge as something more forceful and demanding than those historically and commonly expected expressions of short-lived rebelliousness and deviance. Youth was no longer an exotic, mysterious, and rambunctious stage of development eventually to be superseded by the normal process of maturation; the young appeared as a vital, albeit multiformed, proteanic social category that would make its mark, for better or worse, as an influential social movement. It would be henceforth difficult, if not impossible, to conceive that just as past generations had successfully managed to make a right and proper fit into the social fabric, modern youth would similarly complete the transitional period with little wear and tear on the modern social organization. The massive youth population required reconsideration beyond the simple idea that it was strictly an ecological phenomenon.

At almost the moment when children born a decade or two before were entering their youthhood, a plethora of works concerning every aspect of the "youth phenomenon" also appeared. Articles and reports of all types appeared in magazines, newspapers, journals, and television about youth politics, campus life, alienation, bohemianism, drugs, sexual patterns, and

1

deviance. In terms of public visibility and attention, it was as if a previously vaporous stage of the ages of life described as the innocuous "lost" and "silent" generations had suddenly been invented and singularly fabricated as another journalistic and literary paroxysm for satisfying the cravings of mediaships everywhere. And notwithstanding the possibility that serious and significant changes had occurred in generational succession, youth development, and youth culture, the fact that youth was to be mediaized as a unique "problem" of modern society indicates a revolution, at least to the extent and level of *awareness* in the meaning and importance of being young in the modern world. As it was, whether real or illusory, evolutionary or revolutionary, the public definitions of youth had assisted in transforming it into a major social movement: the youth movement.

Public as well as sociological concern for youth, of course, seemed self-evident; for whatever characteristics are borne by youth of a particular generation, especially if these are oppositional, deviant, and pathological, they augur salient changes in the future of a society. What youth are, society will become. And although this has always been so, its importance had been only occasionally understood.

Still, whereas widespread interest in a human problem may provide the necessary stimulus for an active, energetic, and serious examination of it, it may also prove to be a major impediment to careful study and inquiry. For example, it would be relatively easy to state that modern youth and the modern youth movement represent major transformations, in almost all respects, the summation of which is fundamentally revolutionary. But does an expanded awareness necessarily lead to the conclusion that significant changes have truly taken place? Oddly enough, the sociological response to this question is more complex and includes both negative and affirmative dimensions.

On the one hand, public attention may fairly accurately reflect social reality. This, of course, could be substantiated (or denied) by careful, systematic, empirical research. Since cause and effect is always a historical issue, the empirical problem would be to collect observations of this type that would confirm the extent to which changes have taken place. In all instances, public definitions would be set aside in favor of the careful mapping of things past and present, with the product of these efforts allowing for evolutionary or revolutionary conclusions or, perhaps, without measurable change at all.

On the other hand, public definitions may be the principal precipitant of major social and cultural changes, working in a manner formulated in the W. I. Thomas theorem that "if a situation is defined as real, then its consequences are real." Under these conditions, one must read history with a special scrutiny.

If this seems somewhat far-fetched, perhaps a brief illustration of this process would suggest its importance in major social transformations: Many youths migrated to the East Village in the early 1960s, and although these youths were known to express oppositional values to the dominant culture, little by way of a countercultural structure had evolved, except to the extent that the young merged their orientations with the bohemian traditions that existed prior to their entry into this community. At most, the young were described as a loosely formed collectivity, sharing several variants of a value oppositional theme—which any given observer might elicit after careful questioning. However, 1967 was a year of mass media discovery, and those youths who were there and always known to a few limited *aficionados* of bohemia, were suddenly brought to the attention of an international public. At once, both journalists and social scientists alike adopted the "hippie" appellation and in so doing pressed forward, directing an entirely new youth drama, requiring the articulation and acting out of values, beliefs, and roles that were previously only loosely arranged and structured. Clearly, many of the ingredients for this phenomenon already existed, but through public attention and the insistence on extracting comprehensible information from the youth themselves, a loose form ultimately emerged as a well-structured ideology and "counterculture." Paradoxically, if this countercultural aspect of the youth revolution did occur, the time, place, and form of its occurrence can be attributed in large part to public and media definition. (It might also be of interest to note that as public attention waned, so did the "revolution in hippiedom," although the young and many of their oppositional values can still be observed among the remaining youthful participants in the bohemian life-style and community.) Thus, public attention can be viewed as being significantly implicated in the subsequent transformation of a youth movement.

Surely, in the study of youth, approximations of reality and the reality, magnitude, and direction of change require the most careful research methods and theoretical formulations. It is in this sense that the materials presented in this book revolve about the central ideas of evolution and revolution. An understanding of the changes in youth in modern society demands the introduction of a historical dimension, for history alone will enable a final settlement of the issues. Without such a historical perspective the absence or presence of change will be argued strictly through polemics—and if an overview on the literature of modern youth is permitted, much of the analysis of youth has been framed in the polemics of ideology, criticism, and hope.

In bringing together these several works, drawn from both books and articles authored by specialists with distinctive backgrounds and perspectives on youth studies, an effort has been made to cover a fairly wide range of topics that should allow the reader to take the measure of the youth phenomenon and youth change at different points in history. Although many descriptions of a past era may seem an amusing exercise in nostalgia, it is hoped that the primary issue of change, gradual or rapid, evolutionary or revolutionary, remains at the forefront. In this way, one may ultimately be able to separate the cursory from the profound, the old from the new, the ephemeral from the lasting, and the unreal from the real. Indeed, no simple formula exists for solving these most basic and fundamental issues. But, if the task is the discovery of the future in the present, then a hard and careful look at the past seems the order of the day.

Section I

Historical and Theoretical Issues

INTRODUCTION

In his book *Society, Culture and Personality,* Pitirim A. Sorokin suggests that although both sociology and history are social sciences that study human events as they occur in time and space, they are distinct; the essential distinction between these fields is the generalizing, theoretical, and abstract nature of sociology as opposed to the individualizing, concrete, and unique characterizations that are set forth in history. In a sense, history reports while sociology explains. At first glance it would seem that from this perspective sociology and history are mutually exclusive endeavors; yet all sociological work, insofar as it connects itself to human realities, is always a reporting of moments in history, for history is the stuff of which we have been made. Every human act, once completed, is a historical datum, and whether sociological research employs survey methods, in-depth interviews, or an examination of documents, records, and the like to observe human events, it is at once a slice of human history.

Sociology and history are thus mutually dependent disciplines. Although there is a general recognition of this elementary idea within the social sciences, sociological approaches to the study of youth have too frequently overlooked this wedding of sociology and history. In addition, many observers of contemporary youths have noted that although youths themselves often demand to be the makers of future history, they seem almost unnaturally antipathetic to their historical forebearers and traditions, claiming that since history is flawed history, there are few, if any, lessons to be learned from it.

Unfortunately, this ahistorical orientation pervades much of the commentary on the contemporary youth process. The "youth phenomenon," especially as it is depicted by the mass media, has been given the appearance of having no significant historical counterparts or parallels. At this level of presentation, whatever is contemporary and youthful is perceived as unique and new, at most an invention or accident of the special and unique circumstances of contemporary history. From this perspective, and in its most extreme version, as today's human events unfold, yesterday's events become historically and sociologically obsolete and irrelevant.

Recent history requires a sense of urgency. A multitude of potential dangers are inherent in daily events on the domestic and international scenes. Yet to assume that this urgency precludes serious historical and sociohistorical inquiry, and to treat history as the history of the moment, is to relinquish an important opportunity and avenue for understanding and enlightenment. For if past history has insufficiently abetted contemporary history, perhaps it is because we have failed to use it well.

In the following selections, history, sociohistory, and sociological theory are brought to bear on the study of youth. In each selection historical methods, historical periods, and historical data vary, but each selection attempts to examine through sociological eyes the connections between important historical events and contemporary and fundamental elements of youth.

In the initial selections by Ariès and Seeley, both history and the historical method are reintroduced to the study of youth. With deft and carefully plotted navigation through diverse documents of the Middle Ages, Ariès explores the shifting conceptions, definitions, and significance of the ideas, images, and statuses of youth during and between several centuries of history.

Although Seeley is similarly emphatic about approaching youth through a historical perspective, he further suggests that studies of generational relations along with specific inquiries on the contemporary youth generation must be directed by the view that both the history and life history of adults and youth intercept one another as common history. Although generations may be seen to vary in many respects, they are nevertheless made of whole cloth, sharing a connecting history at any moment in social time. The absence of this dual yet unifying historical dimension, characteristic of many contemporary sociological works on youth, is perceived as a major impediment to both adequate formulation of the youth process as well as the potential diminution of the schisms or gaps that apparently separate generationally contemporaneous youth and adults.

In the application of the broad historical data, Parsons attempts through functional theory in sociology to sketch some of the main structural elements and cultural themes and values of American society, and to relate these to a number of emergent components of the contemporary youth culture. In this systemic orientation to several aspects of modern youth, the primary analytic device is the perception of youthful activities and values as a consequence or product of the larger, dominant cultural and structural systems intrinsic to modern American society. Allen formulates the historical and sociological issue differently, suggesting that youth problems should be viewed from the framework of a historical, structural dialectic of social change. In so doing, she criticizes the functionalist approach found in both Parsons and Eisenstadt (see Section III) as being based upon integrative models of social analysis. She argues that the dialectical framework is more appropriate to the basic conditions of change that characterize both modern society and contemporary youth phenomenon, especially since integrative models do not sufficiently allow for conflict and change as primary historical determinants.

Finally, Bensman carefully details contemporary history as generational history, introducing the notion that basic trends and changes in American occupational structure, the occupational careers of the parents of middle-class youth, and the reorganization of the American class structure are the connecting links to many of the activities and cultural elements exhibited by today's youths.

Centuries of Childhood:
The Ages of Life

Philippe Ariès

The "ages of life" occupy a considerable place in the pseudo-scientific treatises of the Middle Ages. Their authors use a terminology which strikes us as purely verbal: childhood, puerility, adolescence, youth, senility, old age—each word signifying a different period of life. Since then we have borrowed some of these words to denote abstract ideas such as puerility or senility, but these meanings were not contained in the first acceptations. The "ages," "ages of life," or "ages of man" corresponded in our ancestors' minds to positive concepts, so well known, so often repeated and so commonplace that they passed from the realm of science to that of everyday experience. It is hard for us today to appreciate the importance which the concept of the "ages" had in ancient representations of the world. A man's "age" was a scientific category of the same order as weight or speed for our contemporaries; it formed part of a system of physical description and explanation which went back to the Ionian philosophers of the sixth century B.C., which medieval compilers revived in the writings of the Byzantine Empire and which was still inspiring the first printed books of scientific vulgarization in the sixteenth century. We have no intention of trying to determine its exact formulation and its place in the history of science: all that matters here is that we should realize to what extent this science had become common property, how far its concepts had entered into mental habits and what it represented in everyday life.

We shall understand the problem better if we glance through the 1556 edition of *Le Grand Propriétaire de toutes choses.*[1] This was a thirteenth-century Latin compilation which itself repeated all the data of the writers of the Byzantine Empire. It was thought fit to translate it into French and to give it a greater circulation by means of printing. *Le Grand Propriétaire de toutes choses* is an encyclopedia, a sort of Encyclopædia Britannica, but which is not analytical in concept and which attempts to render the essential unity of Nature and God. A treatise on physics, metaphysics, natural history, human physiology and anatomy, medicine and hygiene, and astronomy, at the same time as theology. Twenty books deal with God, the angels, the elements, man and his body, diseases, the sky, the weather, matter, air,

[1] *Le Grand Propriétaire de toutes choses, très utile et profitable pour tenir le corps en santé,* compiled by B. de Glanville, translated by Jean Corbichon, 1556.

water, fire, birds, etc. The last book is devoted to numbers and measures. Certain practical recipes could also be found in this book. A general idea emerged from it, a scientific idea which had become extremely commonplace, the idea of the fundamental unity of Nature, of the solidarity which exists between all the phenomena of Nature, phenomena which could not be distinguished from supernatural manifestations. The idea that there was no opposition between the natural and the supernatural derived both from popular beliefs inherited from paganism and from a science that was physical as well as theological. I am inclined to think that this rigorous concept of the unity of Nature must be held responsible for the delay in scientific development, much more than the authority of tradition, the ancients or the Scriptures. We cannot exert any influence on an element of Nature unless we are agreed that it can be adequately isolated. Given a certain degree of solidarity between the phenomena of Nature, as *Le Grand Propriétaire* postulates, it is impossible to intervene without setting off a chain reaction, without upsetting the order of the world: none of the categories of the cosmos possesses a sufficient autonomy, and nothing can be done in the face of universal determinism. Knowledge of Nature is limited to the study of the relations governing phenomena by means of a single causality—a knowledge which can foresee but cannot modify. There is no escape from this casuality except through magic or miracles. A single rigorous law governs at one and the same time the movement of the planets, the vegetative cycle of the seasons, the connections between the elements, the human body and its humours, and the destiny of a man, with the result that astrology makes it possible to discover the personal effects of this universal determinism. As late as the middle of the seventeenth century, the practice of astrology was sufficiently widespread for the sceptical Molière to choose it as a butt for his raillery in *Les Amants magnifiques*.

The correspondence of numbers seemed to be one of the keys to this profound solidarity; the symbolism of numbers was a commonplace theme in religious speculations, in descriptions of physics and natural history, and in magic practices. For example, there was a correspondence between the number of the elements, the number of man's temperaments, and the number of the seasons: the figure 4. We find it difficult today to imagine this tremendous concept of a massive world in which nothing could be distinguished but a few correspondences. Science had made it possible to formulate the latter and to define the categories which they linked together; over the centuries these correspondences had slipped from the realm of science into that of popular mythology. The concepts born in sixth-century Ionia had gradually been adopted by the ordinary mentality; the categories of antiquo-medieval science had become commonplaces: the elements, the temperaments, the planets and their astrological significance, and the symbolism of numbers.

The concept of the ages of life was also one of the common ways of understanding human biology, in accord with the universal system of correspondences. This concept, which was destined to become extremely popular, did not go back to the great period of ancient science, however. It originated in the Byzantine Empire in the sixth century.[2] Fulgentius found it hidden in the *Aeneid:* he saw in Aeneas's shipwreck the symbol of man's birth in the midst of the storms of existence. He interpreted Cantos II and III as the image of childhood hungering for fabulous tales, and so on. An Arabian fresco of the eighth century already represented the ages of life.[3]

There are countless medieval texts on this theme. *Le Grand Propriétaire de toutes choses* deals with the ages in its sixth book. Here the ages correspond to the planets, and there are seven of them:

> The first age is childhood when the teeth are planted, and this age begins when the child is born and lasts until seven, and in this age that which is born is called an infant, which is as good as saying not talking, because in this age it cannot talk well or form its words perfectly, for its teeth are not yet well arranged or firmly implanted, as Isidore says and Constantine. After infancy comes the second age . . . it is called *pueritia* and is given this name because in this age the person is still like the pupil in the eye, as Isidore says, and this age lasts till fourteen.
>
> Afterwards follows the third age, which is called adolescence, which ends according to Constantine in his viaticum in the twenty-first year, but according to Isidore it lasts till twenty-eight . . . and it can go on till thirty or thirty-five. This age is called adolescence because the person is big enough to beget children, says Isidore. In this age the limbs are soft and able to grow and receive strength and vigour from natural heat. And because the person grows in this age to the size allotted to him by Nature. [Yet growth is over before thirty or thirty-five, even before twenty-eight. And it was probably even less tardy at a time when work at a tender age mobilized the resources of the constitution earlier on.]
>
> Afterwards follows youth, which occupies the central position among the ages, although the person in this age is in his greatest strength, and this age lasts until forty-five according to Isidore, or until fifty according to others. This age is called youth because of the strength in the person to help himself and others, according to Aristotle. Afterwards follows senectitude, according to Isidore, which is half-way between youth and old age, and Isidore calls it gravity, because the person is grave in his habits and bearing; and in this age the person is not old, but he has passed his youth, as Isidore says. After this age follows old age, which according to some lasts until seventy and according to others has no end until death . . . old people have not such good sense as they had, and talk nonsense in their old age. . . . The last part of old age is called *senies* in Latin, but in French there is no separate word for it. . . . The old man is always coughing and spitting and dirtying [we are a long way yet from the

---

[2] Comparetti, *Virgile nel m.e.,* vol. I, pp. 144–155.
[3] Kuseir Amra. Cf. Van Marle, *Iconographie de l'art profane,* 1932, vol. II, pp. 144 ff.

noble old man of Greuze and Romanticism] until he returns to the ashes and dust from which he was taken.

Nowadays we may consider this jargon empty and verbose, but it had a meaning for those who read it, a meaning akin to that of astrology: it called to mind the link which joined the destiny of man to that of the planets. The same sort of sidereal correspondence had inspired another division into periods connected with the twelve signs of the zodiac, thus linking the ages of life with one of the most popular and moving themes of the Middle Ages: the scenes of the calendar. A fourteenth-century poem, reprinted several times in the fifteenth and sixteenth centuries, expounds this calendar of the ages.[4]

> The first six years of life on earth
> We to January would compare,
> For in that month strength is as rare
> As in a child six years from birth.

Or witness this thirteenth-century poem: [5]

> Of all the months the first behold,
> January two-faced and cold.[6]
> Because its eyes two ways are cast,
> To face the future and the past.
> Thus the child six summers old
> Is not worth much when all is told.
> But one must take every care
> To see that he is fed good fare,
> For he who does not start life well
> Will finish badly, one can tell . . .
> When October winds do blow,
> Then a man his wheat must sow
> To feed the other men on earth;
> Thus must act a man of worth
> Who has arrived at sixty years:
> He must sow in young folk's ears
> Wisdom all their hearts to fill,
> And give them charity if he will.

Of the same nature is the correspondence established between the ages of life and the other "fours": *consensus quatuor elementorum, quatuor humorum* (the temperaments), *quatuor anni temporum et quatuor vitae aetatum.*[7] About 1265, Philippe de Novare spoke of the "four times of man's

---

[4] *Grant Kalendrier et compost des bergiers,* 1500 edition, quoted by J. Morawski, *Les douze mois figurez, Archivum romanicum,* 1926, pp. 351–363.
[5] Ibid.
[6] Depicted in the calendars as *Janus bifrons.*
[7] *Regimen sanitatis, schola salernitania,* edited by Arnaud de Villeneuve.

age," [8] namely four periods of twenty years each. And these speculations went on recurring in text after text up to the sixteenth century.[9]

We must try to grasp the fact that this terminology, which seems so futile to us now, expressed ideas which were scientific at the time and also corresponded to a popular and commonplace idea of life. Here again, we come up against great difficulties of interpretation, because today we no longer have this idea of life: we see life chiefly as a biological phenomenon, as a situation in society. Yet we say "Such is life!" to express at once our resignation and our conviction that there is, outside biology and sociology, something which has no name, but which stirs us, which we look for in the news items of the papers, or about which we say: "That's lifelike." Life in this case is a drama, which rescues us from everyday boredom. For the man of old, on the contrary, it was the inevitable, cyclical, sometimes amusing and sometimes sad continuity of the ages of life; a continuity inscribed in the general and abstract order of things rather than in real experience, for in those periods of heavy mortality few men were privileged to live through all these ages.

The popularity of the "ages of life" made the theme one of the most common in profane iconography. They are to be found for instance on some illuminated twelfth-century capitals in the baptistery at Parma.[10] The sculptor has tried to represent at one and the same time the parable of the master of the vineyard and the labourers of the eleventh hour, and the symbol of the ages of life. In the first scene one can see the master of the vineyard laying his hand on a child's head, and underneath an inscription points out the allegory of the child: *prima aetas saeculi: primum humane: infancia.* Further on: *hora tertia: puericia secunda aetas*—the master of the vineyard can be seen putting his hand on the shoulder of a young man who is holding an animal and a bill-hook. The last of the labourers is resting beside his mattock: *senectus, sexta aetas.*

But it was above all in the fourteenth century that the essential characteristics of this iconography became fixed and remained virtually unchanged until the eighteenth century; they can be recognized on capitals in the Palace of the Doges [11] no less than in a fresco of the Eremitani at Padua.[12] First of all the age of toys: children playing with a hobbyhorse, a doll, a windmill, or birds on leashes. Then the age of school: the boys learning to read or carrying book and pen-tray, the girls learning to spin. Next the ages of love or of courtly and knightly sports: feasting, boys and girls walking together, a court of love, and the Maytime wedding festivities or hunt of the calendars. Next the ages of war and chivalry: a man bearing

[8] Charles V. Langlois, *La Vie en France au Moyen Age,* 1908, p. 184.
[9] 1568.
[10] Didron, "La Vie humaine," *Annales archéologiques,* XV, p. 413.
[11] *Ibid.,* XVII, pp. 69, 193.
[12] A. Venturi, "La Fonte di una composizione del guariento," *Arte,* 1914, XVII, p. 49.

arms. Finally, the sedentary ages: those of the men of law, science or learning—the old bearded scholar dressed in old-fashioned clothes, sitting at his desk by the fire. The ages of life did not correspond simply to biological phases but also to social functions; we know that there were some very young lawyers, but in popular imagery learning is an old man's trade.

These attributes of fourteenth-century art are to be found in almost identical form in prints of a more popular, more commonplace type, which lasted with very few changes from the sixteenth century to the beginning of the nineteenth century. They were called the "steps of the ages," because they depicted a row of figures representing the various ages from birth to death, and often standing on steps going up on the left and going down on the right. In the centre of this double staircase, as under the arch of a bridge, stood the skeleton of Death, armed with his scythe. Here the theme of the ages merged with that of death, and it is probably no accident that these two themes were among the most popular: prints depicting the steps of the ages and the dances of death went on recapitulating until the beginning of the nineteenth century an iconography established in the fourteenth and fifteenth centuries. But unlike the dances of death, in which the costumes never changed and remained those of the fifteenth and sixteenth centuries even when the print was produced in the nineteenth, the steps of the ages dressed their characters after the fashion of the day: in the last of the nineteenth-century prints, First Communion costumes can be seen making their appearance. The enduring quality of the symbols is all the more remarkable for that: the child is still there riding his hobbyhorse, the schoolboy carrying book and pen-tray, the handsome couple, with the young man sometimes holding a may-bush in one hand as a sign of the feasts of adolescence and spring, and the man at arms, now an officer wearing the sash of command or carrying a banner; on the downward slope, the costumes have stopped being in fashion or have remained true to the fashions of old; the men of law are still equipped with their procedure-bags, the scholars with their books or their astrolabes, and the churchgoers—the most curious of all these figures—with their rosaries.[13]

The repetition of these pictures, pinned to the wall next to the calendar and in the midst of everyday objects, fostered the idea of a life cut into clearly defined sections corresponding to certain modes of activity, physical types, social functions and styles of dress. The division of life into periods had the same fixity as the cycle of Nature or the organization of society. In spite of the constant evocation of old age and death, the ages of life remained good-natured, picturesque sketches, character silhouettes of a rather whimsical kind.

Antiquo-medieval speculation had bequeathed to posterity a copious

---

[13] The "steps of the ages" was not a theme in popular prints only. It is also to be found in painting and sculpture: in Titian and Van Dyck and on the *fronton* of the Versailles of Louis XIV.

terminology relating to the ages of life. In the sixteenth century, when it was proposed to translate this terminology into French, it was found that the French language, and consequently French usage, had not as many words at its disposal as had Latin or at least learned Latin. The 1556 translator of *Le Grand Propriétaire de toutes choses* makes no bones about recognizing the difficulty: "It is more difficult in French than in Latin, for in Latin there are seven ages referred to by various names, of which there are only three in French: to wit, childhood, youth and old age."

It will be noted that since youth signifies the prime of life, there is no room for adolescence. Until the eighteenth century, adolescence was confused with childhood. In school Latin the word *puer* and the word *adolescens* were used indiscriminately. Preserved in the Bibliothèque Nationale are the catalogues of the Jesuit College at Caen, a list of the pupils' names accompanied by comments.[14] A boy of fifteen is described in these catalogues as *bonus puer,* while his young schoolmate of thirteen is called *optimus adolescens.* Baillet, in a book on infant prodigies, admitted that there were no terms in French to distinguish between *pueri* and *adolescentes.*[15] There was virtually only one word in use: *enfant.*

At the end of the Middle Ages, the meaning of this word was particularly extensive. It could be applied to both the *putto* (in the sixteenth century the *putti* room, the bedchamber decorated with frescoes depicting naked children, was referred to as "the children's room") and the adolescent, the big lad who was sometimes also a bad lad. The word *enfant* ("child")[16] in the *Miracles de Notre-Dame*[17] was used in the fourteenth and fifteenth centuries as a synonym of other words such as *valets, valeton, garçon, fils* ("valet," "varlet," "lad," "son"): "he was a *valeton*" would be translated today as "he was a good-looking lad," but the same word could be used of both a young man ("a handsome *valeton*") and a child ("he was a *valeton,* so they loved him dearly . . . *li valez* grew up"). Only one word has kept this very ancient ambiguity down to our times, and that is the word *gars* ("lad"), which has passed straight from Old French into the popular modern idiom in which it is preserved. A strange child, this bad lad who was "so perverse and wicked that he would not learn a trade or behave as was fitting in childhood . . . he kept company with greedy, idle folk who often started brawls in taverns and brothels, and he never came across a woman by herself without raping her." Here is another child of fifteen: "Although he was a fine, handsome son," he refused to go riding or to have anything to do with girls. His father thought that it was out of shyness: "This is customary in

[14] Bibliothèque Nationale, MSS Fonds Latin, nos. 10990, 10991.
[15] Baillet, *Les Enfants devenus célèbres par leurs études,* 1688.
[16] Translator's note: In the following discussion of terminology (pp. 14–20), wherever the word "child" or "children" is used, the original French source has "enfant" or "enfants."
[17] *Miracles de Notre-Dame,* edited by G. F. Warner, Westminster, 1885. Jubinal, *Nouveau recueil de contes,* vol. I, pp. 31–33, 42–72; vol. II, pp. 244, 356–357.

children." In fact, he was betrothed to the Virgin. His father forced him into marriage: "The child became very angry and struck him hard." He tried to make his escape and suffered mortal injuries by falling downstairs. The Virgin then came for him and said to him: "Dear brother, behold your sweetheart." And: "At this the child heaved a sigh." According to a sixteenth-century calendar of the ages, at twenty-four "a child is strong and brave," and "this is what becomes of children when they are eighteen." [18]

The same is true in the seventeenth century. The report of an episcopal inquiry of 1667 states that in one parish "there is *un jeune enfans* ["a young child"] aged about fourteen who in the year or so he has been living in the aforementioned place has been teaching children of both sexes to read and write, by arrangement with the inhabitants of the aforementioned place." [19]

In the course of the seventeenth century a change took place by which the old usage was maintained in the more dependent classes of society, while a different usage appeared in the middle class, where the word "child" was restricted to its modern meaning. The long duration of childhood as it appeared in the common idiom was due to the indifference with which strictly biological phenomena were regarded at the time: nobody would have thought of seeing the end of childhood in puberty. The idea of childhood was bound up with the idea of dependence: the words "sons," "varlets" and "boys" were also words in the vocabulary of feudal subordination. One could leave childhood only by leaving the state of dependence, or at least the lower degrees of dependence. That is why the words associated with childhood would endure to indicate in a familiar style, in the spoken language, men of humble rank whose submission to others remained absolute: lackeys, for instance, journeymen and soldiers. A "little boy" (*petit garçon*) was not necessarily a child but a young servant, just as today an employer or a foreman will say of a worker of twenty to twenty-five: "He's a good lad." Thus in 1549, one Baduel, the principal of a college, an educational establishment, wrote to the father of one of his young pupils about his outfit and attendants: "A little boy is all that he will need for his personal service." [20]

At the beginning of the eighteenth century, Furetière's dictionary gave an explanation of the usage: " 'Child' is also a term of friendship used to greet or flatter someone or to induce him to do something. Thus when one says to an aged person: 'Goodbye, good mother' ['so long, grandma,' in the modern idiom] she replies: 'Goodbye, my child' ['Goodbye, lad']. Or she will say to a lackey: 'Child, go and get me this or that.' A master will say to his men when setting them to work: 'Come along, children, get to work.' A captain will say to his soldiers: 'Courage, children, stand fast.' " Front-

---

[18] Quoted above, note 4.
[19] A. de Charmasse, *État de l'instruction publique dans l'ancien diocèse d'Autun*, 1878.
[20] J. Gaufrès, "Claude Baduel et la Réforme des études au XVIe siècle," *Bull. Soc. H. du protestantisme français*, 1880, XXV, pp. 499–505.

line troops, those most exposed to danger, were called "the lost children."

At the same time, but in families of gentle birth, where dependence was only a consequence of physical infirmity, the vocabulary of childhood tended rather to refer to the first age. Its use became increasingly frequent in the seventeenth century: the expression "little child" (*petit enfant*) began to take on the meaning we give it. The older usage had preferred "young child" (*jeune enfant*), and this expression had not been completely abandoned. La Fontaine used it, and again in 1714, in a translation of Erasmus, there was a reference to a "young girl" who was not yet five: "I have a young girl who has scarcely begun to talk." [21] The word *petit* or "little one" had also acquired a special meaning by the end of the sixteenth century: it referred to all the pupils of the "little schools," even those who were no longer children. In England, the word "petty" had the same meaning as in French, and a text of 1627 on the subject of school spoke of the "lyttle petties," the smallest pupils.[22]

It was above all with Port-Royal and with all the moral and pedagogic literature which drew its inspiration from Port-Royal (or which gave more general expression to a need for moral discipline which was widely felt and to which Port-Royal too bore witness), that the terms used to denote childhood became common and above all modern: Jacqueline Pascal's pupils at Port-Royal were divided into "little ones," "middle ones" and "big ones." [23] "With regard to the little children," she wrote, "they even more than all the others must be taught and fed if possible like little doves." The regulations of the little schools at Port-Royal stated: "They do not go to Mass every day, only the little ones." [24] People spoke in a new way of "little souls" and "little angels," [25] expressions which foreshadowed the eighteenth century and Romanticism. In her tales, Mlle Lhéritier claimed to be addressing "young minds," "young people": "These pictures probably lead young people to reflections which perfect their reasoning." [26] It can thus be seen that that seventeenth century which seemed to have scorned childhood, in fact brought into use expressions and phrases which remain to this day in our language. Under the word "child" in his dictionary, Furetière quoted proverbs which are still familiar to us: "He is a spoilt child, who has been allowed to misbehave without being punished. The fact is, there are no longer any children, for people are beginning to have reason and cunning at an early age." "Innocent as a new-born child."

All the same, in its attempts to talk about little children, the French

[21] Erasmus, *Christian Marriage.*

[22] J. Brinsley, *Ludus Litterarius,* 1917 edition.

[23] Jacqueline Pascal, *Règlement pour les enfants* (Appendix to the Constitutions of Port-Royal, 1721).

[24] Regulations of Chesney College, in Wallon de Beaupuis, *Suite des Vies des amis de Port-Royal,* 1751, vol. I, p. 175.

[25] Jacqueline Pascal, see note 31.

[26] M. E. Storer, *La Mode des contes de fées (1685–1700),* 1928.

language of the seventeenth century was hampered by the lack of words to distinguish them from bigger ones. The same was true of English, where the word "baby" was also applied to big children. Lily's Latin grammar in English, which was in use from the beginning of the sixteenth century until 1866, was intended for "all lytell babes, all lytell chyldren." [27]

On the other hand there were in French some expressions which seem to refer to very little children. One of these was the word *poupart*. In one of the *Miracles de Notre-Dame* there was a "little son" who wanted to feed a picture of the Infant Jesus. "Tender-hearted Jesus, seeing the insistence and good will of the little child, spoke to him and said: '*Poupart,* weep no more, for in three days you shall eat with me.' " But this *poupart* was not really what the French today call a *bébé:* he was also referred to as a *clergeon* or "little clerk," wore a surplice and served at Mass: "Here there were also little children who had few letters and would rather have fed at their mother's breast than do divine service!" [28] In the language of the seventeenth and eighteenth centuries the word *poupart* no longer denoted a child, but instead, in the form *poupon,* what the French today still call by the same name, but in the feminine: a *poupée,* or doll.

French was therefore reduced to borrowing from other idioms—either foreign languages or the slang used in school or trade—words to denote in French that little child in whom an interest was henceforth going to be taken. This was the case with the Italian *bambino* which became the French *bambin.* Mme de Sévigné also used in the same sense a form of the Provençal word *pitchoun,* which she had doubtless learnt in the course of one of her stays with the Grignans.[29] Her cousin Coulanges, who did not like children but spoke of them a great deal,[30] distrusted "three-year-old *marmousets,*" an old word which in the popular idiom would become *marmots,* "brats with greasy chins who put a finger in every dish." People also used slang terms from school Latin or from sporting and military academies: a little *frater,* a *cadet,* and, when there were several of them, a *populo* or *petit peuple.*[31] Lastly the use of diminutives became quite common: *fanfan* is to be found in the letters of Mme de Sévigné and those of Fénelon.

In time these words would come to denote a child who was still small but already beginning to find his feet. There would still remain a gap where a word was needed to denote a child in its first months of life; this gap would not be filled until the nineteenth century, when the French would borrow from the English the word "baby," which in the sixteenth and seventeenth centuries had denoted children of school age. This borrowing was the last

[27] *I pray you, all lytell babes, all lytell chyldren, lern* . . .
[28] *Miracles de Notre-Dame.*
[29] "You do me an injustice in thinking that I love the little one better than the *pichon* . . ." Mme de Sévigné, *Lettres,* June 12th, 1675; see also her letter of October 5th, 1673.
[30] Coulanges, *Chansons choisies,* 1694.
[31] Claudine Bouzonnet-Stella, *Jeux de l'enfance,* 1657.

stage of the story: henceforth, with the French word *bébé,* the very little child had a name.

Even when a vocabulary relating to infancy appeared and expanded, an ambiguity remained between childhood and adolescence on the one hand and the category known as youth on the other. People had no idea of what we call adolescence, and the idea was a long time taking shape. One can catch a glimpse of it in the eighteenth century in two characters—one literary, as presented by Chérubin, and the other social, the conscript. In Chérubin it was the ambiguity of puberty that was uppermost, and the stress was laid on the effeminate side of a boy just emerging from childhood. Strictly speaking, this was not a new thing: since social life began at a very early age, the full, round features of early adolescence, about the age of puberty, gave boys a feminine appearance. This is the explanation of the ease with which men disguised themselves as women and vice versa in countless baroque novels at the beginning of the seventeenth century—two youths becoming friends when one was a girl in disguise, and so on; however credulous readers of adventure stories have always been, the very minimum of probability demands that there should have been some resemblance between a beardless boy and a girl. However, that resemblance was not presented at the time as a characteristic of adolescence, a characteristic of age. Those beardless men with soft features were not adolescents for they already behaved like fully grown men, fighting and giving orders. But in Chérubin the feminine appearance was linked with the transition from child to adult: it expressed a condition during a certain period, the period of budding love.

Chérubin was not destined to have any successors. On the contrary, it was manly strength which, in boys, would express the idea of adolescence, and the adolescence was foreshadowed in the eighteenth century by the conscript. Witness the text of this recruiting poster dating from the end of the eighteenth century.[32] It is addressed to "shining youth" (*brillante jeunesse*): "Those youths [*jeunes gens*] who wish to share in the reputation which this fine corps has won for itself can apply to M. d'Ambrun . . . They [the recruiters] will reward those who bring them some upstanding men [*beaux hommes*]."

The first typical adolescent of modern times was Wagner's *Siegfried:* the music of *Siegfried* expressed for the first time that combination of (provisional) purity, physical strength, naturism, spontaneity and joie de vivre which was to make the adolescent the hero of our twentieth century, the century of adolescence. What made its appearance in Wagnerian Germany was to enter France at a later date, in the years around 1900. The "youth" which at this time was adolescence soon became a literary theme and a

---

[32] Recruiting poster for the Royal Piedmont Regiment at Nevers, 1789. Exhibition: *L'Affiche,* Bibliothèque Nationale, 1953, no. 25.

subject of concern for moralists and politicians. People began wondering seriously what youth was thinking, and inquiries were made by such writers as Massis and Henriot. Youth gave the impression of secretly possessing new values capable of reviving an aged and sclerosed society. A like interest had been evidenced in the Romantic period, but not with such specific reference to a single age group, and moreover it had been limited to literature and the readers of that literature. Awareness of youth became a general phenomenon, however, after the end of the First World War, in which the troops at the front were solidly opposed to the older generations in the rear. The awareness of youth began by being a feeling common to ex-servicemen, and this feeling was to be found in all the belligerent countries, even in the America of Dos Passos. From that point, adolescence expanded: it encroached upon childhood in one direction, maturity in the other. Henceforth marriage, which had ceased to be a "settling down," would not put an end to it: the married adolescent was to become one of the most prominent types of our time, dictating its values, its appetites and its customs. Thus our society has passed from a period which was ignorant of adolescence to a period in which adolescence is the favorite age. We now want to come to it early and linger in it as long as possible.

This evolution has been accompanied by a parallel but contrary evolution of old age. We know that old age started early in the society of the past. We are familiar with such examples as Molière's old men, who appear to be still young to our eyes. Moreover the iconography of old age does not always represent it in the guise of a decrepit invalid: old age begins with the losing of one's hair and the wearing of a beard, and a handsome old man sometimes appears simply as a man who is bald. This is the case with the old man in Titian's concert, which is also a representation of the ages of life. But generally speaking, before the eighteenth century the old man was regarded as ridiculous. One of Rotrou's characters tries to force his daughter to accept a quinquagenarian: "He is only fifty, and hasn't a tooth in his head. In the whole of Nature there's not a man who doesn't think he was born in the age of Saturn or the time of the Flood. Of the three feet on which he walks, two are gouty. They stumble at every step and are always having to be propped up or picked up." [33] And in another ten years he will look like this sexagenarian in Quinault: "Bent over his stick, the little old man coughs, spits, blows his nose, cracks jokes, and bores Isabelle with tales of the good old days." [34]

Old France had little respect for old age: it was the age of retirement, books, churchgoing and rambling talk. The picture of the whole man in the sixteenth and seventeenth centuries was that of a younger man: the officer in the sash at the top of the steps of the ages. He was not a young man,

[33] Rotrou, *La Soeur*.
[34] Quinault, *La Mère coquette*.

although he would be today. He corresponded to that second category of the ages, between childhood and old age, which in the seventeenth century was called youth. Furetière, who still took very seriously the archaic problems of the division of life into periods, thought up an intermediate concept of maturity; but he recognized that it was not current and admitted: "Jurists see only one age in youth and maturity." The seventeenth century recognized itself in this military youth, as the twentieth century recognizes itself in its adolescents.

Today old age has disappeared, at least from spoken French, where the expression *un vieux,* "an old fellow," has survived with a colloquial, contemptuous or patronizing significance. This evolution has taken place in two stages. First of all there was the venerable old man, the silver-haired ancestor, the wise Nestor, the patriarch rich in precious experience: the old man of Greuze, Restif de la Bretonne and the whole nineteenth century. He was not yet very agile, but he was no longer as decrepit as the old man of the sixteenth and seventeenth centuries. There still remains something of this respect for the old man in the received ideas of the present day. But the fact is that this respect no longer has any object, for in our time, and this is the second stage, the old man has disappeared. He has been replaced by "the elderly man" and by "well-preserved ladies or gentlemen": a concept which is still middle-class, but which is tending to become popular. The technological idea of preservation is replacing the biological and moral idea of old age.

It is as if, to every period of history, there corresponded a privileged age and a particular division of human life: "youth" is the privileged age of the seventeenth century, childhood of the nineteenth, adolescence of the twentieth.

The variations from one century to another bear witness to the naive interpretation which public opinion has given, in each and every period, of its demographic structure, when it could not always form an objective idea of it. Thus the absence of adolescence and the contempt for old age on the one hand, and on the other hand the disappearance of old age—at least as a degradation—and the introduction of adolescence, express society's reactions to the duration of life. Prolongation of the average life-span brought into existence tracts of life to which the scholars of the Byzantine Empire and the Middle Ages had given names even though they had not existed for the generality; and the modern language has borrowed these old terms, which were originally purely theoretical, to denote new realities: the last phase of a long familiar and now forgotten theme, that of the "ages of life."

Adolescence: The Management of Emancipation in History and Life History

John R. Seeley

> Canst thou say in thine heart
> Thou hast seen with thine eyes
> With what cunning of art
> Thou wast wrought in what wise,
> By what force of what stuff thou wast
> shapen,
> and shown on my breast to the skies?
> (from Hertha)

I am often amazed by the degree to which I am put off and put down by the greater part of what I read about adolescence. And the degree of my distress is not generally greatly different whether I read the scientific or the lay press, whether I read in my own narrower field or in those of the allied and associated professions. For wanting from all, to a substantially distorting degree, it seems to me, is a sense of society and a sense of history. The desire for some proper feeling for these is not at all dogmatic. Indeed, the plea for their place is almost purely pragmatic. For a consequence of their slighting is that, cognitively, I can barely recognize, within a great part of these writings, the adolescents I know; and, affectively, I find myself alienated, restive, and uncomfortable in the face of the prevailing posture taken toward them. The wrong—if I am right—is dual: an error in the realm of knowledge, and an offense—if that term is allowable—in the realm of value.

Fundamental to my feeling, I am sure, is the evident self-location of the majority of the authors. Some radically transforming and distorting separation of "themselves" from "the phenomena" has occurred, such as to ensure the virtual disappearance of the appropriate we-perspective—surely the most obvious and self-evident presenting social fact. Even where, as commonly, the treatment is empathic and kindly, what is steadily maintained is an essentially oppositional or counterpositional, narrowed "we" cast over against a similarly contracted "them." At its caricatural extreme we may get the bug-on-a-pin effect, with an object of inspection at one end, and a taken-for-granted, detached, and competent observer-judge at the other.

But "we" know, and "they," the adolescents, know, that affairs are not thus. Whatever else adolescents are, they are *people*—like us. And not only people like us, but people with whom we are most vitally engaged. And not only engaged, but interpenetrated. Not only are they "ours," they are by us and of us: of us in the sense that we sensibly constitute them what they are, even as they simultaneously constitute us what we are. And this is so as far as the relation goes at all, and hence as far as "adolescent" and "adult," as terms, have any operative human or social meaning. It is we (if we must narrow the sense) who call out in them the responses to which in turn we respond, and vice versa. And it is in that conversation of word and act, gesture and realized relation, that the fact and meaning of adulthood and adolescence emerge together and find their reciprocal significance. Within, and only within, that enlarged and inclusive we, thus engaged, do adult and adolescent appear properly—as coemergents and coconstituents. And the matrix—as well as the upshot—of that coemergence and coconstituency is one, single and singular, collaborative, shared history, formation, and fate. It is not that we simply *live with* each other; we *achieve* each other. We are not just, in the going jargon, one "system." We are one we of one substance, one most intimate, society, body corporate, fellowship, community, companionship, and company.

The sense of this overarching membership of one another affects not only the tone and manner of communication, but the very substance of things seen. Any want of an enhanced and lively feel for it will inform and infect reports that get back to the adolescents described, and will thus alter the relation between "us" and "them," and, indeed, so constitute the problems of them-ness and alienation that we shall presently be compelled to deal with. In that next phase our own deliverances, and those of other adults, appreciated and acted upon, will return to us as puzzles and problems whose origins we may then not even or no longer know.

Even neglecting the fatal alteration of affective and affectional realities consequent upon this stance—adults as students taking adolescents as objects of study—there is, in my opinion, a further, fateful distortion in that which the stand was taken to help secure: a balanced, appropriate, reliable, useful appreciation of what is going on and what is likely to occur. For as the most obvious aspect of reality—the overarching unity, our common creation and captivity—is played down or deserted, the adult participants enter with the adolescent into characteristic, shared, neurotic and neuroticizing, alternating fantasies. Adult and adolescent begin to see each other, falsely, in the sadistic mode of victimizers, or the masochistic one of victims. And as both do so, they drive the reality toward the fantasy, so that finally in fact, freedom and agency (that were initially not so distributed) may effectively lie differentially and destructively, decisively more on one "side" than another. If adults do enter into such a pact in irreality with adolescents, both are of course jointly responsible; but, here as elsewhere, some are more jointly responsible, as well as more equal, than others.

Not only are the growing and the grown one we, but we are all engaged together and almost altogether, in one enterprise: the making of history. And outside that recognized historical context, as little of what we are doing is intelligible as would be the case if we tried to understand a person without attending to the fact that he is not merely living out, but *building up,* a life, something that has also its own history: an irreversible, meaningful, patterned, large-scale action in and upon the world, transforming actor, act, and acted-upon, simultaneously and alike.

Once properly appreciated—as caught and caught up in one us, engaged together in the enterprise that is history—the adolescent appears rather differently, and "adolescence" assumes additional and altered meaning. For we now see it as a crucial articulation point or period in the historic as well as the ontogenetic process. At that point, supremely, the new, not only as further biologic fodder or *matériel* for social role playing, but as personal culture changer and pathbreaker, is in preparation and emergence. Adolescence *is* thus what spans the stage of the acted-upon-by-history (the child) and the actor in and upon history (the adult); adolescence is (roughly) what bridges between man as made and man as maker—maker of mind, self, history, culture, society-to-be And the reference is always exquisitely and excruciatingly dual: to the life history and the common history, each of which is context and container for the other. And of that intercept of history and biography, crucial for our understanding of the adolescent and critical for his comprehension also, few speak—so few that we have not even gone through the formality of giving it a name.

Failing such appreciation, adolescence appears variously as a stage or phase, as problem or puzzle or parapathology, as presumed pre-Paradise on the way to an adulthood of a predefined kind in a society of a previsioned character. Given, by contrast, a correct location of each adolescent as at the unique intercept of his history with world history, what is exposed is what is there: an intersecting set of constraints, tasks, and opportunities, additional to, coordinate with, and translatory of the tasks set by the life history, or by the needs of growing up, generically. These constraints, tasks, and possibilities, seen in their general and particular intersections, help make much intelligible that must otherwise appear accidental or remain obscure.

Those who do see thus may see, ostensibly, the same adolescents as others see, in the same numbers, and with, presumably, the same intimacy and similar loving curiosity, but they will see them in a rather different light. So far as I am able, I see them so, though not consistently or adequately. Thus, what I see them doing, thinking, feeling, saying—from Carnaby Street costume to the Berkeley sit-ins, from acute and angry argument with parents to rejection of the educational lockstep and the atomic-competitive ethic—

appears to me, for the most part, to be the relatively rather reasonable response of relatively rather reasonable persons to the problems actually presented to them. *We* are part of those presenting problems; but what we present is not the whole problem. History, too, presents its problems and presses its claims.

When, sometimes angrily, they say that some or all adults are, in the going vocabulary, "square," "not with it," "out of it," they mean, as I hear them, that by providing false contexts, those not clued in read out wrong motives, put the young on with feigned understanding, put them off with phony explanations, or put them down with ill-founded criticism. These, thus misled, divide what should not be divided, and juxtapose what does not belong together.

Thus, they see separately and in disconnection good rebellion and bad rebellion, or, as someone said recently, "the constructive and positive" versus "the negative and passive." In the former category, the speaker evidently encompassed activities from Peace Corps participation to civil disobedience directed to the enfranchisement of Negroes, even over to student struggles to free their universities from the toils of the essentially colonialist regimes that do indeed dominate the most of them. By "negative" and "nonconstructive," he meant to impugn the whole of the drug culture, part of the sex practices, the new language, the redistribution of hair lengths between girls and boys, and so on. Where he would have located the repudiation of ideology, the rejection of the standard materialist package, the abandonment of a rule-oriented modality of judgment, I find it hard to say. What he overlooked entirely is that all of these are parts of wholes that have profound organic connections with each other—even if isolable elements, such as certain varieties of drug use, have far-reaching and different consequences for particular users and parts of the society.

By a similar *tour de force,* "liberals"—and the term is now very nearly a swearword, at least among later adolescents—attempted to separate (or missed the connection between) elements in the nationally celebrated struggles at the University of California at Berkeley in the 1965 academic year. I can no more reconstitute here the entire train of events for those who do not know them than I could hope to tell in brief compass the history of the Vietnam war. But it too was, in the United States, a matter, for a considerable time, of national attention. And it was perhaps the most important sequence of events in American higher education in a decade.

At the height of the controversy—essentially a battle over the status of students, their civil and moral rights, and the nature and morality of the government of the academic community—liberals in numbers were "sympathetic," for a time, with the embattled students. Sympathetic, that is, largely as long as the fight was fought in terms of standard oratorical appeals to unassailable constitutional rights.

But when, toward the "end," a poet sat cross-legged on a plot of grass holding aloft a sign that said simply "Fuck"—and when the leadership of the student movement was drawn into his defense because university administrators falsely implicated them as cause, with his action as consequence— sympathizers in their thousands opted out of even that thin but badly needed support.

I do not here question their right to do—let alone feel—as they please. But their amazement and dismay rested largely upon serious disorientation with reference both to contemporary social connections and to relatively recent historic events. What was really embedded in a rich and intelligible context thus appeared as mere excess or *bizarrerie*. Many who took the poet's act as revelatory—which it was—took it to be "revealing" only in a denigrating sense: the whole prior contest was teleologically reduced to a "dirty word controversy," its original "inner meaning" finally shown forth.

For few, did word and act link up with another, then current, less collapsed, popular slogan, "Make love, not war," even though the poet partly explained his action in such terms. "If I had sat there" he said, "with a sign saying 'Bomb!' or 'Kill!' nobody would have bothered me." No one attended to his wry comment (looking both ways, to the war in Vietnam and the recent horrors on campus): "It's a panacea for all the world's ills." For few, did his act link up with the then recent obscene trial on obscenity charges of a youthful culture hero (Lenny Bruce), who had used (in a night club, and for adults only) "obscene" images to make shockingly alive great and far-reaching social issues. For few again did it link, as an expectable second act, with the stripping in the preceding months from the Berkeley students' University—by its own claim and their concession, acting always *in loco parentis*—of every shard of moral dignity. And hardly any saw it as ·a protest against the misuse of words—to divide, confuse, mislead, and defend the indefensible—that had characterized press and administration pronouncements in the period immediately past. None saw it as an overterse, overcondensed, overdetermined reply, in some sense, to the excessively polished, rounded periods of the Greek Theater performance (whose real meaning was also in a sense "revealed," when carefully concealed campus police rushed from the wings to protect the podium against a student leader who wished to make a rather routine announcement).

The principal object of analyzing this event thus—even though the analysis, incidentally, shows its own bias—is neither to indict nor to praise any of the parties concerned. The poet may have his pathology. Even more tragically, his pathology may have peculiarly cast him for his role, as well as provided him with his insights, prophetic and profane. And so may the officials involved have had their problems and their hangups, their incapacitations, paramount perhaps over good intentions. My purpose is not, here, to judge, but only to insist that the keeping in view of social and historic contexts is vital to the understanding and evaluation of living events, and is evidently much underpracticed.

In a similar fashion, but on a grander scale, a disconnection has, in going lines of explanation, been found or forced, between the "good" activities of Northern white students "laying their bodies on the line" to found freedom schools in Mississippi or to register Negro voters in Alabama, and the "bad" activities involved in the widespread adoption of "hip" language and posture (physical and psychological), the adoption of the uniform of denims and sweatshirts, the elevation of "keeping one's cool" into a major desideratum, and the somewhat successful sabotage of the standard high schools' manpower-procurement schemes and outlooks.

Indeed, one gets the feeling that while the "integration" of American society—across "racial," ethnic, age, sex, class, and other barriers—is, abstractly, widely desired, it is regarded, in its concrete outworkings, as horrific. And it is held horrific because what was originally had in mind by its most vocal liberal proponents was not so much integration as *absorption* —actually the assimilation of all into the subculture of the speaker. (That this is to be desired is no more self-evident than that all forms and varieties of British speech should be lost to pound-note English.) Surely, a genuine integration *must* be preceded by a vast mutual migration of forms, fashions, fads, and values across the pre-existent boundaries, so that, in their collision, recombination, and mutual modification, a culturally creative and fructifying process may freely occur. This presupposes what we see: the migration of practices, views, schemes, and styles from socially below up, instead of merely, as formerly, only from up, down. Hence adolescents, properly about their history's business, will not exhibit, even in well-off Northern white communities, some elements of a culture originating with marginal, Southern Negro jazz musicians, even perhaps in still raw (i.e., unassimilated or unintegrated) form. So the noble freedom schools and the "ignoble" hippy walk may well be aspects of a single movement, an entirely proper response to an entirely urgent historic need.

So also for the very evident *rapprochement* between the sexes. The transforming conquests of technology, the avalanche of affluence resulting, and the emergence into dominance of large-scale ventures based more and more on cooperation, make less and less adaptive and aesthetic the virile Roman virtues. And so, similarly, the overdrawn, overemphasized, too sharply counterposed masculine and feminine role systems, and their corresponding supporting attitude sets, become ever less serviceable. The resultant response of the young is all too visible. But again, critics apparently desire to disjoin what is organically conjoined. They appear to approve the husband who shares with his wife the laundering, dishwashing, and diapering, but to disapprove the appropriate *attendrissement* of the young males. Hence, the critics frown on what is equally relevant and dramatically appropriate, the young males' turning away from mayhem sports, not to mention military exploit, their long hair and generally softened and gentled facial conformation, their cultivation of the inner life at some expense to "achievement," their abandonment of a hard calculus of entitlements in favor of an enlarged sympathy, and their preferential attention, *modo materno,* to need over desert.

Similarly, in the extension of the same sympathy over geographically and socially distant populations. Again the historic need. And again the disallowance of part of a single, a unitary, response. The same sentiment that recoils—and leads to most vocal protest—in reference to the Negro in Birmingham who is mauled by police dogs, trained by police for the purpose, extends of its own nature to the Vietnamese peasant, napalmed or personnel-mined for some unbelievable public benefit. And even those few critics who do follow thus far so often cry violent halt when the same interested and unalienated tolerance extends to those whom the establishment designates as criminal—most especially to those who illegally comfort themselves in their permanent deprivation with such means as are, for them, at hand. The common core of youthful sentiment—again a response to a kind of ecumenicism that history suddenly demands—is a reluctance to legislate for others, even in the heart and mind, particularly beyond necessity. What is involved is not indifference, for each adolescent readily finds and retains his own resonating *entourage.* But there is involved centrally a more humane readiness to accredit (in Polanyi's terms) the hazardous commitment of another, as, at least prima facie, likely to be appropriate to *his* distinct position and possibility.

And so, lastly, for a new union or wedding between *eros* and *agapé.* Nothing seems so visible among the young as a happy heightening and extension and enrichment of the erotic. And nothing is next most visible except the widening and deepening of the empire of goodwill. And nothing, after that, is more obvious, I believe, as one moves around among them, than the way in which these forms of love sustain, feed, and heighten each the other. Thus, typically, the energy for the weary picket line and the strength for the long-drawn sit-in emerge not so much from sexual renunciation and "sublimation," as from the extension and enlargement of a rich and early genitality. Indeed, what is oil to flame, and what flame to oil is a matter for discovery and rediscovery from moment to flowing moment.

Let nothing herein now be taken to detract from what has been elsewhere said and well said. Of course, adolescence is a peculiarly poignant phase in a search for identity. It is only that identity is more than merely the discovery of self; it is self-discovery in relation to what is thus simultaneously made vital and given its meaning: most particularly, in relation to the massive act we call history and the massive "we" that is society. Of course, there is in adolescence pathology and psuedo pathology; but even pathology is often called out by, responds to, and is reinforced by the general history that is container and contained to the personal one. Of course, there is in adolescence much rebellion that would, doubtless, seek some permissible form of expression even in a time that did not so insistently call for the rupture of old forms—from nationalist states that represent clear and present danger to infantilizing schools that prepare for them. These forms, the young feel—and feel, I think, rightly—cannot contain the valuable and vital forces we have ourselves happily set free.

What I plead for, then, in the realm of theory, is the development and recognition of a study: the study of what is to be seen in the simultaneous dual perspective of history and life history. What it calls for practically—as adjunctive to the self-exploration we call psychotherapy and the world exploration we call education—is an enterprise in which we, jointly with them, as one interactive we, explore and explain what is for each of us and each of them the unique intercept of my life with our life, my history with the common history of all of us. For *that* is, I think, peculiarly the locus of large action, the matrix of culture, the growth point of society, and the ground upon which—in adolescence only particularly—personality forms and figures, even as it is figured and formed. Were I speaking to them I would plead for a similar extension and elevation of sight and sympathy. But I should in so doing like to come to them saying that we had seen and sensed them so, cradled in a common concern that is not only paternally ours for them, but properly ours for that us that includes them in a vision appropriate to the principal presenting facts.

Youth in the Context
of American Society

Talcott Parsons

The passage of time has recently been symbolized by the fact that we have elected the first President of the United States to be born in the twentieth century—indeed, well inside it. It is perhaps equally relevant to remark that we have recently entered an era in which a substantial proportion of current youth (rather than children) will experience a major part of their active lives in the twenty-first century. Thus a sixteen-year-old of today will be only fifty-five at the coming turn of the century.

It is possible that the twentieth century will be characterized by future historians as one of the centuries of turmoil and transition—in the modern

Talcott Parsons, "Youth in the Context of American Society," from *Daedalus*. Reprinted by permission of *Daedalus*, Journal of the American Academy of Arts and Sciences, Boston, Mass. (Winter 1962), *Youth: Change and Challenge*, pp. 97–123.

history of the West, perhaps most analogous to the seventeenth. It is also likely, however, that it will be judged as one of the great creative centuries, in which major stages of the process of building a new society, a new culture, will have occurred. The tremendous developments in the sciences and in the technologies deriving from them, the quite new levels of industrialization, and the spread of the industrial pattern from its places of origin, together with the long series of "emancipations" (e.g., women's suffrage and the rapid decline of colonialism) will presumably figure prominently among its achievements. At the same time, it clearly has been and will probably continue to be a century of turmoil, not one of the placid enjoyment of prior accomplishment, but of challenge and danger. It is in this broad perspective that I should like to sketch some of the problems of American youth, as the heirs of the next phase of our future, with both its opportunities and its difficulties.

In the course of this century, the United States has emerged at the forefront of the line of general development, not only because of its wealth and political power but also—more importantly in the present context—because it displays the type of social organization that belongs to the future. Since during the same period and only a little behind our own stage of progress a somewhat differing and competing version has also emerged in the Communist societies, it is not surprising that there is high tension at both political and ideological levels. Obviously, the meaning of American society presents a world-wide problem, not least to its own citizens and in turn to its younger ones: since they have the longest future ahead of them, they have the most at stake.

Some Salient Characteristics of American Society

Before we take up the specific situation of youth, it will be best to sketch a few of the main features of our society and the ideological discussions about them, with special reference to their effect on youth. The structural characteristic usually emphasized is industrialism. It is certainly true that the United States has developed industrial organization and productivity farther than any other society in history. Not only has it done this on a massive scale, both as regards population and area, but it has also attained by far the highest levels of per-capita productivity yet known. The salience of industrialism in turn emphasizes the economic aspects of social structure: a high evaluation of productivity, the free enterprise system, with the private, profit-oriented business firm as a conspicuous unit of organization, and with private consumption prominent in the disposal of the products of industry. This last feature includes both the high levels of current family income and what may be called the "capitalization" of households through the spread of home ownership, the development of consumer durable goods, and the like.

It would be misleading, however, to overstress this economic aspect. Economic development itself depends on many noneconomic conditions, and economic and noneconomic aspects are subtly interwoven in many ways. The same period (roughly, the present century) which has seen the enormous growth of industrial productivity has also seen a very large relative, as well as absolute, growth in the organization and functions of government. The largest growth of all, of course, is in the armed services, but by no means only there. State and local governments have also expanded. Another prominent development has been that of the legal system, which is interstitial between governmental and nongovernmental sectors of society. I mean here not only legislation and the functioning of courts of law but also the private legal profession, with professional lawyers employed in government in various capacities.

A consideration of the legal profession leads to one of the learned professions in general, the educational organizations in which men are trained, and the cultural systems that form the basis of their competence. The most important development has been the growth of the sciences and their application, not only in industry and the military field but also in many others, notably, that of health. Though they are behind their physical and biological sister disciplines, the sciences dealing with human behavior in society have made very great advances, to an altogether new level. To take only the cruder indices, they have grown enormously in the numbers of trained personnel, in the volume of publications, in the amount of research funds devoted to their pursuit, and the like. All this would not have been possible without a vast expansion of the educational system, relatively greatest at the highest levels. By any quantitative standard, the American population today is by far the most highly educated of any large society known to history—and it is rapidly becoming more so.

Furthermore, this has become in the first instance a society of large organizations, though the tenacious survival of small units (in agriculture, but more broadly in retail trade and various other fields) is a striking fact. (It is important to note that the large organization has many features that are independent of whether it operates in private industry, in government, or in the private nonprofit sector.) It is also a highly urbanized society. Less than ten percent of its labor force is engaged in agriculture, and more than half the population lives in metropolitan areas, urban communities that are rapidly expanding and changing their character.

It is also a society with a great mobility as to persons, place of residence, and social and economic status. It is a society that within about eighty years has assimilated a tremendous number of immigrants, who, though overwhelmingly European in origin, came from a great diversity of national, cultural, and religious backgrounds. Their descendants have increasingly

become full Americans, and increasingly widely dispersed in the social structure, including its higher reaches. After all, the current President of the
United States is the grandson of Irish immigrants and the first Catholic to
occupy that office.

Overriding all these features is the fact that this is a rapidly developing
society. There are good reasons for supposing that rapid change is generally
a source of unsettlement and confusion, particularly accentuated perhaps
if the change is not guided by a set of sharply defined master symbols that
tell just what the change is about. The American process of change is of
this type; but we can also say that it is not a state of nearly random
confusion but in the main is a coherently directional process. Since it is
not centrally directed or symbolized, however, it is particularly important
to understand its main pattern.

There has been the obvious aspect of growth that is expressed in sheer
scale, such as the size of the population, the magnitude and complexity of
organization. At the more specifically social levels, however, I should like
to stress certain features of the process that may help to make the situation
of American youth (as well as other phenomena of our time) more understandable. On the one hand, at the level of the predominant pattern, our
value system has remained relatively stable. On the other hand, relative to
the value system, there has been a complex process of change, of which
structural differentiation is perhaps the most important single feature. It is
associated, however, with various others, which I shall call "extending exclusiveness," "normative upgrading," and "an increasing conceptualization
of value patterns on the general level." These are all technical terms which,
if they are not to be regarded as sociological jargon, need to be elucidated.

Values generally are patterned conceptions of the qualities of meaning of
the objects of human experiences; by virtue of these qualities, the objects
are considered desirable for the evaluating persons. Among such objects is
the type of society considered to be good, not only in some abstract sense
but also for "our kind of people" as members of it. The value patterns that
play a part in controlling action in a society are in the first instance the
conceptions of the good type of society to which the members of that
society are committed. Such a pattern exists at a very high level of generality,
without any specification of functions, or any level of internal differentiation,
or particularities of situation.

In my own work it has proved useful to formulate the dominant American
value pattern at this very general level as one of *instrumental activism*. Its
cultural grounding lies in moral and (eventually) religious orientations,
which in turn derive directly from Puritan traditions. The relevance of the
pattern extends through all three of the religious, moral, and societal levels,
as well as to others that cannot be detailed here. It is most important to
keep them distinct, in particular, the difference between the moral and the
societal levels.

In its religious aspect, instrumental activism is based on the pattern Max Weber called "inner-worldly asceticism," the conception of man's role as an instrument of the divine will in building a kingdom of God on earth. Through a series of steps, both in internal cultural development and in institutionalization (which cannot be detailed here), this has produced a conception of the human condition in which the individual is committed to maximal effort in the interest of valued *achievement* under a system of normative order. This system is in the first instance moral, but also, at the societal level, it is embodied in legal norms. Achievement is conceived in "rational" terms, which include the maximal objective understanding of the empirical conditions of action, as well as the faithful adherence to normative commitments. It is of great importance that, once institutionalized, the fulfillment of such a value pattern need not be motivated by an explicit recognition of its religious groundings.

One way of describing the pattern in its moral aspects is to say that it is fundamentally individualistic. It tends to maximize the desirability of autonomy and responsibility in the individual. Yet this is an institutionalized individualism, in that it is normatively controlled at the moral level in two ways. First, it is premised on the conception of human existence as serving ends or functions beyond those of physical longevity, or health, or the satisfaction of the psychological needs of the personality apart from these value commitments. In a sense, it is the building of the "good life," not only for the particular individual but also for all mankind—a life that is accounted as desirable, not merely desired. This includes commitment to a good society. Second, to implement these moral premises, it is necessary for the autonomous and responsible achievements of the individual to be regulated by a normative order—at this level, a moral law that defines the relations of various contributions and the patterns of distributive justice.

The society, then, has a dual meaning, from this moral point of view. On the one hand, it is perhaps the primary field in which valued achievement is possible for the individual. In so far as it facilitates such achievements, the society is a good one. On the other hand, the building of the good society (that is, its progressive improvement) is the primary goal of valued action—along with such cultural developments as are intimately involved in social progress, such as science. To the individual, therefore, the most important goal to which he can orient himself is a contribution to the good society.

The value pattern I am outlining is activistic, therefore, in that it is oriented toward control or mastery of the human condition, as judged by moral standards. It is not a doctrine of passive adjustment to conditions, but one of active adaptation. On the other hand, it is instrumental with reference to the source of moral legitimation, in the sense that human achievement is not conceived as an end in itself but as a means to goals beyond the process and its immediate outcome.

This value pattern implies that the society is meant to be a developing, evolving entity. It is meant to develop in the direction of progressive "improvement." But this development is to be through the autonomous initiative and achievements of its units—in the last analysis, individual persons. It is therefore a society which places heavy responsibilities (in the form of expectations) on its individual members. At the same time, it subjects them to two very crucial sets of limitations which have an important bearing on the problem of youth.

One of these concerns the "moralism" of the value system—the fact that individualism is bound within a strongly emphasized framework of normative order. The achievement, the success, of the individual must ideally be in accord with the rules, above all, with those which guarantee opportunity to all, and which keep the system in line with its remoter values. Of course, the more complex the society, the greater the difficulty of defining the requisite norms, a difficulty which is greatly compounded by rapid change. Furthermore, in the interest of effectiveness, achievement must often be in the context of the collective organization, thus further limiting autonomy.

The second and for present purposes an even more crucial limitation is that it is in the nature of such a system that it is not characterized by a single, simple, paramount goal for the society as a system. The values legitimize a *direction* of change, not a terminal state. Furthermore, only in the most general sense is this direction "officially" defined, with respect to such famous formulae as liberty, democracy, general welfare, and distributive justice. The individual is left with a great deal of responsibility, not only for achieving *within* the institutionalized normative order, but for his own interpretation of its meaning and of his obligations in and to it.

Space forbids detailing the ramifications of this value system. Instead, it is necessary to my analysis to outline briefly the main features of the process of social change mentioned. The suggestion is that the main pattern of values has been and probably will continue to be stable, but that the structure of the society, including its subsystem values at lower levels, has in the nature of the case been involved in a rapid and far-reaching process of change. This centers on the process of differentiation, but very importantly it also involves what we have referred to as inclusion, upgrading, and increasing generalization. I shall confine my discussion here to the structure of the society, though this in turn is intimately connected with problems concerned with the personality of the individual, including his personal values.

Differentiation refers to the process by which simple structures are divided into functionally differing components, these components becoming relatively independent of one another, and then recombined into more complex structures in which the functions of the differentiated units are complementary. A key example in the development of industrial society everywhere is the differentiation, at the collectivity level, of the unit of economic production from the kinship household. Obviously, in peasant economies, production is carried out by and in the household. The development of employing organizations which are structurally distinct from any household is the key new structural element. This clearly means a loss of function to the old undifferentiated unit, but also a gain in autonomy, though this in turn involves a new dependency, because the household can no longer be self-subsistent. The classical formula is that the productive services of certain members (usually the adult males) have been alienated from the organization directly responsible for subsistence and thus lost to the household, which then depends on money income from occupational earnings and in turn on the markets for consumer's goods.

These losses, however, are not without their compensations: the gain in the productivity of the economy and in the standard of living of the household. This familiar paradigm has to be generalized so as to divest it of its exclusively economic features and show it as the primary characterization of a very general process of social change. First, it is essential to point out that it always operates simultaneously in both collectivities and individual roles. Thus, in the example just given, a new type of productive organization which is not a household or (on more complex levels) even a family farm has to be developed. The local community no longer consists only of farm households but also of nonproducing households and productive units— e.g., firms. Then the same individual (the head of the household) has a dual role as head of the family and as employee in a producing unit (the case of the individual entrepreneur is a somewhat special one).

By the extension of inclusiveness, I mean that, once a step of differentiation has been established, there is a tendency to extend the new pattern to increasing proportions of the relevant population of units. In the illustrative case, the overwhelming tendency that has operated for well over a century has been to reduce the proportion of households which are even in part economically self-sufficient, in the sense of a family farm, in favor of those whose members are gainfully employed outside the household. This is a principal aspect of the spread of industrialization and urbanization. The same logic applies to newly established educational standards, e.g., the expectation that a secondary-school education will be normal for the whole age cohort.

Normative upgrading means a type of change in the normative order, to which the operation of units, both individual and collective, is subject. It is a shift from the prescription of rules by a special class or unit in a special situation to more generalized norms having to do with more inclusive classes of units in wider ranges of situations. Thus the law that specifies that a railway engine must be equipped with a steam whistle to give warning at crossings has by court interpretation been generalized to include any effective warning signal (since oil-burning locomotives are not equipped with steam).[1] But in a sense parallel to that in which differentiation leads to alienation from the older unit, normative upgrading means that the unit is left with a problem, since the rules no longer give such concretely un-equivocal guidance to what is expected. If the rule is general enough, its application to a particular situation requires interpretation. Such upgrading, we contend, is a necessary concomitant of the process of differentiation.

When we speak of norms, we mean rules applying to particular categories of units in a system, operating in particular types of situations. For example, individual adults may not be employed under conditions which infringe on certain basic freedoms of the individual. The repercussions of a step in differentiation, however, cannot be confined to this level; they must also involve some part of the value system; this is to say, the functions of the differentiated categories of units, which are now different from one another, must not only be regulated but also legitimized. To use our example again, it cannot be true that the whole duty of the fathers of families is to gain subsistence for their households through making the household itself pro-ductive, but it becomes legitimate to support the household by earning a money income through work for an outside employer and among other things to be absent from the household many hours a week. At the collec-tivity level, therefore, a business that is not the direct support of a household (such as farming) must be a legitimate way of life—that is, the unit that employs labor for such purposes, without itself being a household, must be legitimate. This requires defining the values in terms sufficiently general to include both the old and the new way of life.

The values must therefore legitimize a structural complex by which eco-nomic production and the consumption needs of households are met simul-taneously—that is, both the labor markets and the markets for consumers' goods. For example, this structural complex is of focal importance in the modern (as distinguished from medieval) urban community. The value attitude that regards the rural or the handicraft way of life as morally superior to the modern urban and—if you will—industrial way (a common attitude in the Western world of today) is an example of the failure of the adequate value generalization that is an essential part of institutionalizing the process of structural change.

To sum up, we may state that both the nature of the American value pattern and the nature of the process of change going on in the society make for considerable difficulties in the personal adjustment of individuals. On the one hand, our type of activism, with its individualistic emphases, puts a heavy responsibility for autonomous achievement on the individual. On the other hand, it subjects him to important limitations: he must not only be regulated by norms and the necessity of working cooperatively, in collective contexts; he must also interpret his own responsibilities and the rules to which he is subject. Beyond that, ours is a society which in the nature of its values cannot have a single clear-cut societal goal which can be dramatically symbolized. The individual is relegated to contributions which are relatively specialized, and it is not always easy to see their bearing on the larger whole.

Furthermore, the general erosion of traditional culture and symbols, which is inseparable from a scientific age, makes inadequate many of the old formulae once used to give meaning and legitimation to our values and achievements. This is perhaps true in particular of the older religious grounding of our values.

Not unrelated to these considerations is the very fact of the *relative* success of the society in developing in relation to its values. Not only is there a high general standard of living, which, it should be remembered, means the availability of facilities for *whatever* uses are valued; e.g., increased income may allow for attending prize fights or symphony concerts—a not inconsiderable amount has been going into the latter channel. There is certainly a much better standard of minimum welfare and general distributive justice now than in our past. However much remains to be done, and it is clearly considerable, it is no longer possible to contend that poverty, misery, preventable illness, etc., are the primary lot of the average American. Indeed, the accent has shifted to our duty to the less favored portions of the world. Furthermore, for the average individual, it is probable that opportunity is more widely open than in any large-scale society in history to secure education, access to historically validated cultural goods, and the like. But perhaps it can be seen that, in the light of this all too brief analysis, the great problem has come to be, what to do with all these advantages—not, as has so often been true, how to avoid the worst disasters and take a few modest little steps forward.[2] To be sure, there is a very real danger of the collapse of all civilization through nuclear war; but somehow that danger fails to deter people from making significant investments in the future, not only for themselves as individuals, but also for the society as a whole.

The Position of American Youth

It is in this broad picture of the American social structure and its development that I should like to consider the position of American youth. Contrary to prevalent views that mainly stress the rising standard of living and the allegedly indulgent and easy life, I think it is legitimate to infer that the general trend of development of the society has been and will continue to be one which, by and large, puts greater rather than diminished demands on its average individual citizen—with some conspicuous exceptions. He must operate in more complex situations than before. He attempts to do many things his predecessors never attempted, that indeed were beyond their capacities. To succeed in what he attempts, he has to exercise progressively higher levels of competence and responsibility. These inferences seem to me inescapable when full account of the nature of the society and its main trends of development is taken.

If capacities and relevant opportunities developed as rapidly as do demands, it would follow that life on the average would be neither more nor less difficult. There seems reason to believe that, if anything, demands have tended somewhat to outrun the development of capacities—especially those for orienting to normatively complex situations—and in some respects even opportunities, and that this is a major source of the current unrest and malaise. My broad contention, taking due account of the process of change just outlined, is that this society, however, is one that is relatively well organized and integrated with reference to its major values and its major trends of development. If those values are intact and are by and large shared by the younger generation (there seems to be every indication that they are), then it ought to be a society in which they can look forward to a good life. In so far as their mood is one of bewilderment, frustration, or whatever, one should look for relatively specific sources of difficulty rather than to a generalized malintegration of the society as a whole.

It may be well to set the tone of the following analysis by an example of the ways in which current common sense can often misinterpret phenomena that raise distressing problems. American society, of course, is known for its high divorce rate. Until the peak following World War II, moreover, the trend was upward throughout the century, though since then it has appreciably declined. This divorce rate has widely been interpreted as an index of the "disintegration of the family" and, more importantly, of the levels of moral responsibility of married persons.

That it results in increased numbers of broken families is of course true, though the seriousness of this is mitigated by the fact that most divorces occur between childless couples and that most divorced persons remarry, a large proportion stably. In any case, the proportion of the population of marriageable age that is married and living with their spouses is now the highest it has been in the history of the census.

The main point, however, is that this point of view fails to take into account the increased strain put on the marriage relationship in the modern situation. In effect, it says, since an increased proportion fail in a difficult task relative to those who previously failed in an easier task, this increased rate of failures is an index of a declining level of responsibility; seen in this light, this interpretation is palpably absurd, but if the underlying situation is not analyzed, it is plausible.

The increased difficulty of the task has two main aspects. One is the increased differentiation of the nuclear family from other structures in which it was formerly embedded, notably the farm and other household or family enterprises from which economic support was derived. This differentiation deprives the family and the marriage relationship within it of certain bases of structural support. This is clearly related to the component of freedom mentioned above; the freedom of choice of marriage partners is clearly related to the spread of the view that really serious incompatibility may justify breaking the marriage tie.

The other factor is the enhanced level of expectation in functioning outside the family for both adults and children. For adults, particularly men, the central obligation concerns the levels of responsibility and competence required by their jobs; for children, these requirements of growing up in a more complex and competitive world, going farther in education, and undertaking substantially more autonomous responsibility along the way impose greater demands than before. It is my impression that the cases in which marriage was undertaken irresponsibly are no more numerous than in any other time, and that divorce is not often lightly resorted to but is a confession of failure in an undertaking in which both parties have usually tried very hard to succeed.[3]

I cite this example because it is a conspicuous special case of the more general considerations I wish to discuss. The first keynote here is the rising general level of expectations. The primary reference point, of course, is that of adult roles at their peak of responsibility in middle age. The most prominent example is that of the higher levels of masculine occupational roles, in which (in those with technical emphasis) the requisite levels of training and technical competence are continually rising. With respect to managerial roles, the size and complexity of organizations is increasing, and hence the requirements necessary for their successful management also. Similar things, however, are true in various other fields. Thus the whole range of associational affairs requires membership support for leadership as well as responsible leadership itself, both of which involve complicated responsibilities. These range from the many private associations and "good causes" through participation on boards and staffs (including university departments and faculties) to participation through voting and other forms of exercising public responsibility.

The family in this context is a further case. The feminine role is typically anchored in the first instance in the family. Family duties may not be more onerous in such senses as drudgery and hard work than they were, but they involve a higher level of competence and responsibility, particularly, though not exclusively, in the field of the psychological management of both children and husbands, as well as of selves—the latter because wives are now far more autonomous on the average than they were. What we may call the independence training of children is more delicate and difficult than was the older type of training in strict obedience—that is, if autonomy for the young is to be accompanied by high levels of self-discipline and responsibility. But in addition, the typical married woman participates far more extensively outside the home than she formerly did, and in particular she forms a rapidly increasing proportion in the labor force.

Perhaps the central repercussion of this general upgrading of expectations (and hence of the norms with which conformity is expected) on the situation of youth is in the field of formal education. Here, of course, there has been a steady process of lengthening the average period of schooling, with the minimum satisfactory norm for all approaching the completion of high school, while nearly forty percent of the total age cohort now enter college, and a steadily increasing percentage complete college. Finally, by far the most rapidly growing sector has been that of postgraduate professional education. Uneven as standards are, and unsatisfactory as they are at many points, there is no solid evidence of a general tendency to deterioration and much evidence of their improvement, especially in the best schools at all levels.[4]

It seems fair, then, to conclude that in getting a formal education the average young American is undertaking a more difficult, and certainly a longer, job than his father or mother did, and that it is very likely that he is working harder at it. A growing proportion is prolonging formal education into the early adult years, thus raising important problems about marriage, financial independence, and various other considerations.

Furthermore, he is doing this in a context in which, both within and outside the school, he must assume more autonomous responsibility than did his predecessors. In the school itself—and in college—the slow though gradual trend has been in the direction of a mildly "progressive" type of education, with a diminution of the amount of drill and learning by rote. In certain respects, parents have grown distinctly more permissive within the family and with regard to their children's activities outside. This throws an important stress on the child's relations to his age peers, one that becomes particularly important in adolescence. This is the area least under adult control, in which deviant tendencies can most readily be mutually reinforced, without being immediately checked by adult intervention. This is to say that in general the educational process puts increased demands on the younger group.

Three other factors seem involved in this situation of strain from the combination of enhanced expectations and autonomy. They concern one aspect of the psychological preparation for the tasks of maturing, one aspect of the choices that are open, and one aspect of the situation with reference to normative regulation.

First, with respect to psychological preparation, there seems to have been a trend within the family to *increase* the dependency of the young pre-oedipal child, particularly on the mother, of course. This trend is the consequence of the structural isolation of the nuclear family. There is less likelihood of there being close relatives either directly in the home or having very intensive and continual contact with the family. For middle-class families, the virtual disappearance of the domestic servant has also left less room for a division of responsibility for child care. Further, the proportion of very large families with five or more children has been sharply decreasing, while those with three and four children have been increasing. All these factors contribute to a concentration of relationships within the family and of the parents' (especially the mother's) sanctioning powers—both disciplinary and rewarding.

Psychological theory, however, indicates that under the proper circumstances this enhanced dependency contributes to developing motivations for high levels of achievement. These circumstances include high levels of aspiration for the child on the part of the parents and the use of the proper types of discipline. The essential point is that high dependency provides a very strong motivation to please the parent. This in turn can be used to incite him to learn what the parent sets him, if he is suitably rewarded by parental approval. The general findings of studies on the types of discipline used in middle-class families—the use of the withdrawal of love and approval as the predominant type of negative sanction—seem to fit in this picture.

The dependency components of motivation, however, are seldom if ever fully extinguished. The balance is so delicate in their relation to the autonomous components that it is easily upset, and in many cases this is a source of considerable strain. Attempting to maintain this balance, for example, may very well contribute to the great increase in the practice of "going steady" and its relation to the trend to early marriages. Emerging in adolescence, the dyadic heterosexual relation is the main component of the relational system of youth that articulates most directly with the earlier dependency complex—though some of it may also be expressed in same-sex peer groups, and indeed in "crushes" on the teacher. It is striking that the main trend seems to be toward intensive, and not merely erotic but diffuse, dyadic relations, rather than to sexual libertinism. This is in turn reflected in the emotional intensity of the marriage relationship and hence in the elements of potential strain underlying the problem of divorce.

This brings me to the second of the factors mentioned, the range of choices open. A progressive increase in this range is a consequence of the general process of social change sketched, namely, differentiation in the structure of the society. As this process goes on, types of interest, motivation, and evaluation that were embedded in a less differentiated complex come to be separated out, to become more autonomous and more visible in that they are freed from more ascriptive types of control. Ties to class and family, to local community and region become more flexible and hence often "expendable" as more choices become available.

One of the most conspicuous cases in relation to the present interest is the erotic component of sex relations. In an earlier phase of our society, it was rather rigidly controlled even within marriage, indeed, not infrequently it was partially suppressed. The process by which it has become differentiated, allowing much greater freedom in this area, is closely related to the differentiation of function and the structural isolation of the nuclear family.[5] In a society in which autonomous freedom is so widespread, there is much greater freedom in this field as in many others, not only in practice but also in portrayals on the stage, in the movies and television, and in the press, magazines, and books.

In this connection, since much of the newer freedom is illegitimate in relation to the older standards (normative upgrading and value generalization take time), it is very difficult to draw lines between the areas of new freedom in process of being legitimated and the types which are sufficiently dysfunctional, even in the new state of society, so that the probability is they will be controlled or even suppressed. The adolescent in our society is faced with difficult problems of choice and evaluation in areas such as this, because an adequate codification of the norms governing many of these newly emancipated areas has not yet been developed.

The third factor, that of normative regulations, is essentially a generalization of the second factor. We have maintained (though of course without documentation) that, contrary to various current opinions, the basic pattern of American values has not changed. Value patterns, however, are only part of the normative culture of the society. At the lower levels, both at the more specific levels of values and of what we technically call norms, it is in the nature of the type of process of change we have been discussing that there should be a continual reorganization of the normative system. Unfortunately, this does not occur as an instantaneous adjustment to the major innovations, but is a slow, uneven, and often painful process. In its course, at any one time (as we have noted), there are important elements of indeterminacy in the structure of expectations—not simply in the sense that there are areas of freedom in which autonomous decision is expected, but also in the sense that, where people feel there ought to be guidance, it is either lacking altogether, or the individual is subject to conflicting expectations that are impossible to fulfill all at once. This is the condition that some sociologists, following Durkheim, call *anomie*.

There seems to be an important reason why this source of strain and disturbance bears rather more heavily on the younger generation than on others. This is owing to the fact that the major agents for initiating processes of change lie in other sectors of the society, above all, in large-scale organization, in the developments of science and technology, in the higher political processes, and in the higher ranges of culture. Their impact tends to spread, and there is a time lag in change between the locations of primary change and the other parts of the social structure.

Though there is of course much unevenness, it seems correct to say that, with one major exception, the social structures bearing most directly on youth are likely to be rather far down the line in the propagation of the effects of change. These are the family and the school, and they are anchored in the local residential community. The major exception is the college, and still more, the university, which is one of the major loci of innovation and which can involve its students in the process more directly.

By and large, it seems fair to suggest that adults are on the average probably more conservative in their parental roles than when their children are not involved, and that this is typical of most of their roles outside the family. Similarly, schools, especially elementary and secondary schools, are on the whole probably more conservative in most respects than are the organizations that employ the fathers of their children. In the present phase of social development, another important institution of the residential community, the parish church or synagogue, is probably distinctly on the conservative side as a rule.

This would suggest that, partly as a matter of generation lag, partly for more complex reasons of the sort indicated, the adult agencies on which the youth most depends tend to some extent to be "out of tune" with what he senses to be the most advanced developments of the time. He senses that he is put in an unfair dilemma by having to be so subject to their control.

If we are right in thinking that special pressures operate on the younger generation relative to the general pressures generated by social change, on the other side of the relationship there are factors which make for special sensitivities on their part. The residua of early dependency, as pointed out, constitute one such factor. In addition, the impact on youth of the general process of social differentiation makes for greater differences between their position and that of children, on the one hand, and that of adults, on the other, than is true in less differentiated societies. Compared to our own past or to most other societies, there is a more pronounced, and above all (as noted) an increasingly long segregation of the younger groups, centered above all on the system of formal education. It may be argued especially that the impact of this process is particularly pronounced at the upper fringe of the youth period, for the rapidly increasing proportion of the age cohort engaged in higher education—in college, and, very importantly, in post-graduate work. These are people who are adults in all respects except for the element of dependency, since they have not yet attained full occupational independence.

The Youth Culture

The question may now be raised as to how young people react to this type of situation. Obviously, it is a highly variegated one and therefore occasions much diversity of behavior, but there are certain broad patterns which can be distinguished. These may be summed up under the conception, now familiar to social scientists, of a relatively differentiated "youth culture." Perhaps S. N. Eisenstadt is its most comprehensive student, certainly in its comparative perspective.[6]

It is Eisenstadt's contention that a distinctive pattern of values, relationships, and behavior for youth tends to appear and become more or less institutionalized in societies that develop a highly universalistic pattern of organization at the levels of adult role involvements. Since all lives start in the family, which is a highly particularistic type of structure, there is not only the difficulty of rising to higher levels within the same type of relationship system, but also of learning to adjust to a very different type. What has been discussed above as the enhancement of dependency in early childhood is a special case of this general proposition. Totalitarian societies attempt to bring this period under stringent centralized control through officially organized, adult-directed youth organizations such as the Soviet *Komsomols,* or earlier, the *Hitlerjugend.* In democratic societies, however, it tends to be relatively free, though in our own it is rather closely articulated with the system of formal education through a ramifying network of extracurricular activities.

As a consequence of youth's being exposed to such strains, it might be expected that youth culture would manifest signs of internal conflict and that it would incorporate elements of conformity as well as of alienation and revolt. In nonrational, psychological terms, rather than in terms of rational aims, youth culture attempts to balance its need for conforming to the expectations of the adult agencies most directly involved (parents and the local residential community) with some kind of outlet for tension and revolt and with some sensitivity to the winds of change above and beyond its local situation.

For two reasons, one would expect to find the fullest expression of these trends at the level of the peer group. For one thing, this group is the area of greatest immunity to adult control; indeed, the range of its freedom in this respect is particularly conspicuous in the American case. The other reason is that this is the area to which it is easiest to displace the elements of dependency generated in early experience in the family—on the one hand, because the strong stress on autonomy precludes maintaining too great an overt dependence on parents or other adult agencies, and, on the other, because the competitive discipline of school achievement enforces autonomous responsibility in this area. The peer group then gradually differentiates into two components, one focusing on the cross-sex relationship and one focusing on "activities," some of which occur within the one-sex group, others, relatively nonerotic, in mixed groups.

In general, the most conspicuous feature of the youth peer group is a duality of orientation. On the one hand, there tends to be a compulsive independence in relation to certain adult expectations, a touchy sensitivity to control, which in certain cases is expressed in overt defiance. On the other hand, within the group, there tends to be a fiercely compulsive conformity, a sharp loyalty to the group, an insistence on the literal observance of its norms, and punishment of deviance. Along with this goes a strong romantic streak. This has been most conspicuous in the romantic love theme in the cross-sex relationship, but it is also more generalized, extending to youth-culture heroes such as athletes and group leaders of various sorts, and sometimes to objects of interest outside the youth situation.

It is my impression (not easy to document) that important shifts of emphasis in American youth culture have occurred in the last generation. For the main trend, notably the increasingly broad band we think of as middle class, there has been a considerable relaxation of tension in both the two essential reference directions, toward parents and toward school expectations—though this relaxation is distinctly uneven. In the case of the school, there is a markedly greater acceptance of the evaluation of good school work and its importance for the future. This, of course, is associated with the general process of educational upgrading, particularly with the competition to enter good colleges and, at the next level, especially for students at the better colleges, to be admitted to graduate schools. The essential point, however, is that this increased pressure has been largely met with a positive response rather than with rebellion or passive withdrawal. The main exception is in the lowest sector, where the pattern of delinquency is most prominent and truancy a major feature. This is partly understandable as a direct consequence of the upgrading of educational expectations, because it puts an increased pressure on those who are disadvantaged by a combination of low ability, a nonsupportive family or ethnic background.

As to youth's relation to the family, it seems probable that the institutionalizing of increased permissiveness for and understanding of youth-culture activities is a major factor. The newer generation of parents is more firmly committed to a policy of training serious independence. It tolerates more freedom, and it expects higher levels of performance and responsibility. Further, it is probably true that the development of the pattern of "going steady" has drained off some tension into semi-institutionalized channels— tension formerly expressed in wilder patterns of sexual behavior. To be sure, this creates a good many problems, not only as to how far the partners will go in their own erotic relations, but also possibly premature commitments affecting future marriage. It may be that the pendulum has swung too far and that adjustments are to be expected.

Within this broad framework, the question of the content of peer-group interests is important. What I have called the romantic trend can be broadly expressed in two directions; the tentative terms "regressive" and "progressive" are appropriate, if not taken too literally. Both components are normally involved in such a situation, but their proportions and content may vary. They derive specifically from the general paradigm of social change outlined, the former, at social levels, tending to resist change, the latter to anticipate and promote it.

One of the most striking interests of American youth culture has been in masculine physical prowess, expressed in particular in athletics. It seems quite clear that there has been a declining curve in this respect, most conspicuous in the more elite schools and colleges, but on the whole it is a very general one, except for the cult of violence in the delinquent sector. The cult of physical prowess has clearly been a reflex of the pressure to occupational achievement in a society in which brains rather than brawn come increasingly to count. From this point of view, it is a regressive phenomenon.

The indication is that the lessened concentration on this cult is an index of greater acceptance of the general developmental trend. Alcohol and sex are both in a somewhat different category. For the individual, they are fields of emancipation from the restrictions of childhood, but they are definitely and primarily regressive in their significance for the adult personality. However, as noted, the emancipation of youth in this respect has been connected with a general emancipation which is part of the process of differentiation in the adult society, which permits greater expressiveness in these areas. I have the impression that a significant change has occurred from the somewhat frenetic atmosphere of the "flaming youth" of the 1920's and to some extent of the 1930's. There is less rebellion in both respects, more moderation in the use of alcohol, and more "seriousness" in the field of sexual relations. Youth has become better integrated in the general culture.

On the other side, the progressive one, the most important phenomena are most conspicuous at the upper end of the range, both in terms of the sociocultural level and of the stage of the life cycle. This is the enormous development of serious cultural interests among students in the more elite colleges. The most important field of these interests seem to be that of the arts, including highbrow music, literature, drama, and painting.

The first essential point here is that this constitutes a very definite upgrading of cultural standards, compared with the philistinism of the most nearly corresponding circles in an earlier generation. Second, however, it is at least variant and selective (though not, I think, deviant) with respect to the main trends of the society, since the main developments in the latter are on the "instrumental" rather than the "expressive" side. As to the special involvement of elite youth in the arts, it may be said that youth has tended to become a kind of "loyal opposition" to the main trends of the culture, making a bid for leadership in a sphere important to a balanced society yet somewhat neglected by the principal innovating agencies.

The question of youth's relation to the political situation is of rather special interest and considerable complexity. The susceptibility of youth groups to radical political ideologies, both left and right, has often been remarked. It appears, however, that this is a widely variant phenomenon. It seems to be most conspicuous, on the one hand, in societies just entering a more "developed" state, in which intellectuals play a special role and in which students, as potential intellectuals, are specially placed. In a second type of case, major political transitions and instabilities are prominent, as in several European countries during this century, notably Germany.

Seen in this context, American youth has seemed to be apathetic politically. During the 1930's and 1940's, there was a certain amount of leftist activity, including a small Communist contingent, but the main trend has certainly been one of limited involvement. Recently, there seems to have been a kind of resurgence of political interest and activity. It has not, however, taken the form of any explicit, generalized, ideological commitment. Rather, it has tended to focus on specific issues in which moral problems are sharply defined, notably in race relations and the problems of nuclear war. It does not seem too much to say that the main trend has been in accord with the general political characteristics of the society, which has been a relatively stable system with a strong pluralistic character. The concomitant skepticism as to generalized ideological formulae is usually thought deplorable by the moralists among our intellectuals. In this broad respect, however, the main orientation of youth seems to be in tune with the society in which they are learning to take their places.

The elements in youth culture that express strain because of deviations from the main standards of the adult society are by no means absent. One such deviation is what we have called the "romantic," the devotion to expectations unrealistically simplified and idealized with respect to actual situations. A particularly clear example has been the romantic love complex. It is interesting, therefore, that a comparable pattern seems to have appeared recently in the political field, one that is connected with a pervasive theme of concern: the "meaningfulness" of current and future roles in modern industrial society.

In the field of politics, one not very explicit interpretation of a meaningful role for youth in general is to exert a major personal influence on determining the "big" political decisions of our time. The realistic problem, of course, is the organization of large-scale societies on bases that are not rigidly fixed in tradition, not authoritarian, and not unduly unstable. In this respect, public opinion (though in the long run extremely important) is necessarily diffuse and, with few exceptions, unable to dictate particular decisions. The main policy-making function is of necessity confined to relatively few and is the special responsibility of elected representatives who, in large-scale societies, become professionalized to a considerable degree. The average adult citizen, even if high in competence and responsibility, is excluded from these few. Yet this is not to say that in his role as citizen his responsibilities are meaningless or that his life in general can become meaningful only if his principal concerns (e.g., his nonpolitical job) are sacrificed to the attempt to become a top "influential" in national politics. If this were true, representative democracy as we know it would itself be meaningless. The alternative, however (if large-scale society is to exist at all), is not populistic direct democracy but dictatorship.

This particular syndrome, of course, is a part of a larger one: the general difficulty of accepting the constraints inherent in large-scale organizations—

in particular, the "instrumental" aspect of roles other than those at the highest levels. We have already pointed out some of the features of our developing social system that make this a focus of strain. Equally, through the development of institutionalized individualism, there is a whole series of factors making for an increasing rather than a diminishing autonomy. The question, however, concerns the spheres in which the autonomy of various categories of individuals can operate. Differentiation inevitably entails mutual dependence: the more differentiation, the more dependence. In a system characterized by high levels of differentiation, it is to be expected that organizational policy making will also become differentiated. Hence, only a few will become very intimately concerned with it. The problem of what mechanism can control these few is indeed a complex one which cannot be analyzed here. The political role, however, seems to provide particularly striking evidence of a romantic element in current youth ideology.

Perhaps the most significant fact about current youth culture is its concern with meaningfulness. This preoccupation definitely lies on the serious and progressive side of the division I have outlined. Furthermore, it represents a rise in the level of concern from the earlier preoccupation with social justice—even though the problem of race relations is understandably a prominent one. Another prominent example is the much discussed concern with problems of "identity." This is wholly natural and to be expected in the light of *anomie*. In a society that is changing as rapidly as ours and in which there is so much mobility of status, it is only natural that the older generation cannot provide direct guidance and role models that would present the young person with a neatly structured definition of the situation. Rather, he must find his own way, because he is pushed out of the nest and expected to fly. Even the nature of the medium in which he is to fly is continually changing, so that, when he enters college, there are many uncertainties about the nature of opportunities in his chosen field on completing graduate school. His elders simply do not have the knowledge to guide him in detail.

It is highly significant that the primary concern has been shifting since early in the century from the field of social justice to that of meaningfulness, as exemplified by the problem of identity—except for the status of special groups such as the Negro. In terms of the social structure, this enhances the problem of integration, and focuses concern more on problems of meaning than on those of situation and opportunity in the simpler sense. It is a consequence of the process of social change we have outlined.

It is also understandable and significant that the components of anxiety that inevitably characterize this type of strained situation should find appropriate fields of displacement in the very serious, real dangers of the modern world, particularly those of war. It may also be suggested that the elite youth's resonance to the diagnosis of the current social situation in terms of conformity and mass culture should be expected.[7] Essentially, this diagnosis is an easy disparagement of the society, which youth can consider to be the source of difficulty and (so it seems to them) partially unmanageable problems.

Conclusion

The above analysis suggests in the main that contemporary American society is of a type in which one would expect the situation of youth to involve (certainly, by the standards of the society from which it is emerging) rather special conditions of strain. As part of the more general process of differentiation to which we have alluded, youth groups themselves are coming to occupy an increasingly differentiated position, most conspicuously, in the field of formal education. Though an expanding educational system is vital in preparing for future function, it has the effect of segregating (more sharply and extensively than ever before) an increasing proportion of the younger age groups. The extension of education to increasingly older age levels is a striking example.

The other main focus of strain is the impact on youth of the pace and nature of the general process of social change. This is especially observable in the problem of *anomie*. In view of this change, youth's expectations cannot be defined either very early or very precisely, and this results in considerable insecurity. Indeed, the situation is such that a marked degree of legitimate grievance is inevitable. Every young person is entitled in some respects to complain that he has been brought into "a world I never made."

To assess the situation of American youth within the present frame of reference presents an especially difficult problem of balance. This is an era that lays great stress, both internally and externally, on the urgencies of the times, precisely in the more sensitive and responsible quarters. Such a temper highlights what is felt to be wrong and emphasizes the need for change through active intervention. With reference to the actual state of society, therefore, the tendency is to lean toward a negative evaluation of the status quo, because both the concrete deficiencies and the obstacles to improvement are so great.

That this tendency should be particularly prominent in the younger age groups is natural. It is both to be expected and to be welcomed. The main feature of the youth situation is perhaps the combination of current dependence with the expectation of an early assumption of responsibility. I think that evidence has been presented above that this conflict is accentuated under present conditions. The current youthful indictments of the present state of our society may be interpreted as a kind of campaign position, which prepares the way for the definition of their role when they take over the primary responsibilities, as they inevitably will.

It seems highly probable that the more immediate situation is strongly influenced by the present phase of the society with respect to a certain cyclical pattern that is especially conspicuous in the political sphere. This is the cycle between periods of "activism" in developing and implementing a sense of the urgency of collective goals, and of "consolidation" in the sense of withdrawing from too active commitments and on the whole giving security and "soundness" the primary emphasis. There is little doubt that in this meaning, the most recent phase (the "Eisenhower era") has been one of consolidation, and that we are now involved in the transition to a more activistic phase.

Broadly speaking, youth in a developing society of the American type, in its deepest values and commitments, is likely to be favorable to the activistic side. It is inculcated with the major values of the society, and strongly impressed with the importance of its future responsibilities. At the same time, however, it is frustrated by being deprived of power and influence in the current situation, though it recognizes that such a deprivation is in certain respects essential, if its segregation for purposes of training is to be effective—a segregation which increases with each step in the process of differentiation. A certain impatience, however, is to be expected, and with it a certain discontent with the present situation. Since it is relatively difficult to challenge the basic structure of the youth situation in such respects (e.g., as that one should not be permitted to start the full practice of medicine before graduating from college), this impatience tends to be displaced on the total society as a system, rather than on the younger generation in its specific situation. From this point of view, a generous measure of youthful dissatisfaction with the state of American society may be a sign of the healthy commitment of youth to the activist component of the value system. However good the current society may be from various points of view, *it is not good enough to meet their standards*. It goes almost without saying that a fallibility of empirical judgment in detail is to be expected.

The task of the social scientist, as a scientific observer of society, is to develop the closest possible approach to an objective account of the character and processes of the society. To him, therefore, this problem must appear in a slightly different light: he must try to see it in as broad a historical and comparative perspective as he can, and he must test his judgments as far as possible in terms of available empirical facts and logically precise and coherent theoretical analyses.

Viewed in this way (subject, of course, to the inevitable fallibilities of all cognitive undertakings), American society in a sense appears to be running a scheduled course. We find no cogent evidence of a major change in the essential pattern of its governing values. Nor do we find that—considering the expected strains and complications of such processes as rapid industrialization, the assimilation of many millions of immigrants, and a new order of change in the power structure, the social characteristics, and the balances of its relation to the outside world—American society is not doing reasonably well (as distinguished from outstandingly) in implementing these values. Our society on the whole seems to remain committed to its essential mandate.

The broad features of the situation of American youth seem to accord with this pattern. There are many elements of strain, but on the whole they may be considered normal for this type of society. Furthermore, the patterns of reaction on the part of American youth also seem well within normal limits. Given the American value system we have outlined, it seems fair to conclude that youth cannot help giving a *relative* sanction to the general outline of society as it has come to be institutionalized. On the other hand, it is impossible for youth to be satisfied with the status quo, which must be treated only as a point of departure for the far higher attainments that are not only desirable but also obligatory.

Clearly, American youth is in a ferment. On the whole, this ferment seems to accord relatively well with the sociologist's expectations. It expresses many dissatisfactions with the current state of society, some of which are fully justified, others are of a more dubious validity. Yet the general orientation appears to be, not a basic alienation, but an eagerness to learn, to accept higher orders of responsibility, and to "fit," not in the sense of passive conformity, but in the sense of their readiness to work within the system, rather than in basic opposition to it. The future of American society and the future place of that society in the larger world appear to present in the main a *challenge* to American youth. To cope with that challenge, an intensive psychological preparation is now taking place.

References

1. Willard Hurst, *Law and Social Process in United States History* (Ann Arbor: University of Michigan Press, 1960), ch. 2.
2. To sociologists, the frustrating aspects of a favorable situation in this sense may be summed up under the concept of "relative deprivation." See Robert K. Merton and Paul Lazarsfeld, *Continuities in Social Research: Studies in the Scope and Method of The American Soldier* (Chicago: The Free Press of Glencoe, Illinois, 1950).
3. See Talcott Parsons and Robert F. Bales, *Family, Socialization and Interaction Process* (Chicago: The Free Press of Glencoe, Illinois, 1955), especially ch. 1.
4. For example, I am quite certain that the general level of academic achievement on the part of students of Harvard College and the Harvard Graduate School has substantially risen during my personal contact with them (more than thirty years).
5. The emancipation of components that were previously rigidly controlled by ascription is of course a major feature of the general process of differentiation, which could not be detailed here for reasons of space.

6. S. N. Eisenstadt, *From Generation to Generation* (Chicago: The Free Press of Glencoe, Illinois, 1956). See also his paper in this issue of *Dædalus*.

7. For an analysis of this complex in the society, see Winston R. White, *Beyond Conformity* (New York: The Free Press of Glencoe, 1961).

Some Theoretical Problems in the Study of Youth *

Sheila Allen

Introduction

Young people in industrialized societies share in a common experience of being considered non-adult and are excluded from full participation in adult society. They are admitted into adult status by formal and informal processes, which can be abrupt or gradual and which in Britain take place at different ages in different areas of social activity. This situation is frequently contrasted with non-industrialized societies in which the transition from childhood to adult status is institutionalized and clearly marked by formal ceremonies. This contrast is explained by a variety of factors, such as the reduced significance of kinship based organizations in allocating adult status, the increasing differentiation accompanying the division of labor and the degree and rate of social change. It is also seen as giving rise in industrialized societies to conflict and discontinuity, which are usually characterized in terms of the emergence of youth cultures, youth movements and the problems of youth which are not present in other types of society. The sociological explanations advanced to account for youth problems and cultures contain biological and psychological assumptions as well as assumptions about the nature of the processes and relationships which characterize industrial and non-industrial societies. There is a dominant approach based on integrative models of social analysis in which common value patterns play a major part in articulating social relationships. The problems of youth then become organized into an explanatory scheme in which adjustment to the major value orientations and symbols of a particular society is stressed.

Sheila Allen, "Some Theoretical Problems in the Study of Youth," from *The Sociological Review* (Vol. 16, No. 3, New Series, November 1968), pp. 319–331. Reprinted by permission of the publisher.

* Paper presented to the Yugoslav National Conference of Sociology, Split, Yugoslavia, 16th February, 1968.

The process of such adjustment is assumed to give rise to the problems and stresses of adolescence in modern societies and the coalescence of youth into cultural groups to emphasize "their problematic, uncertain standing from the point of view of cultural values and symbols." [1] This kind of social analysis is derived from the normative functionalist models most highly developed in the work of Talcott Parsons. Criticisms of this approach are increasingly made on the grounds of its theoretical inadequacy; that it stresses stability and continuity, that it is unable to account for structural change and conflict and so on.[2] But so far there is little criticism of the use of concepts and emphases drawn from this approach and applied to the analysis of problems, particularly social problems.

Theoretical Considerations

In investigating the position of colored, immigrant youth in Great Britain this model of an integrative social system articulated through common values is inadequate and moreover misleading. It leads to conceptualizing the problems in terms of value differences and sees the resolution of these problems in terms of adequate socialization for integration into British society. Each of the characteristics, color, immigrant and youth can be the basis of social differentiation. But even where such differentiations exist they cannot explain the behavior of these categories. Indeed in order to understand the operation of these characteristics it is necessary to use a radically different approach.

The social position of youth cannot be separated from the overall social structure in which it is located nor can the approach to youth, as a sociological problem, be understood apart from the general theoretical scheme which is used, implicitly or explicitly, to define and analyze the problem. Perhaps the most thorough-going attempt to deal with the social position of youth in recent years is the work of S. N. Eisenstadt, *From Generation to Generation*.[3] Eisenstadt's analysis of the position of age groups, youth movements and so on seeks on a comparative and historical basis to specify the conditions under which such phenomena will exist. His aim is both theoretical and practical and he claims relevance for his work to the understanding of present day youth cultures and problems. It is my contention that, whatever the merits of Eisenstadt's attempt at a comprehensive analysis of the problem on a theoretical level, and however suggestive his data, his work has little

[1] "Archetypal Patterns of Youth" in S. N. Eisenstadt (Ed.): *Comparative Social Problems*, New York, 1964, p. 140.
[2] See for instance, Hempel: "The Logic of Functional Analysis" in L. Gross (Ed.): *Symposium on Sociological Theory*, New York, 1959, pp. 271 ff. and D. Lockwood: "Some Remarks on the Social System," *British Journal of Sociology*, Vol. VII, No. 2, 1956.
[3] S. N. Eisenstadt: *From Generation to Generation*, Glencoe, 1956.

relevance either to the explanation, in a sociological sense, or to the understanding in a practical social way of the position of youth and the structural conditions of which it is a consequence. It is not my aim to give a textual criticism, which is impossible in a short paper, but to examine the basic assumptions used in this work and in a much more fragmentary way in other work on youth and to discuss an alternative approach which I consider to be more satisfactory theoretically and more relevant in practical approaches to the problem. Eisenstadt states that 'The crucial importance of age relations in all societies and of age groups in all universalistic societies is clearly seen in the fact that the smooth transmission of social heritage, various attempts at change and various manifestations of discontinuity are largely, even if not wholly, effected through them.' [4] Whilst the relations between those of different ages are of significance in all societies, to elevate these relations to a position in which stability, change, continuity and discontinuity are seen to be articulated through them is questionable for simple, relatively static structures; for complex, rapidly changing structures it is extreme sociological naïveté. Social relationships have to be understood as part of a dynamic process, in which social situations are the consequence of structural contradictions operating at different levels and with different intensity. Differentiations such as color, immigrant and youth involve a consideration of the dialectical interrelation of economic, power and ideological structures.

Generational Analysis within a Structural Context

The social world of men is passed on to succeeding generations as an objective social reality which each new generation does not create. Each new generation must individually and collectively live in the world of social relations and through action re-affirm or challenge it. Part of this world is the structure of legitimation passed on for acting in one way rather than another, which is learned within a system of rewards and penalties. But this is not the totality. The externality and objectivity of the world of social relations is not a matter of definition and redefinition by all social groups irrespective of the position in which they find themselves. Age relations (including youth) are part of economic relations and the political and ideological structures in which they take place. It is not the relations between ages which explain change or stability in societies, but change in societies which explains relations between different ages. Karl Mannheim in his generational analysis maintained that generational separation in terms of number of calendar years was an inadequate foundation for an analysis of social

[4] S. N. Eisenstadt: *op. cit.,* p. 323.

process and change. He distinguished between (1) a generational location in which people were located merely by accident of birth and biological rhythm; (2) the generation as actuality, those who shared a common destiny within a generational location and (3) generational unit which participated in this common destiny but responded differently to it.[5] Such distinctions point to the necessity of analyzing sub-groupings within any one generation and the relations between such sub-groups and other age groups in order to explain differential responses.[6] In complex (what Eisenstadt calls universalistic) societies, the experiences of sub-groups with different economic positions, differential amounts of power and differential access to education, housing, occupations, status and so on, cannot be assumed to be similar experiences, either subjectively or objectively, for the members of these groups be they 9, 19 or 90 years of age. In Britain the experience of a 19 year old working class youth is strikingly different from that of a middle- or upper-class person of the same age. This is not simply a difference of economic or social level but a difference which permeates every aspect of life. Comparison of these groups has shown, for instance, a relationship between the forms of language learning and thinking that are acquired through different social environments.[7] Nor does the existence of intergenerational social mobility between classes diminish the differences which exist in the class system. In societies with class systems the position of youth cannot be understood without reference to this system.

I would go further than this and maintain that in no society can we understand the position of youth unless we first ask what structures the everyday lives of members of the society, what groups develop in relation to these structures and what articulates the relational aspects of these groups. That is, we have to have an overall model which will enable us to select and give priority to those parts of the system which are consequential for other parts.[8] In societies without private ownership, and therefore without classes based on the ownership and non-ownership of productive property, it cannot be assumed that all factors have an equal weight in determining life chances and social experience. In such societies generational experience may

[5] Karl Mannheim: "The Problem of Generations," in *Essays on the Sociology of Knowledge,* Paul Keeskmeti (Ed.), London, 1952, pp. 276–320.
[6] Mannheim's explanation is in vague psychological terms, whereas a sociological explanation appears to be more adequate.
[7] B. Bernstein: "Social Class and Linguistic Development: a Theory of Social Learning," in A. H. Halsey *et al.* (Eds.): *Education, Economy and Society,* Glencoe, 1961, pp. 288–314.
[8] For a discussion of this problem of the relation of parts of the system see David Lockwood: "Social Integration and System Integration," in G. K. Zollschan and W. Hirsch (Eds.): *Explorations in Social Change,* London 1964, p. 244–256; A. W. Gouldner: "Reciprocity and Autonomy in Functional Theory," in L. Gross (Ed.): *Symposium on Sociological Theory,* New York, 1959; S. Ossowski: *Class Structure in the Social Consciousness,* London, 1963; and in contrast see T. Parsons: *The Social System,* Glencoe, 1951.

play a more determining rôle in social relations, but this is problematical, a matter for investigation within a framework which hypothesizes the relative autonomy of this factor and others such as sex, region, ethnic and strata or family origins in relation to economic and political power. An empirical enquiry based on a multiplicity of factors, without a systematic consideration of the relations within which these factors are operating, can at best give a partial description of processes; it cannot be the basis of an analysis of social relations. In societies with economic, political, religious, regional and ethnic differentiation the social position of youth is not a unitary phenomenon.

Empirical Studies

A recent survey of much of the existing European and American literature documents clearly how far most research on young people fails to take any account of the realities of the social structure in which the "problem" being investigated is situated.[9] ". . . general studies of adolescence are over-whelmingly concerned with biological and sexual development, and the major social changes are either ignored or discussed briefly and speculatively." [10] Out of eighteen general textbooks on adolescence, for instance, not one emphasized the adjustments necessary in starting work, though in most societies the vast majority of people enter their working lives at this time. Many studies concerned with the transition from school to work rely heavily on the stated aspirations of schoolchildren, rather than investigating the actual experiences of starting work. Others assume adjustment to work involves a "culture shock" deriving from the clash of values between pre-work expectations and the realities of the work situation and discuss this "shock" on the assumption that all school situations and all work situations are the same. In Britain this latter assumption is quite unrealistic; schools are highly stratified and pre-work experience varies not only with type of school, but also with class, neighborhood and family differences, whilst work situations can be differentiated along the lines of occupational and skill level, size, age and social composition of work group and so on. Unless these differences are recognized a blanket assumption about "culture shock"

[9] E. Teresa Keil, D. S. Riddell and B. S. R. Green: "Youth and Work: Problems and Perspectives," *Sociological Review,* Vol. 14, No. 2, July 1966.

I should like to thank the authors for allowing me to see two other papers prepared by them and to record my appreciation for the many discussions I have had, particularly with Mrs. Keil and Mr. Riddell on aspects of some of the problems discussed in this section, both during and after their work on "The Young Worker: Adjustment to Work Situations and Adult Rôles," a research project carried out at the University of Leicester of which I was an investigator from 1962–1964.

[10] *Ibid.,* p. 132.

can only obscure rather than explain the complex processes involved in different transitions from school to work.

Nor is there any agreement in empirical work on what constitutes youth. In Britain this has included the years from twelve to twenty-five or a block of years in between; or the basis has been from puberty to marriage. The right to marry, to vote, to own property, or enter legal agreements, to join the army, or drive a car, or drink alcohol in public and countless other formal rights are products of discrete historical processes and are conferred at a variety of ages with little or no reference to capability or lack of it. Those who attempt to use psychological bases as a guide confer an apparent order on this non-child, non-adult status but increasingly these attempts have been queried.

Although many psychological theories conceive of getting older as a developmental process, often divided into stages whereby human beings pass from immaturity to maturity, much empirical evidence has not supported these simple assumptions. C. M. Fleming comments "the development of the young human being is both more continuous, more complex and more highly differentiated than the psychologists of the past and popular writers of today would lead us to suppose." [11] Peck and Havighurst, who divide development into five stages with ideal-type character-types, found only a quarter of their sample approximated to the level of maturity and these were no more likely to be found among adults than among sixteen year olds. They also reported that a "sizeable minority," "perhaps over 50 per cent" of the adult American population was still in the first two stages of development.[12] Whatever status is given to such findings and to many others,[13] it seems clear that to accept personality development as a linear, inevitable process through which all normally endowed human beings pass to a stage of "adult maturity" is not a useful basis on which to begin to analyze youth. In terms of physical development adolescence may well be the peak period for such development, whilst social development or maturity is assumed to belong to adult status. The "ideal-typical adult" is part of a deeply embedded and pervasive ideological structure. Social adolescence, that is behavior not appropriate for adults, can be created and for the past 200 years societies in Western Europe have been creating adolescents.

The existing work on youth tends to present us with an evergrowing list of factors which seem to be influential but little or no attempt is made to specify their interrelation. In the transition from school to work, for instance, the list grows longer, but we are no nearer explaining the relative

[11] C. M. Fleming: *Adolescence,* London, 1948, Revised ed. 1963.
[12] R. F. Peck and R. J. Havighurst: *The Psychology of Character Development,* New York, 1960.
[13] See, for instance, Percival M. Symonds: *From Adolescence to Adult,* 1961.

significance of school, home, labor market, peer group or work experience in structuring attitudes, behavior and problems in the work situation of adolescents. This ignorance is frequently thought to stem from the difficulties of measuring these influences and the answer to lie in better questionnaire design or interview technique. So that instead of asking "Do you like your job?" and correlating the "Yes," "No" and "Don't Know" with five, fifty or more other variables, we now ask informants to rank money, friends, chances of social mobility and so on, and correlate the answers with job "satisfaction." Whilst it goes without saying that questionnaires and interviews can be technically efficient or inefficient and that a mastery of techniques is a necessity for those who propose to use them, the situation has developed, evident in a wide range of empirical research, where the technique dictates the structure of the research. So much so that for some years in Britain and America the "if it can't be measured, it doesn't exist" kind of sociology was dominant. Such research lends itself to ever more sophisticated statistical handling, but for those who are interested in understanding and explaining social processes it has so far been a peculiarly arid form of endeavor.[14] The dispelling of ignorance will not be achieved through more attention to techniques but through reassessment of the basic theoretical assumptions underlying studies of youth. If empirical research is to be relevant, then structural interrelationships must be recognized and some overall model developed which specifies these in terms of their hypothesized significance. Empirical work would then no longer be an accumulation of *ad hoc* correlations without social meaning and relevance, but a cumulative process in which we progressively identified the conditions under which different forms of social behavior developed. I have been able to mention only a few of the theoretical and methodological deficiencies encountered in most of the studies of youth with which I am familiar. The two outstanding problems which sociologists who are interested in explaining the behavior of young people face if they wish to make use of existing material is, on the one hand, the crude empiricism of much of the work and, on the other, the dominance of a naïve functionalist approach based on integrative models of society.

[14] The remarks by S. M. Miller in relation to aspirations could well be applied to much of the data on occupational choice and satisfaction/dissatisfaction with work. "I think that in social research we have been too prone to accept at face value solicited answers to deceptively simple questions; we have been willing to accept reliable scaleable items and have paid much less attention to the problems of validity. I do not believe that we understand enough about working class people at least to use indiscriminately the questionnaire techniques that are so widespread . . . I just do not understand the results and suspect them to be largely artifacts of sociological research production today." S. M. Miller: "The Outlook of Working Class Youth," a paper presented at the Annual Meeting of the American Sociological Association, Washington, August 31st, 1962.

Youth Viewed as Problematic

When youth is viewed as problematic this has consequences for investigation and for policy recommendations. Such a view is widely held by social workers, educationalists, and youth leaders, who face the task of getting youth to act in certain specifically approved ways, to stay on at school or college, to take and hold certain kinds of jobs, to reject delinquent peers, to become politically involved or whatever the specific problem may be.[15] Such ideological and legal contexts do not bind the sociologist in his analysis. Indeed it is necessary to reject problem-solving perspectives in order to carry out an analysis of the causes and consequences of inter-relations between social groups.[16] In a recent text on social problems, "The selections on youth attempt again to portray *the scope and variety of this problem. . . .* It is only under relatively specific conditions, connected with growing social differentiation, and with the diminution of the rôle of the family, that stage *has crystallized as an area of unmanageable social problems.*" [17] From a social science point of view several questions come to mind. What are the unmanageable social problems of youth? Why is it that youth in some types of societies come to be considered as problematical? Problematical for whom? First it would seem that youth is problematical for adults within given social contexts. On closer inspection these social contexts exist within industrialized societies, with developed patterns of the division of labor which produces groups stratified in accordance with certain economic and technical demands. Second, the problems which arise from this division of labor stem from the contradictions inherent in the structure and are unmanageable within that structure. The unmanageable social problem of unemployed youth in the United States, particularly Negro youth, with its far-reaching consequences seen in their most violent form each summer in many urban centers, can neither be understood nor solved in terms of a youth problem.[18] It is an unmanageable structural problem arising out of economic and social relations, and explanations in terms of the characteristics of youth are less useful for its solution than analyses of the structure of employment and the factors making for differ-

[15] S. M. Miller's paper, "The Outlook of Working Class Youth," *op. cit.* discusses this question with reference to educational drop-outs and the campaign to get young people to stay at school longer.

[16] Social problem oriented sociology would seem to have as one of its primary tasks not the solving of the problem, which in any case is likely to be well beyond the power of the sociologist, but a clarification of the ideological content in the definitions of social problems and the mystification functions of such ideologies.

[17] S. N. Eisenstadt (Ed.): *Comparative Social Problems,* New York, 1964, p. 134 (italics are mine).

[18] Nor as a colored youth problem where race and age differences are adduced as explanations.

ential access to jobs.[19] It is not "deviant" not to be employed, or to take up "delinquent" occupations if jobs do not exist or the achievement of reward is higher in delinquent than non-delinquent occupation. Nor is it "unrealistic" to leave school before completing the course, if continuing your education makes only a marginal difference to your occupational chances as seems to be the case for working class youths in Britain and the U.S. It is a popular belief that longer education brings material and social rewards. This may be so only if the education is well beyond that of others within the group or prior social status, in terms of parental origin, is relatively high. Miller suggests ". . . I believe we would find that graduation does not make a great difference for the working-class boy: it is the linkage of graduation with prior middle-class status that makes the difference in the overall results of high school diplomas to occupations. And I suspect that many working-class boys have some awareness of the facts about them." [20]

The low aspirations of some working class school children have been noted by investigators in Britain, whilst most others aim for a skilled trade, for which apprenticeship rather than longer formal education is the method of recruitment. This latter tendency has also been recorded by investigators in Poland and Germany. In France, on the other hand, handicrafts and small farming are given preference. Mobility aspirations are most frequently reported in work from the United States.[21] In my own research on colored immigrant youth the stated aspirations tend to be higher than for white boys of the same age and education. This may reflect a combination of a lack of knowledge of the processes by which such jobs are obtained and the structural obstacles to such achievement and a high motivation to get out of the narrow job range occupied by most of their parents, some of whom are well qualified for higher status jobs, or it may be due simply to parental pressure. With a structural framework the explanation of the behavior of unemployed youth or those who leave school early would not be presented in terms of a "lack of achievement motivation" or inadequate socialization to "common values" (or heritage), but would first assess the behavior in terms of the realities of the socio-economic situation. The realism or lack of it could then be related systematically to the total social situation in which young people enter work.

A different example of the tendency to reify youth may be found in the political sphere. A variety of characteristics are attributed to present-day youth; in politics the most frequent are apathy and idealism. The process towards political maturity is assumed by many political sociologists in

---

[19] The autobiography of Malcolm X contains very vivid descriptions of the socio-economic dimensions of this problem. *The Autobiography of Malcolm X*, New York, 1964.
[20] S. M. Miller: *op. cit.*
[21] See E. T. Keil *et al.: op. cit.*, p. 120.

Great Britain and the United States to involve compromise. Or put another way, conservatism increases with age. Further assumptions are made that young people are less bound by habit and old political ties than their elders and, therefore, more responsive to political pressures of the moment. Consequently it is argued it is to the young that we must look for one of the principal sources of political change.[22] Various explanations have been put forward to account for the political behavior of youth. Apathy is linked with an "end of ideology" argument; loss of idealism with coming to terms with realities; generational experience, particularly the post-war affluence is used to "explain" both activity and apathy, conservatism and change. The inconsistency of the assumptions, the contradictory nature of much of the data and the non-discriminatory type of explanation raise questions about the usefulness of the category of youth in relation to political behavior. In so far as young people are treated in a similar way, for instance in highly industrialized societies the young are excluded from positions of power, then they can be considered as a meaningful category as a first approximation. Their responses to this exclusion cannot be assumed to be "standard" regardless of their experience. In Britain it may be generally true that young people are "not very interested" in politics and could therefore be described as apathetic. Such "apathy" is not confined to the young. Among those who are active two broad groups which are not necessarily exclusive must be distinguished; those formally linked with the system of parties and those involved in "political" activities. In recent years the second category has included, among others, the Campaign for Nuclear Disarmament, the New Left and groups against the Vietnam War which have generally become known as the "politics of protest" and have largely arisen since the Suez Crisis of 1956. Discussing the political activity of young people, Abrams and Little came to some interesting tentative conclusions.[23] Four out of five activists came from families with records of political activity; seven out of ten support the same party and activism is related not so much to present experience as the experience of two or three generations ago. Support for different parties is related to overall perceptions of British society, particularly the nature of its class system. In overall terms ". . . there is little reason to treat the young in contemporary Britain as a new political generation. The perceptions and orientations of the age group as a whole are organized in an old frame of reference. Young activists, whatever their first hopes, are constrained to work old institutions and accept old possibilities. The pace of change is set by the political parties. . . . British youth has no collective political self-consciousness." [24]

[22] See, for instance, E. E. Maccoby, R. E. Mathews and A. S. Norton: "Youth and Political Change," *Public Opinion Quarterly*, Spring 1954, p. 23.
[23] P. Abrams and A. Little: "The Young Activist in Politics," *British Journal of Sociology*, Vol. XVI, No. 4, December 1965.
[24] *Ibid.*, p. 331.

Put into a more general context, the lack of equality of status, either in controlling the means of power or decision making within a given political structure, is seen clearly between parties and their youth sections in Great Britain. The majority seem to accept this definition of power between youth and adults.[25] Those who try to change the position are likely to find themselves disaffiliated and their section disbanded.[26] The problem of youth is that of being expected to be involved but being powerless. This is not a specific youth problem.

In situations of rapid change where new questions arise which cannot be dealt with by existing institutional arrangements, problems and discontinuities may be seen as, or expressed through, conflicts between generations, but sociologically would be more satisfactorily analyzed in terms of the dialectical relation between existing institutions and changes in structural bases of the society, which affect all ages within the society. For instance, institutional arrangements suitable for revolutionary and immediate post-revolutionary situations are not likely to work as the situation changes and new problems arise. The transformation of society is a continuing process within which constant re-analysis has to be made.[27] To conceptualize it as simply a conflict of views or policies between the "old guard" and the younger generation is to reduce the complexities of social structure to two opposed groups differentiated by age. This is not to say that generational experiences will not differ, and at times may differ markedly, but we add little to our understanding by ascribing such differences to age. When one generation grows up in a world structurally differentiated from the world in which the previous generation was raised, then the questions to be tackled by sociologists concern the identification of the structural differences, the differential impact of these on various sub-groups, and the consequences arising from the lack of congruence between the new problems and the existing institutional arrangements for tackling them. Political apathy or rejection may be a positive symptom of this lack of congruence of political institutions and political problems, and may be as much a characteristic of adults as of youth.

In putting forward a perspective in which the "problems" associated with youth can be seen as more general problems, many areas frequently asso-

[25] F. Musgrove in his work *Youth and the Social Order,* London, 1964, argues that adults impose a special irresponsible status upon the young and then justify their position by denouncing the young for behaving irresponsibly.

[26] The Labor Party has a long history of conflict with its youth section and deep differences on policy questions have led to closing it down on several occasions. With little effort at political education and virtually no attention to policy decisions passed by youth conferences, the conflict continues. The young are expected to work within given policy and without power to change anything.

[27] See W. Hinton: *Fanshen: A documentary of revolution in a Chinese Village,* New York, 1966, for an analysis of the relation between local institutional arrangements and structural change promoted by the Chinese Communist Party in the years before 1949.

ciated with youth have been neglected. The aim of the paper has been, however, not to cover "youth problems" comprehensively but to argue that a new approach to the subject, which puts it firmly into a framework of dialectical structural change, will prove more fruitful both for the analysis of past work and for future research.

American Youth and the Class Structure

Joseph Bensman

The youth revolution, while worldwide in its scope, is a relatively recent phenomenon. The "silent generation" of the 1950s drew the scorn of older leftists who, by and large, have since learned to appreciate the value of silence. The members of the silent generation were criticized as being careerist in orientation, interested only in occupational opportunities, and in making up for losses in their education and training caused by their participation in World War II. The only signs of disenchantment of youths in those years were an increasing tendency on their part to reject business as a career in favor of the professions, teaching, and the arts. Of course, a few became beatniks, "disciples" of Henry Miller and Paul Goodman, and fans of James Dean and Elvis Presley, but their number was small and largely confined to the West Coast.

The "great reawakening" of youth came after 1957 with the emergence of the Southern civil rights movement. The sit-in, the Freedom Ride, the passive resistance originated by Bayard Rustin and black youth, and symbolized and organized by Martin Luther King, gave rise to an explosion of long-repressed idealism and activism, which to many gave promise of unlimited expansion of freedom, euphoria, and personal liberation. John F. Kennedy, especially, captured this enthusiasm in national politics and promised to make it a moving force in American society.

By 1962 the hopes, idealism, and enthusiasm aroused by the civil rights movement were largely crushed by the inability to translate the efforts of the movement and earlier civil rights legislation and legal victories into solid political, economic, or educational gains. In the North, the hopes aroused by that movement were dashed by the inability of black groups to agree upon a viable program that would channel the protests and the

Original article, hitherto unpublished. Copyright © Joseph Bensman, 1971. First publication, in this volume, by permission of the author.

desire for participation into goals that could produce immediate results. The Northern civil rights movements were defeated by the anonymity of their enemies, the bureaucratic, administrative, legalistic, and jurisdictional obstacles to direct action. The passage of laws, and even poverty programs, did not appear to promise direct relief for the blacks' sense of outrage at white school boards, white parents of schoolchildren, and the unions, who were seen as being unresponsive to black demands. Blacks, in their frustration, adopted black nationalist, separatist, and militant slogans and postures. And white youth, whose enthusiasm was aroused by the civil rights movements and the promises implicit in the idealistic rhetoric but small budgets of the Kennedy and Johnson administrations, turned to new causes, but this time with a sense of frustration and increasingly radical aggressiveness directed at the society that had let them down.

These youths now turned in a number of directions. Some white college groups attempted to radicalize the blacks and Third World students, and others turned toward directing self-help programs for the blacks. And in this new activism, some youths discovered that they were being repressed by the universities. From this sense of repression emerged new coalitions and alliances, such as the Free Speech movement that in turn gave rise to other movements aimed at the expansion of freedom, including the Free-Sex and Filthy Speech movements, the antiabortion law movement, and the Women's Liberation movement. Moreover, the "repression" of initial protests gave rise to the discovery of new enemies. In the beginning, these were the universities and the police ("pigs"). But by the mid-1960s, when the escalation of the Vietnamese war in turn escalated the number of young men being drafted, it became possible to put all of one's enemies into one basket: American Imperialism, the military-industrial establishment, the power structure, and the establishment. The establishment was seen as using the university as its research and development branch, as its training center, and as its pool of talent and consultants, thus necessitating either the capture or destruction of the campus. Specific goals of the youth movement now ranged from demands for participatory democracy in the selection, retention, and promotion of staff; student design of curricula; a "voice," up to 50 per cent, in the election of all committees, senates, and other governing structures of the university.

At other times radical students demanded the banning of recruiting officers from Dow Chemical, Inc., and the CIA, the termination of Defense Department, CIA, or NASA sponsored research, or of secret research, the end of the IDA, and the abolition of ROTC, either in total or for credit. These students have also demanded the end of university cooperation with draft boards, and the immediate, unilateral withdrawal of American troops from Indochina. All of these demands were perceived as being connected to their opposition to the Vietnamese war and to the military-industrial complex that presumably initiated and now sustains that war.

In continuing alignment with the Black Revolution, white youths have supported demands for black and Third World studies programs and open-admissions policies, protested against the expansion of the universities into the ghetto, and demonstrated against university construction projects without a full quota of black building workers, even in those areas where skilled black workers were not available for such employment. They have attempted to organize black and Third World university employees, often despite the opposition of those employees.

In addition, certain factions of white middle-class youth, who by now are aging youth, have attempted to organize automobile workers and construction workers as well as the black poor. They have sought confrontation with the "pigs," the military forces, the courts, and the state legislatures, as well as with university officers. When these confrontations have failed, these youths have engaged in direct action, bombings, riots, and provocation. Their tactics have included peaceful protest, and picketing and demonstrations, but have also involved the more conventional strategies such as "militant" protest—forcefully occupying buildings, looting files, burning, rioting, beating, destroying the interiors of buildings, writing graffiti on campus buildings, shouting obscenities, provocatively calling names, and making threats, along with instances of intimidation and personal abuse. In the process, youthful radical groups have achieved many of their specific goals. They have caused significant changes in university ROTC policies, received wider representation in campus government, secured the introduction of new courses in many university departments, and ended parietal rules of social conduct implemented by university administrators.

Other youth groups, less radical and more oriented to peaceful protest and liberal causes and values, have, together with older liberals and leftists, championed the cause and presidential candidacy of Senator Eugene McCarthy in 1968, perhaps forcing President Johnson to withdraw in his campaign for re-election, and forced President Nixon to modify his Vietnam policy. Extremist youth groups have undoubtedly contributed to the backlash sentiments of the white working and lower-middle classes and, thus, to the election of Governor Ronald Reagan in California and President Nixon, and to the support of these classes of Governor George Wallace's presidential candidacy. They have disrupted some universities and helped to reduce others to second-rate status. They have helped to raise the specter of a new "hard hat" militancy, a new form of fascism, and the creation of a new manifest reaction and backlash on the part of the so-called silent majority. The no longer "silent youth" has awakened the no longer "silent majority"; their dialogue is one of riot, violence, and repression.

In the late 1960s and into the 1970s some of the undergraduate new leftists became postgraduates, instructors, lecturers, and assistant professors on the staffs of universities they once helped to disrupt. There they have been joined by older radicals, some who have newly rediscovered a long-past radical youth, and others who link a radical ideology, rhetoric, or posture to their personal ambitions and grievances.

Together, these groups have attempted to "seduce," activate, and lead students in new causes for old ambitions. The students have often been flattered by such attention and have become shock troops of bureaucratic manipulators and adventurers. And it is the students rather than their instructors who are beaten, suspended, or expelled.

As a result, the universities have increasingly been politicized, and political loyalty and activism have often replaced scholarship and intellectual craftsmanship as criteria for advancement, promotion, and tenure.

It is in the undermining of universities that the radical new middle classes have been most effective, and their increased or continued effectiveness could yet result in the destruction of the universities. But as graduates of the youth revolution enter their postgraduate world, the spirit of mindless activism, the desire for relevance, and the demand for a "voice," participation, and control, all may constitute increasing sources of conflict, change, and repression. In virtually every field, including government, the army, the church, social work, law, architecture, as well as all of the academic professions and the new politics, neophytes have demanded that the field be reconstructed to conform to their values, their programs, and their demands for control. If these groups were to succeed in implementing their demands, in imposing their values on the fields, and in restructuring both the organization of the field and its fundamental mission and content, the intended revolutions would be attained.

At present, such demands have not been successful; on the contrary, the "silent majority" has been vocalized, and the activities of the more radical youths have thus resulted in increased repression rather than "liberation."

The Inversion of Values

The sexual revolution, the drug revolution, and the revolutionary youth revolution represent the extremes of a fundamental reversal of values in the middle class.

Sexual freedom, promiscuity, and obscenity have long been regarded, at least stereotypically, as characteristics of the lower classes, whereas the middle classes were regarded as either repressed or hypocritical in appearing to be repressed. The emphasis on public pornography, sexual freedom, and provocative sexuality thus appears to be a break with the middle-class cultural tradition. In the same way, the smoking of "pot," and the addiction to narcotic drugs, with some exceptions (namely medical doctors), originated in the United States among lower-class ethnic minorities, especially among Negro jazz musicians and black "cats" who were *aficionados* of jazz.[1,2] The growth of "pot" usage among white middle-class youth originally resulted from the emulation by white beatniks of the stereotype of the free, loose, "stretched-out," expressive, and sexually uninhibited Negro cat and jazz musician. Recourse to violence was originally deemed to be an attribute of lower-class culture. The middle classes historically shunned personal violence. The radical youth movement uses violence and the provocation to counterviolence as a characteristic political and organizational tactic. Its violence is not "lower class" in the sense that it is related to interpersonal relations. It has now become a political violence.

The middle class characteristically was "law abiding," i.e., its law violation was usually legalistic and abstract, involving the manipulation of the "books" and the law and the perversion of governmental agencies, regulations, and legislative bodies. The new attitude, that the "establishment" is fundamentally immoral, has resulted in an entirely new conception of moral attitudes toward crime. These include the use of other people's credit cards, the charging of phone calls to other people's telephone numbers, the "liberation" of books, as well as the destruction or theft of files and office equipment, and the burning, bombing, and defacing of buildings. Some of these "crimes" are relatively new for the middle classes, but all of them are accomplished within an ideology of moral righteousness and with a sense of personal liberation. Again, this is an innovation in middle-class behavior.

At a deeper level, the middle classes have traditionally been characterized by "impulse control," by the struggle of a rational superego against the irrational, sensual id. The lower classes were often deemed to be subhuman because they were incapable of impulse control, but they were also envied because of their freedom of emotional expression. The "new" freedom of the middle classes rejects, in principle, the norms of impulse control. Thus, sexuality, adherence to drugs, and radical activism ideologize spontaneity, emotionality, sensuality, immediate gratification ("nowism"), and immediate relevancy while rejecting precisely those characteristics that were the hallmarks of their cultural past. In extreme form, many young radicals reject the slow, long-term acquisition of skills that in the long run contribute to the possibility of being personally effective. Perhaps to complete the paradox, it is precisely the militant black "lower classes," especially the Black Muslims and Black Panthers, who have begun to emphasize the discarded values of discipline, control, personal decorum, sobriety in dress, and opposition to drug taking and promiscuity at the same time that the middle classes have discarded these values and forms of behavior. These black movements have adopted these values as a means of achieving personal and organizational effectiveness.

[1] Harold Firestone, "Cats, Kicks and Color," *Social Problems,* 5 (Summer, 1957), pp. 3–13.
[2] Howard S. Becker, *Outsiders* (New York: The Free Press, 1963), pp. 79–95.

But the adoption by white middle-class youth of values and emotional stances previously associated with both the stereotype and reality of the lower classes is not simple emulation, for most white middle-class disaffiliates have little contact with blacks. At most, these disaffiliates are emulating a stereotype and responding directly or indirectly to the new black radical ideologies. We would doubt even this. Ultimately, disaffiliates are responding with a new consciousness of the repressive, the alienating, the unsatisfying conditions within their own families, schools, and communities. They are responding with an ideological and emotional consciousness that makes those conditions, accepted and characteristic of the past, no longer acceptable. The fundamental problem is discerning why at this time this new consciousness has emerged. What are the historical, ideological, cultural, and emotional factors that turn the "silent generation" into a generation that cannot be ignored?

Causes of the New
Middle-Class Revolution

In the following sections, we present some of the hypotheses that have been advanced to explain the new middle-class revolution in sensibilities and values. In general, we recognize that no single hypothesis has been definitively "proved," and we doubt that definitive proof for any one hypothesis as a single cause is possible.

Freudian theory has been advanced to explain the conflict of generations in their struggle against authority and agencies of the parental authority, the schools, teachers, administrators, and the police. The institutions and processes of organized society,[3] according to this theory, are viewed as being representative of parental authority and embody the repressiveness (whether permissive or not) of the parent. The theory is, despite this simplification and, perhaps, vulgarization, capable of almost infinite illustration, exemplification, and extension, yet we would regard it as inapplicable.

We would not argue with the initial Freudian premises on which the theory is based. Oedipal conflict, hostility, and ambivalence to parents and parental surrogates have occurred and do occur with some frequency in a wide variety of cultures and epochs. Because of this very wide range of appearances, the theory does not explain the occurrence at any given time of a particular "youth revolution" nor does it explain the style, form, or content of that revolution. Neither does it explain the immeasurably more frequent eras and epochs in which the "conflict of generations" or youth revolution was not salient. Such a theory, for instance, would not explain the "silent generation" nor the emergence of a youth rebellion in the 1960s and its

[3] Lewis Feuer, *The Conflict of Generations* (New York: Basic Books, Inc., 1969).

continuous evolution in form, style, and content through the 1960s into the 1970s. Historical theories are thus necessary to explain particular revolutions and their particular social and cultural content.

One sociohistorical theory sees the modern youth revolution in terms of historical changes in the significance of youth as a social category. Thus, it is argued that since the late Middle Ages, youth has become increasingly recognized as a separate social category, distinct and different from adulthood and subject to separate definitions, treatment, self-conceptions, and interests.[4] As an element of this changing youth category, it has become possible for youth to think increasingly of itself as a separate class, one with a growing self-consciousness and self-directedness. Moreover, the upper age limit of youth has consistently risen so that at present the dividing line between youth and adulthood is defined by youth at about age thirty. Such a definition is "realistic" since it is at about this age that middle-class youths complete their education, enter the labor market, and become economically self-sufficient, i.e., no longer economically dependent upon their parents.

If this is true, then it is urbanism and industrialism that ultimately contribute to the definition of youth as being "middle-aged" by earlier generational standards. Capital intensification in a postindustrial society makes it possible for youth to remain outside the labor force often until the age of thirty, and the needs for a literate, technically or administratively trained professional and managerial class make the delay in entering into the labor force a positive virtue.

But none of these needs, by themselves, produce a youth revolution. It is also argued that youth matures biologically at the same age (and even earlier) than in the past, but is increasingly treated as "youth": incompetent, unserious, and sexually immature. In earlier times the storms and rages of unfulfilled desire coexisted with a puritanism that was adjusted to early marriage. But at present biological maturity is out of phase with social and economic maturity, and the revolution that ensues is oriented to regain the "natural" advantages of hedonism, license, and sexual freedom. Such a theory by itself might well explain a sexual revolution but not other forms of revolution. In psychoanalytic theory, however, all other revolutions might be derived from youth reaction to the displacement of the "sexual repression" inherent in postponed biological needs. Historically, we know this is not true of the most recent period, and we doubt it was true of earlier periods. Sexual revolutions have existed without political revolution and vice versa. The Bolsheviks were by and large sexual puritans, and the flaming youth of the 1920s were not political revolutionaries.

The Free Sex movement and the Filthy Speech movement emerged at Berkeley after the Free Speech movement. The political movement preceded and was independent of the sexual movement, but political protest gave

[4] Phillipe Ariès, *Centuries of Childhood* (New York: Alfred A. Knopf, Inc., 1962).

legitimacy to all other forms of provocative protest, whether sexual or porno-graphic. Indeed, it appears that sex and pot do not mix well. The latter is often a depressant for the former; but pot may, like alcohol, serve to relieve embarrassment and release inhibitions. It may also induce feelings of satis-faction with sexual performance which in its absence would be otherwise evaluated as less than adequate. A sincere and disciplined commitment to political protest, moreover, requires as much control over sex as it does over the intake of illegal narcotics. The linkage of each movement to the others is, at most, symbolic of an over-all spirit of protest, although of protest by different revolutionary segments of the middle class to different aspects of middle-class culture. Thus, it is youthful revolutionaries who will protest the sexual libertinism and sexual repressiveness of the older middle classes and then indulge in symbolic and provocative sexuality that is less sexual in form than it purports to be.

Yet there is some truth to the argument that extended adolescence causes a number of forms of malaise and discontent that result in provocative political and social rebellion. An extended adolescence intensifies and ex-tends all of the normal problems of youth. Middle-class youths are denied the commitments of having to take and accept a job and a career and of being responsible for oneself and for others, i.e., children or a spouse. Youth spends its youth in "making up" its mind and preparing for respon-sibilities that seem to be forever postponed. The crisis of identity—of deciding who one is, what one wants and will become—and the responsibil-ity for working toward the goal decided on are interminable. And while all of these problems occur at relatively comfortable economic levels, the self-probing, the self-doubt, and the mutual exploration of subjective conscious-ness and ideals are all intensified. The pain and the indecision of probing, waiting, and ruminating are both extended and magnified.

The desire for commitment, for action, and for "reality" are all intensi-fied, and positive goals are provided primarily by a negative reaction to institutions and life-styles that are the source of their inactivity. The protest turns upon the immediate life situation of the protestor, who "naturally" attempts to absolve himself from personal responsibility for his sense of alienation. He seeks to objectify himself, to find specific, objective situations at which to express the protest, and in so doing to find causes to which one can make a commitment. Making a commitment consists of escaping from the subjectivity, the rumination, the indecision of one's situation, of losing self-consciousness, and finding deep, rich emotional experience through which subjective intellectuality is overcome. Political movements, com-munitarian movements, pot, and sex are all means by which one loses self-consciousness. But all of these attempts to "lose oneself" have in common the quality of causing that loss of self to be only a temporary phenomenon: repeated doses are required, and repeated doses have a diminishing effect. The overcoming of radical subjectivism is ultimately accomplished by the total defeat in the attempt, by psychosis, or by the discovery of an objective media in which short-term commitments are exchanged for long-term ones. Long-term commitments allow their possessor to endure short-range self-consciousness for the sake of long-term goals.

Permissive Child Rearing and the Permissive Society

Some sociologists, psychologists, and critics point out that the present generation of middle-class youth is the first generation to be brought up under the several versions of the permissive tenets of Freudian psychology and of Dewey's educational philosophy. They have observed that middle-class youth have been deprived of a sense of limits and authoritative role models, and because of this, of an effective superego. An even more serious result, according to these critics, is that modern middle-class youth have been deprived of the experience and capacity for organizing and disciplining themselves in order to free and overcome the obstacles and constraints that are required in dealing with external reality, an element intrinsic to healthy growth. Because of these defects in the ego, modern youth as a generation is psychodynamically explosive. Minimal frustration incites tantrums, cop-outs, and protests against the very conditions that when mastered allow the achievement of the self-control and discipline necessary to do one's own thing. At one psychological level, tantrums and protests are seen as an attempt to recapitulate, if not retain, the warmth and protected status of infancy. They also secure the attention and concern of neglectful parents who equate permissiveness with indifference and neglect.

The schools, it is argued, contribute to the syndrome by not making objective demands upon the child. Instead, the curricula, especially at the level of the early grades, provide warmth, "relevance," and psychological values instead of the supreme psychological value of the Western tradition—of overcoming the manifest resistances of the external world to their will to shape and control that world from the standpoint of the actor. The schools, according to this argument, do everything but educate, and in their emphasis on psychology and "methods," foster a habit of mind in which self-consciousness, self-manipulation, and the manipulation of others are the ultimate curricula. The concentration on psychology in education results only in the training of amateur psychologists to the neglect of cognitive materials. Thus, in later years when the schools shift their focus to an extreme emphasis on subject matter, the student is totally unprepared. Some students flounder and become early drop outs in either a territorial or psychological sense, and others adjust to the shift in emphasis by developing an amazing ability to master vast amounts of meaningless technical and irrelevant materials, a task performed without grace, pleasure, or interest. Given the joylessness and drudgery of such work, youths continue in this path until they can no longer stomach the indigestible mass of material thrown at them with no apparent purpose and meaning. The threshold of nausea varies from youth to youth, and depending upon age, results in various forms, styles, and content of rebellion and cop-out. Some will disengage at the level of junior high school, others in high school, and still others in college; the swinger makes his semirebellion and cop-out as an adult. But each style of rebellion and cop-out in each age group influences other age groups. Thus, middle-age swingers discover a new youth and new freedom in emulating their children, and middle-class high school and junior high school students, at increasingly younger ages, discover pot, sex, and revolution in emulation of college students. In this sense, the sources of cultural and political rebellion emanate to and from all generational directions.

The theory that locates the new middle-class revolution in Freudian psychology and progressive education is attractive because it links lower-class delinquent behavior with middle-class rebellion. In both cases it is the unavailability of parental models (in one case caused by the absence or unavailability of parents as role models, and in the other case caused by all of these plus overpermissiveness) and a discontinuous, overdemanding, and irrelevant education that causes territorial and psychological reaction and dropping out. For the lower-class youth this results in delinquency, life on the streets, drugs and drift and indulgence in "primary pleasure." For middle-class youth it results in all of these plus a rational, political, or provocative rebellion against the agents and institutions that force them to drop out.

Nevertheless, the analogy can be overdrawn, since black youth and adult movements have been aimed at primarily "copping-in" and sharing the fruits of middle-class success, whereas white middle-class movements have aimed at the opposite result. Both movements, as we have indicated, borrow from and emulate each other, although their goals are ultimately antagonistic.

Taken as a whole, the theories of excessive permissiveness see the middle-class youth revolution as a disease, a psychological disturbance, in which all the manifestations are a reaction formation to psychological and educational theories and practices. The theory neglects the motivation of parents and the structure of society as it has evolved since World War II. It forces us to attribute an enormous importance to psychological and educational theories without concerning ourselves with the social functions and meanings of these theories to the society that adopts them. We shall attempt to probe these meanings in the conclusion of this section.

Television and Mass Communications

It is argued by some observers of the youth scene that the middle-class youth revolution is the product of the first generation of youth that has lived all or the major part of its life in the light of the ever-burning television tube and in the noise from its speakers.

The exact relationship of the specific stimuli in television to the new revolutionary movement is not easy to specify. It is argued, but not provable, that violence seen on television causes acts of violence in the viewer; we shall not dwell on this. It is also argued that long hours spent in front of the television set results in an inability to concentrate and focus one's attention, and eventually causes an inability to compete in those activities that require concentration.

This argument flies in the face of the fact that the vast majority of committed political revolutionaries (but not young hippies) have been good students until the time they developed nausea with society and their family's life-styles.

It is also argued that television provides a premature sophistication, not only in violence and intimations of sex, but also in cynicism about the operation of the adult world. Moreover, it makes available an intimate portrayal of an apparent ease in doing what are often physically and intellectually impossible tasks. The television viewer takes on a blasé attitude toward virtuosity in sport, acrobatics, dance, and all other performing arts. Moreover, in portrayal, the viewer sees the world of the surgeon, the lawyer, the policeman, and others, as a series of triumphs accomplished by otherwise mediocre people. The magic of virtuosity, talent, and technique is removed in part by "behind the scenes" exposure and by overexposure. Such sophistication may be corrosive, if and when it results in a sense of failure and impotence when the youths make some slight starts and then experience difficulties in mastering the techniques that television portrays as easily accomplished and thereby devalues them.

However, this theory explains too much, and ignores those youths who are highly competent and successful up until the time of their rebellion. Another hypothesis concerning the effect of television on youth is more sympathetic. Television portrays, it is argued, most accurately the essence of our society. It exemplifies and portrays the noise, the dirt, the violence, the commercialism, the cynicism, the brutalization, the exploitation, the sexual obsessiveness, and the other negative aspects of our society. According to the argument, television is unable to present whatever is good in society except in cardboardlike, synthetic stereotypes thus emphasizing an exploitative overexposure to evil as compared with the positive values to be found in American society. This hastens the nausea and disgust that underlie the youth revolution, especially when the youths experience that disgust in their personal lives.

Like psychological and educational theories of the youth revolution, the television theory necessitates the elevation of television to the level of major, almost monocausal importance in our society. As far as we know, television reflects basic changes in public opinion and in the structure of society, but does not cause them. Once a cultural trend emerges that is sufficiently strong to attract viewers, the magnates of mass media will hop on the bandwagon in order to profit from it. For the very same reason, they will not innovate themes, ideas, and content (although they will convert new content to the particular forms of its own media). If this is true, television can only accentuate and make manifest trends that develop in other levels of our society.

Television as a media, however, is reputed to contribute to the new sensibility that underlies the youth rebellion. Television as a media has all the attributes of the movie camera and movie editing. It can present montage and kaleidoscopic effects, making its point by the association and disassociation of symbols and images. It can reverse and rearrange the sequence of time. It can construct a logic of its own, a "logic" of combinations of logically unrelated but of emotionally interconnected elements. It combines noise, music, words, and pictures, both live and still. It can employ color effects in color television, as it can combine live shots with animation effects. It suspends conventional literary images and throws a succession of sounds, images, words, noise volume, and music, at the viewer with such rapidity and change of pace that the total sensory receptors (except touch and smell) are at the mercy of the box.

As a result, conventional logic, rationality, and linear thought are overcome. The merely rational, and logical, is tepid and blasé after exposure to the hurly-burly of television. Having been exposed and overcome by such forms of thought, the individual is driven to experience them in his own life. The normal, rational means of personality control in Western society has emphasized rational self-control over these dark and explosive forces in the human psyche. Television, the movies, and the multimedia arts emphasize the orgiastic Dionysian elements in the psyche: the freedom achieved in the release from rational control. This freedom—mind extension—can be sought in LSD, in pot, in primitive music or its equivalents, in dance, and in orgiastic sex.

According to the argument, television, as a media (initially unintentionally), emphasizes those values that long have been suppressed and repressed in rational Western society, especially among the middle classes; but once released on a mass basis (they originally were expressed in modern art, music, literature, and poetry for the "classes"), they became the basis for a self-conscious quest for the nonlinear, the Dionysian, the orgiastic.

Although the argument has power, again, we think that it proves too much. The Dionysian elements in television have tended to emerge after they emerged among middle-class youth itself, and only after highly rational theoreticians told us that they were present in the media.

A final contribution of the mass media to youth rebellions can be found in the movies, especially the relationship of the new sex film and the sexual revolution. The sexual revolution portrayed in the cinema is primarily a product of foreign films. Hollywood, since the creation of the Hays office and until the success of European sex films, had produced an inverted puritanical image of sex in which sexual elements were suggested through subtle, complicated sexual symbolism, but never expressed openly.[5] The American public appeared to accept a portrayal of sexuality that was manifested by its own ambivalence to sex. The rise of television in the late 1940s and early 1950s outcompeted the movies in middle-class respectability, and movie attendance in the early 1950s declined by almost 50 per cent. The importance of European films—French, Italian, and Swedish—all with an increasing emphasis on manifest sexuality, nudity, homosexuality, lesbianism, and perversion, increasingly found a larger and larger market in the United States. After several decades of explicit sexual drought in the public arts, Americans apparently were hungry for public pornography, obscenity, and perversity: thus the European film exports were more successful in America than in Europe. In fact, as the success of such films became increasingly apparent, much of this European film export became specifically directed to the American market.

Off-Broadway theater, radical theater, and resurrected vaudeville shows hopped on the bandwagon, competing with the celluloid nude and lewd with live bodies. The new voyeurism could become more "real," the new obscenity more salient, and physical proximity to the real thing, with or without opera glasses, apparently provides more of a thrill. Radical film makers, using 16-millimeter cameras and new theories of pop art and op art managed to outdo others in public pornography, but in doing so they managed to make sex appear to be boring.

Meanwhile, a new film code was enacted in 1967 that allowed American film makers to compete in the market for the public viewing of nudity, the sexual act, and perversion, if they designated such films as having an "X" rating.

Television, within the limits allowed by fear of protest by those who object to public sex in the living room, has attempted to keep up with the film. In this it has been only partially successful, moving slowly but increasingly to liberate itself from the visual and aural restraints of its past. Television has adopted the sound, the images, the cutting-room techniques of the film, at a more sexually inhibited level than the movies, and yet continues to convey its masked message to the millions.

But whereas the film appears to have had these effects, a fundamental fact remains: Hollywood film makers were driven into manifest portrayals of sex by the "accidental" successes of marginal foreign films not originally geared to the "mass market." The market was only discovered after the fact

[5] Martha Wolfenstein and Nathan Leites, *Movies: A Psychological Study* (New York: The Free Press, 1950).

of the exhibition of such films.[6] The willingness to accept public nudity, public pornography, and public portrayals of the sex act and sexual perversion anticipated those portrayals. At the same time, the ever presence of such portrayals, we would suggest, tends to make the behavior "natural," normal, and legitimate. The dividing line between the public and the private becomes obliterated. The "mystery" of sex is obliterated and the ease of movement into sexual roles is facilitated. At the same time, sex as presented in the media is not yet accepted as totally "natural" to the extent that sex is presented as provocative and aggressive, as an intellectualized sign of liberation, and in a context of self-conscious obscenity and pornography.

In all of this, the movies and the other mass media have accentuated the trend toward greater sexual explicitness but have not created it.

A Proposed Theory of the Middle-Class Revolutions

Each of the theories that have been discussed contributes some elements to a comprehensive theory of the middle-class revolution, but it appears to us that in aiming at exclusivity, all of the theories neglect some factors and overstress others. We would like to attempt to construct a comprehensive theory of the causes of this revolution.

The basis of the youth rebellion, we believe, is to be found not in the youths themselves but in the structure of the American society as it has emerged since World War II, and as middle-class youth is related to that structure. The specific relationship of middle-class youth to its society is, of course, through its parents.

The new middle-class youthful rebel is the child of relatively prosperous, educated, middle-class parents, who are primarily professionals, administrators, and higher-level technicians. They are employed in the vastly expanded governmental and private and service bureaucracies whose growth has mushroomed since World War II. The parents were themselves the children of immigrants and small-town members of the old middle class. After World War II, they received college educations and were able to enter the new middle classes. They tended toward liberal and left-of-center politics, in-

[6] Hollywood film studios always understood the success potential in explicit sexual presentations for the American public; they were hamstrung by powerful anti-obscenity lobbies that had the power to pass restrictive legislation in every state, perhaps in hundreds of municipalities, that would have required making hundreds of versions of the same film in order to pass censorship boards. Of course, this was economically impossible. Oddly, Hollywood (under supervision of the self-censoring Hays office) ordinarily made two versions of every film where sex scenes were included: a suggestive but "cool" version for the domestic market and an explicit and "hot" version for foreign consumption. (See B. Rosenberg and H. Silverstein, *The Real Tinsel* [New York: The Macmillan Company, 1970].)

cluding radicalism and bohemianism, and were aspirants to "higher culture" and intellectual accomplishment. This generational group provided the essential impetus and/or life-style that other nonimmigrant generational peers were eventually swept into. Most were relatively successful by the standards of their own parents. Their success, in the light of the experience of the Great Depression, was unanticipated and unanticipatable, and most were successful in different occupational areas than what was expected in the light of their original cultural and intellectual aspirations. The source of their new success was their ability to serve as technicians, "civil servants," administrators, experts, researchers, and public agents for large-scale organizations that have defined the areas of occupational opportunity in post-industrial society. In a large degree, the new classes were "superclerks" who found little cultural and intellectual autonomy in their work.[7]

The occupational experience produced a sense of cultural deprivation, and as a result, the new middle-class parents attempted in their personal lives to create life-styles that were suffused with cultural pursuits, political liberalism, prestigious leisure (golf, boating, tennis, folk-dancing, country-club sophistication, sophisticated consumption, interior decorating, stereo equipment, art purchasing and the like).

In all of these activities, the parents were handicapped because they were products of small-town American Gothicism and yahooism or of Metropolitan immigrant stock. The ways of life to which they aspired were not "natural" to them, nor were they natural to any but a few upper-class WASPS (White Anglo-Saxon Protestants) in areas of first settlements along the East Coast. Thus, the new middle classes were uncomfortable in their new roles. Moreover, they were uncomfortable as liberals and as "leftists" in work roles that, at most, were ideologically neutral, and in a society that robbed them of their distinction by becoming "liberal" without producing drastic changes.

As parents, the new middle class was permissive, not according to ideological commitments to Freud or Dewey, but to a liberal, permissive way of life. Moreover, in their own intellectual, cultural, and ideological ambivalence, they were, as a whole, not effective as role models. They were committed to higher cultural "values," but not deeply cultured. They were politically liberal and left of center, but worked in organizations that provided them with good livings but were conservative or politically neutral. The "clerical" work they did was not a source of pride and could not provide them with a basis for a source of positive identification for themselves and for their children. Their permissiveness thus consisted in having few deep commitments about which to be "repressive" or restrictive.

Because of their personal problems, divorces, self-preoccupations, or

[7] A more detailed presentation of this argument is to be found in Joseph Bensman and Arthur Vidich, *The New American Society* (Chicago: Quadrangle Press, 1971).

the pursuit of their own pleasures, some parents were unable to make themselves available to their children as positive objects for identification. Some parents surrounded their children with love, warmth, and permissiveness, but relatively few parents were able to provide channels for the disciplined but autonomous expression of the energy and creativity that emerges in the children when the parent provides a protected environment. In part, the lack of restraints—"love is not enough"—blocked the development of identification, of a superego, and of an image of tasks and ideals, media and channels by which one can objectify and discipline the energy that emerges in such a protected environment.

The new middle classes, of course, were interested in many ways in the intellectual, cultural, and political development of their children. First, they were interested in compensating for their own relatively prosperous futility, by exemplifying for their children the political ideals that they themselves did not act upon. They suggested and pressured their young into artistic, cultural, and intellectual achievements, to which their parents in their own lives gave only nostalgic lip service. In so doing, they, with all of their liberalism and permissiveness, attempted to manipulate their children into the pursuit of these "higher goals," providing lessons in music, dance, and painting through specially financed supervision to the point where such parental concern becomes a form of suffocating personality absorption. Moreover, with true middle-class prudence, they attempted to direct these cultural, scientific, and intellectual pursuits of their children into fields and occupations that were profitable or would provide their children with opportunities for economic and social mobility. Within the limits of parental income and the talents or abilities of their children, they aimed their children at the professions and the arts and toward those educational institutions that were most prestigious and conducive to success.

In the midst of this general scramble for educational success, the Soviet launching of Sputnik in the 1950s provided an impetus for increasing the standards and level of training in middle-class high schools. The level of competition increased; standards of performance were strengthened; goals were raised. And the middle-class child, in the midst of this situation, was exposed to and, at least at the unconscious level, saw and understood the underlying dynamics for the new rat race.

The young experienced a discontinuity between the love and warmth and the exploitative pressure on the part of his parents. They saw that activities into which they were pushed by their parents were much more the product of the parents' aspirations than their own. The young were rarely given the opportunity to form their own aspirations, since as soon as they showed a "constructive interest," the parents "took it away" by pressuring them in the direction of that interest. Moreover, the parental interest tended to be fraudulent: parents were more interested in success than in the interest itself.

Moreover, because of the parents' "cop-outs" from their own artistic, intellectual, or political interests, they could not demonstrate in their own lives the consistent rationale or dedication that they expected of their children. To the children, their parents were frauds. Thus, to many of the young, high school work and college work became high-pressure rat races, boring treadmills to no clear or valuable ends. If the child was successful, he might end up like his parents, a superclerk.

Some children could not stand the pressure, even at relatively early ages, and began to "drop out," but the middle-class dropout is relatively sophisticated. He emphasizes the hedonism, the permissiveness, and the cultural style of the parents as sophisticated consumers (but not, of course, as producers). His life-style involves drugs, music, sophisticated sexuality, new hip and beat and mod dress and tonsorial styles. This is provocative to the parents and parental surrogates. It strikes deeply because it attacks the success orientation of the parent and emphasizes, in so doing, his swinging, modish behavior to the exclusion of other values held by the parent.

The dropout demonstrates to the middle-class parents, their hypocrisy, their failure as parents, and the "sellout" of their own values.[8] And parents are defenseless to these psychological attacks because the children use the parents' own weapons and values in their attack. Of course, the children go beyond merely psychological weapons. Pot and hard drugs, music, sexual freedom, new dress styles and language styles have become cultural properties that are all part of a new cultural system and a new mode of sensibility. Once these styles of behavior become culturally standardized and disseminated by the mass media, they become an armory of weapons to be used against parents and the adult establishment. The new cultural styles become supported by peer-group networks, which along with the creation of such almost forgotten territorial bases in North Beach, Haight-Ashbury, the East Village as well as the new urban and rural communes, provided for the young opportunities for flight from the home, the suburbs, the schools, and the whole "fraudulent" middle-class world.

But, contrary to some theorists, it is not failure alone that drives much of middle-class youth to rebellion or revolutionary ideologies. Many of the new revolutionaries have high I.Q.'s and many have had and do have high grades in both their secondary school and college careers. In initially accepting their parents' goals for themselves they became virtually masters at running the rat race. They worked hard and developed the necessary educational and social graces. They engaged in the proper extracurricular activities. They qualified for and were admitted to the best colleges. And at some point in their long-extended educational career they discovered the "meaninglessness" of it all, the tastelessness and the drudgery. They went ber-

[8] See also Kenneth Keniston's *The Young Radicals* (New York: Harcourt Brace Jovanovich, 1968) for further documentation and elaboration of this point.

serk, politically, sexually, and/or culturally. The explanation of this phenomenon, we think, must go beyond that which we have already described.
First of all, middle-class radical youth, as a result of parental training, have
been exposed to the highest ideals of Western society. They have been
exposed to political liberalism and equalitarian ideals. Secondly, unlike their
parents and the working and lower-middle classes, they are not seduced
by the attractiveness of mobility, material success, and "making it." They
have seen these attractions in their homes and are not enchanted by them.
Success does not provide too great a pull on them, since they are already
materially successful in their families. Thirdly, the images of the kinds of
jobs and careers they will graduate into are not very attractive. They will
become, like their parents, superclerks in organizations that provide no
support for their ideals. The channeling of energy, the acquisition of skills,
the drudgery, all serve no useful ends as defined in the higher ideals of a
new upper-middle-class elite.

Thus, the new middle-class prosperity has produced an escalation in the
amount of idealism among increasingly larger segments of youth. The
permissive early environment has led youth to expect an immediate gratification of its wants, but the discontinuity in educational and occupational
demands has led to a sense of anticipatory frustration, or stated differently,
a sense of impotence. Youth wants to change the world to conform to its
higher idealism, but it finds that at every institutional level it must conform
to objective, impersonal, competitive standards that are only geared to
careerist success. The sense of impotence in youth consists of a feeling that
it cannot change the establishment. Youth cannot change the establishment,
but it can perhaps destroy it.

The feeling of disaffiliation, rejection, and revolution is, however, not
purely a personal reaction to parents, schoolwork, and "the establishment."
These personal reactions are given philosophical, social, and ideological
content by reference to the works of older and newly emergent intellectuals
and ideologists: Proudhon, Marx, Bakhunin, Freud, Lenin, Trotsky, Weber,
Sorel, Mao, Mills, Goodman, Brown, Castro, Marcuse, Debray, Guevara,
and Fanon have all articulated images of a repressive establishment or of a
repressive tolerance, or have become interpreted as doing so. They have
provided images of a world free of the tensions, angularities, stress, emptiness, and lack of fulfillment that currently define alienation. Some have
suggested that the only way to create a world free from alienation is to
destroy the present world and replace it with either a Utopian world or a
world that will emerge, free and spontaneous, out of the ashes caused by
revolution. The present world is too corrupt, too bureaucratic, and too
complex to be reformed. Total change and "restructuring" are necessary.

Thus, existential despair is tied to revolution, producing a sense of total
commitment and excitation.

The formula of absolute idealism plus the sense of impotence as a basis for revolutionary nihilism is not new. On the contrary, in the past, wherever the combination expressed in the formula has been experienced as a large-scale phenomenon, it has produced a desire to escape both the boredom and emptiness of daily life by means of exciting and dangerous debauchery and the self-indulgence of alcohol, gambling, and violence. This combination has also resulted in political adventurism that aims to destroy the society that alienates its members and destroys the sense of self.

But in the past, such antisocietal movements have been the products of the lower levels of the upper classes and the upper levels of the middle classes. It is in these groups, freed from the immediate necessities of survival and given the opportunities of maximum ideological and intellectual self-development, where absolute idealism has flourished. But the ruling classes have always produced more children than are able, available, and necessary to rule. The children are made to feel impotent by virtue of their numbers, their ideals, and their lack of specifically useful training. As a result, they turn into a rage against the society, which renders them even more impotent. Such feelings of despair, debauchery, and political adventurism were highly developed among the impotent upper classes of the Golden Age of Athens, in post-Augustan Rome, and among the aristocracies of the *ancien régime* in France, and reached extremes in nineteenth-century Czarist Russia among the Narodniki, and in Berlin between the world wars.

In American society and in much of the Western world today the feelings described have entered the consciousness of the youth of the new middle classes and among the older swingers. The managerial and bureaucratic revolutions and the new prosperity have raised middle-class youth to the level of idealism and impotence that was only experienced by the gentry and aristocracies of the past.

In one sense, this new development represents a failure for all advanced industrial societies, for it means that the parents, society as a whole, and our educational and cultural institutions have failed to provide specific means and ends by which the energy and idealism of youth can be properly channeled. In failing to provide such channels, "society" has left these energies and ideals to be turned against itself. The failure of contemporary society to find or create such channels constitutes a greater problem than has ever occurred in the past because the new middle classes represent a greater percentage of the total population of industrial society than did the gentry and aristocracies of the past.

Some Prospects for the Future

We have indicated that a major contributing factor to the disenchant-ment of youth is its perception of a lack of authenticity, integrity, and honesty among its elders. This lack is evidenced not only by a formless permissiveness of the parents but by the willingness of teachers to "sell out" to whomever has money, power, and authority. College teachers and university officials appear to be willing to sell out to radical youth whenever radical youth appear to have power and stridency and are able to generate a broad base of student support. Some teachers attempt to anticipate the wave of the future, without being able to judge the strength of that wave, and help, at least temporarily, to increase the erosion of that wave. Others ride the wave for other reasons, still others are simply gutless, and some are part of the wave. In most of these cases, the response to the "wave of the future" represents a lack of the teacher's confidence in his own standards. The recovery of standards and an authenticity in exemplifying them would contribute much toward a major solution to the problems of youth. Some intellectuals have recovered a sense of their standards in response to the mindless anti-intellectualism of radical youth. But whether the older generation have, in fact, gone too far in the variety of sellouts of themselves and their own standards, or whether there are any standards left at all, is, at least, an open question. The necessity for adults to provide youth with authentic standards of its own is based upon the need of youth to find ideals and media by which these ideals can be channeled into behavior that objectifies those ideals, consuming energy released by favorable early life, and providing a sense of commitment to long-term tasks. For it is the failure of youth to find such channels that gives rise to its sense of impotence and alienation. We would argue that such channels are not likely to be found in most work that is available to middle- and upper-class youth. The bureaucratic and managerial work in modern industrial society is too narrow, technical, and neutral to express the idealism generated in children of parents who do such work.

Some forms of work do, however, allow for the expression of such ideals. Art, literature, science, music, the humanities, and the arts, when not perverted to commercial ends, provide such channels. However, most of these fields require genuine talent and are thus not available to everyone. Secondly, in all of these fields, the rate of failure is high, and the ability to cope with failure is a resource that few possess. The number of "jobs" available is low, and in a modern setting, many of these "jobs" are as productive of cynicism as no job at all.

Finally, pursuit of literature, the arts, and the intellect have been surrounded by conceptions of gentility, effeteness, and snobbery, so that the intrinsic meaning of the arts as jobs, crafts, and techniques have been lost in such imagery.

Yet it might still be possible to produce meaningful art if training were to commence at sufficiently early ages that the content and techniques of the media could be understood as languages in themselves, i.e., as not being translatable into highly intellectualized, verbal reductions of the media and techniques. Thus, it might be possible for individuals to be trained in the arts before they learn of the arts as "culture," as snobbery, or as an intellectual exercise.

This training might well be applied even at nonprofessional levels, for it is clear that bureaucratic and professional work is not able to absorb the tremendous energies of the new middle classes and that meaningful substitutes are necessary. Art and literature, music and science, have the capacity, even as avocations, of providing the possibilities for limitless self-development, provided that their pursuit is genuine. No other forms of human activity can provide both the continuity and depth and extensive gratification. Sexual, recreational, or culinary gratifications are short in duration and dependent upon the immediate physical condition and age of the consumer. Moreover, they operate under conditions of diminishing returns.

But education in the arts and letters, provided by Philistines as a device for "social planning" for the manipulation of youth—to render youth passive —is not likely to be successful. We elders are not sufficiently capable of practicing deception that successfully conceals ulterior purposes. The Peace Corps, the War on Poverty, and the civil rights movements all appeared initially to be capable of eliciting the energy and enthusiasm of youth. All floundered upon the unwillingness of adult society to go beyond tokenism, manipulation, and symbolic gestures.

Modern industrial society has generated a tremendous reserve of energy and idealism, which, up to now, it has failed to channelize. The very same energy that is capable of producing the greatest good is also capable of producing the greatest self and societal destructiveness. Perverted, it produces a cynicism, which in its highest form, we call swinging. If that society fails to implement the ideals it generates, and fails to produce the specific, concrete channels for implementing those ideals, that energy will either run amok and destroy individuals or the society itself. It can result in a public, social world where the total culture of society, its civilization, is an infinite series of masks that conceal only other masks, and at the bottom only a sense of despair that none of the masks are genuine.

Section II

Youth Development:
Perspectives on
Generations,
Socialization, and
Personality

INTRODUCTION

Generational relations, socialization, and personality are integral components of all human development. *How* these appear and the *ways* they are implemented and experienced will tell us about the kinds of people that eventually emerge in any given society. By focusing on youth as a more advanced stage of development, we may also learn about the kind of society we can expect to evolve in succeeding periods of social history.

In modern society, the period we broadly refer to as youth has no clear-cut and exact chronological boundaries. We commonly suggest that it begins at approximately pubescence, extends through biological adolescence (a period of physical maturation), and in recent times has expanded into a period several years after the completion of biological growth, perhaps as youths see it, until age thirty. On the other hand, specific social institutions are often more exact in distinguishing between youth and adults, but even these institutions are undergoing redefinition and are highly variable. According to the law youthhood (a juvenile or minor) generally ends at age seventeen, political citizenship now begins at eighteen, parental consent for marriage is no longer required at approximately between sixteen and eighteen (differing in various jurisdictions and between male and female), full employment rights begin at age sixteen, voluntary military service is possible at age eighteen, and religious manhood is reached at differing, but earlier times of confirmation.

These wide-ranging definitions of youth indeed imply that mulitple criteria often underlie the approaches and analysis of youth, particularly those inquiries that direct their attention to youth development. Broadly, these criteria emanate from at least three major perspectives: biology, psychology, and sociology, and within each perspective one may discover studies of particular aspects of youth development that also utilize shifting age criteria. So, for example, personality theory may conceive of intellectual maturation (i.e., Intelligence is the relationship between measures of mental age and chronological age) as occurring, or expected to occur, at a time different than emotional maturation. And in sociology, discrepancies between institutional definitions of the termination of youth and broader social redefinitions of youth may require the introduction of a concept such as "extended adolescence," meaning that one is young beyond the age that most social institutions regard as the terminal age of youth.

In fact, modern society's variable, vague, and often confusing classifications of youth may account in part for the considerable attention paid to youth, particularly as this may be said to have generated a large share of the difficulties associated with being youthful in the modern world. Indeed, the realization that youth turmoil was not necessarily a biological invariant inherent to adolescence was stated by the eminent ethnographer Margaret

Mead about four decades ago when she observed that if youth appears to be a developmental no-man's land, then it is modern civilization that is most heavily implicated in this process.[1]

The task, then, in studying the microcosm of coming of age, that is, how people move through a transitional stage before entering adulthood, has been to explicate those elements and conditions that appear to weigh most heavily upon the young during this period. In so doing, a vast body of literature has emerged in which significant efforts have been made to take the measure of human biology, psychology, and social relations, and to examine carefully the impact and dynamic interrelationships that are unique to youthhood. Yet, the difficulty in this task has been that, although each component of development is analytically separable, they are configured in complex humanity and as such have eluded perfect or easy understanding.

The common ground upon which all of the following selections concerning youth development stand is the inclusion of a historical perspective. Whether social history or life history, each author considers the subject of youth development with a sense of the broader social context in which this takes place. Throughout, there is an effort to explore developmental dynamics as generators of healthy and normal outcomes or pathological and deviant products. In this respect, the central language and concepts of these works immediately frame the issues clearly: generational conflict and consensus, continuity and discontinuity, identity formation, crisis and confusion, alienation and commitment, humanization and depersonalization, boredom and aptitude, withdrawal and participation, and cooperative morality and moral anomie.

As the reader will note, although the selections reveal a marked tendency to approach the subject of youth development through observations about abnormal, atypical, deviant, and unhealthy processes, they also insist that the period of youthful growth need not be fraught with anguish and disarray. Whatever might be the variants of growing up and experiencing that time called youth in any given society, these selections underscore the powerful interplay of complex and larger forces impinging on it. They enable us to perceive the essential sweep of both social history and life history, and it is in this sense of generational progression that youth can be said to father the man.

[1] Margaret Mead, *Coming of Age in Samoa* (New York: William Morrow and Co., 1928).

The Sociology of
Parent-Youth Conflict *

Kingsley Davis

It is in sociological terms that this chapter attempts to frame and solve the sole question with which it deals, namely: Why does contemporary Western civilization manifest an extraordinary amount of parent-adolescent conflict? [1] In other cultures, the outstanding fact is generally not the rebelliousness of youth, but its docility. There is practically no custom, no matter how tedious or painful, to which youth in primitive tribes or archaic civilizations will not willingly submit.[2] What, then, are the peculiar features of our society which give us one of the extremest examples of endemic filial friction in human history?

Our answer to this question makes use of constants and variables, the constants being the universal factors in the parent-youth relation, the variables being the factors which differ from one society to another. Though one's attention, in explaining the parent-youth relations of a given milieu, is focused on the variables, one cannot comprehend the action of the variables without also understanding the constants, for the latter constitute the structural and functional basis of the family as a part of society.

* Presented to the American Sociological Society, Philadelphia, Dec. 28, 1939.

Kingsley Davis, "The Sociology of Parent-Youth Conflict," from The American Sociological Review (Vol. 5, No. 4, August 1940), pp. 523–535. Reprinted by permission of the publisher and the author.

[1] In the absence of statistical evidence, exaggeration of the conflict is easily possible, and two able students have warned against it. E. B. Reuter, "The Sociology of Adolescence," and Jessie R. Runner, "Social Distance in Adolescent Relationships," both in Amer. J. Sociol., November 1937, 43: 415–416, 437. Yet sufficient nonquantitative evidence lies at hand in the form of personal experience, the outpour of literature on adolescent problems, and the historical and anthropological accounts of contrasting societies to justify the conclusion that in comparison with other cultures ours exhibits an exceptional amount of such conflict. If this chapter seems to stress conflict, it is simply because we are concerned with this problem rather than with parent-youth harmony.

[2] Cf. Nathan Miller, The Child in Primitive Society, New York, 1928; Miriam Van Waters, "The Adolescent Girl Among Primitive Peoples," J. Relig. Psychol., 1913, 6: 375–421 (1913) and 7: 75–120 (1914); Margaret Mead, Coming of Age in Samoa, New York, 1928 and "Adolescence in Primitive and Modern Society," 169–188, in The New Generation (ed. by V. F. Calverton and S. Schmalhausen), New York, 1930; A. M. Bacon, Japanese Girls and Women, New York and Boston, 1891 and 1902.

The Rate of Social Change

The first important variable is the rate of social change. Extremely rapid change in modern civilization, in contrast to most societies, tends to increase parent-youth conflict, for within a fast-changing social order the time-interval between generations, ordinarily but a mere moment in the life of a social system, become historically significant, thereby creating a hiatus between one generation and the next. Inevitably, under such a condition, youth is reared in a milieu different from that of the parents; hence the parents become old-fashioned, youth rebellious, and clashes occur which, in the closely confined circle of the immediate family, generate sharp emotion.

That rapidity of change is a significant variable can be demonstrated by three lines of evidence: a comparison of stable and nonstable societies;[3] a consideration of immigrant families; and an analysis of revolutionary epochs. If, for example, the conflict is sharper in the immigrant household, this can be due to one thing only, that the immigrant family generally undergoes the most rapid social change of any type of family in a given society. Similarly, a revolution (an abrupt form of societal alteration), by concentrating great change in a short span, catapults the younger generation into power—a generation which has absorbed and pushed the new ideas, acquired the habit of force, and which, accordingly, dominates those hangovers from the old regime, its parents.[4]

The Birth-Cycle, Decelerating Socialization, and Parent-Child Differences

Note, however, that rapid social change would have no power to produce conflict were it not for two universal factors: first, the family's duration; and second, the decelerating rate of socialization in the development of personality. "A family" is not a static entity but a process in time, a process ordinarily so brief compared with historical time that it is unimportant, but which, when history is "full" (i.e., marked by rapid social change), strongly influences the mutual adjustment of the generations. This "span" is basically the birth-cycle—the length of time between the birth of one person and his procreation of another. It is biological and inescapable. It would, however, have no effect in producing parent-youth conflict, even with social change,

---

[3] Partially done by Mead and Van Waters in the works cited above.
[4] Soviet Russia and Nazi Germany are examples. See Sigmund Neumann, "The Conflict of Generations in Contemporary Europe from Versailles to Munich," *Vital Speeches of the Day,* August 1, 1939, 5: 623–628. Parents in these countries are to be obeyed only so long as they profess the "correct" (i.e., youthful, revolutionary) ideas.

if it were not for the additional fact, intimately related and equally universal, that the sequential development of personality involves a constantly decelerating rate of socialization. This deceleration is due both to organic factors (age—which ties it to the birth-cycle) and to social factors (the cumulative character of social experience). Its effect is to make the birth-cycle interval, which is the period of youth, the time of major socialization, subsequent periods of socialization being subsidiary.

Given these constant features, rapid social change creates conflict because *to* the intrinsic (universal, inescapable) differences between parents and children it adds an extrinsic (variable) difference derived from the acquisition, at the same stage of life, of differential cultural content by each successive generation. Not only are parent and child, at any given moment,

FIGURE 1. The Birth-Cycle, Social Change, and Parent-Child Relations at Different Stages of Life *

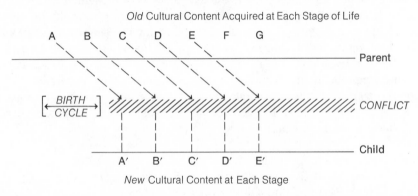

* Because the birth-cycle interval persists throughout their conjoint life, parent and child are always at a different stage of development and their relations are always therefore potentially subject to conflict. E.g., when the parent is at stage *D,* the child is at stage *B.* But social change adds another source of conflict, for it means that the parent, when at the stage where the child now is, acquired a different cultural content from that which the child must now acquire at that stage. This places the parent in the predicament of trying to transmit old content no longer suited to the offspring's needs in a changed world. In a stable society, *B* and *B'* would have the same cultural content. In a changing society, they do not, yet the parent tries to apply the content of *A, B, C,* etc., to the corresponding stages in the child's development, *A', B', C',* etc., which supposedly and actually have a different content. Thus, a constant (the birth-cycle) and a variable (social change) combine to produce parent-youth conflict.

Though the birth-cycle remains absolutely the same, it does not remain relatively the same, because it occupies, as time goes on, a successively smaller percentage of the total time lived. Furthermore, because of the decelerating rate of socialization, the difference in the total amount of cultural content as between parent and child becomes less pronounced. After the period of adolescence, for example, the margin is reduced to a minimum, which explains why a minimum of conflict is achieved after that stage.

in different stages of development, but the content which the parent acquired at the stage where the child now is, was a different content from that which the child is now acquiring. Since the parent is supposed to socialize the child, he tends to apply the erstwhile but now inappropriate content (see Diagram). He makes this mistake, and cannot remedy it, because, due to the logic of personality growth, his basic orientation was formed by the experiences of his own childhood. He cannot "modernize" his point of view, because *he* is the product of those experiences. He can change in superficial ways, such as learning a new tune, but he cannot change (or *want* to change) the initial modes of thinking upon which his subsequent social experience has been built. To change the basic conceptions by which he has learned to judge the rightness and reality of all specific situations would be to render subsequent experience meaningless, to make an empty caricature of what had been his life.

Although, in the birth-cycle gap between parent and offspring, astronomical time constitutes the basic point of disparity, the actual sequences, and hence the actual differences significant for us, are physiological, psychosocial, and sociological—each with an acceleration of its own within, but to some degree independent of, sidereal time, and each containing a divergence between parent and child which must be taken into account in explaining parent-youth conflict.

Physiological Differences

Though the disparity in chronological age remains constant through life, the precise physiological differences between parent and offspring vary radically from one period to another. The organic contrasts between parent and *infant,* for example, are far different from those between parent and adolescent. Yet whatever the period, the organic differences produce contrasts (as between young and old) in those desires which, at least in part, are organically determined. Thus, at the time of adolescence the contrast is between an organism which is just reaching its full powers and one which is just losing them. The physiological need of the latter is for security and conservation, because as the superabundance of energy diminishes, the organism seems to hoard what remains.

Such differences, often alleged (under the heading of "disturbing physiological changes accompanying adolescence") as the primary cause of parent-adolescent strife, are undoubtedly a factor in such conflict, but, like other universal differences to be discussed, they form a constant factor present in every community, and therefore cannot in themselves explain the peculiar heightening of parent-youth conflict in our culture.

The fact is that most societies avoid the potential clash of old and young by using sociological position as a neutralizing agent. They assign definite and separate positions to persons of different ages, thereby eliminating competition between them for the same position and avoiding the competitive emotions of jealousy and envy. Also, since the expected behavior of old and young is thus made complementary rather than identical, the performance of cooperative functions as accomplished by different but mutually related activities suited to the disparate organic needs of each, with no coercion to behave in a manner unsuited to one's organic age. In our culture, where most positions are *theoretically* based on accomplishment rather than age, interage competition arises, superior organic propensities lead to a high evaluation of youth (the so-called "accent on youth"), a disproportionate lack of opportunity for youth manifests itself, and consequently, arrogance and frustration appear in the young, fear and envy, in the old.

Psychosocial Differences: Adult Realism versus Youthful Idealism

The decelerating rate of socialization (an outgrowth both of the human being's organic development, from infant plasticity to senile rigidity, and of his cumulative cultural and social development), when taken with rapid social change and other conditions of our society, tends to produce certain differences of orientation between parent and youth. Though lack of space makes it impossible to discuss all of these ramifications, we shall attempt to delineate at least one sector of difference in terms of the conflict between adult realism (or pragmatism) and youthful idealism.

Though both youth and age claim to see the truth, the old are more conservatively realistic than the young, because on the one hand they take Utopian ideals less seriously and on the other hand take what may be called operating ideals, if not more seriously, at least more for granted. Thus, middle-aged people notoriously forget the poetic ideals of a new social order which they cherished when young. In their place, they put simply the working ideals current in the society. There is, in short, a persistent tendency for the ideology of a person as he grows older to gravitate more and more toward the status quo ideology, unless other facts (such as a social crisis or hypnotic suggestion) intervene.[5] With advancing age, he becomes less and less bothered by inconsistencies in ideals. He tends to judge ideals according to whether they are widespread and hence effective in thinking about practical life, not according to whether they are logically consistent. Furthermore, he gradually ceases to bother about the *untruth* of his ideals, in the sense of their failure to correspond to reality. He assumes through long habit that, though they do not correspond perfectly, the discrepancy is not significant. The reality of an ideal is defined for him in terms of how many

---

[5] See Footnote 11 for necessary qualifications.

people accept it rather than how completely it is mirrored in actual behavior.[6] Thus, we call him, as he approaches middle age, a realist.

The young, however, are idealists, partly because they take working ideals literally and partly because they acquire ideals not fully operative in the social organization. Those in authority over children are obligated as a requirement of their status to inculcate ideals as a part of the official culture given the new generation.[7] The children are receptive because they have little social experience—experience being systematically kept from them (by such means as censorship, for example, a large part of which is to "protect" children). Consequently, young people possess little ballast for their acquired ideals, which therefore soar to the sky, whereas the middle-aged, by contrast, have plenty of ballast.

This relatively unchecked idealism in youth is eventually complicated by the fact that young people possess keen reasoning ability. The mind, simply as a logical machine, works as well at sixteen as at thirty-six.[8] Such logical capacity, combined with high ideals and an initial lack of experience, means that youth soon discovers with increasing age that the ideals it has been taught are true and consistent are not so in fact. Mental conflict thereupon ensues, for the young person has not learned that ideals may be useful without being true and consistent. As a solution, youth is likely to take action designed to remove inconsistencies or force actual conduct into line with ideals, such action assuming one of several typical adolescent forms—from religious withdrawal to the militant support of some Utopian scheme—but in any case consisting essentially in serious allegiance to one or more of the ideal moral systems present in the culture.[9]

A different, usually later reaction to disillusionment is the cynical or sophomoric attitude; for, if the ideals one has imbibed cannot be reconciled and do not fit reality, then why not dismiss them as worthless? Cynicism

[6] When discussing a youthful ideal, however, the older person is quick to take a dialectical advantage by pointing out not only that this ideal affronts the aspirations of the multitude, but that it also fails to correspond to human behavior either now or (by the lessons of history) probably in the future.

[7] See amusing but accurate article, "Fathers Are Liars," *Scribner's Magazine,* March, 1934.

[8] Evidence from mental growth data which point to a leveling off of the growth curve at about age sixteen. For charts and brief explanations, together with references, see F. K. Shuttleworth, *The Adolescent Period,* Monographs of the Society for Research in Child Development, III, Serial No. 16 (Washington, D.C., 1938), Figs. 16, 230, 232, 276, 285, 308.

Maturity of judgment is of course another matter. We are speaking only of logical capacity. Judgment is based on experience as well as capacity; hence, adolescents are apt to lack it.

[9] An illustration of youthful reformism was afforded by the Laval University students who decided to "do something about" prostitution in the city of Quebec. They broke into eight houses in succession one night, "whacked naked inmates upon the buttocks, upset beds and otherwise proved their collegiate virtue. . . ." They ended by "shoving the few remaining girls out of doors into the cold autumn night." *Time,* October 19, 1936.

has the advantage of giving justification for behavior that young organisms crave anyway. It might be mistaken for genuine realism if it were not for two things. The first is the emotional strain behind the "don't care" attitude. The cynic, in his judgment that the world is bad because of inconsistency and untruth of ideals, clearly implies that he still values the ideals. The true realist sees the inconsistency and untruth, but without emotion; he uses either ideals or reality whenever it suits his purpose. The second is the early disappearance of the cynical attitude. Increased experience usually teaches the adolescent that overt cynicism is unpopular and unworkable, that to deny and deride all beliefs which fail to cohere or to correspond to facts, and to act in opposition to them, is to alienate oneself from any group,[10] because these beliefs, however unreal, are precisely what makes group unity possible. Soon, therefore, the youthful cynic finds himself bound up with some group having a system of working ideals, and becomes merely another conformist, cynical only about the beliefs of other groups.[11]

While the germ of this contrast between youthful idealism and adult realism may spring from the universal logic of personality development, it receives in our culture a peculiar exaggeration. Social change, complexity, and specialization (by compartmentalizing different aspects of life) segregate ideals from fact and throw together incompatible ideologies while at the same time providing the intellectual tools for discerning logical inconsistencies and empirical errors. Our highly elaborated burden of culture, correlated with a variegated system of achieved vertical mobility, necessitates long years of formal education which separate youth from adulthood, theory from practice, school from life. Insofar, then, as youth's reformist zeal or cynical negativism produces conflict with parents, the peculiar conditions of our culture are responsible.

[10] This holds only for expressed cynicism, but so close is the relation of thought to action that the possibility of an entirely covert cynic seems remote.

[11] This tentative analysis holds only insofar as the logic of personality development in a complex culture is the sole factor. Because of other factors, concrete situations may be quite different. When, for example, a person is specifically trained in certain rigid, other-worldly, or impractical ideals, he may grow increasingly fanatical with the years rather than realistic, while his offspring, because of association with less fanatical persons, may be more pragmatic than he. The variation in group norms within a society produces persons who, whatever their orientation inside the group, remain more idealistic than the average outsider, while their children may, with outside contacts, become more pragmatic. Even within a group, however, a person's situation may be such as to drive him beyond the everyday realities of that group, while his children remain undisturbed. Such situations largely explain the personal crises that may alter one's orientation. The analysis, overly brief and mainly illustrative, therefore represents a certain degree of abstraction. The reader should realize, moreover, that the terms "realistic" and "idealistic" are chosen merely for convenience in trying to convey the idea, not for any evaluative judgments which they may happen to connote. The terms are not used in any technical epistemological sense, but simply in the way made plain by the context. Above all, it is not implied that ideals are "unreal." The ways in which they are "real" and "unreal" to observer and actor are complex indeed. See T. Parsons, *The Structure of Social Action*, 396, New York, 1937, and V. Pareto, *The Mind and Society*, III: 1300–1304, New York, 1935.

Sociological Differences: Parental Authority

Since social status and office are everywhere partly distributed on the basis of age, personality development is intimately linked with the network of social positions successively occupied during life. Western society, in spite of an unusual amount of interage competition, maintains differences of social position between parent and child, the developmental gap between them being too clear-cut, the symbiotic needs too fundamental, to escape being made a basis of social organization. Hence, parent and child, in a variety of ways, find themselves enmeshed in different social contexts and possessed of different outlooks. The much publicized critical attitude of youth toward established ways, for example, is partly a matter of being on the outside looking in. The "established ways" under criticism are usually institutions (such as property, marriage, profession) which the adolescent has not yet entered. He looks at them from the point of view of the outsider (especially since they affect him in a restrictive manner), either failing to imagine himself finding satisfaction in such patterns or else feeling resentful that the old have in them a vested interest from which he is excluded.

Not only is there differential position, but also *mutually* differential position, status being in many ways specific for and reciprocal between parent and child. Some of these differences, relating to the birth-cycle and constituting part of the family structure, are universal. This is particularly true of the super- and subordination summed up in the term *parental authority*.

Since sociological differences between parent and child are inherent in family organization, they constitute a universal factor potentially capable of producing conflict. Like the biological differences, however, they do not in themselves produce such conflict. In fact, they may help to avoid it. To understand how our society brings to expression the potentiality for conflict, indeed to deal realistically with the relation between the generations, we must do so not in generalized terms but in terms of the specific "power situation." Therefore, the remainder of our discussion will center upon the nature of parental authority and its vicissitudes in our society.

Because of his strategic position with reference to the new-born child (at least in the familial type of reproductive institution), the parent is given considerable authority. Charged by his social group with the responsibility of controlling and training the child in conformity with the mores and thereby insuring the maintenance of the cultural structure, the parent, to fulfill his duties, must have the privileges as well as the obligations of authority, and the surrounding community ordinarily guarantees both.

The first thing to note about parental authority, in addition to its function in socialization, is that it is a case of authority within a primary group. Simmel has pointed out that authority is bearable for the subordinate because it touches only one aspect of life. Impersonal and objective, it permits all other aspects to be free from its particularistic dominance. This escape, however, is lacking in parental authority, for since the family includes most aspects of life, its authority is not limited, specific, or impersonal. What, then, can make this authority bearable? Three factors associated with the familial primary group help to give the answer: (1) the child is socialized within the family, and therefore knowing nothing else and being utterly dependent, the authority of the parent is internalized, accepted; (2) the family, like other primary groups, implies identification, in such sense that one person understands and responds emphatically to the sentiments of the other, so that the harshness of authority is ameliorated;[12] (3) in the intimate interaction of the primary group control can never be purely one-sided; there are too many ways in which the subordinated can exert the pressure of his will. When, therefore, the family system is a going concern, parental authority, however, inclusive, is not felt as despotic.

A second thing to note about parental authority is that while its duration is variable (lasting in some societies a few years and in others a lifetime), it inevitably involves a change, a progressive readjustment, in the respective positions of parent and child—in some cases an almost complete reversal of roles, in others at least a cumulative allowance for the fact of maturity in the subordinated offspring. Age is a unique basis for social stratification. Unlike birth, sex, wealth, or occupation, it implies that the stratification is temporary, that the person, if he lives a full life, will eventually traverse all of the strata having it as a basis. Therefore, there is a peculiar ambivalence attached to this kind of differentiation, as well as a constant directional movement. On the one hand, the young person, in the stage of maximum socialization, is, so to speak, *moving into* the social organization. His social personality is expanding, i.e., acquiring an increased amount of the cultural heritage, filling more powerful and numerous positions. His future is before him, in what the older person is leaving behind. The latter, on the other hand, has a future before him only in the sense that the offspring represents it. Therefore, there is a disparity of interest, the young person placing his thoughts upon a future which, once the first stages of dependence are passed, does not include the parent, the old person placing his hopes vicariously upon the young. This situation, representing a *tendency* in every society, is avoided in many places by a system of respect for the aged and an imaginary projection of life beyond the grave. In the absence of such a religio-ancestral system, the role of the aged is a tragic one.[13]

Let us now take up, point by point, the manner in which Western civili-

---

[12] House slaves, for example, are generally treated much better than field slaves. Authority over the former is of a personal type, while that over the latter (often in the form of a foreman-gang organization) is of a more impersonal or economic type.

[13] Sometimes compensated for by an interest in the grandchildren, which permits them partially to recover the role of the vigorous parent.

zation has affected this *gemeinschaftliche* and processual form of authority.

1. Conflicting Norms. To begin with, rapid change has, as we saw, given old and young a different social content, so that they possess conflicting norms. There is a loss of mutual identification, and the parent will not "catch up" with the child's point of view, because he is supposed to dominate rather than follow. More than this, social complexity has confused the standards *within* the generations. Faced with conflicting goals, parents become inconsistent and confused in their own minds in rearing their children. The children, for example, acquire an argument against discipline by being able to point to some family wherein discipline is less severe, while the parent can retaliate by pointing to still other families wherein it is firmer. The acceptance of parental attitudes is less complete than formerly.

2. Competing Authorities. We took it for granted, when discussing rapid social change, that youth acquires new ideas, but we did not ask how. The truth is that, in a specialized and complex culture, they learn from competing authorities. Today, for example, education is largely in the hands of professional specialists, some of whom, as college professors, resemble the sophists of ancient Athens by virtue of their work of accumulating and purveying knowledge, and who consequently have ideas in advance of the populace at large (i.e., the parents). By giving the younger generation these advanced ideas, they (and many other extrafamilial agencies, including youth's contemporaries) widen the intellectual gap between parent and child.[14]

3. Little Explicit Institutionalization of Steps in Parental Authority. Our society provides little explicit institutionalization of the progressive readjustments of authority as between parent and child. We are intermediate between the extreme of virtually permanent parental authority and the extreme of very early emancipation, because we encourage release in late adolescence. Unfortunately, this is a time of enhanced sexual desire, so that the problem of sex and the problem of emancipation occur simultaneously and complicate each other. Yet even this would doubtless be satisfactory if it were not for the fact that among us the exact time when authority is relinquished, the exact amount, and the proper ceremonial behavior are not clearly defined. Not only do different groups and families have conflicting patterns, and new situations arise to which old definitions will not apply, but the different spheres of life (legal, economic, religious, intellectual) do not synchronize, maturity in one sphere and immaturity in another often coexisting. The readjustment of authority between individuals is always

[14] The essential point is not that there are other authorities—in every society there are extrafamilial influences in socialization—but that, because of specialization and individualistic enterprise, they are *competing* authorities. Because they make a living by their work and are specialists in socialization, some authorities have a competitive advantage over parents who are amateurs or at best merely general practitioners.

a ticklish process, and when it is a matter of such close authority as that between parent and child it is apt to be still more ticklish. The failure of our culture to institutionalize this readjustment by a series of well-defined, well-publicized steps is undoubtedly a cause of much parent-youth dissension. The adolescent's sociological exit from his family, via education, work, marriage, and change of residence, is fraught with potential conflicts of interest which only a definite system of institutional controls can neutralize. The parents have a vital stake in what the offspring will do. Because his acquisition of independence will free the parents of many obligations, they are willing to relinquish their authority; yet, precisely because their own status is socially identified with that of their offspring, they wish to insure satisfactory conduct on the latter's part and are tempted to prolong their authority by making the decisions themselves. In the absence of institutional prescriptions, the conflict of interest may lead to a struggle for power, the parents fighting to keep control in matters of importance to themselves, the son or daughter clinging to personally indispensable family services while seeking to evade the concomitant control.

4. *Concentration within the Small Family.* Our family system is peculiar in that it manifests a paradoxical combination of concentration and dispersion. On the one hand, the unusual smallness of the family unit makes for a strange intensity of family feeling, while on the other, the fact that most pursuits take place outside the home makes for a dispersion of activities. Though apparently contradictory, the two phenomena are really interrelated and traceable ultimately to the same factors in our social structure. Since the first refers to that type of affection and antagonism found between relatives, and the second to activities, it can be seen that the second (dispersion) isolates and increases the intensity of the affectional element by sheering away common activities and the extended kin. Whereas ordinarily the sentiments of kinship are organically related to a number of common activities and spread over a wide circle of relatives, in our mobile society they are associated with only a few common activities and concentrated within only the immediate family. This makes them at once more instable (because ungrounded) and more intense. With the diminishing birth rate, our family is the world's smallest kinship unit, a tiny closed circle. Consequently, a great deal of family sentiment is directed toward a few individuals, who are so important to the emotional life that complexes easily develop. This emotional intensity and situational instability increase both the probablity and severity of conflict.

In a familistic society, where there are several adult male and female relatives within the effective kinship group to whom the child turns for affection and aid, and many members of the younger generation in whom the parents have a paternal interest, there appears to be less intensity of emotion for any particular kinsman and consequently less chance for severe conflict.[15] Also, if conflict between any two relatives does arise, it may be handled by shifting mutual rights and obligations to another relative.[16]

5. Open Competition for Socioeconomic Position. Our emphasis upon individual initiative and vertical mobility, in contrast to rural-stable regimes, means that one's future occupation and destiny are determined more at adolescence than at birth, the adolescent himself (as well as the parents) having some part in the decision. Before him spread a panorama of possible occupations and avenues of advancement, all of them fraught with the uncertainties of competitive vicissitude. The youth is ignorant of most of the facts. So is the parent, but less so. Both attempt to collaborate on the future, but because of previously mentioned sources of friction, the collaboration is frequently stormy. They evaluate future possibilities differently, and since the decision is uncertain yet important, a clash of wills results. The necessity of choice at adolescence extends beyond the occupational field to practically every phase of life, the parents having an interest in each decision. A culture in which more of the choices of life were settled beforehand by ascription, where the possibilities were fewer and the responsibilities of choice less urgent, would have much less parent-youth conflict.[17]

6. Sex Tension. If until now we have ignored sex taboos, the omission has represented a deliberate attempt to place them in their proper context with other factors, rather than in the unduly prominent place usually given them.[18] Undoubtedly, because of a constellation of cultural conditions, sex looms as an important bone of parent-youth contention. Our morality, for instance, demands both premarital chastity and postponement of marriage, thus creating a long period of desperate eagerness when young persons practically at the peak of their sexual capacity are forbidden to enjoy it. Naturally, tensions arise—tensions which adolescents try to relieve, and adults hope they will relieve, in some socially acceptable form. Such tensions not only make the adolescent intractable and capricious, but create a genuine conflict of interest between the two generations. The parent, with respect to the child's behavior, represents morality, while the offspring reflects morality *plus* his organic cravings. The stage is thereby set for conflict, evasion, and deceit. For the mass of parents, toleration is never

---

[15] Margaret Mead, *Social Organization of Manua*, 84, Honolulu, Bernice P. Bishop Museum Bulletin 76, 1930. Large heterogeneous households early accustom the child to expect emotional rewards from many different persons. D. M. Spencer, "The Composition of the Family as a Factor in the Behavior of Children in Fijian Society," *Sociometry* (1939), 2: 47–55.

[16] The principle of substitution is widespread in familism, as shown by the wide distribution of adoption, levirate, sororate, and classificatory kinship nomenclature.

[17] M. Mead, *Coming of Age in Samoa*, 200 ff.

[18] Cf., e.g., L. K. Frank, "The Management of Tensions," *Amer. J. Sociol.*, March 1928, 33: 706–722; M. Mead, *op. cit.*, 216–217, 222–223.

possible. For the mass of adolescents, sublimation is never sufficient. Given our system of morality, conflict seems well nigh inevitable.

Yet it is not sex itself but the way it is handled that causes conflict. If sex patterns were carefully, definitely, and uniformly geared with nonsexual patterns in the social structure, there would be no parent-youth conflict over sex. As it is, rapid change has opposed the sex standards of different groups and generations, leaving impulse only chaotically controlled.

The extraordinary preoccupation of modern parents with the sex life of their adolescent offspring is easily understandable. First, our morality is sex-centered. The strength of the impulse which it seeks to control, the consequent stringency of its rules, and the importance of reproductive institutions for society, make sex so morally important that being moral and being sexually discreet are synonymous. Small wonder, then, that parents, charged with responsibility for their children and fearful of their own status in the eyes of the moral community, are preoccupied with what their offspring will do in this matter. Moreover, sex is intrinsically involved in the family structure and is therefore of unusual significance to family members *qua* family members. Offspring and parent are not simply two persons who happen to live together; they are two persons who happen to live together because of past sex relations between the parents. Also, between parent and child there stand strong incest taboos, and doubtless the unvoiced possibility of violating these unconsciously intensifies the interest of each in the other's sexual conduct. In addition, since sexual behavior is connected with the offspring's formation of a new family of his own, it is naturally of concern to the parent. Finally, these factors taken in combination with the delicacy of the authoritarian relation, the emotional intensity within the small family, and the confusion of sex standards, make it easy to explain the parental interest in adolescent sexuality. Yet because sex is a tabooed topic between parent and child,[19] parental control must be indirect and devious, which creates additional possibilities of conflict.

Summary and Conclusion

Our parent-youth conflict thus results from the interaction of certain universals of the parent-child relation and certain variables the value of which are peculiar to modern culture. The universals are (1) the basic age or birth-cycle differential between parent and child, (2) the decelerating rate of socialization with advancing age, and (3) the resulting intrinsic dif-

---

[19] "Even among the essentially 'unrepressed' Trobrianders the parent is never the confidant in matters of sex." Bronislaw Malinowski, *Sex and Reproduction in Savage Society,* 36 (note), London, 1927, p. 36n. Cf. the interesting article, "Intrusive Parents," *The Commentator,* September 1938, which opposes frank sex discussion between parents and children.

ferences between old and young on the physiological, psychosocial, and sociological planes.

Though these universal factors *tend* to produce conflict between parent and child, whether or not they do so depends upon the variables. We have seen that the distinctive general features of our society are responsible for our excessive parent-adolescent friction. Indeed, they are the same features which are affecting *all* family relations. The delineation of these variables has not been systematic, because the scientific classification of whole societies has not yet been accomplished; and it has been difficult, in view of the interrelated character of societal traits, to seize upon certain features and ignore others. Yet certainly the following four complex variables are important: (1) the rate of social change; (2) the extent of complexity in the social structure; (3) the degree of integration in the culture; and (4) the velocity of movement (e.g., vertical mobility) within the structure and its relation to the cultural values.

Our rapid social change, for example, has crowded historical meaning into the family time-span, has thereby given the offspring a different social content from that which the parent acquired, and consequently has added to the already existent intrinsic differences between parent and youth, a set of extrinsic ones which double the chance of alienation. Moreover, our great societal complexity, our evident cultural conflict, and our emphasis upon open competition for socioeconomic status have all added to this initial effect. We have seen, for instance, that they have disorganized the important relation of parental authority by confusing the goals of child control, setting up competing authorities, creating a small family system, making necessary certain significant choices at the time of adolescence, and leading to an absence of definite institutional mechanisms to symbolize and enforce the progressively changing stages of parental power.

If ours were a simple rural-stable society, mainly familistic, the emancipation from parental authority being gradual and marked by definite institutionalized steps, with no great postponement of marriage, sex taboo, or open competition for status, parents and youth would not be in conflict. Hence, the presence of parent-youth conflict in our civilization is one more specific manifestation of the incompatibility between an urban-industrial-mobile social system and the familial type of reproductive institutions.[20]

---

[20] For further evidence of this incompatibility, see the writer's "Reproductive Institutions and the Pressure for Population," (*Brit.*) *Sociol. Rev.;* July 1937, 29: 289–306.

Continuities and Discontinuities
in Cultural Conditioning

Ruth Benedict

All cultures must deal in one way or another with the cycle of growth from infancy to adulthood. Nature has posed the situation dramatically: on the one hand, the new born baby, physiologically vulnerable, unable to fend for itself, or to participate of its own initiative in the life of the group, and, on the other, the adult man or woman. Every man who rounds out his human potentialities must have been a son first and a father later and the two roles are physiologically in great contrast; he must first have been dependent upon others for his very existence and later he must provide such security for others. This discontinuity in the life cycle is a fact of nature and is inescapable. Facts of nature, however, in any discussion of human problems, are ordinarily read off not at their bare minimal but surrounded by all the local accretions of behavior to which the student of human affairs has become accustomed in his own culture. For that reason it is illuminating to examine comparative material from other societies in order to get a wider perspective on our own special accretions. The anthropologist's role is not to question the facts of nature, but to insist upon the interposition of a middle term between "nature" and "human behavior"; his role is to analyse that term, to document local man-made doctorings of nature and to insist that these doctorings should not be read off in any one culture as nature itself. Although it is a fact of nature that the child becomes a man, the way in which this transition is effected varies from one society to another, and no one of these particular cultural bridges should be regarded as the "natural" path to maturity.

From a comparative point of view our culture goes to great extremes in emphasizing contrasts between the child and the adult. The child is sexless, the adult estimates his virility by his sexual activities; the child must be protected from the ugly facts of life, the adult must meet them without psychic catastrophe; the child must obey, the adult must command this obedience. These are all dogmas of our culture, dogmas which in spite of the facts of nature, other cultures commonly do not share. In spite of the physiological contrasts between child and adult these are cultural accretions.

It will make the point clearer if we consider one habit in our own culture in regard to which there is not this discontinuity of conditioning. With

Reprinted by special permission of The William Alanson White Psychiatric Foundation, Inc., Ruth Benedict, "Continuities and Discontinuities in Cultural Conditioning"; *Psychiatry* (Vol. 1, 1938), pp. 161–167.

the greatest clarity of purpose and economy of training, we achieve our goal of conditioning everyone to eat three meals a day. The baby's training in regular food periods begin at birth and no crying of the child and no inconvenience to the mother is allowed to interfere. We gauge the child's physiological make-up and at first allow it food oftener than adults, but, because our goal is firmly set and our training consistent, before the child is two years old it has achieved the adult schedule. From the point of view of other cultures this is as startling as the fact of three-year old babies perfectly at home in deep water is to us. Modesty is another sphere in which our child training is consistent and economical: we waste no time in clothing the baby and in contrast to many societies where the child runs naked till it is ceremonially given its skirt or its public sheath at adolescence, the child's training fits it precisely for adult conventions.

In neither of these aspects of behavior is there need for an individual in our culture to embark before puberty, at puberty or at some later date upon a course of action which all his previous training has tabued. He is spared the unsureness inevitable in such a transition.

The illustration I have chosen may appear trivial, but in larger and more important aspects of behavior, our methods are obviously different. Because of the great variety of child training in different families in our society, I might illustrate continuity of conditioning from individual life histories in our culture, but even these, from a comparative point of view, stop far short of consistency and I shall therefore confine myself to describing arrangements in other cultures in which training with us is idiosyncratic, is accepted and traditional and does not therefore involve the same possibility of conflict. I shall choose childhood rather than infant and nursing situations not because the latter do not vary strikingly in different cultures but because they are nevertheless more circumscribed by the baby's physiological needs than is its later training. Childhood situations provide an excellent field in which to illustrate the range of cultural adjustments which are possible within a universally given, but not so drastic, set of physiological facts.

The major discontinuity in the life cycle is of course that the child who is at one point a son must later be a father. These roles in our society are strongly differentiated; a good son is tractable, and does not assume adult responsibilities; a good father provides for his children and should not allow his authority to be flouted. In addition the child must be sexless so far as his family is concerned, whereas the father's sexual role is primary in the family. The individual in one role must revise his behavior from almost all points of view when he assumes the second role.

I shall select for discussion three such contrasts that occur in our culture between the individual's role as child and as father: 1. responsible—nonresponsible status role, 2. dominance—submission, 3. contrasted sexual role. It is largely upon our cultural commitments to these three contrasts that the discontinuity in the life cycle of an individual in our culture depends.

1. Responsible—Non-responsible
Status Role

The techniques adopted by societies which achieve continuity during the life cycle in this sphere in no way differ from those we employ in our uniform conditioning to three meals a day. They are merely applied to other areas of life. We think of the child as wanting to play and the adult as having to work, but in many societies the mother takes the baby daily in her shawl or carrying net to the garden or to gather roots, and adult labor is seen even in infancy from the pleasant security of its position in close contact with its mother. When the child can run about it accompanies its parents still, doing tasks which are essential and yet suited to its powers, and its dichotomy between work and play is not different from that its parents recognize, namely the distinction between the busy day and the free evening. The tasks it is asked to perform are graded to its powers and its elders wait quietly by, not offering to do the task in the child's place. Everyone who is familiar with such societies has been struck by the contrast with our child training. Dr. Ruth Underhill tells me of sitting with a group of Papago elders in Arizona when the man of the house turned to his little three-year old granddaughter and asked her to close the door. The door was heavy and hard to shut. The child tried, but it did not move. Several times the grandfather repeated, "Yes, close the door." No one jumped to the child's assistance. No one took the responsibility away from her. On the other hand there was no impatience, for after all the child was small. They sat gravely waiting till the child succeeded and her grandfather gravely thanked her. It was assumed that the task would not be asked of her unless she could perform it and having been asked the responsibility was hers alone just as if she were a grown woman.

The essential point of such child training is that the child is from infancy continuously conditioned to responsible social participation while at the same time the tasks that are expected of it are adapted to its capacity. The contrast with our society is very great. A child does not make any labor contribution to our industrial society except as it competes with an adult; its work is not measured against its own strength and skill but against high-geared industrial requirements. Even when we praise a child's achievement in the home we are outraged if such praise is interpreted as being of the same order as praise of adults. The child is praised because the parent feels well disposed, regardless of whether the task is well done by adult standards, and the child acquires no sensible standard by which to measure its achievement. The gravity of a Cheyenne Indian family ceremoniously making a feast out of the little boy's first snowbird is at the furthest remove from our behavior. At birth the little boy was presented with a toy bow, and from the time he could run about serviceable bows suited to his stature were specially made for him by the man of the family. Animals and birds were taught him in a graded series beginning with those most easily taken, and as he brought in his first of each species his family duly made a feast of it, accepting his contribution as gravely as the buffalo his father brought. When he finally killed a buffalo, it was only the final step of his childhood conditioning, not a new adult role with which his childhood experience had been at variance.

The Canadian Ojibwa show clearly what results can be achieved. This tribe gains its livelihood by winter trapping and the small family of father, mother and children live during the long winter alone on their great frozen hunting grounds. The boy accompanies his father and brings in his catch to his sister as his father does to his mother; the girl prepares the meat and skins for him just as his mother does for her husband. By the time the boy is twelve he may have set his own line of traps on a hunting territory of his own and return to his parent's house only once in several months—still bringing the meat and skins to his sister. The young child is taught consistently that it has only itself to rely upon in life, and this is as true in the dealings it will have with the supernatural as in the business of getting a livelihood. This attitude he will accept as a successful adult just as he accepted it as a child.[1]

2. Dominance—Submission

Dominance—submission is the most striking of those categories of behavior where like does not respond to like but where one type of behavior stimulates the opposite response. It is one of the most prominent ways in which behavior is patterned in our culture. When it obtains between classes, it may be nourished by continuous experience; the difficulty in its use between children and adults lies in the fact that an individual conditioned to one set of behavior in childhood must adopt the opposite as an adult. Its opposite is a pattern of approximately identical reciprocal behavior, and societies which rely upon continuous conditioning characteristically invoke this pattern. In some primitive cultures the very terminology of address between father and son, and more commonly, between grandchild and grandson or uncle and nephew, reflects this attitude. In such kinship terminologies one reciprocal expresses each of these relationships so that son and father, for instance, exchange the same term with one another, just as we exchange the same term with a cousin. The child later will exchange it with his son. "Father—son," therefore, is a continuous relationship he enjoys throughout life. The same continuity, backed up by verbal reci-

[1] Landes, Ruth, *The Ojibwa Woman,* Part 1. Youth—Columbia University Contributions to Anthropology, Volume XXXI.

procity, occurs far oftener in the grandchild-grandson relationship or that of mother's brother-sister's son. When these are "joking" relationships, as they often are, travellers report wonderingly upon the liberties and pretensions of tiny toddlers in their dealings with these family elders. In place of our dogma of respect to elders such societies employ in these cases a reciprocity as nearly identical as may be. The teasing and practical joking the grandfather visits upon his grandchild, the grandchild returns in like coin; he would be led to believe that he failed in propriety if he did not give like for like. If the sister's son has right of access without leave to his mother's brother's possessions, the mother's brother has such rights also to the child's possessions. They share reciprocal privileges and obligations which in our society can develop only between age mates.

From the point of view of our present discussion, such kinship conventions allow the child to put in practice from infancy the same forms of behavior which it will rely upon as an adult; behavior is not polarized into a general requirement of submission for the child and dominance for the adult.

It is clear from the techniques described above by which the child is conditioned to a responsible status role that these depend chiefly upon arousing in the child the desire to share responsibility in adult life. To achieve this little stress is laid upon obedience but much stress upon approval and praise. Punishment is very commonly regarded as quite outside the realm of possibility, and natives in many parts of the world have drawn the conclusion from our usual disciplinary methods that white parents do not love their children. If the child is not required to be submissive however, many occasions for punishment melt away; a variety of situations which call for it do not occur. Many American Indian tribes are especially explicit in rejecting the ideal of a child's submissive or obedient behavior. Prince Maximilian von Wied who visited the Crow Indians over a hundred years ago describes a father's boasting about his young son's intractibility even when it was the father himself who was flouted; "He will be a man," his father said. He would have been baffled at the idea that his child should show behavior which would obviously make him appear a poor creature in the eyes of his fellows if he used it as an adult. Dr. George Devereaux tells me of a special case of such an attitude among the Mohave at the present time. The child's mother was white and protested to its father that he must take action when the child disobeyed and struck him. "But why?" the father said, "he is little. He cannot possibly injure me." He did not know of any dichotomy according to which an adult expects obedience and a child must accord it. If his child had been docile he would simply have judged that it would become a docile adult—an eventuality of which he would not have approved.

Child training which brings about the same result is common also in other areas of life than that of reciprocal kinship obligations between child and adult. There is a tendency in our culture to regard every situation as having in it the seeds of a dominance-submission relationship. Even where dominance-submission is patently irrelevant we read in the dichotomy, assuming that in every situation there must be one person dominating another. On the other hand some cultures, even when the situation calls for leadership do not see it in terms of dominance-submission. To do justice to this attitude it would be necessary to describe their political and especially their economic arrangements, for such an attitude to persist must certainly be supported by economic mechanisms that are congruent with it. But it must also be supported by—or what comes to the same thing, express itself in—child training and familial situations.

3. Contrasted Sexual Role

Continuity of conditioning in training the child to assume responsibility and to behave no more submissively than adults is quite possible in terms of the child's physiological endowment if his participation is suited to his strength. Because of the late development of the child's reproductive organs continuity of conditioning in sex experience presents a difficult problem. So far as their belief that the child is anything but a sexless being is concerned, they are probably more nearly right than we are with an opposite dogma. But the great break is presented by the universally sterile unions before puberty and the presumably fertile ones after maturation. This physiological fact no amount of cultural manipulation can minimize or alter, and societies therefore which stress continuous conditioning most strongly sometimes do not expect children to be interested in sex experience until they have matured physically. This is striking among American Indian tribes like the Dakota; adults observe great privacy in sex acts and in no way stimulate children's sexual activity. There need be no discontinuity, in the sense in which I have used the term, in such a program if the child is taught nothing it does not have to unlearn later. In such cultures adults view children's experimentation as in no way wicked or dangerous but merely as innocuous play which can have no serious consequences. In some societies such play is minimal and the children manifest little interest in it. But the same attitude may be taken by adults in societies where such play is encouraged and forms a major activity among small children. This is true among most of the Melanesian cultures of Southeast New Guinea; adults go as far as to laugh off sexual affairs within the prohibited class if the children are not mature, saying that since they cannot marry there can be no harm done.

It is this physiological fact of the difference between children's sterile unions and adults' presumably fertile sex relations which must be kept in mind in order to understand the different mores which almost always govern sex expression in children and in adults in the same culture. A great many cultures with preadolescent sexual license require marital fidelity and a great many which value pre-marital virginity in either male or female arrange their marital life with great license. Continuity in sex experience is complicated by factors which it was unnecessary to consider in the problems previously discussed. The essential problem is not whether or not the child's sexuality is consistently exploited—for even where such exploitation is favored in the majority of cases the child must seriously modify his behavior at puberty or at marriage. Continuity in sex expression means rather that the child is taught nothing it must unlearn later. If the cultural emphasis is upon sexual pleasure the child who is continuously conditioned will be encouraged to experiment freely and pleasurably, as among the Marquesans;[2] if emphasis is upon reproduction, as among the Zuni of New Mexico, childish sex proclivities will not be exploited for the only important use which sex is thought to serve in his culture is not yet possible to him. The important contrast with our child training is that although a Zuni child is impressed with the wickedness of premature sex experimentation he does not run the risk as in our culture of associating this wickedness with sex itself rather than with sex at his age. The adult in our culture has often failed to unlearn the wickedness or the dangerousness of sex, a lesson which was impressed upon him strongly in his most formative years.

Discontinuity in Conditioning

Even from this very summary statement of continuous conditioning the economy of such mores is evident. In spite of the obvious advantages, however, there are difficulties in its way. Many primitive societies expect as different behavior from an individual as child and as adult as we do, and such discontinuity involves a presumption of strain.

Many societies of this type however minimize strain by the techniques they employ, and some techniques are more successful than others in ensuring the individual's functioning without conflict. It is from this point of view that age-grade societies reveal their fundamental significance. Age-graded cultures characteristically demand different behavior of the individual at different times of his life and persons of a like age-grade are grouped into a society whose activities are all oriented toward the behavior desired at that age. Individuals "graduate" publicly and with honor from one of these groups to another. Where age society members are enjoined to loyalty and mutual support, and are drawn not only from the local group but from the whole tribe as among the Arapaho, or even from other tribes as among the Wagawaga of Southeast New Guinea, such an institution has many advantages in eliminating conflicts among local groups and fostering intra-

[2] Ralph Linton: class notes on the Marquesans.

tribal peace. This seems to be also a factor in the tribal military solidarity of the similarly organized Masai of East Africa. The point that is of chief interest for our present discussion however is that by this means an individual who at any time takes on a new set of duties and virtues is supported not only by a solid phalanx of age mates but by the traditional prestige of the organized "secret" society into which he has now graduated. Fortified in this way, individuals in such cultures often swing between remarkable extremes of opposite behavior without apparent psychic threat. For example, the great majority exhibit prideful and nonconflicted behavior at each stage in the life cycle even when a prime of life devoted to passionate and aggressive head hunting must be followed by a later life dedicated to ritual and to mild and peacable civic virtues.[3]

Our chief interest here, however, is in discontinuity which primarily affects the child. In many primitive societies such discontinuity has been fostered not because of economic or political necessity or because such discontinuity provides for a socially valuable division of labor, but because of some conceptual dogma. The most striking of these are the Australian and Papuan cultures where the ceremony of the "Making of Man" flourishes. In such societies it is believed that men and women have opposite and conflicting powers, and male children, who are of undefined status, must be initiated into the male role. In Central Australia the boy child is of the woman's side and women are tabu in the final adult stages of tribal ritual. The elaborate and protracted initiation ceremonies of the Arunta therefore snatch the boy from the mother, dramatize his gradual repudiation of her. In a final ceremony he is reborn as a man out of the men's ceremonial "baby pouch." The men's ceremonies are ritual statements of a masculine solidarity, carried out by fondling one another's *churingas,* the material symbol of each man's life, and by letting out over one another blood drawn from their veins. After this warm bond among men has been established through the ceremonies, the boy joins the men in the men's house and participates in tribal rites.[4] The enjoined discontinuity has been tribally bridged.

West of the Fly River in southern New Guinea there is a striking development of this Making of Men cult which involves a childhood period of passive homosexuality. Among the Keraki [5] it is thought that no boy can grow to full stature without playing the role for some years. Men slightly older take the active role, and the older man is a jealous partner. The life cycle of the Keraki Indians includes, therefore, in succession, passive homosexuality, active homosexuality and heterosexuality. The Keraki believe that

---

[3] Henry Elkin, manuscript on the Arapaho.
[4] Spencer, B., and Gillen, F. J., *The Arunta;* N.Y., Macmillan, 1927 (2 vols.). Róheim, Géza, Psycho-Analysis of Primitive Cultural Types. *Internat. J. Psychoanal.* (1932) 13:1-224–in particular, Chapter III, on the Aranda, The Children of the Desert.
[5] Williams, Francis E., *Papuans of the Trans-Fly,* Oxford, 1936.

pregnancy will result from post-pubertal passive homosexuality and see evidences of such practices in any fat man whom even as an old man, they may kill or drive out of the tribe because of their fear. The ceremony that is of interest in connection with the present discussion takes place at the end of the period of passive homosexuality. This ceremony consists in burning out the possibility of pregnancy from the boy by pouring lye down his throat, after which he has no further protection if he gives way to the practice. There is no technique for ending active homosexuality, but this is not explicitly tabu for older men; heterosexuality and children however are highly valued. Unlike the neighboring Marindanim who share their homosexual practices, Keraki husband and wife share the same house and work together in the gardens.

I have chosen illustrations of discontinuous conditioning where it is not too much to say that the cultural institutions furnish adequate support to the individual as he progresses from role to role or interdicts the previous behavior in a summary fashion. The contrast with arrangements in our culture is very striking, and against this background of social arrangements in other cultures the adolescent period of *Sturm und Drang* with which we are so familiar becomes intelligible in terms of our discontinuous cultural institutions and dogmas rather than in terms of physiological necessity. It is even more pertinent to consider these comparative facts in relation to maladjusted persons in our culture who are said to be fixated at one or another pre-adult level. It is clear that if we were to look at our social arrangements as an outsider, we should infer directly from our family institutions and habits of child training that many individuals would not "put off childish things"; we should have to say that our adult activity demands traits that are interdicted in children, and that far from redoubling efforts to help children bridge this gap, adults in our culture put all the blame on the child when he fails to manifest spontaneously the new behavior or, overstepping the mark, manifests it with untoward belligerence. It is not surprising that in such a society many individuals fear to use behavior which has up to that time been under a ban and trust instead, though at great psychic cost, to attitudes that have been exercised with approval during their formative years. Insofar as we invoke a physiological scheme to account for these neurotic adjustments we are led to overlook the possibility of developing social institutions which would lessen the social cost we now pay; instead we elaborate a set of dogmas which prove inapplicable under other social conditions.

The Vanishing Adolescent:
ADOLESCENCE:
Self-definition and Conflict

Edgar Z. Friedenberg

One of the most precise clues to what is actually going on psychologically in a culture is its use of language. People only bother to name those aspects of their experience that mean something to them. Those who share the language, therefore, share to some extent a common situation and a common concern.

If a people have no word for something, either it does not matter to them or it matters too much to talk about. If they *do* have a word for something, it is worth asking why they have included in their concept just what they have, and not other aspects which might, from a slightly different point of view, easily have been included. And if they cannot use the words they have without becoming arch, coy, or diffuse—if they cannot discuss a subject of apparent importance to them with vigor and precision—they are clearly in some kind of trouble about it. When experience is deformed by conflict or anxiety, language no longer quite fits. The personal needs of those who are trying to discuss a problem come between their experience and their common symbols, and they find it difficult or impossible to speak about it normally.

Adolescence is one of the topics which is subject to all these difficulties and which is correspondingly difficult to discuss intelligibly in English. Despite our exaggerated concern for and almost prurient interest in the "teenager," we have no neutral term for persons between the ages of, say, fourteen and twenty-one. "Adolescent" has overtones at once pedantic and erotic, suggestive of primitive fertility rites and of the orgies of classical antiquity. "Young person" meets the requirements of British jurisprudence in referring precisely to a portion of this age range, but is too poor in connotations to be a useful phrase in ordinary speech. "Teen-ager" remains the choice for popular usage. It is patronizing, and sounds rather uneasy and embarrassed; but these qualities may add to its appeal, for many of us do indeed respond to adolescence with forced joviality.

There is no English noun which simply identifies precisely persons between the ages of fourteen and twenty-one, leaving the reader free to feel what he pleases about them. This is odd. We have neutral nouns for persons and things that arouse feeling in nearly everyone: child, adult, hangman, cancer, mother, mistress, senator. These are exact; they mean what they mean. They can be dissociated from their connotations if the context demands it. "Teen-ager" cannot be. What does one call an eighteen-year-old girl if one wishes to note that she has triumphed as Joan of Arc or Anne Frank, or written another successful novel? What does one call an eighteen-year-old boy in reporting that he has been killed in a training maneuver at boot camp? Such things do not happen to "teen-agers," absorbed as they are in delinquency and in endless telephone discussions of rock and roll.

Yet, if we have no convenient language for discussing adolescence we seem equally unable to dismiss it. And this too is rather odd. What is there about these eight or so years that lingers so in the psyche? Granted that puberty is a notable event, that the onset of sexual maturity and the bodily changes which ensue are dramatic, and that no language applies its word for "child" to persons beyond the early teens. Nothing so conspicuous demarcates the adolescent from the young adult; yet adults who are no longer young are likely to feel much more at ease with a young man of twenty-five than with a boy of eighteen. They place the two in different classes of humanity, while allotting thirty years, more or less, to middle age. These thirty years also bring changes in personality and body build, but we see them as gradual and have not divided them up with conceptual barriers.

This conception of an upper limit to adolescence is by no means universal. In most primitive cultures—variable as these are—young people are usually initiated into adult life shortly after puberty. They are conducted through *rites de passage* of varying degrees of harshness designed to "separate the men from the boys"; the separation is not a genuine period of adolescence but a brief *interregnum*. Essentially, in such societies, one is either a child or an adult, though adult society is marked by status differences quite as complex and elaborate as ours.

Adolescence is conceived as a distinct stage of life in societies so complicated and differentiated that each individual's social role and function takes years to define and learn. When years of special preparation for adult life are required, these years become a distinguishable period with its own rules, customs, and relationships. The ordeal of the classical British preparatory and public school, for example, could not simply be sweated out in a burst of adolescent pluck; the initiation became a way of life. To instill into youth the complex code of the empire-builder and gentleman so thoroughly that this would be maintained in loneliness and isolation, and even under conditions in which it had become something of a nuisance to all concerned, took time and more than time. It took experience, under discipline, in relating to many different kinds of people whose status with respect to oneself varied sharply. In this way, the schoolboy learned to respond with spontaneous and often deep personal feeling to some of the people and events in his life, while limiting the *range* of his response to persons and situations he had learned to regard as worth noticing.

The British public school, at its most imposing, made adolescence much more than an interregnum. It made it an epoch. Its austerity could be relieved by a sensitive husbanding of sparse human resources; its heroes became myths, and in turn clichés, but the schoolboy had strong feelings about them. The prefect who caned you for specific offenses might, at other times, offer brusque understanding when you seriously needed it. He might also be a sadistic bully, or simply a rather stupid boy who was good at games. There were classmates with whom you could share brief, vivid perceptions and long, comfortable silences, though there were many more with whom you could share nothing. There were masters who had some respect for scholarship and for boys, and there were others who respected neither. All these defined themselves through the years as individuals as well as parts of a system. They could be fought, but there was no getting away from them or erasing your experience with them. At best, they helped the adolescent make himself into a strongly characterized human being who was ready to go on to something more: at worst, their impact made adolescence interminable and their victims permanently fixated "old boys." In any case, they defined the content of adolescence; they gave the adolescent something to be adolescent about.

In a society that sets up special institutions for inducting the young into it, and takes several years doing it, the developmental process that we call adolescence can occur. This institutional provision need not, however, be formal or intentionally planned. A delinquent gang is such an institution. And even institutions as formal and coercive as the classical British public school or the old-fashioned military school influenced their students most strongly in ways that were not consciously planned, though they were certainly the consequence of powerful unconscious intentions.

The unconscious and conscious intentions that dominate a society are, of course, expressed through all its institutions, including those that deal with adolescents. The institutions which mold the adolescence of most young people in technically developed countries today are the instruments of a very different society from that which created the British public school or the military school. They are intended to yield young people predisposed to very different social behavior. They are seldom coercive or immediately painful, but rather informal, democratic, and apparently mild in operation. They make use of sanctions that hardly hurt at all when applied, but that often make their victims ill much later.

The kind of character these institutions—whether the school, the TV, or even the modern army and navy—tend to develop is in many ways the very opposite of that which the British public school, or the old-fashioned school of any kind, sought consciously and unconsciously to produce. All the contemporary institutions that bear on the young, diverse as they seem to be, are united in their insistence on cultivating sensitivity and pliability to the demands and expectations of other persons. Other-direction, adaptability, adjustment, conformity—call it what you will, the idea is familiar enough—is a trait of great short-run, social usefulness in today's relatively open and rootless society; and that society has done a formidable job of creating institutions which mold other-directed and adjustable character structure.

One might expect that the general increase in blandness and good humor which has resulted would also have sweetened the relationship between adults and adolescents; and in many ways it has. There are real friendships between adolescents and adults in contemporary society, especially in America; it is taken for granted that there should be. This would not have been possible earlier, and it is still most unusual in many European or Latin-American countries. It is a basic development in human relations, scarcely less important than the simultaneous improvement in relations among different racial groups, which is resulting from quite similar social changes.

But the modern emphasis on cooperation and group adjustment has also injured the relationship between adolescents and adults in two very significant ways. These are not very widely recognized, but they lie, I believe, at the root of our difficulty in considering adolescence without self-consciousness or conflict. The first of these is rather superficial; the second is much more serious.

The tolerant, reasonable, democratic approach to "teen-agers"—like the comparable approach to formerly discriminated racial groups—is based on a premise of greater respect for them than the earlier attitude of coercive, if paternalistic, dominance. This much is valuable. But the same difficulty arises as in the improvement of interracial relations. In order for this to occur smoothly, the members of the dominant group must like and respect the subordinate group a good deal in the first place. If adults dislike or fear adolescents, the change will make those adults more frightened and more hostile, because it is a very real threat to their continued domination. In today's society they will probably have to be "nice to the kids" despite their fear and hostility; but they will most certainly try to maintain by seduction and manipulation the dominance they previously achieved by coercion and punishment.

This, it seems to me, is what usually does happen. Certainly, there are many exceptions, and the proportion seems to be growing nicely; but I think a detached observer of the behavior and attitudes of school personnel, juvenile court officials, and so forth would probably conclude that, on the whole, these individuals dislike and distrust youngsters more often than they like them. They are often disturbed at the prospect of being involved with young people in any situation that is not under their quite complete control; a dean who has grown accustomed to functioning as a rather fair-minded though rigid martinet is likely to become unscrupulous and conspiratorial if changes in his school force him to act as "adviser" to an ostensibly self-governing student disciplinary committee. Such officials are usually willing to abandon coercive techniques of control in favor of manipulative ones, since these help them preserve a more favorable image of themselves as guides who are liked and accepted by their charges; and, in any case, manipulative techniques work better than coercive ones with modern youngsters, who are usually quite skilled themselves at making tyrants feel guilty. But the teacher, dean, or probation officer who genuinely sees youngsters as persons of dignity equal to himself and who is satisfied to have purely rational authority over them is still rather the exception. The point can be overstressed, and I do not mean to suggest that the planet has become a sort of Madison Avenue streamlined version of Dotheboy's Hall. But the perception of the orientation of the world of adults toward adolescents so well and movingly expressed by Holden Caulfield in *The Catcher in the Rye* seems to me almost wholly valid.

Much of the ambivalence of adults toward "teen-agers" is, I should judge, simply a kind of repressed panic-response to the liquidation of authority over them. It must be understood, however, that the loss of authority is real; the adult empire is tottering. All empires are; this is the era of skepticism about the relationship between authority and status. It is an error, I believe, to interpret what is happening as a decline in respect for authority as such. American youngsters today are generous in according respect to parents, teachers, and other adults who earn it as individuals; and they are far more perceptive of individual quality in their elders than they could possibly have been when all adults were regarded as potentially or actually hostile and dangerous. But it is true that they are less likely to respect an adult today simply because he occupies a position of authority. It is also true that a boy who can be punished for insulting you is far less frightening— even if he is *very* insulting—than a boy who offers out of sheer kindness to share his analyst with you because he has noticed, correctly, that you need help worse than he does.

Adults who do not basically like and respect adolescents—and this includes a large proportion of those who make a career of working with them —are badly frightened by the increasingly democratic relationships between adolescents and adults that are coming to prevail in our society. They have become more tense in their attitude toward youngsters, and contribute greatly to the difficulties of young people in our society. Their manipulative and covert hostility demoralizes adolescents and forms the basis of real personal and social problems. It is easier, and less damaging, for a youngster to face bad grades, disappointment at being passed over for a team or a club, or formal punishment, than it is for him to deal with gossip about his character or his manners, with teachers who pass the word along that he is a troublemaker or that he needs special patience and guidance because his father drinks.

Nevertheless, this is probably not too serious a matter, for it is pretty certain to work itself out in the course of time. Newer and better trained teachers and social workers tend to be of a somewhat different stamp. The youngsters themselves grow more accustomed to respectful handling and more confident of it; they become less rebellious but also less easily diverted from their own moral judgments and decisions. When they *do* nevertheless have to deal with a hostile or tricky adult, they are more likely to know what they want and what they are doing, and can face him coolly. He, in turn, is *not* really confident of himself or his authority, and rapidly becomes more anxious. He may stubbornly refuse to listen; he may lose his temper and really try to hurt them, and this time he may succeed. But he also finds that his efforts to dominate the young cause him more anxiety than he can easily bear. Unless his superiors support him in a counterattack, he is likely to withdraw gradually behind a barrage of indignant complaint. Ultimately, he becomes picturesque; the young may grow quite fond of him.

What is far more serious that the emphasis on cooperation and group adjustment characteristic of modern life interferes specifically with the central developmental task of adolescence itself. *This task is self-definition. Adolescence is the period during which a young person learns who he is, and what he really feels. It is the time during which he differentiates himself from his culture, though on the culture's terms. It is the age at which, by becoming a person in his own right, he becomes capable of deeply felt relationships to other individuals perceived clearly as such.* It is precisely this sense of individuality which fails to develop, or develops only feebly, in most primitive cultures or among lower-status social groups. A successful initiation leads to group solidarity and a warm sense of belonging; a successful adolescence adds to these a profound sense of self—of one's own personality.

Personalization is the métier of adolescence. Of all persons, adolescents are the most intensely personal; their intensity is often uncomfortable to adults. As cooperation and group adjustment become pervasive social norms; as tolerance supersedes passion as the basis for social action; as personalization becomes false-personalization, adolescence becomes more and more difficult. Conceivably, it might become again a rather rare event, having no function in the new world of glad-handing primitives happy among their electronic trinkets. But, for the present at least, the old norms of individual character, personal devotion, particular love and hate retain enough authority to make those who remain faithful to them, as adolescents tend to do, extremely troublesome to their contemporaries.

Adolescents often behave much like members of an old-fashioned aristocracy. They maintain private rituals, which they often do not really understand themselves. They are extremely conservative in their dress and tastes, but the conventions to which they adhere are purely those of their own social group; they try to ignore the norms of the larger society if these conflict with their own. They can be extravagantly generous and extravagantly cruel, but rarely petty or conniving. Their virtues are courage and loyalty;

while the necessity for even a moderate degree of compromise humiliates them greatly. They tend to be pugnacious and quarrelsome about what they believe to be their rights, but naïve and reckless in defending them. They are shy, but not modest. If they become very anxious they are likely to behave eccentrically, to withdraw, or to attack with some brutality; they are less likely to blend themselves innocuously into the environment with an apologetic smile. They are honest on occasions when even a stupid adult would have better sense.

They are therefore at a considerable disadvantage in many relationships of modern life. Modern life is hostile to the aristocratic social principle. Aristocratic attitudes and modes of action snarl its very mainsprings. They interfere with the conduct of practical affairs and impede administrative action. In busy, anxious, and ambitious people, they arouse anger and resentment; but beneath the anger and resentment there is shame and guilt.

Adolescents insult us by quietly flaunting their authenticity. They behave as if they did not even know that passion and fidelity are expensive, but merely assumed that everyone possessed them. This, certainly, is inexcusably valorous; and it is not excused. But it makes us awkward in their presence, and embarrassed in our approach to them.

Not all adolescents, by any means, retain this quality. There are many who learn to soothe adults ruffled by encounters with their more ardent and challenging peers, and charm them on suitable occasions by an ingratiating youthfulness. When a boy or girl is needed for display, they are available; in the same clothes all the others wear, they look a little—not too much—neater. Having them in charge of the school paper and the student government saves a good deal of wear and tear all around; they are described in their school records as having qualities of leadership.

At certain times and places—perhaps here and now—such boys and girls predominate. Processes comparable to natural selection almost insure that they will. Schools nudge them into the pathways believed to lead to success in adult life and rehearse them for it in carefully designed facsimiles of adult institutions. Student life in the modern high school is now conducted through a veritable rat-maze of committees. The big man on campus is a perfectly executed scale model of a junior executive. It may therefore seem either inconsistent or willfully sentimental that I have described my heuristic model of an adolescent as a knight in shining chino pants.

But I think it is valid to maintain this, not just because I have encountered a goodly few such errant defenders of the faith in the course of half a lifetime, but because I am concerned here with a process of growth rather than with a statistical norm. There is certainly no doubt that modern society has power to corrupt, and that it starts early. But the function of adolescence is growth and individuation, and these can be fruitful only if a reasonable and increasing degree of integrity is maintained.

A youngster who has abandoned the task of defining himself in dialectical combat with society and becomes its captive and its emissary may be no rarity; but he is a casualty. There is not much more to be said about him: one can only write him off and trust that the world will at least feed him well if it cannot keep him warm. The promise of maturity must be fulfilled by those who are strong enough to grow into it at their own rate as full bargaining members.

Must there be conflict between the adolescent and society? The point is that adolescence *is* conflict—protracted conflict—between the individual and society. There are cultures in which this conflict seems hardly to occur; but where it does not, the characteristic development of personality which we associate with adolescence does not occur either.

There are cultures, as in Margaret Mead's classic description of coming of age in Samoa, where the young pass delicately as Ariel through puberty into adulthood. But their peoples do not seem to us like adults; they are charming people, but they are from our point of view insufficiently characterized. There is not much difference between them, and they do not seem to make much difference to one another.

In other simple cultures, in which the role of the adult is likewise thoroughly familiar to the child by the time he reaches puberty, the young are initiated into adult life much more harshly. Sometimes the process is more loving than it appears to be, though the very fact that adults find it necessary to inflict it is conclusive evidence of some hostility toward the young. In any case, it is comparatively brief. Some of these cultures are primitive; others are relatively stable subcultures of the Western world like that of British coal miners whose sons are hazed into adult status by their elders when they first enter the mines themselves. But in these as well, the adults seem curiously indistinguishable by our criteria of personality. Differences of temperament and of attitude toward life may be very conspicuous indeed. But they stop short of what we regard as normal variation of human personality; the range is as wide, but not as deep.

And there are other cultures in which there is no conflict because conflict is thoroughly repressed. Not by externally applied brutality—this suppresses; it does not effectively repress. There are adolescents even in totalitarian countries, as the Polish and Hungarian authorities discovered in 1956. But where totalitarianism really sinks in, even the young will be so intensely anxious that no conflict will arise. Only those feelings and attitudes approved by society will then even occur to them as possibilities. There can be no adolescence in *1984*.

Conflict between the individual and society, as Lionel Trilling has so clearly stated in *Freud and the Crisis of Our Culture*,[1] is inherent in the development of personality by the standards of Western man. Freud is still

[1] Lionel Trilling, *Freud and the Crisis of Our Culture* (Boston: The Beacon Press, 1955).

the source of our most tough-minded psychodynamic system, and this point is basic to it. And it is in adolescence that this conflict is critical to individual development. Or to put it another way, and perhaps more truly, adolescence *is* this conflict, no matter how old the individual is when it occurs. Adolescent conflict is the instrument by which an individual learns the complex, subtle, and precious difference between himself and his environment. In a society in which there is no difference, or in which no difference is permitted, the word "adolescence" has no meaning.

But conflict is not war; it need not even involve hostile action. It must, to be sure, produce some hostile feelings, among others. But there need be no intent to wound, castrate, or destroy on either side. Conflict between the adolescent and his world is dialectical, and leads, as a higher synthesis, to the youth's own adulthood and to critical participation in society as an adult. Some of the experiences of adolescence which turn out to be most beneficial to growth are, it is true, painful at the time. Looking for your first job, among strangers; learning that your first love is the girl she is but not the girl you need; getting soundly beaten in your first state-wide track meet when you are used to being the fastest runner in town—none of this is fun. But such experiences are not sickening, heartbreaking, or terrifying because, even at the time, they can be felt as bringing you in closer touch with reality. The pain they produce is somehow accepted as benign, like soreness following unaccustomed physical exercise or the pain of normal childbirth. Growth is more satisfying, and far more reassuring, than comfort; though normal growth is comfortable most of the time.

One cannot, therefore, use the inevitability of conflict in adolescence as a justification for actions which hurt adolescents on the pretext of "toughening them up." If "growing pains" are never sickening, heartbreaking, or terrifying, it is equally true that heartbreak, terror, and a sense of insult and violation contribute nothing to growth. They stunt it or twist it, and the grower is more or less deformed. Perhaps the commonest deformation which these cause in persons too young to know how to handle themselves in pain is apathy.

In their encounters with society, youngsters are frequently badly hurt, and there is no mistaking this kind of agony for growing pains. They are sickened and terrified; they feel their pride break, cringe from the exposure of their privacy to manipulation and attack, and are convulsed with humiliation as they realize that they cannot help cringing and that, in fact, their responses are now pretty much beyond their control. Control once regained is consolidated at a less humane level; there will be no more love lost or chances taken on the adversary.

A number of psychological and social dynamisms can take over at this juncture; none of them is a part of the process of healthy growth, though some at least give time for scars to form so that growth may be resumed later. But most of these defense mechanisms are dangerous in their total context, although they make perfectly good sense in the light of the victim's immediate emotional condition. This is the fundamental dilemma of organism. A severe heart attack is not such a bad idea from the immediate viewpoint of the exhausted heart, if only the rest of the body and the heart itself, as a muscle, were not so thirsty for blood. Somehow, however it has been insulted, the heart must be kept in action, for its own sake as well as for that of the body as a whole; though a wise physician knows when to keep demands on it to a minimum, and also knows that the minimum may still be more than can be borne.

Growth, too, must continue. Apathy, a fawning acceptance of authority, or a hard-eyed campaign of organized delinquency with enough real violence to show you mean business, may all be understood as functional for adolescents bearing certain kinds of wounds. But understandable or not, functional or not, these are dangerous expedients for the young. They may provide cover for the process of healing, and facilitate the formation of strong emotional scar tissue. But they not only lead to more trouble with society; they lead away from the kinds of relationships by which growth continues, and from the kind of self-perception of which growth consists.

Delinquency, apathy, and seductive fawning are not aspects of the essential conflict between youth and society which constitutes adolescence. They are the consequences of the conflict having gone terribly wrong, and a corresponding wisdom and patience—more than is usually available under actual working conditions—are needed to restore it as a fruitful process. For most young people, of course, things do not go terribly wrong. They go moderately wrong, but we nevertheless grow up, more or less, and conduct ourselves toward the next generation in its need with such humanity as we can muster. For the result, no blame attaches. Adam and Eve, at the time that Cain was born, had no opportunity to read the works of Gesell.

I know of no reason to suppose that, at the present time, there is a crisis in our relationship to youth. But if the function of adolescence is self-definition, one would expect it to be very difficult in a society which suffers from a dearth of individuality and in which alienation is a crucial problem. And if the instrument of self-definition is the conflict between the adolescent and a basically humane society—which nevertheless has purposes of its own, and more to do than take care of kids—one would expect the self-defining process to break down as that society became less humane and more manipulative. A society which has *no purposes* of its own, other than to insure domestic tranquility by suitable medication, will have no use for adolescents, and will fear them; for they will be among the first to complain, as they crunch away at their benzedrine, that tranquilizers make you a square. It will set up sedative programs of guidance, which are likely to be described as therapeutic, but whose apparent function will be to keep young minds and hearts in custody till they are without passion.

We have by no means gone so far as yet; but the sort of process of which I speak is already discernible.

Adolescence and the Life Cycle

Erik H. Erikson

As technological advances put more and more time between early school life and the young person's final access to specialized work, the stage of adolescing becomes an even more marked and conscious period and, as it has always been in some cultures in some periods, almost a way of life between childhood and adulthood. Thus in the later school years young people, beset with the physiological revolution of their genital maturation and the uncertainty of the adult roles ahead, seem much concerned with faddish attempts at establishing an adolescent subculture with what looks like a final rather than a transitory or, in fact, initial identity formation. They are sometimes morbidly, often curiously, preoccupied with what they appear to be in the eyes of others as compared with what they feel they are, and with the question of how to connect the roles and skills cultivated earlier with the ideal prototypes of the day. In their search for a new sense of continuity and sameness, which must now include sexual maturity, some adolescents have to come to grips again with crises of earlier years before they can install lasting idols and ideals as guardians of a final identity. They need, above all, a moratorium for the integration of the identity elements ascribed in the foregoing to the childhood stages: only that now a larger unit, vague in its outline and yet immediate in its demands, replaces the childhood milieu—"society." A review of these elements is also a list of adolescent problems.

If the earliest stage bequeathed to the identity crisis an important need for trust in oneself and in others, then clearly the adolescent looks most fervently for men and ideas to have *faith* in, which also means men and ideas in whose service it would seem worthwhile to prove oneself trustworthy. At the same time, however, the adolescent fears a foolish, all too trusting commitment, and will, paradoxically, express his need for faith in loud and cynical mistrust.

If the second stage established the necessity of being defined by what one can *will* freely, then the adolescent now looks for an opportunity to decide with free assent on one of the available or unavoidable avenues of duty and service, and at the same time is mortally afraid of being forced into activities in which he would feel exposed to ridicule or self-doubt. This, too, can lead to a paradox, namely, that he would rather act shamelessly in the eyes of his elders, out of free choice, than be forced into activities which would be shameful in his own eyes or in those of his peers.

Reprinted by permission of the publisher, from Erik H. Erikson, *Identity: Youth and Crisis* (New York: W. W. Norton & Company, Inc., Copyright © 1968), pp. 128–134.

If an unlimited *imagination* as to what one *might* become is the heritage of the play age, then the adolescent's willingness to put his trust in those peers and leading, or misleading, elders who will give imaginative, if not illusory, scope to his aspirations is only too obvious. By the same token, he objects violently to all "pedantic" limitations on his self-images and will be ready to settle by loud accusation all his guiltiness over the excessiveness of his ambition.

Finally, if the desire to make something work, and to make it work well, is the gain of the school age, then the choice of an occupation assumes a significance beyond the question of remuneration and status. It is for this reason that some adolescents prefer not to work at all for a while rather than be forced into an otherwise promising career which would offer success without the satisfaction of functioning with unique excellence.

In any given period in history, then, that part of youth will have the most affirmatively exciting time of it which finds itself in the wave of a technological, economic, or ideological trend seemingly promising all that youthful vitality could ask for.

Adolescence, therefore, is least "stormy" in that segment of youth which is gifted and well trained in the pursuit of expanding technological trends, and thus able to identify with new roles of competency and invention and to accept a more implicit ideological outlook. Where this is not given, the adolescent mind becomes a more explicitly ideological one, by which we mean one searching for some inspiring unification of tradition or anticipated techniques, ideas, and ideals. And, indeed, it is the ideological potential of a society which speaks most clearly to the adolescent who is so eager to be affirmed by peers, to be confirmed by teachers, and to be inspired by worthwhile "ways of life." On the other hand, should a young person feel that the environment tries to deprive him too radically of all the forms of expression which permit him to develop and integrate the next step, he may resist with the wild strength encountered in animals who are suddenly forced to defend their lives. For, indeed, in the social jungle of human existence there is no feeling of being alive without a sense of identity.

Having come this far, I would like to give one example (and I consider it representative in structure) of the individual way in which a young person, given some leeway, may utilize a traditional way of life for dealing with a remnant of negative identity. I had known Jill before her puberty, when she was rather obese and showed many "oral" traits of voracity and dependency while she also was a tomboy and bitterly envious of her brothers and in rivalry with them. But she was intelligent and always had an air about her (as did her mother) which seemed to promise that things would turn out all right. And, indeed, she straightened out and up, became very attractive, an easy leader in any group, and, to many, a model of young girlhood. As a clinician, I watched and wondered what she would do with that voraciousness and with the rivalry which she had displayed earlier. Could it be that such things are simply absorbed in fortuitous growth?

Then one autumn in her late teens, Jill did not return to college from the ranch out West where she had spent the summer. She had asked her parents to let her stay. Simply out of liberality and confidence, they granted her this moratorium and returned East.

That winter Jill specialized in taking care of newborn colts, and would get up at any time during a winter night to bottle feed the most needy animals. Having apparently acquired a certain satisfaction within herself, as well as astonished recognition from the cowboys, she returned home and reassumed her place. I felt that she had found and hung on to an opportunity to do actively and for others what she had always yearned to have done for her, as she had once demonstrated by overeating: she had learned to feed needy young mouths. But she did so in a context which, in turning passive into active, also turned a former symptom into a social act.

One might say that she turned "maternal" but it was a maternalism such as cowboys must and do display; and, of course, she did it all in jeans. This brought recognition "from man to man" as well as from man to woman, and beyond that the confirmation of her optimism, that is, her feeling that something could be done that felt like her, was useful and worthwhile, and was in line with an ideological trend where it still made immediate practical sense.

Such self-chosen "therapies" depend, of course, on the leeway given in the right spirit at the right time, and this depends on a great variety of circumstances. I intend to publish similar fragments from the lives of children in greater detail at some future date; let this example stand for the countless observations in everyday life, where the resourcefulness of young people proves itself when the conditions are right.

The estrangement of this stage is *identity confusion*. For the moment, we will accept Biff's formulation in Arthur Miller's *Death of a Salesman:* "I just can't take hold, Mom, I can't take hold of some kind of a life." Where such a dilemma is based on a strong previous doubt of one's ethnic and sexual identity, or where role confusion joins a hopelessness of long standing, delinquent and "borderline" psychotic episodes are not uncommon. Youth after youth, bewildered by the incapacity to assume a role forced on him by the inexorable standardization of American adolescence, runs away in one form or another, dropping out of school, leaving jobs, staying out all night, or withdrawing into bizarre and inaccessible moods. Once "delinquent," his greatest need and often his only salvation is the refusal on the part of older friends, advisers, and judiciary personnel to type him further by pat diagnoses and social judgments which ignore the special dynamic conditions of adolescence. It is here, as we shall see in greater detail, that the concept of identity confusion is of practical clinical value, for if they are diagnosed and treated correctly, seemingly psychotic and criminal incidents do not have the same fatal significance which they may have at other ages.

In general it is the inability to settle on an occupational identity which most disturbs young people. To keep themselves together they temporarily overidentify with the heroes of cliques and crowds to the point of an apparently complete loss of individuality. Yet in this stage not even "falling in love" is entirely, or even primarily, a sexual matter. To a considerable extent adolescent love is an attempt to arrive at a definition of one's identity by projecting one's diffused self-image on another and by seeing it thus reflected and gradually clarified. This is why so much of young love is conversation. On the other hand, clarification can also be sought by destructive means. Young people can become remarkably clannish, intolerant, and cruel in their exclusion of others who are "different," in skin color or cultural background, in tastes and gifts, and often in entirely petty aspects of dress and gesture arbitrarily selected as the signs of an in-grouper or out-grouper. It is important to understand in principle (which does not mean to condone in all of its manifestations) that such intolerance may be, for a while, a necessary defense against a sense of identity loss. This is unavoidable at a time of life when the body changes its proportions radically, when genital puberty floods body and imagination with all manner of impulses, when intimacy with the other sex approaches and is, on occasion, forced on the young person, and when the immediate future confronts one with too many conflicting possibilities and choices. Adolescents not only help one another temporarily through such discomfort by forming cliques and stereotyping themselves, their ideals, and their enemies; they also insistently test each other's capacity for sustaining loyalties in the midst of inevitable conflicts of values.

The readiness for such testing helps to explain the appeal of simple and cruel totalitarian doctrines among the youth of such countries and classes as have lost or are losing their group identities—feudal, agrarian, tribal, or national. The democracies are faced with the job of winning these grim youths by convincingly demonstrating to them—by living it—that a democratic identity can be strong and yet tolerant, judicious and still determined. But industrial democracy poses special problems in that it insists on self-made identities ready to grasp many chances and ready to adjust to the changing necessities of booms and busts, of peace and war, of migration and determined sedentary life. Democracy, therefore, must present its adolescents with ideals which can be shared by young people of many backgrounds, and which emphasize autonomy in the form of independence and initiative in the form of constructive work. These promises, however, are not easy to fulfill in increasingly complex and centralized systems of industrial, economic, and political organization, systems which increasingly neglect the "self-made" ideology still flaunted in oratory. This is hard on many young Americans because their whole upbringing has made the development of a self-reliant personality dependent on a certain degree of choice, a sustained hope for an individual chance, and a firm commitment to the freedom of self-realization.

We are speaking here not merely of high privileges and lofty ideals but of psychological necessities. For the social institution which is the guardian of identity *is* what we have called *ideology*. One may see in ideology also the imagery of an aristocracy in its widest possible sense, which connotes that within a defined world image and a given course of history the best people will come to rule and rule will develop the best in people. In order not to become cynically or apathetically lost, young people must somehow be able to convince themselves that those who succeed in their anticipated adult world thereby shoulder the obligation of being best. For it is through their ideology that social systems enter into the fiber of the next generation and attempt to absorb into their lifeblood the rejuvenative power of youth. Adolescence is thus a vital regenerator in the process of social evolution, for youth can offer its loyalties and energies both to the conservation of that which continues to feel true and to the revolutionary correction of that which has lost its regenerative significance.

Non-commitment
as a Way of Life

Kenneth Keniston

That consistency and distinctiveness which we have uncovered in the ideology of the alienated cannot be found in a superficial survey of their daily behavior. To be sure, all of these young men were college students, and this fact alone gave a certain regularity to their lives—attending (or deciding to cut) classes, eating their meals in college dining halls, living in college residential houses. But these are the appointed activities of all college students, and in no way distinguish the alienated. In appearance and public manner, they do not differ from other students, apart, perhaps, from a mild predilection for "old clothes"—blue jeans and tattered jackets—which is shared by many but not all their classmates. They are a healthy group of young men, not disabled, infirm, or disadvantaged; they range from tall to short, from fat to thin, from handsome to homely. One once grew a rather scraggly beard and shaved it off soon after, but one brief beard out of twelve is about par for their classmates as a whole.

Seen in the college dining halls, walking to classes, or sitting in seminars and classrooms, these young men do not attract attention. An astute observer might comment that they seem to hold themselves slightly aloof from others at times, and suggest that they were shy or scornful or both; but another observer might be more impressed by their impetuous vehemence in other discussions and find them actively involved with their fellows. To be more ingenious in our search for alienated students, we might visit the campus coffee houses at 11:00 P.M., the cafeteria that has a reputation as a "beatnik" hangout, or the motorcycle and racing car set in the college. In some of these places, we might occasionally find one or two, but even then rather on the peripheries of the group.

A search through the college records would also yield little of note. Like all the students in the college, these young men arrived with test scores and school records which promised outstanding performances and attested to exceptional intellectual abilities; their academic achievements in college had been just about what was predicted for them at the beginning of their freshman year: they are neither "underachievers" nor "overachievers." And if we looked into the formal facts of their family backgrounds, we would find these ran the full gamut of possibilities in the college: average parental income high, as at any private college; parents highly educated (a B.A. and usually graduate work for one or both); typically upper middle-class in background, with a few aspiring young men from working-class homes and a few from more upper-class backgrounds. A slight disproportion of these subjects would mark "no religion" when asked their religious affiliations, but this would be more likely a result of alienation rather than a cause. Among those who were most critical of American popular culture, there would be very slightly more Jews than expected by chance, but the difference is miniscule, and religion would not begin to account for alienation.

A superficial survey of their daily activities would yield equally few results. We might note that none of these young men were engaged in varsity athletics, but their high-school records show somewhat more interest in sports. We might comment on their predilection for the humanities as majors, or the fact that there is an unusual concentration of alienated students at the college residence known for being most bohemian; but all of these facts would be readily expected from what we have learned of their broadly "aesthetic" interests. Despite their distrust of intimacy, they spend about as much time with the opposite sex as do their classmates. And if, by chance, it should occur to us that a group of young men with so oppositional an outlook might have come into open conflict with the "authorities," a search through the college or local police records would yield little result.

In most outward and public respects, then, Inburn is representative of alienated young men in his "typicalness." A more intensive look at the family backgrounds of these young men does indeed uncover special patterns of family relationship and history; but none of these can be related in this group to the usual sociological factors like social class, area of residence, religion, ethnic background, or death or divorce of parents. Quite possibly, were we to restudy these same young men when they were ten years older, we might find that they were doing very different kinds of things than their less alienated fellows. And were we to study the population at large, we would undoubtedly find a connection between social factors (e.g., low socio-economic status) and the amount of alienation present. But among these students, social and religious background have little to do with alienation.

Yet the alienated *are* different from their non-alienated classmates: they usually do the same things but they do them in a special way; they differ not in *what* they do but in *how* they do it. In early adulthood (and probably throughout life), alienation expresses itself most characteristically as a *style of life,* a special attitude brought to ordinary activities, a special relationship to the crucial events of one's life—rather than as any simply identifiable kind of behavior or set of activities. Whatever the alienated do, they do in an alienated way; and by examining their style, we may come to understand better what alienation involves.

Intellectual Passion

I have already noted that the grade averages of the alienated are about what they should be according to pre-admission predictions. As a group, the alienated tend to be, if anything, slightly more able than their classmates, especially on I.Q. tests that measure "verbal" (as opposed to mathematical) aptitudes. And as a consequence, more than half of them are honors candidates in a college where about half of the student body maintains an honors (B) average. But if we look behind these over-all averages, a different picture begins to emerge. The extreme of this trend is one alienated student who announced early in his college career that getting good grades in college was "fantastically easy," and proceeded to take half again as many courses as required. At the end of one term on this schedule, his grades were A, B, B, C, D, and E, which gave him a B average for the four (highest) grades counted. Another student interested in architecture mastered the material in an advanced course in architectural engineering on his own, yet failed completely the required prerequisite for the same course because he disliked the lecturer, text, course, and section man, and consequently did none of his assignments. The course grade, because it was in addition to his required schedule, did not count on his average.

These are extreme results of the characteristic intellectual style of the alienated, a style which involves intensely passionate concentration on a few topics of particular personal importance, coupled with a relative inability to do other work. The special topics which excite the interest of these young men have three common characteristics: they are "far-out," unorthodox, esoteric, and unconventional; they bear a very close though symbolic relationship to the psychic concerns of the young men; and they are seldom academically unimpeachable. One young man, much worried about his ability to stand up under social pressures, became interested in the "brainwashing" of American POW's in Korea, and in a few weeks of total concentration managed to read and master practically everything written on the topic. Another student, in the throes of a conflict with his conventional parents, became interested in the development of criminal outlooks and for a time espoused the view that criminals were merely those who did not conform to conventional middle-class notions of morality. Still other students, concerned with their own fantasies and impulses, find in the study of psychoanalytic writings a way of structuring and organizing their thinking about themselves. The close connection between intellectual pursuit and personal concern is not always obvious to these young men—on the contrary, the obsessive quality of these interests often hides their more personal sources. But to an informed outside observer the connection is sometimes painfully clear.

Total intellectual passions are difficult to reconcile with college requirements, the more so since the timetable of these interests follows the vicissitudes of the psyche and not the established calendar of the academic year. Furthermore, the topics to which the alienated devote themselves are seldom academically respectable: they prefer Sartre to Kant, Ginsberg to the Elizabethan lyricists, and Wilhelm Reich to Pavlov. The assignment of a given writer in a course is often enough to kill any further interest in him among the alienated. One young man developed an intense interest in Shelley and Byron, and devoted many single-minded weeks to studying their work and their lives. But when they were assigned in a literature course, his interest disappeared and he found himself unable to do the assignments. Others react with a less extreme withdrawal of interest, or manage somehow tenuously to relate the requirements of their school work to their own interests; but all share the same predilection for topics at once personally meaningful and as distant as possible from the orthodoxies of the academic establishment.

The academic fate of students so disposed obviously depends in large part on the outlook of their college. In a college with detailed daily assignments and inflexible requirements, they will not prosper. Similarly, in any educational system where orthodoxy is strong, their oppositional streak will lead them into continual conflict with authoritative views and the authorities who support them. In understanding the academic successes of these students, it is important to recall that they attended a college noted for iconoclasm, heterogeneity, and laissez-faire attitude toward its undergraduates. Most of the courses available to these students offered them large freedom to tailor the course to their own needs: by choosing final exam questions on subjects close to their own intellectual passions and by writing term papers on such topics, they were often able to transform characterological necessity into an academic virtue. Even when they could not always do this, their successes in some areas canceled out their failures in others, to yield good over-all performance.

And when all is said and done, the alienated are in many ways extremely rewarding students to teach, partly because of the passion with which they approach any subject that fires their imagination, and partly because of their iconoclasm and questioning outlook. This iconoclasm appeals especially to the often harassed younger teachers on whom the burden of grading usually falls, because it expresses an oppositional streak which must be vigorously suppressed by those negotiating the perilous waters between Ph.D. and tenure. The alienated respond eagerly to challenging teaching; and when they are not challenged, alienated young men, who take the stated goals of most colleges cynically and dislike grades altogether, can approach the grading system with high calculation, doing just enough work to assure an honors grade, or carefully anticipating their likely grades to assure the desired over-all average. Like the student quoted above, many feel that getting grades is a matter of a system to outwit the "System," and that it is really "fantastically easy" if one is willing to make a few small compromises. And when the "heat is on" just before examinations, these students often have an extraordinary capacity for concentration, for completing a series of long-overdue term papers and simultaneously preparing for finals in long-neglected courses.

But for all their adequate if unconventional performance, these are not students who live happily in what must be, even in the most permissive college, a somewhat restrictive environment. As we might infer from their oppositional outlooks, they frequently attack their college, they despise any traces of "college spirit," and above all they question the merit and adequacy of their own participation in the educational process. Here again, the particular college they attended affected their outlook towards it, and probably, indirectly, toward many other things. For the alienated agreed with their classmates in finding their college unusually heterogeneous, unusually un-rigid, unusually free from pressures for conformity either among the students or from the faculty. At other colleges where the hand of student opinion was heavier, where there was a clear definition of the Big Man on Campus, the same young men would doubtless have taken the college itself as one of their primary targets, and might not have so fully developed that more generalized alienation we have seen in their philosophies. But this was seldom possible with these students: the college was so pluralistic and permissive that it tended to absorb and even encourage criticisms. So the discontents of these students could rarely be expended against their college; and when they were dissatisfied with their educations, as they often were, they most often tended to blame themselves. Of twelve alienated students, four withdrew from college before receiving their B.A.'s, and most of the rest seriously considered leaving at one time or another. Their reasons were instructive: they generally felt that they were not "getting what they should" from college; they often recognized that their inability to do assigned work with enthusiasm (if at all) meant they wasted much of their time; and most of them felt that they were seeking something which they had not begun to find in college. Self-blame predominated over blame of the college—as it does in most students who leave college in midstream. Though with one exception they did return after a year or two off, their year of working or wandering changed them relatively little in basic outlook, but merely convinced them that a B.A. was more worth having.

The Detached Observer

The doubts of the alienated about the educational process extended to the extracurricular activities in which they took part. A number of the alienated were involved in such activities; a few held, for a time at least, responsible positions in college organizations—but in their choice of these activities, in the roles they sought out within them, and above all, in the mode of their participation, they retained their alienated style. Alienated students find any institutional involvement complicated and troubled: they are not "joiners," and any hint of pressure leads them quickly to withdraw. They studiously avoided athletic competition (though some had taken part in secondary school athletic competition and one, despite small stature, had been an excellent high-school football player); and they equally consistently eschewed all activities and organizations with any possible taint of "college spirit" or "boosterism." Instead, they found their way into activities where their humanistic or dramatic interests could be expressed.

Some of these activities were quintessentially fugitive, like helping to found the small literary magazines that flourish and quickly die on and around the campus. Others were necessarily short-lived because they were theatrical; taking part in the production of one of the fifty or so plays annually produced by undergraduates also suited the alienated style of total absorption in one passionate endeavor. Other activities were literary in more conventional ways: writing for or editing one of the more established journals published by students. But in each of these activities the alienated tended to bring a particular alienated style. In one case, a young man much interested in the theater always got himself into production positions which, though essential, were nonetheless solitary, and allowed him total autonomy. Another student soon established a bad reputation for himself by becoming intensely involved in the direction of several plays, and after persuading or cajoling others to accept his principles of interpretation, losing interest and withdrawing from the show. Still another wrote for a number of "little magazines" on the campus, but was never willing to become involved in the actual running of the magazines. Another accepted a responsible position on a publication, but failed to meet deadlines and produced half the usual number of issues. And most characteristic of all was the alienated student, elected to an important position in a national organization, who, soon after his inauguration, quit college without warning either to his fellow students or the college authorities—as if "success," commitment, and responsibility had been more than he could bear.

We might well have inferred the principle of their extracurricular activities from the philosophies of alienated students: they dislike and distrust institutional involvements and responsibilities, which make them feel trapped and restricted; they can seldom be happy when truly involved with a group, and only survive on its peripheries. This same principle may help explain why the alienated are not found among the "beatnik" groups on the campus. Almost to a man, they find such groups conformist, sterile, and "not serious"; they scorn those who belong to them. While they are often fascinated by the "beat" style of life, and while many of them may in their own way adopt its characteristics, they are in many ways *too* alienated to be "beatniks"—a stance which, after all, involves accepting an identity, a sense of solidarity, and a set of expectations about one's "beat" behavior.

What do the alienated do with their time, then? As we might expect from their philosophies, they spend much of it alone. They do not distinguish between work and play, and consequently cannot organize their lives around those schedules of "studying" and "goofing off" which many students use to discipline themselves. When the alienated "work," it is usually on some topic of passionate, even obsessional interest to them; they rarely work because they have to, but because they "need" to. Put more precisely, the compulsions which drive them are less often academic requirements than are those of their fellows, and more often inner psychic compulsions only tangentially related to the requirements of the institution. Similarly, their "leisure" activities often have much of the same driven quality, which makes the usual work-play distinctions irrelevant to them. Indeed, what they do when not studying is very similar in psychological meaning to their studies: in both, they try to intensify, deepen, and comprehend their experience.

This cult of experience is sometimes explicit in their philosophies, but its meanings are clearest when we see them in daily activities. For example, as a group, the alienated are wanderers, walkers, and hitchhikers: when confronted with a major or even a minor problem they are likely to "take off," sometimes for a long midnight walk, sometimes for a few years—as with the young man who precipitately left college after being elected to an important office. "Taking off" may mean a voluntary leave of absence for a year, hitchhiking across the country in an unintended imitation of Kerouac (whom they have not read), a long walk along the river, a 3:00 A.M. visit to the burning city dumps which seems to solace the student's nameless rage and anger, an observer's visit to the slums or the red-light district, not for gratification but for something else which they find it hard to describe. But

their descriptions of their wanderings have much in common: in these solitary travels, many find a kind of ecstatic and mystic union with Things, a
Joycean epiphany in which the universe is seen in the garish pennants of a
filling station, childhood memories recaptured by a sudden smell of burning
leaves, or a rapturous moment created by the way the light of the setting
sun falls through an archway onto the grass. It is as if they were seeking
some consoling contact with objects and things, contact more immediate
and embracing than afforded by daily experience, and as if only this contact
could nourish and refresh them.

In all of their wanderings, the alienated remain observers but not participants—or rather, their participation consists of observation. They extend
the role of observer into other areas, and are fascinated by the bizarre, the
unusual, the strange, and the deviant. Recall Inburn, who spent his period
of preparation for examinations recording the memoirs of a call girl. Or
remember the student who talks about his happy contacts with the drunks,
bums, and Brahmin ladies on Beacon Hill, whom he later recollects in tran-
quillity. Another student attached himself peripherally to a group of off-beat
writers who lived near the campus; he limited himself to observing them and
took no active part in their group, although their activities and oddities
obsessed him during many of his waking and sleeping hours. Others approach the bizarre and the deviant more intellectually, as with the student
who made a long study of criminality, or others who became fascinated by
psychosis and perused arcane volumes seeking to understand its significance. In all of these interests, the students are, despite their sideline
position, deeply involved: they identify profoundly with the objects of their
research at the same time that they seek to differentiate themselves from
them.

Only rarely do the alienated shift from the role of observer to that of
participant. A few youths tell us (rather proudly) that they drink to excess,
and recount difficulties encountered in their binges. Others are fascinated,
usually at a distance, by drugs, especially hallucinogenic drugs which promise passage through the "gates of perception" or "expansion of consciousness." Others are fascinated by the experience of psychosis, and wonder
whether they understand what it would be like to be insane. Still others have
indulged in minor thefts, not from need, but for the sake of the experience
of stealing or, as one subject said, "to prove to myself that I didn't feel
guilty." Excessive speed fascinates one or two with a history of speeding
tickets. But in general, as college students, they focused on the perceptual
rather than the active sides of experience; and, paradoxically for so oppositional a group of young men, they were not behavioral non-conformists.
Indeed, the very intensity of their private search for unconventional perceptions and awareness probably lessened their need for public nonconformity.

Their oppositional stance is, however, fully expressed in one of their most characteristic activities: arguing. In intellectual discussions with their peers they are dominant, active, negative, and hostile, constantly interrupting and correcting their fellows, criticizing every point of view brought forward, and impressing their peers with their scornful, contemptuous attitudes. In such discussions, the opposition of the alienated sometimes goes beyond his convictions: he often opposes views with which he fully agrees, merely for the sake of argument. As an informal debater, he tends to be effective, partly because he is articulate and well informed, and perhaps mostly because his position of opposing what others say requires no positive coherent position to back it up. In one experimental situation, however, when alienated subjects were confronted with a single experienced and hostile antagonist who attacked *their* alienated views with great personal bitterness, the same students were thrown off balance and responded rather mildly. Only afterwards, when describing the discussion to a psychologist who did not witness it, did they fully vent their scorn, contempt, dislike, and derision of an assailant who had bested them. This suggests an important fact about the alienated—that they find it easiest to express their hostilities in a large group of people with an abstract topic of discussion; when confronted with only one other person who argues *ad hominem,* they conceal their immediate anger, but later lapse into a slow and enduring burn. On abstract subjects, and when not personally attacked, however, arguing is for the alienated an avocation that goes far beyond challenging views they disagree with: it is a characterological necessity, a part of their self-images; its goal sometimes seems to be more to make a statement about the kind of people they are than to convince anyone else of the rightness of their views.

The Overexamined Life

I have so far emphasized the solitariness of alienated students—their tendency to avoid intimacies and involvements with groups or with people. As a group they spend less time with others, are less intimate with them, become less manifestly involved with groups than do many or most of their peers. To all but their closest friends and acquaintances these students are usually known as aloof and rather negativistic, somewhat scornful, unwilling to be drawn into the activities of others, perhaps condescending. Their acquaintances tend to know relatively little about them, and the alienated usually resist any attempts to break through their armored sense of privacy.

There is, however, another and contrasting side to most of these young men, a side which is very deeply if ambivalently involved with others despite outward appearances to the contrary, a side which prevents any simple characterization of them as aloof, shy, withdrawn, or indifferent to others.

One characteristic type of involvement, seen frequently when such youths become research subjects, involves a simultaneous attraction to and fear of an admired person. One unusually insightful alienated student described his feeling about a graduate student whom he admired in these terms: "Whenever I am with him, he is so enthusiastic about what he is doing that I want to drop everything and follow in his footsteps. It sort of scares me." A similar pattern often emerged with research psychologists whom the alienated came to admire: they would very candidly discuss their worries and anxieties with such men—knowing their confidences would be respected—and seek advice on how to conduct their lives. But if the psychologist responded with anything that could be construed as advice, they would invariably attack it as irrelevant, lacking in understanding, and stupid. Yet paradoxically, despite their sometimes bitter attacks on the research project and on individual members in the project, the alienated seemed more deeply involved in it than most non-alienated students.

All of this suggests that with potentially emulable older men, the alienated are involved in a struggle *against* their own underlying admiration and desire to emulate, a struggle which they must maintain precisely because they are so overwhelming drawn to men who might serve as models for them. Underneath their public face of opposition and negativism, the alienated must often feel their central selves are too weak to tolerate admiration of another person without being totally absorbed by him.

Some of their contemporaries evoke this same mixture of admiration and consequent repudiation by the alienated. Other students who "know where they are headed" are most likely to arouse these feelings. The comments of the alienated about them tend to follow a similar line: on the one hand, they reluctantly admire the purposefulness and lack of vacillation in such young men; but on the other, they deplore what they see as the conventionality, narrowness, and limitation of vision inherent in this purposefulness. Toward other students who are alienated they have less equivocal feelings: they heartily dislike and repudiate anyone else who is alienated, seeing his alienation as sham, hypocrisy, and a cover-up for weakness. In this rejection of the like-minded it is not hard to infer self-contempt: the motives they ascribe to their fellow alienated are those they most fear in themselves. And even in their fierce rejection of the conventional and everyday, we might suspect some fear of their own conventional or conformity-loving potentials.

But the most striking aspect of the involvement of the alienated with others is its ruminative, even obsessional, quality. Virtually no relationship of any duration escapes detailed analysis and examination from every point of view: the character of the other, his motives for liking or not liking the subject, the subject's own motives for entering and continuing the relationship, the effects of the relationship on both parties, etc., etc., etc. Every human encounter has for the alienated an ambivalent quality, so that no judgment can ever be simple and unqualified. Every relationship ultimately becomes a question of identity, of whether to be or not to be like the other person; and since identity is in these young men unsettled and unsure, so are their encounters with others. The result is an overexamined life, wherein every hour spent in any kind of close contact with another demands at least equal time for analysis, questioning, searching for motives, meanings, and effects.

These characteristics are especially prominent with the opposite sex. Rather surprisingly, given their repudiation of intimacy and their agreement with statements like "I don't think I'll ever find a woman who really understands me," the alienated differ not at all from their classmates in the frequency with which they date and in the amount and variety of their sexual experience. As with any group of students, the range of this experience is wide, varying from those who have rarely been out with a girl to those with intense passionate affairs of relatively long duration. Among the majority who as college students date fairly actively, there are several different patterns, each involving intense and ambivalent attachments coupled with much rumination about the relationship. One pattern involves transient encounters with a series of girls, none of whom are found satisfactory for any long-range relationship. If such short-term affairs involve sexual relationships, the subject is very likely to feel extremely guilty about them, believing with a certain mixture of feelings that he ruthlessly exploited the girl. Each new relationship is entered into with the highest of hopes, and every break involves the same intense feeling of disillusionment and even of betrayal—regardless of who initiates the break. Often, such breaks are seen to involve a preferred rival, and the presence of a more successful rival merely adds to the alienated student's feeling of disillusion and defeat.

Another dating pattern involves a more prolonged relationship with a girl described as extremely docile, dependent, passive, compliant, and subservient. One young man describes "teaching" his girl friends how to satisfy him sexually, and implies that his own passivity limits the number of available partners. Another discusses in enthusiastic terms his fiancée's "total" dependence on him, and makes no attempt to hide his enjoyment of his own sense of superiority over her. In these cases, there appears to be little reciprocity between the young man and his girl; the relationship is premised on the availability of a girl who will never be challenging, assertive, or aggressive, or even perhaps, never demand real intimacy.

The final alienated pattern of dating involves an intensely gratifying relationship with a girl who is somehow defined as "forbidden"—whether by virtue of her past, her religion, or merely the student's parents' opposition. Such relationships tend to precipitate violent quarrels and breaks between the student and his family, and he clearly enjoys pitting himself against this segment of the world. However deep and satisfying such relationships are to the students themselves, they are invariably carried on in the shadow of the disapproving family, and one sometimes wonders whether a shift of family policy might not lead to the dissolution of the tie and the search for a new partner even less "suitable." Whatever the motives of the student, it is highly consistent with the alienated style to find someone whom an important part of his world defines as undesirable and to fall deeply in love with her.

In hearing these undergraduates talk about their girl friends and dates, one is again struck with the amount of ambivalence and examination of relationship that goes on. Their partners sometimes complain to them that they "pick them to pieces," and this is true. However much they may seek and occasionally find intimacy, it is threatening: they find it difficult to trust the object of their love unless she is either totally dependent on them, or else somehow defined as undesirable. Thus, their continual dissection of all relationships has a fearful quality, as if they needed continually to reexamine the trustworthiness of the other and reassure themselves that the relationship was not harming them. In all of their encounters, they retain the same agonizing combination of desire for closeness and fear of it; and the ways they deal with this ambivalence—the way they choose their potential intimates and the way they deal with those to whom they might be close—often merely serve to confirm their view that intimacy is the prelude to disappointment and disillusion.

The Fragmented Self

If we ask how the alienated describe themselves and how they perform on psychological tests, we find a similar set of distinctive alienated qualities. In interviews as on questionnaires, the alienated make no bones about their own confusions, angers, anxieties, and problems. These are not young men who conceal their own unpleasant motives and fantasies from themselves or others: given a list of symptoms, worries, anxieties, and concerns, they will check all they possibly can, as if to boast of their superior honesty with themselves. They tell us that they are confused, anxious, nervous, irritable, hostile, angry, impulsive, depressed, and dejected. They say they are suspicious, lacking in will power, resentful, unfriendly, and jealous. They experience time as confused and disorganized, as the arena for decline and decay; consequently, they have few long-range plans. They question their ability to cope with life, they feel unfulfilled in their work and at the college, they say they are rarely themselves with other people; they describe themselves as philosophically confused and disoriented. Indeed, given any list of "socially undesirable" characteristics, the alienated affirm that they possess them. And on interviews, once the ice has been broken, they talk freely about their disturbing feelings, fantasies, and dreams; they sometimes worry aloud about their ultimate sanity; they ask reassurance as to their normality.

How we are to understand these results? One possibility is, of course, that the alienated are indeed incredibly disturbed young men, neurotic, apprehensive, and confused. And as we will see, there is some evidence to support this view. But at the same time, we must recall that most of our definitions of "mental health" (like most of the tests by which we try to measure it) are based on traditional American notions that the "mentally healthy" are those optimistic, practical, unapprehensive, "reasonable," forward-looking men and women who people our cultural Hall of Fame. Insofar as a young man rejects these definitions of the good life, he will (by definition) be "unhealthy" in the terms of his culture. Thus, at least a part of the appearance of mental unbalance in these young men may come from their rejection of the very premises by which mental health is usually defined.

A related factor in understanding the "mental unhealth" of the alienated is their relative lack of repression. Most "good adjustment" in America presupposes a "healthy" amount of repression, suppression, and denial of unpleasant thoughts, feelings, and fantasies—an "accentuation of the positive," a determined effort to see the bright side of things and of oneself and not to dwell on the sordid, unpleasant, hostile, or nasty side. Much of this repression, this "not noticing," is involuntary, for from an early age American children are usually taught to suppress their open complaints and direct aggressions, finding more suitable and sublimated expressions. Such feelings do not, of course, disappear, but they do in time tend to disappear from the consciousness of those who have them. In a youth who will not or cannot repress, such motives will be far more accessible to awareness, and therefore more available for reporting to psychologists and on personality questionnaires. Seen this way, the man or woman with great insight into his own motives—including the bad ones—will often appear more "neurotic" on tests than the man without awareness of precisely the same motives.

The alienated, then, whose lives are overexamined, who make a virtue, even a fetish, of complete and ruthless honesty with themselves about their most undesirable qualities, and for whom awareness and self-understanding are central goals, show up poorly on personality tests partly because they lack the ability to repress or the desire to put up a "good show." It is more important to them to admit—or to exaggerate—their problems and thus to retain their tenuous inner conviction of honesty with themselves and with others about themselves, than it is to appear "normal," a classification they despise. In psychological research one quickly learns to distrust "objective" test scores and look at behavior, for it often happens that an individual with extremely "healthy" test scores can be in reality far more disturbed than a man who checks all the symptoms but somehow copes with life.

We can explain away some of the appearance of poor psychological health in these young men by recognizing their awareness of and exaggeration of their symptoms, and perhaps by refusing, with them, to accept conventional views of "good mental health." Yet behaviorally this remains an unusually confused, disoriented, and unhappy group of young men. The defiant public face of scorn and opposition soon gives way to clear unhappiness, depression, self-doubt, and apprehensiveness. And beneath their assertions that "suffering is the primary source of wisdom" they are not totally reconciled to their discontents. Though they proclaim that unhappiness is the lot of any man honest enough to face reality and himself as he is, they find it hard to suppress their own suspicions that it may be something about *them*—rather than the human condition—that makes them so miserable.

To put their plight in a phrase, they suffer from what the psychoanalyst Erik Erikson has called "identity diffusion"—from an intense feeling of the precariousness and disunity of the self, from doubt about their own continuing capacity to "cope," coupled with a relentless search for some trustworthy foundation for selfhood. Their use of intellect is in the service of this quest for understanding and meaning for the sake of ultimate selfhood. Their dissatisfaction with their education is coextensive with an inability to find in college any solid sense of who they are and where they stand. The search for identity pervades their wandering, their seeking some renewing contact with Things, their simultaneous refusal of the identity of a "beatnik" and their need to define themselves as "one who opposes." And in their fear of being overwhelmed by their own admiration, in their scorn both for those who resemble them and for those who are different, in the wariness and distrustfulness with which they approach reciprocity and intimacy of any kind—in all these we can infer the same fragility of self.

Strong in opposition, these young men are weak in affirmation; unable to articulate or even to know what they stand for, they have little sense of self to stand on. For the achievement of identity requires in every young man and woman an implicit set of goals and standards—usually those provided by society—which tell him who he is, where he stands, whence he comes and whither he goes. Even those who find some principle in whose name they reject their society can find personal meaning in their allegiance to that principle and in solidarity with others who are faithful to it. But rebels without a cause can only stand against, not for; and even their opposition is diffuse and unspecific. The price they pay for this opposition, a price exacted by all societies (which must refuse sanctioned identity to their opponents), is inner confusion, disunity, and fragmentation. For this reason if for no other, it is far easier psychologically to be a revolutionary with a program than an alienated youth with only a vague set of rejections.

Growing Up Absurd

Paul Goodman

Aptitude

Our subject is the present waste of human resources. Yet this waste is nothing new. Considering our wonderful faculties and powers, people on the average have never accomplished much. Regarded just as machines of virtue, pleasure, wisdom, battle, or friendship, we have always operated at a tiny fraction of capacity. This is evident if we contrast how people usually hang around with how people come across in emergencies, or when they are enthusiastic, or when they are calmly absorbed. Children find the average inactivity very painful and they nag, "What can I do? Tell me something to do." Adolescents are restive hanging around, and they think up ways to make trouble. Adults are inured to it, and Schopenhauer claimed that boredom is a metaphysical attribute of the World as Will.

Psychologically, we define boredom as the pain a person feels when he's doing nothing or something irrelevant, instead of something that he wants to do but won't, can't, or doesn't dare. Boredom is acute when he knows the other thing and inhibits his action, e.g., out of politeness, embarrassment, fear of punishment or shame. Boredom is chronic if he has repressed the thought of it and no longer is aware of it. A large part of stupidity is just this chronic boredom, for a person can't learn, or be intelligent about, what he's not interested in, when his repressed thoughts are elsewhere. (Another large part of stupidity is stubbornness, unconsciously saying, "I won't, you can't make me.")

Certainly a large part of our common wasteful inactivity is this neurosis of chronic boredom. Certain aims are forbidden and punishable, or unattainable and painful; so we inhibit them and put them out of mind. In a vicious circle, the repression then makes the idea of the aims seem threatening: the aims are now rejected also in ourselves. So we are bored and inactive. We see how boredom easily turns into apathy, the lack of incentive.

At first this Sunday-afternoon neurosis, of lively children brought to a pause, is worse among the middle class than among the poor, for the middle class is less permissive, it has stricter standards to maintain and more expensive furniture to protect. But by adolescence it is generally evident in all classes of the young, hanging around, reading comic books, or watching TV. It is evident in their notion of what is acceptable behavior in their groups, in their sexual paranoia, in their inability to think up anything interesting. Their hearts are elsewhere and they don't remember where. Many boys are afraid to be alone with themselves, because they might masturbate, which in itself may be an activity of boredom.

All this has long been with us, and formerly perhaps it was worse than it is now, for now there is more permissiveness for small children and more rationality about sexuality. In this chapter, however, I want to discuss another factor altogether: *ineptitude,* not knowing *how;* the situation in which, even if they know their aims, children don't know the means or can't manage the means. I propose that in this respect our present system is uniquely bad and getting worse. For ironically, just in our times, when science and technology are so advanced, this factor of ineptitude also increases, and children become practically more stupid.

It is notorious that the physical plant and social environment have grown out of human scale. To achieve simple goods it is often necessary to set in motion immense masses. In scarcity, where the means are unavailable, we wistfully renounce the ends. In an abundant economy, there is a plethora of means of what a person doesn't really want. Middle-class parents know from bitter experience that billions of dollars are spent annually for children's toys and teen-age junk that are not really wanted and lie idle. But furthermore, even if the end is desirable, the means often become so complicated that one is discouraged from starting out. For instance, it's too complicated on a hot day to travel two hot hours to get to a cool place when so many others have had the same idea that it's hot there too. To adults, such complicated means are irritating and take the joy out of life. To children growing up, they are disastrous because they make it impossible to learn by doing. The sense of causality is lost. Initiative is lost. And one ends with the idea that nothing can be changed.

We must remember that to children the city plan and social plan we present them with are like inevitable facts of nature. Unless they have architects or builders in the family, they cannot realize that the buildings were drawn by somebody on a piece of paper and could have been different. Unless their parents teach them otherwise, they believe that compulsory school attendance is a divine creation and it is a sin to be absent.

It is, of course, very difficult to judge the environment concretely from the child's point of view. Thus, living in a big city does not as such make a child inept, though any city has very complicated means. The city is short on farm work, swimming holes, and animals to trap; but it has docks, freight-car yards, labyrinthine basements, pavements to chalk up, and subway trains to play tag on. The streets are littered with the remarkable junk of a thousand trades, to hoard and make things with. The ingenuity of New York ball games adapted to various improbable fields and obstacles is a model of rule making and rational debate that any senate might emulate: it sizes up the situation, argues, decides, and gets things done that work. The *London Street Games* compiled by Norman Douglas is no contemptible manual of traditional culture. History teaches that cities have made people smart because of their mixed peoples, mixed manners, and mixed learning. On the whole, cities have probably trained more intelligent children than the country. But we must remember, too, that until recently cities have been continually replenished from the country. City people had country cousins, and drew on both influences. There could be a powerful educative effect if a country boy came to the city and was exposed to bewildering new ways, or if a city boy visited the country and was exposed to space, woods, and cows.

There is probably a point of complexity at which, cut off from the country, the city ceases to advance beyond country backwardness; it becomes impractical and begins to induce its own kind of stupefaction and ineptness. The endless city-spread of suburbs makes the real farming and open country unavailable. The city becomes the only world, getting duller as one leaves the center, through first the inner ring of blight and then the deadly dormitories and suburbs.

Within the big metropolises at present, industry and commerce are shut off and concealed. The freight yards go underground. Manufacture is in great walled plants on the outskirts. In New York, even the Hudson River and its ships are cut off by impassable through-highways, and stupid planning has provided a mile of child-useless landscaping, so that few kids get down to the river any more to fish. The newer high dwellings make the streets inaccessible to small children. The automobiles make the streets dangerous.

Also the streets are strange, because there is a loss of neighborhood. This is due not only to bad planning but to the greatly increased mobility of families. Children are torn from their school chums and this destroys culture. For instance, the street games and game songs that I remember, in New York 1911–1921, were the ancient London (Dublin?) games; and this tradition has now considerably faded. But it is not easily that a new child-tradition could develop, especially among minorities of various cultures. Quite the contrary, history and bad social planning have conspired to create in New York huge income and cultural ghettos—it makes no difference whether low-income or high-income; children of all classes are equally deprived of the human community. Whereas mixing sharpens intelligence, any segregated differences create prejudice and make people stupid.

The very space has been crushingly pre-empted. The cars in New York seem finally to have discouraged many of the ball games; we see boys going a mile to find a Sunday-deserted parking lot to play stickball which previously they played on their own street with the small children chosen in. With increasing traffic, the policing is more strict. In Los Angeles 40 per cent of the area will be swallowed up by the cloverleaves and express highways so that people can drive bumper to bumper in and out of Los Angeles! This is certainly out of human scale and is a dead loss for skating and bicycles. In Northern cities, the snow is never allowed to pile up; city sleighing is finished. The streamlined functional architecture is bare of useful stoops.

In brief, concealed technology, family mobility, loss of the country, loss of neighborhood tradition, and eating up of the play space have taken away the real environment. The city, under inevitable modern conditions, can no longer be dealt with practically by children.

> Consider the dehumanizing complexity of the city just as a problem in municipal administration. In New York City "in charge of housing are many agencies, some for housing the poor, some for housing generally, some agents of the city, but others agents of the state and federal governments. They are, in part, the Housing Authority, the Mayor's Commission on Slum Clearance and Urban Renewal, the Comptroller's Office, the Board of Estimate, the Bureau of Real Estate, the Department of Buildings, and the State and Federal Housing Agencies. Meantime, unco-ordinated with these, there are agencies in charge of location of schools (Board of Education), and playgrounds and parks (Parks). Transportation by rail falls to the Transit Authority, but if it is automotive it may fall to the Port Authority (for certain highways, tunnels, and bridges) or the Triborough Authority (for other highways, etc.). When cars are moving or parked in the streets they belong to the Traffic Department, and safety in general belongs to the Police. Nobody as such attends to the specific relation of workers and their particular industries, the cause of all this commuting, but there are zoning laws for broad kinds of occupancy, under the City Planning Commission. Neighborhood quarrels, family disruption, delinquency, etc., might be handled by the Police and various social agencies. Other departments, too, have a hand in the community planning of New York, e.g., Public Works; Gas, Water and Electricity; etc.
>
> It seems reasonable to ask if the integration of these functions is not relevant? but nobody is in charge of that. To give a partial list: housing, slum clearance, location of industries, adequate schools and teachers, transportation, clear streets, traffic control, social work, racial harmony, master planning, recreation. The list could be long extended, not to speak of a beautiful city and local pride. Apart from such a unified view, the solution of this or that isolated problem inevitably leads to disruption elsewhere. Escape thoroughfares must aggravate central traffic. Slum clearance as an isolated policy must aggravate class stratification and delinquency. New subways aggravate conurbation. "Housing" makes for double-shift and overcrowded classrooms. No master plan guarantees foolishness like the Lincoln Square project. These consequent evils produce new evils among them. . . .
>
> (*Communitas,* Appendix D.)

Even so, confusing as these factors are and much as they cut down the available child-games and child-objects, it is hard to know what things look like from the child's-eye view. For instance, the new public housing seems after a few years to swarm like any old-fashioned slum and is perhaps developing its own worthwhile child culture. At first, active boys shunned the official playgrounds, but now, driven by necessity, they have agreed to take them over and turn them to their own uses, games, adventure, necking, and battle.

My guess is that, in city, suburb, and small town, the chief unambiguously retarding influence of the complicated technology acts on the children through the ineptitude of the grownups—just as the stultifying effect of the movies is *not* that the children see them but that their parents do, as if Hollywood provided a plausible adult recreation to grow up into.

People use machines that they do not understand and cannot repair. For instance, the electric motors: one cannot imagine anything more beautiful and educative than such motors, yet there may be three or four in a house, cased and out of sight; and when they blow they are taken away to be repaired. Their influence is then retarding, for what the child sees is that competence does not exist in ordinary people, but in the system of interlocking specialties. This is unavailable to the child, it is too abstract. Children go shopping with Mama; but supermarket shopping for cellophane packages is less knowledgeable and bargainable than the older shopping, as well as providing tasteless Texas fruit and vegetables bred for nonperishability and appearance rather than for eating. Cooking is more prefabricated. Few clothes are sewn. Fire and heat are not made. Among poor people there used to be more sweated domestic industry, which didn't do the adults any good but taught something to small children. Now, on the contrary, the man and perhaps the woman of the house work in distant offices and factories, increasingly on parts and processes that don't mean anything to a child. A child might not even know what work his daddy does. Shop talk will be, almost invariably, griping about interpersonal relations. If the kid has less confidence that he can make or fix anything, his parents can't either; and what they do work at is beyond his grasp.

Parents, especially fathers, feel that this way of life offers too little to their children, especially the sons. They tend to blame it on the city—just as many dog lovers will not keep dogs in the city. Some guiltily give the kids more money to go to the movies. Others choose the suburbs, where they can putter and fix, even though they thereby limit their own lives in other ways. We must return to the meaning of this fateful move.

Let me give a dismal illustration of the case at its worst. At an underprivileged school in Harlem, they used to test the intelligence of all the children at two-year intervals. They found that every two years each advancing class came out ten points lower in "native intelligence." That is, the combined efforts of home influencing and school education, a powerful combination, succeeded in making the children significantly stupider year by year; if they had a few more years of compulsory home ties and compulsory education, all would end up as gibbering idiots. In this same school a new principal, with a better staff, more personal attention to the kids, and more progressive methods—and also willing to give his own time for social work among the parents—has reversed the trend. One method to remedy stupidity that he swears by is to invite the free expression of criticism and hostility, e.g., "Write a composition telling why you hate your father—why you hate school—why you hate me."

It was just to this deepening crisis of boredom, lack of personal engagement, cultural irrelevance, and ineptitude, in conditions of mass industry and mass education, that the movement called progressive education addressed itself. It is now moribund, but it can be revived. Its history in our century, however, is immensely instructive.

The pragmatism, instrumentalism, and technologism of James, Dewey, and Veblen were leveled against the abuses and ideals of the then dominant class: the Four Hundred and the Robber Barons—academic culture, caste morals and formal religion, unsocial greed. The philosophers were concerned about abundant production, social harmony, practical virtues, and more honest perception and feeling, which would presumably pertain to the rising group of technicians, social-scientific administrators, and organized labor. (As a symbol of the "leisure-class culture" that they were attacking, they chose the "classical" culture of Greece, founded on slavery.) In that early turn of the century, these philosophers failed to predict that precisely with the success of the managers, technicians, and organized labor, the "achieved" values of efficient abundant production, social harmony, and one popular culture would produce even more devastatingly the things they did not want: an abstract and inhuman physical environment, a useless economy, a caste system, a dangerous conformity, a trivial and sensational leisure. (So that now we tend to think of the Greek polis as an "integral community," making a public use of leisure and having a perfected education of the whole man, whereas we have fragments.)

Yet midway in this transition from the old tycoon-and-clergyman culture to the new managerial organization, there was crystallized a practical method of education with the defects of neither extreme (and in many ways strangely like Greek education); and it was given a sounding board especially by the daring Twenties. Progressive education drew on every radical idea since the middle of the eighteenth century, in pedagogy, politics, socialist and communitarian theory, epistemology, esthetics, anthropology, and psychiatry. It was as if progressive education resolved that *in the education of the children there should be no missed revolutions and no unfinished situations.*

In its heyday, progressive education was not sectarian. Different schools laid the emphasis in different places—Dewey was more experimental, Russell more rational, Neill more sex-reformist, the people around Goddard and Antioch more communitarian, Berea more "handicrafts," Black Mountain more "creative," Muste and Fincke more political-economical, and so forth. But I think that almost all schools would have accepted, in varying degrees, all of the following positions:

To learn theory by experiment and doing.
To learn belonging by participation and self-rule.
Permissiveness in all animal behavior and interpersonal expression.
Emphasis on individual differences.
Unblocking and training feeling by plastic arts, eurhythmics and dramatics.
Tolerance of races, classes, and cultures.
Group therapy as a means of solidarity, in the staff meeting and community meeting.
Taking youth seriously as an age in itself.
Community of youth and adults, minimizing "authority."
Educational use of the actual physical plant (buildings and farms) and the culture of the school community.
Emphasis in the curriculum on real problems of wider society, its geography and history, with actual participation in the neighboring community (village or city).
Trying for functional interrelation of activities.

This is not a perfect educational program. It lacks grandeur and explosive playfulness. It lacks religious quiet. And it is weak in the models of the humanities. But there cannot be a "perfect" educational system, for each system must meet its social situation. In a period like ours, of transition, uprootedness, inhuman scale, technical abstractness, affectlessness, and conformity, *no lesser program is seriously conservative of human resources.* Our official public educators are not serious in their concern for human resources, or they would use this program.

There has always been one criticism of progressive education that must be answered, namely, that it is weak in curriculum, in cultural and scientific content. I think this is a misunderstanding. There *is* only one curriculum, no matter what the method of education: what is basic and universal in human experience and practice, the underlying structure of culture. This philosophic content fans out as speech, as finding where you are in space and time, as measuring and structuring, and being a social animal. It may be called English, geography and history, arithmetic, music and physical training; or Greek, history, logic, and Rugby; or trivium and quadrivium (plus games); or literature, social studies, science, and eurhythmics. It is the same basic curriculum; the differences are in method, and they concern how to teach the curriculum and make it second nature to the students, unblocking rather than encumbering, and bringing out the best. The curriculum is only superficially what "a man ought to know"; it is more fundamentally how to become a man-in-the-world. The method must vary with what good or bad habits and powers the young have come with in various situations. The curriculum certainly cannot vary with what is temporarily convenient for a bad society (the definition of a bad society being one that is not educational). Not to teach the whole curriculum is to give up on the whole man.

For instance, in our present Cold War debate about teaching science, Dr. Kvaraceus, the National Education Association's expert on delinquency, warns us that geometry is "too hard" for most, and that to insist on it for all will produce failure and truancy. But this is not the progressive educator's way of looking at it. Is it that geometry is too hard, or that the aim of teaching is not bona fide, being rapid technical know-how rather than humane understanding? Is it that the method is irrelevant to the aptitude and ineptitude that the children have come with? What dismays me in thinking like that of Dr. Kvaraceus is that it disregards our duty to geometry as such as a worth-while human object, our duty to Euclid, Kepler, and Einstein. The result of his attitude is that these champions will not be champions for all men. We are in a sad dilemma if, as is the case, kids don't learn because it is not humanly worthwhile to learn, they have no deep motivation; and then, to keep them in school we have to cut down on the few subjects that are humanly worthwhile. The question cannot be whether to teach science or to whom, for what is man without science? but how to teach it in various circumstances.

At the other pole from Dr. Kvaraceus, the recent public alarm about Sputnik has led to Dr. Conant's quasi-official and vastly circulated reports on the high schools. But *because* the concern is not serious but is simply fear of the Russians, the reports show such little pedagogic imagination that they are a minor national disaster. Dr. Conant's philosophy is expressed in the sentence:

> Attention has been centered for so long on the individuality of each child that [educators] resist any idea that a new national concern [defense against Russia] might be an important factor in planning a high school program. [From *The Child, the Parent, and the State.*]

What an extraordinary thought, that there could be a conflict between the unfolding individuality and the achievement of habits of science! When Dr. Conant proposes that the bright upper fraction of the students be somehow induced to take hard programs—for everywhere large percentages of the brightest shirk the hard courses or quit school—he does not ask what is *at present* lacking in their motivation. He objects to treating education in a vacuum, but he treats our national needs in a vacuum. Will the incentive to fight an atomic war, or a Cold War, match the social apathy and cynicism of these boys? More important, Dr. Conant does not seem to wonder why there are so few (15 per cent) who are "academically talented." Does he think that the general dullness of the high school population has occurred in a void? Contrast a remark on the same subject by the Dean of Teachers College, John Fischer: "I have a strong suspicion that we have learned little about the abilities of human beings. I suspect they are greater than most people assume." If one is concerned about conserving human resources, this would seem to be the obvious first approach: to find why most are so inept and to invent techniques to unblock them, to increase the pool of the "academically talented." Perhaps the conventional school itself is not such a good idea, especially if the "national need" is for creative scientists; for at the point in their careers at which these boys are tested (say ages twelve to fifteen), the "brightness" of the 15 per cent might or might not indicate a profound feeling for the causes of things; it is largely verbal and symbol-manipulating, and is almost certainly partly an obsessional device *not* to know and touch risky matter, just as Freud long ago pointed out that the nagging questions of small children are a substitute for asking the forbidden questions.

If these are the important kinds of issues—motivation, unblocking ability, deep-rootedness of learning—a little *more* attention to the individuality of the child, and some more progressive education, might suit the national need. It might even speed up the invention of rockets. . . .

Let us return to the thread of our argument. Besides the out-of-scale physical environment and its complicated techniques, the social environment too is baffling and produces ineptitude and loss of the sense of causality.

Think of a child trying to cope with Property Rights, a most abstract notion. There is no problem when it is a case of something being used by somebody else, when Jack tries to take Bobby's shovel out of his hand and Bobby clouts him over the head with it or complains to authority in no uncertain terms. The puzzlement comes when the shovel is idle and Mama says, "You mustn't use that shovel, it's Bobby's." What impresses the child is no precise idea, but the grownup's tone of conviction. The child "believes," though there is no evidence of his senses. It is the beginning of what Marx called the fetishism of commodities. What is sickening is that it is just this kind of influencing that is wanted by priests, mayors, and tavern philosophers who declare that more home influence is the remedy for our troubles of youth.

But the social relationships of the grownups themselves are out of human scale, for in the corporate system of organization the puzzling has become altogether mysterious. It is disturbing to a child to sense that his mother is under the unseen thumb of religion or his father of the boss. But the top managers in our semimonopolies are quite anonymous. This is part of the new managerial code, as described by *Fortune* itself. A child cannot use them as model heroes, for they are invisible. This is why Jackie Robinson's proposal to import the TV personalities as ersatz models is so unfortunate, for these visible "heroes" are puppets. With the increasing concentration of management and control, as A. A. Berle has pointed out, there is less relation even to Property Rights.

Consider it. If one is put upon or abused, with whom shall he be angry? One cannot vent rage against an abstract system. But there is no need to vent feeling, for it is a matter of the grievance committee and other regular channels. In the Middle Status, the heart of the organized system, the situation is not the same as in a bureaucracy, with which it is usually compared; for a bureaucracy has a written code and a definite pecking-order; but the organization protects everybody's personal dignity, and its subtle interpersonal feuding and competition cannot be codified, for it is without any objective utility to give a principle. Even that mighty system the State is more material: it has banners, soldiers, elections, postmen, police. In a child it rouses awe and fear. But the organized system exists only in the bland front of its brand-name products and advertising. There is no knowing how it is run or who determines.

It is in these circumstances that young persons grow up convinced that everything is done with mirrors, by "influence." Not even the personal influence of nepotism, but something more like the astrological influence of the planets. The sense of initiative, causality, skill has been discouraged. Merit is a trait of "personality." Learning is the possession of a Diploma. Usefulness is a Union Card. Justification is Belonging. . . .

We have in America a mystique of "production" and a man engaged in "production" is highly esteemed. In *The Affluent Society,* J. K. Galbraith shows that this attitude is entirely specious. Of five ways in which production can be increased: (1) except in wartime we do not try to increase the labor supply; (2) we do not try to encourage new enterprises; (3) in most industries, we do not try for technological innovation. All the stress is laid on (4) full employment, and (5) efficient use of present capital.

But this economist does not even bother to mention the factor of productivity that concerns us here: (6) to increase the aptitude and skill of each lad. Indeed, as we have tried to show, rather than encouraged it is systematically retarded. It would not today be said, as it used to be, that the Americans are born mechanics. Among the model heroes of the young we do not think of Edison, Burbank, Ford, Steinmetz, and so forth. It is anachronistic to mention their names.

The juvenile literary and pictorial image of the inventor and scientist has correspondingly changed. Two generations ago it was a kindly bumbling old fool, unkempt but stubborn and brave, and with a light of divine truth in his eyes. A generation ago science began to be altogether strange and the scientist began to be a surgeon with rubber gloves or a cold maniac with diabolic power in his eyes. But this stereotype is forbidden today, for strategic reasons, and the scientist is now a young, neatly dressed, co-operative Organization Man holding up some apparatus that proves his role, but nothing in his eyes at all, at all. But he *is* having fun.

The claim of the organized system is that research and invention are in their nature increasingly corporative and anonymous, and this produces great results. That is debatable. I doubt that very much is corporatively invented which is not pretty directly dictated by managerial need and policy, whereas the essence of invention is to be hitherto-unthought-of—though, of course, there occurs the rich comedy of administrators anxiously waiting for mathematicians to turn up with something "useful," and never knowing what goes on behind those spectacles. (I have a mathematician friend who bills his firm for overtime because he tends to think of things in bed about 2:00 A.M. and his attitude is that they can take it or leave it.) Certainly the following example is not *un*typical: A gifted food chemist puts in six months developing a formula; he is successful and the product is going to be pushed with a million-dollar campaign; it is, in his opinion, *identical* with ——— Mayonnaise, the popular brand. (In this case the scientist suddenly decided to quit and to set himself up as an independent consultant, hoping that people would come in with real problems.)

Proof on this kind of issue is difficult. On the one side, the corporations, having pre-empted much of the talent, point proudly to inventions made under their auspices, as if they might not have been made anyway. On the other side, their opponents argue from inventions-that-have-not-been-made, a peculiar metaphysical category, e.g., "If all the capital and research had not gone into internal combustion engines, by now we should have much superior steam or electric cars." It may be said definitely that research entailing million-dollar equipment and vast samplings of the populace cannot be carried on without corporative or state sponsorship; yet many would deny that this style of research, and expense of social wealth, is so fruitful as the old American shoestring operator or the seventeenth-century gentleman-philosopher with his dumb-bunny apparatus and towering intellect. We certainly have at present the dismal situation that the most imaginative men are directed by a group, the top managers, who are among the least, hard-working though they may be. Also, inventions made outside the organization are notoriously bought up and withheld or otherwise sabotaged by the organization. (To my conscience, this practice, of keeping basic new ideas in limbo until it is profitable to exploit them, is immoral and disruptive of the community of mankind far more than rigged quiz shows, but it comes from the same box, whose label is Intellect Bought.)

So we return to the President of Merck and Company, who, hauled before a Senate investigation on charges that Merck and its semimonopolistic "competitors" were criminally overpricing drugs, *warned* the Senators that they might "upset the delicate balance we have been able to develop over the years between the quest for scientific knowledge on the one hand and the drive for financial success on the other."!! *Quo usque tandem.*

The situation of a young fellow is ironical. If he has reached college age and has technical aptitude, the most desperate attempts are made to get him for this or that firm. They pay for his schooling and guarantee him a job. Meantime, the systematic behavior of those firms has been to baffle aptitude in the young and to limit it where it has survived.

It is in this context that we must listen to Dr. Conant's recommendations for the high school: the selection of the academically talented, the top 15 per cent, to major in a program of mathematics and sciences. No effort is made to increase the pool of ability; and the public schools are, effectually, to be used as apprentice training grounds for the monopolies and the armed forces.

The Antinomian Personality: The Hippie Character Type *

Nathan Adler

Most observers of the contemporary scene concede that we are in the midst of a crisis. It is a crisis of values. Among its symptoms are changing personality configurations manifested in the new ideology and culture of the "drop-out"; the epidemic diffusion of drug abuse; the changing patterns and the blurring of differentiated sex roles; the enthusiastic propagation of the Hippie ethos in both its evangelical and apocalyptic forms.

We are confronted here with more than the changing of the guard as a new generation enters Bohemia or with altering patterns that represent merely superficial permutations in fashion. We are confronted here with the crystallization of a specific personality configuration. Some of its characteristics are the widespread use of drugs, a commitment to Utopian colonies and communes, and a search for a "tribalism" as a commitment that dis-

Reprinted by special permission of The William Alanson White Psychiatric Foundation, Inc., *Psychiatry* (Vol. 31, 1968), pp. 325–338. This article also appears in, *The Underground Stream: Papers on the Antinomian Personality and the New Life Style* by Nathan Adler (New York: Harper & Row, Publishers, 1972). By permission of the author.

* I am indebted to Professor Theodore R. Sarbin who urged me to prepare this chapter and who, as always, gave generously of his time and his critical thoughtfulness.

dains and repudiates social action. It is accompanied by the development of an "underground" press that propagandizes the new ethos and a shift in the acceptable public boundaries of the erotic and the pornographic. The apparent coherence and internal consistency of this Hippie configuration of conduct and value requires a structural as well as a dynamic account, and suggests that it should be evaluated as a social type. The thesis of this paper is that given certain social contexts, familiar components of Hippie conduct comprise a type which has emerged many times in past history. The history of this character type suggests "antinomian" as a metaphor to distinguish it from others.

The emergence of the Hippie personality has been forced upon public attention by the increasing numbers of young people who have manifested its principal symptoms. For example, in a twenty-year practice of psychotherapy, I rarely encountered the drug user, except within the clearly deviant population of the state prison. Within the last five years, however, not a day has passed that two or three of my patients have not acknowledged or contemplated the use of marijuana, methedrine, LSD, or other hallucinogenic substances. Drug use has shifted from a lower-class culture to the suburban middle class; estimates of high school and college use of marijuana are consistently reported in the range of 25 to 50 percent, and use of LSD has been estimated as at least 10 percent on some college campuses. During this period the drug culture has diffused down from the college campus and is increasingly reported as a problem in junior high schools.

It is customary to try to explain the Hippie phenomenon by references to war and the threat of war; the danger of nuclear annihilation of all mankind; the affluent society; changing family patterns—explanations that are repeatedly used for everything that is amiss and that, since they explain everything, explain nothing in a systematic and theoretically relevant way.

The word "antinomian," which I am introducing in an attempt better to understand the Hippie personality, typically appears in a theological vocabulary [1] and its relevance in a secular setting may not be immediately apparent. Its initial use implied an interpretation of the antithesis between moral law and gospel. [2] Antinomianism designated those values and behaviors that challenged ecclesiastical authority and questioned the moral law—hence its appropriateness for current unconventional behavior. Antinomianism has a long history in many settings, and to suggest that the term be transposed into a contemporary, secular setting is to emphasize the continuities between those earlier times and our own. The employment of the label also stresses the fact that particular conduct and personality modes can and do recur under specific ecological conditions.

[1] Ronald A. Knox, *Enthusiasm, A Chapter in the History of Religion, with Special Reference to the 17th and 18th Centuries;* Oxford, Galaxy Books, 1961.
[2] Namely, that faith alone is sufficient justification without adherence to moral law, the legitimacy of whose sanctions is not acknowledged.

Our predecessors formulated their orientation, values, and conduct within a theological metaphor system construed as sin and salvation, good and evil, revelation, and so forth. Later, the configuration of similar values and conduct, elaborating commitments to enthusiasm, transcendence, faith, and ardor, was expressed within a romantic metaphor system.[3] Today our experiences and orientations are conceptualized within a technological metaphor system. We focus, for example, upon the pharmacology of "mind-expanding" drugs and the presumed effects of the electronic revolution upon media and upon ourselves. We tend to see our problem as unique. Because we are insensitive to history and to the ready assimilation of metaphor to myth, we tend to overlook the underlying correspondences between our technological metaphors and other vocabularies and metaphor systems.

But, though the metaphors change, similar themes recur. Religious and existential issues become paramount. "Self-actualization" and "transcendence" become dominant motives. Teeny-boppers speak of the unity of mankind and of the need for fusion, as if they were Sufis or adherents of Meister Eckhart. There is manifest a defusion of the ego and an intensified narcissism which withdraws from the world into a quietist orientation, to self manipulation, and to the amplification of sensory inputs and modalities as adaptations to the experience of alienation. Such stress and these themes cohere in a configuration which constitutes the antinomian personality.

The Antinomian Personality

Personality is elaborated within a matrix of values. The personality type which I call "antinomian" is manifested by one whose frame of reference is threatened or has been disrupted. He therefore suffers from a breakdown in the balance of his control and release mechanisms and from the permeability of his body boundaries. As a result, the autistic components in his perception become more dominant and the range of his receptivity and response is modified.

There is a diffusion of identity in which the self-object relation becomes unstable and in which the discrete interrelation of self and objects, an achievement of maturity and differentiation, is replaced by their fusion. This behavior is made up of components that are subsumed also in psychiatric categories as manic and depressive and fugue-like states. It involves a hyper-vigilance, an incoherent, inconsistent scanning that may use sexual activity, drugs, religious exercises, fasting, hunger, or other triggers as part of an effort to reestablish an enduring, consistent orientation.

The antinomian fears diffusion and depersonalization. He seeks out haptic

---

[3] Eugene N. Anderson, "German Romanticism as an Ideology of Cultural Crisis," *J. History Ideas* (1941) 2:301–317. J. L. Talmon, *Romanticism and Revolt, Europe 1815–1848;* New York, Harcourt, Brace & World, 1967.

irritations to overcome boredom and insensibility. He plays at throwing away what is lost to maintain the illusion of self-determination and freedom; and through "trips" to the interior, through pantheistic fusion, or through sadistic and masochistic ventures he attempts to demonstrate a capacity to control self and objects and to reinstate both self and object constancy.

The sense of his isolation and separation leads him to see the distal world as alien and detached from himself. The bridge between the self as spectator and the self as actor is down. There is a confusion between what is agent and what is agency.

In this situation and with such needs, the physical, the visceral, and the concrete are of greater moment than the abstract, the generalized, and the cognitive. The antinomian personality values most the immediate and the vivid, the uninhibited and the outrageous. Feeling, texture, touch, warmth become more important than central modes which are more likely to make for a discrete self differentiated from objects. Visual modes are manipulated and distorted by drugs and by fasting so that the discrete components melt, merge, and fuse.

The antinomian personality, as a construct, is to be differentiated from the sociological terms of "anomie" or "anomia." [4] The latter terms are conceived of as referring to a deficiency state, as a lack or absence of specific values or adaptive conduct. As the term is here intended, the antinomian personality implies an alternative mode of adjustment rather than a deficiency state. The personality is recognized by a particular set of role behaviors that enables the individual to cope with cognitive, affective, and social strains.

The Uses of Theories of Types

Traits and role behaviors tend to cluster and to hang together. The recognition of this fact has been asserted in a long tradition, from the literary characterology of Theophrastus through the explanations of conduct via typologies based upon physical elements, humors, clinical syndromes, somatotypes, erogenous zones, and other categories. There has been a persistent effort to determine organizing principles that order diverse, varying needs, motives, traits, elements, and factors into structured types.

The formulation of typologies or of modalities assumes no reification. It need imply no underlying organismic substrate. It is the function of a typological construct to integrate apparently disparate bits of data into continuities that demonstrate the interrelation of the parts. Ultimately such a theoretical formulation should account for variability and deviation from

[4] Leo Srole, "Social Integration and Certain Corollaries: An Exploratory Study," *Amer. Sociol. Review* (1956) 21:709–716.

the type and make possible prediction and deduction from the type to its component parts.

Typological constructs make possible the assignment or classification of data into different categories. They may cut across other typologies and other category systems. What is relevant is their utility for economically ordering data and for revealing new relationships, standardized, institutionalized ways in which people act. Such roles as "pure" cases at the extreme ends of the continuum represent typologies as ideal types. The abstractions permit grouping the data. They encourage comparison and contextual scanning. Typing, as Adorno said, does not merely order diversity; typing makes it possible to conceptualize diversity and to reach beyond the descriptive level for inferences that may have explanatory power.[5]

Changing Times and Changing Types

Social and political events confront us with problems and provoke questions that impel psychologists to revise their constructs and research strategies. For example, the pragmatic need to identify and cope with prejudice and the fascist mentality of the 1940's led Adorno and his colleagues to conceptualize the authoritarian personality. They demonstrated that traits such as conventionality, submissiveness to authority, aggressiveness, projection, and manipulativeness appeared to be functionally interrelated. Rather than appearing as isolated traits, they interacted dynamically within a *process.* The work that grew out of this investigation stimulated research for more than a decade. It focused attention on authoritarianism as an adaptive technique and as a character structure.[6]

The fact that with changing social conditions new configurations of behavior emerge and new roles are institutionalized does not necessarily imply the appearance of new traits. The newly prevalent behavior may have been endemic or latent in many persons, and may have required only a stimulus to become active. Instances of deviance may now find social support so that behavior which formerly was an isolated characteristic can be

---

[5] Adorno, building his case for the authoritarian personality, said, "People form psychological classes inasmuch as they are stamped by variegated social processes," and further maintained that the critique of topology should note that many people are not and have never been individuals. They remain standardized and with little individuation. It is by now a cliché to observe, for example, that nonconformist styles in clothes and hairdress have themselves become uniforms. Theodore W. Adorno et al., *The Authoritarian Personality;* New York, Harper, 1950; p. 744.

[6] In contrast to the Authoritarian Low, who, though he is anti-authority, has an internalized father image and a strong superego, Adorno also noted the existence of an Impulsive Low, whom he identified with actors, circus folk, vagrants, libertines, addicts, prostitutes, etc. He commented, "There is reason to assume that the Impulsive Low represents a syndrome of its own." This was a group he identified as weak both in ego and in superego. See footnote 5; p. 776.

confirmed as a role. Given the appropriate circumstances, latent structures and recessive or marginal behavior find socially channelled outlets. The endemic becomes epidemic.

If it is the case that such behaviors persist and recur, the study of their manifestation may help to clarify determinants of the self and of roles enacted to validate one's assigned or adopted status. It should illuminate from another view the development and the meaning of deviance. In arguing the case for an antinomian personality, differentiated from other typological modalities, it should be clear that the construct is not annulled by variability of some of the associated elements or by differing social settings in which the construct is employed.[7]

In some of these differentiated constructs it is possible that identical traits may have been included. These common traits may endure and rise in different configurations as facets of the same underlying process. Laboratory science leads to other typologies than the molar constructs of social science or clinic. Yet, there may be an underlying communality, manifested consistently in different settings where the focus is on different aims, which recurs in such typological constructs.[8] All of these constructs and variables may represent partial approaches to the same ongoing functional process.

Preoccupation with the authoritarian personality has now been replaced by concern with new styles and patterns of conduct: the politics of "dropping out," the resurgence of religious interests, the psychedelic cults of "mind expansion," the ideology of drug abuse, and other components of the Hippie ethos. These activities, values, acts, and roles seem to comprise a unified and integrated system of conduct. Significant psychological data will, however, not be recovered if we limit our attention to circumscribed variables, such as the pharmacological properties of drugs, or if we confine our studies to the peripheral transactions of the human organism.

---

[7] Typologies are construed in differing settings to meet varying goals. Thus, typologies have been concerned with the classification of diseases, perceptual styles, temperaments, morphological somatotypes. In medicine and psychiatry the aim is to meet problems of diagnosis, prognosis, and classification of diseases and problems of institutional management. Kraepelin and Lombroso elaborated psychiatric typologies. Some typologies remain more descriptive than explanatory while others seek to link variables in a higher order inference. The fact that currently the disease model itself is under serious scrutiny and challenge does not necessarily invalidate the earlier constructs. It suggests only that the same data can be ordered in new ways, encompassing a wider range of variables to reveal new meanings and relationships.
[8] Such as: Suggestibility Type vs. Non-Suggestibility Type (P. Janet, *Les Obsessions et la Psychosthenie;* Paris, Alcan, 1903); Syntropic Type vs. Idiotropic Type (F. L. Wertheimer and F. E. Hesketh, *The Significance of the Psychical Constitution in Mental Disease;* Baltimore, Williams and Wilkins, 1926); B-Type vs. T-Type and Disintegrate Type vs. Integrate Type (E. R. Jaensch, *Eidetic Imagery;* New York, Harcourt Brace, 1930); Field Dependent Type vs. Field Independent Type (H. A. Witkin et al., *Psychological Differentiation;* New York, Wiley, 1962); Low Body Barrier Type vs. High Body Barrier Type (Seymour Fisher, "Body Attention Patterns and Personality Defenses," *Psychol. Monogr.: General and Applied* [1966] 80 [9]); and many other studies.

Historical studies may be more appropriate and fruitful for personality theory than the variables psychologists customarily employ. Psychology, as a science, deeming *Verstehen* and *Geisteswissenschaft* suspect, has confined itself to a naive physicalism and has been reluctant to employ the study of history as a means of illuminating the dark corners of present-day conduct. If psychologists have grudgingly made a place for historical models in idiographic studies, there still is no sign that they can conceive of a nomothetic enterprise concerned with historical parameters that would not stray and become lost within the ambiguous boundaries of *Verstehenpsychologie*. This exposition of the argument for the antinomian personality is an attempt to demonstrate the utility of historical research for social psychology and personality theory.

Changing Times and Recurrent Types

Viewed as an exclusively contemporary occurrence, Hippie conduct and the values associated with it are too easily rationalized or dismissed as the antics of the lunatic fringe. But when the deviant conduct is examined as a modern version of earlier modes of behavior, not only does the investigation become more relevant, but also it leads to significant theoretical implications. The antinomian personality, it becomes manifest, recurs in specific stressful settings of social instability and crisis, where it serves the same adaptive function.

If one reviews such phenomena as the decline of Rome after the third century A.D.,[9] and the heretical movements prevalent at the time, if one follows the various streams that led to the development of nationalism and that culminated in the Reformation,[10] if one scrutinizes the values, roles, and social changes that developed as a response to the Industrial Revolution, to the French Revolution, and to the Napoleonic Wars [11]— usually identified as the Romantic movement in Germany, England, France, and Middle Europe—one will find the recurrence of similar value systems. In all of them a common theme appears, one which is manifested again in the Hippie scene today. They all show identical modes of adaptation as a response to similar kinds of social stress. One need not imply an Eternal Return or assume a Viconian theory of historical cycles to maintain that there are historical regularities or to argue that social crisis in different historical periods may produce similar values and similar modes of adjustment.

When roles lose their congruence, when the world's responses are no

[9] E. R. Dodds, *Pagan and Christian in an Age of Anxiety;* Cambridge Univ. Press, 1965.
[10] George H. Williams, *The Radical Reformation;* Philadelphia, Westminster Press, 1962.
[11] See Talmon, in footnote 3.

longer reliable and contradict the individual's expectations, specific behaviors emerge as an attempt to maintain an optimal degree of arousal or activation. In the effort to maintain orientation and overcome the threat of diffusion of the self, of fugue states or a depersonalization, characteristic activities and roles are elaborated. In our time and in the earlier periods to which I referred above, the recurrence of similar needs and contexts, whether in an ecclesiastical or in a secular setting, has produced similar adaptive techniques that have led to the same personality configuration. Similar needs seem to provoke similar responses.

In a stable, orderly world what is construed as "human nature" appears self-evident and lawful. Parts seem related to the whole. Morale is high and an optimistic, naturalistic, and rational orientation is dominant. In times of social instability and crisis, when morale is low, the sense of order is lost and perspectives are fragmented and violated. It is the recognition of order and the incorporation of values that constitute the armature on which the self and its identity are built and that determine the orientation of the individual. If this armature collapses, if the relationship between the individual and his community is no longer viable, confirming information is unavailable and the threat of depersonalization arises. A new scaffold for the self becomes necessary; other manipulations of sensory and perceptual inputs are required to stabilize and master the threatened self.

The sense of identity depends upon experiencing consistency in the self, finding congruence in multiple roles, and receiving from the world a reliable response that consistently confirms and validates the self. It is from this consistency and this reliability that the individual construes the ground for his orientation, through which he monitors his experience, receiving, integrating, and feeding back stimuli from central, proximal, and distal worlds. He establishes the range in which impulses are controlled and released. He chooses modes of regulation and accommodation, either ascetic systems of control or ecstatic systems of release. He develops cognitive and perceptual styles that augment or reduce the reception of stimuli. In a consistent and reliable world the individual achieves a discrete, analytic, rational orientation which enables him to discriminate subject and object and to manage an effective commerce between them. When such a world and such an orientation are disrupted, autistic components become dominant and synesthetic and nonrational modes that fuse sensory modalities prevail. Tactile and haptic perceptions become more necessary and more valued than visual orientations.[12]

Some individuals in such stress and conflict are unable to maintain the organization of their world. In their search for order and security they seek a lost Golden Age and long to return to the wonder and innocence of child-

[12] Wylie Sypher, *Four Stages of Renaissance Style, Transformations in Art and Literature, 1400–1700;* Garden City, N.Y., Doubleday, Anchor, 1955; pp. 14–27.

hood. Fleeing from memories they reject and from a future they dread, they enshrine the present moment and make a cult of immediacy. Since time perspective can serve as a locus of control of the self, this shift to "now or never" helps them to anchor a self which repudiates control, tolerates no delay, and typically challenges the "Establishment," whose conventions and authority they deny. In periods of transition and instability, as these people find their mobility blocked, they respond with passive resistance or with rebellion. In a world that disrupts orientation, a nihilistic posture by irreverence or by denial questions the validity of any order.

In losing his sense of order the antinomian also loses his own boundaries. He asserts the primacy of the "natural" self and of its impulses and desires, rejecting counsels of discrimination and control. Whether the behavior is due to a stimulus hunger or a hyperirritability, whether it expresses a need to augment or to avoid stimuli, the antinomians seek the excessive and the extravagant. In self-assertion they hope to regain lost anchorage and orientation points. Pantheistic cosmic expansion, erotic moment, manipulations of immediacy—all are attempts to bind the self and to reinstate its boundaries. Theirs is a rage for order.

The Gnostics, Hippies of Religion

The writings of Marcus Aurelius anticipate and document the decline of the Roman Empire. He records the existential anguish familiar in our time. He speaks of Man, standing on a knife-edge between two voids, naught but smoke to be blown away. Life seems derealized. The self is a puppet, a stringed marionette; Man is an actor playing roles that are so many external masks. Life is perceived as "games," dream, and delusion, in the same way that in our time some speak of "games," "trips," and "happenings," and even of game theories of war, and of psychotherapy.

When Aurelius wrote, the Pax Romana was coming to an end. The barbarians were at the gates. It was a time of runaway inflation, of recurrent epidemics, of personal disaster, and of sacked cities. There were portents of doom, rumors of invasions from other worlds, and fear of the world's end.

It was in such apocalyptic times that the Gnostic heresies arose as social movements.[13] Gnosis refers to knowledge, but not as an analytic and cognitive process. It implies, instead, Illumination, Revelation, and Intuition as the basis of a truer, purer, and better knowing. The Gnostic heretical cults rejected the authority of church and law and devised new strategies to achieve salvation. These movements rejected the worldly life and turned to the interior self for truth. Scorning established institutions they insisted on direct and personal access to insight and to God. They defended faculties

[13] Hans Jonas, *The Gnostic Religion* (2nd ed.); Boston, Beacon Press, 1963.

that they deemed to be superior to reason and to order. Liturgy and ritual had lost meaning for them; they reached out for a pantheistic fusion and unity with nature or for a total escape from the bondage of this evil world.

The members of these Gnostic sects founded utopian communities and colonies; they aspired to a "self-actualization" in which they would free the "pneuma," as pure spirit, from its bondage in the contemptible body. They spoke in tongues, joined cults of love, and sought ecstasy as a steady state.

The Gnostics believed that through spiritual exercises they achieved union with the Holy Ghost and that for them sin was no longer possible. Therefore they were absolved of obligation to the moral law. Libertine excesses degraded both the evil body and the scorned world. In avoiding procreation and rejecting marriage they hastened release from the fleshly prison and accelerated the return to the Godly spirit. In rejecting all that was worldly they spurned the ornate, both in the rituals and imagery of the church and in their personal lives. They affirmed, instead, a simplification of values, rites, and dress. In their zeal some became ascetic. Others permitted themselves all indulgences and perversions as an expression of their contempt for the world and themselves.

One of the earliest Gnostic sects, the Manichaeans,[14] devised ceremonies of preparation and initiation. As an elect, they separated themselves from the worldly; they ritualized diets that would purify them and assure visions. They roamed the countryside as wanderers, beggars, and vagabond preachers. Pacifists, they repudiated the killing even of animals. They refused to work or to comply with secular regulations and lived instead on charity. The Manichaean Church, too passive and too nonresistant, was easily suppressed. Although it failed to survive the severe repression that it provoked, its name became generic for the Gnostic heretical movements that recurred in the succeeding centuries.

All of these movements distrusted rational analysis and relied on inspiration. They felt that the New Jerusalem was imminent. Women often were prominent and found in these cults the opportunity for a radical change in their status and their mobility.

While some Gnostic groups affirmed passive resistance, others became militant warriors. Some counseled civil disobedience, denounced wealth, and condemned the nobles, while others encouraged a quiet, meek, and sober demeanor. Their civil disobedience led them to poaching, pranks, outrages, and rebellion.

These heretical movements first found a mass base among the poor peasants, who found alien and unconsoling the Christianity imposed upon them by their lords. Much later, diffused by itinerant weavers, but still within a theological framework, these movements reflected the first stirrings of a nascent nationalism, struggling against the feudal lords and the church.

[14] Steven Runciman, *The Medieval Manichee;* Cambridge Univ. Press, 1947.

They were known by various names—Manichaeans, Bogomils, Cathars, Patarenes, Albigensians, Waldensians.[15] In these and other variants the Gnostic ethos persisted and converged into the reformation. Its proponents were imprisoned, burned at the stake, weighted and drowned in rivers. The Gnostic values ran like an underground stream, but in stressful times the antinomian values surfaced again, the stream found new beds and cut deeper gorges. This stream disappeared as a society became tranquil and stable, or lingered in isolated pools, but when social crisis returned it appeared again.

In Wycliffe's fifteenth century England [16] the Lollards struck Oxford University. Parents feared to send their sons and the University enrollment declined. The Lollards inveighed against war, against capital punishment, and against the Univeristy "Establishment." So great was the uproar that ex-students and nonstudents a half a millennium ago were forbidden by the administration to speak on campus unless they first obtained the Bishop's approval, even as at Berkeley campus recently all nonstudents were barred.

The Anabaptist cults of the Peasant Wars in Luther's Germany [17] asserted similar values, roles, and personality styles as they rejected the "Establishment" and fought the overorganization of the Church. Runciman asserts that in all Gnostic movements the goal is to destroy, to repudiate, and to reject rather than to atone, redeem, and heal.[18] The established order is always construed as an order of evil that ought to be outraged, violated, and met with mocking self-indulgence and contempt. Membership in the cults is achieved by insight and by initiation. It requires separation from the world by a journey or by a drug. One follows the leader, the spiritual guide, the Elect, and is granted membership in a spiritual aristocracy.

When rituals atrophy and are emptied of their power there is no Elect and no spiritual aristocracy other than the Establishment and its hierarchy. Disaffected individuals again find self-confirmation and recover a source of meaning and a ground for the self in new rites of initiation and a new sense of membership. A new revelation, a new "trip" creates a new Elect and offers to marginal and declassed people a new vehicle of both mobility and esteem.

Romanticism as a Secular Variant

Generations of "flower children," the "innocent," the "guileless," the "pure in heart," who do not speak with the forked tongues of the adult world and its Establishment, recur in ages of transition and anxiety. Burned at the

[15] Norman Cohn, *The Pursuit of the Millenium;* New York, Harper Torchbooks, 1961.
[16] G. M. Trevelyan, *England in the Age of Wycliffe, 1368–1520;* New York, Harper Torchbooks, 1963.
[17] See footnote 10.
[18] See footnote 14.

stake by the Dominicans, impaled on Turkish swords, the Gnostic movement returns in new cults with new names. The underground stream rises in occult rites and Kabbalah, in witchcraft, and in its secular form as a Romantic movement. As a referent for "alienation" may be cited the loss of the sacred, the profanation of Man, the experience of finding oneself sundered, observer and actor split, spectator and participant as two separate masks and each in amnesia.[19] Involved in alienation is a sense of apathy and of passivity as one impotently confronts an overwhelming power seen as Fate. Unable to effect one's self-determination, one responds with inertia or with hyperactivity.[20]

The Romantic movement became dominant in the first half of the nineteenth century. For some decades, even before the turn of the century, a reaction to the Enlightenment and a rejection of its values were already manifest. Romanticism was a response to the transition and social crisis brought about by the Industrial Revolution, the French Revolution, and the Napoleonic Wars, and it was an accommodation to this crisis. The word "Romantic," with its source among the Cathars and the Albigensians, binds the earlier Gnostic groups and the new secular coteries. As a movement it is an adaptive response to the critical conditions in which it develops; it is liable, too, to the same pathologies and excesses of the antinomian mode. If the orderly and the reasonable too often do deteriorate into the dull, the shallow, and the complacent, the Romantic repudiation often turns into silliness, indulgence, mocking extravagance, outrage, and the loss of standards.

In the Romantic movement, as in the Gnostic, Truth is achieved by vision rather than by "dry" analysis, rationality, and calculation. The intense Part is more valued than the ordered Whole; the central focus is on emotion, imagination, and vision. "The heart," said Pascal, lost in an indifferent Universe, "has its reasons that the Reason does not know." [21] Common sense appears trivial and banal and only through the Act and the Deed can one wrest significance and redeem meaning. Freedom and the gratuitous act are preferred to convention, balance, and restraint. The Romantic trusts his own feelings rather than rules; peak experiences of vision, choice, gesture, and action alone can overcome quotidian dullness; these experiences and acts contain their own justification, independent of consequences.

Sensibility and insensibility, as de Sade noted, are close to one another.

[19] "All sacred things must have their place. . . . being in their place is what makes them sacred, for, if they were taken out of their place, even in thought, the entire order of the Universe would be destroyed. Sacred objects therefore contribute to the maintenance of order in the Universe by occupying places allocated to them." Claude Lévi-Strauss, *The Savage Mind;* Univ. of Chicago Press, 1967; p. 10.

[20] Keniston's study of alienation notes the same factors described in the antinomian personality—the same yearning for fusion, the cult of immediacy, and self-fragmentation, the same ideology of sentience and groping for pantheistic unity. But Keniston limits himself to the contemporary crisis alone, and does not call attention to the historic parameter. Kenneth Keniston, *The Uncommitted;* New York, Delta, 1965.

[21] Blaise Pascal, *Pensées;* New York, Dutton, 1960; IV, p. 277.

The Romantic craves sensation, makes a cult of sentiency, and hones his appetite for the exotic and the macabre. He seeks emotion for emotion's sake, explores the extravagant, experiments with obscure and violent feelings, and finds special Truths in madness [22] and in polymorphous perversions. The Romantic spiritual or physical tourist, remarks a scholar of the period,[23] seeks out periods and places that are extraordinary and exotic, where habits are likely to be strange or horrible, and motives passionate and unusual. The Romantic reasserted the primacy of intuitive, emotional, and inspirational values. He renewed the quest for that fusion, enthusiasm, and "organic" unity of which, undone by Newton's image of the Universe, he had been deprived.

Just as Huizinga [24] remarked on the compulsive weeping in the waning Middle Ages, so Taine in his record of the *ancien regime* [25] describes new fashions of weeping, swooning, and enthusiasm as characteristic behavior. Nostalgia, boundless and without referent, becomes a central motif. Faced with the Industrial Revolution and with Blake's "Satanic mills," a zeal for folk art and for simple rural Arcadian values is reaffirmed. The Enlightenment asserted the primacy of Reason, the universality of natural law; it optimistically assumed an immanent progress as it construed a mechanistic universe. The Romantics denied and rejected such assumptions.

Changes from a classic to a Romantic orientation are not merely matters of changing taste. Wolflin, for example, in his *Principles of Art History,* notes the recurrence of the classical and the Romantic, but seems to make them merely formal issues.[26] But to assume that these are merely stylistic changes, to see form as fad, is too shallow. Such a view fails to recognize that changes are adaptive and functional; they reassert values as to the nature of man, of society, and of the universe, and involve a change in orientation intended to master experience and to enable men to cope with loss, crisis, and stress.

In the age of the Enlightenment, order, regularity, rules, etiquette, style, and ceremonial were central values. A world seen as orderly and meaningful finds its rituals and ceremonials viable, its discipline appropriate, and the legitimacy of the disciplining agents established and acknowledged. The need for conformity seems to be self-evident and in the "nature" of things. Decorum and decency are deemed appropriate. Such is a classical world. It may not be irrelevant to our purposes to note that propriety and proprium, as a referent to the self, or to *amour-propre,* share a common root.

[22] Consider in this context the existential, phenomenologic antipsychiatry of Laing. R. D. Laing, *The Politics of Experience;* New York, Pantheon Books, 1967.
[23] G. S. R. Kitson Clark, "The Romantic Element, 1830–50," in *Studies in Social History,* edited by J. H. Plumb; Toronto, Longmans, Greene, 1956.
[24] J. Huizinga, *The Waning of the Middle Ages;* London, Arnold, 1937.
[25] Hippolyte Taine, *The Ancient Regime,* translated by John Durand; New York, Smith, 1931.
[26] Heinrich Wolflin, *Principles of Art History;* New York, Dover, 1932.

But the antinomian, whether as Gnostic, as Romantic, or in his contemporary reincarnation as Hippie, lives in a habitat of forms and rituals that have been depleted of value and meaning. He finds forms exhausted or banal. When he permits himself an emotional statement, it often is either ecstatically ineluctable, or "camp" and mocking of all sentiment as sententious. Man is the measure, but the deranged self becomes an unreliable gauge and perception is construed as hyperbole.

If the Enlightenment valued clarity, rationality, and order, the Romantics sought the allusive and the synesthetic,[27] the intuitive and the passionate. The Enlightenment confirmed the social man, but the ideal of the Romantics was the isolated wanderer, the lone melancholy rebel. If the Enlightenment embellished thought with ceremonial and activity with ritual, the Romantics opposed rules and regulations. If the Enlightenment asserted the primacy of the group and the civility of life, the Romantics repudiated the mediocrity of the herd and affirmed the impulsive, the spontaneous, and the novel. They chose the irrational, the mystic, and the ecstatic, which they contrasted with an arid, abstract, analytic intellectualism.[28] Romanticism opposed the mechanistic universe with a supernatural world of visions; against consciousness and rationality, it lauded the virtues of the unconscious and the bizarre. The Romantic self, alienated by and in recoil from a mechanical paradigm, saw nature instead as a benign mother or as a dark, threatening, chaotic witch.

In their dreams the Romantics took "trips" to Xanadu or imagined the life of the Red Indian in the forests of North America before he had known the white man. If they could not find a Golden Age in the past or the future, they built Ivory Towers to escape the drab actuality of steaming factories and city slums.

It has been argued that German, French, and English Romanticism each had different goals, the former reactionary and conservative, and the latter

[27] Referring to synesthetic imagery in the course of a comment on Baudelaire, Adorno maintains that it fulfills a specific function. "By clouding the division between different realms of sense perception, they simultaneously try to efface the rigid classification of different kinds of objects, as it is brought about under the practical requirements of industrial civilization. They rebel against reification." (See footnote 5; p. 746.) But Adorno fails to appreciate that also involved in the synesthetic and the syncretistic is the need to blur the differentiation between subject and object and that the need for fusion and for ego inflation is also a motive.

[28] Wordsworth spoke of "that false secondary power by which we multiply distinctions." (William Wordsworth, *The Prelude, or Growth of a Poet's Mind*, text of 1805, edited by E. De Selincourt; London, Oxford Univ. Press, 1933; Book II, p. 26.) And Coleridge said, ". . . self-consciousness is not a kind of *being*, but a kind of *knowing*, and that too the highest and furthest that exists for us." He also spoke of "the sacred power of self-intuition." (Samuel Taylor Coleridge, *Biographia Literaria;* New York, Holt and Williams, 1872; Thesis X, pp. 361–362.) And Blake, contemptuous of self-control, said, "Those who restrain desire, do so because theirs is weak enough to be restrained; . . ." (William Blake, *The Marriage of Heaven and Hell;* London, Chatto and Windus, 1911; p. 49.)

two progressive and liberal. Despite their disparate goals, what binds them into a common movement is the identical commitment to enthusiasm, intuition, and irrationality; the preference for extremist solutions as adaptive behavior. With the attrition of traditional values about the nature of society and the universe, with the collapse of customary social and psychological assumptions, the antinomian maneuver recurs. It is the identity of style and of response that makes for the commonality of the variant forms of the Romantic movement, that links the earlier Gnostics with the contemporary hipsters.[29]

It is noteworthy too that for Wordsworth, Blake, and their cohorts a central motive was their disappointment with and revulsion against the French Revolution. Today's drug scene can also be understood in part as a recoil from and repudiation of politics, as a consequence of disillusionment with the Russian and Chinese revolutions and the rejection of the rational, secular values these revolutions affirmed. The "egg head" is discredited not only by the Philistines. The visionaries of Bohemia are anti-mind, too.

The former antinomians—the Gnostics, the Anabaptists, and the Romantics—like today's antinomians, sought ways to outrage and provoke the Establishment. Uncouth behavior becomes a way of saying "No!" to the system, separating oneself from Philistines and "squares" by bizarre and extravagant costumes and by strange hairdresses and beards. Gautier, in the period between the Revolutions of 1848 and the Paris Commune, paraded in a red waistcoat, and "Pope" Enfantin masqueraded in splendid costumes. In Germany, Father Jahn, bearded, dressed in leather, carrying staff and guitar, gathered youthful disciples who burned books and practiced physical and spiritual exercises.[30] Were those costumes used to achieve distance from the world of factory and finance and to provoke the Philistines, or was the masquerade a maneuver to demonstrate that the isolation in which these career-hungry intellectuals lived was intentional and really brought about by themselves?

The Hippie as Antinomian

We again live in an epoch of wars and revolutions. Established institutions and values crumble and are repudiated. The British Empire is at an end

---

[29] Among the contemporary hipsters it is necessary to note role differentiations, too. As a social movement it absorbs ambulatory schizophrenics who in an earlier time might have been "hoboes" or solitary eccentrics; young adolescent experimenters with roles; and a range of role commitments, all antinomian, from those who assert values of gurus and mystics like Alan Watts and Timothy Leary, of shamanism and Indian tribalism like Allen Ginsberg and Gary Snyder, to Merry Pranksters whose aim is *epater le bourgeois* like Ken Kesey, self-conscious Albigensians like the Diggers, hooligans like the Hell's Angels, homosexuals, Bohemians, and bored middle-class sensation tasters.

[30] Peter Viereck, *Metapolitics, the Roots of the Nazi Mind;* New York, Capricorn Books, 1961.

and American claims as the heir apparent are not being honored. Radicals shaken by the Khrushchev revelations and the internecine struggles of the Russians and the Chinese are dismayed as they see these revolutions, too, devour their children.

Major breakthroughs in technology and new sources of energy introduce a new industrial revolution. Racial groups demand civil rights and disrupt customary roles and power relations. Bureaucratic governmental and corporate structures depersonalize human relations and confront people only in "rational" functions rather than as human respondents. Alienation, a cry that arose among the French *cognoscenti* of the Resistance, has become the code word of intellectuals around the world.

In our own country, and also in Europe as it is Americanized, youth lives in an ambiguous adolescence with no meaningful and significant institutional roles to define and structure its status. Under the constant shadow of the military draft, immobilized in indecision, lingering in school not for chosen vocations but for draft deferments, they are dangling men. Satiated with violence, they unblinkingly read in the daily news about "kill ratios," and they endure a war whose moral basis has been questioned as no other in recent times. Protests appear ineffective. The vast bureaucratic and corporate world continues in its course, indifferent as the stars to all protest and dissent. Again apocalyptic visions emerge; forebodings of the end of the world, of flying saucers and the threat of invasion from other planets.

Now, as in other periods when a society was in transition, we see the re-emergence of the antinomian personality, who scorns his Establishment as evil and corrupt, who deplores the aimless, trivial preoccupations of family and business life, and repudiates forms and rituals he finds empty and dead.

The current antinomian style is expressed in the contemporary preoccupation with drugs as a gimmick of transcendence and as a social movement. It finds expression in the theological assertion that "God is dead," in the development of sexual freedom leagues sponsoring orgiastic communions and challenging traditional sexual roles, in the growth of homosexual communities, and in new art forms, such as the Theater of the Absurd, the spontaneous "Happening," the drama that abandons the proscenium separating stage and audience, and all the graphic arts which reflect the diffusion and breakdown of objects and of orientation to them.[31]

---

[31] In this context one can question McLuhan's argument that the synesthetic and syncretistic modes and the new tribalism can be seen as products of electronic technology which has displaced visual linear perception. (Marshall McLuhan, *The Gutenberg Galaxy;* Univ. of Toronto Press, 1962.) They can also be seen as additional evidence of antinomian fusion, which typically rejects visual perspectives and the constancy of objects.

In 1887 and 1888, long before the new electronic technology could modify perception, Nietzsche correlated nihilism with a sensibility that had become more irritable; with the exposure to intensified and desparate impressions: "The tempo of this influx *prestissimo;* the impressions erase each other; . . . Men unlearn spontaneous action, they merely react to stimuli from the outside." (Friedrich Nietzsche, *The Will to Power,* edited by Walter Kaufmann; New York, Random House, 1967, p. 47.)

There is renewed interest in the Kabbalah, in Tarot cards and in astrology as one attempts to read one's fate in an indifferent universe. The antinomian ethos reaches beyond the obvious hipster and Bohemian cults. Current philosophical and scientific models in part reflect these values, whether as ideological positivism that stems from the anguish of uncertainty, or in the current modishness of phenomenology as a method and as a philosophy. The phenomenologist is acutely aware of the diverse and protean forms of appearance. These seem to him to negate any sense of continuity, structure, or order other than that created by the self, and he beats against the walls of his solipsistic universe.

This ethos leads to the search for a "Psychology of Being," to the quest for "peak" experiences, and to the ideology of self-actualization.[32] The cultivation of idiosyncracy becomes an honored vocation. When institutions fail, when boundaries break or become permeable, when external frames of reference lose their validity, impulses and drives within the individual expand in disarray and overcome controls. The inflated individual is then compelled to find a new principle of order and control within himself.

He experiments with the fragmentation of perception of objects and of self. He explores thresholds of pain, light, and sound, seeking a way out of his constant refractory phase. He seeks to bind and sustain a sense of immediacy. He embarks on a subversive program of willful, deliberate derangement in the hope that he can purge the accidental, the banal, and the trivial and renew the world. Since external sources of identity have been discredited and their authority is no longer honored, the antinomian seeks to establish and maintain his identity by a hyper-irritation of the self. Unlike Descartes, he may say, *"Coitus, ergo sum."*

There is a rupture between the world outside and inner experience. The desolate unconscious is projected into the outer world. Now, as before, when the antinomian has become modal, mysticism and transcendence, "kicks"

Unlike McLuhan, whose focus is technological, Nietzsche described the centripetal forces leading to disintegration of the self as a factor in the encroaching nihilism. He described the loss of aim, unity, and "truth," which made the world appear valueless. He noted the sense of emptiness and the attempt to overcome it by intoxication, hedonism, enthusiasm, mysticism, and "the voluptuous enjoyment of eternal emptiness." (p. 20) He remarked upon "The multitude and disgregation of impulses and the lack of any systematic order among them. . . ." (p. 28), and of the despair that follows upon the experience of being powerless against men, so that one reduces all problems to questions of pleasure and displeasure.

[32] Self-actualization is more a new politics of despair than a psychology, whether it is sponsored by Maslow or by Norman Brown. It is a revolt against "repression," which, as Marcuse has noted, "promotes existence in that immediacy which, in a repressive society, is bad immediacy. It isolates the individual . . . encourages nonconformity and letting go in ways which leave the real engines of repression in the society entirely intact. The desublimation involved in this sort of self-actualization is itself repressive inasmuch as it weakens the necessity and the power of the intellect." Robert Paul Wolff, Barrington Moore, Jr., and Herbert Marcuse, *A Critique of Pure Tolerance;* Boston, Beacon Press, 1965; p. 114.

and ecstasy become dominant aims. The Hippies seek a Golden Age to renew the lost innocence of childhood, or to find the purity of the ancient apostles, or the integrity of the noble savage. They synthesize an Indian tribalism as an identity. Thoreau becomes their patron saint and they leave the cities to live in the wilderness or in utopian communities.[33]

The Romantics demonstrated that the sad, melancholy, isolated rebel could also become the conspirator who took up arms. He could swing in cataclysmic conversions between the poles of Revolution and Restoration. What begins as Byronic or Promethean defiance and self-assertion can for some culminate in a Bonapartist ideology and the solace of the corporate state.[34] The turn to populism and to folk ballads is an attempt to renew a national myth as one form of identity. The antinomian longs for relationship and unity and seeks to fuse himself with a group, a leader, a cult of friendship and "love" that can overcome his uncertainty and supply him with support. In scorning corruption, in rejecting the smug, the complacent, and the unjust, he may glorify whatever he finds that gives him again a sense of relatedness. He may find this in the church or in the state.

Conclusion

I have presented evidence that the personality configuration and the values that have emerged within the contemporary Hippie movement are not new. They have appeared many times in the past, as for example in the Gnostic and similar religious heresies, and in the Romantic movement. In each case this personality configuration, which I have denoted as the antinomian personality, arose in a time of social crisis and transition, when old values

---

[33] The Six Day School at Mendocino, California, announces in a descriptive leaflet that it "offers a course in Primitive Home Economics to equip students with practical know-how in the maintenance of a wilderness household; the preparation of wholesome natural foods, wood-stove cookery, treadle sewing machine operation, the making of soap and candles, and the utilization of herbs as food and medicine. Both of the primitive courses are intended to help man work with nature rather than against her." There is also a course in "Primitive Trades and Tools" that offers "indoctrination" in the use and care of the tools and materials of wilderness living. Curriculum includes "chain-saw, blacksmithing, tree felling, and well digging." Courses are also offered in "Tarot, Kabbalah, and Astrology."

[34] Adorno (see footnote 5; p. 763) describes a type he identifies as the "Condottiere" who appears in the setting of the increased insecurity of postwar existence. He is nihilistic and is convinced that chance alone matters. Out of work, rootless, he is often an adventurer, an air ace or motor racer. These people become "born leaders of the unemployed." Captain Roehm, a leading storm trooper, called himself a *"hochverrater."* They demonstrate an "enthusiasm" for youth and an appetite for excesses— heavy drinking, homosexuality, and acts of violence. They are not as rigid as the authoritarian personality and are not submissive to authority. They manifest resistance to it, maintaining an irrational and blind hatred of *all* authority; yet at the same time, there is a potential readiness to capitulate and to join hands with the hated "strong" man.

and behavior controls were no longer adequate and new ones had not yet emerged to take their place. The antinomian mode, with its characteristic emphasis on intuition, immediacy, self-actualization, transcendence, and similar themes familiar in Hippie conduct, is an adaptive style manifest in transitional periods.

The typological construct of the antinomian personality permits a modal differentiation of a specific configuration of personality. It should be useful in clarifying and making more precise clinical diagnosis, and in elucidating the structure and context of deviance. If it is confirmed, in research studies that will control values and perceptual modalities as dependent variables, it should prove of value to personality theory. It should encourage the use of semantic analysis and of other techniques in the examination of historical documents, not only to test the argument developed here, but also to demonstrate the values of historical parameters for personality theory. In a practical sense, the confirmation of this typological construct should make it possible to avoid counterfeit issues and pseudo-problems in meeting the polemics of the proponents of "psychedelic" ideologies.

Moral Socialization
and Moral Anomie

Bernard Rosenberg and Harry Silverstein

However anomic or alienated a person may be, he is never totally lacking in a sense of good and evil. That sense may outlast all capacity to communicate with other human beings; it can animate a psychotic (and in catatonic schizophrenia it can throttle, silence, and paralyze him) despite his narcissistic isolation from everyone else. Indeed, conceptions of right and wrong, of good and evil, are everpresent in any population of human beings regardless of how fully or superficially they have been socialized. Consequently, it is not surprising that we should have found these terms, applied by and to boys and girls, so meaningful and so productive for our purposes.

A Chicago boy says, "A good person don't do nothin'. A bad person does anything;" vivid definitions so polarized that, armed with them, he is able to be contemptuous of the former while dissociating himself from the

Reprinted by permission of the publisher, from Bernard Rosenberg and Harry Silverstein, *The Varieties of Delinquent Experience* (Lexington, Mass.: Ginn & Company, a Xerox Company, Copyright © 1969) pp. 139–162.

latter. We would expect respondents of any type to deny their wickedness (and they do so less than we would expect). We would also expect them to affirm their virtue (but if so, here again we are being too simple-minded). One finds rationalizations before the fact ("techniques of neutralization" as David Matza and Gresham Sykes have dubbed them) [1] and rationalizations after the fact used to justify disapproved conduct. They are often the same rationalizations that Matza and Sykes find among juvenile delinquents. We find them just as often among nondelinquents. No one, not even in the community of saints Emile Durkheim once asked his readers to envisage, where venial sins become deadly sins, can always bring value and action into perfect harmony. Furthermore, one man's value is another man's poison —neither has much to do with law-abiding or law-breaking behavior. All young people within society are somehow responsive to its controls; only the presocialized and the asocialized, for example, small children, mongoloid idiots, and psychotics, are somewhat less so. In gross terms, we may say that juvenile delinquents like juvenile nondelinquents are socialized, one no more or less than the other. To say this is not to deny that delinquents break rules which nondelinquents obey. But why they do certain things or abstain from doing them does not seem to us to be normatively determined.

The pioneer work of Mead, Cooley, Freud, Durkheim, and Piaget [2] has conditioned students of the subject to assume that socialization and normative determination are identical. Yet it is possible to be both socialized and anomic, to be conformist and normless. That this condition obtains in the large middle reaches of American society most of us have taken for granted, at least since David Riesman wrote *The Lonely Crowd*.[3] By middle-class other-direction, Riesman can only have meant a specific state of socialized deregulation such that Americans, as they responded less and less to inner promptings, came, through imitation, to look and act more and more alike. Widespread conformity may issue from circumstances that foster *socialization into anomie,* with people seeking surface cues to replace the norms they no longer internalize. Such conformity, with standard deviation, is observably present in the American middle class. No one should be astounded that it is also observably present in the American underclass.

Of late, and with good reason, much has been made of the identity crisis facing middle-class Americans. Large numbers of them have been plagued by the question of who they are and what they are. Is there any reason for

[1] David Matza and Gresham M. Sykes, "Juvenile Delinquency and Subterranean Values," *American Sociological Review,* XXVI (October, 1961), pp. 712–719.

[2] George Herbert Mead, *Mind, Self and Society* (Chicago: University of Chicago Press, 1934); Charles Horton Cooley, *Social Organization: A Study of the Larger Mind* (New York: C. Scribner, 1916); Sigmund Freud, *A General Introduction to Psychoanalysis* (New York: Liveright Publishing Co., 1935); Emile Durkheim, *Rules of Sociological Method* (Chicago: University of Chicago Press, 1938); Jean Piaget, *The Moral Judgment of Children* (London: K. Paul, Trench, Trubner and Co., Ltd., 1932).

[3] David Riesman, *The Lonely Crowd* (New Haven: Yale University Press, 1950).

sociologists to doubt a priori that this anxiety is society-wide? Why should one suppose that lower-class persons have been unaffected by the general dislocation and wholesale deracination of our times? On the contrary, if many a middle- and upper-class person cannot locate his "true self" nor any active superego in his multiple self, then how much more likely are people at a lower level to be afflicted in the same way. Such piecemeal evidence as we have indicates that they are. If so, then conscience, that heavy burden of prescriptions and prohibitions, is dead or dying from top to bottom in a society that has lost its bearings. Scratch the system anywhere (as Reisman and more recently, Kenneth Keniston did with college students,[4] as we do with youth in the slums), and unless we are much mistaken, you will find something like social psychopathy. Given their superior education, members of the middle class can verbalize the problem with greater skill than those who have had to attend slum schools. Given their superior income, they can seek professional help and psychiatric solace. A psychoanalyst like Allen Wheelis, judging by the vague malaise and diffuse contents of his own affluent patients, is able to offer a superb portrait of their trouble (and his) in a book appropriately entitled *The Quest for Identity*.[5] Following classical Freudian procedure, he peels off one layer of consciousness after another, only to encounter a great void. It is the same void we have encountered over and over among our economically impoverished subjects.

The externals, the trappings, the phenotypic representations are as various as the colors on a spectrum; and the genotype, moral anomie itself, transcends them all. Sexual, chronological, socioeconomic, ethnic, racial, and regional differences persist. We must reckon with them in attempting to make any sensible analysis or useful prediction: and to do so is to negate the culture of poverty as a viable concept. Microsociologically, it breaks down into too many important variables, but by the same token, macrosociologically, poverty as such loses all significance. Nearly thirty years ago, Edwin Sutherland dispelled the notion that poverty, or traits associated with poverty, caused crime.[6] He acknowledged that poor and disreputable people commit crimes—while drawing attention to the fact that rich and reputable people also commit crimes. Offenders in the upperworld and in the underworld, he pointed out, were internally differentiated into groups of abortionists, fee splitters, pickpockets, confidence men, and so forth. At the same time Sutherland contended, they were all subject to two major forces which he designated as: differential association and social disorganization. Sutherland's insights have yet to be exhausted even in criminology proper. It is nevertheless possible and desirable to carry them farther afield. If we retain differential association as more or less equivalent to socialization, and alter the amorphous "social disorganization" into anomie, much can be learned

[4] Kenneth Keniston, *The Uncommitted* (New York: Harcourt, Brace & World, 1965).
[5] Allen Wheelis, *The Quest for Identity* (New York: Norton, 1958).
[6] Edwin H. Sutherland, *White Collar Crime* (New York: Dryden Press, 1949).

about American society and all of its subgroups. With this conceptual scheme, we need not slight real and vital differences; Sutherland knew that embezzlement and misrepresentation had to be distinguished from bootlegging and safe-cracking; criminality and delinquency, like life style in general, is obviously class-typed. To study the unlawful acts of corporation executives is one thing; to study racketeering in the organized underworld is another. Still, a judicious application of the scheme makes it possible to trace a red thread of common processes through the whole system.

Independently written reports on our three groups of poverty-stricken, ethnically diversified youth, highlight that red thread—the more so for self-evaluation (good boy–bad boy, good girl–bad girl) since its presence is not nearly so marked in any other area of the inquiry. Here perhaps we come to the heart of the matter: there is a certain sameness of responses that rules out "blind" attribution of origin. Those who hold to the "culture of poverty" theory might claim further support for their position in these findings. On the other hand, following Sutherland, we suspect that our data point to something more like a universal phenomenon. To proceed additively by piling one variable on top of another, using poverty as a base, has so far proved to be sterile in criminological research. Practically everybody violates the criminal law; some poor people do not; many rich people do. Selective sanctions are another matter. Poverty substantially accounts for *punishment,* but it is no more criminogenic than wealth. Crime, as an American way of life, is deeply and systemically embedded in the social fabric. Why that should be so is, ultimately, something we need to know. For the present, it behooves serious investigators to move modestly in a broader Copernican direction, and to separate common from discrete conditions while striving to attain a more appropriate general theory.

Images of the Self

We have discovered that the terms, good boy and bad boy (as well as good girl and bad girl), no matter what connotations they may have for the public at large, are loaded with meaning for young people. They—and as it turned out, their older siblings and their parents—responded without hesitation to questions we raised about the content and the significance of these words. Their answers provide considerable insight into the adolescent's self-image and his image of others—plus further light on prevailing systems of morality.

At one extreme, we behold the oversocialized boy or girl who is utterly incapable of making his own independent judgments of good and bad. He unquestioningly accepts the visible and official, the certified and respectable judgments of society. He does this even when negative judgments are passed on *him,* and even when he considers himself innocent of accusations on

which those judgments are based.[7] Consider the case of a New York boy
who has been consigned to a school for "the emotionally disturbed," and
who for that reason alone, declares himself to be bad:

> [Do you think you are a bad boy?]
> Yeah.
> [Why?]
> Because I'm going to a 600 school.
> [And that makes you a bad boy?]
> I wouldn't be going there if I wasn't a bad boy.
> [Well, why did they send you there?]
> They said I was smoking cigarettes. They said I was trying to choke
> other boys. They said I was throwing firecrackers out the bathroom
> window. They said I was hitting the teacher.
> [And were you doing all those things?]
> I didn't throw firecrackers out the window. I didn't try to choke no
> guy. I didn't smoke no cigarette. I did hit the teacher—after she
> scratched me in the face . . . and twisted my arm around. I tried to
> break away, and then I went like that, and I hit her in the lip.

Knowledge of his own conduct, in this case, of his own innocence, is
eclipsed by an authoritative judgment to the contrary. He reasons: since I
have been relegated to a school for bad boys, I *am* a bad boy. The frequency
with which boys and girls manifest such logic has been duly noted most
recently by John M. Martin and Joseph P. Fitzpatrick in their excellent
handbook, *Delinquent Behavior:* ". . . When we, by gossip or rumor, label
a particular child a "bad boy"; when we, as a term of disapprobation, call
(by word or deed) a young man a "hoodlum," we may very well be
contributing to establishing him as such, both in his own mind (because
what he thinks he is depends heavily upon what others say he is), and in
the minds of others such as parents, friends, peers, local shopkeepers,
policemen, and school teachers who treat him according to some status and
role. Once the status-role of bad boy, delinquent or hoodlum has been
assigned, and perhaps reinforced by an arrest or two, and possibly even a
trip to juvenile court and '12 and 6' (18 months) at the local training school
or reformatory, then the Dramatization of Evil ('tagging, defining, identify-
ing, segregating, describing, emphasizing, making conscious and self-conscious') is nearly complete. Our young man *is* a hood: others think he is a
hood; he thinks he is a hood; others exclude him from many legitimate roles
in school, work, friendships, and even the armed forces. At best he is
permitted only menial or illegitimate roles; if his offense is reprehensible
enough, nothing is left open to him—he is a pariah, literally an outlaw." [8]

Conversely, a favorable self-image may be preserved regardless of actual

---

[7] For a general discussion of "deviance by definition," see Edwin M. Lemert, *Social
Pathology* (New York: McGraw-Hill, 1951); Howard S. Becker, *Outsiders* (New
York: Free Press of Glencoe, 1963).

[8] John M. Martin and Joseph P. Fitzpatrick, *Delinquent Behavior: A Redefinition
of the Problem* (New York: Random House, 1966), 81–82.

misbehavior, so long as heteronomous youth is able to avoid a head-on collision with official society. The oversocialized boy, once branded as bad, so brands himself:

> [Are you a good boy or a bad boy?]
> Now that I'm in trouble, I'm a bad boy.
> [But you say you didn't steal anything.]
> Yeah, but I'm still in trouble.

The rule of moral expediency, by which our youth are governed, is not differentiated by sex. For this reason, a New York girl who thinks sexual promiscuity is wrong, makes her objection to it on purely pragmatic grounds. She feels that "scheming around" with boys produces too great a loss of face. Once your sexual availability is well known, "Around our neighborhood, they just put you aside," you are disesteemed and your marriageability is reduced. Getting pregnant is a real problem, but it becomes catastrophic if you do not know which of several boys has caused your plight. Therefore, be virtuous.

An adolescent unwed mother flatly asserts that, "There is no good girls really," and then, a little later, softens her indictment, for she means, "There isn't any good, *good* girls." Finally she clarifies her view (much as we would and as well as we could): "I mean, you find girls who are obedient, but you will not find girls who are good."

Although in the framework of goodness, girls stress appearance, manners, clothes, cleanliness more than boys do, they are also more wary about mere facade—which is a snare and a delusion:

> There's girls that they go to school regularly, and they stay clean. They keep out of trouble. They never have to go to court. That's what we consider a good girl. But, usually those good girls are the ones that have the devil in them. They're the ones that turn out to be no good.

The same idea expressed by another girl:

> The good girls are supposed to be the quiet ones. We say, the quiet ones are the sneaky ones. They're always sneaking on their mother and everything. But a bad girl tells her mother what she does. She don't hide it. Like some girls are quiet, and they say, "Oh, I don't do this. I don't drink or anything," but . . . they do it all. You know, and they're supposed to be so good and high and mighty.

An occasional youngster (more often female than male) will seek absolution by shifting blame onto others who have corrupted him or her. Evil consists less in doing bad than in teaching it, or taunting and coercing others into it:

> Like robbing. Someone tells you, "We're going to rob a place," and you listen, not knowing what he knows, that you're going to end up in jail or in a home, telling you, "Oh, you're a punk or a fool," or some-

thing like that, you know, if you don't do it. . . . And the only one that's bad is the one teaching the other one. He knows he's doing wrong, but he thinks he's going to get someplace by getting the other guy to go along.

Thus do the Children of Darkness corrupt the Children of Light. Theirs is an unpardonable offense, for they prey upon the innocent:

Rita got me to go to this hardware, you know, and I thought me and her were good friends. But, anyhow, she said she'd beat me up if I didn't go to the hardware and steal this glue. She said she'd beat my head in. So, I mean I was scared of her at the time. I did what she told me to. And my mother never found out until she went and told my mother, and I said, "Mother what am I supposed to do?"

Mother told her. "Golly, she. . . . You should of seen what she done to me. I thought she was going to beat me to death." In short, a girl shoplifts in order to escape physical assault; the act is revealed to a stern mother—and results in physical assault. In this game of heads I win, tails you lose, the offender is able to picture herself as a victim—not of such grand abstractions as "society," but of those in her immediate surroundings.

Wrongdoing may be avoided even under intense peer-group pressure, but only, or most effectively, if one is heavily fortified by fright, which is a substitute for—or gets to be equated with—conscience. In Chicago, a girl who never goes shoplifting herself, admits that she once went along with a friend. "She done it, but I didn't. . . . And she got caught. . . . They called her parents, who weren't home, and then they called the cops. The cops came and got her, but they made me go home. They said I didn't do anything." Why didn't she do anything? "Because I was scared. I just knew I'd get caught." Finally, as an afterthought: "I would have had a guilty conscience, you know."

For most of our adolescents, very little is intrinsically wrong. From this point of view, immorality consists not so much in certain acts, but in the *discovery* of those acts. Evil stems more from detection than from commission. Nothing has happened until it is known to have happened by those who are authorized to make one's private actions into public scandals. This attitude is precisely the one Branislaw Malinowski delineated years ago in describing Trobriand Islanders,[9] whose youth went unpunished for the violation of sacred sexual tabus—unless they were given publicity, which insured remorseless punishment. Early in his fieldwork, Malinowski witnessed the suicide of a young Trobriand boy who had been denounced by a rival for having breached the incest tabu. The boy felt no great guilt and suffered no special shame for criminal conduct known to many; its exposure

[9] Branislaw Malinowski, *Crime and Custom in Savage Society* (London: K. Paul, Trench, Trubner and Co., Ltd., 1926).

and public condemnation, required him to climb a tall tree and plunge to his death. Malinowski, as he dug deeper and deeper into Trobriand society, learned that this case was paradigmatic. His nonliterate people, young and old alike, were no more slavishly bound to law, with all its supernatural sanctions, than modern man. Either could "do" anything, neither could survive the inexorability of justice after certain unforeseeable forces actuated people to make an issue of everyday transgressions.

Malinowski's analysis fits our data much better than the work of most professional criminologists. It also makes our respondents look statistically normal. In all probability, most people, while undersocialized in the sense that they do not have well-developed superegos, are oversocialized in the sense that their self-image is not distinguished from their social image. If, consciously or unconsciously committed to this oversocialized conception of ethics, they are nothing but what society says they are. When they see themselves exactly as others see them, there is no self except "the looking-glass" self.

Crime statistics are notoriously misleading because they grossly distort the nature and the incidence of unlawful deviation in any American community. In addition, crime statistics fail to reflect the social pathology of any particular individual. Nevertheless, it is obvious that whether or not a teen-ager is branded as a delinquent will be of the utmost importance to him. For self-perception and the perception of others, this circumstance may well be decisive.

There are those in our sample who, although they have committed only very petty offenses, and these but rarely, characterize themselves as "bad" solely because they were apprehended. Being "caught" means that henceforth they are assigned, and they accept, their status as delinquents. Invert the situation and it still holds: career delinquents whose behavior patterns are consistently unlawful (through their possible involvement in the drug traffic or the numbers racket), who have escaped arrest (sometimes by chance, often as a result of protection)—overwhelmingly define themselves as "pretty good," "just like everybody else," and "not so bad," and the like. Appearances are widely understood to be deceptive, but they eventually merge with reality, the truth will out, and that truth is external to the individual. In the long run, there is no difference between the social self and the private self. That this conviction should prevail at a developmental stage in which young people are struggling to attain the definitive boundaries of their identity is no small issue.

A View of the World

The adolescent tends not only to draw his self-image from the salient institutional world that encapsulates him, he simultaneously perceives the pecking order of that world in much the same terms. Self-definition, which originates outside his own consciousness, is projected back onto the external world of significant and insignificant others. A formula emerges. Slightly simplified it reads, "What *I* am, others are too."

For example, a young Washington girl who has had many illicit sexual relationships and regards herself as both good and bad, when asked what a good girl is, says, "I don't think there are any good girls." The interview proceeds:

> [You don't think there are any?]
> I don't know of any. All the girls I thought were good and pure and never had anything to do with boys, I found out they weren't doing anything but fooling the public.
> [Just like everybody else?]
> Yeah. They just kept everything secret. But sooner or later people find out.

Again, from the same group, a self-confessed but so far unlabeled pathological deviant who asserts, like many of his peers, that he is both good and bad, states:

> I've done a whole lot of things that was wrong. I have raped people. I have did everything.
> Even bad children got some good in them. . . . I've got a little bit of good. I mean I got good.
> What's good? I'm living and I eat. I mean, I do things for people. Like if somebody says, "Look, I need food. I'm hungry," I give 'em money. I say, "Here."

Then, to round out his ruminations:

> Everybody is doing something wrong.

When placed in the dominant moral calculus, this thought may be translated as, "Everybody runs the risk of getting caught." And, since he has avoided arrest, he is innocent, an evaluation in which he believes that his mother concurs.

Once its explicitness has been established time and again, all ambiguity about the moral criterion disappears, and it is as freely applied to others as to oneself. Here are illustrative excerpts that deserve to be quoted at some length. From New York:

> [Would you say that you're a good boy?]
> Yeah.
> [Nothing bad about you?]
> No.

[Then these things like hitting a teacher and carrying a gun are not bad?]
No.
[Smoking pot is not bad?]
No.
[What would you say a bad boy is?]
Always getting into trouble, always getting sent up.
[If you don't get caught, then you are not a bad boy?]
No.
[You're only bad if you get caught?]
Yeah.
[Why does that make you bad? You don't have much luck?]
Mostly luck.
[Then the difference between a good boy and a bad boy is luck?]
Yeah.
[Do you really believe that?]
Yeah.
[You mean if you killed someone and got away with it, you wouldn't be bad?]
You're good, sure.
[Well, what's the worst thing that anybody can do?]
What do you mean?
[To anybody else.]
Mostly beat them up.
[Not kill them?]
No.
[Why is it worse to beat them up than to kill them?]
Because, it hurts, man, it pains.

Some of this may be synthetic, merely put on to deceive the interviewer. That it nonetheless has some substance we learn from the startling responses to another question along the same lines, namely, "Which is worse: smoking pot or mugging?" put to teen-agers in New York who by and large insist that marijuana is harmless. A majority claim that smoking pot is worse than mugging. The reason is simple: if you are caught smoking pot, even though you injure no one, the sentence is stiffer than if you are caught mugging and inflicting an injury on someone else.

For our population, badness isn't all that bad, and goodness isn't all that good. Thus this exchange in Chicago:

[How do you feel about some of the things that you've been doing, like burglary, breaking in on people's homes? Does that bother you at all?]
It don't bother me that much, when I'm broke. If I had money I wouldn't ever do it.
[While you were working, did you ever do anything like that?]
Naw. When I was working I stayed drunk all the time.
[Why would you stay drunk all the time?]
Something to do. Go to the show Friday, play poker Saturday. Then get drunk. Not every week, I didn't do that.

> [Do you ever think that some of the things the guys do, like robbing and burglarizing, is bad?]
> I used to tell 'em about that—when I never done it before. . . . I said, "Now, what's you go and do that for?" They didn't think nothin' of it— I did that until I started going. I never did go in; I just stayed outside. I don't think that's so bad but still it's the same thing as going in.
> [Would you say that anybody who does that is bad then?]
> Not really that bad.

If a violation of the law seldom induces guilt, it sometimes produces exultation. A boy who believes that, "No one's good, and a lot of people [like himself] are bad," likes to "hit" cabs, skirting danger, courting trouble, "feeling good inside" when he has had a close shave: "Watching a guy get mad and letting him chase you. That's what I like." The experience is just "scary" enough to make it thrilling; burglary, which "can get you into more trouble," is less appealing for that reason. But moderately risky lawbreaking yields legitimate kicks. There is the pure pleasure of outrunning and out-witting a respectable antagonist, of robbing kids who have better clothes, of boasting that: "We *all* bad."

For something about goodness is suspect. Good guys are. "Them cats with their hair real short. They wear white gym shoes and look pretty good all day. They're frail, in other words . . . Everybody got their own styles, I guess. Frails like to be frails, and we like to be like we are." Lengthy concrete, referential lists of bad behavior, overlapping legal classifications, are easy to elicit. A bad boy steals, cusses, drinks, rapes, fights, sniffs glue, takes drugs. He talks back to his mother, stays out late at night. A bad girl "puts out" for anyone and everyone. Getting caught and being punished for such acts makes youth bad. What then is goodness? The question baffles many respondents, causing some who are otherwise voluble to be tongue-tied. To be good is to be nice, to obey, to have manners. But "good" is most often defined negatively as the opposite of "bad." It is an abstract category with little behavioral content, an "act" of omission. Not being bad is being good. Not to steal, not to fight, not to look for trouble is to be good. After having dilated at length on bad behavior, one Washington youth, generally articulate and sensitive to questioning, is stymied.

> [What's your definition of a good boy?]
> Well, let's just say it's the opposite of that [a bad boy].
> [How about girls? How would you define a good girl?]
> [Laugh] That's very hard for me to put into words. I mean I couldn't really answer that—so I might as well not talk, 'cause I'm liable to get tumbled up with words. I couldn't answer that. Not right now. I mean it would really take some thought. I possibly could if I tried, but right off the bat, I couldn't say.

To a New York boy, the good kid is one who, "Don't do nothing. He be good. He don't carry nothing on him." We wonder if he ever met a kid like that: "No." Are there any really good kids on the street? "Yeah. They little kids, two, three years old. They can't do nothing. Carry a knife, maybe they could pick it up, but they couldn't put it in their pocket." Not to be bad is to be good—and to be good is hardly to be anything at all. Good boys and girls are formless, featureless, passive receptors; they "keep to themselves"; they are "quiet"; they "stay alone"; they "don't hang around with other kids"—which makes them apparitions, ciphers, shadows, isolates hovering outside the mainstream of youthful activity. Those who are "bad" act bad; those who are "good" do not act; they scarcely exist. Inaction leads to inanition as goodness is purified and etherealized into nothingness.

While the good is impalpable and unreal, the bad can be seen everywhere. And to have been very bad, to have been through the crucible, has its advantages. A young lady who is still in her teens, but raising an illegitimate child asserts that, "I'm not too good now, but I'm an angel compared to what I used to be. I smoke reefers once in a blue moon. Before it was every day . . . I come out into the street and I hang around with my friends and we drink and we have times together. But it's not like it was when I went out with a crowd of girls looking for fights." All "the stupid things" she used to do helped her to grow up fast, taught her about life, made it possible for her to improve later on, to stay human, to be realistic after she "grew up and matured a little bit mentally." Nor does she regard her experience as unusual:

> Oh, no, there's a lot of girls like that. Take my cousin. She was one of the biggest hoodlums on this street, and now if you see her . . . She's so sophisticated that you'd never think that she was the President of the Sweethearts [Gang]. She looks very decent compared to what she used to be when she was a teen-ager.

Another girl describes her friends as "half-and-half." As for herself, "I can't say I'm good and I can't say I'm bad because I got good and bad in me." We pursue the matter:

> [Would you say you're better than you used to be?]
> Yes.
> [Were you good or bad before?]
> I was terrific.
> [Terrific?]
> I was bad, very bad.

The equation of "very bad" and "terrific" slips out, interlarded with a little laughter, and then, more seriously: "Well, I don't go stealing all the time any more. And I'm more matured than I used to be. I mean, you know, I act ladylike. I used to act like a hoodlum, a girl that just stayed in the street any time. Not now . . . As the years go by you get more matured."

Unknown or unpunished deviation is widely viewed, then, as a stage one passes through and outgrows all the more swiftly for having experienced it in the first place. Objectively, we have good reason to know something most of our informants tell us, that, "There's no difference whatsoever," in the acts of boys and girls who get stigmatized as delinquents and those who do not. Or as one New York girl puts it: "There's some that do things worse than those that get police records, and there's kids that don't have police records at all that do some of the funniest things." Another girl whose boy-friend had been sent away to a training school, deplores his desire for notoriety:

> He's always looking for bad stuff. He tries to be known. When you try to be known, you have a record. You go to jail. That makes you a *big* boy. You have a rep and you say, "Oh, I been to jail."

In a large part of this milieu, recognition comes with "bigness," "knowness" and "badness." And "goodness" exacts a toll perhaps as high as "badness."

The Moral Code

The polarization of these concepts, put into reciprocal action terms, does not appear to be simply a semantic device. Almost every decision to classify specific acts under one or another of the mutually exclusive categories emanates from standards located in semisacred American institutions: the school (whence comes self-assessment of intelligence and achievement potential), the law, and the family. Reference to God or Church or revered spiritual leaders as sources of moral judgment are noticeably scarce. In no instance do our respondents allude even remotely to theological or broadly ideological considerations. Deviation and conformity are perceived in strictly concrete behavioral forms—underscoring the morally anomic condition operative in this population.[10]
Self-evaluation goes like this:

> I know I'm not the . . . you know, most honest person in the world. But I ain't really dishonest. I mean I'm a little dishonest. . . . I don't suppose I'm that dishonest. I never steal from my friends, and I never steal from my brother.
> [What kinds of faults do you have?]
> Burglarizing homes, that's a fault . . . no good. I don't know. Stay out late. That's a bad thing. My aunt, she'll ask me to be in by 11:00 P.M. Sometimes I do, sometimes I don't come in till 1, 2, that's bad.

[10] It is the same condition, with the same nonideological focus, similarly oriented to the present, which Kenneth Keniston reports for his "alienated" and "over-privileged" Harvard students. See *The Uncommitted* (New York: Harcourt, Brace and World, 1965).

Another youth:

> I'm pretty good, I guess.
> [How about your stealing?]
> I just call it borrowing, ambushing. I just borrowed it for the time being.
> I'm a good burglar, I'm smart, I ain't got caught yet.
> [What are your bad points?]
> Fightin', cards—losing. Unlucky at cards and girls.

A "good Chicago boy" tells us:

> I don't sniff glue or take dope or nothin' like that. I don't go around
> robbin' and doin' stuff like that on purpose. At least, not all the time.
> Don't hang around in gangs. . . .
> [What is a good boy?]
> Does everything his mother and father asks, he respects 'em, respects
> the teachers, respects who he works with.

A seventeen-year-old boy says:

> I'm in between. No one's good and lot of people are bad, I'm closer
> to being bad. I'm stupid.
> [Probe as to nature of peer group.]
> We all bad, we don't do things on the side of the law. Good boys stay
> inside the law.

An experienced burglar and leader says:

> . . . good and bad I guess . . . bad when I'm taking things. Good
> when I'm stayin' away from people's stuff . . . just average.
> [What is a good boy?]
> . . . probably call 'em a giant boob . . . but he's a lot smarter boob,
> 'cause at least he knows he's never gonna get in trouble.

As we have already suggested, institutional sources for standards are more
often explicitly cited by girls,.to explain their conformity, than by boys. The
girls mention personal attributes, such as clean clothes, neat and conservative dress, nice speech, friendliness, warmth, and empathy, as distinctive
criteria used to assess their worth as well as that of others, to a greater
degree than the boys.

> You don't run around with the bad kind of people, and always listen
> to your elders, which can explain everything to you if you listen just
> right. I'm really in between . . . no angel, but I go to school every
> day, and I don't hang around with boys by myself, don't run out in
> the middle of the street and stuff like that. Sometimes I don't listen to
> Mom, I'll fuss back at my sister when she starts fussin'. [Respondent
> never steals] because I just didn't wanta lose my reputation. . . . I'm
> the only one of my whole family that's never ditched school or any-
> thing.

What's the difference between a good and a bad girl?

> The way she talks . . . around the boys. Some of these girls that are
> in school, they don't care what they say, some of 'em take . . . dope.
> A lot of the kids around school, you can just tell, by lookin' at 'em
> in their actions, sometimes, that they do.
> [Good] . . . someone that can talk to people and that's got a real nice
> personality and doesn't hang around with the wrong crowd or some-
> thing like that. They're always saying something that's not nice to hear
> or something. And it's not only the girls, it's to the boys.
> One that doesn't cuss and smoke and steal anything, stuff like that.
> Girls that goes around and steals every time you turn around and is
> cussing all the time, and takes things that doesn't belong. Flirt with
> boys.
> If they're dressed nice, have clean things and have clean body. . . .
> She'd be all sloppy, wouldn't comb her hair, wear all sloppy dresses,
> wouldn't be clean and would be stealing, and hittin' others.

Only one female youth offered anything like a sociocultural explanation for
girls that are bad:

> Some experience she had that influenced her . . . lead her to start
> drinking, smoking, swearing, sexual things not out of love but just out
> of sex.

These examples clearly indicate that our youth only exceptionally offer an
explanation for their good or bad attributes. Moreover, there is an extreme
lack of self-denigration. No one is in a repenting mood; there is no quest
for a psychic solution which would resolve inner conflicts and feelings of
ambivalence or assuage the imperceptible sense of guilt brought on by their
confessions.

Our cluster of good-bad questions produces something like a bell-shaped
curve. A few see themselves and their associates as all bad ("there's no
such thing as a good kid"), and a few are oblivious to anything but "good
kids" like themselves. But, overwhelmingly, their answers are mixed: "I'm
somewhere in between," "I'm not exactly an angel," "Sometimes I'm good
and sometimes I'm bad," "I'm not good and I'm not bad," "I'm half-and-
half," "I consider myself bad and good," "I'm normal—some ways good,
some ways bad," and so on and on. Moreover, the child who thinks he is
such a mixture, thinks the same of everyone else. (However, that bell-shaped
distribution of self-definition corresponds more to adjudicative definition,
the social labeling, than the deviant behavioral patterns of action.)

There is an overarching attitude toward this mixed interpretation of
human nature, namely, the unquestioning but abstract acceptance of parental codes. Adherence to those codes produces the good, their violation the
bad in all of us. Guilt and shame, insofar as they exist, are the products of
disobedience. Failure to heed *mother* is the source of all further transgres-

sions. To an out-of-wedlock mother we interviewed, no girl is wholly good because none is completely honest. At least this is her spontaneous opinion; it means a good girl would "never have told even a little lie." She would never have stolen or fought or "schemed" but, above all, she would "always, always have been obedient." We want to know whether she is describing a girl or an angel, and she responds, "Well, that's what I'm trying to say— there is no good girl." It is easier for her to delineate the "real bad girl" as follows:

> She has no respect for anybody, always fighting, cursing—can't control her tongue, drinking, smoking, looking for trouble. . . . She's always trying to throw herself at boys, trying to be very sexy, trying to show everything she's got, but she ain't got nothing. . . . She has sex with different people and is proud of it, she broadcasts it. . . .

The portrait is consistently harsh, and her self-portrait is only a little softer: "I have some good things and a lot of bad things in me." Whichever way the balance tips, a girl is undone finally by disregarding *mother*. She herself could have been redeemed at the penultimate moment by paying proper heed to maternal advice:

> When I was engaged to X, he used to come to my house and take me out. Once I took the ring off and threw it at him, because I got sick of hearing him say I was always playing with him. So my mother picked the ring up and she put it back on my finger. And then he said it again, and I took it off, and threw it at him. Then he started crying—so I told him. "Why should you cry over a girl who is always playing with you?" And that's one thing I did wrong 'cause at the time I didn't know I was two months pregnant. I should have waited 'cause my mother had gave me permission when I was sixteen that we could get married. Me, the fool, I couldn't wait.

"Being nice with mother," "Doing like she says"—boys and girls repeatedly, ritualistically, repeat some such maxim. Although fathers or father substitutes are called upon to act as disciplinarians in the administration of corporal punishment, it is the mother who symbolizes morality. It is from her lips that the admonitions, which are later ruefully recollected, have fallen. Few can bring themselves to criticize mothers who are described elsewhere by the same respondents as having lived far from exemplary lives and who in many cases are represented by youngsters as having driven them to such hysteria and rage as to produce the very behavior which is forbidden. Only one male informant in his twenties has sufficient detachment to turn the tables, charging the mothers more than their progeny with irresponsibility:

> A lot of the mothers on our street are not married. They just want to live with a man. They have kids and don't really watch out for them.

> They let their kids play out in the street. There's no recreation area—
> and no one to come or give them, or even to look at them. No one
> gives them a start.

The same informant (a young man who thinks his salvation lay in being
sent away from the street to Catholic schools even though the same exile
had no such salutary effect on his numerous brothers and sisters) also
adopts a heterodox position—but one that is much more baffling—on the
subject of "taking things from little kids." This offense is widely regarded
as more heinous than any other—so that boys who brag about stealing from
other boys say they make it a point of honor not to steal from smaller ones.
After awhile, in answer to our question. "What's the worst thing a boy can
do?" we came to expect the frequent retort, "Take things from little kids."
Whether this answer was truthful or not is another matter. It may only have
been offered by way of consolation, to establish that the respondent was not
utterly depraved. In any case, our more adult informant replies, "Well, I
think that the worst thing he could do is, at the age of sixteen, have a child
from a girl and quit school and not work and go on living with his
parents. . . ." A formidable bill of particulars, and not surprising, as this
exchange is:

> [How about taking things from smaller kids?]
> Well, that's something no one can change. It's happening and it always
> will be happening.
> [But isn't that very bad?]
> Well, it's one of the things I wouldn't consider bad. I call that one of
> the normal things in the world.

The logic here is even more involuted:

> [Suppose a little kid has money and a big kid comes over and grabs it?]
> Well, this is what makes these kids of today very slick and very clever.
> It's the first point of learning. When you own something, you must
> keep it to yourself. If I walked down the street showing everybody that
> I have five dollars, I wouldn't blame that person for taking it. If a young
> kid walks around tempting somebody, I think that somebody should
> take it away from him.

This is of a piece with his view that big kids should slap little kids who
"decide they're getting wise" and keep them in line that way, an extension
of the punitive technique already in force. The view is important because
it comes from a truly rehabilitated "bad boy" who plans to devote himself
to community service by keeping others from going astray. He is capable
of real sensitivity:

> Kids go to school in this neighborhood, and the teachers speak to them
> very cruelly. And the kid who comes from Puerto Rico, how you speak

to him is how he learns to speak back. And a lot of them get emotionally disturbed. So they come home, and their parents may be about five feet four, and the kid happens to grow up a little bit taller or the same size. He goes to school—and the school teaches him different things than the parents who have no education. So the kid is outslicking his own parents.

These are shrewd observations and they have some diagnostic value. The bewilderment and insecurity of parents—and the decay of their authority in a foreign environment—are certainly symptomatic of deregulation or anomie. A generalized moral vacuum is created when parents lose confidence in old but no longer appropriate norms which they cannot successfully transmit any more than teachers are able to convey the values of modern urban middle-class society. Absorbing fragments of both, the child of either sex is ordinarily socialized to the point where he can experience conflict—while lacking psychic resources to resolve it. He is erratically but steadily punished and seldom rewarded. And yet, it is possible to emerge, to rise a bit above this bind, only to favor, as our reformed gang boy does, still more physical punishment. He would have the fathers "take out a belt and whack the kids" more than they now do.

We discover in all this a kind of *moral absolutism* or *moral realism,* the term used by Jean Piaget to indicate an early stage in child development, presumably replaced at a later stage by *moral relativism;* the awareness that rules are man-made and flexible.[11] For example, in the first stage a child fails to distinguish between acts committed with malice aforethought and those that are accidental. Therefore, he is inclined to judge himself more severely than he is judged by those who have attained a higher degree of maturity. Few residents of our study blocks seem to have moved much beyond moral absolutism, applied to themselves. Tired professionals, schoolteachers, caseworkers, clergymen—also apply it to them. The punitive law of Emile Durkheim is much more apparent in this world than the *cooperative* or *restitutive law* he took to be characteristic of modern civilization.[12] Exasperated adults, exasperated "do-gooders," and the children who seek to please or to defy them, are caught in the same net. Confusing neglect, dismay, and capricious punishment with permissiveness, they flay one and reinforce the other—its demonstrated ineffectiveness notwithstanding.

"Good and bad boy," as well as "good and bad girl," have personal meanings with objective correlatives we hope to work out more fully on further study and more analysis. For the largest proportion of youth, we believe that the adjectives will have to be hyphenated. Most of them, like most of the rest of us, are, as they contend, good-and-bad. It should be possible to construct a continuum embracing the whole juvenile population.

[11] Jean Piaget, *The Moral Judgment of Children* (London: K. Paul, Trench, Trubner and Co., Ltd., 1932).
[12] Emile Durkheim, *The Division of Labor in Society* (New York: Macmillan, 1933).

We are sure that wherever specific individuals are ultimately placed on this continuum, there will be no significant correspondence between it and the official delinquent-nondelinquent records. If this is true, then as conscientious social scientists, we will have to set administrative records aside as irrelevant to our task, as a "will-o'-the-wisp" whose pursuit has led us down one blind alley after another. Henceforth, it will be necessary to study the slum child—good, bad, or indifferent—in all his complexity as a human being. To assume this burden is to relinquish a statistical artifact—and good riddance to it!

Section III

Youth Culture, Subculture, and Counterculture

INTRODUCTION

It is axiomatic in the field of sociology to state that man is a complex creature who expresses himself and organizes his world through the use of multiple signs, symbols, and languages. Man's unique capacity for symbolization seems infinite, and no event or experience can long withstand the natural thirst to construct some abstract representation, perhaps a word, to at least denote and eventually share these experiences with other men. In this sense, man is the symbol-bearer, the creator and carrier of culture.

In practice, the study of culture is considered an essential and basic key to understanding man's complex and varied patterns of behavior. Whereas human biology and psychology are seen to predispose and broadly direct human actions, culture enables us to specify our experiences, relationships to events, and relations to one another. Thus, observations about culture also include the study of culturally determined behavior and interactions as they occur within the context of specific human groupings.

When one speaks of a *complex* society, it is in large part a recognition of society's multiculturedness or cultural pluralism. Complexity suggests that the cultural elements, beliefs, values, and norms are unevenly and variably distributed among different segments of a societal population. Although broad and common cultural themes, a common language root, and the identification of one's common nationality with others may exist, smaller, specialized groupings, segments, and strata of society develop distinctive cultural elements that render their relatively unique experiences in the world both meaningful and useful.

In any society where youth emerges beyond a theoretical and abstract life-stage and becomes a vital and significant social reality distinguishable from other age-groupings, there is also the emergence of a concomitant youth culture. This culture of youth might well be conceptualized as subcultural in nature in that it is comprised of universal as well as unique cultural elements that reflect the special experiences of the generationally young. Moreover, youth culture in complex societies can be expected to be highly pluralistic, so that the study of youth culture will concern itself, at least initially, with descriptions of the many youth subcultures that may develop in a given society. In short, the study of youth culture inquires into the quality, type, content, and structure of the multiple subcultures that are unique to members of the youth generation.

That youth cultures are not created in a vacuum seems self-evident; they are recognized as extensions and variants of the dominant cultural and social conditions in which they arise. For example, in Hollingshead's material on youth cliques, one can immediately observe the direct connection between the larger social class system of Elmtown and the attitudes, values, preferences, and relationships that are mirrored by the young in this community. The culture of Elmtown's youth may thus be summarized as

186

generationally continuous with the class structure of the adult generation.

Societies and communities that reproduce relatively continuous generational waves and behavioral similarities are not ordinarily concerned with youth as a significant problem, except perhaps to note that this is an integral aspect of all evolving societies. From this perspective, if youth culture is at all variant and distinctive, it is conceived as a function of the incomplete, underdeveloped, and imperfect character of youth socialization to the wider culture in which youth have been reared. It is expected also that upon reaching the age of adulthood, youth will ultimately succeed in incorporating those beliefs, values, and norms that are central to the dominant cultural system.

However, youth cultures become sociologically more problematical if they contain cultural elements that seem antithetical and oppositional to those held by their progenitors. It is at this point that youth cultures are conceptualized as conflict subcultures, contracultures, or countercultures, suggesting at once that cultural reproduction is flawed by mutant, revolutionary forms.

Studies of youth culture, then, inevitably range between the evolutionary and revolutionary quality of both content and character, attempting at the same time to locate and explain the causes and consequences of that culture. These studies, however, are impeded by one factor that seems well supported by historical observations of youth: youth cultures have an ephemeral, wispy, and faddist quality, so much so that *succeeding generations of youth* also appear largely discontinuous with one another. Thus, serious concern with youth culture and its significance for social change is diluted by this apparent cultural transience, which is often interpreted as part of the playful, ludic nature of being young, whereas cultural maturation is seen as a surer solution to this youthful deviance.

The following selections represent several complementary approaches to the study of youth culture, subculture, and counterculture. Hollingshead explores the relationship between social class, youth groupings, and youth culture; Bernard examines in detail the content of youth culture in different institutional and social settings; both report on a historical period that for some may seem ancient, but is only a generation or two in the past.

Berger views youth culture from a wider cross-generational perspective and introduces the notion that the interplay between youthfulness and youth culture is not limited to chronological age but by common generational elements. Eisenstadt offers an opportunity to observe the development, content, and quality of modern youth groups in a comparative framework and emphasizes the larger contextual social factors in which these have emerged.

Finally, although their approaches, conceptions, and explanations may differ somewhat, Keniston, Matza, and Roszak all concern themselves with the issues of deviant subcultural or countercultural developments among modern youth. These presentations reflect the most common, widespread concern about the nature of modern society and the unique forces and influences that, at least for some, have seemingly transformed sizable segments of the youth population into a social movement of major significance.

Cliques and Social Class in Elmtown

August Hollingshead

Cliques and Clique Relations

> This school is full of cliques. You go into the hall, or the Commons Room [between classes or at noon], and you will find the same kids together day after day. Walk up Freedom Street at noon, or in the evening, and you'll see them again. These kids run in bunches just like their parents. This town is full of cliques, and you can't expect the kids to be any different from their parents.

This opinion, expressed by a high school teacher, is also expressed by many Elmtowners. Frequently, the question is asked, "Have you run into those bunches in the high school?" Another common comment is, "You can't understand those kids unless you can get into their gangs."

Systematic observation over a six-month period confirmed these and similar remarks. Persistent study revealed the vast majority of a particular boy's or girl's waking hours are spent in the company of a few pals. When he leaves home in the morning he generally walks or rides to school with them. In and around the high school he can be seen talking, laughing, walking, playing with them. Through the day he is with them whenever some formal demand on his time, such as classes or the job, frees him for informal activities. Before school opens in the morning little groups of friends can be seen talking together, laughing over some joke or prank, planning future activities, or reliving past ones through talk and shared memories. Later the same little band of boys or girls can be seen going to class together. At noon they may be seen going to or from lunch, and usually together; if they pack their lunch they may be grouped in a corner of the Commons Room or in the Central School gymnasium.

After school two or three out of a group of five or six may go uptown to the pool hall if boys, or to the drug store or bowling alley if girls. The same two or three boys or girls may be seen early in the evening on their way to a show or a friend's home. This persistent relationship between a few boys or a few girls which carries over from one activity to another throughout the day, and day after day, is the most obvious thing about the behavior patterns of the high school pupils.

Reprinted by permission of the publisher, from August B. Hollingshead, *Elmtown's Youth* (New York: John Wiley & Sons, Inc., Copyright © 1949), pp. 204–210; 217–220.

These small, informal groups, which we shall call *cliques,* consume most of the interest, time, and activities of the adolescents. We shall call the more or less permanent ties the members of a clique have with one another a *clique relation* to differentiate it from other kinds of social relationships. The clique relationship exists only through the social relations the members of a clique maintain with each other. A clique relationship lasts as long as a person is a member of the clique, whereas social relationships in the clique are ephemeral, multiform, and almost infinite in number.

A clique comes into existence when two or more persons are related one to another in an intimate fellowship that involves "going places and doing things" together, a mutual exchange of ideas, and the acceptance of each personality by the others. Perhaps the most characteristic thing about the clique is the way its members plan to be together, to do things together, go places together. Within the clique, personal relations with one another involve the clique mates in emotional and sentimental situations of great moment to the participants. Confidences are exchanged between some or all members; often those very personal, wholly private, experiences that occur in the family which involve only one member may be exchanged with a best friend in the group. Relations with the opposite sex, with adults, and with young people outside the clique are discussed and decisions reached on the action to be taken by the clique, or by a particular member involved in a situation.

Membership is voluntary and informal; members are admitted gradually to a pre-existing clique and dropped by the mutual consent of its participants. Although there are no explicit rules for membership, the clique has a more or less common set of values which determines who will be admitted, what it does, how it will censure some member who does not abide by its values.

As the clique comes to be accepted by other cliques as a definite unit in the adolescent society it develops an awareness of self, a "we feeling," sentiments and traditions which impel its members to act and think alike. Its members frequently identify their interests with the group in contrast to the interests of the family, other cliques, the school, and society. Generally clique interests come before those of the individual member or any outside group or interest. This attitude often results in conflicts between the clique and the family, between the clique and the school, or between the clique and the neighborhood. If this conflict element becomes the *raison d'être* of the group, the clique develops into the gang.[1]

The impact of clique controls on the adolescent produces a sense of his

[1] The clique and the gang are closely related social forms, the essential difference between the two being the importance placed upon predacious activity that almost invariably leads to conflict in the gang. The clique is a socially accepted group which normally does not develop conflict relations to the point where an undeclared war exists between itself and society or, for that matter, other cliques.

personal importance in his relations with other members, as well as with persons outside the clique, for the clique has a powerful emotional influence on him which he tends to carry over into outside social relations, using it to bolster his own conception of himself. Each member has a group status derived from his ability to achieve some thing or to contribute some thing to the well-being of the clique. This group-derived status is often valued very highly by the boy or girl. Thus, the clique is a powerful influence in the life of the person from its formation in the pre-adolescent years until it is dissolved by the development of the dating pattern.

Outsiders, especially parents and teachers, often fail to realize the meaning which the clique has for its members; consequently there is a tendency for them to deprecate it. This may produce more resistance and withdrawal into the sanctuary of the clique on the part of the adolescent, for, in a conflict situation that involves him as a member of the group, the youngster tends to look to the clique for support. The adolescent, bolstered by his sense of belonging to a group that backs him in his efforts to emancipate himself from adult and institutional controls, feels a sense of power, of belonging, of security, and consequently makes decisions in collaboration with his clique mates he would never make alone, as long as his decisions meet with clique approval. Each member of the clique, reinforced by the presence of his "pals" and their agreement that some line of action is desirable or undesirable, that something must be done or undone, produces a cohesive social situation in which the clique acts as a unit. Controls operating in the clique tend to produce uniformity of thought and action on the question at issue. Individuals who do not go along with the decision of the majority are coerced into acquiescence or ostracized, since deviation is tolerated only within narrow limits. Adherence to the group code is guarded carefully by the clique's members, for cliques develop reputations and have favorable or unfavorable status attached to them by other cliques, parents, teachers, preachers, and adults on the basis of their membership and activities.

Number, Type, and Size of Cliques

The 259 cliques we studied are divided into three types on the basis of where they functioned. *School cliques* are composed of either boys or girls who associate with each other around school. Their membership can be seen between class periods, during the last quarter hour of the lunch hour, or immediately after school, participating in the activity of the moment. There are 106 school cliques which have from two to nine members for boys, two to twelve for girls; the modal size for both sexes is five members. *Recreational cliques* function in various situations away from school. Their members are only slightly different from the school cliques, but in a typical recreational clique some members of the school clique are missing. The place of the missing boy or girl may be taken by a person who belongs to another school clique, but for recreational purposes this person participates with a clique with which he does not associate around school. Sometimes a large school clique splits into two recreational cliques. The 120 recreational cliques are smaller than the school cliques. They range in size from two to seven members and have a modal membership of four for both the boys and the girls. *Institutional cliques* are seen in specific non-school situations such as Sunday School, young people's meetings at the churches, Boy Scouts, and Campfire Girls. Thirty-three institutional cliques are known to exist, thirteen of boys and twenty of girls. They are smaller than the others, ranging from two to five members each. The modal membership is three for the boys and four for the girls.

Exactly one-fourth of the students live in the country, but only fifteen cliques (6 per cent) are composed exclusively of rural boys or girls. These cliques tend to be neighborhood- as well as school-oriented because of the distance they live from school and from each other. The rural cliques are smaller in size than the cliques made up of town or mixed town-country adolescents. They average (mode) three members, whereas the others have five members. However, what the town adolescent does with his three or four pals, the country youth does with one or two, for the quality and function of the relationships entailed in the smaller cliques are not different from those in the larger ones. Moreover, since in general the interests of the country youth are not essentially different from those of town dwellers, we shall dismiss the town-country dichotomy without further consideration.[2]

Who Cliques with Whom

Evidence accumulated from parents and children indicates that parents consistently try to limit their children's friendship ties to certain boys or girls, usually, however, without too much success. Social pressures in the adolescent group operate far more effectively, and with greater subtlety, to channelize friendships within limits permitted by the social system of both the adult and the adolescent social worlds than the hopes, fears, and admonitions of anxious parents. This dual process is illustrated in the materials given [on page 192 of the present book].

Joyce Jenson, class III,[3] was discussing her friend Gladys Johnson, class

[2] All cliques were analyzed by X^2 to determine if any significant difference exists between (1) size and class in school and (2) size and prestige class. None was found.
[3] Editor's note: Hollingshead stratified the population of Elmtowners into five prestige classes with class I at the top and class V at the bottom. Roughly, class III was composed of small businessmen, farmers, or salaried white-collar workers. For a complete description of class measurements and characteristics see, *Elmtown's Youth,* Chapters 1 and 5.

III, when she laid bare a number of factors which regulated the group relations of the adolescents.

> We influence each other a lot. She influences me almost as much as my parents do. I listen to them, especially when it comes to choosing friends, but I don't agree with everything they tell me. I've had them really give me the dickens about going around with some girls I wanted to go with or maybe Gladys did. Most parents don't want their kids running around with certain other kids, and they'll give them advice and they'll follow it or they won't, but when my folks put the foot down on me I listen.
>
> I know that the folks give me good advice, but sometimes they just don't understand what kids want to do, and they think we ought to act like they acted twenty years ago. My parents, especially my mother, influence me in what I do, but Gladys probably influences me as much or more.
>
> I don't want to run any of the kids down, but there are certain girls here who are just not my type, and they're not Gladys' type; they'd like to run around with us, but we don't let them.
>
> Pauline Tryon [class IV] and her bunch would like to run around with us, but we turn our backs on them because they run around all night, cut school, and hang out down at the Blue Triangle.
>
> There are some kids we'd like to go around with, but they don't want us to go with them. Gladys and I would like to go around with "Cookie" Barnett [class II] and her bunch, or the G.W.G.'s, but they snub us if we try to get in on their parties, or dances, or date the boys they go with.

Gladys revealed the close reciprocal relation between these girls, and how they reacted upon each other in different situations when she said:

> I have one very close friend, Joyce Jenson. We met four years ago and we've been going around together since. We plan our clothes, we talk about what we're going to do, and we study together. We come to school together, we take the same courses, we visit each other at home, we go to church together, we plan church parties, and so on. Of course, we don't agree 100 per cent on everything, but we've made up our minds when we don't agree that one is going to dominate the other. Sometimes she dominates me and sometimes I dominate her. If we decide we want to go to a church party, well, maybe I won't want to go, but I'll go because she really wants to go. Then maybe we'll decide to go to a show. Sometimes she won't want to go because she doesn't like the show, but she'll go because I've gone to the church party with her.

This is typical of the interaction between adolescent personalities in the intimate relationships of the clique and the still closer, and more pervasive, ties that hold best friends together. . . .

Reputation in the Student Group

Once an adolescent is identified as a member of a particular clique, the reputation of the clique tends to be attached to him by adolescents outside the clique, by teachers, and by other adults who know the youngster and his clique mates. Cliques develop their reputations through the extracurricular activities their members participate in, as well as through what they do away from school, particularly in their leisure time. The students use dozens of clichés to categorize a particular boy's or girl's reputation, or clique affiliation; but they have one common element, namely, they are symbolic of the esteem or disesteem in which the person or his clique is held by the speaker. Often this evaluation is shared commonly in the adolescent group. The function of these clichés is to place a clique in the informal structure of the adolescent social world. Some of these referential statements are given here to indicate their nature; some apply to individuals, others to cliques.

> Bill is a trouble maker, and his gang is just like him.
> Perk's a good, ambitious kid, but Plug's kind of dumb. He comes from an unfortunate family.
> Hank is one of our leading playboys; he belongs to the elite.
> Bob's in a wild gang; they have rotten reps. No respectable girl will go with them.
> John's bunch are "clippers"; none of our group [Lutheran girls] will go with them.
> Sleepy's a "grubby," I don't know whether he's dumb or just not interested in school.
> Joe's a "lone duck." His only friend is a "bush ape" from east of town.
> Those kids have gone to the dogs. [Said in reference to a clique of class IV girls who attended public dances, drank, and petted indiscriminately.]
> "Doc" has a bad rep. He works in a carnival in the summer; from what he says, I don't imagine he'd feel out of place in one.
> Eleanor's one of the faster girls.
> They're all nice kids in Mary's bunch.
> Little Butch's gang are "grubbies."
> That's the big-bang athletic bunch; they belong to the elite around here. [The reference is to the clique of Frank Stone, Jr.]
> Those kids are all jerks. [Said by a class IV girl in reference to a clique of class IV girls of whom she did not approve.]
> The G.W.G.'s are our "four hundred."
> Ola's bunch are nice, harmless kids who don't have many dates.
> Kink runs with the kids who are never much of this or much of that. [This is in reference to a large clique of class III boys.]
> You know, they're good kids. [A clique of class IV girls in Home Makers.]
> They are awfully sweet kids but not active in school. [Another group of III's and IV's.]

They are pretty fast, and we leave them alone. . . . Those kids are not accepted at all. [These comments apply to a mixed clique of class III and class IV girls.]

Gabby acts like a wild animal; I guess she just hasn't been told or raised. [A class V girl.]

Some of the kids think Pansy is crazy, but I think she is just queer. [Statement made about a class V girl by a representative of class III.]

The athletes rate tops with everybody. You see, they're our heroes! [A class IV girl's estimate.]

The Polish kids live across the tracks and have bad reps. Annie and Romine are "Poles" but they're different. Annie is a nice kid; she's pretty, dresses slick, and she's bright. [From a class III girl who lived in the older residential area.]

Everything is wrong with the kids May runs with. First, they live down by the old tannery. They're not clean, they don't dress well. Their hair isn't fixed right. Then May can't live her sisters' reps down. [Said by a class III girl with reference to a class V girl and her clique.]

Jane's a Lutheran that's gone wild.

Janet's a big girl [class IV] and she doesn't dress right; so she just isn't accepted. [Said by another class IV girl.]

Emma's another one that's isolated. She has a rotten "rep" too.

That's the Lutheran crowd. Those kids stick together like glue.

Jerry belongs to the Catholic bunch.

Nadine is a farm kid.

There are two kinds of farm kids—those who associate with any body, and those who stick with the farm kids.

Careful grooming, proper language, and character traits such as honesty are accepted by the vast majority of students as desirable qualities. Other personal traits, such as "Jim's a swell fellow: he'll never pass you up without speaking," "Tom'll help anybody with their math," "Alice won't cheat, but she won't tell on you if she sees you copying an answer," are rated as valuable characteristics by most students. Participation in athletics rates high among both boys and girls. However, if a boy on an athletic team breaks training rules, he is generally condemned, but he does not lose the rating of a "big bang" unless he is singled out as the scapegoat for the loss of a game. Other extracurricular activities have various ratings. To be a member of the Drama and Debating Club places one among the elite, but to be a prominent member of the Home Economics Club means little, except that the girl is probably a "good kid." Actually, the "Home Ec" girls occupy a lower rating than they might otherwise enjoy simply because they are identified as "Home Ecs." Personal behavior such as carrying tales, malicious gossip, drinking, or smoking in public, among the girls, places the individual in an unenviable category among most of the other students.

Teen-Age Culture: An Overview

Jessie Bernard

The 1961 teen-agers were born between 1942 and 1948. They are there-fore, the war babies and the postwar babies, the advance guard of the great baby boom. Many are atomic-age youngsters, born after Hiroshima and Nagasaki.

There were an estimated 19 million teen-agers in 1959.[1] About one seventh of them were nonwhite, mostly Negro. Most of them, over 57 per cent, lived in cities; only about 21 per cent lived on farms. The others, about 22 per cent, lived in rural nonfarm communities.

Chronological and Cultural Teen-Age

Not all teen-agers participate in the teen-age culture. Those who are in civilian labor force (4,419,000 in January 1961), who are in the armed services (about 904,000), or who are married (about 1,206,000 in 1959)—something like 6½ million all told—are chronologically, but not necessarily culturally, teen-agers. They are neophytes in the adult culture of our society. They may share some aspects of teen-age culture, but, for the most part, they are expected to perform adult roles in adult dress. Teen-age culture is essentially the culture of a leisure class.

CLASS SELECTIVITY BY AGE

The figures just given are important because they reflect a class selectivity in teen-age culture by age. Youngsters of lower socioeconomic classes are in the teen-age culture only in their early teens. They are more likely than children of higher socioeconomic class to enter the labor force or the armed forces or to get married soon after high school and, thus, to disappear into the adult world. This exit from the teen-age world by youngsters of lower class background means that those who remain are disproportionately from the higher socioeconomic class background.

Jessie Bernard, "Teen-Age Culture: An Overview," from *The Annals of the Ameri-can Academy of Political and Social Science* (Vol. 338, November 1961), pp. 2–12. Reprinted by permission of the publisher and author.

[1] This figure includes Alaska but not Hawaii. It was arrived at by assuming that the proportion of 13- and 14-year-old youngsters in the 10–14 age bracket was the same in 1959 as in 1950 and applying it to 1959 estimates.

TABLE 1—Proportion of Teen-Agers in School
by Sex, 1959

	14–15 Years of Age	16–17 Years of Age	18–19 Years of Age
Males	97.8%	84.8%	45.6%
Females	97.0%	81.0%	29.2%

The drastic nature of this class selectivity by age in teen-age culture can be seen in the proportions of the several age groupings that are in school and, hence, able to participate in it. In 1959 the proportions of teen-agers still in school were as shown in Table 1.

Practically all children, then, regardless of class, are in the teen-age culture of the younger years; less than half are in the teen-age culture of the later teens. By and large, therefore, the teen-age culture of the younger years is more colored by lower socioeconomic class standards; that of the later years, by higher. And, as contrasted with, let us say, thirty years ago, the lower socioeconomic classes are of increasing importance.[2] It should be noted, also, that later teen-age culture is predominantly a male phenomenon. The teen-age culture of the early teens is, therefore, a lower-middle class phenomenon, in which girls are equally involved with boys; that of the later teens is an upper-middle class phenomenon, in which young men outnumber young women by about half. The differences are mainly in matters of taste. Money is required in both lower and higher class teen-age cultures. The differences arise in the ways the money is spent.

A Product of Affluence

Our teen-age culture—in contradistinction to the teen-age culture of the past or of other societies—is a product of affluence. It is possible because our society can afford a large leisure class of youngsters not in the labor force but yet consumers on a vast scale, or, if in the labor force, free to spend their earnings on themselves.[3] And they spend it primarily on clothes,

[2] The proportion of teen-age males in school rose between 1930 and 1958 from 93 to 99 per cent for 14-year-olds, from 85 to 96 per cent for 15-year-olds, from 66 to 88 per cent for 16-year-olds, from 47 to 74 per cent for 17-year-olds, and from 31 to 43 per cent for 18-year-olds.

[3] Young women under 20 spend $4½ billion dollars, and, as one of the editors of *Seventeen* points out, they have no income taxes, no rent, no insurance premiums to take out of this sum; they have it all for themselves. Sigana Earle, in a talk at the Michigan Home Economics Association convention, April 30, 1960, at Michigan State University.

cosmetics,[4] recreational paraphernalia, records, cars, travel, and other leisure class goods and services.[5]

MATERIAL ASPECTS

Clothes are an important part of teen-age culture. Industry first discovered the profitable teen-age consuming market in this area. Clothes were once sized and styled very simply—little-girl dresses, for example, until about age thirteen or fourteen and misses' and women's thereafter. The common lament of mothers and their teen-age daughters was that there was nothing suitable for the in-between age—once called the awkward age—when the girl was no longer a child but not yet a woman. Once industry discovered this market, the teen-age girl became one of the most catered-to segments of the buying public. Deb, sub-deb, sub-teen, and scores of other categories were developed, sized, and styled—by the most talented designers—for her. Her figure, not that of the mature woman, became the norm of fashion. An analogous development occurred for boys, who once jumped from knickers to long trousers in one dramatic leap. "Ivy league" is now as important in clothes for teen-age boys as Jonathan Logan is for girls. Leather jackets and chinos are equally standard for the younger or lower socioeconomic class boys.

The importance of clothes in teen-age culture in the case of girls is illustrated by the following document:

> A girl should dress as the other girls do but with just a touch of individuality. If she is considered a good dresser, she wears labels. Her dresses are Lanz or Jonathan Logan. She wears shoes by Capezio for people who dare to be different. Her skirts are Pendleton and the right length and the sweaters to match are Garland. Her coat is a Lassie, and no good dresser uses any make-up but the current fad which usually alternates between Revlon and Coty. All of these labels show (1) that she has money, (2) that she is allowed to spend it on her choices, and (3) that those choices are ones of quality.

The automobile is another basic trait in the material culture of teen-agers. It is taken for granted that every teen-ager will learn to drive and that, if he does not have a car of his own, individually or as member of a group, he will certainly have access to one. In one community, a car-dealer takes it for granted that when a boy reaches the age of sixteen he will be in the market for a used car. There were some 1½ million cars owned by teen-agers in 1960. The number of licensed drivers was, of course, much greater—some 5.9 million in 1958, or 7.2 per cent of all drivers—and they

[4] Allegedly $20,000,000 is spent annually on lipstick, $25,000,000 on deodorants, and $9,000,000 on home permanents.
[5] They spent 38 per cent of their money on such items as transportation, grooming, books, newspapers, magazines, school supplies; 25 per cent on food; 16 per cent on entertainment; 15 per cent on clothes; and 9 per cent on sports. *Life Magazine,* August 29, 1959, pp. 78–85.

did 5 per cent of all driving done.[6] The psychological and social problem aspects of the automobile are important but do not concern us here; the cultural aspect, however, is interesting and relevant: [7]

> . . . automobiles have become a factor of great importance in adolescent culture. For example, in many cities it is an accepted pattern that in order to date a girl, a boy must be able to provide a car for transportation; she may not go in a cab or allow herself and her date to be driven by parents. To many boys the car itself becomes a dominant motivating force. Having acquired a car for transportation, socialization, and dating, a boy becomes so involved in its care and upkeep he has little time or interest left for other activities. . . . "For many, the clubhouse on wheels is a medium for holding a party. . . ."

Popular records—$75,000,000 worth annually—constitute another important trait in teen-age culture; the contents will be analyzed below. Bongo drums, athletic equipment, high fidelity phonographs, travel, camping are other elements which loom large in the material aspect of teen-age culture.

To get these clothes, cars, bongo drums, record players, and cosmetics to the teen-agers, an enormous market has developed. It amounted to an estimated $10 billion in 1959 and was expected to reach twice that amount by 1970.[8] The girls in this market have been called the "teen tycoons," the "more groups":[9]

> They do and feel *more* than anybody else. They eat *more*. . . . They wear *more*—high school and college girls buy 889 million dollars worth of clothes in the 60-day back-to-school period. They give *more* parties —at least once a month 7½ million girls get together for some kind of social event and spend over 432 million dollars a year on party foods. . . . These girls are a power to reckon with.

". . . A POWER TO RECKON WITH"

The existence of this great leisure class with so much buying power at its disposal has had profound repercussions on the relationships between teenagers and the adult world. They have had to be catered to. The values of teen-age culture become a matter of concern to the advertising industry. What teen-agers like and want, what they think is important. As contrasted with the traditional agencies charged with socializing youngsters, the advertisers and the mass media flatter and cajole. They seek to create desires in order to satisfy, rather than, as the parent, teacher, or minister must often do, to discipline, restrict, or deny them. The advertiser is, thus, on the side of the teen-ager. "The things bought are determined by what the

[6] Ross A. McFarland and Roland C. Moore, "Youth and the Automobile," in *Values and Ideals of American Youth,* Eli Ginzberg, ed. (Columbia University Press, 1961), pp. 171, 172.
[7] *Ibid.,* pp. 173, 176.
[8] *Life Magazine,* August 29, 1959, pp. 78–85.
[9] Sigana Earle, of *Seventeen, loc. cit.*

child wants rather than by what the parents want for him." [10] Coffee is encouraged, as is smoking, if not—as yet—drinking. In fact, the rebound of the cigarette industry after the first cancer scare in the 1960's has been attributed to a big increase in teen-age smokers.[11] The teen-age press—to be commented on in greater detail [on page 200 of the present book] reflects values and standards which teen-agers select for themselves, rather than those selected for them. They have the money to call the tune; they are "patrons" of the arts and must, therefore, be catered to.

The coalition of advertisers and teen-agers is, thus, buttressed not only by psychological props but also by economic ones. For, "if parents have any idea of organized revolt, it is already too late. Teen-age spending is so important that such action would send quivers through the entire national economy." [12] Many parents feel that they are dealing with a piper who, though never pied, nevertheless draws children after him. The teen-ager's "relentless consumption"—to use Keynes' phrase—is essential to the economy, and it is they who direct it, not their parents.

Nonmaterial Traits

The language of teen-agers serves to maintain barriers between them and the outside world. This language may vary from community to community and from class to class. The following expressions were current on one campus in 1961: "clod," a person who is socially unacceptable by real collegiates; "tweedy," fashionably dressed; "tweeded down," dressed up; "rough and tough," well-accepted individual; "whip," to transport one's self; "roomy," roommate; "wheels," a car; "zowies," happy surprises; "tough dresser," a stunning dresser; "mickey mouse," anything easy, as a college course.

The values and preoccupations of teen-age culture may be discovered by analyzing those aspects of the mass media beamed directly to them: teen-age periodicals and popular records.[13] The "tribal customs" of teen-age culture can best be observed in the teen-age hangout.

[10] *Chicago Tribune,* reporting on Park Forest, cited in *Population Bulletin,* October 1960, p. 140.

[11] Joseph Welch once pointed out that, in the tobacco advertisements beamed at teen-agers, the choice seems to them to be between brands rather than between smoking and not smoking. *New York Times,* February 26, 1961.

[12] *Life Magazine,* August 29, 1959, p. 78.

[13] Teen-agers share with adults moving pictures and television programs. These media must reach as wide a public as possible, adult as well as adolescent; no American studio specializes in pictures for young people only. Although teen-agers go to movies about twice as often as the 20–29 age group and three times as often as the 40–49 age group, their taste is not markedly different from that of adults of the same class. Television viewing declines between childhood and adolescence; preferences for blood-and-thunder, mysteries, cowboy stories, comedy, family programs remain but make way in part for sports and adult drama. See George Gerbner, "Mass Communications and the Citizenship of Secondary School Youth," mimeographed report for the Interdisciplinary Study Group, Tufts Civic Education Center.

Teen-agers constitute an important set of publics as well as of markets. Children who used to have a hard time coming by pennies now have quarters and half dollars to spend on a bewildering variety of periodicals beamed primarily at them. These range from highly technical magazines for hot rod and railroad buffs all the way to lonely hearts-type magazines for shy little girls. Photography, sports, athletics, as well, of course, as pornography, have their publics also. The teen-type magazine, characterized usually by the term "teen" in its title, reveals the major positive—fun and popularity—and negative—overweight or underweight and adolescent acne—values of its readers. How to be attractive in order to be popular in order to have fun is the major burden of their contents. The teen-type magazine differs from its slick counterparts—*Seventeen* and *Mademoiselle,* for example—in a way analogous to the way true-story magazines for adult women differ from the service-type women's magazines. The class background of these differing publics is revealed in the relative sophistication of the content, as well as in the nature of the advertising. The values, however, are the same in both class levels—beauty, fun, popularity.

Popular songs, almost exclusively a teen-age cultural trait, have been subjected to content analysis by several researchers. One author finds that they fit neatly into what he calls the drama of courtship. There is a Prologue which emphasizes wishing and dreaming. Act I deals with courtship, and songs in this category constitute about a third of all popular songs. Five scenes deal respectively with: direct approach, sentimental appeal, desperation, questions and promises, impatience and surrender. Act II, contributing about 8 per cent of all lyrics, is on the honeymoon. The downward course of love, including about 14.5 per cent of the songs, is depicted in four scenes of Act III: temporary separation, hostile forces, threat of leaving, and final parting. Then, alas, Act IV concerns All Alone, about a fourth of the songs, in three scenes: pleading, hopeless love, and new beginnings.[14] He found remarkable similarities wherever he turned for materials, the Hit Parade, lists of Song Hits, Country Song Roundup, or Rhythm and Blues. In all categories, courtship and downward course of love songs accounted for well over half of all songs.

The values of teen-age culture are also reflected in what is rewarded among high school students. Schools differ markedly, but there is great uniformity in one respect: athletic ability is far more rewarded and prized than intellectual ability.[15] James Coleman believes one factor involved is that, when an athlete shows great achievement, the school and the community share the honor; when a bright student shows great achievement, he

---

[14] Donald Horton, "The Dialogue of Courtship in Popular Songs," *American Journal of Sociology,* Vol. 62 (May 1957), p. 575.
[15] These studies are summarized in *Recognition of Excellence* (Glencoe: Free Press, 1960), pp. 57–63.

does it as an individual and he alone shares the honor; he may even be viewed as a rate-buster.[16]

Tribal Customs

Contrary to the pattern of past generations, present-day teen-age boys and girls do not pass through a stage of withdrawal from one another. It has been found that as early as the fifth or sixth grades the sexes are already interested in one another; dating may begin as early as age ten or eleven. This teen-age culture already has a set of sex mores of its own. Kissing games—spin the bottle and post office—are very old; they antedate current teen-age culture by many years. What is new is parental acceptance by many, grudging in some cases, but resigned. Kissing games are supplemented by parking as soon as the boys acquire cars. Along with parking goes the custom of "bushwacking" or "hunting"; peers find the parked cars and flash their headlights on the petting couple.

Group norms may be observed in the hangout, as values can be noted in the mass media. In the early teens, the hangout may be a local malt shop or soda fountain. If the community provides a canteen, it may take the place of a hangout, but it is not the same thing, because it is supervised by adults.

The hangout can be usefully analyzed in terms of the framework of "the establishment," as suggested by Erving Goffman:[17]

> A social establishment is any place surrounded by fixed barriers to perception in which a particular kind of activity regularly takes place. . . . Any social establishment may be studied profitably from the point of view of impression management. Within the walls of a social establishment we find a team of performers who cooperate to present to an audience a given definition of the situation. This will include the conception of own team and of audience and assumptions concerning the ethos that is to be maintained by rules of politeness and decorum. . . . Among members of the team we find that familiarity prevails, solidarity is likely to develop, and that secrets that could give the show away are shared and kept. A tacit agreement is maintained between performers and audience to act as if a given degree of opposition and of accord existed between them. . . .

In the teen-age hangout, the "teams" are likely to be the boys on one side and the girls on the other. One study found that going to hangouts—drug-

---

[16] James S. Coleman, "The Adolescent Subculture and Academic Achievement," *American Journal of Sociology,* Vol. 65 (January 1960), pp. 346–347.
[17] Erving Goffman, *The Presentation of Self in Everyday Life* (Garden City, N.Y.: Doubleday Anchorage, 1959), p. 238.

store, fountain bar—almost equalled pleasure-driving in terms of numbers of participants involved.[18]

Work in Teen-Age Culture

The teen-ager participates in the economy primarily as a consumer. It is true that teen-agers work very hard—customizing automobiles, for example, or organizing and soliciting members for fan clubs—and it is conceivable that such work might have a market. But it is usually not marketed and, therefore, not subjected to the discipline of the adult work world. When the teen-ager sells his labor in the market, he is participating in adult culture, not his own.

When he does participate in the labor market, it is likely to be as a marginal producer, usually in part-time jobs which articulate well with the other demands of teen-age culture and, therefore, do not remove him from it. Certain occupations are characteristically teen-age. The paper route, odd jobs such as cutting lawns and shoveling snow, and baby sitting are standard teen-age jobs. Between high school and college, summer jobs may be in the adult world and constitute a first introduction to its demands. Some kinds of jobs at supermarkets are sometimes reserved for teen-agers. But, for many teen-agers, the typical job is at a summer camp or resort; and most of these articulate well with the other demands of teen-age culture and, therefore, do not remove the worker from its impact.[19]

The Political Values

Teen-age culture provides for an absorbing way of life. It is fairly well insulated against outside forces except those beamed directly at it. One of the commonest characteristics of American teen-agers, in fact, has been that, in alleged contrast to those of some other societies, they are politically apathetic. Interest in politics is not an integral part of teen-age culture.[20]

When pressed for opinions on political questions by adults, however, teen-agers reply in ways which reflect, as clearly as other aspects of their culture, a distinct class bias. Polls of high school students during the 1940's

[18] George Gerbner, *op. cit.*, p. 10.

[19] In 1937–1938, the most frequent part-time jobs of boys were paper boys, sales clerks, filling-station attendants, theater ushers and assistants, and delivery jobs. For girls, the commonest part-time jobs were sales clerks, housework, nursemaids, waitresses, musicians, and music teachers. In 1942, 28.7 per cent of a sample of boys and 9.0 per cent of a sample of girls had after-school jobs; 41.6 per cent and 12.5 per cent respectively had Saturday jobs; and 57.6 per cent and 14.4 per cent had summer jobs. Miller and Form, *Industrial Sociology* (New York: Harper, 1951), Chap. 16. For an excellent analysis of "culture shock" as the teen-ager moved from his school culture to the work culture, see pp. 610–632.

[20] But note current trends in teen-type magazines described on page 200.

and 1950's with respect to political opinions and attitude corroborate with almost uncanny accuracy the conclusion which Seymour Lipset arrived at after analyzing adult voting behavior.[21] With respect to government control, that is, lower class teen-agers are more likely than upper class teen-agers to be "liberal"; but, with respect to civil liberties and race relations, they are more likely to be reactionary (see Table 2).

TABLE 2—Teen-Age Political Opinion Related
to Socioeconomic Class

Issue	Per Cent Upper Income Group Teen-Agers	Per Cent Lower Income Group Teen-Agers
Civil Liberties and Race Relations		
Democratic institutions depend on free business enterprise	64%	54%
Democratic institutions depend on freedom of the press	47	42
Unwarranted search and seizure is permissible	11	26
Third degree is permissible to gain criminal confessions	53	59
Taking the Fifth Amendment is acceptable	28	39
Wiretapping is not acceptable	37	29
School desegregation is approved	46	38
Disturbances and pupil strikes to prevent desegregation are disapproved	70	50
Government Control of Economy and Private Ownership		
Government should have control of railroads and airlines	11	26
Basic industries should be owned by government	14	21
Large unused estates should be divided among the poor for farming	48	63
Slum clearance should be privately controlled	18	16
Private ownership and/or control is advocated for:		
Peaceful uses of atomic energy	25	13
Electric power from rivers and dams	26	18
Electric power from steam plants	55	38
Oil resources	53	49
Nativism		
Immigration should be restricted	35	42
Foreign countries have little to contribute to American progress	10	19

Source: H. H. Remmers and D. H. Radler, *The American Teen-ager* (Indianapolis: Bobbs-Merrill, 1957), pp. 208 ff.

[21] Seymour Martin Lipset, *Political Man* (Garden City, N.Y.: Doubleday, 1960), Chap. 4.

Class and Teen-Age Culture

Hollingshead reported more than a decade ago on the pervasiveness of class in high schools in the 1940's.[22] Teen-age society is still stratified and class still pervades teen-age culture. By and large, the cleavage still divides high school students into the college preparatory or academic students and the vocational or commercial students. All aspects of teen-age culture—like political attitudes referred to [above, pp. 202–203 of the present book]—differ for the different classes—taste in moving pictures and dress, hangouts, dancing, and dating practices. The ideal-typical girl is different. The following reports document these differences.

CLASS AND MOVING PICTURES
IN TEEN-AGE CULTURE

My town had three movies, two of which showed grade A movies while the third showed grade F—cowboy and horror movies. Two different classes of boys and girls attended these features. In the grade F theater one would find the "cats" of the town, mostly boys. Conduct in this movie could be characterized by whistling, throwing empty candy boxes, and placing feet on chairs. Loud conversations also could be heard.

In the grade A movie houses one usually saw the girls and boys of middle-class families. Of course, while these individuals did not attend the horror shows in the other theater, once in a while the "other element" would attend the better movies. Personal conduct in the grade A movies was opposite to that in the grade F movies—no throwing boxes, placing of feet on chairs, engaging in loud conversations. Once in a while the boys might whistle, though.

CLASS AND DRESS

From my experience, I've found that the clothes a boy wears definitely elevate or lower his social status. When a boy dresses in the current fashion, it shows that he knows what's going on and is not "out of it." On first impression, a boy is rated on his appearance—either tweedy or cloddy, as the case may be.

To rate well socially, a boy should look as tweedy as possible. This means wearing tan raincoats, crew-neck sweaters, button-down oxford cloth shirts, khaki, corduroy or flannel pants, and loafers or sneakers. Not only must he wear these clothes, but he must choose the correct style in each. Sweaters should be in neutral or dark shades, shirts are white, blue, or pinstriped, and the pants are continental or at least tapered and slim in the legs.

A boy may be considered a clod if he wears flannel or non-button-down shirts, baggy pants or deviates from the traditional crew-neck style sweaters. Shoes with laces (oxfords) worn with casual clothes are also in poor taste.

[22] A. B. Hollingshead, *Elmtown's Youth* (New York: Wiley, 1949).

A girl may also be socially rated as to the clothes she wears. Girls dress to look tweedy or collegiate. Tweedy girls wear button-down blouses or round or pilgrim collar blouses, pleated, bandstand, or flared skirts, wool crew-neck or fur-blend sweaters, knee socks and loafers. . . . Girls should beware of rayon-type or felt skirts which are too long, wing collar blouses, banlon sweaters, and low socks. Sneakers are being replaced by loafers in the really "in" groups. The goal is to look simple, the characteristic of tweediness. Most of the kids I know feel that sharp clothes indicate a hip personality.

CLASS AND HANGOUTS

In my town of 20,000 people, there were two main hangouts for the teen-agers. The YMCA recreation room was a place where one could snack, watch TV, play ping pong and dance to juke box music. But it was more of a canteen, I guess, than a real hangout. It was considered a nice place for the kids to go. Most of the girls and boys would usually drop in after school for an hour or two in the evening. Since the canteen was a part of the Y, it was considered quite respectable.

Another gathering place for the students was a little drug store. The boys and girls who frequented this particular drug store were the smokers and drinking set of the school. They were considered to be off-limits by the more respectable students. Perhaps not strictly off-limits —one could talk to them, but, on the other hand, interdating would not occur. This element of our town, while they did attend the Y-teen dances, also had their own little restaurant dancing spot where they would go on weekdays and week ends. It was not considered such a good place to go. One needed transportation to get to this second hangout.

CLASS AND THE IDEAL-TYPICAL GIRL

The girls who are high school cheerleaders and those who are high school majorettes differ markedly in background, appearance, and personality. The cheerleader is typically an academic student preparing for college and representing the middle and upper class. . . . She is a clean-cut, all-American girl. . . . She is not made up nor does she wear her hair in anything but a simple, classic, schoolgirl hairdo. . . . She is a breathing replica of a *Seventeen* model. . . . She belongs to the right clubs and dates a football hero or the student body president. She is in the know but not conceited about her position. . . . As a rule she doesn't associate with the majorettes.

The majorettes, who lead the band, seldom lead the school. They are usually commercial students who are planning to be secretaries. Most of them are from lower middle or upper lower classes. Their attitude toward school is poor and, as a result, their grades are low. Or, if their grades are good, they are discounted by the fact that they are in a commercial curriculum.

The twirlers are opposite in appearance, also, to the cheerleaders. They are pretty but in a gaudy way. Their hairdos and make-up are overdone and in poor taste, and they wear tight and often suggestive clothing that suggests cheapness. As a rule, they are not the popular girls nor do they try to be. Often being a majorette is their only activity. . . .

Because the cheering squad was so selective and enviable, many very capable girls who qualified were disappointed each year because they failed to make it. A group of these girls, who wanted to be in on things at school knew that they couldn't make cheering yet wouldn't settle for being a majorette. They began to organize a marching squad which would be chosen on the same criteria as the cheering squad except that these girls would do precision drills with the band. At first their group was small and only performed at talent shows and the like. But it soon became a part of pep rallies. . . . These girls formed their own in-group and at last have status almost equal to the cheerleaders and far above the majorettes.

Related to these class distinctions is the existence of alienation among teen-agers. There are the clods, the outs. And they constitute a sizeable proportion of the high school population. One study, for example, found that there were 22 per cent who felt left out of things, 11 per cent who felt "different," 44 per cent who seldom had dates, 13 per cent who felt they were not wanted, 20 per cent who felt lonesome, and 25 per cent who felt ill at ease at social affairs.[23] This alienation occurred in all classes, but it was more common in teen-agers with low income backgrounds than it was in those with high income backgrounds.

The College Level

Up to now, the class selective factor has operated to weed out teen-agers with lower class backgrounds from the older teen-age culture, leaving the upper middle class teen-agers as bearers of teen-age culture at the college level. Typically, it took the form of the so-called "rah-rah" culture.

Today, however, many young people from lower socioeconomic class background also go to colleges and universities. Some are absorbed into the collegiate culture. But many others have a strong vocational orientation. They do not participate in the old collegiate culture; they are preparing for adult roles. And even students from upper class backgrounds now find that they must take higher education more seriously. The tendency is, therefore, for teen-age culture to end with high school for an increasing number of young people. The forces at work making for this result have been analyzed by Clark and Trow, whose findings we follow here.

They distinguish four models of student cultures, namely: collegiate, vocational, academic, and nonconformist.

The collegiate culture is the world of football, Greek letter societies, cars, and drinking. Courses and professors occupy a dim background position. This culture is not hostile to the college; it is only indifferent and resistant

[23] H. H. Remmers and D. H. Radler, *The American Teen-ager* (Indianapolis: Bobbs-Merrill, 1957), pp. 80–85.

to serious demands and involvement in intellectual activities. "This culture is characteristically middle and upper middle class—it takes money and leisure to pursue the busy round of social activities—and flourishes on, though is by no means confined to, the resident campuses of big state universities." [24]

The vocational culture tends to prevail in urban colleges and universities attended by the children of lower middle class families. Because many of these students are married and working hard, their culture is not teen-age in character. They are customers not in a luxury market but in a diploma market. "They buy their education somewhat as one buys groceries," to use an idea of Riesman and Jencks. "If the symbol of the collegiate culture is the football and fraternity weekend, the symbol of this vocationally oriented culture is the student placement office." [25]

The academic culture has learning and knowledge and ideas as a central set of values. "The distinctive qualities of this group are (a) they are seriously involved in their course work beyond the minimum required for passing and graduation and (b) they identify themselves with their college and its faculty." [26] No more than the vocational culture, therefore, is this one teen-age in its essential characteristics.

The nonconformist culture belongs to the intellectual, radical, alienated Bohemian. The authors who distinguish it concede that it is elusive, that it may be merely a residual category, difficult to distinguish from the academic culture. "The academic cultures we speak of include students with intellectual interests as well as grinds submissive to the demands of the faculty. When students' intellectual interests are not merely independent of but also at odds with the curriculum, they often form the nucleus of what we have called 'nonconformist' cultures, which however also include styles and interests that are by no means intellectual. In our typology, the members of the academic subcultures tend to link their interests to the curriculum; the nonconformist pursue theirs outside it." [27]

It is the conclusion of Clark and Trow that, because of the career demands in large bureaucratic organizations whose hiring staffs scrutinize transcripts and evaluate grades, the characteristically teen-age or collegiate culture is now on the decline. As more and more children of lower middle class background go to college and as the demands of society call for greater

[24] Burton R. Clark and Martin Trow, "Determinants of College Student Subculture," in *The Study of College Peer Groups: Problems and Prospects for Research,* a volume based on the work of the seminar sponsored by the Social Science Research Council, Ann Arbor and Berkeley, 1959–1960 (mimeographed), p. 2. See Davie and Hare, "Button-down Collar Culture: A Study of Undergraduate Life," *Human Organization,* Vol. 14 (Winter 1956), pp. 13–20, for a picture of collegiate culture.
[25] Clark and Trow, *op. cit.,* p. 6.
[26] *Ibid.,* p. 7.
[27] *Ibid.,* p. 8. See David Matza's selection, "Subterranean Traditions of Youth" for an analysis of nonconformist culture.

training, the vocational and academic cultures wax. "Both the vocational and the academic orientations are 'adult' in a way that the collegiate culture is not." [28]

ETHNICITY AND RACE

Our discussion so far has emphasized class and age differences in teen-age culture. Ethnicity and race are also significant factors, closely related to class. The child of the recent immigrant is pulled between the ethnic culture of his family, which is separatist in effect, and the teen-age culture of his peers. After two or three generations, the ethnic factor all but disappears. Not so the racial factor. The Negro teen-ager is in many ways an even newer phenomenon than the white teen-ager today. It is only very recently that a substantial middle class could afford to keep children in high school, let alone college. The upper level teen-age Negro finds himself caught in two intersecting cultures. The clash is between the traditional values professed by American society which he now studies in school and the discriminating culture he still sees in operation around him. In 1960 the Negro college student decided to do something about it.

Conclusion

This overview of teen-age culture is presented as an introduction to the several facets of teen-age culture. No forecast of future trends is attempted. The whole phenomenon of teen-age culture may be moving down, so far as age is concerned. As the collegiate culture of the eighteen- and nineteen-year-olds wanes, we note that entrance into teen-age culture occurs at an earlier age than in the past—cosmetics and brassieres at younger ages, for example, as well as dating. Teen-age culture may come to refer to those in the ten to eighteen age bracket rather than to those in the thirteen to twenty age bracket.

But so long as our society can afford a large leisure class, profitable to exploit, teen-age culture will continue. The specific contents, it may safely be predicted, will certainly change. And in 1981 many of the current teen-age generation will be bragging of their pioneer experiences in the Peace Corps and be clicking their lips in disapproval and harking back nostalgically to the good old days of the 1960's when the songs and dances were so much more attractive than those of today.

[28] *Ibid.,* p. 16.

On the Youthfulness
of Youth Cultures *

Bennett M. Berger

For more than twenty years now, sociologists have increasingly concerned themselves with the study of "youth culture." Talcott Parsons' very influential article, published in 1942,[1] with its much quoted characterization of youth culture as "more or less specifically irresponsible" has become a point of departure for an enormous amount of research and discussion on youth. Parsons' characterization of youth culture, however, inadvertently suggests that whatever it is that constitutes the "youthfulness" of youth culture may have less to do with chronology than with culture. To characterize youth culture as "irresponsible" or to describe its "dominant note" as "having a good time" or to say that it has "a strong tendency to develop in directions which are on the borderline of parental approval or beyond the pale . . ." (note 1) clearly excludes those large numbers of adolescents who have had no important experience in anything remotely resembling such a milieu. Many, and probably most young persons, while they experience the classic problems of adolescent psychology described in the textbooks, seem to make their way through to full adult status without grave cultural damage, without getting into serious trouble, without a dominating hedonism, and without generalized attitudes of rebellion toward parents and the world.

These introductory remarks are not intended as a preface to a "defense" of adolescents against the bad press they have been getting in recent years. I intend, rather, to suggest that (1) "youth culture" should refer to the normative systems of *youthful* persons, not necessarily of young ones; and (2) since whatever it is that is normatively distinctive about youth culture is probably not characteristic of all or even most adolescents, it is not attributable solely or even primarily to chronological age; and hence (3) that the definitive characteristics of youth culture are relevant to groups other than the age-grade we call adolescence.

While Frederick Elkin and William A. Westley believe they have exploded "The Myth of Adolescent Culture" [2] with survey data showing that a sample

From Bennett M. Berger, "On The Youthfulness of Youth Cultures," from *Social Research* (Autumn, 1963), pp. 319–342. Reprinted by permission of the publisher and the author.

* Author's Note—A revised version of a talk given at the annual banquet of Alpha Kappa Delta, Purdue University, May 19, 1961.
[1] "Age and Sex in the Social Structure of the United States," *American Sociological Review* (October 1942).
[2] *American Sociological Review* (December 1955).

of middle class adolescents comply with the norms of deferred gratification, get along well with their parents, without hostility or resentful feelings that "they don't understand us," what they have actually done is present evidence that certain adolescents do not share the norms of youth culture. By thus implicitly distinguishing the facts of chronological age from the phenomena of culture, they invite us to consider the hypothesis that what we are in the habit of calling "youth culture" is the creature of some young and some not so young persons. If hedonism or irresponsibility or rebelliousness are essential features of youth culture, then it may be unwise as well as unnecessary to restrict the consideration of youth culture to adolescent groups—since these qualities are dominant in several adult groups as well; and the fact that this is so is probably not fortuitous. I am suggesting, in short, that youthfulness, like fertility, is unequally distributed in society, and not satisfactorily explained by reference to chronological age. This essay is an attempt to explore theoretically some of the conceptual problems that an investigation of the structure and dynamics of youth culture will encounter.

Youth Cultures of the Young

TWO IMAGES OF THE YOUNG: "TEEN-AGERS" AND "AMERICAN YOUTH" [3]

To begin, let us note a recurrent ambiguity in the images with which American adolescents are usually conceived. The "teen-agers" are those who, in Dwight McDonald's apt enthnography,[4] spend an hour a day on the phone and two hours a day listening to disc jockeys; they are the most assiduous movie-goers in the nation, preferring especially films about monsters, rock and roll music, and teen-agers like themselves. More than half of them "go steady" and practice the sexual or proto-sexual intimacies implied by that phrase. The boys are very car-conscious, and spend a good deal of their leisure reading about, talking about, and working on hot rods. They read *Mad,* and its imitators *Frenzy* and *Think;* they don't read the Bible, don't go to church regularly, are bored by politics, ignorant of the Bill of Rights, and so on.

If one shifts one's perspective for a moment, and begins to think of the adolescents who populate Boy Scouts, Youth for Christ, 4H clubs, Future Farmers of America, and other groups of this sort, McDonald's characterization (based in part upon the results of Remmers' work [5] and Eugene Gilbert's youth polls) has a rather jarring effect. These doers of good deeds

[3] I am indebted to Barbara Williams for the terms of this distinction.
[4] See his two-part "profile" of Eugene Gilbert in *The New Yorker* (November 22 and 29, 1958).
[5] H. H. Remmers and D. H. Radler, *The American Teenager* (Indianapolis, Ind.: The Bobbs-Merrill Co., 1957).

and raisers of prize pigs and winners of essay contests on Americanism are clearly not the adolescents who have seemingly become a permanent "problem" on the American scene.

"Teen-agers" and "American youth" are, of course, images, and as such, they may be little more than stereotypes; we may, and likely will, find rock and rollers belonging to the FFA. But it is also likely that these distinctive images express differences in social and demographic variables like class, region, ethnicity, and religion. In any case, the initial distinction between "teen-agers" (the adolescents publicly worried about) and "American youth" (the adolescents publicly praised) does suggest the useful banality that some adolescents engage in ways of life essentially at odds with or indifferent to the official desires and expectations of "responsible" adults, whereas other adolescents comply with or actively pursue the aims and expectations set down for youth by adult authorities.

TRANSITIONAL STAGE AND SUBCULTURE

One way of extending this distinction between types of adolescents is to contrast two ideas that are frequently used in psychological and sociological discussions of youth. Most standard works on the social psychology of adolescence speak of it as a "transitional stage" between childhood and adulthood, a period of years ridden with conflicts and tensions stemming partly from an acceleration in the individual's physical and cultural growth but also from the age-grading norms of our society that withhold from adolescents most of the opportunities, rights, and responsibilities of adults. When sexual desires are more powerful than they will ever again be, sexual opportunities are fewest; obedience and submission are asked of adolescents at precisely the time when their strength, energy, and desire for autonomy are ascendant; responsible participation in the major institutions are denied them at the moment when their interest in the world has been poignantly awakened.[6] Such tensions, generated by our age-grading system and exacerbated by a decline in parental control and a world in a state of permanent crisis, are frequently cited as the major source of adolescent difficulty. Conceived as a "transitional stage," adolescence is a very difficult period; it is described—and caricatured—as a time of awkwardness and embarrassment and trouble and pain—something to be got out of as soon as possible by orienting oneself primarily toward eventual membership in the adult community.

For many years, apparently, this conception of adolescence as a difficult transitional stage was the dominant framework in which adolescent prob-

[6] These are a few of the "discontinuities" made famous by Ruth Benedict in her celebrated article "Continuities and Discontinuities in Cultural Conditioning," *Psychiatry* (May, 1938). See also Kingsley Davis' related discussions: "Adolescence and the Social Structure," *The Annals* (November 1944) and "The Sociology of Parent-Youth Conflict," *American Sociological Review* (August 1940).

lems were discussed. As recently as 1944, Caroline Tryon could write, "we have a tendency to disregard or to minimize the educational significance of the child's experience in his peer group." [7] Today, this statement strikes the eye as incredible; certainly it is no longer true. Very few contemporary discussions of youth fail to mention the significance of the involvement of young persons in their own age-graded peer groups. The emphasis in these discussions, however, is quite different from that contained in discussions of adolescence as a transitional stage; the stress is on the orientation of adolescents to their peers. From this perspective emerged the idea of an adolescent subculture [8] as a "way of life" relatively autonomous, and controlled internally by a system of norms and sanctions largely antithetical or indifferent to that offered by parents, teachers, and clergymen—the official representatives of the adult world.

By itself, the subcultural view of adolescence suggests nothing *inherently* transitional, except in the sense that all experience is transitional, representing, as it does, the passage from what one was to what one is about to become. But oddly enough, it is precisely this element that is missing from the conventional usage of the concept of "transitional stage." To suggest that adolescence is "a stage they go through"—something that adolescents "grow out of," is to violate much of what we know about the permanent effects of socialized experience. It is as if adolescence, frequently designated "the formative years," formed nothing, but was simply a rather uncomfortable period of biding one's time until the advent of one's twenty-first birthday or that one's graduation from school induces the adult world to extend a symbolic invitation to join it. But if the transitional view of adolescence minimizes the permanent influences of adolescent experience, the subcultural view exaggerates the degree to which adolescents create an insulated, autonomous milieu in which they may with impunity practice their anti-adult rites. No large scale study of high school youth, for example, has successfully demonstrated the existence of a really deviant system of norms which governs adolescent life. [9]

The point I wish to stress here, however, is that our understanding of the varieties of adolescent experience depends heavily upon whether adolescent group life is primarily conceived in the vocabulary of developmental psychology as a transitional stage, or in the sociological vocabulary of subcultures. Conceived as a transitional stage, adolescence is typically described

[7] Caroline Tryon, "The Adolescent Peer Culture," *43rd Yearbook of the National Society for the Study of Education* (Chicago, Ill.: University of Chicago Press, 1944).
[8] This is not the place to go into the problems of applying the concept of "subculture," developed on ethnic models, to age groups. See, however, J. Milton Yinger, "Contraculture and Subculture," *American Sociological Review* (October 1960) and my own comments in "Adolescence and Beyond," *Social Problems* (Spring 1963).
[9] The most ambitious attempt to demonstrate this is James Coleman, *The Adolescent Society* (Glencoe, Ill.: The Free Press of Glencoe, 1961).

in ways which make its termination devoutly to be wished.[10] When adolescence is discussed in subcultural terms, no such implication is carried with it. The literature on youth culture most consistently describes it in terms of hedonistic, irresponsible, and "expressive" behavior. Although most adults may believe that this behavior and the norms that constrain it *ought* to be terminated at the threshold of adulthood, it is by no means self-evident that a group which can "get away with" a life of hedonism (read: fun, kicks), irresponsibility (read: freedom, license), and expressiveness (read: immediate gratification, ego enhancement) may be expected to terminate it easily in exchange for the mixed blessing of recognition as adults, and the sometimes baleful responsibilities that this entails. Objectively—and at the very least, adolescence is a portion of a life lived—*formative* attitudes and orientations, talents and commitments, capacities, *and incapacities* develop that affect adolescents' various modes of adaptation into adult worlds, which more or less facilitate or obstruct their eventual recruitment into a specific adult milieu. If the child is father of the man, an understanding of the varieties of experience adolescents undergo, the varieties of milieu they touch, should contribute to the understanding of the kind of adults they are likely to become—and *not* to become.

CHRONOLOGICAL AGE AND YOUTHFULNESS

Before attempting to describe the groups that might fit the categories of "teenagers" and "American youth," and the groups that might be usefully analyzed with the concepts of "transitional stage" and "subculture," I wish to make explicit one more distinction alluded to earlier, and conceptually parallel to the two sets of distinctions I have already made. To say that youthfulness is far from perfectly correlated with chronological age is to imply that some adolescents are more youthful than others. Once the distinction is made, we can speak categorically of youthful young men, unyouthful young men, youthful old men and unyouthful old men. This fourfold classification suggests, perhaps oversharply, that chronological age and the culture-personality variables associated with it may be analytically separated. To render the distinction fruitful, however, it is necessary to specify what is meant by youthfulness. Rather than approach this problem directly, it may be wiser to do it indirectly, by contrasting with it the relative lack of youthfulness in "American youth."

In this connection, let me draw attention to a recent book called *The Vanishing Adolescent* in which Edgar Friedenberg argues that adolescence

[10] The characterization of adolescence as "the awkward age" full of pimples and embarrassment has validity only for the very early teen years. It may merely be a survival from a period when adolescents were completely dependent and completely subordinate. Today, high school students, free and relatively affluent, frequently feel that they are currently living what they expect will be the best years of their lives.

as a stormy decade of identity-seeking and as a distinctive stage of human development is disappearing in the United States largely as a result of premature socialization primarily in the high schools.[11] Without digressing into a discussion of Friedenberg's thesis, we *can* say that we have all known adolescents of the kind about which he is concerned. They do well enough in school, are "well-adjusted," popular with their peers, have few great conflicts with their parents or other authorities, and in general have few if any serious quarrels with the value system into which they are being socialized or with the institutions representing these values. Grant this image some validity; then let us ask: in what sense are these young persons youthful? Certainly they are young and probably inexperienced in the affairs of the world. But adolescents who respond docilely to the expectations of school authorities, who accept as legitimate the limits imposed on them by their parents,[12] who engage in the activities that are deemed appropriate by adult authorities, are more aptly described as going through the final phase of their pre-adult socialization, as junior grown-ups, rather than as incarnations of youthfulness. For when, in common usage, we describe persons as "youthful," we mean not primarily that they are obviously young, and hence relatively naïve and inexperienced; we mean that they tend to manifest certain qualities in their behavior, and that although these qualities do seem to be empirically *associated* with tender years, they are not *exclusively* age-graded. Regardless of chronological age, youthful persons tend to be impulsive, spontaneous, energetic, exploratory, venturesome, and vivacious; they tend to be candid, colorful, blunt in speech (having not acquired the skill and habit of dissimulation); they are often irreverent, frequently disrespectful; extreme, immoderate, they know no golden mean; they are "action seekers" [13] rather than seekers of stable routine. They joke a lot; the play motif dominates much of their activity—which they tend to transform into games, even in the most apparently unpropitious of circumstances. Lacking caution and judiciousness, they tend to throw themselves with full passion and sexually alert intensity into those activities that promise thrills and excitement, which they tend to pursue with little regard for consequences.

Notice that these are primarily the qualities of persons, not roles, and certainly not rationalized, bureaucratic roles—although they may become quasi-institutionalized as "deviant" roles. Notice too that they are all very active—one might say erotic. When abstracted from behavior and become

---

[11] Edgar Friedenberg, *The Vanishing Adolescent* (Boston, Mass.: The Beacon Press, 1959).

[12] There actually are many adolescents who respond to questionnaires with the opinion that teenagers are not really old enough to smoke or drink or in general to know what is good for them.

[13] The term "action seeker" is taken from Herbert Gans' characterization of some working-class Bostonians. See his *The Urban Villagers* (New York: The Free Press of Glencoe, 1962).

conscious, qualities such as these assert themselves on *ideological* grounds. When, that is, they take on the character of moral imperatives, we can properly speak of a system of subcultural norms.[14] Such norms underlie the content of youth culture. Clearly, they are dangerous: from the perspective of the major institutions of social order, youthfulness is excess; it is implicit or incipient disorder; for society, it is a "problem" that requires handling, control, co-optation, or channeling in socially approved directions.

Society has at its disposal a great armory of means to control this implicit threat of disorder. I mean not the police and the courts or the more informal sanctions wielded by parents and other authorities; I mean the community youth center, the chaperoned dance, organized sports, school-sponsored extracurricular clubs, and the junior auxiliaries of business, religious, fraternal and veterans' associations—for adults have learned that adolescents will frequently accept from their peers the same norms they may reject from adults. But the effectiveness of these organizational weapons in coping with youth varies with the location of particular youths in the social structure. Where, for example, adult leadership is poor and community facilities limited, as in urban slums and certain new suburbs; or where sudden discontinuities in style of life create inter-generation tensions and anxieties, and disqualify parents as models worthy of emulation and respect, as frequently occurs in immigrant or highly mobile families; or where failure or anticipated failure in academic competition leaves the failer with the perception of a bleak future and with no approved alternative sources of self-respect, as frequently occurs among ethnic and working class boys in schools dominated by middle-class norms—where these and other early experiences of incipient social disaffection can mobilize ideological supports and some degree of structural insulation from the major institutions, there we are likely to find fertile ground in which the seeds of youthful excess and disorder can grow, and, eventually, bear the exotic flower called "youth culture."

VARIETIES OF YOUTH CULTURE

The flower has many blooms; the varieties of youth culture are as wide as the variety of cultural contexts and opportunity systems offered by a pluralistic society. At its broadest and most innocuous, the youth cultures of the young touch the fringes of what is called "teenage culture": popular songs, rock and roll, disc jockeys, juke boxes, portable phonographs, movie stars, dating, and romantic love; hot rods, motorcycles, drag racing, and sports cars, panty raids and water fights, drive-in hamburgers and clandestine drinking, football games, basketball games, dances and parties, and clubs and cliques, and lovers' lanes. At its delinquent extreme, youth culture

[14] For modern formulations of this ideology, see Norman Brown, *Life Against Death* (New York: Random House, 1960); Herbert Marcuse, *Eros and Civilization* (Boston, Mass.: The Beacon Press, 1959); and Paul Goodman, *Growing Up Absurd* (New York: Random House, 1960).

is black leather jackets, gang rumbles and switch blades, malicious mischief, and joy riding in stolen cars. Politically, it is expressed in sit-ins, freedom rides, peace marches, and folk songs; it is jazz at Newport, vacations at Fort Lauderdale—and their attendant riots. And it is also bohemians and beatniks and beards and hipsters, and coffee shop desperadoes plotting everything from literary magazines to assaults on the House Committee on UnAmerican Activities.[15]

I intend by this apparently formless catalogue of symbols to suggest how wide a variety of group styles and expressions the youth cultures of the young include. Intimations [16] of youth culture will be found more frequently among "teen-agers" than among "American youth," more frequently among "conflict" and "retreatist" delinquent gangs than among the "rational" criminal delinquents,[17] more among "bohemian" and "collegiate" undergraduates than among academically or vocationally oriented college students,[18] and more among politically militant and extreme student groups than among the student adherents of "moderate" sentiment within the two major political parties. The wide social spectrum represented by these groups should reassure the skeptical that I have no ideological axes to grind; few of those prone to moral judgments of youth could unambiguously approve or disapprove of *all* of these groups at the same time. But what delinquents and bohemians and campus radicals and even some high school hot rodders and college fraternity boys have in common is, I am suggesting, their youthfulness, that is, their tendency to behave in patterned ways normatively hedonistic, irresponsible, and expressive.

In spite of the wide variety of dissimilar forms in which it is expressed, it seems reasonable and useful—and also more objective—initially to designate this normative behavior as "youthful" (rather than, say, "deviant" or "delinquent" or "alienated"—although it may *become* these) because it is in large part the autonomous creature of sub-societies of the recalcitrant young. Although, as I have suggested previously and will argue at some length later, it is also selected from, supported by, and modeled after a long cultural tradition, nourished by several contemporary subcultures of adults, and is hence in principle viable into adulthood and beyond. The youth cultures of the young are an adaptive response by *some* adolescents to problems presented to them by their parent society and culture (for example, con-

[15] For a very similar formulation, see David Matza, "Subterranean Traditions of Youth," *The Annals* (November 1961) in which Matza argues that radicalism, bohemianism, and delinquency are the three basic forms which subterranean traditions (that is, subcultures) of youth take.
[16] I say "intimations" because "teen-age culture" is what David Matza calls a "conventionalized version" of what I would call a genuine youth culture.
[17] See Richard Cloward and Lloyd Ohlin, *Delinquency and Opportunity*, (Glencoe, Ill.: The Free Press, 1960) for a discussion of these types of gangs.
[18] See the typology of college student orientations in Martin A. Trow and Burton Clark, "Determinants of College Student Subcultures," in *The Study of College Peer Groups*, T. M. Newcomb and E. K. Wilson, eds. (Forthcoming)

tradictions or imbalances in norms, blockage of opportunity, inadequately defined roles, ambiguities of age-grading, the prospect of meaningless work), and the forms they take in specific groups reflect a choice from traditions available to them. To see the matter this way takes account of both the autonomous character of the subculture and its linkage to important traditions which antedate it. The significance of the adjective in the term "youth culture," however, rests not in the fact that many of its participants are young, but in the fact that their selective interaction with one another, under the difficult conditions generated by our age-grading norms and in contexts that limit the exercise of adult supervision and control, may sustain a set of more or less counter-norms which encourage and support, however ambivalently, a pattern of behavior at odds with the official norms of the culture in which it is located, but *adaptive* in the sense that it can provide— not just temporarily—a more or less viable way of life.

Adult Youth Cultures

THE PRESERVATION OF YOUTH CULTURE:
ITS LINKS WITH THE ADULT WORLD

Earlier, I criticized the usage of the concept of "transitional stage" because it did not sufficiently specify the differential impact of adolescent experience upon subsequent careers. We already know that adolescents eventually become adults; but we do not know much about the ways in which variations in adolescent experience affect subsequent adult adaptations. The concept of "transitional stage" is often employed largely as a palliative for society's functional problems of recruiting and integrating youth into adult worlds: if it's merely "a stage they're going through," then adults need not frankly confront the problems their behavior raises because, after all, "they'll grow out of it."

Most of them, it is true, do grow out of it, and the fact that they do is testimony not only to the power of adult agencies of socialization but to the vulnerability to co-optation of "teen-age culture"—to its lack of resources to sustain it in crisis and insulate it from attack.[19] But some do not or cannot grow out of it. What becomes of those young persons whose "youthful rebelliousness" turns out to be not "a stage they're going through," but a series of subculturally rewarding experiences that subjectively validate their

---

[19] It is this lack which distinguishes "teen-age culture" from more genuine subcultures such as ethnic communities, delinquent gangs in urban slums, and bohemias. Ethnic communities frequently have a full blown institutional structure to shield its members from the society's encroachments; delinquent gangs emphasize the inviolability of "turf" for good sociological reason; bohemias are usually ecological communities as well as subcultures, and even political radicals have, at the very least, a strong ideology to sustain them. Teen-agers have very little.

initial opposition to or irritation with the official demands of adults? And what becomes of those whose participation in political, delinquent, and bohemian forms of youth culture leaves permanent stigmata that render them permanently visible to a henceforth skeptical and suspicious world? Delinquency statistics, the "beatnik" craze, student militance and riots suggest that for substantial numbers (how many, no one knows) adolescence is not simply an awkward but benign transitional stage, and it is these facts to which we refer when we speak of youth and their growing up as a "social problem." To the extent that we can conceive of growing up as a *career* (and in this psychoanalytical age it is not difficult to do so), "*not* growing up" (that is, the preservation of the essential features of youth culture in later life) can also be considered as a career. Although there is a certain joylessness in the idea of "maturity" (identified, as it is, with sober responsibilities and solemn commitments), there are relatively few niches in the adult social structure where "youthfulness" does not receive severe negative sanctions, and those adolescents whose peer group experience has developed in them trained incapacities for growing up or perhaps even conscientious objections to it may be expected to gravitate toward them.

Those adolescents among whom youthful attributes are weakest—for example, those studied by Elkin and Westley, the prematurely socialized type described by Friedenberg, and the bulk of adolescents only superficially involved in teen-age culture—will probably have the least difficulty in making the transition to the typical adult careers offered in a highly industrialized, bureaucratized society. On the other hand, those in whom youthful attributes are strong will have the greatest difficulty in making those sacrifices of youthfulness that most executive and professional and other prestigious adult careers require.

What kinds of adult occupations and milieu are likely to reward or at least to tolerate youthfulness, and thus normatively support an attempt not to grow up or an inability to grow up? If it is true that some adolescents are more youthful than others, it is also true that some adults are more youthful than others, and it is likely that some of the important forces that sustain youthfulness in those who are no longer young may be found in the norms of the occupations they choose (or which choose them) and in the milieu that those norms help create.[20] What are some of these types of occupations?

YOUTHFUL CAREERS

I submit the following short list for illustrative purposes. My best hope is that it will be taken as suggestive of one way of theoretically linking the content of adolescent youth cultures with important subterranean or deviant

[20] Statuses other than occupational ones, of course, may also help sustain youthfulness: bachelor, divorcé(e), student, for example. Periodicals such as *Esquire* and *Playboy* are apparently directed at youthful adult audiences, and an analysis of their readers might provide evidence of youthful adult statuses.

traditions in the adult world, and hence of linking certain kinds of youthful experience in the adolescent milieu with the subsequent taking up of adult careers.

Bohemian business. By bohemian businessmen, I mean the proprietors or managers of small enterprises that cater to the needs, tastes, and desires of bohemians. These enterprises range all the way from those that are central to bohemian subcultures (*espresso* coffee houses, small art galleries, sandal and leather shops, pottery shops, jewelry shops, and so on) to other marginal businesses serving other markets as well ("art" theaters, paperback bookstores, small night clubs specializing in modern jazz, accessory and specialty shops for women, and so on). Wherever a "deviant" community exists (in this case a bohemian community), a business community is likely to exist to supply the wants that symbolize and define its deviance—in a sense analogous to that in which organized crime is symbiotically inter-related with government, law enforcement agencies, and parts of the legitimate business community. Bohemian business enterprise is one of the relatively few types of careers available to persons who, having had their basic orientations to the world shaped by experience in an adolescent subculture, have developed trained incapacities for pursuing more conventional kinds of business or professional or "bourgeois" careers—although the ironic and economically "reactionary" character of bohemian enterprise is that it gives its entrepreneurs the status of shopkeeper.

But their status as shopkeepers is less important and less revealing than the fact that they are likely to be bohemians. Bohemian businessmen, that is, are more like their customers than like other small businessmen. Even in their strictly economic capacities, bohemian businessmen are likely to reflect the habits of their customers. They may, for example, be expected to keep irregular hours, to open their shops late in the day, and remain open late in the evening. Located primarily in the "Latin quarter" of large cities or near university campuses, they frequently take long summer vacations or move their shops to summer resorts of the "art colony" type. They are not likely to keep rigorous books and their prices are frequently not standardized—sometimes because their wares are not. Often, they do not have a primarily commercial or instrumental orientation to what they sell, but rather an expressive one.[21] Dealing mainly in beauty—in esthetic objects or experience—they are not likely to think of themselves primarily as businessmen, but either as craftsmen or as esthetic functionaries performing services for the community of avant-garde good taste. However they think of themselves, bohemian businessmen (recruited largely from the student bohemian world

---

[21] As an example a customer walks into an "art mart" to purchase a teapot that goes with a set of china that the customer knows the shop stocks. With some hauteur, the proprietress informs the customer that she does not sell the teapot (although she sells all the other pieces in the set) because it is "poorly designed."

of craftsmen, failed or insufficiently talented artists, and hangers-on and camp followers of the cultural avant-garde) live in a milieu that tolerates and rewards a youthful adaptation to the world. Bohemian business offers a moderately viable niche in the adult world for those unable or unwilling to grow out of youth culture.

Perhaps an *image* of a viable niche in the world would be a more accurate statement. For it is, of course, true that the actual opportunities for a successful career in bohemian business are probably not very good. Although it is a theoretically open milieu, the rate of business failure seems high, and the population of bohemia is probably not large enough to support the commercial enterprises of very many of those young persons who are more or less successfully resisting or evading middle-class socialization. Nevertheless, the image of an adult bohemian life is culturally fertile and ambiguously seductive to many. Bohemia is always newsworthy; its consistent coverage in the mass media, its consistent status as a "tourist attraction" means that it is of great interest to the vicarious lives of large numbers of people. For every core bohemian there are probably five fringe bohemians; for every fringe bohemian there are probably five "weekend bohemians"; and for every weekend bohemian there are probably scores of Walter Mittys each of whom might be secretly flattered to have one of his perhaps idiosyncratic habits labeled "bohemian" by a suspicious and surly neighbor. My point is simply that although full-time bohemianism as a career may not be viable very long for very many, its part-time or fantasy appeal is apparently much stronger than the actual opportunities it offers. But it is the existence of this appeal and the ambiguous possibilities represented by it that enable it to serve for the youthful as a *milieu of orientation* tolerant of their behavior and to which they may look for permanent sustenance.

Show business. Many actors, singers, dancers, musicians, comedians, and other entertainers inhabit a world suffused by the myth of youth—a world in which grandmothers and grandfathers are noted for their sex appeal. The professional milieu of jazz musicians interpenetrates with the hipster and bohemian varieties of youth culture, bonded by a common antipathy to "squares." Much like the jazz milieu, the world of the off-Broadway theater is heavily populated with aspiring actors and actresses, committed to their expressive art, who live on the fringe of bohemia. The celebrity world of Hollywood stars is, for public consumption at least, "La Dolce Vita," with its dominating motifs of sex, speed, alcohol, drugs, and perversion set in a context of luxury. Most of the "new" American comedians have come up from the dark basement clubs catering to bohemian-intellectual audiences into the bright glare of the legitimate stage and the TV studio to continue, somewhat diluted, their savage satires of the routine, the usual, the ordinary (that is, the "adult")—but now to the masochistic audience upon whose lives and opinions their material is based. Finally, teen-age pop singers, despite their ritual affirmation of God, Home, and Mother, and their pious promises to "continue their education" (directed, one supposes, at the parents of their admirers), create a professional image compounded of thinly disguised erotica and forlorn adolescent alienation, and, with the help of publicity, transform their slum or otherwise poverty-stricken backgrounds into a romantic determination to "be somebody." ("I want to become a really good actor instead of just a teen-age singer.")

That show business careers and similar occupations are in fact subject to much the same economic circumstances and bureaucratic controls as are other occupations, and that many show folk in fact live model middle-class lives are less important than the carefully nurtured Dionysian images of show business life, the persistent myth that careers are made "overnight," that its durable stars are ageless, and that "expressive" opportunities are offered by the public spotlight. Like other "creative" occupations, show business tends to be tolerant of irregular, spontaneous, unpredictable, exhibitionistic behavior—indeed, these are sometimes built into the very conditions of employment; more, show business expects this kind of behavior, and sometimes rewards it (in publicity, if nothing else—and publicity is seldom nothing else), at least among its stars. The hedonism and public irresponsibility of show business celebrities is disingenuously mythologized as "artistic temperament," suggesting that in those industries in which "creativity" is a basic commodity, perversities of other sorts must also be accepted: great beauty, great talent, great acclaim imply great vices. Thus Ava Gardner (a living Lady Brett) leaves a trail of discarded lovers across the bull rings of Spain; thus Maria Callas sails the Mediterranean in her Greek billionaire's yacht, telling the press at Riviera ports that they are "just friends"; thus Ingrid Bergman illegitimately conceives a child on a volcanic Aegean island to the merely temporary dismay of her fans; thus Lana Turner rears a daughter who becomes the killer of her mother's gangster-lover; thus Eddie leaves Debbie for Liz and Liz leaves Eddie for Richard to a breathless watching world of column readers. Billie Holiday, the greatest jazz singer of the era, wasted from years of addiction to heroin, dies under guard in a hospital; idols of teen-age girls get picked up for homosexuality; Dean Martin nurtures a lucrative public image built on a reputation for alcoholism, and the Frank Sinatra clique spread across the night life of the country their money, their liquor, their arrogance, and their talent to delight the press.

With this newsreel, I intend neither a documentation of the lurid nor a righteous cry of decadence but only a vivid suggestion that, manufactured or not, the image of show business careers exists in a milieu in which Dionysian excess has a long tradition and an honored place—a cautious and implicit honor (given its dependence on the whims of public opinion), but a milieu in which one neither loses face nor gets fired for scandalous behavior, a milieu in which the only bad publicity is no publicity at all. The extremes to which the public behavior of show business celebrities is constrained are, like that of gang delinquents, justified by the "rep" it engenders; the Dionysian comings and goings of middle-aged Frank Sinatra and his middle-aged friends are apparently regarded by the public with the same chuckling benignity reserved for the pranks of teen-agers. There is a normative kinship between the Dionysian motifs of the celebrity world of show biz and the hedonistic, expressive values of youth culture. A substantial part of the material content of youth culture is provided and sustained by the industries of mass entertainment and a large part of the entertainment business depends upon youth for its markets. Notice also that show business careers (and satellite show business careers such as disc jockeying and modeling) are virtually the *only* occupations or occupational images offered to adolescents in the pages of the "teen-age magazines." Like bohemian business, show business offers the image of a career to talented young people with trained incapacities for business or the bureaucratized professions. People with "artistic talent" have, according to legend, no "business sense," and show business careers are often said to require the kind of single-minded dedication that is unable even to imagine another kind of future. Like bohemian business, show business tolerates or rewards a youthful orientation to the world and offers the inducement of "romantic" or "glamorous" careers to those unable or unwilling to "grow up." [22]

Like bohemian business too, show business has an important component of vicarious appeal; there is a sense in which show business is everyman's vicarious business; there are probably thousands of Americans who sit in front of their TV sets quietly confident that they can sing as well, dance as well, tell jokes as well, ride a horse and sling a gun as well as those merely lucky ones on the screen. Show business not only involves the audience in the imaginary worlds it creates, it involves them vicariously in show business itself. This may be one of the reasons for the proverbial interest of Americans in the private lives of celebrities, and why professional, in-group banter and jokes about show business is virtually the only kind of esoteric humor of interest to out-groups. So that in addition to the promise of an actual career, show business, again like bohemia, offers an abundance of vicarious careers to the imperfectly socialized, and is thus, in an oddly perverse sense, functional to the extent that, by mollifying largely unfulfilled yearnings for a freer, more spontaneous that is, more youthful life, it softens the tensions and frustrations engendered by socialization without internalization. Like the Horatio Alger myth, which told us that we too could succeed, the myths of the adult milieu which combine the exciting with the unsavory

---

22 Moss Hart, who should know, writes, "I would hazard a guess . . . that the temperament, the tantrums, and the utter childishness of theater people in general, is neither accidental nor a necessary weapon of their profession. It has nothing to do with so-called 'artistic temperament.' The explanation, I think, is a far simpler one. For the most part they are impaled in childhood like a fly in amber." Moss Hart, *Act One* (New York: Random House, 1959).

tell us that our lives need not be routine and colorless. The Alger myth
succored an age of economic growth preoccupied with objective success;
the youthfulness myth succors an age of psychology preoccupied with subjective "fulfillment."

Working-class occupations. Many of the adolescents whom I have called
"youthful"—the high school rebels, the flouters of adult authority, the
claimers of autonomy for adolescents—are likely to be of working-class
background, especially ethnics, culturally "deprived," without much talent,
who drop out of high school or do poorly in it, and are probably headed
not for the glamorous careers I have mentioned but for the lower reaches
of the manual labor force. Nevertheless, there are good reasons for believing
that many working-class occupations and the subcultural norms associated
with some of them are more supportive of youthful orientations than most
middle-class occupations.

Several otherwise disparate intellectual traditions converge in their characterizations of working-class life in terms akin to my conception of youthfulness. The Marxist tradition, for example, confers upon labor the innocent
dignity of useful work, the tragedy of exploitation and alienation, and the
heroic mission of carrying within it the seeds of a bright and revolutionary
future. Having nothing to lose but their chains, the proletariat can take
dramatic and passionate steps in its own interest. Sabotage, walkouts,
general strikes, the Marxist myth of a militant working class—bold, defiant,
resentful of its oppressors, impatient to bring down the system of authority
which victimizes it—strikingly partakes of much the same spirit and imagery
as rebellious adolescents *vis-à-vis* the world of adults. Both groups claim for
themselves, in the strident tones characteristic of those without a parliamen-
tary voice, autonomy, freedom from their illegitimate subordination to an
authority they never chose, that consigns them to a future they do not want.

There is also a literary tradition more than 150 years old that bestows
upon laborers—especially rural laborers—greater energy, vitality, and
sexuality than the pale, thin, beardless, repressed pencil pushers who inhabit
the offices of the world. In this literary tradition, workers are impulsive,
strong, intuitive, passionate—capable of great anger and great tenderness;
above all, they are, like adolescents, *personal,* largely alienated from and
disgusted with the rationales and rationalizing of the impersonal bureaucratic world.

Paralleling these two romanticisms of working-class life is a third intellectual tradition that emphasizes the common values and long history of
both the highest and the lowest classes of traditional Europe, which the
despised, calculating minds of the *arriviste* middle class could never share:
aristocrats and peasants share a tendency to violence, to alcoholic excesses,
and to blood sports. This kinship between the highest and the lowest may
be rather forced, but the peculiar combination of aristocratic and vulgar
motifs, or élite and egalitarian themes which crystallize around a disdain

for middle-class life has persisted for nearly 200 years.[23] The intellectual core of this tradition is the belief that the powers, privileges, and immunities of aristocratic life, and the passion, desperation, and anarchy of life in the depths are both preferable to the calculated moderation and mediocrity inherent in bourgeois definitions of maturity and responsibility. Each extreme is, in its different way, transcendent; the middle class is forever earthbound. Translating this tradition into my own terms, the lower classes and the upper classes are more youthful than the middle class.

Finally, recent empirical descriptions of working-class culture by sociologists lend considerable support to these romanticized versions of working-class life. These studies show a highly remarkable but generally unremarked upon similarity to standard descriptions of youth culture. Thus workers tend to be hedonistic, unable to plan ahead or defer gratification; they are highly expressive rather than instrumental in their basic orientations, given to violent and extreme views, irrational, anti-intellectual, "person-centered" (rather than "role-centered"), and generally neglectful of their civic responsibilities.[24] Certain working-class occupations, then, especially *lower* ones, are likely to require much less in the way of sacrifice of youthfulness than most other occupations, and it should come as no surprise that recalcitrant youth without academic ability or usable deviant talents should gravitate toward these jobs.

Conclusion

What I have offered here is in a sense a conceptual model for the analysis of adolescent behavior and the youthful adult milieu to which, under certain conditions, it may lead. There are youthful occupations and milieu other than those I have described. I have not, for example, mentioned free lance art or the military or professional sports, nor have I mentioned several niches in the academic and intellectual worlds that support youthful orientations. But I think that by now my major point should be clear: I have tried to suggest that the successful socialization of children into the dominant

---

[23] Especially strongly in the bohemian literary tradition from, say, Diderot to Norman Mailer. One is reminded that "teddy boys" affect the garments of Edwardian gentlemen and the manners of hoodlums. Leslie Fiedler has argued at some length that "highbrow" and "lowbrow" culture have more in common than either has with "middlebrow" culture. See his, "Both Ends Against the Middle," reprinted in Rosenberg and White (eds.) *Mass Culture* (Glencoe, Ill.: The Free Press, 1957).

[24] See, for example, William F. Whyte, *Street Corner Society*, (Chicago, Ill.: University of Chicago Press, 1943); S. M. Miller and Frank Riessman, "The Working Class Subculture," *Social Problems* (Summer 1961); Richard Hoggart, *The Uses of Literacy* (London: Chatto and Windus, 1957); A. K. Cohen and H. M. Hodges, "Characteristics of the Lower-Blue-Collar Class," *Social Problems* (Spring 1963); Herbert J. Gans, (Note 13), and Seymour Martin Lipset, "Working Class Authoritarianism," in *Social Controversy*, W. Petersen and D. Matza, eds. (Belmont, Calif.: Wadsworth Publishing Co., 1963).

value system is always problematic especially in pluralistic societies, that recalcitrance can be spotted early, and that what I have called youth culture begins when adolescent rebellion against dominant adult norms takes on ideological supports from existing deviant traditions. For many adolescents, of course, this is only "a stage they go through," and most of them eventually internalize or at least comply with the norms constrained on them by the major agencies of socialization. At the same time, it is important to recognize that many adolescents do not, that the experience of many in adolescent subcultures shapes their futures by incapacitating them for bureaucratic roles. Most of these, it is true, wind up at the lower end of the occupational hierarchy, especially those who are unable to survive high school. But those who do survive and who are fortunate enough to discover the other face of their trained incapacities—in college or elsewhere—are uniquely enabled to take advantage of the few sheltered places a pluralistic society offers in its occupational structure which will permit them, as adults, to sustain that normative variation without which pluralism is emptied of its cultural meaning. This leaves a society highly differentiated on the level of social structure but homogeneous on the level of culture.

With this analysis, I am not offering only a more differentiated view of socialization—substituting a frame of reference emphasizing conformity to milieu rather than to general cultural norms. I mean also to emphasize that groups differ in the extent to which they tolerate or encourage normative dissension, and the extent to which this is true is directly relevant to the *roles* that inveterate dissenters can find in the social structure. In groups which require a high degree of uniformity, dissenters are constrained to yield or to withdraw from active participation; but in groups that place a high value on innovation—and many youthful groups are prominent among these— dissenters are much more likely to be able to retain the privileges of active association.[25]

This analysis also bears upon the problem of adaptation to failure, and casts a little light on the ingenious way in which society provides for the comfort of its failures while using its own failure to socialize some of its members as a way of easing the tensions engendered by its excessive success with others: those who are relegated to the bottom of the occupational heap, for example, are heir to a ready-made ideology, a myth that invidiously contrasts their own vigor, vitality, and authentic humanity with the repressions, the desk-boundless, and the futile status-seeking of the successful. Society uses the luckier ones too—those who are able to find loftier, more glamorous, youthful adult niches. These feed the vicarious appetites of the nation, and are living testimony to the bored, the alienated from work, and the otherwise vaguely dissatisfied that exciting careers *do* exist. And the definition of these careers as newsworthy by the mass media peculiarly fits them for the strategic role they play in the vicarious lives of others.

[25] For empirical data on this point, see Yrjo Littunen, "Deviance and Passivity in Radio Listener Groups," *Acta Sociologia* (Vol. 4).

From Generation to Generation: Youth Groups in Modern Societies

S. N. Eisenstadt

Modern Societies

In the following pages we shall give brief descriptions of various types of youth groups, organizations and movements existing within various sectors of modern societies. We shall, first, describe, very briefly, some types of more informal youth groups—types that are very well known in the relevant literature. We shall then proceed to describe, in somewhat greater detail, some examples of the more organized youth movements.

INFORMAL YOUTH GROUPS IN VARIOUS SECTORS OF MODERN SOCIETIES

The informal or semiformal youth group is very widespread in most sectors of modern societies, and is to be found in all European countries, in the U.S., etc.[1] Despite many local differences some general types can be discerned. Such groups are usually formed within a given neighborhood, or near a school or a place of work. They consist of boys (and sometimes girls), of a given age group. There usually is a difference between pre-adolescent and adolescent groups. The former may be more heterosexual, while the latter are mostly composed only of members of one sex, although they may engage, as a group, in various activities with a parallel group of the other sex.[2] These groups may develop a strong, although informal, organization of their own, with various "secret rites," with special officers, etc. Such a development is most conspicuous in various fraternities and sororities; but it exists also, even if in an embryonic form, in other groups of such kind.[3] Such youth groups may, in some instances, be affiliated with a certain formal organization—either a school or some youth organization or movement: Scouts, a youth organization of a political party or religious organization, a sports organization, etc. In that case the various small local or neighborhood groups are interwoven into a wider framework. In that case they evince some of the organizational characteristics of the more organized youth movements to be described later. But even in these cases the small youth group has a very strong autonomy and solidarity of its own and does not always fully accept the directives of officials of the central organization. This is especially evident in the strong adherence to its in-

Reprinted by permission of the publisher, from S. N. Eisenstadt *From Generation to Generation* (New York: The Macmillan Company, The Free Press of Glencoe, 1956), pp. 92–114.

formal leadership as opposed to the "official" leadership set up from above. But the latter do play, nevertheless, an important role in the life of the group—even if not always fully accepted. The extent of organization, and especially the values of these groups vary greatly according to the class and ethnic composition of the group. It is interesting to note that most of such informal groups are usually homogeneous from the point of view of class and ethnic affiliations.[4]

Thus, for instance, in one of the studies dealing with middle-class youth-groups the following were found to be its most important values:

> The principal values of the adolescent peer culture were social participation, group loyalty, and individual achievement and responsibility. As a means of social participation, such social skills as dancing are desirable, as well as a supply of spending money and good clothes. Group loyalty took the form principally of loyalty to the high school and its activities, but church youth groups and the informal cliques of the adolescent social world also commanded loyalty. Individual achievement and responsibility meant, for most young people, doing well in school, getting a part-time job, and being a responsible member of several clubs or other organizations.
>
> The high school was the principal locus of the adolescent peer culture. School dances, athletic contests, hay rides, and club activities, as well as study halls and classrooms, are the places where boys and girls learn how to behave socially and morally as young men and women.
>
> Thus the two most powerful groups in the school, the teachers and the leading clique among the adolescents, worked pretty much together in setting standards. Most of the students followed their lead. Only in the sphere of relations between boys and girls was there any considerable conflict between teachers and parents, on the one hand, and adolescents, on the other hand. . . .
>
> To achieve success in the adolescent peer culture, a boy or girl must stay in school, be a reasonably good student, take part in school activities, and go to the school dances and parties. In the process of adjusting successfully in these ways, he would be learning middle-class morality. The majority of young people attempted to fit themselves into this situation.[5]

While the organizational framework of the group and the values of various upper- and middle-class youth may differ from place to place, and from country to country, yet their main values and orientations seem similar. In some places there may be a greater emphasis on "sports" and "games," and a very strongly organized hierarchical self-government of the boys (like in the English public schools)—while in others there may be a stronger emphasis on various collective values and political, religious and community-oriented activity may be found.

Despite the close relation between the values of the youth group and youth culture and those of the strata to which they belong, there usually exists also a very strong difference in emphasis between the two. Although

the extent of the difference may vary greatly from place to place, to some
extent it exists everywhere. It is perhaps most pronounced in certain groups
of American youth, among whom a distinctive youth culture has developed
which has been analyzed in the following way by T. Parsons:

> By contrast with the emphasis on responsibility in the adult role the
> orientation of the youth culture is more or less specifically irresponsible.
> One of its dominant notes is "having a good time" in relation to which
> there is a particularly strong emphasis on social activities in company
> with the opposite sex. A second predominant characteristic on the
> male side lies in the prominence of athletics, which is an avenue of
> achievement and competition which stands in sharp contrast to the
> primary standards of adult achievement in professional and executive
> capacities. Negatively, there is a strong tendency to repudiate interest
> in adult things and to feel at least a certain recalcitrance to the pres-
> sure of adult expectations and discipline. In addition to, but including,
> athletic prowess the typical pattern of the male youth culture seems to
> lay emphasis on the value of certain qualities of attractiveness, es-
> pecially in relation to the opposite sex. It is very definitely a rounded
> humanistic pattern rather than one of competence in the performance
> of specified functions. Such stereotypes as the "swell guy" are significant
> of this. On the feminine side there is correspondingly a strong ten-
> dency to accentuate sexual attractiveness in terms of various versions
> of what may be called the "glamor girl" pattern. Although these pat-
> terns defining roles tend to polarize sexually—for instance, as between
> star athlete and socially popular girl—yet on a certain level they are
> complementary, both emphasizing certain features of a total personality
> in terms of the direct expression of certain values rather than of instru-
> mental significance.[6]

While such a strong difference in emphasis may be perhaps found only in
very specific groups, the general emphasis on diffuse and solidary relations,
on ascribed mutual acceptance of the members, and a concomitant somewhat ambivalent attitude towards the adult world can be found in most
such youth groups. In some cases which will yet be analyzed in greater
detail, this ambivalent attitude may express itself in an intensification of
political activity.

The pattern of youth groups among skilled workers, etc., differs mainly
from the former in the following points:

The life span which these groups cover is usually somewhat shorter (as
the marrying age is lower), there is a stronger emphasis on the instrumental
aspects of school life (e.g., vocational education), a smaller extent of organization in cliques, clubs, etc., a smaller emphasis on athletics and organized
sports (although there exists a very strong evaluation of physical prowess
and skill), and a relatively weaker attachment to youth organizations and
movements, to political organizations, etc.—unless these are specific working
youth movements. We do also find among them a greater emphasis on
attendance at movies, some drinking parties, etc.—and a relatively high

evaluation of various leisure-time activities which render direct expressive satisfactions.[7]

The picture of youth groups within lower sectors of society, which tend, especially in the U.S., to coincide with specific ethnic groups, is somewhat different.[8] The main differences may perhaps be summarized, very generally, in the following way. Lower-class boys and girls, especially among children of unskilled workers, spend a much greater part of their time outside of the home than do middle-class adolescents. The activities of the group encompass many more aspects and spheres of life, and home is more of a hotel-and-eating-place. These groups are usually affiliated to a lesser degree with either adult-sponsored organizations (Boy Scouts, clubs, etc.) or established institutional fields of activities (such as the school, etc.); and are much more separated from the sphere of official organization. On the other hand, paradoxically enough, the tension between adults and children of the lower classes is smaller—or at least of a different kind—than that evinced in the middle-class youth groups and youth culture. While there exist many concrete tensions between parents and children, even giving rise to running away from home, etc., these tensions do not necessarily involve an ambivalent attitude towards the whole cultural world of the parents as adults, and does not necessarily define the life of youth and adolescents as entirely different from those of the adults. In many ways the pattern of behavior prevalent in these groups—emphasis on drinking, some gambling, various types of unorganized recreation, unplanned spending of money, earlier sexual experience and sometimes perhaps some extent of promiscuity, great extent of aggressiveness, etc.—is to some extent a continuation of the pattern of adult life within these sectors; or at least there is a stronger emphasis on some of the patterns of behavior accepted in the adult group, and not a distinctive opposition to it.

Another very important and prevalent type of youth group, in America and in many other countries, is the group of juvenile delinquents, the "gang." [9] Since it has been described so often there is no need to give any details here, and some general characteristics will suffice at this point. The "gang" may originate either within the framework of ambivalent "youth cultures," or within some of the lower-class groups. Its main characteristics are the following:

The activities of its members are usually directed towards the open violation of the mores and norms of the society in which they live—stealing, pilfering, various types of aggressive behavior, whether group or individual —acts which may be directed towards adults as persons or towards social and cultural norms and symbols. We may distinguish several types of such groups, especially from the point of view of their relations with the adult world:[10]

a. Those groups which are more or less connected with deviant adult organized groups—crime syndicates, etc.—and who are highly organized, possess a strong internal status symbol hierarchy and status differentiation patterned after that of the adult criminal sector.

b. Those who are more in touch with the law-abiding adult world, and live, as it were, in a state of constant tension and dual norms. Within these groups membership fluctuates considerably between the delinquent and nondelinquent spheres, and the degrees of internal organization and structure.

c. Those groups of delinquents who are out of touch with any section of the adult world and outside adult control, and which, consequently, evince the maximum degree of internal aggression and other deviant traits.

A sociologically important characteristic of these groups is that their deviancy is oriented more towards the normative means of the societies than to their ends, which they seek to attain by uninstitutional means. This tendency is usually coupled with a strong ideological emphasis on the distinct characteristics of the youth and the "strong man" which differentiate him from the established, conforming values of the adult world. It seems that in this ideological emphasis these groups are in some respects more akin to the middle-class "youth culture" than to some parts of the working- or lower-class youth group. The same may be said, in broad lines, of their internal structure; these groups —as do the middle-class "youth culture" groups—usually evolve a status system of their own, which allocates prestige according to their own specific goals and value emphasis. . . .

ISRAEL'S VOLUNTARY YOUTH MOVEMENTS [11]

A large part of the adolescent population in Israel participates in special youth organizations and youth movements. These groups begin to recruit children at a relatively early age—nine to ten years—but their activities reach their peak in the adolescent period. It has been estimated that about 30 per cent of the adolescents in the country are organized into these movements; but the number of those who have passed through them is much greater, and they touch, in one way or another, upon the social life of almost every boy and girl. Three main types may be discerned: (a) The pioneering type, which emphasizes Zionist and social ideals and whose manifest aim is to make its members into members of agricultural communal and co-operative settlements; (b) the "working youth" movement, whose main aim is the educational and occupational advancement of its members; and (c) a chiefly recreational type with strong emphasis on sport and leisure-time activities. There are, altogether, about nine to ten movements. Enrollment in them is voluntary, being effected through canvassing, informal social influences (whole groups of friends joining the same movement, etc.), membership shifting with a strong persistent nucleus.

The most distinctive type of all is the "pioneering" type, which is historically connected with Zionist youth movements in the Diaspora.

All of the pioneering movements have central organizations, affiliated either with political parties or in a more general way with the General Federation of Labor. The central staff, which is composed of young adults, comprises members of agricultural settlements who either volunteer for or are assigned this duty, and a more urban nucleus. Both groups are paid some salary or emolument. Sometimes the chief instructors live in a "commune" in town as a sort of preparation for settlement work, and at the same time perform their duties as instructors (*madrichim*). This, however, holds true mainly of the central and older instructors, while instructors of young groups are themselves usually members of older groups and are still in school.

The members of the movement are organized into small, local groups composed of twenty–thirty members, several of these groups into a "regiment," and these finally into a "stratum," according to age groups. Each small group has its own organization—an instructor, secretary, treasurer, etc.—and the same applies at the higher level, though with a much greater degree of formal organization.

The final age group of organization is the *garin hachshara* (training nucleus), the small group (usually composed of school-age adolescents) which actively prepares itself for life in the settlement. The membership of these groups is, however, very small in proportion to the total membership of any of the movements, as only a few members are actually prepared to go out and be "pioneers," a great majority of them dropping out on the way.

The main activities of the members are: (1) social and sport (excursions); (2) cultural; and (3) inculcation of the pioneering and social ideology of their specific movement. They also perform some more general functions, such as fund-collecting for the National Funds, etc., and, in the days of the Mandate, paramilitary and political functions such as helping the *Haganah* (Defense Army), etc. While most of their time is actually spent in social and cultural activities, dancing, etc., they emphasize strongly their negative attitude towards mere "recreation," and particularly that of the "salon" type. Thus they put greater emphasis on folk dances, unsophisticated relations between the sexes, etc., and have a definite ascetic aversion to smoking, gambling, fancy dress, etc. (Khaki shorts are a typical part of their dress.) Their entire ideology emphasizes that they, as youth, have more opportunities—and the consequent duty—to realize the basic pioneering values, etc., than the adults, who have already been contaminated by their worldly pursuits (all these emphases differ, of course, among the various movements). Within the more recreational types of youth movements and within the "border type," the Scouts, the development of individual character, of manly and civic virtues, is particularly emphasized. Within the more pioneering types these values are inseparably interwoven with more social goals: serving the country, realizing the distinctive common goals of the Zionist movement and its various parts (especially pioneering values), and the belief that youth is more apt to realize these values than adults. Because of this they are not usually over-enthusiastic about direct leadership by adults. Even when thoroughly loyal to the political cause of a given party, they regard the adult leadership distantly, without attempting effective, primary communication towards the rank and file of the youth. They are led mainly by slightly older coevals of their organization. The success of a given group, stratum, etc., is to a very large extent dependent on the existence of a gifted leader-instructor who can directly and personally appeal to the youth. Official status is not enough; "personality" is what counts most, with a strong leaning towards a charismatic type. Such a leader should "practice what he preaches," and it should be known that he intends to go out pioneering. Otherwise half his attraction is lost, whatever his official status within the overall organization.

This fact constitutes one of the main difficulties and permanent critical points of the movements. As the members advance in age, more and more feel disinclined to become pioneers, while at the same time they still perform various tasks in the movement and are socially strongly attached thereto. There are never enough pioneer-instructors to lead in pioneering, and after the peak of activity in middle adolescence the enthusiasm for the instructor fades a bit, as they approach maturity and enter upon the threshold of adult life and occupational achievement.

While membership in youth movements usually ceases in the first stages of adulthood—except for a small band of officials, etc.—the comradeship established in them is of longer standing, continuing into adult life and sometimes forming the basis for adult cliques in various spheres of life.

Within the organization there is strong emphasis on common rituals, and particularly on those of passage from one stratum to another, from one age grade to another. But the strongest cohesion is usually that of the smaller group or at the most of the entire "regiment," the country-wide groups meeting only on special occasions, excursions, festivities, etc.

THE FREE GERMAN YOUTH MOVEMENT [12]

Among the various types of age and youth groups of modern society, the German youth movements have occupied a prominent and special place, serving in a way as a prototype of rebellious youth, of a specifically juvenile social movement. It is difficult to give a clear, brief picture of these movements, because they varied in detail and changed greatly in the course of their development. We shall, then, give here a mere outline of some of the most important features of the movements in a very cursory way.

The first German youth movement, which later developed into the *Wandervogel*, began at the end of the nineteenth century in one of the new industrial centers of Prussia-Steglitz. It started as a camp of school youths, led by a young leader, who sought to free themselves from the "suffocating" atmosphere of the bureaucratic formal school structure and of the home. At first its activities were concentrated mainly on going on excursions in the country, behaving generally in a way contrary to the prevailing mores of bourgeois life, such as going on these excursions on Sunday mornings, wearing light, sports clothes, spending the whole day in the country among "haystacks," singing folk songs, and generally disengaging themselves from the atmosphere of home and school life. Soon many such groups were formed in different parts of Prussia and Germany, showing that there existed some general tension and some preconditions for their emergence. At first their numbers were not large, and a contact based to a very large extent on the personality of their leader and his driving force was established between the various groups. At first the movement did not have any aims which could specifically define the scope of its activities. There were no definite activities, but all the activities of the members were directed towards the achievement of a new way of life, the development of a new type of person who could shake off all the trimmings of contemporary society, emphasizing only the inner nature of man, his innermost self. Although these attitudes were mainly individualistic, preparing, as it were, an individualistic escape within a small circle of friends, they slowly acquired a more community-oriented, nationalistic meaning and emphasis. The escape to nature, the emphasis on asceticism (abstention from drinking, smoking, etc.), the "roaming about" (hence the famous name of "Roamers," the "Wandervogel") slowly acquired a folkist, nationalistic meaning and became a yearning for the establishment of a true national community (*Gemeinschaft*), in place of the artificial one existing at that time. The entire ideology—or ideologies—of the movement were greatly influenced by the romantic movement, and the similarities between the two are obvious. The whole attitude of the movement towards the established social order was very ambivalent: On the one hand, an attempt to separate its members from society and a negative attitude towards its values and norms; on the other, an attempt to recreate society and a utopian emphasis on common values and spirit. "It (the youth movement) was purely secular but was colored by religious or mystic enthusiasm. . . . It sought to create true and free individuals but at the same time was agitated by a longing for a new and true country, a *Gemeinschaft*, which should be both a symbol of the rebirth of the nation and the only place where such freedom could be made universal. It fought against all established authority but it longed for a new authority, for a real *Fuehrer* instead of established bureaucratic leadership." [13] The revolt against authority—parents, teachers, officials—gradually gave rise to an ideology in which youth was set apart as a separate distinct type of human being, the only type within which this full realization of humanity can be achieved. Through various stages it developed into an ideology of "youth culture" (*"Jugendkultur"* [14]), as a distinct type of social and cultural life. The first full declaration of youth's distinctiveness and its right to shape its own destiny was made at the Hohe Meissner rally in

1913, where it was declared that: "Free German Youth, on their own initiative, under their own responsibility, and with deep sincerity, are determined independently to shape their own lives. For the sake of this inner freedom they will under any and all circumstances take united action." [15]

Despite some common basic characteristics, the German youth movement never acquired nationwide comprehensive unity of organization. Developing slowly from small bands of "roamers" into a wider movement, it was riven by various schisms and quarrels which undermined its unity. These rifts were caused mainly by dissension from the charismatic qualities of its first leadership, the rise of new leaders, and constant quarrels among them. Numerous attempts to unify the different parts of the movement were never totally successful and internal dissension continued throughout the history of the movement. Behind these quarrels were hidden, however, some crucial issues which faced the movement. The first was involved in the movement's attitude towards its contemporary social order. The early sectarianism involved a complete separation from society—a separation which became more difficult with the advancing age of the members. At the same time the religious zeal of the movement necessarily involved a "missionary" trend—a wish to instill the spirit of the movement into all spheres of life; into the fields of politics, social movements and education. This dilemma between withdrawal and alienation aiming at the domination and transformation of social life became particularly acute with the passage of time, as many institutions sponsored by the youth movements—youth hostels, etc.— were adopted by various youth welfare organizations, schools, etc. From the political point of view the problem became more acute after World War I and the Revolution. The second main issue which faced the movement was caused by the growing up of members and by the relative bureaucratization of the movement, which necessarily meant a loss of the primary élan and charismatic identification with a leader and within the group.

Dissension within the movement developed to an even larger extent after World War I, as political activity and interest in politics increased, and political parties began to encroach more and more on the sphere of youth movements. The internal tension and ambivalence of the youth movements' ideology and attitudes was not resolved, becoming accentuated by postwar disillusionment, until the movements were abolished, and, in a way, absorbed by the Nazi youth movement.

THE KIBBUTZ [16]

We shall now describe the patterns of group-life existing among the children in a Kibbutz. As we have already indicated, they live most of their life apart from the adults. They sleep and eat and study in houses of their own. Their life is organized in definite groups which are usually constituted on the basis of *age differences* instead of "ages," because the absolute age level may not be fixed and varies according to circumstances to the number

of children of a given age now living in a Kibbutz, etc. The relative difference of ages (younger—older) is, however, almost always maintained.
Each group leads its own life in school and at home and has its own autonomous arrangements and institutions. Usually it has its own living rooms,
dining room and services, its own instructors and sometimes even teachers.
(In one Kibbutz, for instance, the distribution of age groups has been as
follows: five groups, corresponding to the school grades, each comprising
children with two years' difference in age, from six-and-one-half up to
sixteen-and-one-half.) The basic principles and framework of the children's
work, studies and life are set up by the General Assembly on the recommendation of the educational committee, to be implemented by the teachers, instructors, etc. The working out of these principles and their application to
daily routine and problems are left to them and to the "autonomous" institutions of the age group. The life of the age group as an entity is centered
around three poles: (a) School—education, comprising most of the usual
subjects with strong emphasis on agricultural and technical education and
on the ideological basis of the pioneering Zionist movement. Here they are
taught by teachers who quite often divide their time between different age
groups, according to their special professional qualifications. In the younger
age groups, however, it is usually so arranged that one *main* teacher is
assigned to a class, with only a small degree of outside help for some special
subjects. (b) Work—usually every group (or two groups together) has some
small plot of land allotted to it for cultivation, and the elder groups also
usually participate, to different degrees, in the work of the various economic
branches of the settlement. In these matters every age group has its own
committee, which arranges the division of labor, the allotment of different
tasks to different children, etc. This committee is usually guided by the
group's own instructor (*madrich*), who also acts as an intermediary with
the heads of the different economic branches of the settlement. On its own
plot of land the group is usually advised by its instructor and by the various
experts or teachers of different agricultural subjects. (c) The social and
cultural life of the group—the most important of them are: library and
newspaper distribution, editing of own newspaper, arrangement of games
and festivals (it is very important and interesting to note that on almost
all festive occasions—Sabbath, the various holidays, etc.—the children
do not participate in the general festival but arrange special festivals
for themselves, in which the adults participate at most as spectators,
the only notable exception being the Passover "Seder," the culminating
feast of the year, in which children and adults participate together), various
discussions, disposition of their communal property and various scouting
activities. (These usually form part of the youth movement to which all the
children officially belong.) All these activities are organized by the children
themselves, guided and advised by their instructors (sometimes children of
older age groups). Almost every activity is organized and supervised by an

elected committee of the children, and the number of committees is usually
large so as to enable the greatest number of children to participate. (In some
Kibbutzim the number of committee members among the children comprises
more than half of the total number of children.) Parallel to life in the adult
section, the supreme authority here is the assembly of all of the children.
Assembly meetings are very frequent. Almost all members take part in all
of the activities carried on by the age group. The whole group is quite often
summoned by the instructors to discuss various problems arising out of their
common life. This is utilized as a very important educational means, especially for the inculcating of the various ideological foundations and practical norms of Kibbutz life. The main pedagogical means is the open
explanation and discussion, skillfully guided by the instructor or teacher. In
this way the acceptance of various behavioral norms is based on active
group participation, and carries with it the whole weight of group approval.
It is thus quite natural that one of the most important occasions for a meeting of the whole group and a full discussion is the unruly and undisciplined
behavior of one of its members, a quarrel with a teacher or an instructor.
Such quarrels may give rise to various tensions, especially as the children
are wont to complain of unjustified disciplinary measures, scolding, or harsh
words from the teachers, etc. If such a matter cannot be settled by one of the
older children, more influential committee members, etc., or the instructor,
then a general meeting of the whole group is called and both parties lay
their case before it and a full-fledged discussion arises. This discussion,
however, is guided by the teacher or instructor so as to lead at least to the
full explanation of the behavior of both parties and to the resumption of the
approved group behavior. Quite often the adult member involved in the case
may be censured for deviating from the proper and ascribed modes of behavior. Whatever the exact outcome of such a discussion may be, it is always
intended to serve as an occasion for catharsis on the one hand, and as a
guide to the inculcation of group norms on the other.

A very important feature of the children's life is the transition from one
age group to another. It does not, however, involve a change of personnel,
as it is the whole group that changes its status. The identity of the group
is usually preserved throughout the children's life span (as children).

Almost every group has its own name (usually a name of an animal, plant
or tree; sometimes a name designating an activity, such as fishing, singing,
etc.). This name does *not* change while the group passes from one grade to
another, and so the group's preservation of its identity receives a definite
symbolic expression. The exact age grades may differ from Kibbutz to Kibbutz, but the main outlines exist in almost all Kibbutzim; they comprise
about four or five age grades, varying according to school-age, scouting
performances, relative age, etc. The transition of a group from one grade
to another is quite often a festive occasion, organized in a rather ceremonial
fashion, in which all other age groups and the adults participate as on-

lookers. The transition from one age group to another, which is in many places linked together with transition from one school grade to another—although usually almost automatic—is dependent on various performances and achievements of the group, either in the school, in work or in scouting activities. Almost all the activities of the group during the preceding months are directed towards the successful performance of these activities. Thus the transition ceremony comes as a culminating point of a long period of rather hectic activity. The most important of the ceremonies is the graduating ceremony, when the children acquire the status of pre-adults (candidates for full membership in the Kibbutz), or immediately to full adult status. (There exists no fixed and ascribed norm in all the settlements in regard to this matter. Some insist on a transitory period of "candidacy," while others do not.) The degree and intensity of ceremony on these occasions varies in different Kibbutzim. Some of them have different graduation ceremonies and ceremonies for acceptance as full members, and some do not. In other words, in some places the young men and women are accepted as a *group* of new members, while in others this acceptance bears a more individual character. The element of ceremony and festivity exists, however, in almost all settlements.

There is one more aspect of the age group that should be emphasized, and that is that boys and girls participate equally in the same groups. There are no separate groups for the sexes. They also live in the same buildings, although usually in separate rooms. This characteristic also stems from the ideological bases of the pioneering movement, but its full understanding can be achieved only through the analysis of its place in the social structure.

THE KOMSOMOL [17]

The Komsomol is the overall official children's and youth organization of the U.S.S.R., organized by the Government and the Communist Party.

The process of official, semi-political training starts in the kindergarten, where play, singing and story-telling are used for the inculcation of patriotic feeling. The child is first enrolled in the "Little Octobrists," where his education in civic responsibilities begins. At the age of nine, he becomes eligible for membership in the "Young Pioneers," where his political education begins to assume more significant proportions. Membership in the Young Pioneers is virtually universal in the eligible age group (nine to fifteen). The drive to affiliate is so great in the early, impressionable years that the threat of exclusion is frequently a sufficient sanction to discipline the most unruly. Entrance into the Pioneers is the occasion for an impressive initiation ceremony replete with symbolism.

Once enrolled in the Pioneers, the new member becomes part of a "link" of eight to twelve youngsters who elect their own leader. The "links" are united in a "brigade" with approximately forty members in the same or adjoining classes. Each brigade chooses its "council" of five to represent it and functions under a Komsomol leader who is designated to supervise and direct brigade activities. These activities vary with the age level of the Pioneers. In the younger classes, political indoctrination at meetings largely takes the form of tales of the childhood of Lenin or Stalin or stories of heroism on the part of young Pioneers in the war against the Nazis. With older children, political instruction becomes more pointed.

Political instruction in the narrow sense, however, is only one part of the Pioneer program. There are also a variety of organized activities such as excursions for nature study, to museums and points of historical interest, athletic competitions, literary, dramatic and musical evenings, and opportunities to pursue hobbies at school or at the so-called Houses of Pioneers, which are set aside as centers of Pioneer extra-curricular programs. There is the requirement to engage in socially useful work, which may embrace such diverse activities as helping to edit a wall newspaper for Pioneers, gathering scrap, working in the school garden or on a neighboring Kolkhoz, or even helping combat "religious prejudices" in the home. The tendency of these extra-curricular activities to compete with and even interfere with school programs has led to periodic protests by Soviet school authorities against overburdening the child with outside activities. The present tendency is to integrate Pioneer activities as closely as possible with the school, to emphasize classroom obligations as the first responsibility of the Pioneer, and to arrange the Pioneer program so that it supports, rather than comes into conflict with, the school curriculum.

At the age of fourteen the child becomes eligible for membership in the Komsomols, provided, of course, that he can fulfill the conditions for admission. These conditions include recommendation by one member of the Communist Party or two Komsomols who have themselves been members of the organization for at least one year. Recommendation by the council of a Pioneer brigade counts as the equivalent of one recommendation by a Komsomol member.

Enrollment in the Komsomols is thus a much more selective process than membership in the Pioneers. Whereas the Pioneers operate as a virtually universal organization for all children in the eligible age group, not more than half of the students in the upper three classes of the ten-year school ordinarily join the Komsomols, and only about a quarter of those in the eligible age group (fourteen to twenty-six) become Komsomol members. The Komsomol is the reservoir from which Party members will be recruited; and in the eyes of the Party leadership at least, this is the period of tutelage when qualifications and political ardor can be tested.

The organization of the Komsomols is closely modeled on the hierarchical pattern of the big brother, the Party. At the bottom of the pyramid are the primary organizations in factories, collective farms, state farms, educational and other state institutions. Each primary organization must have at least three members and is established with the consent of the district or town committee which supervises it. Where the primary organization consists of more than a hundred members, it may be broken down into subgroups in shops of a factory, different faculties of a university, etc. Where the group has less than ten members, a secretary is selected to provide leadership. In large groups a committee or bureau as well as a secretary serves as the directing nucleus. Both perform their Komsomol duties in addition to their regular employment. Full-time Komsomol secretaries are ordinarily assigned by the central apparatus only to important enterprises or institutions where there is a substantial membership and a program of work requiring the exclusive attention of a Komsomol functionary. In most cases the primary Komsomol organizations operate under the control of the district or town Komsomol committees and their secretaries; but in the armed forces and in institutions where special political sections have been established, the line of responsibility leads directly to the head of the political section, or his assistant in charge of Komsomol activity.

At the district or town level, supervisory power is concentrated in a committee which in turn elects a bureau and a number of secretaries. The next higher levels in the Komsomol hierarchy are the regional and republic organizations. Here the basic pattern of organizations is essentially the same as below. At this level secretaries are required to be Party members with at least three years' experience in the Komsomol. Operating under them are substantial staffs of full-time Komsomol functionaries with specific responsibilities running the gamut of the organization's activities.

The central administrative organization of the Komsomol consisted in 1949 of a Central Committee of 103 members and forty-seven candidates, a control commission of thirty-one members, a bureau of eleven members, five secretaries, and a large secretariat, all of whom operate under the general direction of the First Secretary. Theoretically, the highest organ in the Komsomol is the All-Union Congress, which, according to the Rules, is required to meet at least once every three years. Until the Tenth Congress in 1936, meetings were held with reasonable regularity.

While the responsibilities of the Komsomol organization embrace a wide range of diversified activities, the emphasis, in contrast to the Pioneers, is much more heavily on politics. These activities include:

1. Political instruction of Komsomol members;

2. Political instruction and leadership supplied by the Komsomols to the Pioneers, to non-affiliated youth, and to other groups;

3. Military and para-military training and physical culture and sports;

4. Leadership and assistance in carrying out governmental and Party programs;

5. Social and cultural activity.

The political indoctrination of all Komsomol members is a central concern of the Party. As has already been observed, it begins seriously with the Pioneers and increases in scope and intensity as children grow older.

The various age groups existing in modern societies have some basic characteristics in common:

I.

Age is here a criterion of group membership, although it is not very strictly defined or adhered to. Youth groups extend usually through adolescence and very early adulthood only and membership in them is not universal, nor equally distributed in all sectors of the society.

II.

Within all modern youth groups, the small primary groups forms the basic nucleus of the organization—a nucleus which may or may not be incorporated in wider formal organizations.

III.

All modern youth groups perform mostly preparatory tasks and concentrate on recreational and cultural activities of their members. They regulate only the internal relations of their members and their behavior, but not their overall behavior nor that of other members of the society.

In addition to these common characteristics, each of the types presented evinces some characteristics of its own. The most important of these are:

THE INFORMAL AND SEMI-FORMAL YOUTH
GROUPS AND YOUTH CULTURE:

1. Small extent of institutionalization, although most of their activities are legitimate. (This does not, of course, hold true with reference to the juvenile delinquents group.)

2. No unified organization, although similar development in many parts of the country. A formal, unified hierarchy may exist in the case of youth organizations and movements. Groups based mostly on membership usually homogeneous from the point of view of class and ethnic group affiliation.

3. Corporate organization into small groups and cliques with various organization and informal status systems of their own. Differing extents of cohesion and stability.

4. Large extent of autonomy, tempered by some very general adult supervision.

5. Most activities centered on recreation, heterosexual relations (in the

later stages of adolescence) and general emulation of certain aspects of adult culture.

6. Ambivalent attitude towards adult culture, strong emphasis on overall, diffuse humane characteristics in opposition to more specific achievements, and on physical prowess, early maturity. Despite this there exists, in most cases, ultimate acceptance of adult values (with the exception, of course, of the gangs, etc.).

THE GERMAN YOUTH MOVEMENT:

1. Lack of institutionalization and a strong element of deviancy, rebellion against established social order.

2. Corporate groups, but without unitary organization; parallel developments in different parts of the country.

3. Close relations between various groups, but no full unification; continual rifts and schisms.

4. Organization into close, sectarian groups with high degree of internal solidarity and identification, strong identification with a charismatic leader. Complete autonomy; group led by the leader, with a strong element of homosexual identification.

5. Manifold activities—mainly recreation, cultural and educational.

6. Completely negative attitude towards existing patterns of authority, and a specific romantic youth ideology which sets youth up as a different—and the only complete—free human being.

7. Despite these attitudes, a strong yearning towards an authoritative charismatic leadership, national folk community and strong community orientation.

8. Movement originated among adolescents but slowly developed into a more adult group, thus facing its perpetual crisis because of its adherence to and emphasis on "youth ideology."

In comparison with these characteristics we find among the

ISRAEL YOUTH MOVEMENTS:

1. Institutionalization and legitimacy.

2. Country-wide organization, but with smaller groups constituting the main foci of social life and solidarity.

3. Organizational hierarchy and collective passage of group from one grade to another.

4. General principles and programs of activities drawn up by the (mostly adult) leaders of the various movements, which are affiliated with political parties, social movements, etc. Despite this, great extent of social autonomy of the smaller groups.

5. Relation between adult leaders and rank and file constitutes one of the main points of tension in the movements.

6. Values of the movements do not constitute a negation of those of adult society, but rather an emphasis of them.

7. The movements develop a general ideology of youth as the potentially better realizers of the basic values of the society.

The Komsomols and the Kibbutz youth groups show these different characteristics:

1. Overall, unified, country- (or community-) wide organization.

2. Organizational hierarchy and collective passage of groups from one grade to another, directed by the adult society, with different degrees of internal social autonomy (greater in the Kibbutz).

3. Identity of values with those of the adult society, age group life constituting mainly preparation for full membership in adult society.

4. Particularly strong emphasis on the collective, common values of the society.

The foregoing descriptions have given an overall picture of the main types of age groups and of some of their basic differences. While all of them have some basic common characteristics—the age criterion, the basic nucleus of a primary group, some general attitudes to the social structure in which they are formed, etc.—yet there are many outstanding differences between them. We have seen that they differ in the extent of the explicitness of the age criterion, in the extent to which they are universal in any given society, in the age spans they cover. They differ in their internal structure, in the extent of existence of a unitary hierarchy of age groups, of corporate organizations; in their relations to other age groups and generations and in the extent of their autonomy and autocephaly. They differ in the type of tasks which are allocated to them, in the extent to which they regulate the behavior of their own members and of other members of the society and in the extent to which they are conformists to the main values of society, or deviate from them.

References

1. The descriptive material is abundant. See for instance: R. Landis, *Adolescence and Youth*, New York, 1947; K. Davies, *Modern American Society* (*Readings in the Problems of Order and Change*), 1948, pp. 627–667; H. Bell, *Youth Tell Their Story*, Washington, 1938; N. McWill and E. Matthews, *The Youth of New York City*, New York, 1940.

    The best systematic descriptions are those of: A. B. Hollingshead, *Elmtown's Youth*, New York, 1949; R. L. Havighurst and H. Taba, *Adolescent Character and Personality*, New York, 1949; K. Davis, "Adolescence and the Social Structure," *op. cit.*

2. See *op. cit.* and W. F. Whyte, *Street Corner Society*, Chicago, 1943.

3. See J. Bossard, *Parent and Child*, New York, 1953, and B. Bettelheim, *Symbolic Wounds*, *op. cit.*, especially pp. 98–100.

4. See Hollingshead, *op. cit.*; Havighurst, *op. cit.*; W. F. Whyte, *op. cit.*

5. Adapted from R. Y. Havighurst and H. Taba, *op. cit,* pp. 35–41.

6. T. Parsons, "Age and Sex in the Social Structure of the United States," in *Essays in Sociological Theory,* Glencoe, 1949.

7. On literature on working-youth movements, see in detail ch. III, note 112, *From Generation to Generation.*

8. See on this: W. F. Whyte, *Street Corner Society, op. cit.;* A. Davies and J. Dollard, *Children of Bondage,* Washington, 1940.

   The literature on English and European Youth is mostly descriptive. See for instance: B. Reed (ed.), *Eighty Thousand Adolescents, A Study of Young People in the City of Birmingham,* 1950.

   Most relevant material is summarized in M. Fleming, *Adolescence,* London, 1948.

9. On juvenile delinquency and delinquent groups in general, see: Tappan, P. W., *Juvenile Delinquency,* New York, 1949; Reckless, W., *The Crime Problem,* New York, 1950; Sellin, Th., *Culture Contact and Crime,* New York, 1938.

   One of the first vivid descriptions is the famous book by F. Trasher, *The Gang,* Chicago, 1927.

   An interesting analysis is to be found in: S. Kobrin, "The Conflict of Values in Delinquent Areas," *American Sociological Review,* vol. 16 (1951), pp. 653–661.

10. See on this R. Merton, "Social Structure and Anomie," in *Social Theory and Social Structure, op. cit.,* pp. 125 ff.

11. The Israeli material is based on researches of the Research Seminar in Sociology of the Hebrew University, Jerusalem. The first phase of the research has been summarized by the author in S. N. Eisenstadt, "Youth Culture and Social Structure in Israel," *The British Journal of Sociology,* June, 1951. The second phase has been summarized by J. Ben-David, "Participation in Youth Movements and Social Status," *Megamoth,* 1954 (Hebrew). Further reports will be published subsequently.

12. The literature on German youth movements is boundless. The following should be consulted at this stage: H. Becker, *German Youth, Bond or Free,* London, 1946; R. Schmid, German Youth Movements, A Typological Study, Ph.D., University of Wisconsin, 1939; Ch. Lütkens, *Die Deutsche Jugendbewegung,* Frankfurt/Main, 1927; H. Blueher, *Der Charakter der Jugendbewegung,* Lauenberg, 1921.

13. H. Kohn, "Youth Movements," *Encyclopedia of the Social Sciences.*

14. The term "Jugendkultur" has been coined by G. Wyneken. See, for instance, G. Wyneken, *Schule u. Jugendkultur,* Jena, 1919.

15. This phase is fully analyzed by H. Becker, *op. cit.,* ch. II.

16. The description of the Kibbutz age-grades is adopted from the author's *Age Groups and Social Structure, an analysis of some aspects of socialization in the communal and cooperative settlements in Israel,* Jerusalem, 1950, pp. 56.

17. The description here is adapted from H. Fainsod, "Youth Under Dictatorship," *American Political Science Review,* 1951.

Alienation and American Society

Kenneth Keniston

Youth Culture as Enforced Alienation

What we call "youth culture"—the distinctive values, outlooks, manners, roles, activities, and behavior patterns of youth considered as a separate age group—is not a uniquely American phenomenon. In other technological societies, national variants of youth culture are increasingly visible. But in America, the most advanced of the technological nations, youth culture shows its greatest scope and development. Here, youth culture involves not only the privileged and educated, but all sectors of society; it includes not only our "teen-agers," but many who are advanced into their twenties. And though we commonly take it for granted that youths should exhibit special and often erratic, bizarre, and deviant behavior simply because of their age, not all societies make this assumption. On the contrary, in many, adolescents are seen primarily as young adults or as old children: they are expected to exhibit no distinctive behavior by simple virtue of their age. Even in our own country two generations ago, youth was largely defined as a time of apprenticeship: adolescence was a matter of "learning the ropes" and memorizing the map and the timetable for the road of success ahead. Gawky, awkward adolescence was a phase to be outgrown as quickly as possible.

Some few Americans still retain this view of youth, but most of us do not. Increasingly we expect that youth will have a special culture of its own, with characteristics that are those of neither childhood nor adulthood. Our language reflects this expectation: we seldom speak colloquially of "youths" or "adolescents"—terms that implicitly suggest the transition to adulthood—but rather of "teen-agers," "hoods," and "beatniks," all of whom are seen as ensconced in a world of their own with a world view of their own. Increasingly, we expect adolescents and young adults to behave in idiosyncratic ways which are symptomatic of their age.

The growth and dominance of youth culture in America means that most young Americans spend their formative years in a special culture only peripherally related to the adult world. We expect teen-agers to be different, and they come to expect it of themselves as well. Most adults view a youth of seventeen with a firmly established adult outlook as someone who is "too old for his years." The values and behaviors of the youth culture are rarely explicitly anti-adult, but they are explicitly non-adult; and the dominant virtues of adolescent society are not those of the adult world. This means that the average young American must undergo two major transitions en route to adulthood: first he must move from childhood to the youth culture, learning its ways and adapting to its requirements; and later, when he "drops out" of the youth culture or is expelled by commencement, he must make a second transition into the "real" world of grownups.

To be precise, we should speak of many "youth sub-cultures" which share common characteristics rather than of one embracing youth culture, for under this rubric we must subsume a great many different groups, variously labeled "typical teen-agers," "rock-and-rollers," "Joe College students," "youthful beatniks," and so on. F. Scott Fitzgerald's picture of Princeton before and after the First World War has come to epitomize one of the earliest American youth cultures, that of "flaming youth." In our own day, we have more various and contrasting versions, ranging to the black-jacketed delinquent to the oversensitive Catcher in the Rye, from the misunderstood James Dean to the fun-and-football fraternity man. A few of these sub-cultures are clearly alienated, like the delinquent gang or the youthful beat world; and if we are not to prejudge the issues of the tie of youth cultures with alienation, we must consider the other, more socially acceptable versions. Writing of these more than twenty years ago, Talcott Parsons suggested that they shared an emphasis on physical attractiveness, irresponsibility, lack of interest in adult things, and interest in athletics; but to this list we must now add further characteristics.

Let us take, then, as the most articulate form of the youth culture, the relatively unalienated group from which our alienated students were drawn, and attempt to characterize some of their dominant views and outlooks. And let us concentrate on those of their views which seem especially distinctive to this age group. This composite portrait, then, will be one of "elite youth," of those who have the ability to "fit in," of those whom society has fully embraced, of those from whom tomorrow's leaders will likely be drawn.

Few of these young men and women have any doubt that they will one day be part of our society. They do not actively or enthusiastically *choose* to be part; rather they unreflectively assume that they *will* be part; and problems of "choosing" conventional adulthood, so central to the alienated, rarely even occur to them as such. They wonder about where they will fit, but not about whether. They take it for granted that they will one day "settle down"; and if it troubles them, they push it out of their minds or consider it a problem to be solved by finding a suitable wife and career. By and large they "approve" of American society if asked, though normally they do not think in these terms. Society is simply there.

But at the same time, these young men and women often show a lack of deep commitment to adult values and roles. They are not alienated as are beatniks, delinquents or our group of alienated students. Rather, they view the adult world they expect to enter with a subtle distrust, a lack of high expectations, hopes, or dreams, and an often unstated feeling that they will have to "settle" for less than they would hope for if they let themselves hope. A surprising number, despite their efforts to get good grades so that they can get into good graduate schools and eventually have good careers, despite their manifest desire to do well in the existing social order, nonetheless view it, in Paul Goodman's phrase, as "an apparently closed room with a rat race going on in the middle." Whether they call it a rat race or not is immaterial (though many half-jokingly do); the point is that they expect little in the way of personal fulfillment, growth, or creativity from their future roles in the public world. Essentially, they recognize that adulthood is a relatively cold, demanding, specialized, and abstracted world where "meaningful" work is so scarce they do not even ask for it. Thus, the majority stay "cool" when it comes to the "real world"; and "coolness" means above all detachment, lack of emotion, absence of deep commitment, not being either enthusiastic *or* rejecting of adulthood.

Toward their parents, who are psychologically the most crucial exemplars of adulthood, most students show a similar lack of conscious or articulate involvement. They are neither ardently devoted nor explicitly rebellious. Indeed, many a youth is so distant from his parents, in generational terms if not in affection, that he can afford to "understand" them and show a touching sympathy for their tentative efforts to guide and advise him. His parents, too, usually sense their distance, fear that they are "dated" or "square," and become reluctant to interfere by imposing their own values and styles of life where they might be inappropriate. The result is frequently an unstated gentleman's agreement between the generations that neither will interfere with the other. To be sure, beneath this agreement, most students are deeply and usually unconsciously involved in relinquishing their ties of personal dependency on their parents; and many of the 10 to 20 per cent of students who avail themselves of psychiatric help when it is available are concerned with this problem. But dependency is not commitment; dependency *on* parents is often the greatest problem where commitment *to* what they stand for is impossible.

Most youths approach the wider world, social problems, political events, and international affairs with a comparable lack of deep involvement. There are notable exceptions in the civil rights movement, as among other student activists, but they are very few in number. The vast majority are well informed and uninvolved. Ultimately, most students feel a strong underlying sense of social powerlessness which dictates this lack of involvement. Few believe that society could, much less should, be radically transformed; most consider the world complex far beyond their power to comprehend or influence it; and almost all see the stage of history and social change as inhabited by vast impersonal forces which are quite beyond human control. The more sophisticated are sometimes drawn to Toynbeean or Spenglerian theories of the rise and fall of civilizations; the less sophisticated subscribe to theories of "the market"; and almost no one thinks that he, even in concert with his fellows, could alter the irrevocable course of events by so much as an iota.

The adult world, then, as seen from within the youth culture, inspires neither enthusiasm nor deep commitment. Most youths expect to be of it, but not for it or "with it." In fact, most do not expect very much at all of adulthood: they think about it rarely and ask little of it. Instead, their dominant focus is on the present, on the years of the youth culture itself, on high school or college life and on the pleasures to be derived therein. To be sure, many take courses whose goal is ultimately vocational: to become an engineer, a teacher, or a doctor; but most spend little time (as little as possible) thinking about what a career will involve. Instead they live within the present, for the present; the future will take care of itself.

Until that happens, the youth culture provides a distinctive and separate world, many of whose central themes are familiar from our survey of the motifs of alienation. One such theme is an emphasis on the present, on experience. In its most extreme form, this is the intense and obsessive alienated search for sentience; beatniks characteristically define experience as "kicks"—speed, sex, and stimulation. But most college students seek milder forms of experience: good times, girl friends, fun with the gang, the exploration of nature, happy days in summer, even art, music, and poetry. The American myth of "carefree college days" is dominated by an eternal present where things are done "just for the fun of it." For some students, the present means a bull session with the gang or a shopping expedition with the girls; for others, it means an opportunity to experiment, to make tentative commitments, to try on roles or selves with the option of returning them if they do not fit. The disappearance of the Protestant ethic among college students has entailed the demise of the concept of a "life work"; in place of yesterday's Horatio Algers are today's more easy-going, relaxed young men and women who are learning how to enjoy themselves.

Yet this cult of the present has a hidden rationale, the search for identity. Consciously, this search is usually defined as a question about "what to do with my life," that is, about careers and vocations. But less consciously the cult of the present, the freedom of the youth culture to experiment, and its authorization from adult society to postpone binding commitments—all allow young men and women time to confront the difficult freedoms, choices, and selections their society demands of them. Adolescence in America is considered a place for legitimate "role-playing," for testing alternatives, for provisional commitments followed by a loss of interest, for overwhelming enthusiasm followed by total apathy. In a few students, especially at the most demanding colleges, problems of choice and commitment may reach full consciousness; and there, many a graduating senior on the eve of graduation wonders "Who am I?" in a cosmic as well as a vocational sense. And at a few "elite" colleges, "I'm having an identity crisis," becomes the proud self-justification of any self-conscious youth. Though it can be ex-

ploited and caricatured, resolving this "identity crisis" is indeed a central
function of the youth culture as a whole, which allows what Erik Erikson
calls "a psychosocial moratorium" on adult commitments, and gives time
and room for role-playing and experimentation.

The very discontinuity of the youth culture with the demands of adult
society allows youth a "breathing space" between childhood and adulthood,
time to try to resolve the developmental discontinuities between these two
stages of life, and, above all, space to try to achieve some sense of inner
unity, self-sameness, and continuity that promises to endure despite continual social change, to cohere despite the dissociative demands of our
society. By providing a waiting room before adulthood, the youth culture
offers a protected space in which to do the psychological work which adulthood presupposes. Most of this work is done unconsciously and quietly,
"acted out" on the stage of college activities, summer jobs, going steady,
and a continuing reassessment of one's links to the personal past. The youth
culture permits experimentation in the service of unconscious choice, exposure to experience for the sake of selection, and trial commitment in the
interest of future self-definition. Acute self-fragmentation, the alternative to
success in these pursuits, only rarely occurs. But the problem of identity is
there for all.

Much of this unconscious work ultimately involves redefining one's relationship to one's parents, to childhood, and to the childhood self. Those who
founder often do so because the backward pulls of childhood are too strong.
Like the alienated, they unconsciously find the fantasy of childhood embeddedness more compelling than the "cold adult world." Given the pull of
childhood dependencies, alienation is but one possibility; others are so
normal that we scarcely note them at all—the almost inevitable homesick-
ness of freshmen, a tendency to alternate between nostalgic idealization of
one's parents and acute embarrassment at their limitations, a readiness to
plunge into some substitute and often premature intimacy with a girl, a
reactive assertion of independence, masculinity, toughness, and autonomy
from parents. College students are normally prone to become excessively
dependent upon advisers, counselors, and even upon psychotherapists, who
at best duplicate the role of the "good mother" by exploiting their patients'
involvement with them in order to promote their eventual disengagement.
The underlying fantasy of fusion often finds partial expression in fusion with
some college group—a fraternity, a "crowd," a set of dorm mates, a sorority
—all of which can inspire almost mystical feelings of solidarity, self-sacrifice,
and devotion despite their actually limited goals and even meretricious
values. At some colleges, this adolescent potential for self-surrender is
channeled into "college spirit," which can bring unashamed tears to the eyes
of a football player who would die rather than weep for his mother. The
dependency and need for embeddedness fostered by our small intimate
families must somehow be dislocated from mother, family, and childhood

until it can be refocused on the second true love of one's life. The youth culture abets this rechanneling.

Though the youth culture permits narrowly defined forms of solidarity and surrender to a group, it enjoins against overt idealism, especially in any Utopian cause. It is normal to be loyal to college and fraternity, but not to an ideology. Even those who hanker after political careers rarely admit ideological commitment. To remain "popular" and "normal," they must avow a healthy cynicism, professing politics a "job like any other" and disavowing any intent to "change the world." Whatever one's real purposes (and these often are idealistic), the youth culture requires that one not admit to noble motives. Thus, young men and women who devotedly trudge each week to dismal mental hospitals to work with and sometimes save "hopeless" chronic patients will more often say that they "want the experience" or are "testing themselves" than they will confess to a genuine desire to help or serve. And a youth who joins the Peace Corps will often find it easier to term his decision a way of "solving his identity crisis" than to admit his Utopian hopes and goals. Idealistic motives and Utopian aspirations extend out of the youth culture into the wider society, and thus fall under the injunction to "coolness." Furthermore, because their childhoods often leave them so full of deep and sentimental nostalgias, American young men are fearful of all that might appear sentimental. Since once, in the distant and repressed past, it was so good to be cared for and enfolded, young Americans (and especially young men) are anxiously fearful of seeming "suckers," of being "taken in," of being embraced by any embracing cause.

Yet beneath this apparent cynicism there usually lies a deeper search for commitments of ultimate worth and value. When something like the Peace Corps comes along, a surprising number, disavowing idealism, are willing to join this idealistic cause. Philosophical or religious inquiry offers an avenue to commitment for a few; and others turn to the study of psychology, which seems to promise the "discovery" of positive values within the psyche. The arts, drama, poetry, music—all of which are undergoing a revival on better college campuses—also offer solace, if not purpose. And above all in the civil rights movement an increasing, though still small, number of students (most of whom are not ideologically alienated) can find a creative channel for their idealism. The struggle for equality for Negro Americans, like the Peace Corps, offers a vehicle for the expression of idealism without ideology, a simple moral commitment to work for the welfare of one's fellow men.

But for the great majority, commitment is sought and found in individual private experience—in leisure, in comradeship, in sports, in a girl. All of these commitments, which David Riesman calls "privatism," involve turning away from the wider social and public world toward the more manageable domain of personal life. Whatever dim glimmerings of Utopian spirit are visible in the youth culture can be seen largely as diffused through these privatistic pursuits. The Utopian quest, the search for positive values so clearly seen in the alienated, is here muted into the precursor of the ethic of family and fun in adulthood.

Yet we should recall that permission is granted to remain in the youth culture only so long as academic requirements are met. Those who quit, drop out, or are failed out, either enter adulthood forthwith or must enter upon serious delinquency or the "beat" world. The power of exclusion is a powerful sanction, and it is one reason Americans often prefer education to the "real world" for so many years. By indirectly encouraging prolonged education, this requirement also promotes the high-level ego training of precisely the kind our society requires: higher education is especially designed to inculcate and develop the specialized cognitive skills needed for success in American society. The price of admission and permission to stay in the youth culture is steadily rising academic performance: the most talented and hard-working can therefore stay the longest. The liberal arts colleges usually attended by such eager and able students explicitly disavow any intent at providing vocational training. They explicitly aim at training the mind, at developing powers of analysis, criticism, selection, and organization, at encouraging independent work and study—in short, at developing and defining ego skills that will be useful no matter what the job and even if its requirements change. The freedom of the youth culture is purchased at the price of the continuing acquisition of the ability to meet our society's ego demands.

The elite youth culture I have characterized is thus closely related to the major themes of alienation and to the central demands of American society. This group of talented young Americans, most of whom are not alienated, nonetheless show in their youth culture comparable themes to those found among the alienated: a preoccuption with the present, a concern with the search for identity, many symptoms of continuing problems of dependency, a quest for positive values which aborts in private commitment, and a preoccupation with the ego demands of our technological society. There are enormous differences between a college booster and an Inburn; but they have their underlying similarities as well.

More important, however, than any similarities between the themes of alienation and the motifs of the youth culture is the fact that the youth culture as a whole *requires* a refusal of conventional adulthood for the time one is in it. Its values are discontinuous with those of adulthood: it is not a simple transition or apprenticeship between the child and the man. In one sense, then, we normally *expect* its members to be alienated: not to undertake irrevocable adult commitments, to experiment and experience, to live in the present, to be irresponsible and carefree, to value and create color and excitement, to be physically daring and sexually attractive. All of these qualities are secondary, subordinated, or actively discouraged in adult society. Furthermore, youth culture and adulthood are defined as irreconcilable: any youth who is prepared to make an immediate commitment to adulthood *must* leave the youth culture, *must* stop his education, and *must* enter the world of grownups.

The youth culture therefore permits American youth as a whole to be "institutionally" alienated without having to be personally alienated. It provides a socially supported period when the average young man or woman simply finds it impossible to enter the adult world. It therefore points to the unreadiness, psychological and ideological, of most young Americans to accept adult commitments and to meet the difficult ego demands of our society. By "taking off the pressure" for a period ranging from five to fifteen years, the youth culture permits most youths to remain uninvolved in the adult world without having to take an open stand against it. By sanctioning and even requiring *de facto* alienation, it removes the need in most youths for a more focused and articulated alienation from adulthood. And it takes the pressure off longest for those on whom adult pressures will eventually be greatest: the highly educated, of whom most will be later required.

The relation of youth culture and alienation is therefore paradoxical. Youth is defined in America as a stage of systematic disengagement from conventional adulthood; the values of the youth culture involve a lack of any deep commitment to adult society, parents, and the adult world. But at the same time the socially supported alienation of the youth culture acts to absolve most young men and women of any need for personally repudiating conventional adulthood: their membership in the youth culture does it for them. During this long moratorium on adulthood, young Americans must undertake a series of major psychological transitions: they must attempt to abandon childhood identifications and commitments for the more selective and partial identifications of adulthood and for commitments that promise to weather the ravages of chronic social change. They must make the many choices our society demands and integrate them into one coherent sense of self. Perhaps most difficult psychologically, they must gradually renounce their ties of dependency on their first families and free themselves to form new ties to adult social groups and their own families. Somehow, usually without much conscious thought, they must find where they stand ideologically—*what* if anything they stand for, *how much* they will stand for, and *where* they stand. And simultaneously, they must develop to the limit of their ability and patience their capacity to meet the stringent demands of our society.

All of this means that most American youths have a double orientation to adulthood. On the one hand, they see themselves as free and feckless participants in the youth culture, by virtue of that fact committed (for the time being) to non-adult values and distrustful of the adult world. On the other hand, most take for granted that they will one day enter adulthood and see themselves as preparing themselves for it. Many of the controversies over the real nature of American youth—over whether it is irresponsible and hedonistic or sober and dedicated—stem from this double orientation. Some observers see one face of youth, and other observers the other; and both observers often mistake the part for the whole.

Such oversimplification is especially hard to avoid because young people themselves present now one and now another face, all the while maintaining there is no more than meets the eye. Not that they deliberately deceive older people as to what they are like—on the contrary, when a young man or woman is with representatives of the adult world (teachers, ministers, admissions officers, poll takers) he not only acts like a future citizen of America, he really *feels* that way. And the same youth under other circumstances— when with friends, at Daytona Beach or Newport, in campus coffee houses, fraternities, sororities, or dormitories—really *feels* like a hood, a beatnik, a college Joe or a Deke. But in each of these stances some of the same ambivalence exists, despite the frequent insistence of the young (with a characteristic adolescent combination of ambivalence and intolerance for ambivalence) that there is only one side of the coin.

Compared to the extreme group we have studied, then, their classmates are "alienated" as members of the youth culture but rarely as individuals. Our society evokes scant enthusiasm in them; but since it need not be actively confronted, it evokes little overt or articulate rejection. In many ways, the alienated are alienated because they have not been able to *use* the youth culture to escape the pressures of adult society. For them, there *is* no moratorium on the demands of adulthood; these demands continually push at them, epitomized by parents, teachers, and images of the "cold adult world." Paradoxically, though they vociferously reject conventional adulthood, the very act of rejection also makes them more continually concerned with it than are their less alienated fellows.

Subterranean Traditions of Youth

David Matza

The rebellious character of youth has periodically troubled serious-minded adults since the appearance of modern civil life. While the major purpose of this paper is to describe some patterns of youthful rebelliousness, and not to inquire into their causes, it will be useful to begin with a brief discussion

David Matza, "Subterranean Traditions of Youth," from *The Annals of the American Academy of Political and Social Science* (Vol. 338, November 1961), pp. 103–118. Reprinted by permission of the publisher and the author.

of some theories regarding youth's vulnerability to rebelliousness, and the evidence on which theories presumably rest.

The Vulnerability of Youth

The primary object of Kingsley Davis' two essays on youth written some twenty years ago was to explain the rebelliousness of youth in modern society as contrasted with the docility allegedly found in more primitive societies.[1] Among the reasons given was the fact that, although parents and youth remain together, the viewpoints of parents are primarily shaped during their own childhood; thus, friction is likely whenever the rate of change in customary attitudes is rapid. Furthermore, Davis suggested that the contemporary domination of the principle of merit results in tension and frustration by providing the basis for dispute regarding rightful incumbency in scarce positions and relative claims over scarce rights and perquisites. Moreover, he argued that adults tend to realism because of their greater stake in the system and because they are implicated in the compromises necessary in any ongoing social order. Youth, standing outside the establishment and not responsible for its defects, is likely to oscillate between what seems to adults an overdemanding idealism and a merciless cynicism.

Other writers have indicated additional sources of tension in the position of youth. Benedict, Erikson, Bloch and Niederhoffer, and many others, have stressed the crisis of identity inherent in a society which defines adolescence and youth ambiguously.[2] Parsons has emphasized the effects of an adult stress on performance.[3] Some have stressed the frustrating effects of a puritanical repression of sexuality, and others, of the post-Kinsey era, lament the effects of the stimulation provided by a sex-obsessed culture.[4] Whatever the difference in opinion regarding the source, there seems to be a general consensus that something requires explaining, and this something usually turns out to be youthful rebelliousness.

Most empirical evidence seems to support this consensus, provided we limit our assertions in two ways. First, we may not contend that extremist versions of youthful rebelliousness characterize anything like a majority of the youthful population. Rather, it seems that the great majority of Ameri-

[1] Kingsley Davis, "Sociology of Parent-Youth Conflict," *American Sociological Review*, Vol. 5 (August 1940) and "Adolescence and the Social Structure," *The Annals of the American Academy of Political and Social Science*, Vol. 236 (November 1944).
[2] Ruth Benedict, "Continuities and Discontinuities in Cultural Conditioning," *Psychiatry*, May 1933; Erik Erikson, in *New Perspectives for Research in Juvenile Delinquency*, eds. Helen Witmer and Ruth Kotinsky (Publication No. 356; Washington, D.C.: Children's Bureau, 1956); Herbert Bloch and Arthur Niederhoffer, *The Gang* (New York: Philosophical Library, 1958).
[3] Talcott Parsons, "Age and Sex in the Social Structure of the United States," *American Sociological Review*, October, 1942.
[4] Pitrim Sorokin, *The American Sex Revolution* (Boston: Sargent, 1956).

can youth behave either in a conventional manner [5] or participate in conventional versions [6] of deviant youth traditions; this, despite the fact that many youths are vulnerable to rebelliousness. Second, there seems no reason to believe that there have been any long-run increases or decreases in rates of youthful rebelliousness during the modern era. Rather, it seems likely that rates of some forms of youthful rebelliousness have increased somewhat over the last twenty-five years, whereas rates of other forms have declined. Even in those modes of rebelliousness like delinquency, where rates during the last twenty-five years have apparently increased, there is some evidence that rates fifty years ago were higher than those currently experienced. [7] During the decade of the fifties, a decline in youthful radicalism gave rise to the feeling that an age of conformity was upon us. There seems no firm ground for this suspicion. Periods of prosperity have often signaled a decline in radical activity.

What may we contend? First, within the life cycle, the apex of rebelliousness is reached during the period of youth, before and after which rates of rebelliousness seem considerably lower. [8] This holds, by hypothesis, for the three modes of youthful rebelliousness to be discussed in this selection: delinquency, radicalism, and Bohemianism. This means that the youthful

---

[5] Frederick Elkin and William A. Westley, "The Myth of Adolescent Culture," *American Sociological Review,* December 1955; also, Bennett M. Berger, "On the Youthfulness of Youth Cultures."

[6] Conventional versions of deviant traditions are discussed in the final section of this paper.

[7] Negley K. Teeters and David Matza, "The Extent of Delinquency in The United States," *The Journal of Negro Education* (Summer 1959), pp. 210–211; also, Henry McKay's unpublished data on Chicago delinquency rates, cited in Albert K. Cohen and James F. Short, "Juvenile Delinquency," in *Contemporary Social Problems,* eds. Robert K. Merton and Robert A. Nisbet (New York: Harcourt, Brace and World, 1961), p. 84.

[8] Evidence of this using national delinquency statistics may be found in most standard textbooks and the *Uniform Crime Reports* of any year. For instance, Cohen and Short, *op. cit.,* p. 85. More reliable evidence of "maturational reform," based on cohort analysis, appears in William McCord, Joan McCord, and Irving Zola, *Origins of Crime* (New York: Columbia University Press, 1959), p. 21; Jessie Bernard, *Social Problems at Midcentury* (New York: Dryden, 1957), pp. 421, 444; W. H. Dunham and M. E. Knauer, "The Juvenile Court and its Relationship to Adult Criminality," *Social Forces,* March 1954. The evidence for radicalism and Bohemianism is necessarily more impressionistic. For supportive but inconclusive evidence of "maturational defection" in radicalism, see Gabriel A. Almond, *The Appeals of Communism* (Princeton: Princeton University Press, 1954), pp. 218–220; James A. Wechsler, *The Age of Suspicion* (New York: Random House, 1953), p. 84; Robert E. Lane, *Political Life* (Glencoe: Free Press, 1959), pp. 216–217; Morris L. Ernst and David Loth, *Report on the American Communist* (New York: Holt, 1952). For impressionistic evidence on the drifting from Bohemianism with the gaining of adulthood, see Thomas Parkinson, "Phenomenon or Generation," in *A Casebook on The Beat,* ed. Thomas Parkinson (New York: Crowell, 1961), pp. 277–278; Albert Parry, *Garrets and Pretenders: A History of Bohemianism in America* (New York: Covici-Friede, 1933), p. 12.

spirit of rebelliousness coincides more or less with chronological youth.[9] Second, we contend that because of the persistent vulnerability of youth, traditions of each mode have emerged; distinctive viewpoints have remained relatively stable in content and location.[10] And, finally, that these traditions of youthful rebelliousness—delinquency, radicalism, and Bohemianism— are in the nature of subterranean traditions in American life.

The Subterranean Tradition

The major contribution of sociology to the understanding of deviance has consisted of two fundamental insights. First, persistent deviance is typically not a solitary enterprise; rather, it requires and most often receives group support. Second, deviance does not typically represent an historical innova- tion; rather, it has a history in particular neighborhoods and locales. Thus, the individual deviant is linked to the society in minimal fashion through companies of deviants and through localized traditions. To speak of sub- terranean traditions is to extend the notion of linking to the wider social system; it is to posit connections between localized deviant traditions and the broader traditions of conventional society. The notion of subterranean implies that there is an ongoing dialectic between conventional and deviant traditions and that, in the process of exchange, both are modified.[11]

Subterranean traditions of youth have a number of common aspects which suggest a definition of the concept. First, they are traditions which are pub- licly denounced. Second, the extreme versions of these traditions are adhered to by only a small proportion of the youthful population. Third, these tradi- tions are familiar to and tolerated by broad segments of the adult population. Fourth, conventional versions of these traditions are experienced by broad

---

[9] Bennett Berger, *op. cit.*, rightly distinguishes between youthfulness in the spiritual sense and chronological youth. He suggests that there is no necessary correlation between the two. I agree but suggest that there is a rough empirical correlation.

[10] The content of these viewpoints will be discussed. With regard to stable ecological anchoring, the evidence varies in reliability. The ecological anchoring of the delinquent tradition has been documented in Clifford H. Shaw and Henry D. McKay, *Juvenile Delinquency and Urban Areas* (Chicago: University of Chicago Press, 1942); Albert K. Cohen, *Delinquent Boys* (Glencoe: Free Press, 1955). The widespread impression that youthful radicalism has been stably located on the campuses of a handful of typically large, prestigious, and cosmopolitan universities and colleges receives ade- quate documentary confirmation in Robert W. Iversen, *The Communists and the Schools* (New York: Harcourt, Brace, 1959), Chap. 6. The widespread impression that American Bohemianism has located in run-down sections of large cities or in areas adjacent to cosmopolitan campuses remains largely undocumented. However, there seems no urgent reason to question this impression.

[11] Reinhard Bendix and Bennett Berger, "Images of Society and Problems of Concept Formation in Sociology," in *Symposium on Sociological Theory,* ed. Llewellyn Gross (Evanston: Row, Peterson, 1959).

segments of the youthful population. Fifth, these traditions are viewed with ambivalence in the privacy of contemplation by a majority of adults, and, thus, public reactions are subject to faddish oscillation ranging from sympathetic tolerance to outright suppression.[12] To point to the existence of subterranean traditions is to suggest that no one in any society is fully socialized or fully respondent to public expectations;[13] as a consequence, whenever there are available counterthemes, there will be varying degrees of indulgence in these traditions ranging from relatively complete immersion to occasional vicarious appreciation.

Subterranean Traditions of Youth

Delinquency, radicalism, and Bohemianism are the extremist versions of subterranean youth traditions. They impart a spirit of rebelliousness and impetuosity that seems consistent with the sort of tensions ordinarily attributed to the position of youth. These kinds of behavior exhibit what is frequently termed immaturity or irresponsibility.[14] However, the lumping together of delinquency, radicalism, and Bohemianism requires more systematic justification. Thus, it will be useful to briefly discuss their similarities, over and above their apparent temperamental affinity, and to specify the differences between them.

SIMILARITIES

First, the traditions in question seem to have a greater appeal to youth than to the population at large. Second, all three have distinct anticivil implications, at least over the short run. All three are "threats" to the stability and order of an ongoing system. Third, all three are specifically antibourgeois, although in different ways. The delinquent, for instance, does not denounce bourgeois property arrangements, but he violates them. He does reject the bourgeois sentiments of methodism and routine, particularly as they are manifested within the school system. The Bohemian's attitude toward bourgeois property arrangements is typically one of indifference, although he is appalled by the commercialization ordinarily associated with these arrangements. His ire is especially reserved for the puritanical and methodical elements of the bourgeois ethos. Moreover, the Bohemian is typically antagonistic to recent trends in bourgeois society. He is opposed to

---

[12] Fads often involve the brief elevation of modified elements of subterranean traditions, most notably Bohemian traditions, to the status of eccentric but partially acceptable behavior. Perhaps the classic example of this in the United States was the "Trilby" fad in the 1890's when a modified form of female Bohemianism came in vogue. For a discussion of "Trilby," see Parry, *op. cit.*, Chap. 9.

[13] Dennis Wrong, "The Oversocialized Conception of Man in Modern Sociology," *American Sociological Review*, April 1961.

[14] Parsons, *op. cit.*

the mechanized, organized, centralized, and increasingly collectivized nature of modern capitalism. The radical tradition envisages a less general denunciation. Particularly in the varieties of revolutionary Marxism, which represent the most important examples of modern radicalism, the primary focus of radical attack has been on the capitalist system of political and economic domination and on the imperialist role allegedly played by such systems in international affairs. The methodical, the puritanical, and, especially, the industrial aspects of the bourgeois order have been more or less embraced.

Thus, we see that each subterranean tradition has been hostile to the bourgeois order, but each has followed a somewhat different line of attack.

DIFFERENCES

First, delinquency differs from both radicalism and Bohemianism with respect to the specific age of vulnerability. However, the stage of education seems a more decisive point of division than age per se. Delinquency is a high school phenomenon; it seems most pronounced among that section of youth which terminates its education during or at the end of high school. Radicalism and Bohemianism, particularly in the United States, are apparently enmeshed within the system of higher education. Its adherents are typically drawn from those whose education terminates during college, with the attainment of a bachelor's degree, or with some graduate work of indeterminable duration.

Second, they differ with respect to the degree of self-consciousness attained. Radicalism and Bohemianism are intellectually self-conscious and represent explicit and reasonably coherent critiques of modern society; the delinquent critique tends to be implicit. Furthermore, radicalism and Bohemianism possess a written literature: delinquency is almost by necessity an oral tradition.

Third, the modes of rebelliousness differ with respect to their ambitions. Delinquency has no designs on society; there is no desire on the part of delinquents to reconstruct it. Thus, in Merton's terms, they are aberrant.[15] Radicals, on the other hand, wish to reshape society in the form of their own ideological predilections. Thus, they are the archetype of Merton's nonconformist.[16] Bohemians fall somewhere between, typically wishing to develop a private and insulated way of life but rarely having any aspiration to convert the rest of society.

Fourth, the modes of rebelliousness differ with respect to assessments regarding their moral worth. In the case of delinquency, the judgments of its adherents seem to coincide with those belonging to conventional society.[17]

---

[15] Robert K. Merton, "Social Problems and Sociological Theory," in *Contemporary Social Problems, op. cit.,* pp. 725–727.
[16] *Ibid.*
[17] Gresham M. Sykes and David Matza, "Techniques of Neutralization," *American Sociological Review,* December 1957.

There is no serious belief in either camp in the moral value of the delinquent enterprise. On the other hand, there has been considerable dispute regarding the moral value of radicalism and Bohemianism. Many intellectuals attribute varying degrees of moral value to them; those of lesser intellect have probably been less generous. Moreover, radicals and Bohemians, unlike delinquents, are convinced of the moral value of their enterprises.

Despite these differences, we have suggested that there is a spiritual affinity between delinquency, radicalism, and Bohemianism; all are modes of youthful rebelliousness. Each represents a subterranean tradition of American youth. Thus, an analysis of youthful deviance requires an examination of each tradition. It is to that task that we now turn.

Delinquency: Spirit and Substance [18]

There are many perceptive accounts describing the behavior of juvenile delinquents and their underlying values.[19] Although there have been important differences of opinion in the interpretation of this material and in the relative stress placed on various components, there exists a striking consensus on the content of delinquent values. Three themes describing the spirit of the delinquent enterprise and two defining its substance, or business, seem implicit in these accounts.

The distinctive feature of the spirit of delinquency is the celebration of prowess. Each of the themes in the delinquent tradition develops an aspect of the meaning of prowess. First, delinquents are deeply immersed in a restless search for excitement, "thrills" or "kicks." According to the delinquent code, the approved style of life is an adventurous one. Activities pervaded by displays of daring and charged with danger are highly valued in comparison with more mundane and routine patterns of behavior. Although delinquent acts do not exhaust the field of adventurous activities,

---

[18] The following section is, with slight modification, based on David Matza and Gresham M. Sykes, "Juvenile Delinquency and Subterranean Values," *American Sociological Review,* forthcoming.

[19] Frederic M. Thrasher, *The Gang* (Chicago: University of Chicago Press, 1936); Clifford R. Shaw and M. E. Moore, *The Natural History of a Delinquent Career* (Chicago: University of Chicago Press, 1931); Albert K. Cohen, *Delinquent Boys, op. cit.;* Albert K. Cohen and James F. Short, "Research in Delinquent Subcultures," *The Journal of Social Issues,* Vol. 14 (1958), No. 3; Walter Miller, "Lower Class Culture as a Generating Milieu of Gang Delinquents," *The Journal of Social Issues,* Vol. 14 (1958), No. 3; Solomin Kobrin, "The Conflict of Values in Delinquent Areas," *American Sociological Review,* Vol. 16 (1951); Harold Finestone, "Cats, Kicks and Color," *Social Problems,* Vol. 5 (1957); Richard A. Cloward and Lloyd E. Ohlin, *Delinquency and Opportunity* (Glencoe: The Free Press, 1960); H. Bloch and Arthur Niederhoffer, *The Gang, op. cit.;* Beatrice Griffith, *American Me* (Boston: Houghton Mifflin, 1948); Sheldon and Eleanor Glueck, *Unraveling Juvenile Delinquency* (New York: Commonwealth Fund, 1950).

they make up an important component of activities that may be feasibly viewed as adventurous. The fact that an activity involves breaking the law is often the fact that lends it its air of excitement. In fact, "kicks" or "action" may come to be defined with clear awareness as "any action tabooed by 'squares' that heighten and intensifies the present moment of experience and differentiates it as much as possible from the humdrum routines of daily life." [20] In courting physical danger, experimenting with the forbidden, and provoking the authorities, the delinquent is not simply enduring hazards; he is creating them in an attempt to manufacture excitement. For many delinquents, "the rhythm of life fluctuates between periods of relatively routine and repetitive activities and sought situations of greater emotional stimulation." [21]

Second, to attain prowess is to seek and receive the material rewards of society while avoiding, in the manner of a leisure class, the canons of school and work with their implicit commitments to methodism, security, and routine. Thus, delinquents commonly exhibit a disdain for "getting on" in the realms of school or work. In its place, there is a sort of aimless drifting or grandiose dreams of quick success.

However, the delinquent must be financed if he is to attain the luxury of the sporting life. Although some writers have coupled the delinquent's disdain of work with a disdain of money, it seems unlikely that money is renounced in the delinquent code; it would seem more accurate to say it is treated in a special way. Money is valued, but not for purposes of a careful series of expenditures or long-range objectives. Money, for the delinquent, is luxury and not regular income; and the modesty of the sums involved, for what are, after all, children, has obscured this fact. Money is viewed as something to be squandered in gestures of largesse, in patterns of conspicuous consumption. An age-old method of facilitating this is gambling among peers. A major function of this sort of gambling, whatever its motive, is to redistribute scarce finances so that, over the long run, each member of the group may play at luxury. This hardly exhausts the ways in which prowess may be used in the sudden acquisition of "large" sums of money. The other techniques involve incursions on the world of outsiders—the victims.

Simple expropriation—theft and its variants—must be included, of course; but it is only one of a variety of ways of "scoring" and does not always carry great prestige in the eyes of delinquents.[22] Other forms of prowess include chicanery or manipulation which may take the form of borrowing from social workers or more elaborate forms of "hustling"; an emphasis on "pull," frequently with reference to obtaining a "soft" job assumed to be available only to those with influential connections. Thus, there are a variety of means,

[20] Finestone, *op. cit.*
[21] Miller, *op. cit.*
[22] Finestone, *op. cit.*

ranging in legality from theft to the holding of a soft job, all of which are exhibitions of prowess, all of which may be applied in the pursuit of luxury.

A third theme running through the accounts of juvenile delinquency centers on aggression. This is the third component of prowess. The code of the warrior, which in many ways the delinquent code reflects, calls for an aggressive manliness, a reluctance to accept slights on one's honor.[23] The delinquent's readiness for aggression is particularly emphasized in the analysis of juvenile gangs in the slum areas of large cities. It is in such gangs that we find the struggles for "turf," and, thus, it is in these cases that the applicability of the warrior code is most apparent. Cloward and Ohlin have pointed out that we can be led into error by viewing these conflict-oriented delinquents as typical of all delinquents.[24] Yet, the gang delinquent's use of violence for the maintenance of honor, or "rep," and the proof of courage, or "heart," seems to express in extreme form the idea that aggression is a demonstration of toughness and, thus, of masculinity; and it is this idea which pervades delinquent thought. Whatever the degree of differentiation among delinquent subcultures, the concept of *machismo*,[25] of the path to manhood through the ability to take it and hand it out, is foreign to the average delinquent only in name.

Finally, let us turn to the substance of delinquency—the business of the delinquent enterprise. The substance of delinquency is defined by the legal code and contains two major elements. First, there is victimization. This includes larceny and all of its variants, assaults on persons or on property, that is, vandalism, and a host of less frequently committed offenses, all involving victims. Second, there are status offenses, activities which are expressly prohibited for juveniles but which may be performed by adults, within limits, with legal impunity. This includes truancy, drinking, gambling, driving cars, runaway, indulgence in sex, and, in some jurisdictions, smoking, swearing, staying out late, and a host of vaguely defined forms of misconduct. However, while these activities are officially delinquent, the law, particularly at the level of police enforcement, exhibits considerable discretionary tolerance with regard to youngsters exhibiting these forms of behavior, particularly if their dossiers are otherwise clean.[26]

[23] Joseph Margolis, "Juvenile Delinquents: Latter-Day Knights," *The American Scholar,* Spring 1960.
[24] Cloward and Ohlin, *op. cit.*
[25] Griffith, *op. cit.*
[26] Though it may appear obvious or unimportant, it is crucial to specify the substance of delinquency as well as its spirit. The basic process involved in the conventional versions of each tradition is the fortuitous stripping away of its most odious features. Thus, for instance, the conventional version of delinquency, teen-age culture, involves a continuing flirtation with its tolerable components; and among these tolerable components are the status offenses, to be discussed.

Student Radicalism: Spirit and Substance

Compared to the many accounts of delinquency, there are relatively few systematic descriptions of student radicalism in the United States.[27] Enough exists, however, to proceed with a tentative description of this tradition.[28]

Radicalism among students did not begin in the decade of the Thirties, although there is little question that it reached its height during that period. The Intercollegiate Socialist Society was organized in 1905, and by 1921 Calvin Coolidge decried student radicalism.[29] Despite the internecine struggles within the revolutionary socialist movement since 1905, some aspects of the radical tradition have remained relatively stable. What are the stable components of modern student radicalism?

First, there is the vision of apocalypse.[30] This refers to "the belief that the evil world as we know it, so full of temptation and corruption, will come to an end one day and will be replaced by a purer and better world." [31] This tradition has its origins in the apocalyptic outlook of the prophets of the Old Testament and has been passed down through the early Christians and adherents of heretical sects. Its modern recipients, suggests Shils, are "the modern revolutionary movements and above all the Marxian movements." [32] The tradition is best reflected in "doctrinaire politics, or the politics of the ideal." [33]

Whatever its general importance in revolutionary socialism, the politics of the ideal seems peculiarly well suited to the predispositions of youthful rebelliousness. This sort of politics seems perfectly consistent with Davis' description of youth's mixture of idealism and cynicism. In the politics of the ideal, perception and assessment become bifurcated with respect to idealism and cynicism. On this side of the apocalypse, one views and interprets events critically and cynically; on the other side, or in some contemporary foreshadowing of the future, one views and interprets events idealistically and generously.

The second component of the spirit of student radicalism is populism. "Populism is the belief in the creativity and in the superior worth of the

---

27 The most detailed and documented account is found in Iversen, *op. cit.;* for a good impressionistic account, see Wechsler, *op. cit.*

28 While the Communists have never had a monopoly on student radicalism, their influence, particularly during the Thirties and early Forties, was considerable. Our discussion will focus primarily on Communists partially because of their prominence and partially because their activities have been best documented. See Iversen, *op. cit.,* Chap. 6.

29 Iversen, *op. cit.,* p. 13.

30 Edward A. Shils "The Traditions of Intellectuals," in *The Intellectuals,* ed. George de Huszar (Glencoe: Free Press, 1960), pp. 55–61.

31 *Ibid.*

32 *Ibid.*

33 *Ibid.*

ordinary people, of the uneducated and the unintellectual." [34] Because of the central role of populism in modern radicalism, revolutionary movements have tended to equate the apocalypse with the liberation of the folk. The particular folk celebrated has varied: in the Russian social revolutionary movement, it was the peasant; in traditional Marxism, it is the industrial proletariat; in the anarchism of Bakunin, it tended to be the *lumpenproletariat*. American student radicalism, largely unaware of these esoteric distinctions, has tended to lump these populist ideals together, arriving at a compote consisting of migrant farm workers, unskilled and semiskilled industrial workers, and Negroes.

Among students, the appeal of populism is not simply an outgrowth of traditional radical propensities. Just as the apocalyptic mentality has a special appeal to youth, so, too, does populism. Students have a special affinity for populism because it serves an important function; populism, for students, is an effective attack on the presumption of professorial authority and a neat way of defending against unflattering assessment. For the radical, and for the Bohemian, too, a belief in populism allows students who perceive themselves as vanguard or avant garde to deflect the contrary judgments of their academic elders.

A third component of the student radical spirit is evangelism. Evangelism refers to excursions made by sectarians to the outside world for the purpose of recruiting sympathizers, supporters, and members. It is an intensively active sort of belief. Thus, it is well suited to the exuberance and impetuosity characteristic of rebellious youth. Evangelism plays an especially important role since, compared to Bohemianism, radicalism would otherwise be too serious an enterprise to compete effectively for rebellious youth. Evangelism notwithstanding, student radicalism remains chronically vulnerable to Bohemianism within its ranks.[35] Thus, evangelism seems as important in the bolstering of internal enthusiasm as in its alleged purpose of gaining new adherents. By encouraging excursion, it allows student radicals to stray from the routine of the radical enterprise,[36] and challenges their capacities for argumentation, intimidation, persuasion, and seduction.

The substance of student radicalism is unconventional political action. Its round-of-life consists of taking stands on concrete issues, circulation of petitions, distribution of leaflets, sale of literature, raising funds, demonstrations and rallies, frequent meetings, discussions, debates, and the like. The mundane character of most of these activities is more or less obscured by the

---

[34] *Ibid.*

[35] The evidence for this is indirect but suggestive. The fear that Bohemianism is infecting the youth is a persistent fear among adult radicals. The classical radical case against Bohemian corruption was made by Lenin in his "sex is not a glass of water" dictum; the classical radical case for Bohemian joy was made by the anarchist Emma Goldman.

[36] For a discussion of the monotonous character of the round of student radical life, see Wechsler, *op. cit.*

context within which they are viewed. This context is provided by the general characteristics of unconventional politics.

Radical politics is extremist rather than moderate.[37] It is less attentive than conventional politics to the administrative bylaws which govern collegiate activity. Thus, elements of excitement and risk are introduced. Moreover, radical politics is revolutionary rather than simply reformist. A revolutionary orientation adds meaning and drama to concrete activities, and it provides a basis for vicarious excitement by requiring identification with actual revolutions taking place elsewhere. Furthermore, radical politics is ideological rather than "market" [38] politics, and, thus, a sense of moral superiority attaches to the activities of the enterprise. Finally, radical politics is year-round rather than seasonal, and, thus, imparts a sense of urgency rarely apparent in conventional politics. In summary, each of the characteristics of unconventional politics conspires to transform the mundane to the extraordinary. Thus it is that what appears to the uninitiated a serious and dull business is converted to an enterprise with some appeal for rebellious youth.

Bohemianism: Spirit and Substance

Bohemianism is a socioartistic enterprise which appeared as a widespread phenomenon in the first part of the nineteenth century in France.[39] Since then, it has spread to many parts of the world, particularly Europe and the United States. Despite indigenous sources in the United States and despite internal influences, the periods of rise and fall have coincided fairly well with its cycles in France.[40] Beat, the most recent expression of American Bohemianism, is best viewed as a response to recurrent internal conditions which have typically favored its resurgence, most notably prosperity of the postwar variety and as a reflection of developments on the French scene, most notably the emergence of *café* existentialism.

The failure to understand the traditional character of Bohemianism in selected American locales and the failure to see its ebb and flow as a reflection of recurrent social process, internal and external, has been largely responsible for alarmist interpretations of beat. Beat has been viewed, alternatively, as a sign of incipient nihilist rebellion and a symbol of hedonistic withdrawal from public life. It has been interpreted as a symptom of some deeper malady and a dark foreboding of what is to come. Interpretations of this sort should be expected whenever deviant patterns are not viewed in

---

[37] Seymour M. Lipset, *Political Man* (New York: Doubleday, 1960).
[38] Daniel Bell, *End of Ideology* (Glencoe: Free Press, 1960).
[39] Parry, *op. cit.,* ix.
[40] Parry, *ibid.*

their historical context.[41] What are the persistent components of the Bohemian tradition, and why may beat be properly viewed as its most recent American expression?

ROMANTICISM

The first and major component of Bohemianism is romanticism. Romanticism, suggests Shils, "starts with the appreciation of the spontaneous manifestations of the essence of concrete individuality. Hence it values originality . . . that which is produced from the 'genius' of the individual (or the folk), in contrast with the stereotyped and traditional actions of the philistine." [42] The commitment to spontaneity and originality has had many manifestations among traditional Bohemians, particularly in the graphic arts.[43] Among beats, however, greater stress has been placed on development of originality and spontaneity in other art forms. Most notable among these have been the celebration of improvisation in modern jazz, poetry, and the novel. For this reason, and for others, jazz and jazz musicians have occupied an exalted role in the beat point of view. Kerouac, the most notable literary exponent of improvisation, has occupied a similarly exalted position.[44]

The exaltation of spontaneity in artistic endeavor is reflected in the Bohemian view of the folk. Bohemianism, like radicalism, has a distinctive form of populism, which is best termed "primitivism." Its authentic folk hero is, of course, the gypsy. Due, perhaps, to the gypsy's chronic unavailability, it was not long before the notion of primitive folk was expanded to include more visible groupings. The closest approximation that could be found in urban society was the *lumpenproletariat,* and it is this group that has occupied a central place in the Bohemian's primitivist mystique.[45] In the modern rendition of Bohemianism, the mantle of idealized folk has largely fallen on the lower-class Negro.[46] However, the Negro is not the first American ethnic group to be granted this dubious honor. East European Jews, too, were perceived by previous Bohemians as the incarnation of primitive folk.[47]

Closely connected to the celebration of the primitive is the tradition of dedicated poverty. "A neighborhood where the poor live, the poor who are

[41] John P. Sisk, "Beatniks and Tradition," in Parkinson, *op. cit.*
[42] Shils, *op. cit.,* p. 57.
[43] Harold Rosenberg, *The Tradition of the New* (New York: Horizon, 1959); also, William Barrett, *Irrational Man* (New York: Doubleday, 1958), Chap. 3.
[44] Jack Kerouac's major publications include *On the Road* (New York: Viking, 1957); *Dharma Bums* (New York: Viking, 1958); *The Subterraneans* (New York: Grove, 1958); *Excerpts from Visions of Cody,* 1958 (no further citation).
[45] See the critique by Jean Malaquais of Norman Mailer's "White Negro," in *Dissent,* Winter 1958.
[46] The most explicit statement of this view is found in Norman Mailer, "The White Negro," *Dissent,* Summer 1957.
[47] See Parry, *op. cit.,* p. 35, for a Bohemian's description of East European Jews on the Lower East Side in 1910 that is indistinguishable from the way in which lower-class Negro life is currently romanticized.

resigned to their poverty, is the best environment in which to live 'the life.' This is a cardinal principle which the beat share with the Bohemians of the past." [48] Although the dedication to poverty is, in part, a natural outgrowth of a commitment to primitivism, it is simultaneously a conscious way of avoiding the corrupting influence of the commercial world. Among beats, dedicated poverty is taken for granted. It is hardly a subject for debate. What is discussed are "ways of 'making it' . . . with as little commercial work as possible, or ideally, with no commercial work at all." [49]

A final aspect of romanticism seems wholly consistent with primitivism. It consists of a more or less complete rejection of bureaucratic-industrial society. This may be referred to as medievalism and is best described as an apocalyptic view without the apocalypse. Medievalism accepts the first part of the apocalyptic formula, man's fall from grace,[50] but makes no provision, as in radicalism, for man's redemption.[51]

In many respects, the beat's medievalism is similar to a more conventional intellectual view embodied in the theory of mass culture. Shils suggests: [52]

> The critical interpretation of mass culture rests on a distinct image of modern man, of modern society and of man in past ages. . . . According to this view, the ordinary consumer of popular culture is something new in the world. He is a "private atomic subject," utterly without religious beliefs, without any private life, without a family that means anything to him; he is standardized, ridden with anxiety, perpetually, in a state of exacerbated unrest, his life emptied of meaning, trivialized, alienated from his past, his community, and possibly from himself, cretinized and brutalized.

Thus, the beat's rejection of modern life [53] is linked to the larger society through its affinity with the theory of mass culture, just as it is linked to the past through the tradition of what we shall call morose Bohemianism.

EXPRESSIVE AUTHENTICITY
AND THE BOHEMIAN MOODS

The second component of the Bohemian tradition is the insistence on the expression of authentic inner feelings. Thus, Bohemianism has been marked

[48] Laurence Lipton, *The Holy Barbarians* (New York: Messner, 1959), p. 59.
[49] *Ibid.*, p. 54.
[50] Typically dating from the Industrial Revolution.
[51] Its only vision of apocalypse is the atomic holocaust, which, in a strict sense, is no apocalypse at all since there is little promise of redemption. See Gene Feldman and Max Gartenberg, *The Beat Generation and the Angry Young Men* (New York: Dell, 1958), p. 12.
[52] Edward A. Shils, "Daydreams and Nightmares," *Sewanee Review,* Fall 1957, pp. 596–600.
[53] For a somewhat obscene statement of the beat's rejection of modern progress, see Jack Kerouac, *Dharma Bums, op. cit.,* pp. 38–39; for a discussion of Poe and his rejection of society, see Parry, *op. cit.,* Chap. 1.

by an intense moodiness. Mood is not to be suppressed or obscured; rather, it is to be indulged, pursued, and exhibited. Mood is a crucial part of inner, or authentic, experience and, thus, deserves unhampered expression. Because of the dedication to the full expression of mood, Bohemianism has always been somewhat perplexing to the outsider who expects some consistency of temperament to accompany a reasonably coherent viewpoint.

Bohemianism has long had two faces which, although they are often combined in the career of the same person, have been manifested in two roughly differentiated streams. There is frivolous Bohemianism, reminiscent in many respects of aristocratic "dandyism"; and there is morose Bohemianism, initiated by Poe and popularized by Baudelaire.[54] After Baudelaire, the two moods persist and are reflected in beat in the modern distinction between "hot" and "cool." [55]

> By 1948 the hipsters, or beatsters, were divided into cool and hot. Much of the misunderstanding about . . . the Beat Generation . . . derives from the fact that there are two distinct styles of hipsterism; the cool today is your bearded laconic sage . . . before a hardly touched beer in a beatnik dive, whose speech is low and unfriendly, whose girls say nothing and wear black: The "hot" today is the crazy talkative shining-eyed (often innocent and open-hearted) nut who runs from bar to bar, pad to pad, looking for everybody, shouting, restless, lushy, trying to "make it" with subterranean beatniks who ignore him. Most beat generation artists belong to the hot school. . . . In many cases the mixture is 50–50. It was a hot hipster like myself who finally cooled it in Buddhist meditation, though when I go in a jazz joint I still feel like yelling "Blow, baby, Blow!"

Thus, in the insistence on the authentic display of mood, and in the development of frivolous and morose subtraditions, Bohemianism has pushed to the limits of human expression. It has had a manic and a depressive character.

MONASTICISM

Even for the morose, however, the solitary life receives little authorization in the Bohemian view. The unfriendly, laconic sage in Kerouac's description had, after all, "made the scene." Bohemias must have "scenes," since Bohemianism has always referred to a collecting of like-minded eccentrics.[56]

Monasticism, which refers to the formation of insulated communities of adherents, is an explicit attempt on the part of Bohemians to regain the sense of community which, according to their ideology, no longer exists in the broader society.[57] The clubs, *cafés,* dives, or pads, which are their monas-

---

54 Parry, *op. cit.,* pp. 11–12.
55 Jack Kerouac, "The Origins of the Beat Generation," in Parkinson, *op. cit.,* p. 73.
56 For a discussion of the importance of "scenes," see Francis Rigney and L. Douglas Smith, *The Real Bohemia* (New York: Basic Books, 1961), Chap. 1; also Lipton, *op. cit.,* Chap. 1; and Parry, *op. cit.*
57 It is because of their peculiar commitment to community that beats often sound like "squares."

teries, are places where the bonds of familiarity can be assumed and, except for the danger of the police interloper, one hardly need "check out" a scene before feeling secure in it. However, not all are welcome in the places of congregation. Monasticism refers to communities of authentic adherents. Thus, theirs is an exclusive community. Bohemians are not evangelist; on the contrary, the newcomer must prove in a variety of ways that he belongs.[58]

Bohemians have long realized that both the unauthentic (pretenders or "phonies") and the outright conventional (tourist or "squares") are greatly fascinated by the Bohemian life.[59] But because of their stress on authenticity, Bohemians have been guarded in their relations with phonies and squares. Moreover, they are guarded because they have been dimly aware of the fate that, sooner or later, befalls all Bohemians. The monasticism of Bohemians, coupled with the persistence with which the squares and phonies discover their haunts, has meant that virtually no Bohemian "monastery" could long survive. Moreover, Bohemian neighborhoods, too, made up of garrets and *cafés,* in traditional Bohemian parlance, or pads and scenes, in modern Bohemian parlance, have been short-lived. When the phonies and squares arrive, some of the most zealous Bohemians leave. From that point on, the process seems irreversible; the phonies move in, the rents increase, many of the remaining Bohemians are forced to leave, and a new pseudo-Bohemia, in the manner of Greenwich Village, is created.[60]

SUBSTANCE

The "business" of Bohemianism has two important and interrelated elements. First, there is the creation of unconventional art which may be distinguished from the conventional variety in three major ways. It is disaffiliated from the major institutions which provide the machinery for the production and distribution of art. Among these institutions are the modern university, with its direct and indirect subsidization of the arts, and the modern industries of mass communication which, alternatively, deal commercially in art (publishing firms) or deal in commercialized art (advertising). Second, stylistic innovation is characteristic of Bohemian art. In each of the arts, the Bohemian has been an experimenter in new styles of expression.

The third feature of unconventional art applies to its subject matter. Bohemian art has frequently dealt with the forbidden, the censorable. In his attempt to plumb the depths of human existence, the Bohemian has often been guilty of equivocation, of confusing or equating the two meanings of "depths." This equivocation was an outgrowth of the Bohemian's peculiar style of populism in which authentic life coincides with primitive life, with life as it is lived in the lowest orders of society and the underworld. His own

[58] Rigney and Smith, *op. cit.*
[59] Rigney and Smith, *op. cit.,* p. 181.
[60] Parry, *op. cit.,* p. 58; Rigney and Smith, *op. cit.,* Chaps. 10–11.

descent into the lowest orders, resulting from his dedicated poverty, allowed him to extend the province of his subject matter in an important manner. If the Bohemian feared the *lumpenproletariat,* or if he discovered that their behavior was not always censorable, he could always turn to what is, after all, the most frequent subject matter of Bohemian art—Bohemians. This was fortunate, for if Bohemian life was not sufficiently censorable, there was always the possibility of making it so.

This brings us to the second and interrelated element of the Bohemian enterprise, the pursuit of unconventional personal experience. It is interrelated, because, whatever its motive among Bohemians, it has persistently performed a crucial function for young, aspiring painters, poets, sculptors, and novelists. It has provided them with a subject matter to which to apply their variable talents.

In the pursuit of unconventional personal experience, there is no assurance of success. Some sorts of experience involve higher risks of failure than others—the pursuit of sexual conquest, for instance, is less likely to culminate successfully than the use of alcohol to lessen inhibitions. Thus, a cataloguing of the forms of experience traditionally pursued by Bohemians should not be mistaken for an accurate rendition of what Bohemians typically do. More time seems spent in pursuit than in actual experience.[61]

Two sorts of unconventional experience are pursued. First, there is the pursuit of hedonistic experiences which overlap considerably with activities that are currently deemed illegal in the United States. These are generally nonvictimizing offenses; included are such offenses as sexual excess, homosexuality, intemperate use of alcohol, disturbing the peace, use of narcotics, and speeding in automobiles. Many of these activities received celebration among Bohemians during the nineteenth century.[62] Thus, it should not be assumed that beats have attained a new threshold of hedonistic experience.

Second, there is a quest for transcendence. This is closely related to the problem of creativity and represents an experimenting with the limits to which human perception may be pushed. It is as an attempt to transcend the mundane limits on human perception that we can best understand three highly esoteric activities of beats: religious mysticism as manifested in Buddhist meditation, or the "Zen kick";[63] the flirtation with and acceptance of psychosis, or the "insanity bit";[64] and the hallucinogenic use of drugs.[65]

---

[61] Most novels of beat life written by beats, or those close to beats, confirm this point. Kerouac's novels particularly, may be taken as accurate replicas of beat life. Also, see Chandler Brossard, *Who Walk in Darkness* (New York: New Directions, 1952).

[62] Parry, *op. cit.,* p. 11.

[63] Kerouac, *Dharma Bums, op. cit.*

[64] Seymour Krim, "The Insanity Bit," in *The Beats,* ed. Seymour Krim (Greenwich: Fawcett, 1960).

[65] Lipton, *op. cit.,* p. 178.

Rebellious Youth: Restoration and Prevention

The integration of rebellious youth into conventional society hardly seems possible, particularly in view of the eccentricities inherent in each of the subterranean traditions. Yet, the great majority of vulnerable youth are barely touched by these traditions in their full-blown forms and, of those that are, the great majority seem able to re-enter conventional life with the attainment of social adulthood. Two questions must, therefore, be posed. Why, given the vulnerability of youth to modes of rebelliousness, do so few participate in full-blown deviant traditions? And by what process are those who do participate reintegrated into society? The first is the problem of prevention, the second of restoration.

Our concern, here, is not with programmatic solutions which, with respect to the problems of youthful rebelliousness, seem ineffective or nonexistent.[66] Instead, we are interested in a process on which the integration of youth seems far more dependent, and that is the crescive and unintended formation of arrangements which fortuitously expedite integration. One such arrangement may be found in the existence of conventional versions of subterranean traditions.[67]

Conventional versions are reasonable facsimiles of subterranean traditions in which their most offensive features are stripped away or tempered. As indicated, this is not by design, but as a result of emergent syntheses of conventional and rebellious sentiments or as a consequence of the fortuitous existence of independent traditions.

A conventional version of the delinquent tradition is what has come to be called teen-age culture. Here we find an emphasis on fun and adventure; a disdain for scholastic effort; the more or less persistent involvement in "tolerated" status offenses like drinking, gambling, occasional truancy, "making out" in the sense of sexual conquest, driving cars before the appropriate age, smoking, swearing, and staying out late. The elements of the delinquent tradition that are lacking or tempered are those that are least tolerated. Aggression is considerably tempered, but there is a persistent concern with the credentials on masculinity and femininity. Victimizing crimes are stripped away, and the forms of prowess used for getting money to play at luxury are usually limited to the "conning" of parents.

---

[66] The only subterranean tradition for which there is an ongoing correctional apparatus specializing in the restoration of youth is delinquency. Even in that case, however, there is considerable uncertainty as to whether the fact of official correction or the quality of that correction has any effect on the chances of reforming. See Edwin Powers and Helen Witmer, *An Experiment in the Prevention of Delinquency: The Cambridge-Somerville Youth Study* (New York: Columbia University Press, 1951).

[67] Talcott Parsons, *The Social System* (Glencoe: The Free Press, 1951), pp. 305–306; also, Paul Goodman, *Growing Up Absurd* (New York: Random House, 1960); also, Bennett Berger, *op. cit.*

Many youngsters who would otherwise be vulnerable to the appeals of delinquency get caught up in the teen-age round-of-life. Because it has many inherent satisfactions, it tends to maintain the loyalty of its adherents. Furthermore, since it is allegedly capable of deflecting studious teen-agers, it is probably at least as effective in deflecting youngsters who are prone to a tradition with which it has far greater affinity. Moreover, it is likely that the greatest proportion of ex-delinquents do not fully reform and become "good boys" in the adult and scholastic sense of the term; more likely, they pass into the ranks of "corner boys" of the lower and middle classes. Thus, although teen-age culture may sometimes act as a preparation for the delinquent tradition, as its critics would have it, there seems little doubt that it often serves the functions of prevention and restoration.

A conventional version of the radical tradition may be found in the long-standing American posture of "doing good." This is a kind of inchoate and uninformed liberalism. It is vaguely radical in that it, too, laments the corruption of society and looks forward to improvement, but it does not envisage apocalypse. It, too, is populist, but only in the limited sense of being for the underdog. It, too, believes in evangelism, but the most frequent expression of its evangelism is guilty inaction. Though this group has long been recognized as a source of sympathizers for radical organizations, its functions in preventing radicalism by providing a tenable alternative, a facsimile, for rebelliously inclined and idealistic youth has been frequently overlooked; so, too, has its function in the restoration of radical youth. It is not likely that the greatest number of ex-radicals become either McCarthyites or liberal anti-Communists; more likely, they slip into inactivity, pass into ranks of those committed to doing good, and neutralize the guilt of persistent political inactivity by pointing to the demands of scholarship.

In the Bohemian case, we must proceed cautiously. Because of the great emphasis placed on authenticity and, thus, the great sensitivity and hostility to phonies, the integrative effects of the conventional versions of Bohemianism may be partially neutralized. It is, perhaps, for this reason that Bohemians seem to linger further into the reaches of chronological adulthood than radicals or delinquents. A Bohemian, because of the stress on authenticity, is more likely than the radical or the delinquent to perceive the "duplicity of social systems" that lies behind each of the facsimiles. While this almost certainly holds with respect to the function of restoration, it is likely that conventional versions serve to deflect youth who are vulnerable to Bohemianism without yet being aware of its esoteric details. Nonetheless, we must leave open the possibility that, because of the stress on authenticity, there can be no effective facsimile of Bohemianism.[68] Thus, it is with some hesitation that we suggest that fraternity life may be viewed as a conventional

[68] This does not mean that Bohemians cannot be restored to conventional society. There are other integrative processes. Bennett Berger points to the integrative effects of "youthful" roles within the adult system. See Berger, *op. cit.*

facsimile of frivolous Bohemianism and that student intellectuals stand in a similar relation to morose Bohemianism. Fraternity life frequently has a quality that is reminiscent of the most frivolous sorts of Bohemianism. There is the congregating and singing in student taverns, the round of larks and pranks, the aversion for cerebral activity, the exclusiveness and fraternalism of Bohemian monasticism, the pursuit of "weak" and typically inoffensive "kicks." The affinity between student intellectualism and morose Bohemianism may be found in the following: the student intellectual is concerned with creativity and free expression, which may be taken as a tempering of the Bohemian's commitment to unconventional art; he is concerned with integrity, which may be viewed as a routinized form of expressive authenticity; he is unwilling to join his conventional classmates in the celebration of material success, which is a tempered form of the Bohemian's dedication to poverty; he is prone to the medievalist view of Bohemians while rejecting primitivist populism; and, finally, he is temperamentally given to seriousness, which is a tempered version of the Bohemian's moroseness.

Our brief discussion of the integration of youth has focused on one set of mechanisms. These mechanisms, however, operate within a context of two other important features of modern society. First, there is the widespread sentiment of adult tolerance. Though the strength of this sentiment varies through time and by section of the population, there is a significant and influential portion of adult opinion that is ready to embrace prodigal youth if and when they return. Second, there is the waning of the tensions and frustrations making for youthful rebelliousness resulting from the onset of adulthood and the gaining of "first-class citizenship." As important as these are, they are not sufficient to provide a basis for the integration of youth. There is the further necessity for some systematic arrangement to exist through which the integrative potential of adult tolerance and social maturation of youth may be realized. One such arrangement may be found in the fortuitous existence of conventional versions of the subterranean traditions of youth.

The Making of a Counter Culture:
An Invasion of Centaurs

Theodore Roszak

> In the "today," in every "today," various generations coexist and the
> relations which are established between them, according to the different
> condition of their ages, represent the dynamic system of attractions and
> repulsions, of agreement and controversy which at any given moment
> makes up the reality of historic life.[1]

If we agree with Ortega that the fitful transition of the generations is a
significant element in historical change, we must also recognize that the
young may do little more than remodel the inherited culture in minor or
marginal ways. They may settle for alterations that amount to a change of
superficial fashion, undertaken out of mere pique or caprice. What is special
about the generational transition we are in is the scale on which it is taking
place and the depth of antagonism it reveals. Indeed, it would hardly seem
an exaggeration to call what we see arising among the young a "counter
culture." Meaning: a culture so radically disaffiliated from the mainstream
assumptions of our society that it scarcely looks to many as a culture at all,
but takes on the alarming appearance of a barbaric intrusion.

An image comes at once to mind: the invasion of centaurs that is recorded
on the pediment of the Temple of Zeus at Olympia. Drunken and incensed,
the centaurs burst in upon the civilized festivities that are in progress. But a
stern Apollo, the guardian of the orthodox culture, steps forward to ad-
monish the gate-crashers and drive them back. The image is a potent one,
for it recalls what must always be a fearful experience in the life of any
civilization: the experience of radical cultural disjuncture, the clash of irreconcilable conceptions of life. And the encounter is not always won by
Apollo.

Toynbee has identified such cultural disjunctures as the work of a dis-
inherited "proletariat," using as his paradigm the role of the early Christians
within the Roman Empire—a classic case of Apollo being subverted by the
unruly centaurs. The Christian example is one that many of the hip young
are quick to invoke, perhaps with more appropriateness than many of their
critics may recognize. Hopelessly estranged by ethos and social class from

[1] José Ortega y Gasset, *Man and Crisis,* trans. Mildred Adams (London: Allen &
Unwin, 1959), p. 45.

the official culture, the primitive Christian community awkwardly fashioned of Judaism and the mystery cults a minority culture that could not but seem an absurdity to Greco-Roman orthodoxy. But the absurdity, far from being felt as a disgrace, became a banner of the community.

> For it is written [St. Paul boasted] I will destroy the wisdom of the wise, and will bring to nothing the understanding of the prudent. . . . For the Jews require a sign, and the Greeks seek after wisdom. . . . But God hath chosen the foolish things of the world to confound the wise; and God hath chosen the weak things of the world to confound the things which are mighty. (I Cor. 1:19, 22, 27)

It is a familiar passage from what is now an oppressively respectable source. So familiar and so respectable that we easily lose sight of how aggressively perverse a declaration it is . . . how loaded with unabashed contempt for a long-established culture rich with achievement. And whose contempt was this? That of absolute nobodies, the very scum of the earth, whose own counter culture was, at this early stage, little more than a scattering of suggestive ideas, a few crude symbols, and a desperate longing. It was the longing that counted most, for not all the grandeur of Greco-Roman civilization could fill the desolation of spirit Christianity bred upon. Since we know now with an abundance of hindsight what the Christian *scandalum* eventually led to, the comparison with the still fledgling counter culture of our youth is bound to seem outlandish. But then, all revolutionary changes are unthinkable until they happen . . . and then they are understood to be inevitable. Who, in Paul's time, could have anticipated what would come of the brazen hostility of a handful of scruffy malcontents? And what would the nascent Christian movement have looked like under the merciless floodlights of any then-existing mass media? Would it even have survived the saturation coverage?

Perhaps the young of this generation haven't the stamina to launch the epochal transformation they seek; but there should be no mistaking the fact that they want nothing less. "Total rejection" is a phrase that comes readily to their lips, often before the mind provides even a blurred picture of the new culture that is to displace the old. If there is anything about the ethos of Black Power that proves particularly attractive even to young white disaffiliates who cannot gain access to the movement, it is the sense that Black Power somehow implies an entirely new way of life: a black culture, a black consciousness . . . a black soul which is totally incompatible with white society and aggressively proud of the fact. Black Power may build any number of barriers between white and Negro youth, but across the barriers a common language can still be heard. Here, for example, is Bobby Seale of the Oakland Black Panthers speaking to a meeting of the Center for Participative Education held at the University of California at Berkeley in September 1968. The crisis at hand stemmed from a decision of the UC regents to deny a Black Panther spokesman access to the campus. But for Seale, as for the students, the issue had deeper cultural implications. Everything—the meaning of authority, of personal identity, of Judeo-Christian ethics, of sexual freedom—was somehow involved in this single act of administrative censorship.

> Archie and Jughead never kissed Veronica and Betty. Superman never kissed Lois Lane. We are tired of relating to comic book conceptions. Adam should have defended the Garden of Eden against the omnipotent administrator. Life, liberty, and the pursuit of happiness don't mean nothing to me if I can't go home and feel safe with my wife in bed replenishing the earth.[2]

At first glance, it may not be apparent what sentiments of this kind (and they were the substance of the address) have to do with an issue of academic freedom. But Seale's audience had no trouble understanding. They readily recognized that authoritarianism in our society operates overtly or subtly at every level of life, from comic strip imagery to Christian theology, from the college classroom to the privacy of the bedroom—and they were prepared to discard the culture that relied on such sleazy coercion, root and branch.

Or to take another example of these apocalyptic yearnings that beset our young. When the Antiuniversity of London, the first English version of our free universities, was opened in early 1968, its prospectus was filled with courses devoted to "anti-cultures," "anti-environments," "anti-poetry," "anti-theatre," "anti-families," and "counter institutions." Seemingly nothing the adult society had to offer any longer proved acceptable. The super-heated radicalism of the school was eventually to reach such a pitch that even the age-old student-teacher relationship came under fire as an intolerable form of authoritarianism. So it too was scrapped, on the assumption that nobody any longer had anything to teach the young; they would make up their own education from scratch. Unfortunately—but was the misfortune more comic or more tragic?—the school failed to survive this act of radical restructuring.

Such white-hot discontent always runs the risk of evaporating into a wild, amorphous steam—so that it becomes difficult to tell the chiliastic illuminations from mere inanities. The typical fare offered at the Antiuniversity can be sampled in one of the "courses," called "From Comic Books to the Dance of Shiva: Spiritual Amnesia and the Physiology of Self-Estrangement." (Again one notes the bizarre but cunning association of the comic strip and high religion.)

> Description of course: A free-wheeling succession of open-ended situations. Ongoing vibrations highly relevant. Exploration of Inner Space,

[2] From a recording of the address presented over KPFA (Berkeley) on September 24, 1968.

> de-conditioning of human robot, significance of psycho-chemicals, and
> the transformation of Western European Man. Source material: Artaud,
> Zimmer, Gurdjieff, W. Reich, K. Marx, Gnostic, Sufi, and Tantric texts,
> autobiographical accounts of madness and ecstatic states of conscious-
> ness—Pop art and twentieth century prose.

Heavy weather indeed. But altogether representative of the free-university
style. Often enough, such madcap brainstorming under the auspices of instructors hardly out of their teens degenerates into a semi-articulate, indis-
criminate celebration of everything in sight that is new, strange, and noisy;
a fondling of ideas that resembles nothing so much as an infant's play with
bright, unfamiliar objects. The appetite is healthily and daringly omniv-
orous, but it urgently requires mature minds to feed it. But to make my own
point of view quite clear from the outset, I believe that, despite their follies,
these young centaurs deserve to win their encounter with the defending
Apollos of our society. For the orthodox culture they confront is fatally and
contagiously diseased. The prime symptom of that disease is the shadow of
thermonuclear annihilation beneath which we cower. The counter culture
takes its stand against the background of this absolute evil, an evil which
is not defined by the sheer *fact* of the bomb, but by the total *ethos* of the
bomb, in which our politics, our public morality, our economic life, our
intellectual endeavor are now embedded with a wealth of ingenious rationali-
zation. We are a civilization sunk in an unshakeable commitment to geno-
cide, gambling madly with the universal extermination of our species. And
how viciously we ravish our sense of humanity to pretend, even for a day,
that such horror can be accepted as "normal," as "necessary"! Whenever
we feel inclined to qualify, to modify, to offer a cautious "yes . . . *but*" to
the protests of the young, let us return to this fact as the decisive measure
of the technocracy's essential criminality: the extent to which it insists, in
the name of progress, in the name of reason, that the unthinkable become
thinkable and the intolerable become tolerable.

If the counter culture is, as I will contend here, that healthy instinct which
refuses both at the personal and political level to practice such a cold-
blooded rape of our human sensibilities, then it should be clear why the
conflict between young and adult in our time reaches so peculiarly and
painfully deep. In an historical emergency of absolutely unprecedented
proportions, we are that strange, culture-bound animal whose biological
drive for survival expresses itself *generationally*. It is the young, arriving
with eyes that can see the obvious, who must remake the lethal culture of
their elders, and who must remake it in desperate haste.

To take the position I assume here is undeniably risky. For once a cultural disjuncture opens out in society, nothing can be guaranteed. What
happens among the minority that finds itself isolated by the rift is as apt to
be ugly or pathetic as it is to be noble. The primitive Christian absurdity can

be credited at least with the capacity to produce mighty works of intellect and mystic insight, as well as an ideal of saintly service. On the other hand, the alienated stock clerks and wallpaper hangers of post-World War I Germany sullenly withdrew to their beer halls to talk imbecile anthropology and prepare the horrors of Buchenwald. So, too, contemporary America's isolated minorities include the Hell's Angels and the Minutemen, from whom nothing beautiful or tender can be expected.

And our alienated young: how shall we characterize the counter culture they are in the way of haphazardly assembling? Clearly one cannot answer the question by producing a manifesto unanimously endorsed by the malcontented younger generation: the counter culture is scarcely so disciplined a movement. It is something in the nature of a medieval crusade: a variegated procession constantly in flux, acquiring and losing members all along the route of march. Often enough it finds its own identity in a nebulous symbol or song that seems to proclaim little more than "we are special . . . we are different . . . we are outward-bound from the old corruptions of the world." Some join the troop only for a brief while, long enough to enter an obvious and immediate struggle: a campus rebellion, an act of war-resistance, a demonstration against racial injustice. Some may do no more than flourish a tiny banner against the inhumanities of the technocracy; perhaps they pin on a button declaring "I am a human being: do not mutilate, spindle, or tear." Others, having cut themselves off hopelessly from social acceptance, have no option but to follow the road until they reach the Holy City. No piecemeal reforms or minor adjustments of what they leave behind would make turning back possible for them.

But where is this Holy City that lies beyond the technocracy—and what will it be like? Along the way, there is much talk about that, some of it foolish, some of it wise. Many in the procession may only be certain of what it must *not* be like. A discerning few have a shrewd sense of where the technocracy leaves off and the New Jerusalem begins: not at the level of class, party, or institution, but rather at the non-intellective level of the personality from which these political and social forms issue. They see, and many who follow them find the vision attractive, that building the good society is not primarily a social, but a psychic task. What makes the youthful disaffiliation of our time a cultural phenomenon, rather than merely a political movement, is the fact that it strikes beyond ideology to the level of consciousness, seeking to transform our deepest sense of the self, the other, the enviroment.

The psychiatrist R. D. Laing captures the spirit of the matter when he observes: "We do not need theories so much as the experience that is the source of the theory." Such a distinction between theory and experience, challenging as it does the validity of mere analytical clarity as a basis for knowledge or conviction, cannot help but carry an anti-intellectual tone.

The tone becomes even more pronounced when Laing goes on to define the goal of "true sanity" as being

> in one way or another, the dissolution of the normal ego, that false self competently adjusted to our alienated social reality: the emergence of the "inner" archetypal mediators of divine power, and through this death a rebirth, and the eventual re-establishment of a new kind of ego-functioning, the ego now being the servant of the divine, no longer its betrayer.[3]

When psychiatry begins to speak this language, it moves well beyond the boundaries of conventional scientific respectability. But if the dissenting young give their attention to figures like Laing (he is one of the leading mentors of Britain's burgeoning counter culture), it is surely because they have seen too many men of indisputable intelligence and enlightened intention become the apologists of a dehumanized social order. What is it that has allowed so many of our men of science, our scholars, our most sophisticated political leaders, even our boldest would-be revolutionaries to make their peace with the technocracy—or indeed to enter its service so cheerfully? Not lack of intellect or ignorance of humane values. It is rather that technocratic assumptions about the nature of man, society, and nature have warped their experience at the source, and so have become the buried premises from which intellect and ethical judgment proceed.

In order, then, to root out those distortive assumptions, nothing less is required than the subversion of the scientific world view, with its entrenched commitment to an egocentric and cerebral mode of consciousness. In its place, there must be a new culture in which the non-intellective capacities of the personality—those capacities that take fire from visionary splendor and the experience of human communion—become the arbiters of the good, the true, and the beautiful. I think the cultural disjuncture that generational dissent is opening out between itself and the technocracy is just this great, as great in its implications (though obviously not as yet in historical import) as the cleavage that once ran between Greco-Roman rationality and Christian mystery. To be sure, Western society has, over the past two centuries, incorporated a number of minorities whose antagonism toward the scientific world view has been irreconcilable, and who have held out against the easy assimilation to which the major religious congregations have yielded in their growing desire to seem progressive. Theosophists and fundamentalists, spiritualists and flat-earthers, occultists and satanists . . . it is nothing new that there should exist antirationalist elements in our midst. What *is* new is that a radical rejection of science and technological values should appear so

[3] R. D. Laing, *The Politics of Experience and The Bird of Paradise* (London: Penguin Books, 1967), p. 119.

close to the center of our society, rather than on the negligible margins. It is the middle-class young who are conducting this politics of consciousness, and they are doing it boisterously, persistently, and aggressively—to the extent that they are invading the technocracy's citadels of academic learning and bidding fair to take them over.

The task of characterizing the non-intellective powers of the personality in which our young have become so deeply involved is far from easy. Until the advent of psychoanalysis, the vocabulary of our society was woefully impoverished when it came to discussion of the non-intellective aspects of life. The mystics and Romantics who have worked most closely to the dark side of the mind provide us with a repertory of brilliant metaphors and images to explain their experience. Similarly, the Hindu and Buddist traditions contain a vocabulary of marvelous discrimination for speaking of the non-intellective consciousness—as well as a number of techniques for tapping its contents. But the scientific intelligence rejects metaphor and mystical terminology the way a vending machine tosses out counterfeit coins (with a single revealing exception: the metaphor of natural "law," without which the scientific revolution might never have gotten off the ground). It leaves us devoid of language as soon as we enter that province of experience in which artists and mystics claim to have found the highest values of existence. Even psychoanalysis has been of little help in the discussion of the non-intellective, mainly because its approach has been burdened with a mechanistic vocabulary and an objective stand-offishness: a prying examination from the "outside," rather than a warm experiencing from the "inside." In reviewing the intellectual history of the generation that saw the appearance of Freud, Sorel, Weber, and Durkheim—the first generation to undertake what it hoped would be respectably scientific research into man's irrational motivations—H. Stuart Hughes observes:

> The social thinkers of the 1890's were concerned with the irrational only to exorcize it. By probing into it, they sought ways to tame it, to canalize it for constructive human purposes.[4]

As the spell of scientific or quasi-scientific thought has spread in our culture from the physical to the so-called behavioral sciences, and finally to scholarship in the arts and letters, the marked tendency has been to consign whatever is not fully and articulately available in the waking consciousness for empirical or mathematical manipulation, to a purely negative catch-all category (in effect, the cultural garbage can) called the "unconscious" . . . or the "irrational" . . . or the "mystical" . . . or the "purely

[4] H. Stuart Hughes, *Consciousness and Society* (New York: Vintage Books, 1958), pp. 35–36. Only Bergson and Jung, among major thinkers of the period outside the arts, treated the non-rational side of human nature with an intuitive sympathy. But who, in the scientific community or the academy, any longer regards them as "major thinkers"?

subjective." To behave on the basis of such blurred states of consciousness is at best to be some species of amusing eccentric, at worst to be plain mad. Conversely, behavior that is normal, valuable, productive, mentally healthy, socially respectable, intellectually defensible, sane, decent, and practical is supposed to have nothing to do with subjectivity. When we tell one another to "be reasonable," to "talk sense," to "get down to brass tacks," to "keep one's feet on the ground," to "stick to the facts," to "be realistic," we mean that one should avoid talking about one's "inner" feelings and look at the world rather in the way an engineer looks at a construction project or a physicist views the behavior of atomic particles. We feel that worthwhile things come of such a state of mind—knowledge, solutions to problems, successful projects, money, power—whereas only some manner of unproductive self-indulgence comes of wallowing in "mere feelings." The more sophisticated may admit the legitimacy of allowing artists to moon and daydream. But the world, as every practical man knows, can do without poems and paintings; it can scarcely do without dams and roads and bombs and sound policy. Art is for the leisure hours: the time left over from dealing with realities and necessities.[5]

What is said here is meant only to suggest the difficulty the counter culture faces in simply trying to designate its project. It has removed itself to a position so wide of our cultural mainstream that it can scarcely speak without seeming to fall into a foreign tongue. In a world which more and more thinks of society as the subordinate adjunct of a gigantic technological mechanism requiring constant and instantaneous co-ordination from the center, the young begin to speak of such impracticalities as "community," and "participative democracy." Thus they revert to a style of human relations that characterizes village and tribe, insisting that real politics can only take place in the deeply personal confrontations these now obsolete social forms allow. Where are they to find understanding for such a homely ideal in a world dominated by vast political abstractions decked out in glittering propagandistic symbols, slogans, and statistical measures: nation, party, corporation, urban area, grand alliance, common market, socio-economic system . . . ? The lively consciousness of men and women *as they are*

[5] One might expect some softening of this compulsively utilitarian rationality to stem from the new and now lavishly subsidized field of sleep research, which tells us of the absolute necessity of non-intellective experience. For a fascinating survey of this work, see Gay G. Luce and J. Segal, *Sleep* (London: Heinemann, 1967). Whatever else the sleep researchers may prove, however, they have already revealed the pathos of a society that must have it demonstrated by way of encephalographs and computers that the relaxation of rational consciousness and the experience of dreaming are vital to healthy life. But they do so seemingly without any awareness of the part science, with its militant intellectuality, has played in obscuring this fact. It is this blind spot which will probably lead to their research, like all science worth its subsidies these days, being used for idiotic ends. For example, Herman Kahn and Anthony Wiener, in their book *The Year 2000* (New York: Macmillan, 1967) give us a prognosis of "programmed dreams." Another instance of the technocratic principle: never let happen naturally and enjoyably what can be counterfeited by the technicians.

in their vital daily reality is missing from our culture, having been displaced by these grandiose figments. To assert that the essence of human sociability is, simply and beautifully, the communal opening-up of man to man, rather than the achievement of prodigious technical and economic feats—what is this but to assert an absurdity?

Further, what is it to assert the primacy of the non-intellective powers but to call into question all that our culture values as "reason" and "reality"? To deny that the true self is this small, hard atom of intense objectivity we pilot about each day as we build bridges and careers is surely to play fast and loose with psychopathology. It is to attack men at the very core of their security by denying the validity of everything they mean when they utter the most precious word in their vocabulary: the word "I." And yet this is what the counter culture undertakes when, by way of its mystical tendencies or the drug experience, it assaults the reality of the ego as an isolable, purely cerebral unit of identity. In doing so, it once again transcends the consciousness of the dominant culture and runs the risk of appearing to be a brazen exercise in perverse nonsense.

Yet what else but such a brave (and hopefully humane) perversity can pose a radical challenge to the technocracy? If the melancholy history of revolution over the past half-century teaches us anything, it is the futility of a politics which concentrates itself single-mindedly on the overthrowing of governments, or ruling classes, or economic systems. This brand of politics finishes with merely redesigning the turrets and towers of the technocratic citadel. It is the foundations of the edifice that must be sought. And those foundations lie among the ruins of the visionary imagination and the sense of human community. Indeed, this is what Shelley recognized even in the earliest days of the Industrial Revolution, when he proclaimed that in the defense of poetry we must invoke "light and fire from those eternal regions where the owl-winged faculty of calculation dare not ever soar." [6]

---

[6] Shelley's magnificent essay "The Defence of Poetry" could still stand muster as a counter cultural manifesto. If only our technicians, our scientists, our experts of all description could be brought face to face with such statements! Surely that would do the trick.

Section IV

Youth and the
Sex Revolution

INTRODUCTION

One of the most difficult sociological realms of study is the empirical analysis of human sexual practices and sexual relations. By nature and custom, sexuality is both private and secret, so much so that whatever data are eventually collected are subjected to the most severe tests of factual reliability.

Our knowledge of human sexual behavior is ordinarily derived from statistically biased samples or highly idiosyncratic clinical reports and, hence, is extremely limited when utilized for the purpose of generalizing about larger societal populations. Thus, in the absence of direct, comprehensive, reliable, and representative data, much of the information necessary for us to speak confidently about modern *sexual practices* has emanated from surveys of *sexual attitudes and values.* In this framework, attitudes about behavior become *indexes* of the behavior, and through an indirect approach, it enables observations and theory construction about an otherwise seemingly unobservable phenomenon.

Although it is common practice in sociology to study *either* human values *or* behavior related to these values, and consequently assume that the measure of one is also the measure of the other, the hazards of this process are perhaps no better illustrated than in the study of sexuality.[1] For in the history of modern sociological studies of sex practices until the 1940s, it was assumed that the sexual behavior of Americans fairly well conformed to the puritanical sexual codes observed to be shared by the majority of this society's members. Of course, there was knowledge of deviance from these codes, but this was regarded as the exception to the rule. In 1948 Alfred C. Kinsey and his associates, despite sampling and other methodological imperfections, exploded that myth in their initial, rather grandiosely entitled work *Sexual Behavior in the Human Male.* If any sociological lesson was to be learned from this effort, it was that reliance on data about attitudes and values often tells us little about human practices and relationships; the ultimate sociological paradox is, in fact, the limited convergence and correlation between the two.

Yet, important lessons are sometimes easily forgotten. More than two decades have passed since the publication of Kinsey's work, and almost everywhere the sex revolution is trumpeted as a fact of modern life. But what is the evidence of this revolution and what are its dimensions? In general, there appears to be good reason to believe that there have been significant changes in values toward sexuality: overall, a toleration of sexual deviance from puritanical codes, and a freedom from censorship in media presentations. It is not clear, however, that this revolution in

[1] Note: For an incisive critique of this practice and related implications for the study of delinquency and delinquent subcultures, see David Matza, *Delinquency and Drift* (New York: John Wiley & Sons, Inc., 1966).

values has equally affected all segments of society; many individuals still reject the newly found toleration and liberalism. Youths appear heavily implicated in a large share of the sex-value revolution, although even among the young, there is an unequal distribution of removal from sexual puritanism.

On the other hand, many observers still question the supposed revolutionary changes in sexual practices, particularly among the young. Again, with limited and skewed data, it appears that changes in practices may be occurring, but these changes are much slower and have failed to keep apace of the revolution in sexual values. In a sense, whereas sexual values have been revolutionized, sexual practices have slowly evolved. And, given the youthful impetus to changing sexual mores, while adding a broad historical skepticism, perhaps the apparently revolutionary process is little more than a short-lived and temporary phenomenon.

Despite the methodological and consequent theoretical problems of studying sexuality, at least two major areas of study do not provide great obstacles. One of these is the study of nonsexual components of sexual relations. Waller's article on rating and dating is the classical example of this study. In it he describes the varying social bases of courtship practice among the young. Both Reiss and Bell contribute significantly to the study of changing sexual standards and values among youths, and attempt to identify the institutional and social sources of these changes and their implications for youthful behavior, particularly its less than revolutionary magnitude.

And finally, Winick explores changing sexual identity as it appears to be evolving in modern times, suggesting through an analysis of changing names, dress, appearances, and media representations that the sexes are moving toward a single gender, described as the process of desexualization. If he is correct in his observations, then perhaps an unexpected dimension of revolutionary sex practices has already begun to arise.

The Rating and Dating Complex

Willard Waller

Courtship may be defined as the set of processes of association among the unmarried from which, in time, permanent matings usually emerge. This definition excludes those associations which cannot normally eventuate in marriage—as between Negro and white—but allows for a period of dalliance and experimentation. In the present paper we propose to discuss the customs of courtship which prevail among college students.

Courtship practices vary from one culture group to another. In many cultures marriage eventuates from a period of sexual experimentation and trial unions; in others the innocence of the unmarried is carefully guarded until their wedding day. In some cultures the bride must be virginal at marriage; in others this is just what she must not be. Sometimes the young are allowed no liberty of choice, and everything is determined for them by their elders. Sometimes persons marry in their own age group, but in other societies older men pre-empt the young women for themselves. Although there are endless variations in courtship customs, they are always functionally related to the total configuration of the culture and the biological needs of the human animal. It is helpful to remember that in a simple, undifferentiated, and stable society a long and complex process of choosing a mate is apparently not so necessary or desirable as in our own complex, differentiated, and rapidly changing society.[1]

The mores of courtship in our society are a strange composite of social heritages from diverse groups and of new usages called into existence by the needs of the time. There is a formal code of courtship which is still nominally in force, although departures from it are very numerous; the younger generation seems to find the superficial usages connected with the code highly amusing, but it is likely that it takes the central ideas quite seriously. The formal code appears to be derived chiefly from the usage of the English middle classes of a generation or so ago, although there are, of course, many other elements in it.

From Willard Waller, "The Rating and Dating Complex," *The American Sociological Review* (American Sociological Association, Vol. 2, No. 5, October 1937), pp. 727–734. Reprinted by permission of the publisher.

[1] James G. Leyburn quotes an old-fashioned Boer mother who said, "I am sick of all this talk of choosing and choosing. . . . If a man is healthy and does not drink, and has a good little handful of stock, and a good temper, and is a good Christian, what great difference can it make to a woman which man she takes? There is not so much difference between one man and another." (*Frontier Folkways,* p. 129.) Such an attitude was possible in Boer society as it is not in ours.

The usual or intended mode of operation of the formal mores of court-ship—in a sense their "function"—is to induct young persons into marriage by a series of progressive commitments. In the solidary peasant community, in the frontier community, among the English middle classes of a few decades back, and in many isolated small communities in present-day America, every step in the courtship process has a customary meaning and constitutes a powerful pressure toward taking the next step—is in fact a sort of implied commitment to take the next step. The mores formerly operated to produce a high rate of marriage at the proper age and at the same time protected most individuals from many of the possible traumatic experiences of the courtship period.

The decay of this moral structure has made possible the emergence of thrill-seeking and exploitative relationships. A thrill is merely a physiological stimulation and release of tension, and it seems curious that most of us are inclined to regard thrill-seeking with disapproval. The disapproving attitude toward thrill-seeking becomes intelligible when we recall the pur-pose of such emotional stirrings in the conventional mores of courtship. Whether we approve or not, courtship practices today allow for a great deal of pure thrill-seeking. Dancing, petting, necking, the automobile, the amuse-ment park, and a whole range of institutions and practices permit or facilitate thrill-seeking behavior. These practices, which are connected with a great range of the institutions of commercialized recreation, make of courtship an amusement and a release of organic tensions. The value judg-ment which many lay persons and even some trained sociologists pass upon thrill-seeking arises from the organizational mores of the family—from the fact that energy is dissipated in thrills which is supposed to do the work of the world, i.e., to get people safely married.

The emergence of thrill-seeking furthers the development of exploitative relationships. As long as an association is founded on a frank and admitted barter in thrills, nothing that can be called exploitative arises. But the old mores of progressive commitment exist, along with the new customs, and peculiar relationships arise from this confusion of moralities. According to the old morality a kiss means something, a declaration of love means some-thing, a number of Sunday evening dates in succession means something, and these meanings are enforced by the customary law, while under the new morality such things may mean nothing at all—that is, they may imply no commitment of the total personality whatsoever. So it comes about that one of the persons may exploit the other for thrills on the pretense of emotional involvement and its implied commitment. When a woman exploits, it is usually for the sake of presents and expensive amusements—the common pattern of "gold-digging." The male exploiter usually seeks thrills from the body of the woman. The fact that thrills cost money, usually the man's money, often operates to introduce strong elements of suspicion and antagonism into the relationship.

With this general background in mind, let us turn to the courtship practices of college students. A very important characteristic of the college student is his bourgeois pattern of life. For most persons, the dominant motive of college attendance is the desire to rise to a higher social class; behind this we should see the ideology of American life and the projection of parents' ambitions upon children. The attainment of this life goal necessitates the postponement of marriage, since it is understood that a new household must be economically independent; additional complications sometimes arise from the practice of borrowing money for college expenses. And yet persons in this group feel very strongly the cultural imperative to fall in love and marry and live happily in marriage.

For the average college student, and especially for the man, a love affair which led to immediate marriage would be tragic because of the havoc it would create in his scheme of life. Nevertheless, college students feel strongly the attractions of sex and the thrills of sex, and the sexes associate with one another in a peculiar relationship known as "dating." Dating is not true courtship, since it is supposed not to eventuate in marriage; it is a sort of dalliance relationship. In spite of the strength of the old morality among college students, dating is largely dominated by the quest of the thrill and is regarded as an amusement. The fact that college attendance usually removes the individual from normal courtship association in his home community should be mentioned as a further determinant of the psychological character of dating.

In many colleges, dating takes place under conditions determined by a culture complex which we may call the "rating and dating complex." The following description of this complex on one campus is probably typical of schools of the sort:

> X College, a large state-supported school, is located in a small city at a considerable distance from larger urban areas. The school is the only industry of the community. There are few students who live at home, and therefore the interaction of the young is but little influenced by the presence of parents. The students of this college are predominantly taken from the lower half of the middle classes, and constitute a remarkably homogeneous group; numerous censuses of the occupations of fathers and of living expenses seem to establish this fact definitely. Nevertheless, about half of the male students live in fraternities, where the monthly bill is usually forty-five or fifty dollars a month, rarely as high as fifty-five. There is intense competition among the fraternities. The desire for mobility of class, as shown by dozens of inquiries, is almost universal in the group and is the principal verbalized motive for college attendance.
>
> Dating at X College consists of going to college or fraternity dances, the movies, college entertainments, and to fraternity houses for victrola dances and "necking"; coeds are permitted in the fraternity parlors, if more than one is present. The high points of the social season are two house parties and certain formal dances. An atypical feature of this

campus is the unbalanced sex ratio, for there are about six boys to every girl; this makes necessary the large use of so-called "imports" for the more important occasions, and brings it about that many boys do not date at all or confine their activities to prowling about in small industrial communities nearby; it also gives every coed a relatively high position in the scale of desirability; it would be difficult to say whether it discourages or encourages the formation of permanent attachments. Dating is almost exclusively the privilege of fraternity men, the use of the fraternity parlor and the prestige of fraternity membership being very important. Freshman men are forbidden by student tradition to have dates with coeds.[2]

Within the universe which we have described, competition for dates among both men and women is extremely keen. Like every other process of competition, this one determines a distributive order. There are certain men who are at the top of the social scramble; they may be placed in a hypothetical Class A. There are also certain coeds who are near the top of the scale of dating desirability, and they also are in Class A. The tendency is for Class A men to date principally Class A women. Beneath this class of men and women are as many other classes as one wishes to create for the purposes of analysis. It should be remembered that students on this campus are extremely conscious of these social distinctions and of their own position in the social hierarchy. In speaking of another student, they say, "He rates," or "He does not rate," and they extend themselves enormously in order that they may rate or seem to rate.

Young men are desirable dates according to their rating on the scale of campus values. In order to have Class A rating they must belong to one of the better fraternities, be prominent in activities, have a copious supply of spending money, be well-dressed, "smooth" in manners and appearance, have a "good line," dance well, and have access to an automobile. Members of leading fraternities are especially desirable dates; those who belong to fraternities with less prestige are correspondingly less desirable. I have been able to validate the qualities mentioned as determinants of campus prestige by reference to large numbers of student judges.

The factors which appear to be important for girls are good clothes, a smooth line, ability to dance well, and popularity as a date. The most

---

[2] Folsom, who has studied this same process, has come to essentially similar conclusions concerning the exclusion of certain persons from the dating process: "This factor is especially prominent in state universities with a vigorous fraternity culture and social stratification. Such institutions are attended by students from an unusually wide range on the social scale; there is a tendency to protect one's social ranking in college through a certain snobbishness, and there is also a great drive toward social climbing. Fraternities are important agencies in this struggle for prestige. The fraternities and sororities apply considerable pressure to the 'dating' of their members. One gets merits, whether formally recorded or not, for dating with a coed of a high-ranking fraternity, demerits for association with a non-fraternity person. The net result of this competition might seem to be to match each person with one of fairly equal rank, as happens in society in general. But there is another result. It is to discourage matching altogether among the lower ranks. The fire of competitive dating burns hot at the top, smoulders at the bottom. The low-ranking student often has more to gain by abstaining from dating than from dating with a person of his own rank." (J. K. Folsom, *The Family*, p. 341.)

important of these factors is the last, for the girl's prestige depends upon dating more than anything else; here as nowhere else nothing succeeds like success. Therefore the clever coed contrives to give the impression of being much sought after even if she is not. It has been reported by many observers that a girl who is called to the telephone in the dormitories will often allow herself to be called several times, in order to give all the other girls ample opportunity to hear her paged. Coeds who wish campus prestige must never be available for last minute dates; they must avoid being seen too often with the same boy, in order that others may not be frightened away or discouraged; they must be seen when they go out, and therefore must go to the popular (and expensive) meeting places; they must have many partners at the dances. If they violate the conventions at all, they must do so with great secrecy and discretion; they do not drink in groups or frequent the beer-parlors. Above all, the coed who wishes to retain Class A standing must consistently date Class A men.

Cressey has pointed out that the taxi-dancer has a descending cycle of desirability. As a new girl in the dance hall, she is at first much sought after by the most eligible young men. Soon they tire of her and desert her for some newer recruit. Similarly the coed has a descending cycle of popularity on the campus which we are describing, although her struggle is not invariably a losing one. The new girl, the freshman coed, starts out with a great wave of popularity; during her freshman year she has many dates. Slowly her prestige declines, but in this case only to the point at which she reaches the level which her qualities permanently assure her. Her descent is expedited by such "mistakes," from the viewpoint of campus prestige, as "going steady" with one boy (especially if he is a senior who will not return the following year), by indiscretions, and by too ready availability for dates. Many of the girls insist that after two years of competitive dating they have tired of it and are interested in more permanent associations.

This thrill-dominated, competitive process involves a number of fundamental antagonisms between the men and the women, and the influence of the one sex group accentuates these. Writes one student informant, a girl, "Wary is the only word that I can apply to the attitude of men and women students toward each other. The men, who have been warned so repeatedly against coeds, are always afraid the girls are going to 'gold-dig' them. The coeds wonder to what degree they are discussed and are constantly afraid of being placed on the black list of the fraternities. Then too they wonder to what extent they can take any man seriously without being taken for a 'ride'." Status in the one-sex group depends upon avoiding exploitation by the opposite sex. Verbatim records of a number of fraternity "bull sessions" were obtained a few years ago. In these sessions members are repeatedly warned that they are slipping, those who have fallen are teased without mercy, and others are warned not to be soft. And almost all of the participants pretend a ruthlessness toward the opposite sex which they do not feel.

This competitive dating process often inflicts traumas upon individuals who stand low in the scale of courtship desirability. "While I was at X College," said a thirty year old alumnus, "I had just one date. That was a blind date, arranged for me by a friend. We went to the dorm, and after a while my girl came down and we were introduced. She said,

'Oh, I'm so sorry. I forgot my coat. I'll have to go get it.' She never came down again. Naturally I thought, 'Well what a hit I made!' " We have already seen that nonfraternity men are practically excluded from dating; it remains to note that many girls elect not to date rather than take the dates available to them. One girl writes as follows: "A girl's choice of whom to fall in love with is limited by the censorship of the one-sex group. Every boy that she dates is discussed and criticized by the other members of the group. This rigid control often keeps a girl from dating at all. If a girl is a member of a group in which the other girls are rated higher on the dating scale than she, she is often unable to get dates with boys who are considered desirable by her friends. In that event she has to decide whether to date the boys that she can and choose girl friends who would approve, or she must resign herself to not dating."

Since the class system, or gradient of dating desirability on the campus, is clearly recognized and adjusted to by the students themselves, there are interesting accommodations and rationalizations which appear as a result of inferior status. Although members of Class A may be clearly in the ascendant as regards prestige, certain groups of Class B may contest the position with them and may insist upon a measuring stick which will give them a favorable position. Rationalizations which enable Class D men and women to accept one another are probably never completely effective.

The accommodations and rationalizations worked out by one group of girls who were toward the bottom of the scale of campus desirability are typical. Four of these girls were organized in one tightly compact "bunch." All four lived off campus, and worked for their room and board. They had little money to spend for clothes, so there was extensive borrowing of dresses. Members of the group co-operated in getting dates for one another. All of them accepted eleventh hour invitations, and probably realized that some stigma of inferiority was attached to such ready availability, but they managed to save their faces by seeming very reluctant to accept such engagements, and at length doing so as a result of the persuasion of another member of the bunch. The men apparently saw through these devices, and put these girls down as last minute dates, so that they rarely received any other invitations. The bunch went through "dating cycles" with several fraternities in the course of a year, starting when one of the girls got a date with one member of the fraternity, and ending, apparently, when all the girls had lost their desirability in that fraternity.

Partly as a result of the unbalanced sex ratio, the boys of the group which we are discussing have a widespread feeling of antagonism toward the coeds. This antagonism is apparently based upon the fact that most of the male students are unable to date with coeds, at least not on terms acceptable to themselves. As a result of this, boys take great pride in the "imports" whom they bring in for house parties, and it is regarded as slightly disgraceful in some groups to date a coed for one of the major parties. Other men in the dateless group take on the role of misogynists—and read Schopenhauer.

During the winter term the preponderance of men assures to every coed a relatively high bargaining power. Every summer witnesses a surprising reversal of this situation. Hundreds of women school teachers flock to this school for the summer term, and men are very scarce;

smooth, unmarried boys of college age are particularly scarce. The
school-teachers are older than the boys; they have usually lost some of
their earlier attractiveness; they have been living for some months or
years within the school-teacher role. They are man-hungry, and they
have a little money. As a result, there is a great proliferation of highly
commercialized relations. The women lend their cars to their men
friends, but continue to pay for repairs and gasoline; they take the boys
out to dinner, treat them to drinks, and buy expensive presents for
them. And many who do not go so far are available for sex relations
on terms which demand no more than a transitory sort of commitment
from the man.

The rating and dating complex varies enormously from one school to
another. In one small, coeducational school, the older coeds instruct the
younger that it is all right for them to shop around early in the year, but
by November they should settle down and date someone steadily. As a
result, a boy who dates a girl once is said to "have a fence around her,"
and the competition which we have described is considerably hampered
in its operation. In other schools, where the sex ratio is about equal, and
particularly in the smaller institutions, "going steady" is probably a great
deal more common than on the campus described. It should be pointed out
that the frustrations and traumas imposed upon unsuccessful candidates
by the practice of "going steady" (monopolistic competition) are a great
deal easier to bear than those which arise from pure competition. In one
school the girls are uniformly of a higher class origin than the boys, so that
there is relatively little association between them; the girls go with older
men not in college, the boys with high school girls and other "townies." In
the school which is not coeducational, the dating customs are vastly different,
although, for the women at least, dating is still probably a determinant of
prestige.

True courtship sometimes emerges from the dating process, in spite of
all the forces which are opposed to it. The analysis of the interaction
process involved seems to be quite revealing. We may suppose that in our
collegiate culture one begins to fall in love with a certain unwillingness, at
least with an ambivalent sort of willingness. Both persons become emotionally involved as a result of a summatory process in which each step power-
fully influences the next step and the whole process displays a directional
trend toward the culmination of marriage; the mores of dating break down
and the behavior of the individuals is governed by the older mores of progressive commitment. In the fairly typical case, we may suppose the interaction to be about as follows: The affair begins with the lightest sort of
involvement, each individual being interested in the other but assuming
no obligations as to the continuation of the affair. There are some tentatives
of exploitation at the beginning; "the line" is a conventionalized attempt
on the part of the young man to convince the young woman that he has
already at this early stage fallen seriously in love with her—a sort of

exaggeration, sometimes a burlesque, of coquetry—it may be that each person, by a pretence of great involvement, invites the other to rapid sentiment-formation—each encourages the other to fall in love by pretending that he has already done so. If either rises to the bait, a special type of interaction ensues; it may be that the relation becomes exploitative in some degree and it is likely that the relationship becomes one in which control follows the principle of least interest, i.e., that person controls who is less interested in the continuation of the affair. Or it may be that the complete involvement of the one person constellates the other in the same pattern, but this is less likely to happen in college than in the normal community processes of courtship.

If both persons stand firm at this early juncture, there may ensue a series of periodic crises which successively redefine the relationship on deeper levels of involvement. One form which the interaction process may assume is that of "lover's quarrels," with which the novelists have familiarized us. A and B begin an affair on the level of light involvement. A becomes somewhat involved, but believes that B has not experienced a corresponding growth of feeling, and hides his involvement from B, who is, however, in exactly the same situation. The conventionalized "line" facilitates this sort of "pluralistic ignorance," because it renders meaningless the very words by means of which this state of mind could be disclosed. Tension grows between A and B, and is resolved by a crisis, such as a quarrel, in which the true feelings of the two are revealed. The affair, perhaps, proceeds through a number of such crises until it reaches the culmination of marriage. Naturally, there are other kinds of crises which usher in the new definition of the situation.

Such affairs, in contrast to "dating," have a marked directional trend; they may be arrested on any level, or they may be broken off at any point, but they may not ordinarily be turned back to a lesser degree of involvement; in this sense they are irreversible. As this interaction process goes on, the process of idealization is re-enforced by the interaction of personalities. A idealizes B, and presents to her that side of his personality which is consistent with his idealized conception of her; B idealizes A, and governs her behavior toward him in accordance with her false notions of his nature; the process of idealization is mutually re-enforced in such a way that it must necessarily lead to an increasing divorce from reality. As serious sentimental involvement develops, the individual comes to be increasingly occupied, on the conscious level at least, with the positive aspects of the relationship; increasingly he loses his ability to think objectively about the other person, to safeguard himself or to deal with the relationship in a rational way; we may say, indeed, that one falls in love when he reaches the point where sentiment-formation overcomes objectivity.

The love relationship in its crescendo phase attracts an ever larger proportion of the conative trends of the personality; for a time it may seem to absorb all of the will of the individual and to dominate his imagination completely; the individual seems to become a machine specially designed for just one purpose; in consequence, the persons are almost wholly absorbed in themselves and their affair; they have an *egoisme à deux* which verges upon *folie à deux*. All of these processes within the pair-relationship are accentuated by the changes in the attitude of others, who tend to treat the pair as a social unity, so far as their association is recognized and approved.

Sexual Codes in Teen-Age Culture

Ira L. Reiss

Teen-age sexual codes reflect quite clearly the bold outlines of adult sexual codes. The high degree of conformity in teen-age culture increases the observability of teen-age beliefs and adds to our understanding of adult beliefs. The teen-ager exists in a world somewhere between youthful idealism and adult realism, and his sexual codes reflect this state of being. In a very real sense, he is a marginal man with one foot in the world of the child and the other foot in the world of the adult.[1]

The teen-ager is at the stage at which it is vitally important for him to learn how to exist in society independent of his parents. For this reason, he transfers his dependence to his peers and strives to learn from them the secrets of entrance into the adult world. One would think that this vaguely defined status of "almost adult" would lead to confusion and weak statements of belief. To a large extent, this is the case, but, nevertheless, it is equally true that it leads to dogmatic statements of belief and a search for conviction through conformity. Teen-agers translate and adapt the sexual codes of adults to fit their particular circumstance and state of mind.[2]

Ira L. Reiss, "Sexual Codes in Teen-Age Culture," from *The Annals of the American Academy of Political and Social Science* (Vol. 338, November 1961), pp. 54–62. Reprinted by permission of the publisher and the author.

[1] Albert J. Reiss, "Sex Offenses: The Marginal Status of the Adolescent," *Law and Contemporary Problems,* Vol. 25 (Spring 1960), pp. 309–334.

[2] Of course, there is a biological basis for sexual behavior, but social scientists seem generally agreed that the specific way the sexual drive expresses itself is learned. The wide variety of sexual codes throughout the world testifies to the fact that whatever differences exist biologically between men and women can be compensated for by cultural training. The best brief source for cross-cultural information is Clellan S. Ford and Frank A. Beach, *Patterns of Sexual Behavior* (New York, 1954). For a discussion of this entire issue, see Ira L. Reiss, *Premarital Sexual Standards in America* (Glencoe, Ill., 1960), Chap. 1.

Going Steady

When unchaperoned dating gained prevalence in the early part of this century, it involved a much more rapid change of dating partners than occurs today. Nevertheless, by the time of World War II, going steady had taken root, and, today, it seems that slightly more than half of the high school students have some going-steady experience. Even among the early teen-agers, possibly one quarter go steady.[3]

Class differences are important in examining the going-steady complex. It seems that those high school people who go steady and plan to go to college are not likely to marry their high school steadies, and those who are from lower economic classes and who do not plan to go to college are much more likely to marry their high school steadies.[4] Thus, in looking at the custom of going steady, one must realize that there are different subtypes and that the consequences differ for each type.

Although a psychologist may point to the security of going steady as its chief reason for being, as a sociologist, I would point out how Western society has, for centuries, been developing an association of sexual behavior with mutual affection. This association is hard to achieve in casual dating; but, in steady dating, sex and affection can quite easily be combined, and, in this way, a potential strain in the social system is reduced. Another area of strain which is reduced by going steady is the conflict a girl may feel between her desire for sexual experience and her desire to maintain her reputation. For many, sexual behavior is made respectable by going steady.[5] In these ways, one may say that no other dating custom is quite as central to the understanding of teen-age sexual codes as going steady.

Girls' Sexual Codes

One of the most popular sexual codes among teen-age girls is petting-with-affection. This code is a modern day subtype of our formal abstinence standard. This subtype of abstinence seems extremely popular among high

---

[3] For evidence, see Maureen Daly, *Profile of Youth* (Philadelphia, 1951), p. 30. It may be well to note here that the author has conducted a pilot study to test the hypothesis that the advent of the junior high school has spread heterosexual knowledge and behavior to younger age groups and thus encouraged earlier dating. In support of this, one may cite Dr. J. B. Connat's belief that the junior high imitates the high school in its social characteristics. In addition, the anticipatory socialization of sex games like "spin the bottle," "post office," and "flashlight" begin today prior to junior high levels and thus prepare students for dating in junior high. The author's evidence indicates a connection between junior high school and early dating patterns.

[4] Robert D. Herman, "The Going Steady Complex: A Re-Examination," *Marriage and Family Living,* Vol. 17 (February 1955), pp. 36–40.

[5] For evidence on this point, see Winston W. Ehrmann, *Premarital Dating Behavior* (New York, 1959), p. 141.

school couples who are going steady. Such couples feel it is proper to engage in heavy petting if they are going steady, the justification being that they are in love or at least extremely fond of each other. The petting-with-affection sex code probably grew along with the going-steady custom; they both illustrate adaptations of our dating institution to the newer unchaperoned dating circumstances.

What evidence do we have for such petting behavior among teen-agers? Though surely not perfect, the most extensive study of sexual behavior is that done by the Institute for Sex Research, formerly headed by Alfred C. Kinsey and now run by Paul H. Gebhard. It should be noted that the Kinsey studies are most valid for urban, white, northeastern, college-educated people, and, thus, great care must be taken when applying the results to other groups. The reader should keep in mind the tenuousness of any such generalizations made in this paper.

Kinsey's data show that, of the females who were twenty years old or older when interviewed, about one fifth to one fourth admitted they had petted to orgasm while still in their teens. Most of this behavior occurred between the ages of sixteen and twenty. About three-quarters of all the girls twenty years old or more admitted being aroused by some form of petting or kissing in their teens, and approximately 90 per cent stated they had at least been kissed during their teens.[6]

Those girls who marry in their teens start their petting and kissing behavior earlier than those who marry later. In general, the few years previous to marriage are by far the most sexually active for girls. Lower class females marry earlier, and, thus, they are more active in their teens and are more likely to marry their teen-age steadies.

These rates are averages for Kinsey's entire sample of several thousand females; were we to take only the females born in more recent decades, the rates would be considerably higher. For example, of those females born before 1900, only 10 per cent ever petted to orgasm in their teens, whereas, of those girls born in the 1920s, almost 30 per cent, or three times the proportion, petted to orgasm in their teens.[7]

It seems clear that we have developed not only new dating forms such as going steady but also, as we have seen, new sexual codes to go with them. These new codes allow females much more freedom in heavy petting, provided affection is involved. Of course, other girls, particularly in the early teens, adhere to standards which only permit kissing, and a few others adhere to standards which allow full sexual relations, but, by and large, petting-with-affection seems the increasingly popular sex code for high school girls.

The most recent evidence of the nature of teen-age sex codes also sup-

[6] Alfred C. Kinsey and Others, *Sexual Behavior in the Human Female* (Philadelphia, 1953), Chap. 7.
[7] *Ibid.*, p. 244.

ports these contentions. This evidence comes from research which the author is engaged in at present.[8] Some preliminary reports on this study were made in the author's book *Premarital Sexual Standards in America*. The study involves 1,000 high school and college students, most of whom are teen-agers. Although final analysis of the study has not been completed, it is clear that petting-with-affection is an extremely popular code with teen-age girls, particularly with the teen-agers who are high school juniors and seniors.

Finally, one should note that, in my own study and in the Kinsey study, religion was another key factor affecting girls' sexual beliefs and behaviors. Those girls who were devout in their religion were much more conservative in their sexual behavior and belief. Religion was not as strong a factor for boys and did not control their behavior as much. As we shall see, amount of education was the key determinant for male sexual behavior.

Boys' Sexual Codes

Among the teen-age boys, we find a quite different code dominant. Abstinence is given some form of lip service, particularly among the more highly educated classes, but, by and large, it is not an operational code; it is not adhered to in the behavior of the majority of the teen-age boys. Even among the males destined for college, about half have coitus in their teens; among those who stop their education in high school, about three-quarters have coitus in their teens, and, among those whose education stops before high school, about eight-tenths have coitus in their teens. Thus, it is clear that the majority of all males, in this sample of Kinsey's, at least, experienced full sexual relations before reaching twenty years of age.[9]

For teen-age girls, the rate of nonvirginity appears to be considerably lower. Kinsey reports approximately 20 per cent nonvirginity for females by age twenty. Of course, the greater liberality of the boys does not involve a single standard; that is, they are predominantly adherents of the double standard which allows boys to have coitus but condemns girls for the same thing. This is an ancient standard reaching back many thousands of years in Western culture. It is by no means a universal standard, however, for we do find many cultures where the sexes are treated equally.[10]

Although in recent generations, due to our greater equalitarianism and the evolving nature of the dating institution, the double standard seems to have been weakened sharply, it is still quite dominant among teen-age

---

[8] This investigation is supported by a Public Health Service research grant (M-4045) from the National Institute of Mental Health, Public Health Service.

[9] Alfred C. Kinsey, *Sexual Behavior in the Human Male* (Philadelphia, 1948), p. 550.

[10] For a full discussion of this standard, its historical sources and reasons for being, see Ira L. Reiss, *Premarital Sexual Standards in America* (Glencoe, Ill., 1960), Chap. 4.

boys. The greater freedom allowed the male child in almost all areas of life constantly buttresses this standard and makes it seem obvious to teen-agers. Teen-agers are not sufficiently objective or sophisticated to be bothered by the contradictions in this or any other sexual code. For example, if all women abided fully by the double standard, then no men could, for the men would have no partners! Thus, this code operates only to the extent that someone violates it.

Some of these double standard teen-age boys will condemn a girl who accepts petting-with-affection, for they believe heavy petting is improper for girls. However, my own data indicate that most of these teen-age males will accept heavy petting in a going-steady relationship. They, of course, allow themselves to go further and may try to have coitus with a steady in order to see if she is a "good" girl. It is not unusual to find a relationship either broken up or its affectionate nature altered if a girl gives in to her double standard steady. Such condemnatory behavior on the part of double standard males keeps many girls from going as far sexually as they might want to. Thus, the double standard male eliminates many potential sex partners because of the attitude he takes toward such sex partners.

Teen-age double standard males are often stricter than their older brothers who accept coitus for a girl when she is in love and/or engaged. These teen-age males are supported in this rigidity by the conformity of their peer group. Double standard males typically view the act of coitus as a conquest, as a source of peer group prestige. Thus, they are quite prone to tell their friends all of the details of any affair. This characteristic tends further to discourage females from yielding to double standard males. Instead, the girl is encouraged to be, in part at least, a tease, that is, to show just enough sexual activity to keep the male interested but not enough to arouse his condemnation. Sexual behavior in this sense involves a great deal of the aspect of a game. Sex comes to be used as a power leverage to control the relationship. Under such circumstances, sexual desire is developed so sharply in the male and so differently in the female that the male wants the female to be both sexually active and sexually pure. Under such conditions, sexual behavior can only with great difficulty relate directly to feelings of affection.[11] This is particularly true for the act of coitus. In fact, one finds very often an inverse relation, in that boys prefer to have coitus with girls they do not care for, because they regard the girls they do care for as "too good" for such behavior. Girls, too, may control their sexual reactions, particularly with someone they care for, until they are sure they will not be condemned for their sexual response.

Thus, in the area of coitus among teen-agers, the double standard does seem to block the association of sex and affection. However, one should

---

[11] Lester Kirkendall has conducted extensive research on the nature of the interaction process in sexual relations, and his evidence to date seems to support my position here. He will soon publish a book on this topic.

quickly add that, on the level of petting, sex and affection can more easily be combined, for this behavior is much more likely to be accepted for both sexes by both males and females.

Minor Standards

There are minor teen-age standards which are more permissive than petting-with-affection or the double standard. For the older teen-ager, the most popular minor standard is what I shall call permissiveness-with-affection.[12] This standard accepts full sexual intercourse for both boys and girls, provided they are involved in a stable, affectionate relationship. The degree of stability and affection required varies among adherents from feeling strong affection to being in love and engaged. Some teen-age couples who are going steady have coitus in accord with this standard. The situation here is quite different from that of the double standard boy and his girl friend, for, in permissiveness-with-affection, both the boy and girl accept for each other what they are doing. They combine sex with affection and use affection as one of the key justifications of the sexual act.

There is a class difference in sexual standards among boys. My evidence indicates that the lower classes are more likely to be strong supporters of the double standard, while the upper classes, though still mostly double standard, contain a large proportion of boys who are not so dogmatic in their beliefs and a minority who accept permissiveness-with-affection. In general, the upper classes seem to stress equality of the sexes and the importance of affection more than the lower classes. A permissiveness-without-affection code seems more widespread at the lower levels.

Age is a crucial factor among teen-agers. Teen-agers under sixteen are much more likely to accept only kissing than are older teen-agers, who may accept petting or coitus. As noted earlier, religion does not restrict sexual behavior as much among boys as it does among girls. Education is a more important factor, with the more highly educated groups being the most conservative.

Promiscuity

The newspapers from time to time pick up stories of high school "sex clubs" and other forms of promiscuous teen-age sexual behavior.[13] The available evidence indicates that promiscuous coitus is common predominantly for double standard males and a few females. Promiscuous coitus is

---

12 Ira L. Reiss, *op. cit.,* Chap. 6, for a full discussion of this standard.
13 For a book containing many of these "stories," see Shailer U. Lawton, M.D., and Jules Archer, *Sexual Conduct of the Teen-Ager* (New York, 1951).

not common on an equalitarian basis, that is, where both male and female accept the behavior as right for each other. Our culture has stressed the association of sex-with-affection to such an extent that it is difficult, at least for many females, to violate this association in coitus. In the case of petting, one finds more likelihood of violation of this norm by both men and women, but, in the case of coitus, it is much more often violated by males. Ehrmann's study of 1,000 college students supports this difference between male and female sexual activity and attitudes.[14] Females, in addition to associating love with sexual behavior more than males, also have more nonsexual motives for sexual behavior, such as the desire to please the boy or to cement a relationship.[15]

During the teens, the sexual outlets of boys and girls differ considerably. The chief outlet for girls seems to be masturbation and petting, whereas for boys the chief outlets include coitus at the fore. In Kinsey's sample, about one third of the girls masturbated to orgasm in their teens, while over 90 per cent of the boys have so masturbated in their teens.[16] Despite their high rate of masturbation, males also have a high rate of coitus. The lower class boys rely less on masturbation and petting and more on coitus for their sexual outlets than do those boys who go to college.

The teen-age girl today is still typically the much more conservative partner and the guardian of sexual limits. However, she appears increasingly to be a half-willing guardian who more and more seeks her self-satisfaction and strives to achieve sexual equality.[17]

There is a general trend in American society toward more equalitarian and more permissive sexual codes in all areas.[18] This is true for teen-age sexual codes, too. The growth within abstinence of petting-with-affection is one sign of this increasing equalitarian and permissive force. Also, within the double standard, one finds increased willingness by males to accept some coitus on the part of females, especially if it occurs when the girl is in love and/or engaged. Finally, in the minor standard of permissiveness-with-affection, one sees this trend in the increased strength of this standard among teen-agers, particularly among older, college teen-agers. And these trends toward equalitarianism and permissiveness seem even stronger among older dating couples in their twenties. The teen-agers are relatively new at

[14] Ehrmann, *op. cit.*, pp. 263–266.

[15] Lester A. Kirkendall and A. E. Gravatt, "Teen-Agers' Sex Attitudes and Behavior," in Evelyn M. and Sylvanus M. Duvall (eds.), *Sexways in Fact and Faith* (New York, 1961), pp. 115–129.

[16] Kinsey, *Sexual Behavior . . . Female, op. cit.*, p. 173. See also William R. Reevy, "Adolescent Sexuality," in A. Ellis and A. Abarbanel, *The Encyclopedia of Sexual Behavior* (New York, 1961), pp. 52–67.

[17] For an interesting article discussing shifts in male and female attitudes, see J. P. McKee and A. C. Sherriffs, "Men's and Women's Beliefs, Ideals and Self Concepts," in Jerome M. Seidman (ed.), *The Adolescent* (New York, 1960), pp. 282–294.

[18] One of the major efforts of my book is to demonstrate the evidence for this trend. See Ira L. Reiss, *op. cit.*, Chap. 10.

sexual behavior, and they, at first, grab the basic outlines of the older couples' codes. With the passage of time, they come to behave in a somewhat more equalitarian and permissive manner.

In my current research, there is evidence that the real change-over in a teen-ager's sexual code is more one of integrating attitudes and changing overt behavior than of changing basic attitudes. In short, it seems that a person holds his basic sexual attitudes in rudimentary form in his teens, but he is not fully ready to act upon them and has not fully learned how to combine these values into a coherent code of living. As he learns to do this, his behavior changes and so does his awareness of his beliefs and their unity, but his basic beliefs may well remain the same. This entire area of how our sexual beliefs are formed and how they change is in need of more careful study. My own research is aimed at probing some aspects of this problem.

Parents are prone to be most aware of what they consider excessive sexual behavior, for they are concerned about the consequences of such behavior as they may affect their children. Thus, parents complain about sexual acts of which they become aware, and they often believe teen-agers are sexually promiscuous. Actually, according to our best estimates, the real increases in teen-age sexual behavior over the last generation are not in the area of sexual intercourse but rather in the area of petting and in the public nature of some petting behavior.[19] Thus, these parents of today have probably had similar rates of coitus but perhaps lower rates of petting. In addition, one should note that the petting behavior today very often is not promiscuous but occurs in a stable affectionate relationship.

Youth Culture: Tame or Wild?

About twenty years ago, Kingsley Davis and Talcott Parsons wrote of a youth culture and of a parent-youth conflict and, in doing so, implied in part that youth culture was largely irresponsible, impulsive, and antiadult.[20] Many people have come to share this view and to expect rather extreme sexual behavior from teen-agers. I myself formerly accepted this view of the teen-ager as valid. However, after examining the evidence in the key areas of teen-age sexual behavior, I must admit that I can no longer accept such a conception of youth culture without serious modification and qualification. I would submit that the vast majority of our approximately twenty million teen-agers are not only not extreme but are quite conservative and re-

[19] Kinsey, *Sexual Behavior . . . Female, op. cit.,* pp. 275, 339 *passim.*
[20] Kingsley Davis, "The Sociology of Parent-Youth Conflict," *American Sociological Review,* Vol. 5 (October 1940), pp. 523–535; Talcott Parsons, "Age and Sex in the Social Structure of the United States," *American Sociological Review,* Vol. 7 (December 1942), pp. 604–616.

strained in the area of premarital sexual codes and behavior when we compare them to their older brothers and sisters.

There is evidence to show that teen-agers are unsure of how far to go sexually, that they feel ill at ease on dates, and that they are concerned with such "tame" issues as whether one should kiss good night on a first date.[21] A recent study showed that teen-agers rate themselves lower in comparison to adults than adults rate them. Teen-agers in this study rated adults considerably higher than themselves on most all "good" qualities.[22] These are hardly the attitudes of an arrogant or antiadult youth. They seem more those of a group desirous of becoming like adults and striving toward that goal.

Further, when we look at the rates of female petting to orgasm in the Kinsey studies, we find considerably more of this behavior among girls in their twenties than among girls in their teens. The coitus rate for females doubles between the ages of twenty and twenty-five. Masturbation rates also increase considerably after the teens.[23] In all these ways, the teen-agers seem more conservative than those individuals who are in their twenties.

August Hollingshead's excellent study of a midwest community also gives evidence on the conservatism of youth. He found a very close correspondence between social class of parents and social class of teen-ager's dating partners. In this study, too, we are given a picture of youth culture that is very much like adult culture in its status consciousness. Hollingshead and others have also noted the fact that a large proportion of the teen-age population is virtually not involved in any dating. A good estimate for the high school age group would be that about one third of the boys and one fifth of the girls are not involved in dating.[24]

Venereal Disease and Pregnancy

Let us now examine two key indices, venereal disease and pregnancy, which should give us additional insights into the behavior of teen-agers. Teen-agers do have significant rates of venereal disease and illegitimacy. However, the press has largely exaggerated such rates. The teen-age rate of venereal disease for ages fifteen to nineteen is only about a third of the rate for the twenty to twenty-four age group and is also lower than that of the twenty-five to twenty-nine age group.[25]

[21] H. H. Remmers and D. H. Radley, *The American Teen-Ager* (Indianapolis, 1957), pp. 83, 225–236.
[22] R. D. Hess and I. Goldblatt, "The Status of Adolescents in American Society," in Seidman, *op. cit.*, pp. 321–333.
[23] Kinsey, *Sexual Behavior . . . Female, op. cit.*, Chaps. 5 ,7, 8.
[24] August B. Hollingshead, *Elmtown's Youth* (New York, 1949), p. 227. See also Maxine Davis, *Sex and the Adolescent* (New York, 1960), p. 136.
[25] T. Lefoy Richman, *Venereal Disease: Old Plague—New Challenge* (Public Affairs Pamphlet No. 292; New York, 1960), p. 7. For more technical data, see T. Lefoy Richman (ed.), *Today's Venereal Disease Control Problem* (New York: American Social Health Association, 1961), especially pp. 36–43.

There has been a slight rise in the number of teen-age venereal disease cases in recent years, and this has received much publicity. It is quite likely that the actual rates for teen-agers are not higher and that this slight increase is due to the greater number of teen-agers today. More than 80 per cent of the venereal disease reported is from older groups of people. Finally, the rate of venereal disease among teen-agers is not evenly distributed in the teen-age group. As far as we can tell from reported cases, it is highly concentrated in the lower social classes.[26]

When one examines the national figures for unwed mothers, one finds that 40 per cent are teen-agers. Here, too, several qualifications are needed. First, most of these reported cases are Negro, and class status in general is low. The upper classes, according to Paul Gebhard's recent study, are much more willing to resort to abortion.[27] The upper classes, also, have a greater ability to stay out of public statistics and may, thus, show lower rates. According to Clark Vincent's study, when upper class females become pregnant before marriage, it is more likely to be the result of a love affair, whereas, when lower class females become pregnant, it is more likely to be a result of a casual affair.[28] Thus, there are important class differences here, too.

When we compare teen-age unwed motherhood with that for girls in their twenties, we find that the older girls have about the same proportion of the illegitimate children. We also find that the teen-age rates are not increasing as much as the rates for older groups. For example, in 1940 teen-age mothers were 46 per cent of the total; in 1957 they were 40 per cent.

Thus, from the evidence of national figures, it seems reasonable to conclude that it is a small and specific segment of the teen-age population that becomes involved with venereal disease or premarital pregnancy. Furthermore, the people in their twenties seem somewhat more likely to be involved in such circumstances. Also, these older couples are much more involved in adult culture in terms of their occupations and their nearness to marriage, and yet their sexual behavior is less conservative.

A warning must be added at this point concerning the venereal disease rates and unwed motherhood rates. They are far from perfect indices and, as mentioned, many higher class people manage to be excluded from them because they can afford more private means of coping with their problems. However, to the extent that we use these rates, we fail to find support for the charges made about teen-agers. It is no doubt true that teen-agers are irresponsible in the sense that they seek "to have a good time," but I would suggest that, in the area of sexual codes and behavior, the evidence shows more conservatism and responsibility than one might otherwise suspect. It

[26] Richman, *Venereal Disease* . . . , *op. cit.,* pp. 6, 20.
[27] Paul H. Gebhard and Others, *Pregnancy, Birth, and Abortion* (New York, 1958), pp. 45, 160.
[28] Clark E. Vincent, "Illegitimacy in the United States," in Duvall (eds.), *op. cit.,* p. 143.

may be well to avoid the over-all impressions given by a general use of the term "youth culture" as described by Parsons. Here, as elsewhere, qualification and specific research is a step toward better theoretical formulation and better understanding.

A Final Overview

What has occurred in teen-age sexual codes in recent generations is a working out of sexual practices acceptable to teen-agers. Many of these practices are at the level of petting. In short, as unchaperoned dating came into vogue and as adolescence became more prolonged due to our specialized industrial culture, young people worked out additional sexual codes to supplement and modify the older codes of abstinence and the double standard. There always were people who engaged in coitus; today there are more, but, for girls in their teens, it is still a minor activity. When we look at petting, we note something different, for here we see a much more continuous and current change among teen-agers—it is here in this middle ground that teen-agers have come to accept a petting-with-affection standard. The equalitarian and permissive aspects of this standard in many cases lead at later ages to acceptance of the more radical permissiveness-with-affection standard. However, during the teens, petting-with-affection is probably the major standard involved in stable affectionate relationships at middle and upper class levels.

At the present time, it is impossible to predict precise changes in sexual codes. This is especially true because, as we have seen, there are differences according to social class, religion, educational level, and so forth. But one can say that all the signs indicate a continued trend toward equalitarian and permissive codes. The trend seems to be toward that which now obtains in the Scandinavian countries, with the inclusion of sex education in the schools and with permissive attitudes on the formal as well as covert levels. This does not forebode the end of the double standard, for the double standard is still deeply rooted in our male dominant culture, but it does mean a continued weakening of the double standard and more qualifications of its mandates.

Teen-agers are a paradoxical group, They are not as wild as their parents or they themselves sometimes think. Teen-agers do want independence. But, judging by their sexual codes, they want independence from their parents, not from the total adult culture.

Parent-Child Conflict
in Sexual Values

Robert R. Bell

The old cliché that as one grows older he becomes more conservative may be true, if premarital sexual values held by parents are compared with the values they held when they were younger. In this paper, the interest is in the nature of sex value conflict between parents and their unmarried late adolescent and young adult children. Our discussion will focus on values held by parents and by their unmarried children toward premarital sexual intimacy.

Conceptually, our approach focuses upon values related to a specific area of sexual behavior held by individuals from two very different role perspectives. The perspectives differ because parents and children are always at different stages in the life cycle, and while parents are highly significant in the socialization of their children, other social forces increasingly come to influence the child as he grows older. The various social values that influence the child's sexual behavior are often complementary, but they may also be contradictory. Furthermore, various types of influences on the acceptance of a given set of values may operate on the child only during a given age period. For example, the youngster at age fifteen may be influenced by his age peers to a much greater extent than he will be at age twenty.

Given their different stages in the life cycle, parents and children will almost always show differences in how they define appropriate behavior for a given role. Values as to "proper" premarital sexual role behavior from the perspective of the parents are greatly influenced by the strong emotional involvement of the parent with his child. Youth, on the other hand, are going through a life cycle stage in which the actual behavior occurs, and they must relate the parent values to what they are doing or may do. There is a significant difference between defining appropriate role conduct for others to follow and defining proper role conduct to be followed by oneself. Even more important for actual behavior, there is often more than one significant group of role definers to which the young person can turn to as guides for his sex role behavior. Therefore, our discussion will focus more specifically on parent values related to premarital sexual intimacy, the peer group values of youth, and how these two different age groups, as role definers, influence the sexual values and behavior of unmarried youth.

From Robert R. Bell, "Parent-Child Conflict in Sexual Values," *The Journal of Social Issues* (The Society for the Psychological Study of Social Issues, Vol. XXII, No. 2), pp. 34–44. Reprinted by permission of the publisher.

For several reasons, our discussion will center primarily on the middle class. First, this class level has been highly significant in influencing changes in general sexual values and behavior. Second, and on a more pragmatic level, what little research has been done on parent-child conflict over sexual values has been done with middle-class groups. Third, the general values of the middle class are coming to include an increasing proportion of the American population. This also suggests that the values and behavior of college youth are of increasing importance as this group continues to expand in size and influence within the middle class.

A further limit is that our main focus is on the generational conflict between mother and daughter. The history of change in sexual values in the United States has been complexity interwoven with the attainment of greater sex equality and freedom by the female (2). Also, the relationship between the mother and daughter tends to be the closest of the possible parent-child relationships in the family socializing of the child to future adult sex roles. Furthermore, whatever the value system verbalized and/or applied by the girl, she often has more to gain or lose personally than the boy by whatever premarital sexual decisions she makes.

We also believe that any analysis of conflict over premarital sex between generations should center on *value* changes rather than *behavioral* changes. On the basis of available evidence, it appears that there have been no significant changes in the *frequency* of premarital sexual petting or coitus since the 1920s. Kinsey has pointed out that "there has been little recognition that the premarital petting and coital patterns which were established then (1920s) are still with us" (15, p. 300). Therefore, it is important to recognize that the parents and even some of the grandparents of today were the youth who introduced the new patterns of premarital sexual behavior about forty years ago.

Parent Values About Premarital Sex

The transmission of sexual values by parents to their children is only a small part of all parent values passed on during the family socialization process. Most parents do a more deliberate and comprehensive job of transmitting values to their children in such areas as educational attainment, career choice, religious beliefs, and so forth than they do with reference to any aspect of sexual values. Often when parents do discuss sex with their children it may be from a "clinical, physiological" perspective with overtones of parental embarrassment and a desire to get a distasteful task over with.

But perhaps more important than the formal confrontation between the parent and child in sexual matters are the informal values transmitted by the parent. In the past girls were often taught that premarital sexual deviancy was dirty and shameful, and that nonconformity to premarital sexual chastity values would mean suffering great personal and social shame. This highly negative view of premarital sex is undoubtedly less common today, but the newer, more "positive" values may also have some negative consequences. Very often today the mother continues to place great value on the daughter's virginity, and stresses to the daughter the great virtues of maintaining her virginity until marriage. But the "romantic" view of the rewards for the girl who waits for coitus until after marriage are often highly unrealistic and may sometimes create problems by leading the girl to expectations that cannot be realistically met in marital sex. Morton Hunt writes with regard to this approach that "if the woman has been assured that she will, that she ought, and she *must* see colored lights, feel like a breaking wave, or helplessly utter inarticulate cries, she is apt to consider herself or her husband at fault when these promised wonders do not appear" (13, 114). Whether or not the "romantic" view of marital sex is presented by her mother the girl often encounters it in the "approved" reading list suggested by the adult world, which tells her about the positive delights of waiting for sex until after marriage. So, though premarital sexual control may be "positive" in that it is based on rewards for waiting, it can be "negative" if the rewards are unrealistic and unobtainable.

For many parents, a major problem as their child moves through adolescence and into early adult years centers around how much independence to allow the child. Because they often recall the child's younger dependency, it may be difficult to assess the independency of the same child who is now older. Also, over the years the growing child has increasingly become involved with reference groups outside—and sometimes competing with—the family. In other words, the self-role definitions by the child and the parents' definitions of the child's role undergo constant change as the child grows older. For example, "The daughter in her younger years has her role as daughter defined to a great degree by her mother. But as she grows older she is influenced by other definitions which she internalizes and applies to herself in her movement toward self-determination. The mother frequently continues to visualize the daughter's role as it was defined in the past and also attaches the same importance to her function as mother in defining her daughter's role. But given the rapid social change associated with family roles the definer, as well as the definitions, may no longer be institutionally appropriate" (5, 388).

Parents may also be biased in their definitions of their child as less mature than they, the parents, were when they were the child's age. One can not recall experiences earlier in the life cycle free from influence by the events that have occurred since. This may result in many parents' thinking of their younger selves as being more mature than they actually were. At the same time the parents' view of their child's degree of maturity may be biased by their recall of him when he was younger and less mature. Thus, from the parents' perspective they may recall themselves as youngsters within the context of what has occurred since (more mature) and may see their offspring within the context of their earlier childhood (less mature).

There also may be some symbolic significance for parents who must define their children as having reached the age when something as "adult" as sexual behavior is of relevance. In part, viewing one's children as too young for sexual involvement may contribute to the parents' feeling young, while seeing their children as old enough to be involved in sexual activity may lead to some parents feeling forced to view themselves as aging. For example, the comment about a man seen out with a young woman that "she is young enough to be his daughter" may have implications for his self-role image if the young woman *is* his daughter. We have little research data on how the aging process of parents influences their definitions of appropriate behavior for their young adult children.

In general, it is probable that most parents assume that their children, especially their daughters, accept the traditional restrictive values about premarital sexual behavior unless they are forced to do otherwise. Also, because of the great emotional involvement of parents with their own children, there is a common parental tendency to attribute sexual "immorality" to other youngsters. For many parents to face the possibility that their children do not conform to their values is to suggest some failure on the part of the parents. Often, rather than admit failure, the parents may define their children as having been forced to reject the parent values by other social influences or that their children have willfully let them down.

Youth Views About Premarital Sex

The importance of age peer group influence on the values and behavior of young people has been shown by a number of social scientists (see: 6, 9, 10, 11, 12, 14, 19, 20, 21, 22). Because youth subcultures are to some degree self-developing, they often have conflict points in relation to some dominant adult values. However, the inconsistency and lack of effective adult definitions for adolescent behavior have also contributed to the emergence of youth subcultural values. That adults often view the adolescent with indecision as to appropriate behavior means that sometimes given adolescent behavior is treated one way at one time and in a different way at another time. Since the young person desires some decisiveness and precision in his role definitions, he often develops his own role prescriptions. Often when he creates his own role expectations, he demands a high degree of conformity by other adolescents as "proof" of the rightness of his definitions. It is ironical that the adolescent often thinks of himself as a social deviant. What he fails to realize is that his adolescent group deviates from the adult world, but that the requirements for conformity within his youth subculture are very strong (1, 369–374).

Youth subcultures have developed great influence over many aspects of premarital male-female interaction. The patterns of dating and courtship, appropriate behavior, success and failure are for the most part patterns defined by the youth group and not by the adult world. Yet, heterosexual relationships of youth are often based on adult role patterns, and they are therefore an important part of the youth world because they are seen by the youth as symbolizing adult status. To many young people, who are no longer defined by the adult world as children, but are not yet given full status as adults, their involvement in what they see as adult roles is important to them in seeking for adult status and recognition.

A part of the American youth subculture has been the development of new values related to premarital sexual intimacy. Reiss suggests that "It might well be that, since the 1920s, what has been occurring is a change in attitudes to match the change in behavior of that era" [premarital sexual behavior] (16, 233). The evidence suggests that for at least some college students new sex norms are emerging at the various stages of dating and courtship. One study found that "on the dating level necking is the norm for females and petting for males. During going steady and engagement, petting seems to be acceptable for both sexes. This would suggest that the young people both act and accept a higher level of intimacy than has generally been suggested by courtship norms." (3, 63).

In the past, emphasis was placed on the girl's virginity at the time of marriage; but today, many young people may only emphasize her being a virgin until she is in love, which may mean at the stage of going steady or engagement (8, Ch. 5 and 16, Ch. 6). If the girl is in love, some premarital sexual relations may be acceptable by peer group standards, although the dominant adult values—that love *and* marriage are basic prerequisites for coitus—continue. In the United States love as a prerequisite for sexual relations has long been a necessary condition for most middle-class females. The condition has not changed; rather, the point in the court-ship-marriage process where it may be applied to sexual involvement has shifted. Hence, the major point of parent-child conflict over premarital sex centers around the parent value that one should be in love *and* married before entering coitus and the modified value system of youth that an emotional and interpersonal commitment is important, but that this may occur before marriage.

There are two recent studies that provide some evidence on the nature of generational conflict; one study is of youth and adults in general and the other study is specifically concerned with mothers and their daughters. Reiss, in his extensive study of premarital sexual permissiveness, provides data on values held by adults as contrasted with values in a sample of high school

and college students. The respondents were asked to express their beliefs
about different combinations of intimacy and degree of interpersonal commitment for both unmarried males and females. Respondents were asked
if they believed petting to be acceptable when the male or female is engaged. In the adult sample the belief that petting during engagement was
acceptable for the engaged male was the response of 61 per cent, and for the
engaged female the response was 56 per cent. Of the student responses 85
per cent approved for the engaged male and 82 per cent for the engaged
female (17, 190–191); thus adult attitudes about petting during engagement
were more conservative than those of the student population. It may also
be noted that for both the adult and student groups there was a single
standard—that is, the acceptance rates were essentially the same for both
males and females.

Reiss also asked his respondents if they believed full sexual relations to
be acceptable if the male or female were engaged. Approval was the response given by 20 per cent of the adult group for males and 17 per cent
for females. In the student group acceptance was given by 52 per cent for
the male and 44 per cent for the female (17, 190–191). Here, as with
petting, there are significant differences between the adult and the student
samples, and once again both respondent groups suggest a single standard
of acceptance or rejection for both males and females.

A study by Bell and Buerkle compared the attitudes of 217 coeds with
those of their mothers. Both mothers and daughters were asked to respond
to the question, "How important do you think it is that a girl be a virgin
when she marries?" Of the mothers, 88 per cent answered "very important,"
12 per cent "generally important," and 0 per cent "not important"; compared to 55 per cent, 34 per cent and 13 per cent of the daughters (4, 391).
Both the mothers and daughters were also asked: "Do you think sexual
intercourse during engagement is: very wrong; generally wrong; right in
many situations?" The percentages for each response category were 83
per cent, 15 per cent and 2 per cent for the mothers; and 35 per cent, 48
per cent, and 17 per cent for the daughters (4, 391).

Both of the questions show sharp differences between the value responses
of the mothers and daughters with reference to premarital chastity. Many
mothers were undoubtedly influenced in their responses by having a daughter
in the age setting where the questions had an immediate and highly emotional application. Nevertheless, the differences in mother and daughter
responses indicate that the area of premarital sexual behavior is one of
potentially great conflict. One means of minimizing conflict is for the daughter not to discuss her sexual values or behavior with her mother. In the
Bell and Buerkle study it was found that only 37 per cent of the daughters,
in contrast with 83 per cent of the mothers, felt daughters should freely
answer questions from their mothers in regard to attitudes toward sexual
intimacy (4, 392).

The area of sexual values appears to be highly influenced by emotion, especially for the mother with reference to her daughter. Generational conflict with regard to premarital sexual intimacy has a variety of implications. First, the conflict in values clearly suggests that the traditional morality is often not socially effective as a meaningful determinant of behavior. Social values have behavioral influence when they emerge as social norms with significant rewards and punishments. In the case of sexual norms, however, there are rarely clearly articulated rewards, or positive consequences, for the conforming individual. In almost all situations the effectiveness of sexual norms is dependent upon their negative sanctions, or punishments. For example, the traditional norm of female premarital chastity bases its behavioral influence primarily on negative consequences for the girl who fails to conform. This negative means of control is most commonly found as a part of the adult value system. In effect, the major sanctions over premarital chastity are based upon punishments for the girl and for her family if she deviates. Yet, in most cases the girl who has premarital coitus is not discovered by her parents or by the community. The real danger for the girl often centers around premarital pregnancy, because if that occurs and becomes known there can be no denying premarital coitus. Vincent has suggested that an important part of the negative sanction toward premarital pregnancy is not the pregnancy itself, but rather that it symbolizes premarital coitus *and* getting caught (23, Ch. 1).

The available studies indicate that fear of pregnancy is not the major deterrent for most girls (7, 344 and 15, 315). The personal values of the girl appear far more important in restricting her from engaging in premarital coitus. Yet, within the privacy of the youth world, there may operate for some girls certain values positive toward premarital coitus. For example, there may be a strong emotional desire and commitment to the boy and a positive feeling by the girl of wanting to engage in greater sexual intimacy.

There is a tendency by parents, as well as by many who give professional advice, to overlook the pleasurable aspects of sex at all ages, especially for the young who are experiencing sexual pleasure for the first time. Undoubtedly many girls engage in premarital sexual intimacy to "compensate" for some need and many may suffer some negative consequences. But it is foolish to state categorically that the "artificial" setting of premarital sex always makes it negative and unpleasant for the girl. We would be much more honest if we recognized that for many girls premarital coitus is enjoyable and the participants suffer no negative consequences. This was illustrated in the Kinsey research; it was found that "69 per cent of the still unmarried females in the sample who had had premarital coitus insisted they did not regret their experiences. Another 13 per cent recorded some minor regrets" (15, 316). Kinsey also found that "77 per cent of the married females, looking back from the vantage point of their more mature experience, saw no reason to regret their premarital coitus" (15, 316).

The Extent of Generational Conflict

With the evidence suggesting strong conflict between generations with regard to premarital sexual values, our final consideration is: how permanent is this generational conflict? We can provide some evidence on this question by examining the values of college-educated females of different ages. This appears justified because higher educated females are generally the most liberal in their views about sexual rights and expectations for women.

The evidence suggests that the premarital sexual liberalism of the college girl may be a temporary phenomenon. The coed's sexual liberalism must be seen as related to the interactional context of her being emotionally involved, and to a future commitment to an on-going paired relationship. The Bell and Buerkle study (4) found that the values of daughters toward the importance of premarital virginity were very similar to those of their mothers, until they had spent some time in college. However, at "around age twenty there emerge sharp differences between mothers and daughters in regard to premarital sexual attitudes. Behavioral studies indicate that it is at this point that sexual activity is greatly intensified, perhaps because it is at this age that college girls are entering engagement. A suggested pattern is that the college girl of twenty or twenty-one years of age, in her junior or senior year and engaged, has a strong 'liberal' pattern toward premarital sexual behavior and attitudes" (4, 392 and 18, 696).

We can get some indication of the persistence of premarital sexual liberalism by comparing the values of mothers by education. In the mothers' views as to the importance of premarital virginity it was found that the college educated mothers were actually as "conservative" as those mothers with lower levels of education (4, 392). It is quite possible that in the future the coeds will become as conservative as the college educated mothers. This may occur when the coed's attitudinal rationales are not related to herself, but as a mother to her own daughter. It is therefore possible that the "sexual emancipation" of the college girl exists only for a short period of time, centering mainly around the engagement years.

Yet, even if the girl becomes more conservative as she grows older, and especially with reference to her own daughter, her temporary "liberalism" probably is contributing to some shift in adult values about premarital sexual intimacy. Certainly, today's parental generation accepts greater sexual intimacy as part of the premarital heterosexual relationship. Probably most parents assume that their adolescent and young adult children are engaging in necking and even some petting. Most parents, as long as they don't actually see the sexual intimacy, don't concern themselves about it. However, to suggest that parents may be more liberal (or tolerant) of premarital sexual intimacy does not necessarily suggest that parents are liberal if the intimacy reaches coitus.

It also appears that there has been some reduction in the severity of negative sanctions by parents if the daughter deviates and is caught. Among middle-class parents today it may be less common to reject the unwed daughter if she becomes pregnant than in the past, and more common for the parents to help her. This is not to suggest that today's parents offer any positive sanctions for premarital pregnancy, but that they may be able to adapt (often painfully) to it, rather than respond with high rejection and anger.

If our suggestion is correct (that parents take a less totally negative view of "discovered" premarital coitus), then this further suggests that traditional sexual values are being altered, since, as we have suggested, in the past the values of premarital chastity were primarily based on the negative consequences for those who deviated and were caught. If these negative consequences have been reduced, then the social force of the traditional values has been reduced as a means utilized by parents to control premarital sexual deviancy.

Conclusions

Based on the available evidence, there are several general speculations that may be made about future generational conflict over premarital sex. In general we would suggest that conflict between parents and their adolescent-young adult children with regard to premarital sexual intimacy may decrease in the future, because of several trends.

1. The trend in the United States is toward a more liberal view of sexual behavior in general. This is reflected in the generally accepted professional opinion that the woman has a right to sexual satisfaction, and that sexual satisfaction is a desirable end in itself. The trend toward a belief in a single sexual standard for both men and women, even though within the setting of marriage, is bound to influence the beliefs and behavior of the unmarried. For the unmarried, there may be an increasing tendency to attach less importance to the marriage act as the arbitrary dividing line between socially approved and socially disapproved sexual intimacy.

2. Since the evidence suggests that over the past three or four generations the rates of female premarital coital experience have not changed, and since the younger generation has developed some value frameworks for its behavior, modification of traditional values and behavior may increasingly influence the values of parents to be more liberal. That is, it may become increasingly difficult for many parents to hold their children to a set of conservative values which they, the parents, did not hold to when they were younger.

3. Parents seem increasingly unwilling to strongly punish their daughters

who sexually deviate and are caught. This parental reduction of punishment may be influenced by the increasing public attention directed at such social problems as illegal abortion. For example, many parents may be more willing to accept and help an unmarried pregnant daughter than take the risk of her seeking out an illegal abortion. The possible negative consequences of abortion may appear more undesirable than the premarital pregnancy.

4. Less generational conflict will occur if parents know less about the sexual activities of their children. A great part of the social activity of young people is carried out in the privacy of their age peer setting; what they do in the way of sexual intimacy is increasingly less apt to be noted by their parents. With the development and marketing of oral contraceptives, the risks of premarital pregnancy will be greatly reduced. In the future the rates of premarital coitus may remain the same, but with the chances of pregnancy reduced parents may be less aware of their children's premarital coitus.

Over time, then, the values of parents and the adult community in general may become more liberal and the conflict between generations reduced. (There seems little possibility that the opposite will occur; i.e., the younger generation's reducing the conflict by becoming more conservative.) But in the meantime, and certainly in the near future, it appears that parents and their children will continue to live with somewhat different value systems with regard to premarital sexual values. Parents will probably continue to hold to traditional values, and assume that *their* child is conforming to those values unless his actions force them to see otherwise. The youth generation will probably continue to develop their own modified value systems and keep those values to themselves, and implicitly allow their parents to believe they are behaving according to the traditional values of premarital sexual morality. For many parents and their children, the conflict about premarital sex will continue to be characterized by the parent's playing ostrich and burying his head in the sand, and the youth's efforts to keep the sand from blowing away.

References

1. Bell, Robert R. *Marriage and Family Interaction,* Homewood, Ill.: The Dorsey Press, 1963.
2. Bell, Robert R. *Premarital Sex in a Changing Society,* Englewood Cliffs, N.J.: Prentice-Hall, (in press).
3. Bell, Robert R. and Leonard Blumberg. "Courtship Stages and Intimacy Attitudes," *Family Life Coordinator,* 1960, 8, 60–63.
4. Bell, Robert R. and Jack V. Buerkle. "Mother and Daughter Attitudes to Premarital Sexual Behavior," *Marriage and Family Living,* 1961, 23, 390–392.
5. Bell, Robert R. and Jack V. Buerkle. "Mother-Daughter Conflict During The 'Launching Stage,'" *Marriage and Family Living,* 1962, 24, 384–388.

6. Bernard, Jessie (Ed.). "Teen-Age Culture," *Annals of the American Academy of Political and Social Science*, November, 1961, 338.
7. Burgess, Ernest and Paul Wallin. *Engagement and Marriage*, Philadelphia: J. B. Lippincott, 1953.
8. Ehrmann, Winston. *Premarital Dating Behavior*, New York: Henry Holt, 1959.
9. Ginsberg, Eli. *Values and Ideals of American Youth*, New York: Columbia University Press, 1962.
10. Gottlieb, David and Charles Ramsey. *The American Adolescent*, Homewood, Ill.: The Dorsey Press, 1964.
11. Grinder, Robert. *Studies in Adolescence*, New York: Macmillan, 1963.
12. Hechinger, Grace and Fred. *Teen-Age Tyranny*, New York: Crest, 1962.
13. Hunt, Norton M. *The Natural History of Love*, New York: Alfred A. Knopf, 1959.
14. Kelley, Earl C. *In Defense of Youth*, Englewood Cliffs, N.J.: Prentice-Hall, 1962.
15. Kinsey, Alfred C., Wardell B. Pomeroy, Clyde E. Martin and Paul H. Gebhard. *Sexual Behavior in the Human Female*, Philadelphia: W. B. Saunders, 1953.
16. Reiss, Ira L. *Premarital Sexual Standards in America*, Glencoe, Ill.: The Free Press, 1960.
17. Reiss, Ira L. "The Scaling of Premarital Sexual Permissiveness," *Journal of Marriage and the Family*, 1964, 26, 188–198.
18. Reiss, Ira L. "Premarital Sexual Permissiveness Among Negroes and Whites," *American Sociological Review*, 1964, 29, 688–698.
19. Remmers, H. H. and D. H. Radler. *The American Teenager*, New York: Charter, 1957.
20. Seidman, Jerome. *The Adolescent*, New York: Holt, 1960.
21. Smith, Ernest A. *American Youth Culture*, New York: The Free Press, 1963.
22. Symonds, P. M. *From Adolescent to Adult*, New York: Columbia University Press, 1961.
23. Vincent, Clark. *Unmarried Mothers*, Glencoe, Ill.: The Free Press, 1961.

The New People:
Childhood, A Journey
with New Maps

Charles Winick

> Father calls me William,
> Mother calls me Will,
> Sister calls me Willie,
> But the fellers call me Bill.[1]

The confusion of sex roles that pervades our environment would be meeting more opposition if our young people had not previously been prepared for the change. The culture which reflects our social system, which is part and parcel of personality itself, demands that childhood reflect our new values.

The authors of the nursery rhyme ("Natural History") could once have easily answered questions like "What are little boys made of?" and "What are little girls made of?" Such positive responses cannot be given lightly today. A number of milestones on the once familiar road of child development have been knocked down, including traditional name preferences, dolls, children's involvement in fairy tales, and established identities and roles of children. Each of these changes seriously affects how a child assimilates traditional ideas of masculinity and femininity. The nursery and playroom provide ample evidence.

From Dick and Jane
to Leslie and Tane

As Jack Paar once admitted, he had answered his daughter's puzzlement as to why she was named Randy with a counter-question: "Why don't you ask your mother George?" [2] A few years before his quip, Americans were discussing two prominent women called Pat and Jackie. Our new enthusiasm for given names that are not necessarily associated with either sex is important because personality may be shaped, reinforced, and reflected in a

[1] Eugene Field, "Jest 'Fore Christmas," in *The Writings in Prose and Verse of Eugene Field*. Vol. 4, Poems of Childhood. New York: Scribner's, 1894.
[2] March 6, 1964, on the Jack Paar program.

name. The individuality of a given name can be seen in the great painters whose signatures consisted only of their first names. Vincent Van Gogh, Rembrandt Harmenszoon van Rijn, and Michelangelo Buonarroti underscored their given names' uniqueness, even if others shared the family name.

The associations of names, often half-conscious, came from such wildly diverse sources as novels, historical figures, movie stars, comic strip heroes, religious leaders, friends and relatives, even places and pleasures.[3] They identify a person's family, reinforce his status, link him with a culture hero, provide a tie between tradition and the individual, and help to position him in society. A person's name carries his spirit and clothes him, just as the "soul is forme and doth the body wear," in Spenser's lovely phrase.

A given name is the only thing of value in our society which may be taken from anywhere, without asking. Everyone must have a given name, perhaps the one aspect of popular culture that touches us all. In several religions, to be dead is to have no name. Although a name does not necessarily influence self-identity, its ability to identify a person makes it easier for his attitudes toward a name to become closely related to feelings about himself.

As a child becomes aware of his name, between the ages of one and two, the fantasies forming around it tend to become deeply involved in the development of his idea of self. The given name is recognized as part of one's self long before the family name. Many children assume fantasy names because of concern about whether they have the "right" name. Children constantly test the effects of a name, and their ability to do so determines the extent to which they can accept it and its connotations.

Some rather striking effects of names on their owners are suggested by a finding that Harvard students with unusual names are significantly represented among students with superior personality, neurotics, and flunk-outs.[4] Another study concludes that boys with peculiar first names are more disturbed than those with ordinary names.[5] Such findings could, of course, result less from any intrinsic properties of a name than the attitudes toward a child that originally led the parents to select a particular name.

It is not unreasonable, then, to suspect that names given to children will reflect our culture's neuterization and what is becoming the game of sexual identity. One way of measuring this is to note birth announcements and to compare the names of the children with their parents'. In a large sample of birth announcements between 1948 and 1963, over one-fifth (21.3 per cent) of the children's names were not found among the parents', and three

[3] Daniel Adelson, "Attitudes toward First Names," *International Journal of Social Psychiatry,* Special Edition I, Section A, 1964, pp. 81–86; William F. Murphy, "A Note on the Significance of Names," *Psychoanalytic Quarterly,* 26, 1957, pp. 91–106.
[4] B. M. Savage and F. L. Wells, "A Note on Singularity in Given Names," *Journal of Social Psychology,* 27, 1948, pp. 271–272.
[5] Albert Ellis and R. M. Beechley, "Emotional Disturbance in Children with Peculiar Given Names," *Journal of Genetic Psychology,* 85, 1954, pp. 337–339.

kinds of names accounted for practically all of the difference: surnames used as given names, names linked with both sexes, and those having no established connotations.[6]

The surname as given name was originally a device to give a mother's maiden name to her son. The practice was once popular in the South, where a given name like Page, Saunders, Mallory, Logan, or Pierce was not uncommon even for a girl. Its previously established surname use tends to give such names a genderless quality.

The largest category of new names consisted of those given to both sexes. Some names have historically been given to either sex, e.g., Maria in Latin countries. England has had generals and admirals named Vivian, Jocelyn, and Joyce. But such established historical trends in other countries are quite different from our recent increase in ambisexual names.

One reason for the increase could be a more liberal interpretation of how names may be derived from religious sources. American Catholics still relate a child's baptismal name to a saint, who is a prestigious and protective model and guiding figure for the child. But today, a saint's name may appear on the baptismal certificate (e.g., Anastasia) and a related but secular name on the birth certificate (e.g., Stacey). Another approach is to add a saint's name to a secular one, so that Dana on a birth certificate might become Dana Anne at baptism. Jewish parents interpret the requirement to relate a name's initial letter to a deceased ancestor in an increasingly free manner.

---

[6] It was hypothesized that the names given to children would reflect our culture's tendency toward depolarization of sex. Birth announcements between the current and preceding generations appearing in *The New York Times* over a fifteen-year period (1948–1963) were analyzed, in terms of a comparison between names of the children and their parents.

A listing was made of every third one of the 43,337 children whose births were announced during this period. The frequency of occurrence of each name found among the 14,446 newborn, along with the incidence of the names of their parents, was tabulated. There were 816 different given names in the 14,446 that were sampled.

It was possible to prepare a table consisting of five columns, with the first containing the name, the second the number of fathers with the name, and the third column the number of mothers who had the name. The fourth column represented the number of boy children who had the name, and the fifth the number of girl children with the same name.

With a frequency count in each of the five columns it was possible to use a chi-square test in order to compare the distribution of parents' versus children's names to see whether they were significantly different, with the 5 per cent level representing significance of difference. All differences cited in the text were significant at the 5 per cent level or better. The chi-square test was used because it is nonparametric and makes no assumptions about the existence of a normal or Gaussian distribution pattern in the universe of names published in the newspaper.

The same kind of analysis was conducted to measure the extent to which the names were sex-linked. It was assumed that the expected distribution for a name is to have it ascribed only to persons of one sex, with no persons of the opposite sex possessing it. This would be true if names had a unimodal distribution by sex. To the extent that the statistical analysis indicated significant differences from such a distribution, such differences would suggest that the names are being assigned to boys and girls on a basis other than the 100 percent ratio.

An ancient Hebrew name like Rachel may appear on family records but metamorphose into Robin on a birth certificate.

Another sanction for names that could be used by either sex is the growing number of prominent persons with such names: Alexis (Smith, Johnson), Babe (Didrickson, Ruth), Connie (Francis, Mack), Dale (Evans, Robertson), Dana (Wynter, Andrews), Gene (Tierney, Tunney), Jan (Sterling, Murray), Jean (Seberg, Shepherd), Jeff (Donnell, Chandler), Jo (Stafford, Davidson), Joey (Heatherton, Adams), Joyce (Brothers, Cary), Kay (Kendall, Kyser), Lee (Remick, Tracy), Leslie (Caron, Howard), Loren (MacIver, Eisely), Lynn (Fontanne, Riggs), Michael (Strange, Wilding), Noel (Adam, Coward), Pat (Carroll, Boone), Ray (Dooley, Milland), Ruby (Keeler, Goldstein), Shelley (Winters, Berman), Shirley (MacLaine, Povich), and Vivian (Blaine, Fuchs).[7]

There is a busy traffic in names from one sex to the other. Kipling's Kim was a man, but in America three famous actresses bear the name (Hunter, Novak, Stanley). Miss Novak has indicated the confusion caused by her name: "I like Kim. . . . I see a little boy or girl with a shining face looking you straight in the eye." [8] Dana and Robin, once used for boys, have become very popular for girls. A number of names (Shirley, Leslie, Michael, Sidney) that are still masculine in England are used for both sexes in this country. Many other previously masculine names are now shared with women, but fewer feminine names have been taken by men (e.g., Winifred).

Children born in the last twenty years are more likely than their parents to have similarly pronounced names, differentiated only by spelling, e.g., Barrie-Barry, Claire-Clair, Jessie-Jesse, Rae-Ray, Sydney-Sidney. The popularity of such names has further contributed to blurring of sex differences. Some formerly sex-linked names have become homophonic, with Jessica, for example, becoming Jessie.

Unfortunately, ambiguous names continue to plague draft boards—women constantly receive notices to report for military duty. Such names have also led some steamship lines—inadvertently—to pair a man and woman in the same cabin. Another side of the problem is illustrated by a young man originally named Leslie Towne Hope, who has become better known as Bob Hope. After falling hopelessly in love with a young kindergarten classmate called Leslie, he renamed himself Lester in order to assert his maleness. Names' ability to convey problems in sexual identity is suggested in two films released during the war year of 1943. Both had heroines called Charlie and a third heroine was called Chris.[9] The films were released when men were away from home and women assumed many

---

[7] Jo Hubbard Chamberlin, "I'm Tender About Gender," *Coronet,* February 1960, pp. 55–57; the woman's name, of course, precedes the man's.
[8] Ezra Goodman, *The Fifty Year Decline and Fall of Hollywood.* New York: Simon and Schuster, 1961, p. 281.
[9] James Agee, *Agee on Film.* New York: McDowell Obolensky, 1958, p. 29.

previously male tasks. Such sexual confusion has become routine in today's movies, with Irving an attractive blonde in *Breakfast at Tiffany's,* and Charlie the heroine of *Good-bye, Charlie.*

Still a third category of children's names that differed significantly from parents' consisted of those that were freshly minted and lacked established connotations, e.g., Tane, Abar. The increase in names without antecedents among the New People may well support Ortega y Gasset's observation on the tendency of the masses to avoid history, since not using names from the past represents an excellent way of losing identification with it. After all, a name connected with nothing in particular involves loss of a ready-made identity.

The parents who made Washington the most popular post-Revolutionary boy's name were expressing admiration for the first president and a belief in contagious magic. The unfortunate child saddled with a name which has historical connotations may identify with or rebel against them. But even more importantly, beliefs about the sort of personality associated with a name may strongly influence otherwise latent traits.[10]

In the 1948–1963 sample and in earlier large-scale studies, unusual names were twice as frequent among girls as boys. Fathers have more to say about sons' than daughters' names and naturally seem to prefer more ordinary first names. Women carry and enjoy less common names.[11] Their favoring relatively unusual names is contrary to the stereotype about women being less adventurous and more conforming than men.[12] Some mothers may select masculinized or ambisexual names for daughters as an expression of identification, rivalry, or ambivalence.

All three name types found in children—surnames, ambisexual, and those without connotations—have neuter qualities. Such names may have a variety of effects on their innocent young bearers. Latent anti-masculine tendencies of a boy or anti-feminine tendencies of a girl may be reinforced. Other persons may look for sexual ambivalence in a person with such a homogenized name and the name can cause its owner to react against such tendencies.

Even the sounds of names are significant. Many neuter names have more sibilants and liquids than guttural consonants. They tend to be shorter than the parents' and many have become thinner: Mark becomes Marc and John's son is Jon.

An attempt is sometimes made to distinguish sex by pronunciation. A boy Cecil may have the first vowel short but a girl often has it long. A male

[10] G. Jahoda, "A Note on Ashanti Names and Their Relationship to Personality," *British Journal of Psychology,* 45, 1954, pp. 192–195.
[11] H. L. Mencken, *The American Language:* Supplement II. New York: Alfred A. Knopf, 1956, p. 472; L. Allen, V. Brown, L. Dickinson, and K. C. Pratt, "The Relation of First Name Preferences to Their Frequency in the Culture," *Journal of Social Psychology,* 14, 1941, pp. 279–293.
[12] Alfred I. Kolatch, *These Are the Names.* New York: Jonathan David Co., 1948.

Leslie can be identified by a sibilant *s* while a female might have the *s* pronounced like a *z*. For most ambisexual names, however, such distinctive pronunciation for either sex is not possible.

Other related trends reinforce the new generation's neuter names. There is a growing penchant for initials that do not stand for anything, like Harry S. Truman's middle initial. Many young people have added such initials in recent years. Among the prominent men who prefer to be identified by their initials are former presidents Kaufman Thuma Keller of Chrysler Corporation, Cyrus Rowlett Smith of American Airlines, and toymaker Alfred Carlton Gilbert. Actress K. T. Stevens is known by her initials, presumably inspired by great admiration for Katie Hepburn.

The homogenization of names can be seen in the LBJ brand. The name of each member of the First Family has similar syllabication and initials. Although the similarity among the Johnson names may inspire some names with identical syllabication and initials on the banks of the Pedernales, it has not become a national consensus and it is unlikely that many children have been named after the President and First Lady. There was not one Lyndon or Lady Bird in a large sample of children born in New York City in 1964, although a substantial number in previous years had been named after presidents or their wives.[13] The very homogenization of the First Family names could make it more difficult for parents to be emotionally involved with any one Johnson and to reflect such identification in naming a child than was possible with White House occupants who had more singular names.

Homogenization of names is also encouraged by the growing popularity of neutral diminutives and nicknames: Jerry, Bobbie, Jo, Willie, Mickey, Rusty, Bunny, Jackie, and Billie can identify either gender. Governor Nelson Rockefeller is called Rocky and his wife is known as Happy, but many a happy woman is nicknamed Rocky, e.g., Gary Cooper's widow. Happy is also a popular name for men, e.g., sportscaster Happy Felton.

Even famous athletes compound the confusion through neuter nicknames or diminutives. Consider a baseball team which included Ruby Gomez, Nellie Fox, Elly Howard, Sal Maglie, Babe Ruth, Lena Styles, Birdie Tebbets, Vickie Power, Gussie Triandos, and Gene Woodling.[14] Such neutering of sports figures' names is relatively unexpected because athletes often have complex and non-euphonious names. Typical are Zoilo Versalles of the Minnesota Twins, Felipe Alou of the Atlanta Braves, Yelberton A. Tittle of the New York Giants, Erich (pronounced Eerish, not Eric) Barnes of the Cleveland Browns, Vada Pinson of the Cincinnati Reds, and jockeys Angel, Ishmael, and Mario Valenzuela and Braulio Baeza.

The same name may even belong to two people of different sex and in

[13] Bureau of Records and Statistics, New York City Health Department, Report on Preferred Names for 1928, 1948, and 1964, dated April 28, 1965.
[14] John G. Fuller, "Trade Winds," *Saturday Review*, October 19, 1963, p. 8.

different fields of endeavor: Terry Moore, a brilliant center fielder for the St. Louis Cardinals, and also a prominent actress. Such ambiguity may increase the difficulty of a boy or girl Terry in finding an appropriate resonance for his or her name.

But how are ambiguous names regarded by others? The connotations of six first names were investigated by personal interviews. Two were unequivocally masculine (William and John), two were clearly feminine (Mary and Elizabeth), and two of the recently popular ambiguous names were rotated from a roster of six (Dale, Dana, Leslie, Lynn, Robin, Tracy) that had not differentiated sex in our study of birth announcements. The majority of both younger (17–30) and older (31–50) adults who were interviewed failed to associate the ambiguous names with either one sex or the other, although neither group had any such difficulty with the traditional names. The younger persons were better able to relate a range of personality characteristics to the ambiguous names but tended to ascribe non-sex-linked qualities to them.[15]

The new American propensity for neuter names is not found in England, which does favor names that are connected with movie stars but clearly communicate the sex of their owners. A study of names given to workers and their children in London found sharp differences between generations. Older parents tended to name their children after themselves, with most (58 per cent) husbands and many (38 per cent) wives passing on their own names. Few (20 per cent) of the youngest husbands and none of the wives conveyed their names to children. The inherited names tend to be simple (John, George, James, Mary, Alice, Ada), but Hollywood's influence here can be seen in the post-World War II children (Glenn, Gary, Maureen, Lana, and Linda).[16]

Although the incidence and neuter qualities of recent American names were unequivocal, the names of parents who submitted birth announcements might themselves have differed from their own parents'. When files of the same newspaper were studied and similar comparisons made for 1923–1938, some 19.4 per cent of the names of children born during the earlier period differed from their parents'—but only 3.1 per cent were surnames, sexually ambiguous, or lacking in connotations. Then and now, the great

---

[15] It proved possible to conduct interviews with a probability sample of adults between the ages of 17 and 50 about the connotations of these names. The sample, interviewed in connection with a larger study, consisted of 983 women and 957 men in the metropolitan New York area. In order to avoid any influence of the positioning of the ambiguous names in the total list, their sequence in the list was systematically rotated. The subject was handed a card on which the name had been typed and asked, "Could you please describe the kind of person that someone with this first name is likely to be?" He was encouraged to respond until he commented on both the sex as well as the personality characteristics of the name. He was then shown the next card in the series, until he had responded to all six cards.

[16] Michael Young and Peter Willmott, *Family and Kinship in East London.* London: Routledge and Kegan Paul, 1957, p. 10.

majority of parents seem loyal to established names, but perhaps one-fifth are responsive to other possibilities.

Yet, it is possible that people who arrange newspaper birth announcements may not be representative of the general population. There is no complete directory of the children born during the period studied, but spot checks with hospital birth records and school records substantially confirmed the incidence of neuter names. Why are they in the air at this time? Because like all names, they express attitudes toward the self, one's own sex, the opposite sex, and toward sexuality itself.[17] To a parent, such names may seem to be one way of being different, although, sadly, they provide still more evidence of conformity. They may also represent, along with spelling changes like Edythe for Edith, a desire to provide a classier name and identity for the New People who can expect to enjoy the age of affluence.[18]

Barbie as Baby Doll

The extraordinary popularity of *Lolita,* written by a middle-aged Russian émigré who would hardly have known any American girls of his heroine's age, suggests how ready the American public was to accept the idea of a sexually precocious young girl. The witty story of Humbert's becoming the victim of his twelve-year-old mistress was published in 1958, just one year after the introduction of the first mannequin doll and one year before Barbie, the most successful such doll. Four years before *Lolita, Susan Slept Here* had been the first movie to discover the power of the sexually emancipated teen-ager. Its aggressive girl delinquent moves in with a disillusioned script writer, deftly eliminates his fiancée, and marries him.

The great popularity of the mannequin doll is noteworthy because it mirrors an acceleration of social and sexual development and because doll

[17] Manuel Prenner, "Ora Jones Married Ora Jones," *American Speech,* 17, 1942, pp. 84–88. It is possible that such attitudes are especially important in large cities and may be less significant in rural areas. Dr. Earle H. MacCannell of Portland State College was able to identify the sex of 99 per cent of the children born in Chelan County in 1954 (a rural area in the state of Washington) by their given names (personal communication).

[18] Intersexual first names represent the most obvious use of names to express crisscrossing of sex roles. A subtler approach is found in retention of a clearly sex-linked name like John or Mary, but selecting it from an ancestor related to the opposite sex. A study of middle-class Chicago families in the 1950's concluded that their sons were more apt to be named for maternal grandparents and maternal collateral kin and less likely to be named for paternal relatives than in the 1920's. Girls were more likely to be named for paternal grandparents and paternal collateral kin and less apt to derive names from maternal grandparents and aunts than in the 1920s. Such a tendency, like the popularity of neutral names, could become even more conspicuous as our culture sidesteps toward depolarization. See Alice S. Rossi, "Naming Children in Middle Class Families," *American Sociological Review,* 30, 1965, pp. 499–513.

play is traditionally so important. Dolls represent the largest single category of expenditure of the $2.68 billion that Americans spent on toys during 1966. The more than twenty million girls of doll age in the United States average two new dolls a year and devote more play time to them than to any other toy.

Children can magically and easily transfer the qualities of living persons to their dolls. A passion for dolls is strongest between seven and ten, reaching a climax between eight and nine.[19] The old-fashioned rubber baby doll was practically indestructible. Simple, without gadgetry, it represented an ideal object for creative fantasy play that could later help a little girl to become comfortable in the role of mother. Simple dolls tend to elicit the fullest response. Elaborate mechanical dolls that sucked, drank from bottles, wet diapers, cried, kissed, waved, and burped have also been popular but tend to stifle rather than stimulate creative impulses. A gimmicky baby doll may be so robotlike and have such specific physical detail that imaginative play is difficult.

Many girls learned to sew by working on doll clothes. By taking care of her doll, a girl could project into the future and see herself as mother. At the same time, the child could identify with the doll, since both were being taken care of by a mother. The baby dolls looked young enough for such identification and projection. Long before Freud, Victor Hugo wrote: "The doll is one of the most imperious necessities, and at the same time one of the most charming instincts of female childhood."

The ability that dolls once had to evoke such rhapsodic responses and help a girl ultimately to prepare for active nurturing motherhood became historical with the extraordinary popularity of mannequin dolls. They have far outsold their predecessors and radically changed the satisfactions provided by dolls. Every fourth girl between four and twelve owned a Ginny mannequin doll by the mid-1950s, when another popular favorite was Betsy McCall, whose extensive wardrobe included mink stoles and muffs.

The prototype teen or full-figured doll was introduced in 1957, and Barbie appeared in 1959, followed in two years by Ken, her male consort. Three Barbies have been sold for every Ken. An average of over six million mannequin dolls have been sold each year for a decade. A minimum standard wardrobe for Barbie costs an elegant $588. Auxiliary equipment includes a car, ranch house, and fashion wigs that can be dyed. The mannequin dolls have very adult and sophisticated clothes, and one of their contributions to acceleration of young girls' social development has been a sparking of interest in grooming and fashion. Little girls have been buying a weekly average of 125,000 dresses for fashion dolls, including costumes for cocktails, dancing, and traveling. A girl can purchase a *boutique* shop,

---

[19] A. Caswell Ellis and G. Stanley Hall, "A Study of Dolls," in Hall, *Aspects of Child Life and Education*. New York: D. Appleton, 1921, pp. 157–204.

with her doll as the proprietress. To complete the adult charade, Ken's chums include Ricky and Allen, Barbie has relatives, and her "best friend" is a doll called Midge. The girl with a Barbie can get a Midge and practice the game of competing with Ken as the target. Ten or fifteen years later, our Barbie may find that it's not all that simple. Her expectations may prove inadequate because love cannot, like Barbie's wardrobe, be purchased at the corner store.

What is the effect of these mannequin dolls on their millions of owners between four and twelve? Such girls may be less able to achieve the emotional preparation for being a wife and mother that they received from baby dolls. Barbie is a sexy teen-ager. A girl who projects and sees her doll as a mother figure is seeing her mother as a teen-ager, which is certainly confusing. If the youngster identifies herself as the mother, then she is taking care of a child who is already an adolescent.[20]

The role of the new woman in the larger world is suggested in fashion doll owners' play, which typically involves social activities for the doll and her escort. The girl selects a situation and dresses her doll accordingly. If she owns a male doll, he is also dressed—just as if she could control the way the man in the mating game would dress. She also gains experience in mixing with the opposite sex and competing for a male. On the make, in control of the situation, she is preparing herself to be the aggressive woman who flourishes in novels, plays, and movies. On television, her most obvious expression is *The Dating Game,* which is so successful that it can be seen weekdays and Saturday. Its format involves a girl who puts questions to a panel of three young men, evaluates their answers, and then selects one who will accompany her on a date. By the time the Barbie owner reaches the age at which she can actually participate in dating, she is likely to have a definite idea of just how her escort will play his part. For this mechanical bride, little will be left to chance or to disturbing human impulses.

Alas, many a young man, already two years slower in achieving puberty, may well be overwhelmed by his date's aggressiveness. For the Barbie-weaned girl, a relationship with the opposite sex may not be marvelous and exciting; it could rather be a routinized aspect of our culture's material assembly line, lacking mystery or momentum because of its predictable outcome. The Barbie girl may learn to expect to be valued because of her ever-increasing wardrobe and ability to manipulate her father and, later, husband into buying clothes and more clothes. During the latency years, she is being introduced to precocious sexuality, voyeurism, fantasies of seduction, and conspicuous consumption.[21]

As the sexy automatized doll displaces the baby doll, some effects may be seen in recent studies of figure drawings by girls from twelve to sixteen.

---

[20] Mariann A. Winick, "Little Girls and Their Dolls." Unpublished manuscript.
[21] "A Psychiatrist in Toyland," KMPC, Los Angeles, February 27, 1966.

Although such a tendency was not reported before the mannequin doll's popularity, girls now frequently draw male figures with feminine characteristics.[22] The girls are aware of basic sexual differences but insist on tagging the male with feminine qualities—a symbolic castration. Their confusion about boys' appearance may be related to some characteristics of the dolls. Barbie has a very substantial bosom, but Ken has no visible genital signs of masculinity. Many girls who have put Ken's head on Barbie do not appreciate the significance of Barbie's bosom or hair. They will find Ken-Barbie in the flesh when, in later years, they look for "men" and discover how many have feminine characteristics.

So much time separated the nine-year-old with an old-fashioned baby doll from her role as mother that she could enjoy fantasies about motherhood and not be concerned about doing something about them. But the distance in years that separates a Barbie fan from a socially active ten- or eleven-year-old girl is frighteningly slight, and she can easily translate doll-play fantasies into real social life. The girl's confusion of fantasy with reality was only increased when stores began selling "Barbie-coordinated fashions" that could be worn by the dolls' owners.

Barbie's wardrobes, homes, stores, playrooms, automobiles, and other elaborate equipment are an elaborate and rigid script for fantasies. Mannequin dolls' great popularity comes directly from their provision of vicarious experiences which are far beyond the emotional ability of their owners. One unanticipated consequence is that more and more teen-age girls who have gone through a Barbie phase later buy stuffed baby dolls in an apparent attempt to make up for earlier deprivation of symbolic motherhood via a baby doll. There is already some evidence that the teddy bear frequently ends up as the third person in the honeymoon bed.

We can only speculate on the ultimate effects of play with a doll that is relentlessly geared toward courtship rather than motherhood. Children can confirm their sense of identity by play with dolls, which is a "royal road" to understanding the infantile ego's efforts to come to terms with the real world and the other components of self.[23] The small world of toys that the child can manage is a harbor to which she can return for the purpose of redefining her ego, but mannequin dolls can accelerate psychosexual development and transform doll play into a turbulent and disruptive voyage.

Barbie and her counterparts are so recent that there really has not been enough time to assess their ultimate results. But there is already good reason to fear that some effects on many young girls were not anticipated by their purchasers, any more than Rabbi Löw could predict how much trouble would result from his golem, which followed instructions until the charm was removed from its mouth. The rabbi originally used the golem

[22] Dr. Jacob Goldstein, personal communication.
[23] Erik H. Erikson, *Childhood and Society*. New York: Norton, 1950, pp. 182, 194, 202, 209.

with good intent, just as parents want to please their daughters. Premature learning of later social roles, however, could cast a shadow into the later life of many a child who is currently enjoying her Barbie.

A parable with some ominous implications for the future may be divined in the history of the wheel's development in Mexican culture. Wheels were never used to lighten labor or to facilitate transportation in pre-Conquest Mexico, although archeologists have found children's wheeled pull toys from the same period. The Barbie craze may be predicting later trends in adult life, just as wheeled pre-Conquest toys were precursors of later developments.[24] The Mexicans regarded their children's play with wheeled toys as a game without implications for adult life and American parents view the fantasy play that Barbie provides as a curiosity without practical consequences. Although nothing in play is final and play itself usually occurs within the charmed circle of reversibility, Barbie may be providing experiences that are ultimately irreversible. . . .

Playing and Wearing Roles

At a government conference on recruiting women scientists, a major toy manufacturer stressed that "we need to develop new lines of toys which have no 'sex,' which would appeal equally to girls as well as boys. Giant magnifiers, our lens comparer, incubators, stethoscopes, flexible mirrors, etc., are precisely such items. . . . Let us start recruiting women scientists . . . during the years from two to seven." [25] Science-oriented, neuter toys are receiving more attention as playthings specifically designed for each sex decline in popularity.

Play preferences of boys and girls now overlap at a relatively early age, in addition to traditional shared sports like hiking and roller-skating. Girls are learning to play with model cars, Erector sets, baseball equipment, and guns, and are "pretend" space travelers or western heroes. High-riser bicycles, with handlebars resembling the horns of a longhorn steer, are rapidly eliminating the need for boys and girls to own different bicycles. Pangloss's buttockless people would have been delighted with the very high thin seat that tops the high risers' small frames and wheels. The crossbar connecting the seat of a boy's model with the steering apparatus is low enough not to injure a girl while she is mounting or dismounting. As a result, many girls are now using their brothers' high-riser bicycles, and sales of girls' models have declined.

Just as the profile of boy and girl cycling on their high risers is indistinguishable at a distance, the profile of school studies for both sexes shows

[24] Gordon F. Ekholm, "Wheeled Toys in Mexico," *American Antiquity*, 11, 1946, pp. 222–228.
[25] *Help Them to Grow Every Day*, Catalog of Creative Playthings, 1964, p. 27.

much overlap. A number of schools offer boys sewing in the fifth and sixth grades. Many eighth-grade boys learn cooking, while girls study tool and die work, plumbing repairs, metalcrafts, and lathe work. Both sexes are taught to type in high school.

Once upon a time, young people used to have masculine or feminine fountain pens. Boys' pens were long and stubby while girls' tended to be thin and short, but the use of standardized ball-point pens has largely erased these differences. Sex differences in handwriting were easily communicated by nib pens, but are now relatively difficult to identify because ball points make strokes of uniform width.

Young people of each sex are more likely than ever before to have read books formerly associated with the other sex. Girls who never owned a *Nancy Drew* story may have read *Treasure Island* or *Huckleberry Finn.* Many boys who are oblivious to the appeal of the *Hardy Boys* enjoy *Heidi* or *Peter Pan.* Some very successful recent books have a girl hero but seem of equal interest to both sexes, like *Island of the Blue Dolphins* and *The Moon Spinners.* Except for boys' interest in sports, both sexes are now almost equally interested in all categories of books, although there were distinct reading preferences even twenty-five years ago.

Television programs watched by children also seem to be devoid of qualities that appeal to one sex or the other. The most extensive study of television and children found little support for the view that girls are more squeamish than boys in connection with violence. Other studies concluded that middle-class adolescent girls took greater responsibility than boys for aggressive action toward a frustrating authority.[26] The girls will probably be even more forceful in the era of the mannequin doll.

In the past, parents tended to punish boys more often than girls with beatings and other physical measures. Recently the frequency with which such punishment is administered to boys and girls has become less distinguishable. Many a mother who never was physically disciplined as a girl has spanked her daughter, perhaps reluctantly at first, as she has learned to make few distinctions between measures applied to sons and daughters. Twenty-five years ago, when little girls were perhaps still believed to be made of "sugar and spice and all things nice," Talcott Parsons could accurately observe that "there is really no feminine equivalent of the expression 'bad boy.' "[27] But today we do not hesitate to speak of and punish a "naughty" or even "bad" girl. Contemporary parents are more willing than

[26] Hilde T. Himmelweit, A. N. Oppenheim, and Pamela Vince, *Television and the Child.* New York: Oxford University Press, 1958; Leonard M. Lansky, Vaughn T. Crandall, and Jerome Kagan, "Sex Differences in Aggression and Its Correlates in Middle Class Adolescents," *Child Development,* 32, 1961, pp. 45–58. Eleanor E. Maccoby et al., *The Development of Sex Differences* (Stanford: Stanford University Press, 1966) provides the most thorough coverage of this subject.

[27] Talcott Parsons, "Age and Sex in the Social Structure," *American Sociological Review,* 7, 1942, pp. 604–616.

the previous generation to recognize that their daughters can behave unpleasantly and even destructively.

The formerly considerable gap that once separated the allowances given to girls from those received by boys has been dwindling steadily as girls have been getting more money from parents. Eleven-year-old girls in one study received 76¢ a week while boys of the same age averaged 97¢ a week.[28] Girls of thirteen tend to get and spend more money than boys and many fourteen-year-old girls expect allowances to be large enough to cover their wardrobe expenses. Barbie owners are especially likely to press for money for clothes.

Many other lines of evidence support the view that a wide range of forces is helping to cast boys and girls in the same mold. Even before a name is selected, the blurring of sex differences may begin. Parents once bought pink for a girl and blue for a boy. The pink-clad girl was "darling" and "beautiful" and the boy in blue was "handsome" or "strong." Although pink is still restricted to girls, blue is now worn by infants of either sex. But an even more important change is the popularity of maize, aqua, pale green, gray, and other neutral colors for both boys and girls. The near-disappearance of clothing differences should prepare the toddler for later blurring of visible signs of masculinity and femininity.

The signs are even disappearing from diapers. A diaper folded in front conveyed masculinity and one folded in the back connoted femininity, because of differences in the direction of the child's urination. In the last fifteen years, this difference has almost vanished, as a result of the disposable diaper and the "ready fold" with a rectangular panel along its center, both front and rear.

Diapers are only the beginning and children soon learn to wear other desexualized clothing. Identical coats and jackets are favored by both boys and girls.[29] Colors like sage seem to have been created because children of either sex wear similar clothing. As designer John Stephen summed it up: ". . . the hottest story in young fashion: boy/girl, his/hers, either/or clothes and haircuts." [30]

Even in the first years of school, girls wear trousers so often that some school systems have required them to wear dresses. Young boys' footwear is almost indistinguishable from their sisters'. Boys' sneakers were formerly ankle-high, but today are often cut as low as girls'. Many a boy strolls down the street in sneakers and bobby sox interchangeable with his sister's. Little boys and their sisters wear shoes of similar colors. Brown boys' shoes have gone the way of the black or white that formerly accounted for most little girls' footwear. Ten years ago, the Mary Jane that once was available

---

[28] Judith Kranes, "What About Children's Allowances?", *Understanding the Child,* 26, 1957, pp. 13–17.
[29] "Report on Children's Wear," *New York Times,* August 11, 1963, Section 6, Part 2.
[30] Dick Schaap, "Tomorrow the World," *New York Herald Tribune,* August 6, 1965.

only in black patent leather or white kid blossomed forth in a variety of colors and fabrics on young feet.

Boys are letting their hair grow longer. Now that girls are cutting their hair shorter, they are relatively unlikely to have the pigtails that boys of an earlier generation used to enjoy pulling. The ambisexual Oliver haircut, which represented one mark of a well-dressed young person, led logically to the Beatle non-haircut. The many other similarities in the appearance of boys and girls provide a bridge to adult clothing and help to explain why leading designers of women's clothes, like Courrèges and Gernreich, have been so successful in creating children's wear. Parents in our psycho-analytically sophisticated times are so tolerant of neutering that they permit crisscrossing of sex roles in children's appearance that would have been considered pathological just one generation ago.

The word "sissy," which derives from "sister," was once a terrible fate for a young man. With so many boys resembling and adapting clothes from their sisters, perhaps "sissy" should be retired. The phrases used to describe boys' wear sound as if they have been taken directly from women's fashion magazines ("the ultimate in wash 'n' wear," "the elegance of simplicity").

By 1963, young girls began saying good-bye to ruffles and bows and adopted the little-boy look. Now that a typical girl's costume consists of a shirt with a bib front and suspenders, worn with a boy's cap, there would seem to be considerable understatement in a report that identified twelve as the age at which a girl begins to raid her brother's wardrobe.[31] Girls' clothing is sold in quantities commensurate with the proportion of girls in the population. Boys' costumes are, however, sold in much greater quantity than the proportion of boys, suggesting that girls are far more likely than boys to dress in the others' costumes.

Over a generation ago, when writing anonymously, three times as many girls as boys wished to be of the opposite sex.[32] The many traditional boys' attributes that have been taken over by girls make it likely that fewer girls would express such a wish today, and in a more recent investigation, only 40 per cent more girls than boys wanted to be of the opposite sex.[33] If current trends toward role reversal continue, and literary critics continue to raise questions about Huck Finn's masculinity, more boys than girls will soon be expressing a desire to change gender.

---

[31] *New York Times,* August 11, 1963, *op cit.*
[32] Reik, *op cit.,* p. 117.
[33] Study conducted by the author in the metropolitan New York area in 1956 with 1,203 high school students. The questions were put to young people who were being interviewed as part of a larger study. See Charles Winick, "Tendency Systems and the Effects of a Movie Dealing with a Social Problem," *Journal of General Psychology,* 68, 1963, pp. 289–305.

Section V

Youth, Politics,
and the Campus

INTRODUCTION

If any one event in recent history could be designated as the catalyst of the contemporary youth movements, it would most likely be the campus disruptions that occurred at Berkeley in 1964. As almost all observers (including the authors presented here) have noted in discussions about the accelerated attention paid to youth during the 1960s, prior to Berkeley, youth in general, and students in particular, seemed to be engaged in the expected minor, relatively quiet, and therefore invisible forms of normal "abnormality"; Berkeley signaled a new voice, a collective identity, and a thrust that not only changed the face of campus life and campus politics, but spread contagiously to other segments of the American youth culture.

The oddity about Berkeley and subsequent student confrontations, demonstrations, and riots was the fact that American universities in the preceding decades were relatively serene, undisturbed, and insulated sanctuaries in which students and faculty relations at most rose to the level of vigorous discussion and criticism; the university in those years was a training ground for the future expertise and leadership in American social institutions. Or so it appeared. If social change was to come in modern society, it would take the form of reasoned and intelligent progress led by those youth who were sufficiently advantaged to have learned the quality and manners of civility within the halls of higher education. No other institution seemed so entirely safe from the mundane, divisive world.

Yet, the ingredients for political turmoil in the universities already existed. Universities had rapidly grown into huge, impersonal administrative structures called multiversities; college students were among the original standard-bearers of the civil rights movement; and the larger political climate of the 1950s and 1960s, from the Cold War to the Vietnam War, allowed few youths to be impervious to at least a broad form of politicization. Whereas American universities retained a tradition of apoliticalness, universities throughout the world were often primary institutions of political dialogue, conflict, and change.

In addition, college students were an effectively disenfranchised campus group with little role or responsibility for determining the kind of education they would receive. Administrators and faculties saw no imperative need to alter the political hierarchy of the campus, for it would be like turning the world on its head if students were allowed to make decisions that by definition they were unqualified to make—especially since various and sundry political channels were open and available for those potential activists who desired them. Although it was clear to many that political inequities concerning youth existed outside the campus (such as the right to vote only upon reaching the age of twenty-one), sufficient opportunities for political expression were still perceived.

Of course, few of these traditions and views have since gone untouched.

330

Depending upon one's ideological perspective, changes in the political structure of the campus, voting rights, and the political influence of youth have been described as negligible or significant, reformative or radical, evolutionary or revolutionary. The Amercian university is now a different, if not entirely transformed place, and that difference is to be found in the events and conditions of the 1960s. The fact that the 1970s have begun with relative quiet and almost undetectable political activity on the campuses suggests several possible explanations, any of which may assume greater validity as the political history of the decade unfolds: (1) a new, different youth generation has come to the campus, and this generation's student is essentially apolitical and apathetic; (2) the campus political leadership of the 1960s has graduated both to adulthood and to outside political groups, effectively dissipating the active leadership that had been present for a period of approximately six years; (3) the political and educational gains and changes of the 1960s were sufficient to transform radical confrontation to quiet reform; (4) the antichange forces on campus have developed successful strategies and measures to quickly weed out potential sources of conflict; (5) the traditionalist views on higher education within the academic sanctuary have convinced youth that political strife has no place on the campus; (6) the same ingredients and causes that existed in the 1950s and early 1960s still exist but lay dormant during a brief period of strategic retrenchment; (7) campus problems resulting from political confrontation were far too costly compared to the gains subsequently made, and thus youthful political expression will find either new strategies or another area outside the university; (8) and, finally, the larger political climate has now lost its previous sense of urgency, particularly as a result of modifications of both foreign and domestic policy.

Indeed, predictions about complex events are most difficult, if not impossible to make, the best evidence for which can be found in the fact that few prognosticators thought it possible that the college campus would quickly return to a state of normal quietude at the turn of this decade.

Students and Politics
in Comparative Perspective

Seymour Martin Lipset

Ten years ago, hardly anyone devoted himself to research on students and politics. Today hundreds of scholars are analyzing student political movements, behavior, and attitudes. It is evident that student activism and the importance of students in politics long antedates the current interest. Students were a key element in the Revolutions of 1848 in Germany and Austria, and student activism stimulated the "Professors' Parliament," which almost succeeded in toppling several monarchs. In Czarist Russia, students spearheaded various revolutionary movements, and the university campus was a major center of revolutionary activity. In the East European countries, where education was limited to a small proportion of the population, students were often the carriers of modern ideas of liberty, socialism, industrialization, and equality of opportunity.

The important role of students in the movements for national independence in the developing areas also goes back a half century or more. In Imperial China, students were crucial to the Imperial effort at modernization, but at the same time spread republican and radical ideas throughout the society. Students helped overthrow the dynasty in 1911, and were thereafter one of the elements continually pushing China toward modernization and radical ideologies. In other Asian and African countries, students were often a central element in anticolonial struggles. Particularly important were the "returned students"—those individuals who had lived and studied abroad, mostly in Europe, and returned home with ideas of modernization and Marxism, socialism and struggle. International student meetings were held as early as the 1920's, and such men as Nehru of India and Hatta of Indonesia were profoundly influenced by these student organizations and movements.

Scholars in the past paid relatively little attention to the rather major role students played in reform and radical movements, in part because student movements are quite transitory in character and have left fewer records than adult organizations. Moreover, to stress the role of youth and students, rather than that of the social classes or religion, seemed in a sense to underemphasize the seriousness and significance of the happenings and to turn them into "children's crusades."

Then, too, from the Marxist perspective, intellectuals and students are

Seymour Martin Lipset, "Students and Politics in Comparative Perspectives," from *Daedalus*. Reprinted by permission of *Daedalus,* Journal of the American Academy of Arts and Sciences, Boston, Mass. (Winter 1968) Students and Politics.

not significant independent social forces. Rather, they have been viewed as vacillating, unreliable, "*petit-bourgeois* elements" who are inclined to shift with the prevailing ideological winds. Although students have played a rather major role in supporting various Communist movements at different times, the Party has tended to deprecate their role.

The greater willingness to recognize the political role of students stems, in part, from the awareness by many on the left that other social forces are not always available for support. The organized workers of the developed countries of Europe and America, for example, have become a conservative force, as C. Wright Mills has pointed out. Trade unions and labor-based parties have been integrated into an institutional system of representation and collective bargaining. As such, they are not concerned with policies and programs that may upset the political pattern. The orthodox (pro-Russian) Communist Parties in many countries have also become part of the regular system of representation and no longer advocate use of extralegal and extra-parliamentary tactics. In Latin America, they oppose the guerrilla tactics fostered by Castroites and Maoists.

Mills saw in the intellectuals and students a major potential mass base for new revolutionary movements. They have *remained* a source of new radical leadership and mass support, while other elements of society have not. Thus, more attention is being focused on the American student move-ment at present than occurred during the 1930's, even though the move-ment was larger in both absolute and proportionate terms in the thirties. But beyond the emergence of an intellectual concern with the politics of students, well-publicized events of the past decade have illustrated the significance of student politics. Student demonstrations and movements played a consider-able role in the overthrow of Perón in Argentina in 1955; the downfall of Pérez Jiménez in Venezuela in 1958; the successful resistance to Diem in Vietnam in 1963; the massive riots against the Japan-U.S. Security Treaty in Japan in 1960 which forced the resignation of the Kishi govern-ment; the anti-Sukarno movement in Indonesia in 1966; the October demon-strations for greater freedom in Poland in 1956; and the 1956 Hungarian Revolution. It is important to note, however, that although students may be catalysts for political action, they can seldom bring a revolutionary move-ment to fruition. In Korea, students began the movement that succeeded in toppling the Rhee government in 1960, but they relied on popular pressure and the army to make their movement successful.

Although much of the recent writing on student politics has focused on leftist activist groups, it is also important to analyze the strength and activities of traditional and conservative groups as well. Opinion data for various countries assembled by Glaucio Soares indicate that the left-wing students are in a minority, often very small, even in countries where leftist demonstrations have made international headlines. Even though university campuses provide a significant proportion of the future radical leadership, as well as the mass base for antigovernment demonstrations, most students are not involved in such activities. In most countries, the vast majority of students are apolitical and tend to endorse the moderate or even conservative parties. In the United States today, the largest campus political groups are the Young Democrats and Young Republicans, which have a total combined membership of under 250,000 members, as contrasted to 7,000 members of the new-left Students for a Democratic Society (SDS). A recent (1967) U. S. survey of American college students reports that a plurality favors the Republicans for the 1968 Presidential Election. Four national surveys conducted during 1965 and 1966 found that from two thirds to three quarters of American students support the Vietnamese war.

Influences derivative from university experiences are, of course, not the sole or even primary determinants of student political beliefs. Family perspectives often influence students' orientations. The high correlation between the political stance of students and that of their parents would imply that the children of poorer families should be more leftist than those of the more well-to-do, since socio-economic class and political choice are generally related in this way. Although research in various countries tends to validate the generalization, it does not, for a number of reasons, apply this simply to student populations. Students from relatively poor families tend to come from that minority within the lower strata which is strongly oriented toward upward mobility and the values of the privileged. Hence, their parents are often among the more politically conservative of their class. Moreover, upwardly mobile students who represent the first generation of their family attending university tend to be vocationally oriented. They are more likely to be found in fields that lead to professions. This strong concentration on careerist professional objectives, plus the need to have a job during the school term, results in these students being less available for political or other extracurricular activities than those from more privileged backgrounds.

In Scandinavia, a student of working-class origins is likely to shift from a Social Democratic family orientation to a conservative one. There is less probability that a student from a conservative middle-class background will shift to left-wing parties. Recent American data suggest the reverse finding. Attendance at university is stronger in pressing well-to-do students to a position to the left of their parents, than in moving those from less-privileged Democratic and liberal families to the right. Such findings should be subjected to more precise specification as to type of school attended and academic discipline studied. The greater shift to liberalism among the more well-to-do in the United States may reflect the high proportion attending the better universities, which characteristically have the most creative, intellectually oriented, and liberal faculties. Conservative students on such campuses experience a political atmosphere hostile to their family political beliefs.

Well-to-do parents are also among the better educated. Particularly is this so among professionals. Increased education is associated in most underdeveloped countries with approval of modern, as contrasted with traditional, values and in the developed societies with belief in "noneconomic liberalism" —support for civil liberties for unpopular minorities, internationalism, and so forth. These orientations are generally fostered by the more liberal or leftist campus groups. Matters related to economic class are less salient sources of campus politics than noneconomic ones. Students in the United States, for example, are much more concerned with civil rights for Negroes or political rights on campus and in the larger society, than with the power of trade unions or the consequences of different systems of taxation on economic growth.

Many of those who experience a tension between the political atmosphere of the university and their family tradition escape the choice by abstaining from politics, by accepting the doctrine that school and politics do not mix. Most students from conservative backgrounds remain in this tradition. In countries where there is a visible difference in the dominant political orientation of universities, continuity in family political orientation may be facilitated by the process of conscious selection of universities because of their political reputations. In Latin America, conservative privileged families will often send their children to schools with a conservative or apolitical reputation, such as the Catholic or other private universities. Unfortunately, there is little reliable information on this subject.

American research findings suggest that there is congruence between the characteristic political orientation of different disciplines and the political beliefs of entering students who plan to major in them. Conservatives are more likely to study engineering or business, and liberals the humanities or social sciences. Such selection reflects the extent to which varying political orientations influence students to opt for different career goals. Leftists, particularly those from well-to-do and well-educated families, are inclined to favor academic fields concerned with social and political issues or careers in the arts, social work, scholarship, and public service.

Academic ecology, the social environment in which a student happens to find himself by virtue of his choice of university or academic field, tends to be more important than his class background in affecting his opinions. The faculty within which students are enrolled seems more predictive of their political stance than class origins. In various Latin American countries, the differences among universities in their modal political choice are greater than the social-class variation within them. Nevertheless, those who bring strong traditionalist values with them to the university are more likely to remain conservative and apolitical than others. This may be seen most strongly in the role of religion. In the Catholic countries of Latin America and Europe, practicing Catholic students are much more conservative than nonbelievers. Thus, reported differences in family religious practices are highly predictive in this respect. Similar findings have been reported for India. In the United States, Catholics and evangelical Protestants are also among the most conservative groups in the university.

Minority-majority social status also seems more important than economic class background in affecting student propensity for action. In Germany and Austria, for example, students from minority groups (Jews and Slavs) and from the lower-middle class spearheaded the Revolution of 1848. Students from minority ethnic backgrounds were also active in the pre-revolutionary Russian student movement as well. Today in the United States, Britain, and Argentina, Jews contribute heavily to the membership and support of activist left groups.

In many of the developing countries and in nations like Belgium and Canada, there are often deep cleavages that prevent a sense of community among the students. Religious divisions, regional, linguistic, caste, racial, and tribal differences often severely inhibit the growth of national student movements devoted to societal objectives, or even to university reform. In a number of countries, divergent student groupings based on such variations are locked in conflict. In India students have taken to the streets because of religious or linguistic differences. In Indonesia, student groups are often organized on the basis of religious or regional affiliation.

The varying demands that universities make on students also affect the possibilities for political participation and the political climate on the campus. The examination system used is a key factor in determining student political activism. In the American system, for example, students are generally required to take examinations at regular intervals and to maintain at least minimal academic standards to stay in school. They may take part in extracurricular activities, political or other, but these are at the expense of their studies. In Latin America, where examinations are not so important or may be postponed, such sanctions do not exist.

In many countries, it is possible to predict accurately the cycle of student activism on the basis of examination schedules. In India, students do not generally study until a month before the annual examinations. Thus, most students have a very substantial amount of free time during the year. In Latin America, many student leaders are able to maintain their status within the university for years by postponing their examinations and devoting themselves full-time to political activity.

Entrance requirements to a university may also affect political reactions. The Japanese and American patterns place great emphasis on getting into the best universities and require high-school students to work long hours under considerable psychic pressure. These patterns clearly affect the way some students behave after they are admitted to the university. A great deal of Japanese and American student activism is concentrated in the freshmen and sophomore years, which may reflect the students' reaction to being released from the pressures of entrance anxiety. Upperclassmen tend to be more liberal in their attitudes than lower-division groups, but to give less time to politics. Presumably years of university attendance are associated both with greater liberalism and more concern with preparing for jobs or admission into good graduate schools.

The greater activism of lowerclassmen may also reflect the liberating influences of the university. Students often express their newly found freedom by engaging in various forms of "nonconformist" behavior. Regardless of class in school, students living away from home, either in dormitories or in private accommodations, are more likely to participate in activist politics than those commuting from home. Moreover, Berkeley data suggest that "new" students—whether freshmen, juniors, or graduate students—are more likely to be activists than students who have been in residence for some time. In other words, recent transfer students contribute disproportionately to the activist core. This raises a general question about transferring from one campus to another. A campus is not always a community in which students remain for the entire period of their education and in which they are gradually socialized into the community norms. Frank Pinner suggests that young people, particularly students, join organizations or integrated collectivities because they have just left their families, their home town, or friends and are anxious, disoriented, and lonely. They find in organizational life—particularly in movements that have a sense of commitment, purpose, and high intimacy—a kind of replacement for the collectivity they have just left. This factor, which would apply more to the new than to older students, would also vary by country and university system. It would depend, in part, on what proportion of students live at home or close to home.

Opinions as to the place of politics in the university are inherently related to feelings about the larger society. Those—whether of the extreme left or right—who believe that drastic changes are necessary, that major evils exist, or that the basic verities are under attack will feel that students and faculty ought to be deeply involved in politics. Conversely, moderate conservatives and liberals are more likely to accept President Benitez's formula that a university is a "house of study," rather than a "house of politics." Conservatives, as believers in the *status quo,* will generally be even less active politically than liberals or moderate leftists. Glaucio Soares's Brazilian data indicate that conservative students not only are not interested in politics, but often "perceive student politics as an undue interference with their studies." The leftists, on the other hand, feel that they have a duty to be politically engaged and that the university should be an agency of modernization and radical change. As Soares puts it, conservatives argue that the political and academic roles should be compartmentalized, while leftists seek to integrate the two. This means, of course, that under current conditions in most countries, the student left will mobilize a much greater proportion of its potential strength for politics than will the moderates or the rightists.

Most of the recent writing on student activism tends to ignore the phenomenon of rightist activism. Indeed, although many students are conservatives, there has been little rightist campus activism since the 1930's. As a result, little material has been published concerning the activities of the extreme rightist student groups of the 1920's and 1930's in much of Europe. German and Austrian students were on the left during the early-nineteenth century, but many turned to rightist nationalism in the late-nineteenth and early-twentieth centuries. Anti-Semitism and extreme nationalism were characteristic of many of the more politically sophisticated German fraternities, and Nazism had great appeal in the universities in the 1930's. French Fascism, strong during the interwar period, received considerable support from university students. Many of the student groups active during the 1930's in Latin America had strong Fascist views, due mainly to the influence from Spain and Italy, while German Nazi influence was strong in some Arab movements. In the colonial areas, nationalist movements often looked with favor on Hitler and Mussolini because of their opposition to the imperialist powers of Western Europe. Although ideological issues were confused, university students tended to accept some aspects of Fascist ideology, particularly the stress on militant nationalism and race pride and the concern with militaristic thinking.

From a functional point of view, such "rightist" behavior is quite similar to contemporary left-wing styles of politics. Rightist students were nationalistic, anti-authority, and concerned with the seeming inferiority of their nation within the world community. The subtleties of ideology were not meaningful to the rightist student movements of the 1930's. There was often a mixture of rightist and Marxist rhetoric, which combined notions of racialism with ideas of "proletarian" and exploited nations.

As Frank Pinner suggests, student organizations may, for analytical purposes, be divided into two categories: *transgressive* groups, which are directed mainly against the authority structures of their societies, and *traditional* groups, which socialize their members into their role as conventional citizens of the society. A similar distinction can be made in the role of the university itself. On the one hand, universities are centers of innovation where scholars are expected to challenge the traditional truths of their fields and receive the highest rewards for work which is sharply innovative. On the other, they are schools with faculties of teachers and, thereby, part of the socialization process of their society. Universities and the subdivisions within them vary in the extent to which they emphasize these functions. Many parts of the unversity, particularly the professional schools, are essentially concerned with a socialization function—training students in socially useful skills. The so-called liberal-arts subjects, on the other hand, tend to value scholarly innovation and competence in research more highly. Thus, transgressive student groups are more likely to be found among liberal-arts students than among those in professional schools, such as engineering, education, or business. In Latin America and other countries, universities that are affiliated to religious bodies tend to have little student activism. In Japan and the United States, the most important centers of scholarship tend also to be the strongholds of transgressive student movements.

It is possible to differentiate further among transgressive social movements: Some are concerned with changes in basic social *values* (ultimate ends or conceptions about basic social institutions) and others with affecting *norms* (means to attain agreed upon social values).

Movements concerned with value change are more prevalent and stronger in the underdeveloped countries than in the developed ones. Talcott Parsons and S. N. Eisenstadt have suggested the need to look at the magnitude of the differences between the values of the adult and youth generations in varying types of societies. They indicate that generational conflict is caused, at least in part, by sharp value differences among generations, and that such cleavages—particularly between the better educated (younger on the average) and the uneducated (older)—are great in modernizing societies, but relatively minor in the developed societies.

Similarly, the difference between the values of the university and those of society is considerable in backward societies and small in developed societies. Michio Nagai has argued, for example, that the university is basically universalistic and meritocratic, even in societies that are neither universalistic nor meritocratic. On the one hand, the university judges people, events, and research on the basis of objective achievement criteria, and, on the other, it values freedom of inquiry and discussion. Thus, when we speak of a university anywhere in the world, we have a similar model in mind, no matter how far reality may deviate from that model. The norm of academic freedom is basic to the idea of the university. The tension between university and society will, therefore, be great in authoritarian societies, considerable in emerging and developing nations, which are normally quite particularistic, and relatively small in the developed democratic societies. Faculty and students will reflect the depth of these tensions in their behavior. One should expect *value* conflicts (differences about ends) between student movements and the society in emerging or authoritarian nations and more normative conflicts in developed societies. Education, particularly university education, is inherently a modernizing force, and hence in underdeveloped countries it will be in conflict with those elements seeking to maintain traditional values and institutions. In the democratic developed states, the society more generally accepts the values of universalism, achievement, and freedom.

These distinctions help to account for the varying emphases on ideology among student movements. In general, ideological concerns have declined among student activists in advanced industrialized countries during the postwar period, as compared to the 1930's, but have remained important in many of the developing countries. Nationalism, which involves a concern for modernizing and industrializing, is also particularly important in developing countries. Even such relatively non-leftist groupings as the Philippine student movement and the militant KAMI organization of Indonesia are extremely nationalistic. The ideological concerns of student groups in the emerging nations reflect their interest in value change in the larger society. They are at odds with any forces that support traditional values or stand in the way of rapid economic growth.

In the West, however, where the tension between social values and the political concerns of students is less manifest, even the relatively small radical student movements do not show a strong attachment to formal ideologies. Thus, pragmatism and a preoccupation with specific issues characterize its student politics. This obtains even in Eastern Europe, perhaps because ideologies would be difficult to voice. Students there have been a key element in demanding liberalization in the name of the manifest socialist values and have argued for a nondogmatic approach to society and politics. Even the French Communist students have been in the forefront of revolt against the ideological commitments of the parent Party. Scandinavian students have campaigned for individual freedom and an end to social regulations, particularly those related to sex.

In many countries, one may find some version of the maxim: "Anyone under twenty who is not a radical [socialist, Communist, anarchist] does not have a heart; anyone over forty who still is one does not have a head." There is a notion that it is normal, appropriate, and morally correct for young people to be radicals or revolutionaries. Indeed, many societies treat radical youth, particularly students, as if they believed this maxim. They permit students a degree of political freedom, even license, to violate the norms and laws of society without being punished, or with less punishment than is generally meted out to others. Thus, Berkeley students who surrounded a police car and held it captive for thirty hours were neither arrested nor otherwise sanctioned. Even in authoritarian countries like Czarist Russia, Communist Poland, or Franco Spain, student oppositionists have been treated more lightly by the authorities than have other organized opponents. Sentences against student revolutionaries are usually mild compared to those given non-students.

This tolerance reflects, in part, the fact that university students are often the children of the "elite." The vast majority of the offspring of the privileged strata go to university. This elite finds it difficult to employ stringent measures against its own children. In Cuba, the Batista regime was undermined, in part, because some of the young people with Castro in the mountains were the children of Cuban upper-class families. Members of the Havana elite exerted tremendous pressure on Batista to quit because they wanted their children back from the mountains alive. In recent years, many of the trials of student activists in Spain have involved at least one son of an important family. In this context, the Spanish courts have been faced by two conflicting forces: the particularism of the society, which requires that an offender who belongs to a privileged family be treated lightly, and the universalism of the law, which implies that all those who commit similar offenses be treated in the same way. Most of the punishments of Spanish students have, therefore, been relatively mild.

Nations may also be differentiated by their varying conceptions of youth. Revolutionary ideologies are generally positive toward youth. Hence, the vitality of revolutionary ideologies may be measured by the extent to which they still identify virtue with youth. One of the best pieces of evidence that the American revolutionary tradition is still viable is the prevalent belief in youth, which interestingly the Russians no longer have. The United States is very much a youth culture; it stresses the truism that the young will inherit the world and are probably on the side of justice and progress, as opposed to adults. Many adults thus feel youth should be encouraged in their disdain for the old, in their advocacy of progress and change. Older people consequently lack assurance when debating with youth. It is significant that the Soviet Union has sharply modified the belief in youth that prevailed immediately after the Revolution. Stalin eliminated the notion that youth is right in its conflicts against the older elements, and his successors have not reinstated it. Mao Tse-tung, in his seventies, however, is attempting to emphasize the role of youth as the main source of support for a continuing revolutionary ideology in China.

Authoritarian systems like Fascist Italy or Communist Cuba have, however, been interested not in encouraging students to be critical of the system, but in using "youth" as a social base to support a supposedly "revolutionary" regime against conservative adults. They have hoped to inhibit adult opponents by impressing on them the idea that they represent a historic anachronism. A stress on the worth of youth politics in a democracy may bring to reform movements the support and encouragement of students and other youth. Conversely, it may inhibit some adults who disagree from strongly resisting the proposals of activist students.

Michio Nagai has suggested that as societies "modernize," their universities necessarily move from a diffuse to a specific relationship with both the state and religion. The growth of the scholarly and research function has required universities to separate themselves from the clergy and the politicians. The university must be free to find and teach what is scientifically "true," without concern for the reactions of religious or political establishments. The norm of academic freedom assumes that these outside bodies will leave the university alone. Conversely, if the university insists on freedom from external interference, from being criticized or coerced by those not involved in scholarly pursuits, the norm implies that it must abstain as a university community from attacking others.

The extent to which universities have differentiated themselves from society will, of course, differ. The Confucian ethic stresses the linkages between scholarship and the state. Chinese, Japanese, and Korean scholars were civil servants and supporters of the state. They maintained a relationship with the state similar to that between the religious scholars and the church in the West. In more recent times, universities in the East, particularly state universities, have been expected to be agents of state purposes. Nagai concludes that the considerable involvement of students in the political life of these countries is to some extent linked to the continued strength of Confucian values.

Similarly, in many developing countries the national emphasis on economic development and modernization overrides the idea of the completely autonomous university. Various sections of the governing elite, as well as many faculty members and students, believe that the university should serve the national interest of fostering development. They do not think the nation can afford the "luxury" of supporting pure scholarship which is not related to development objectives, nor can students or faculty isolate themselves from active involvement in politics. These are, of course, highly debated issues in many of the countries, but insofar as the university is perceived as serving political objectives, it necessarily becomes a source of political stimulation.

The effort to separate the university from extramural influences has been most successful in the developed countries of Western Europe and the English-speaking world. The university gradually freed itself from political and religious interference in the late-nineteenth and twentieth centuries. In recent decades, however, the growing role of the university as the key center of research and development for the public sector has necessarily involved it in political controversy. Governments and scholars have broken down the barriers between politics and science by using academics as temporary government officials or as consultants. Scientists have not been able to escape taking responsibility for the social and political uses of their discoveries. Physicists have had to take a position on the various controversies concerning the military uses of atomic energy, academic economists have been called on to take part in the debates on national economic policy, and sociologists and psychologists are involved in issues concerning race relations, education, and the culture of poverty.

Seemingly, the process that brought about increased differentiation between the academy and other institutions has been reversed. The growing complexity of modern society has challenged the effort to segregate the university as an "ivory tower," seeking primarily to serve scholarly ends. As the university in the West becomes a "multiversity," to use Clark Kerr's term, it will continue to be a center of political agitation, as those who favor or disagree with specific endeavors seek to use or attack it. The growing involvement of the Western university as the research arm of the governing elite has, for example, led some critics to view it as a "tool" of the establishment. Universities have nevertheless generally remained as major sources of criticism, despite their growing ties to government. In France, where all universities are state controlled, faculty and students were in the forefront of the opposition to the Algerian war. In the United States many have been the principal centers of support for the Negro struggle for equality and an important source of protest against the Vietnam war.

Student politics is also affected to a considerable degree by the social position and political values of the country's intellectual community. The position of the English intellectuals vis-à-vis power in the political establishment differs from that of the French or the American intellectual. The English have been included in effective political life; the French are outside it. In the United States, intellectuals have great power as experts, but there is no intellectual political community comparable to that in Britain. In many ways, the "nonexpert" American intellectual, similar to the French, has high status but little power and views himself as alienated from the power structure, while the American academic "expert," like the English, has considerable status and power and is more likely to identify with the political-decision makers.

The attitudes of intellectuals and of students toward the national *status quo* are, moreover, not simply a function of their position within the society. More than any other group, intellectuals tend to have an international reference group. To use Merton's distinction between "cosmopolitans" (oriented to outside groups for standards of comparison) and "locals" (concerned with the evaluations of the community within which one resides), intellectuals are clearly more likely to be cosmopolitans. As such, they will be aware of the shortcomings of their nation compared with the standards of the leading countries. The intellectuals and academics of the underdeveloped countries generally realize that they are at the summits of nations or university systems that are considered "backward." This awareness heightens their desire to foster change within their own society and increases their resentment against local or foreign groups that inhibit modernization. The intellectuals in Central and Eastern Europe in the nineteenth century regarded their countries as backward compared to France and Britain, and many of them supported radical political movements.

Intellectuals who are resentful of their society often stimulate rebellious "apprentice intellectuals"—students. In many countries professors see themselves as a deprived stratum, one which is not given the rewards of working conditions appropriate to their role. This sense of resentment will vary, of course, both within nations and among them. Students, particularly in the better universities, are more prone to rebel when the faculty are relatively incompetent in their teaching and show authoritarian tendencies. Student indiscipline in India has been linked with the low salaries, long hours, and bad working conditions of the faculty. The historic pattern of the "part-time" professor in Latin America is a crucial factor in the lack of commitment to scholarly endeavors and values by many students. The very bad faculty-student ratio of French universities and the low salaries of Japanese professors, which require them to find other sources of remuneration, have been cited as factors lowering the educational level of the institutions of higher education and encouraging protest movements.

Student political patterns are also determined, in part, by variations in political institutions. As Robert Scott points out, the lack of political stability in much of Latin America has stimulated student activism, since the possibility of successful agitation has been substantial, and students have occasionally been able to exert political leverage on weak governments. In Scandinavia, on the other hand, as Erik Allardt and Richard Tomasson indicate, the stability and legitimacy of the established political structures have discouraged student activism, and national politics is not generally seen as a legitimate domain of student concern. The same pattern can be seen in other politically stable nations.

Confrontation politics is characteristic of polities in which students, and other groups as well, lack legitimate channels of communication to authority. Clark Kerr has observed that political groups turn to activist demonstrations when they find themselves ignored by the adult power structure. Nevertheless, the existence of student militancy, in and of itself, does not necessarily indicate that such channels do not exist. Youth generally lack a long time-perspective; they tend to become quickly frustrated if their demands are not met immediately. Hence, even in countries with reasonably good channels of political communication, students may turn to confrontation politics if their political idealism has been activated by a major moral issue. For example, American students concerned with civil rights for Negroes or with ending the Vietnam war have not been satisfied with communicating with authority. Whether such alienation becomes pervasive and long-term will be related to the reality of the democratic institutions. In stable democracies, student unrest tends to be a temporary phenomenon.

The pressures on higher educational institutions to expand have been tremendous, but countries have responded to them differently. The military government of Burma has used severe repressive measures to keep the university population limited. In other nations—notably, the Philippines, Korea, India, the United States, and Japan—rapid educational expansion has caused substantial strains on the educational system and may be a factor in student unrest. The arts and law faculties, which rely on lectures and do not need laboratories, can expand most rapidly. Classes are simply enlarged. The effect of expansion has varied considerably within university systems. Educational standards have fallen most rapidly in the liberal arts, as have elite occupational opportunities. In many countries, students in the sciences are often able to obtain remunerative jobs in expanding technological fields, while liberal-arts graduates face an oversupply, which has led to educated unemployment and political unrest.

There is no clear-cut simple relationship between size or rate of expansion of the student body and patterns of political behavior. The emergence of large student populations on one campus or within given cities, particularly national capitals, has facilitated student activism. It has become relatively easy to mobilize a visibly large protest demonstration. A small minority of the students in Buenos Aires, Mexico City, Berkeley, Calcutta, Tokyo, or Paris can constitute an impressive protest in absolute numbers. The creation of "University Cities" in places like Caracas or Paris has increased the potential for mass student action. On the other hand, in nations in which there is only one university and the student body is small and homogeneous, a small group of activists can have an impact on the ideological climate of the national student body and on political events. This was true in the Congo after independence in 1960. The growth of the student population increases the size of the minority available for activist protest and makes for a more heterogeneous student body, one which may sustain competing campus political groupings.

In many countries, the university system is completely state-financed; in others, both in the developed and underdeveloped world, the universities are divided among public, private, and religious schools. Such differences permit substantial variation in quality among institutions. Universities with religious affiliations not only tend to recruit from the most traditionalist sectors of society, but their administrations and faculties are more likely to ban politics than are those in secular universities. Nippon University, the largest private university in Japan, prohibits participation in the *Zengakuren,* the national student union. Other private universities like Waseda, which have a history of student activism, were originally established as a means of training opposition to the governmental elite educated in the University of Tokyo. In the Philippines, the extensive system of private colleges includes many "diploma mills" designed to get students, often from less-well-to-do families, through a nominal university education as quickly and easily as possible. As might be expected, there is little student politics in these institutions.

"Statistically significant" relationships found in one country need not hold up in others. There are, for example, interesting variations concerning the effects of different disciplines on politics. Disciplines tend to be identified with student activism and leftist ideas in some countries, but not in others. Medicine has a leftist aura in various Latin countries in the Americas and Europe, but is traditionally quite conservative in most of northern Europe and the Anglophonic world. In the Catholic world, this orientation seems to stem from the historic conflict between science and the church, a tension relatively absent from the politics of most Protestant countries. Where economics is taught as an extremely technical, mathematically based subject, those who concentrate in the field are less radical than where it remains concerned with qualitative and historical institutional analysis. Similarly, in some countries "law" means a pre-professional discipline or a professional field as it does in the United States; in other places, it denotes a broad social-science or philosophical training. Consequently, the behavior of law students may vary considerably from country to country.

One may also differentiate between subjects that lead to explicit role models and those which involve diffuse objectives. (Pre-professional subjects have explicit role models, while some of the humanities and social-science subjects have diffuse postgraduate role expectations.) Glaucio Soares has distinguished between students whose role image is that of the intellectual as against those who conceive of themselves as scientists or professionals. These images are highly predictive of political orientations. Those with an intellectual role identity are much more leftist and activist than those who identify as scientists or professionals.

This difference is, of course, a subjective one. In every discipline, those who think of themselves as intellectuals rather than professionals are more politically activist. It also works out objectively, in terms of the types of disciplines. Those disciplines that are thought of as "intellectual"—the humanities and most of the social sciences—are more activist and leftist than those that are oriented toward the professional or scientific world. In Puerto Rico, almost all the supporters of the radical and nationalist FUPI (pro-independence) movement have come from the social sciences and have seen themselves primarily as intellectuals, with strong ambitions toward writing and journalism. Chile and Argentina have demonstrated similar patterns. Most of the activists in the Indian and Indonesian student movements, particularly during the nationalist periods, came from the liberal arts. In the United States, the activists in groups like the Students for a Democratic Society tend to be in the social sciences and humanities and to see themselves as intellectuals rather than as professionals.

Thus, differences in the political behavior of students in different universities or countries may be linked to variations in the fields in which they specialize. Certain schools deal primarily with liberal-arts subjects; others, like the University of Moscow, are essentially institutes for technology and science. Most underdeveloped countries, particularly in Latin America, tend to have proportionally fewer students enrolled in technical and vocational subjects. (In some, however, like Israel and Nigeria, the proportion is quite high.) The Communist countries rank highest in proportions of students engaged in vocational and professional training, which may contribute to the relative political passivity of their student bodies.

The political orientations of professors and their students do not necessarily vary in the same way. There is a congruence in some fields. In such professional schools as engineering, education, or business, faculty and students are both relatively conservative. In other areas, such as mathematics or molecular biology, they tend to be relatively leftist. In still others, particularly sociology or political science and especially in the better universities, the students tend to be to the left of the faculty. Where discrepancies between faculty and student orientations exist, the student and the faculty often differ in their conceptions of the subject. Thus, students view some of the social sciences as fields concerned with remedying "social problems." As scholarly disciplines, however, they are essentially concerned with the elaboration of knowledge within scientifically rigorous conceptual frameworks and methodology. Since social scientists see crucial political questions as having complex causes and different solutions, they tend to refrain from endorsing simple solutions. Thus, political concerns motivate many students to major in the social sciences, while the canons of scholarship press social scientists to refrain from taking public political positions. Natural scientists or humanists, on the other hand, may take political positions without reference to their special roles as scholars. Politically motivated students who hold to an "ethic of ultimate ends," which requires a total commitment to furthering politically desirable goals, will not understand nor sympathize with Max Weber's insistence that introducing one's personal values into scientific analysis undermines the ability to understand the facts. Accepting Weber's position often places social scientists in conflict with their best students, who see any faculty reluctance to link scholarly and political roles as cowardly.

These are some of the issues with which any analysis of the role of students in politics and higher education must deal. The university is premised on the belief that "knowledge will make man free" and will increase his ability to control and to better his environment. Those interested in the role of students in politics are obligated to avoid using their special competencies and knowledge as weapons in ongoing campus politics. To separate one's role as scholar and citizen is often difficult. In this case, it is almost impossible.

Bibliographical Note

This selection is a condensation of an effort to sum up the various issues presented in the analysis of student politics that have arisen in the work of the Comparative Student Politics Project of the Harvard Center for International Affairs. I have drawn on various papers delivered at the San Juan Conference on Students and Politics, many of which are included in this issue of *Dædalus*. Papers reported on in San Juan which deal with Latin America are published in a special issue of *Aportes* (No. 5 [July, 1967]). Other publications of the project which contain articles and materials referred to here are S. M. Lipset (ed.), *Student Politics* (New York, 1967), and S. M. Lipset and Aldo Solari (eds.), *Elites in Latin America* (New York, 1967). A detailed bibliography of articles, books, and theses is Philip G. Altbach, *Select Bibliography on Students, Politics, and Higher Education* (Cambridge, 1967).

Class and Politics
in the Family Backgrounds
of Student Political Activists *

David L. Westby and Richard G. Braungart

Recent years have seen the growth and projection of student groups into national politics with an intensity and impact never before experienced in American history. This abrupt turn from the often-criticized juvenile college culture of earlier years has provided sociologists with opportunities to study social movements without leaving their own bailiwick.

Much of the research on student youth movements has found its theoretical point of departure in socialization theory in that it attempts to explain political beliefs and action in terms of family-based experience and family structure.[1] Thus, Maccoby, Mathews, and Morton, in a study of 339 first-time voters, explain the "political conformity" exhibited by some members of their sample in terms of the degree to which their parents exercised control over their youthful activities.[2] In somewhat similar fashion, Middleton and Putney, in a study of 1440 college youths, endeavored to demonstrate that those "rebelling" against the political positions of their fathers were more estranged from their fathers, especially if the fathers were interested in politics.[3] Generally, the focus of research in this area, with its concentration on socialization patterns in the family, seems to neglect the older class-based model of political beliefs which assumes that the latter are primarily a function of the stratification system.[4]

From David L. Westby and Richard G. Braungart, "Class and Politics in the Family Backgrounds of Student Political Activists," *The American Sociological Review* (American Sociological Association, Vol. 31, No. 5, October 1966), pp. 690–692. Reprinted by permission of the publisher and the authors.

* Revised version of a paper read at the meetings of the Eastern Sociological Society in Philadelphia, Penn., April, 1966.
[1] The general importance of the family in the continuity of party and voting traditions is, of course, a well-established generalization in political sociology.
[2] Eleanor Maccoby, Richard Mathews, and Anton Morton, "Youth and Political Change," *Public Opinion Quarterly*, 18 (Spring, 1954), pp. 23–39.
[3] Russell Middleton and Snell Putney, "Student Rebellion Against Parental Political Beliefs," *Social Forces*, 41 (May, 1963), pp. 377–383.
[4] See, for instance, Paul Lazarsfeld, Bernard Berelson, Hazel Gaudet, *The People's Choice*, New York: Duell, Sloan & Pearce, 1944; Phillip Converse, "The Shifting Role of Class in Political Attitudes and Behavior," in Eleanor Maccoby *et al.*, *Readings in Social Psychology*, New York: Holt, Rinehart and Winston, Inc., 1947; Richard Centers, *The Psychology of Social Class*, New York: Russell & Russell, 1961; and Herbert Hyman, *Political Socialization*, New York: The Free Press of Glencoe, 1959. Of course, practically everything in the Marxist tradition takes this view.

The present study, based on a relatively small number of student activists, suggests that the class and party of the student's family of orientation may be significant factors in understanding at least certain features of the student movement. It should be clear that we regard the findings presented here as suggestive for further research and definitely not sufficient to establish valid generalizations.

Method

Our study focused on "left" and "right" activists in a large public institution in the eastern United States, and was conducted during the spring of 1965. The data reported here deal with class and party backgrounds of the membership bodies of two campus activist organizations, SENSE (Students for Peace) and the Young Americans for Freedom (Y.A.F.), which may be taken to represent the extremes of political opinion on the "left" and "right" respectively. There are other activist groups at the institution in question, especially on the left, but their membership is heavily overlapping with that of SENSE.[5]

A questionnaire was administered *en masse* to each of the two groups. The first part of the questionnaire consisted of items tapping class backgrounds and related variables, while the second part was composed of a twenty-two-item Likert-type attitude scale dealing with attitudes toward the present war in Vietnam.[6] The questionnaire was administered to twenty-nine students at a SENSE meeting, to nineteen students at two Y.A.F. meetings, and to one hundred and five students in an introductory sociology class. A few members were absent from these meetings and there is reason to believe that those missing were less extreme and less active.

Findings

Tables 1 through 3 present the origins of SENSE and Y.A.F. members. Table 1 shows a significant difference in median income for the two groups, while Table 2 gives the social class distribution for the two groups,

---

[5] That these two groups represent the extremes of political opinion was demonstrated in a series of attitude items dealing with the present administration policy in Vietnam. The groups took overwhelmingly opposed positions on this controversial political issue, while a control group composed of a class of Sociology I students, roughly representative of the student body, fell in between the two, although somewhat closer to Y.A.F. than to SENSE. Mean scores on the attitude scale items, which ranged from 22 (most liberal) to 110 (most conservative), were: SENSE, 37; Sociology I, 72; Y.A.F., 85.

[6] An example of how a typical attitude scale item distributed itself over our three groups may be seen in the following table.

utilizing the Hollingshead Two-Factor Index. The predominantly upper-middle-class high-income origins of SENSE members contrast sharply with the generally low-income and lower-middle- or working-class backgrounds of Y.A.F. members. We shall briefly consider these findings in the light of current stratification theory.

Table 1. Distribution of Student Activists by Annual Family Income

	SENSE		Y.A.F.	
Family Income	*N*	*%*	*N*	*%*
Above median	19	68	4	24
Below median	9	32	13	76
	—	—	—	—
	28	100	17	100

$\chi^2=8.36$, d.f.$=1$, p$<$.005.
Median income: SENSE, \$12,232; Y.A.F., \$6,625.

TABLE 2. Distribution of Student Activists by Hollingshead's Two-Factor Index of Social Class

	SENSE		Y.A.F.	
Social Class	*N*	*%*	*N*	*%*
I, II	15	52	5	26
III	10	35	7	37
IV, V	4	13	7	37
	—	—	—	—
	29	100	19	100

$\chi^2=4.60$, d.f.$=2$, p$<$.10.

TABLE 3. Distribution of Student Activists by Political Affiliation of Parents

Political Affiliation of Parents	SENSE		Y.A.F.	
	N	*%*	*N*	*%*
Democrat, Socialist	17	68	5	29
Republican	8	32	12	71
	—	—	—	—
	25	100	17	100

$\chi^2=6.03$, d.f.$=1$, p$<$.01.

Note: A few parents could not be classified by political affiliation because they had none or were independent.

Question 9: Vietnam is historically and geographically an Asian country and should therefore be allowed to develop autonomously within the Asian sphere of influence and power.

Response	SENSE		Soc. I		Y.A.F.	
	N	%	N	%	N	%
Agree	24	83	24	23	2	11
Uncertain	5	17	22	21	5	26
Disagree	..	..	59	56	12	63
	29	100	105	100	19	100

$\chi^2 = 47.18$, d.f.$= 4$, p$<.001$.

Twenty-one of the 22 attitude questions were significant at the .001 level. The remaining attitudinal comparison was significant at the .02 level. The composite political attitude scale developed for this study had an internal consistency of .92 as determined by a Pearson product-moment correlation coefficient using a Spearman-Brown correction.

That "revolutionary reactionaries," to use Clinton Rossiter's term, or adherents to the "radical right," should be drawn from the lower-middle and working classes is not surprising if one accepts the "status politics" theory of Hofstadter and others.[7] The "status politics" theory suggests that extreme "right" activists, or "pseudo-conservatives" as Hofstadter prefers to call them, are generally found within status-threatened groups. It is precisely the lower-middle and working classes that are least secure and tend to feel threatened by the upward thrust of new minorities. As Hofstadter wrote in his seminal discussion, "conformity is a way of guaranteeing and manifesting respectability among those who are not sure that they are respectable enough." [8]

Upper-middle-class status, on the other hand, typically provides the social and economic security that is lacking in the lower-middle and upper-working classes. These latter strata provide a kind of protective belt insulating the upper-middle classes from any immediate challenge on the part of militant lower-status groups. As members of a fully "arrived" stratum, upper-middle-class individuals can afford the luxury of "deviance" from straight-line conformist politics, especially if their position is relatively well-established, and their mobility not too recent.[9]

[7] Richard Hofstadter, "The Pseudo-Conservative Revolt—1955," in Daniel Bell (ed.), *The Radical Right,* New York: Doubleday, 1962, pp. 63–80. In the same volume, see also S. M. Lipset, "The Sources of the 'Radical Right'," and "Three Decades of the Radical Right; Coughlinites, McCarthyites, and Birchers," pp. 259–377.

[8] Hofstadter, *ibid.,* pp. 76–77. Our data on the marital status of parents also seem to support the insecurity—conformity relation. Eight Y.A.F. students (46 per cent) came from homes with divorced or widowed parents, while this was true of only 2 (6 per cent) of SENSE members.

[9] We should note that whenever such insulation is absent, as in certain Northern suburban areas and in the South generally, the upper-middle class is as susceptible to right-wing extremist forms of politics as any other group.

While this interpretation may seem plausible, it casts a very wide net for a few small fish. Classes are enormous aggregates, while student activists are a small segment of the student body at at any university or college. It is important to try to demonstrate which factors *within strata* are decisive in their influence on political action at the extremes of the political spectrum. Table 3 gives the political affiliations of the students' parents and shows a pronounced relationship between left activism and Democratic or Socialist background on the one hand, and Republican background and right activism on the other. In other words, families of SENSE members are predominantly high-status Democrats while Y.A.F. members come mainly from low-status Republican families. Within each stratum, it seems, it is party identification and presumably the accompanying ideological orientation that are the more particular factors that predispose students toward political extremism.

Finally, despite their opposed ideological stances, these two groups are similar in one respect—they both exhibit a kind of inconsistency or absence of crystallization. Lenski and others have presented evidence that such types are more insistent upon or receptive to change, more radical as it were, than the highly crystallized.[10] Both the far left and far right press for policies and actions representing considerable departure from those current today.

Generally, student activists seem to be expressing ideological positions that, though extreme, are in the main consistent with the political orientations of their families. It may be that activists are rebelling against their parents, but, if so, it seems to be in a highly selective way in which the intersection of the class structure and the political system is a powerful predisposing force. We think that researchers of the student movement would do well to consider the class and political backgrounds of their subjects.

[10] Gerhard Lenski, "Status Crystallization: A Non-Vertical Dimension of Social Status," *American Sociological Review,* 19 (August, 1954), pp. 405–413. "Crystallization" is defined as the degree to which positions within two or more ranking systems are congruent. Thus, a white Anglo-Saxon, Protestant doctor making $30,000 a year could be said to be highly crystallized, whereas a Negro doctor making $4,000 would be uncrystallized.

The Sources of Student Dissent

Kenneth Keniston

The apparent upsurge of dissent among American college students is one of the more puzzling phenomena in recent American history. Less than a decade ago, commencement orators were decrying the "silence" of college students in the face of urgent national and international issues; but in the past two or three years, the same speakers have warned graduating classes across the country against the dangers of unreflective protest, irresponsible action and unselective dissent. Rarely in history has apparent apathy been replaced so rapidly by publicized activism, silence by strident dissent.

This "wave" of dissent among American college students has been much discussed. Especially in the mass media—popular magazines, newspapers and television—articles of interpretation, explanation, deprecation and occasionally applause have appeared in enormous numbers. More important, from the first beginnings of the student civil rights movement, social scientists have been regular participant-observers and investigators of student dissent. There now exists a considerable body of research that deals with the characteristics and settings of student dissent (see Lipset and Altbach, 1966; Block, Haan and Smith, forthcoming; Katz, 1967; Peterson, 1967 for summaries of this research). To be sure, most of these studies are topical (centered around a particular protest or demonstration), and some of the more extensive studies are still in varying stages of incompletion. Yet enough evidence has already been gathered to permit tentative generalizations about the varieties, origins and future of student dissent in the nineteen sixties.

In the remarks to follow, I will attempt to gather together this evidence (along wtih my own research and informal observations) to provide tentative answers to three questions about student dissent today. First, what is the nature of student dissent in American colleges? Second, what are the sources of the recent "wave of protest" by college students? And third, what can we predict about the future of student dissent?

Two Varieties of Dissent

Dissent is by no means the dominant mood of American college students. Every responsible study or survey shows apathy and privatism far more dominant than dissent (see, for example, Newsweek, 1965; Katz, 1965;

Reed, 1966; Peterson, 1966; Block, Haan and Smith, forthcoming). On most of our twenty two hundred campuses, student protest, student alienation and student unrest are something that happens elsewhere, or that characterizes a mere handful of "kooks" on the local campus. However we define "dissent," overt dissent is relatively infrequent and tends to be concentrated largely at the more selective, "progressive," and "academic" colleges and universities in America. Thus, Peterson's study of student protests (1966) finds political demonstrations concentrated in the larger universities and institutions of higher academic calibre, and almost totally absent at teachers colleges, technical institutes and non-academic denominational colleges. And even at the colleges that gather together the greatest number of dissenters, the vast majority of students—generally well over 95 percent—remain interested onlookers or opponents rather than active dissenters. Thus, whatever we say about student dissenters is said about a very small minority of America's six million college students. At most colleges, dissent is not visible at all.

Partly because the vast majority of American students remain largely uncritical of the wider society, fundamentally conformist in behavior and outlook, and basically "adjusted" to the prevailing collegiate, national and international order, the small minority of dissenting students is highly visible to the mass media. As I will argue later, such students are often distinctively talented; they "use" the mass media effectively; and they generally succeed in their goal of making themselves and their causes highly visible. Equally important, student dissenters of all types arouse deep and ambivalent feelings in non-dissenting students and adults—envy, resentment, admiration, repulsion, nostalgia and guilt. Such feelings contribute both to the selective over-attention dissenters receive and to the often distorted perceptions and interpretations of them and their activities. Thus, there has developed through the mass media and the imaginings of adults a more or less stereotyped—and generally incorrect—image of the student dissenter.

THE STEREOTYPED DISSENTER

The "stereotypical" dissenter as popularly portrayed is both a bohemian and political activist. Bearded, be-Levi-ed, long-haired, dirty and unkempt, he is seen as profoundly disaffected from his society, often influenced by "radical" (Marxist, Communist, Maoist, or Castroite) ideas, an experimenter in sex and drugs, unconventional in his daily behavior. Frustrated and unhappy, often deeply maladjusted as a person, he is a "failure" (or as one U. S. Senator put it, a "reject"). Certain academic communities like Berkeley are said to act as "magnets" for dissenters, who selectively attend colleges with a reputation as protest centers. Furthermore, dropouts or "nonstudents" who have failed in college cluster in large numbers around the fringes of such colleges, actively seeking pretexts for protest, refusing all compromise and impatient wtih ordinary democratic processes.

According to such popular analyses, the sources of dissent are to be found in the loss of certain traditional American virtues. The "breakdown" of American family life, high rates of divorce, the "softness" of American living, inadequate parents, and, above all, overindulgence and "spoiling" contribute to the prevalence of dissent. Brought up in undisciplined homes by parents unsure of their own values and standards, dissenters channel their frustration and anger against the older generation, against all authority, and against established institutions.

Similar themes are sometimes found in the interpretations of more scholarly commentators. "Generational conflict" is said to underly the motivation to dissent, and a profound "alienation" from American society is seen as a factor of major importance in producing protests. Then, too, such factors as the poor quality and impersonality of American college education, the large size and lack of close student-faculty contact in the "multiversity" are sometimes seen as the latent or precipitating factors in student protests, regardless of the manifest issues around which students are organized. And still other scholarly analysts, usually men now disillusioned by the radicalism of the 1930's, have expressed fear of the dogmatism, rigidity and "authoritarianism of the left" of today's student activists.

ACTIVISM AND ALIENATION

These stereotyped views are, I believe, incorrect in a variety of ways. They confuse two distinct varieties of student dissent; equally important, they fuse dissent with maladjustment. There are, of course, as many forms of dissent as there are individual dissenters; and any effort to counter the popular stereotype of the dissenter by pointing to the existence of distinct "types" of dissenters runs the risk of oversimplifying at a lower level of abstraction. Nonetheless, it seems to me useful to suggest that student dissenters generally fall somewhere along a continuum that runs between two ideal types—first, the political activist or protest, and second, the withdrawn, culturally alienated student.

The activist. The defining characteristic of the "new" activist is his participation in a student demonstration or group activity that concerns itself with some matter of general political, social or ethical principle. Characteristically, the activist feels that some injustice has been done, and attempts to "take a stand," "demonstrate" or in some fashion express his convictions. The specific issues in question range from protest against a paternalistic college administration's actions to disagreement with American Vietnam policies, from indignation at the exploitation of the poor to anger at the firing of a devoted teacher, from opposition to the Selective Service laws which exempt him but not the poor to—most important—outrage at the deprivation of the civil rights of other Americans.

The initial concern of the protester is almost always immediate, ad hoc and local. To be sure, the student who protests about one issue is likely to feel inclined or obliged to demonstrate his convictions on other issues as well (Heist, 1966). But whatever the issue, the protester rarely demonstrates because his *own* interests are jeopardized, but rather because he perceives injustices being done to *others* less fortunate than himself. For example, one of the apparent paradoxes about protests against current draft policies is that the protesting students are selectively drawn from that subgroup *most* likely to receive student deferments for graduate work. The basis of protest is a general sense that the selective service rules and the war in Vietnam are unjust to others with whom the student is identified, but whose fate he does not share. If one runs down the list of "causes" taken up by student activists, in rare cases are demonstrations directed at improving the lot of the protesters themselves; identification with the oppressed is a more important motivating factor than an actual sense of immediate personal oppression.

The anti-ideological stance of today's activists has been noted by many commentators. This distrust of formal ideologies (and at times of articulate thought) makes it difficult to pinpoint the positive social and political values of student protesters. Clearly, many current American political institutions like de facto segregation are opposed; clearly, too, most students of the New Left reject careerism and familism as personal values. In this sense, we might think of the activist as (politically) "alienated." But this label seems to me more misleading than illuminating, for it overlooks the more basic *commitment* of most student activists to other ancient, traditional and credal American values like free speech, citizen's participation in decision-making, equal opportunity and justice. In so far as the activist rejects all or part of "the power structure," it is because current political realities fall so far short of the ideals he sees as central to the American creed. And in so far as he repudiates careerism and familism, it is because of his implicit allegiance to other human goals he sees, once again, as more crucial to American life. Thus, to emphasize the "alienation" of activists is to neglect their more basic allegiance to credal American ideals.

One of these ideals is, of course, a belief in the desirability of political and social action. Sustained in good measure by the successes of the student civil rights movement, the protester is usually convinced that demonstrations are effective in mobilizing public opinion, bringing moral or political pressure to bear, demonstrating the existence of his opinions, or, at times, in "bringing the machine to a halt." In this sense, then, despite his criticisms of existing political practices and social institutions, he is a political optimist. Moreover, the protester must believe in at least minimal organization and group activity; otherwise, he would find it impossible to take part, as he does, in any organized demonstrations or activities. Despite their search for more truly "democratic" forms of organization and action (e.g., participatory democracy), activists agree that group action is more effective than purely individual acts. To be sure, a belief in the value and efficacy of political action is not equivalent to endorsement of prevalent political institutions or forms of action. Thus, one characteristic of activists is their search for new forms of social action, protest and political organization (community organization, sit-ins, participatory democracy) that will be more effective and less oppressive than traditional political institutions.

The culturally alienated. In contrast to the politically optimistic, active, and socially concerned protester, the culturally alienated student·is far too pessimistic and too firmly opposed to "the System" to wish to demonstrate his disapproval in any organized public way.[1] His demonstrations of dissent are private: through nonconformity of behavior, ideology and dress, through personal experimentation and above all through efforts to intensify his own subjective experience, he shows his distaste and disinterest in politics and society. The activist attempts to change the world around him, but the alienated student is convinced that meaningful change of the social and political world is impossible; instead, he considers "dropping out" the only real option.

Alienated students tend to be drawn from the same general social strata and colleges as protesters. But psychologically and ideologically, their backgrounds are often very different. Alienated students are more likely to be disturbed psychologically; and although they are often highly talented and artistically gifted, they are less committed to academic values and intellectual achievement than are protesters. The alienated student's real campus is the school of the absurd, and he has more affinity for pessimistic existentialist ontology than for traditional American activism. Furthermore, such students usually find it psychologically and ideologically impossible to take part in organized group activities for any length of time, particularly when they are expected to assume responsibilities for leadership. Thus, on the rare occasions when they become involved in demonstrations, they usually prefer peripheral roles, avoid responsibilities and are considered a nuisance by serious activists (Draper, 1965).

Whereas the protesting student is likely to accept the basic political and social values of his parents, the alienated student almost always rejects his parents' values. In particular, he is likely to see his father as a man who has "sold out" to the pressures for success and status in American society: he is determined to avoid the fate that overtook his father. Toward their mothers, however, alienated students usually express a very special sympathy and identification. These mothers, far from encouraging their sons towards independence and achievement, generally seem to have been over-solicitous and limiting. The most common family environment of the alienated-student-

[1] The following paragraphs are based on the study of culturally alienated students described in *The Uncommitted* (1965). For a more extensive discussion of the overwhelmingly anti-political stance of these students, see Keniston (1966) and also Rigney and Smith (1961), Allen and Silverstein, 1967, Watts and Wittaker, 1967, and Wittaker and Watts, 1967.

to-be consists of a parental schism supplemented by a special mother-son alliance of mutual understanding and maternal control and depreciation of the father (Keniston, 1965a).

In many colleges, alienated students often constitute a kind of hidden underground, disorganized and shifting in membership, in which students can temporarily or permanently withdraw from the ordinary pressures of college life. The alienated are especially attracted to the hallucinogenic drugs like marijuana, mescalin and LSD, precisely because these agents combine withdrawal from ordinary social life with the promise of greatly intensified subjectivity and perception. To the confirmed "acid head," what matters is intense, drug-assisted perception; the rest—including politics, social action and student demonstrations—is usually seen as "role-playing." [2]

The recent and much-publicized emergence of "hippie" subcultures in several major cities and increasingly on the campuses of many selective and progressive colleges illustrates the overwhelmingly apolitical stance of alienated youth. For although hippies oppose war and believe in inter-racial living, few have been willing or able to engage in anything beyond occasional peace marches or apolitical "human be-ins." Indeed, the hippies's emphasis on immediacy, "love" and "turning-on," together with his basic rejection of the traditional values of American life, inoculates him against involvement in long-range activist endeavors, like education or community organization, and even against the sustained effort needed to plan and execute demonstrations or marches. For the alienated hippie, American society is beyond redemption (or not worth trying to redeem); but, the activist, no matter how intense his rejection of specific American policies and practices, retains a conviction that his society can and should be changed. Thus, despite occasional agreement in principle between the alienated and the activists,

---

[2] The presence among student dissenters of a group of "nonstudents"—that is, dropouts from college or graduate school who congregate or remain near some academic center—has been much noted. In fact, however, student protesters seem somewhat *less* likely to drop out of college than do nonparticipants in demonstrations (Heist, 1966), and there is no evidence that dropping out of college is in any way related to dissent from American society (Keniston and Helmreich, 1965). On the contrary, several studies suggest that the academically gifted and psychologically intact student who drops out of college voluntarily has few distinctive discontents about his college or about American society (Suczek and Alfort, 1966; Pervin et al., 1966; Wright, 1966). If he is dissatisfied at all, it is with himself, usually for failing to take advantage of the "rich educational opportunities" he sees in his college. The motivations of student dropping out of college are complex and varied, but such motivations more often seem related to personal questions of self definition and parental identification or to a desire to escape relentless academic pressures, than to any explicit dissent from the Great Society. Thus, although a handful of students have chosen to drop out of college for a period in order to devote themselves to political and societal protest activities, there seems little reason in general to associate the drop-out with the dissenter, whether he be a protester or an alienated student. The opposite is nearer the truth.

cooperation in practice has been rare, and usually ends with activists accusing the alienated of "irresponsibility," while the alienated are confirmed in their view of activists as moralistic, "up-tight," and "un-cool."

Obviously, no description of a type ever fits an individual perfectly. But by this rough typology, I mean to suggest that popular stereotypes which present a unified portrait of student dissent are gravely oversimplified. More specifically, they confuse the politically pessimistic and socially uncommitted alienated student with the politically hopeful and socially committed activist. To be sure, there are many students who fall between these two extremes, and some of them alternate between passionate search for intensified subjectivity and equally passionate efforts to remedy social and political injustices. And as I will later suggest, even within the student movement, one of the central tensions is between political activism and cultural alienation. Nonetheless, even to understand this tension we must first distinguish between the varieties of dissent apparent on American campuses.

Furthermore, the distinction between activist and alienated students as psychological types suggests the incompleteness of scholarly analyses that see social and historical factors as the only forces that "push" a student toward one or the other of these forms of dissent. To be sure, social and cultural factors are of immense importance in providing channels for the expression (or suppression) of dissent, and in determining *which* kinds of dissenters receive publicity, censure, support or ostracism in any historical period. But these factors cannot, in general, change a hippie into a committed activist, nor a SNCC field worker into a full-time "acid-head." Thus, the prototypical activist of 1966 is not the "same" student as the prototypical student bohemian of 1956, but is rather the politically aware but frustrated, academically oriented "privatist" of that era. Similarly, as I will argue below, the most compelling alternative to most activists is not the search for kicks or sentience but the quest for scholarly competence. And if culturally sanctioned opportunities for the expression of alienation were to disappear, most alienated students would turn to private psychopathology rather than to public activism.

Stated more generally, historical forces do not ordinarily transform radically the character, values and inclinations of an adult in later life. Rather, they thrust certain groups forward in some eras and discourage or suppress other groups. The recent alternation in styles of student dissent in America is therefore not to be explained so much by the malleability of individual character as by the power of society to bring activists into the limelight, providing them with the intellectual and moral instruments for action. Only a minority of potential dissenters fall close enough to the midpoint between alienation and activism so that they can constitute a "swing vote" acutely responsive to social and cultural pressures and styles. The rest, the majority, are characterologically committed to one or another style of dissent.

The Sources of Activism

What I have termed "alienated" students are by no means a new phenomenon in American life, or for that matter in industrialized societies. Bohemians, "beatniks" and artistically inclined undergraduates who rejected middle-class values have long been a part of the American student scene, especially at more selective colleges; they constituted the most visible form of dissent during the relative political "silence" of American students in the 1950s. What is distinctive about student dissent in recent years is the unexpected emergence of a vocal minority of politically and socially active students.[3] Much is now known about the characteristics of such students, and the circumstances under which protests are likely to be mounted. At the same time, many areas of ignorance remain. In the account to follow, I will attempt to formulate a series of general hypotheses concerning the sources of student activism.[4]

It is abundantly clear that no single factor will suffice to explain the increase of politically motivated activities and protests on American campuses. Even if we define an activist narrowly, as a student who (a) acts together with others in a group, (b) is concerned with some ethical, social, ideological or political issue, and (c) holds liberal or "radical" views, the sources of student activism and protest are complex and inter-related. At least four kinds of factors seem involved in any given protest. First, the individuals involved must be suitably predisposed by their personal backgrounds, values and motivations. Second, the likelihood of protest is far greater in certain kinds of educational and social settings. Third, socially directed protests require a special cultural climate, that is, certain distinctive values and views about the effectiveness and meaning of demonstrations, and about the wider society. And finally, some historical situations are especially conducive to protests.

---

[3] Student activism, albeit of a rather different nature, was also found in the nineteen thirties. For a discussion and contrast of student protest today and after the Depression, see Lipset (1966a).

[4] Throughout the following, I will use the terms "protester" and "activist" interchangeably, although I am aware that some activists are not involved in protests. Furthermore, the category of "activist" is an embracing one, comprising at least three sub-classes. First, those who might be termed *reformers,* that is, students involved in community organization work, the Peace Corps, tutoring programs, Vista, etc., but not generally affiliated with any of the "New Left" organizations. Second, the group of *activists proper,* most of whom are or have been affiliated with organizations like the Free Speech Movement at Berkeley, Students for a Democratic Society, the Student Non-violent Coordinating Committee or the Congress on Racial Equality or the Vietnam Summer Project. Finally, there is a much publicized handful of students who might be considered *extremists,* who belong to doctrinaire Marxist and Trotskyite organizations like the now-defunct May Second Movement. No empirical study with which I am acquainted has investigated the differences between students in these three sub-groups. Most studies have concentrated on the "activist proper," and my remarks will be based on a reading of their data.

The Protest-Prone Personality

A large and still-growing number of studies, conducted under different auspices, at different times and about different students, presents a remarkably consistent picture of the protest-prone individual (Aiken, Demerath and Marwell, 1966; Flacks, 1967; Gastwirth, 1965; Heist, 1965, 1966; Lyonns, 1965; Somers, 1965; Watts and Whittaker, 1966; Westby and Baungart, 1966; Katz, 1967; and Paulus, 1967). For one, student protesters are generally outstanding students; the higher the student's grade average, the more outstanding his academic achievements, the more likely it is that he will become involved in any given political demonstration. Similarly, student activists come from families with liberal political values; a disproportionate number report that their parents hold views essentially similar to their own, and accept or support their activities. Thus, among the parents of protesters we find large numbers of liberal Democrats, plus an unusually large scattering of pacifists, socialists, etc. A disproportionate number of protesters come from Jewish families; and if the parents of activists are religious, they tend to be concentrated in the more liberal denominations— Reform Judaism, Unitarianism, the Society of Friends, etc. Such parents are reported to have high ethical and political standards, regardless of their actual religious convictions.

As might be expected of a group of politically liberal and academically talented students, a disproportionate number are drawn from professional and intellectual families of upper middle-class status. For example, compared with active student conservatives, members of protest groups tend to have higher parental incomes, more parental education, and less anxiety about social status (Westby and Braungart, 1966). Another study finds that high levels of education distinguish the activist's family even in the grandparental generation (Flacks, 1967). In brief, activists are not drawn from disadvantaged, status-anxious, underprivileged or uneducated groups; on the contrary, they are selectively recruited from among those young Americans who have had the most socially fortunate upbringings.

BASIC VALUE COMMITMENTS OF ACTIVISTS

The basic value commitments of the activist tend to be academic and non-vocational. Such students are rarely found among engineers, future teachers at teachers colleges, or students of business administration (see Trent and Craise, 1967). Their over-all educational goals are those of a liberal education for its own sake, rather than specifically technical, vocational or professional preparation. Rejecting careerist and familist goals, activists espouse humanitarian, expressive and self-actualizing values. Perhaps because of these values, they delay career choice longer than their classmates (Flacks, 1967). Nor are such students distinctively dogmatic, rigid or authoritarian. Quite the contrary, the substance and style of their beliefs and activities tends to be open, flexible and highly liberal. Their fields of academic specialization are non-vocational—the social sciences and the humanities. Once in college, they not only do well academically, but tend to persist in their academic commitments, dropping out *less* frequently than most of their classmates. As might be expected, a disproportionate number receive a B.A. within four years and continue on to graduate school, preparing themselves for academic careers.

Survey data also suggest that the activist is not distinctively dissatisfied with his college education. As will be noted, activists generally attend colleges which provide the best, rather than the worst, undergraduate education available today. Objectively then, activists probably have less to complain about in their undergraduate educations than most other students. And subjectively as well, surveys show most activists, like most other American undergraduates, to be relatively well satisfied with their undergraduate educations (Somers, 1965; Kornhauser, 1967). Thus, dissatisfaction with educational failings of the "impersonal multiversity," however important as a rallying cry, does not appear to be a distinctive cause of activism.

In contrast to their relative satisfaction with the quality of their educations, however, activists *are* distinctively dissatisfied with what might be termed the "civil-libertarian" defects of their college administrations. While no doubt a great many American undergraduates distrust "University Hall," this distrust is especially pronounced amongst student protesters (Kornhauser, 1967; Paulus, 1967). Furthermore, activists tend to be more responsive than other students to deprivations of civil rights on campus as well as off campus, particularly when political pressures seem to motivate on campus policies they consider unjust. The same responsiveness increasingly extends to issues of "student power": i.e., student participation and decisions affecting campus life. Thus, bans on controversial speakers, censorship of student publications, and limitations on off-campus political or social action are likely to incense the activist, as is arbitrary "administration without the consent of the administered." But it is primarily perceived injustice or the denial of student rights by the Administration—rather than poor educational quality, neglect by the faculty, or the impersonality of the multiversity—that agitates the activist.

Most studies of activists have concentrated on variables that are relatively easy to measure: social class, academic achievements, explicit values and satisfaction with college. But these factors alone will not explain activism: more students possess the demographic and attitudinal characteristics of the protest-prone personality than are actually involved in protests and social action programs. Situational, institutional, cultural and historical factors (discussed below), obviously contribute to "catalysing" a protest-prone personality into an actual activist. But it also seems that, within the broad demographic group so far defined, more specific psychodynamic factors contribute to activism.

ACTIVISTS . . . NOT IN REBELLION

In speculating about such factors, we leave the ground of established fact and enter the terrain of speculation, for only a few studies have explored the personality dynamics and family constellation of the activist, and most of these studies are impressionistic and clinical (e.g. Coles, 1967; Ehle, 1965; Draper, 1965; Fishman and Solomon n.d., 1964; Gastwirth, 1965; Newfield, 1966; Schneider, 1966; Solomon and Fishman, 1963, 1964; Zinn, 1965). But certain facts are clear. As noted, activists are *not,* on the whole, repudiating or rebelling against explicit parental values and ideologies. On the contrary, there is some evidence that such students are living out their parents' values in practice; and one study suggests that activists may be somewhat *closer* to their parents' values than nonactivists (Flacks, 1967). Thus, any simple concept of "generational conflict" or "rebellion against parental authority" is clearly oversimplified as applied to the motivations of most protesters.

ACTIVISTS . . . LIVING OUT PARENTAL VALUES

It does seem probable, however, that many activists are concerned with *living out expressed but unimplemented parental values.* Solomon and Fishman (1963), studying civil rights activists and peace marchers, argue that many demonstrators are "acting out" in their demonstrations the values which their parents explicitly believed, but did not have the courage or opportunity to practice or fight for. Similarly, when protesters criticize their fathers, it is usually over their fathers' failure to practice what they have preached to their children throughout their lives. Thus, in the personal background of the protester there is occasionally a suggestion that his father is less-than-"sincere" (and even at times "hypocritical") in his professions of political liberalism. In particular, both careerism and familism in parents are the objects of activist criticisms, the more so because these implicit goals often conflict with explicit parental values. And it may be that protests receive both covert and overt support from their parents because the latter are secretly proud of their children's eagerness to implement the ideals they as parents have only given lip-service to. But whatever the ambivalences that bind parents with their activist children, it would be wrong to over-emphasize them: what is most impressive is the solidarity of older and younger generations.

Activists . . . Family Structure

While no empirical study has tested this hypothesis, it seems probable that in many activist-producing families, the mother will have a dominant psychological influence on her son's development. I have already noted that the protester's cause is rarely himself, but rather alleviating the oppression of others. As a group, activists seem to possess an unusual *capacity for nurturant identification*—that is, for empathy and sympathy with the underdog, the oppressed and the needy. Such a capacity can have many origins, but its most likely source in upper-middle class professional families is identification with an active mother whose own work embodies nurturant concern for others. Flacks' finding that the mothers of activists are likely to be employed, often in professional or service roles like teaching and social work, is consistent with this hypothesis. In general in American society, middle-class women have greater social and financial freedom to work in jobs that are idealistically "fulfilling" as opposed to merely lucrative or prestigious. As a rule, then, in middle-class families, it is the mother who actively embodies in her life and work the humanitarian, social and political ideals that the father may share in principle but does not or cannot implement in his career.

Given what we know about the general characteristics of the families of protest-prone students, it also seems probable that the dominant ethos of their families is unusually equalitarian, permissive, "democratic," and highly individuated. More specifically, we might expect that these will be families where children talk back to their parents at the dinner table, where free dialogue and discussion of feelings is encouraged, and where "rational" solutions are sought to everyday family problems and conflicts. We would also expect that such families would place a high premium on self-expression and intellectual independence, encouraging their children to make up their own minds and to stand firm against group pressures. Once again, the mother seems the most likely carrier and epitome of these values, given her relative freedom from professional and financial pressures.

The contrast between such protest-prompting families and alienating families should be underlined. In both, the son's deepest emotional ties are often to his mother. But in the alienating family, the mother-son relationship is characterized by maternal control and intrusiveness, whereas in the protest-prompting family, the mother is a highly individuating force in her son's life, pushing him to independence and autonomy. Furthermore, the alienated student is determined to avoid the fate that befell his father, whereas the protesting student wants merely to live out the values that his father has not always worked hard enough to practice. Finally, the egalitarian, permissive, democratic and individuating environment of the entire family of the protester contrasts with the overcontrolling, over-solicitous attitude of the mother in the alienating family, where the father is usually excluded from major emotional life within the family.

These hypotheses about the family background and psychodynamics of the protester are speculative, and future research may prove their invalidity. But regardless of whether *these* particular speculations are correct, it seems clear that in addition to the general social, demographic and attitudinal factors mentioned in most research, more specific familial and psychodynamic influences contribute to protest-proneness.

The Protest-Promoting Institution

However we define his characteristics, one activist alone cannot make a protest: the characteristics of the college or university he attends have much to do with whether his protest-proneness will ever be mobilized into actual activism. Politically, socially and ideologically motivated demonstrations and activities are most likely to occur at certain types of colleges; they are almost unknown at a majority of campuses. The effects of institutional characteristics on protests have been studied by Cowan (1966) and Peterson (1966), and by Sampson and by Brown (1967).

In order for an organized protest or related activities to occur, there must obviously be sufficient *numbers* of protest-prone students to form a group, these students must have an opportunity for *interaction* with each other, and there must be *leaders* to initiate and mount the protest. Thus, we might expect—and we indeed find—that protest is associated with institutional size, and particularly with the congregation of large numbers of protest-prone students in close proximity to each other. More important than sheer size alone, however, is the "image" of the institution: certain institutions selectively recruit students with protest-prone characteristics. Specifically, a reputation for academic excellence and freedom, coupled with highly selective admissions policies, will tend to congregate large numbers of potentially protesting students on one campus. Thus, certain institutions do act as "magnets" for potential activists, but not so much because of their reputations for political radicalism as because they are noted for their academic excellence. Among such institutions are some of the most selective and "progressive" private liberal arts colleges, major state universities (like Michigan, California at Berkeley and Wisconsin) which have long traditions of vivid undergraduate teaching and high admissions standards (Lipset and Altbach, 1966) and many of the more-prestigious private universities.

Once protest-prone students are on campus, they must have an opportunity to interact, to support one another, to develop common outlooks and shared policies—in short, to form an *activist sub-culture* with sufficient mass and potency to generate a demonstration or action program. Establishing "honors colleges" for talented and academically motivated students is one particularly effective way of creating a "critical mass" of protest-prone students. Similarly, inadequate on-campus housing indirectly results in the development of off-campus protest-prone sub-cultures (e.g., co-op houses) in residences where student activists can develop a high degree of ideological solidarity and organizational cohesion.

But even the presence of a critical mass of protest-prone undergraduates in an activist sub-culture is not enough to make a protest without leaders and issues. And in general, the most effective protest leaders have not been undergraduates, but teaching assistants. The presence of large numbers of exploited, underpaid, disgruntled and frustrated teacher assistants (or other equivalent graduate students and younger faculty members) is almost essential for organized and persistent protest. For one, advanced students tend to be more liberal politically and more sensitive to political issues than are most undergraduates—partly because education seems to have a liberalizing effect, and partly because students who persist into graduate school tend to be more liberal to start than those who drop out or go elsewhere. Furthermore, the frustrations of graduate students, especially at very large public universities, make them particularly sensitive to general problems of injustice, exploitation and oppression. Teaching assistants, graduate students and young faculty members also tend to be in daily and prolonged contact with students, are close enough to them in age to sense their mood, and are therefore in an excellent position to lead and organize student protests. Particularly at institutions which command little institutional allegiance from large numbers of highly capable graduate students (Lipset and Altbach, 1966) will such students be found among the leaders of the protest movement.

THE ISSUES OF PROTEST

Finally, issues are a necessity. In many cases, these issues are provided by historical developments on the national or international scene, a point to which I will return. But in some instances, as at Berkeley, "on-campus" issues are the focus of protest. And in other cases, off-campus and on-campus issues are fused, as in the recent protests at institutional cooperation with draft board policies considered unjust by demonstrating students. In providing such on-campus issues, the attitude of the university administration is central. Skillful handling of student complaints, the maintenance of open channels of communication between student leaders and faculty members, and administrative willingness to resist public and political pressures in order to protect the rights of students—all minimize the likelihood of organized protest. Conversely, a university administration that shows itself unduly sensitive to political, legislative or public pressures, that treats students arrogantly, ineptly, condescendingly, hypocritically or above all dishonestly, is asking for a demonstration.

Thus one reason for the relative absence of on-campus student protests and demonstrations on the campuses of private, non-denominational "academic" colleges and universities (which recruit many protest-prone students) probably lies in the liberal policies of the administrations. As Cowan (1966) notes, liberal students generally attend non-restrictive and "libertarian" colleges. Given an administration and faculty that supports or tolerates activism and student rights, student activists must generally find their issues off-campus. The same students, confronting an administration unduly sensitive to political pressures from a conservative board of regents or State legislature, might engage in active on-campus protests. There is also some evidence that clever administrative manipulation of student complaints, even in the absence of genuine concern with student rights, can serve to dissipate the potentialities of protest (Keene, 1966).

Among the institutional factors often cited as motivating student protest is the largeness, impersonality, atomization, "multiversitification" etc., of the university. I have already noted that student protesters do not seem distinctively dissatisfied with their educations. Furthermore, the outstanding academic achievements and intellectual motivations of activists concentrate them, within any college, in the courses and programs that provide the most "personal" attention: honors programs, individual instruction, advanced seminars, and so on. Thus, they probably receive relatively *more* individual attention and a *higher* calibre of instruction than do non-protesters. Furthermore, protests generally tend to occur at the best, rather than the worst colleges, judged from the point of view of the quality of undergraduate instruction. Thus, despite the popularity of student slogans dealing with the impersonality and irrelevance of the multiversity, the absolute level of educational opportunities seems, if anything, positively related to the occurrence of protest: the better the institution, the more likely demonstrations are.

Nor can today's student activism be attributed in any direct way to mounting academic pressures. To be sure, activism is most manifest at those selective colleges where the "pressure to perform" (Keniston, 1965b) is greatest, where standards are highest, and where anxieties about being admitted to a "good" graduate or professional school are most pronounced. But, contrary to the argument of Lipset and Altbach (1966), the impact of academic pressure on activism seems negative rather than positive. Protest-prone students, with their superior academic attainments and strong intellectual commitments, seem especially vulnerable to a kind of academic professionalism that, because of the enormous demands it makes upon the student's energies, serves to cancel or preclude activism. Student demonstrations rarely take place during exam periods, and protests concerned with educational quality almost invariably seek an improvement of quality, rather than a lessening of pressure. Thus, though the pressure to perform doubtless affects *all* American students, it probably acts as a deterrent rather than a stimulus to student activism.

DEPRIVATION OF EXPECTATIONS

What probably does matter, however, is the *relative* deprivation of student expectations (see Brown, 1967). A college that recruits large numbers of academically motivated and capable students into a less-than-first-rate education program, one that oversells entering freshmen on the virtues of the college, or one that reneges on implicit or explicit promises about the quality and freedom of education may well produce an "academic backlash" that will take the form of student protests over the quality of education. Even more important is the gap between expectations and actualities regarding freedom of student expression. Stern (1967) has demonstrated that most entering freshmen have extremely high hopes regarding the freedom of speech and action they will be able to exercise during college: most learn the real facts quickly, and graduate thoroughly disabused of their illusions. But since activists, as I have argued previously, are particularly responsive to these issues, they are apt to tolerate disillusion less lightly, and to take up arms to concretize their dashed hopes. Compared to the frustration engendered by disillusionment regarding educational quality, the relative deprivation of civil libertarian hopes seems a more potent source of protests. And with regard to both issues, it must be recalled that protests have been *fewest* at institutions of low educational quality and little freedom for student expression. Thus, it is not the absolute level either of educational quality or of student freedom that matters, but the gap between student hopes and institutional facts.

The Protest-Prompting Cultural Climate

Even if a critical mass of interacting protest-prone students forms in an institution that provides leadership and issues, student protests are by no means inevitable, as the quiescence of American students during the nineteen fifties suggests. For protests to occur, other more broadly cultural factors, attitudes and values must be present. Protest activities must be seen as meaningful acts, either in an instrumental or an expressive sense; and activists must be convinced that the consequences of activism and protest will not be overwhelmingly damaging to them. During the 1950s, one much-discussed factor that may have militated against student activism was the conviction that the consequences of protest (blacklisting, F.B.I. investigations, problems in obtaining security clearance, difficulties in getting jobs) were both harmful to the individual and yet extremely likely. Even more important was the sense on the part of many politically conscious students that participation in left-wing causes would merely show their naiveté, gullibility and political innocence without furthering any worthy cause. The prevailing climate was such that protest was rarely seen as an act of any meaning or usefulness.

ACADEMIC SUPPORT . . .

Today, in contrast, student protesters are not only criticized and excoriated by a large segment of the general public, but—more crucial—actively defended, encouraged, lionized, praised, publicized, photographed, interviewed and studied by a portion of the academic community. Since the primary reference group of most activists is not the general public, but rather that liberal segment of the academic world most sympathetic to protest, academic support has a disproportionate impact on protest-prone students' perception of their own activities. In addition, the active participation of admired faculty members in protests, teach-ins and peace marches, acts as a further incentive to students (Kelman, 1966). Thus, in a minority of American colleges, sub-cultures have arisen where protest is felt to be both an important existential act—a dignified way of "standing up to be counted" —and an effective way of "bringing the machine to a halt," sometimes by disruptive acts (sit-ins, strikes, etc.), more often by calling public attention to injustice.

UNIVERSALISM . . .

An equally important, if less tangible "cultural" factor is the broad climate of social criticism in American society. As Parsons (1951, 1960), White (1961), and others have noted, one of the enduring themes of American society is the pressure toward "universalism," that is, an increasing extension of principles like equality, equal opportunity, and fair protection of the law to all groups within the society (and in recent years, to all groups in the world). As affluence has increased in American society, impatience at the slow "progress" of non-affluent minority groups has also increased, not only among students, but among other segments of the population. Even before the advent of the student civil rights movement, support for racial segregation was diminishing. Similarly, the current student concern for the "forgotten fifth" was not so much initiated by student activists as it was taken up by them. In this regard, student activists are both caught up in and in the vanguard of a new wave of extension of universalism in American society. Although the demands of student activists usually go far beyond the national consensus, they nonetheless reflect (at the same time that they have helped advance) one of the continuing trends in American social change.

A contrasting but equally enduring theme in American social criticism is a more fundamental revulsion against the premises of industrial—and now technological—society. Universalistic-liberal criticism blames our society because it has not yet extended its principles, privileges and benefits to all: the complaint is injustice and the goal is to complete our unfinished business. But alienated-romantic criticism questions the validity and importance of these same principles, privileges and benefits—the complaint is materialism and the goal is spiritual, aesthetic or expressive fulfillment. The tradition of revulsion against conformist, anti-aesthetic, materialistic, ugly, middle-class America runs through American writing from Melville through the "lost generation" to the "beat generation" and has been expressed concretely in the bohemian sub-cultures that have flourished in a few large American cities since the turn of the century. But today, the power of the romantic-alienated position has increased: one response to prosperity has been a more searching examination of the technological assumptions upon which prosperity has been based. Especially for the children of the upper middle-class, affluence is simply taken for granted, and the drive "to get ahead in the world" no longer makes sense for students who start out ahead. The meanings of life must be sought elsewhere, in art, sentience, philosophy, love, service to others, intensified experience, adventure—in short, in the broadly aesthetic or expressive realm.

DEVIAN VIEWS . . .

Since neither the universalistic nor the romantic critique of modern society is new, these critiques affect the current student generation not only directly but indirectly, in that they have influenced the way many of today's college students were raised. Thus, a few of today's activists are children of the "radicals of the 1930s" (Lipset and Altbach, 1966); and Flacks comments on the growing number of intellectual, professional upper middle-class families who have adopted "deviant" views of traditional American life and embodied these views in the practices by which they brought up their children. Thus, some of today's activists are the children of bohemians, college professors, etc. But in general, the explanation from parental "deviance" does not seem fully convincing. To be sure, the backgrounds of activists are "atypical" in a statistical sense, and thus might be termed empirically "deviant." It may indeed turn out that the parents of activists are distinguished by their emphasis on humanitarianism, intellectualism and romanticism, and by their lack of stress on moralism (Flacks, 1967). But it is not obvious that such parental values can be termed "deviant" in any but a statistical sense. "Concern with the plight of others," "desire to realize intellectual capacities," and "lack of concern about the importance of strictly controlling personal impulses"—all these values might be thought of as more normative than deviant in upper middle-class suburban American society in 1966. Even "sensitivity to beauty and art" is becoming increasingly acceptable. Nor can the socio-economic facts of affluence, freedom from status anxiety, high educational levels, permissiveness with children, training for independence, etc. be considered normatively deviant in middle-class America. Thus, the sense in which activists are the deviant offspring of sub-culturally deviant parents remains to be clarified.

PSYCHOLOGICAL FLEXIBILITY . . .

Another explanation seems equally plausible, at least as applied to some student activists—namely that their activism is closely related to the social and cultural conditions that promote high levels of psychological flexibility, complexity and integration. As Bay (1966) has argued, social scientists may be too reluctant to entertain the possibility that some political and social outlooks or activities are symptomatic of psychological "health," while others indicate "disturbance." In fact, many of the personal characteristics of activists—empathy, superior intellectual attainments, capacity for group involvement, strong humanitarian values, emphasis on self-realization, etc.— are consistent with the hypothesis that, as a group, they are unusually "healthy" psychologically. (See also Heist, 1966, and Trent and Craise, 1967.) Similarly, the personal antecedents of activists—economic security, committed parents, humanitarian, liberal and permissive home environments, good education, etc.—are those that would seem to promote unusually high levels of psychological functioning. If this be correct, then former SDS president Tom Hayden's words (1966) may be a valid commentary on the cultural setting of activism:

> Most of the active student radicals today come from middle to upper middle-class professional homes. They were born with status and affluence as facts of life, not goals to be striven for. In their upbringing, their parents stressed the right of children to question and make judg-ments, producing perhaps the first generation of young people both affluent and independent of mind.

In agreeing with Bay (1967) that activists may be more psychologically "healthy" as a group than nonactivists, I am aware of the many difficulties entailed by this hypothesis. First, complexity, flexibility, integration, high levels of functioning, etc. are by no means easy to define, and the criteria for "positive mental health" remain vague and elusive. (See Jahoda, 1958.) Second, there are obviously many individuals with these same "healthy" characteristics who are not activists; and within the group of activists, there are many individuals with definite psychopathologies. In any social move-ment, a variety of individuals of highly diverse talents and motivations are bound to be involved, and global descriptions are certain to be oversim-plified. Third, the explanation from "psychological health" and the explana-tion from "parental deviance" are not necessarily opposed. On the contrary, these two arguments become identical if we assume that the preconditions for high levels of psychological functioning are both statistically and nor-matively deviant in modern American society. This assumption seems quite plausible.

Whatever the most plausible explanation of the socio-cultural sources of activism, the importance of prevailing attitudes toward student protest and of the climate of social criticism in America seems clear. In the past five years a conviction has arisen, at least among a minority of American college students, that protest and social action are effective and honorable. Furthermore, changes in American society, especially in middle-class child rearing practices, mean that American students are increasingly responsive to both the universalistic and romantic critique of our society. Both strands of social criticism have been picked up by student activists in a rhetoric of protest that combines a major theme of impatience at the slow fulfillment of the credal ideals of American society with a more muted minor theme of aesthetic revulsion at technological society itself. By and large, activists respond most affirmatively to the first theme and alienated students to the second; but even within the student protest movement, these two themes coexist in uneasy tension.

The Protest-Producing Historical Situation

To separate what I have called the "cultural climate" from the "historical situation" is largely arbitrary. But by this latter term I hope to point to the special sensitivity of today's student activists to historical events and trends that do not immediately impinge upon their own lives. In other nations, and in the past, student protest movements seem to have been more closely related to immediate student frustrations than they are in America today. The "transformationist" (utopian, Marxist, universalistic or democratic) aspirations of activist youth in rapidly developing nations often seem closely related to their personal frustrations under oppressive regimes or at "feudal" practices in their societies; the "restorationist" (romantic, alienated) youth movements that have appeared in later stages of industrialization seem closely connected to a personal sense of the loss of a feudal, maternal, and "organic" past. (See Lifton, 1960, 1963, 1964.) Furthermore, both universalistic and romantic youth movements in other nations have traditionally been highly ideological, committed either to concepts of universal democracy and economic justice or to particularistic values of brotherhood, loyalty, feeling and nation.

ANTI-IDEOLOGICAL . . .

Today's activists, in contrast, are rarely concerned with improving their own conditions and are highly motivated by identification with the oppressions of others. The anti-ideological bias of today's student activists has been underlined by virtually every commentator. Furthermore, as Flacks notes, the historical conditions that have produced protest elsewhere are largely absent in modern America; and the student "movement" in this country differs in important ways from student movements elsewhere. In many respects, then, today's American activists have no historical precedent, and only time will tell to what extent the appearance of organized student dissent in the 1960s is a product of locally American conditions, of the psychosocial effects of a technological affluence that will soon characterize other advanced nations, or of widespread changes in identity and style produced by psycho-historical factors that affect youth of all nations (thermonuclear warfare, increased culture contact, rapid communications, etc.).

SENSITIVITY TO WORLD EVENTS

But whatever the historical roots of protest, today's student protester seems uniquely sensitive to historical trends and events. In interviewing student activists I have been impressed with how often they mention some world-historical event as the catalyst for their activism—in some cases, witnessing via television of the Little Rock demonstrations over school integration, in another case, watching rioting Zengakuren students in Japan protesting the arrival of President Eisenhower, in other cases, particularly among Negro students, a strong identification with the rising black nationalism of recently independent African nations.

Several factors help explain this sensitivity to world events. For one, modern means of communication make the historical world more psychologically "available" to youth. Students today are exposed to world events and world trends with a speed and intensity that has no historical precedent. Revolutions, trends, fashions and fads are now world wide; it takes but two or three years for fashions to spread from Carnaby Street to New York, New Delhi, Tokyo, Warsaw, Lagos and Lima. In particular, students who have been brought up in a tradition that makes them unusually empathic, humanitarian and universalistic in values may react more intensely to exposure via television to student demonstrations in Japan than to social pressures from their fellow seniors in Centerville High. Finally, this broadening of empathy is, I believe, part of a general modern trend toward the *internationalization of identity*. Hastened by modern communications and consolidated by the world-wide threat of nuclear warfare, this trend involves, in vanguard groups in many nations, a loosening of parochial and national allegiances in favor of a more inclusive sense of affinity with one's peers (and non-peers) from all nations. In this respect, American student activists are both participants and leaders in the reorganization of psycho-social identity and ideology that is gradually emerging from the unique historical conditions of the twentieth century (Lifton, 1965).

A small but growing number of American students, then, exhibit a peculiar responsiveness to world-historical events—a responsiveness based partly on their own broad identification with others like them throughout the world, and partly on the availability of information about world events via the mass media. The impact of historical events, be they the world-wide revolution for human dignity and esteem, the rising aspirations of the developing nations, or the war in Vietnam, is greatly magnified upon such students; their primary identification is not their unreflective national identity, but their sense of affinity for Vietnamese peasants, Negro sharecroppers, demonstrating Zengakuren activists, exploited migrant workers, and the oppressed everywhere. One of the consequences of security, affluence and

education is a growing sense of personal involvement with those who are
insecure, non-affluent and uneducated. . . .

References

Aiken, M., Demerath, N. J., and Marwell, G. Conscience and confrontation:
some preliminary findings on summer civil rights volunteers. University of
Wisconsin, 1966. (mimeo)

Allen, M., and Silverstein H. Progress report: creative arts—alienated youth
project. New York: March, 1967.

Bay, Christian. Political and apolitical students: facts in search of theory.
Journal of Social Issues, 1967, **23**, (3).

Bernreuter, Robert G. The college student: he is thinking, talking, acting. *Penn
State Alumni News*, July, 1966.

Block, J., Haan, N., and Smith, M. B. Activism and apathy in contemporary
adolescents. In J. F. Adams (Ed.), *Contributions to the understanding of
adolescence*. New York: Allyn and Bacon, forthcoming.

Brown, Donald R., "Student stress and the institutional environment," *Journal
of Social Issues* (1967), **23:** 92–107.

Coles, Robert. Serpents and doves: non-violent youth in the South. In Erik
Erikson (Ed.), *The challenge of youth*. New York: Basic Books, 1963.

Coles, Robert. *Children of crisis*. Boston: Little, Brown, 1967.

Cowan, John Lewis. Academic freedom, protest and university environments.
Paper read at APA, New York, 1966.

Draper, Hal. *Berkeley, the new student revolt*. New York: Grove, 1965.

Ehle, John. *The free men*. New York: Harper and Row, 1965.

Erikson, Erik H. (Ed.), *The challenge of youth*. New York: Basic Books, 1963.

Fishman, Jacob R., and Solomon, Frederic. Psychological observations on the
student sit-in movement. *Proceedings of the Third World Congress of
Psychiatry*. Toronto: University of Toronto/McGill, n.d.

Fishman, Jacob R., and Solomon, Frederic. Youth and social action. *Journal
of Social Issues*, 1964, **20**, (4), 1–28.

Flacks, Richard E. The liberated generation: an exploration of the roots of
student protest. *Journal of Social Issues*, 1967, **23**, (3).

Gastwirth, D. Why students protest. Unpublished paper, Yale University, 1965.

Hayden, T. Quoted in *Comparative Education Review*, 1966, **10**, 187.

Heist, Paul. Intellect and commitment: the faces of discontent. *Order and
freedom on the campus*. Western Interstate Commission for Higher Education and the Center for the Study of Higher Education, 1965.

Heist, Paul. The dynamics of student discontent and protest. Paper read at APA,
New York, 1966.

Jahoda, Marie. *Current concepts of positive mental health*. New York: Basic
Books, 1958.

Katz, J. The learning environment: social expectations and influences. Paper
presented at American Council of Education, Washington, D.C., 1965.

Katz, J. The student activists: rights, needs and powers of undergraduates. Stanford: Institute for the Study of Human Problems, 1967.

Keene, S. How one big university laid unrest to rest. *The American Student,* 1966, **1,** 18–21.

Kelman, H. D. Notes on faculty activism. *Letter to Michigan Alumni,* 1966.

Keniston, Kenneth. American students and the 'political revival.' *The American Scholar,* 1962, **32,** 40–64.

Keniston, Kenneth. *The uncommitted.* New York: Harcourt, Brace and World, 1965a.

Keniston, Kenneth. The pressure to perform. *The Intercollegian.* September, 1965b.

Keniston, Kenneth. The faces in the lecture room. In R. S. Morison (Ed.), *The American university.* Boston: Houghton Mifflin, 1966a.

Keniston, Kenneth. The psychology of alienated students. Paper read at APA, New York, 1966b.

Keniston, Kenneth, and Helmreich, R. An exploratory study of discontent and potential drop-outs at Yale. Yale University, 1965. (mimeo)

Kornhauser, W. Alienation and participation in the mass university. Paper read at American Ortho-Psychiatric Association, Washington, D.C., 1967.

Lifton, Robert Jay. Japanese youth: the search for the new and the pure. *The American Scholar,* 1960, **30,** 332–344.

Lifton, Robert Jay. Youth and history: individual change in post-war Japan. In E. Erikson (Ed.), *The challenge of youth.* New York: Harper and Row, 1963.

Lifton, Robert Jay. Individual patterns in historical change. *Comparative Studies in Society and History.* 1964, **6,** 369–383.

Lifton, Robert Jay. Protean man. Yale University, 1965. (mimeo)

Lipset, Seymour M. Student opposition in the United States. *Government and Opposition,* 1966a, **1,** 351–374.

Lipset, Seymour M. University students and politics in underdeveloped countries. *Comparative Education Review,* 1966b, **10,** 132–162.

Lipset, Seymour M., and Altbach, P. G. Student politics and higher education in the United States. *Comparative Education Review,* 1966, **10,** 320–349.

Lipset, Seymour M., and Wolin, S. (Eds.), *The Berkeley student revolt.* Garden City, New York: Doubleday, 1965.

Lyonns, G. The police car demonstration: a survey of participants. In S. Lipset and S. Wolin (Eds.), *The Berkeley student revolt.* Garden City, New York: Doubleday, 1965.

Michael, Donald Nelson. *The next generation, the prospects ahead for the youth of today and tomorrow.* New York: Vintage, 1965.

Miller, Daniel R., and Swanson, Guy E. *The changing American parent.* New York: Wiley, 1958.

Miller, Michael, and Gilmore, Susan (Eds.). *Revolution at Berkeley.* New York: Dell, 1965.

Newfield, Jack. *A prophetic minority.* New York: New American Library, 1966.

Newsweek. Campus, 1965. March 22, 1965.

Parsons, Talcott. *The social system.* Glencoe, Ill.: Free Press, 1951.

Parsons, Talcott. *Structure and process in modern societies.* Glencoe, Ill.: Free Press, 1960.

Paulus, G. *A multivariate analysis study of student activist leaders, student government leaders, and non-activists.* Cited in Richard E. Peterson, *The student Left in American higher education.* Draft for Puerto Rico Conference on Students and Politics, 1967.

Pervin, Lawrence A., Reik, L. E. and Dalrymple, W. (Eds.). *The college drop-out and the utilization of talent.* Princeton: Princeton University, 1966.

Peterson, Richard E. *The scope of organized student protest in 1964–65.* Princeton: Educational Testing Service, 1966.

Peterson, Richard E. The student Left in American higher education. Draft for Puerto Rico Conference on Students and Politics, 1967.

Reed, M. Student non-politics, or how to make irrelevancy a virtue. *The American Student,* 1966, **1,** (3), 7–10.

Rigney, Francis J., and Smith, L. D. *The real bohemia.* New York: Basic Books, 1961.

Schneider, Patricia. A study of members of SDS and YD at Harvard. Unpublished B. A. thesis, Wellesley College, 1966.

Solomon, Frederic, and Fishman, Jacob R. Perspectives on the student sit-in movement. *American Journal of Ortho-Psychiatry,* 1963, **33,** 873–874.

Solomon, Frederic, and Fishman, Jacob R. Youth and peace: a psycho-social study of student peace demonstrators in Washington, D.C. *Journal of Social Issues,* 1964, **20,** (4), 54–73.

Somers, R. H. The mainsprings of the rebellion: a survey of Berkeley students in November, 1964. In S. Lipset and S. Wolin (Eds.), *The Berkeley student revolt.* Garden City, New York: Doubleday, 1965.

Stern, G. Myth and reality in the American college. *AAUP Bulletin* Winter, 1966, 408–414.

Suczek, Robert Francis, and Alfert, E. Personality characteristic of college drop-outs. University of California, 1966. (mimeo)

Trent, James W., and Craise, Judith L. "Commitment and conformity in the American college." *J. Social Issues* (1967), **23:** 34–51.

Trow, Martin. Some lessons from Berkeley. Paper presented to American Council of Education, Washington, D.C. 1965.

Watts, William Arther, and Whittaker, D. Some socio-psychological differences between highly committed members of the Free Speech Movement and the student population at Berkeley. *Applied Behavioral Science,* 1966, **2,** 41–62.

Watts, William Arther, and Whittaker, D. Socio-psychological characteristics of intellectually oriented, alienated youth: a study of the Berkeley nonstudent. University of California, Berkeley, 1967. (mimeo)

Westby, D., and Braungart, R. Class and politics in the family backgrounds of student political activists. *American Social Review,* 1966, **31,** 690–692.

White, Winston. *Beyond conformity.* Glencoe, Ill.: Free Press, 1961.

Whittaker, D., and Watts, W. A. Personality and value attitudes of intellectually disposed, alienated youth. Paper presented at APA, New York, 1966.

Wright, E. O. Student leaves of absence from Harvard College: A personality and social system approach. Unpublished paper, Harvard University, 1966.

Zinn, Howard. *SNCC, the new abolitionists.* Boston: Beacon, 1965.

Social and Cultural Meanings of Student Revolt: Some Informal Comparative Observations *

Richard Flacks

The phenomenon of student rebellion has in the past few years come to appear international in scope. During this period, student demonstrations and strikes have paralyzed universities and shaken the political systems in societies as far apart, culturally and geographically, as Japan and France, Mexico and West Germany, Italy and Brazil, Czechoslovakia and the United States.

The simultaneity of these outbursts and the similarities in style and tactics of the student movements have led many observers to assume that there is a world-wide revolt of the youth, which is new historically, and which derives from a single set of causes.

It is obvious, however, that student movements, acting in opposition to established authority, are not at all new. For example, student revolutionary activity was a constant feature of Russian life during the nineteenth century. It played a major role in the revolution of 1848 in Central Europe. The communist movements in China and Vietnam grew out of militant student movements in those countries. In Latin America, student movements have been politically crucial since the early part of this century. Youth and student movements were a dramatic feature of life in pre-World War I Germany; the Zionist movement among European Jews had its roots in the German youth movement. Since World War II, student movements have helped bring down regimes in Asia and Latin America. It is clear that the events of recent months are in certain respects merely further expressions of a long tradition of student rebelliousness (Cf. Altbach, 1967, for an overview of this tradition).

But just as it would be a mistake to think that the student revolts are historically new, it would also be an error to uphold the conventional wisdom which asserts that youth are "naturally" rebellious, or idealistic. There are, of course, good reasons for believing that some segments of the youth are

Richard Flacks, "Social and Cultural Meanings of Student Revolt: Some Informal Comparative Observations." Reprinted by permission of *Social Problems,* The Society for the Study of Social Problems, and the author (Vol. 17, No. 3, Winter 1970), pp. 340–357.

* Paper prepared for presentation at meetings of American Association for the Advancement of Science, Dallas, Texas, December 1968.

likely to be particularly disposed to revolt, particularly attracted to new ideas, particularly prepared to take direct action in behalf of their ideals. But it is by no means true that rebellious, experimental, or idealistic behavior is a general characteristic of young people—indeed, it is probably the case that in any historical period the majority of the young, as Bennett Berger has remarked, are not "youthful." Moreover, it is even less true that youthful impulses in support of radical change inevitably take the form of distinct, autonomous political movements against the established political system. For instance, such movements have been quite rare in the U.S. and other advanced Western countries until the present decade. Although significant minorities of students and other young people have been active participants in movements for social change in the U.S., Britain, France, and the smaller capitalist democracies, these societies have not had movements created by and for youth, independent of adult organizations, containing a strong element of rebellion not only against injustice but against the authority of the older generation. The feeling that there is something new about generational revolt is not accurate in global terms; but it is substantially correct for societies like our own.

There is a need for a theoretical framework to account for the emergence of oppositional movements among youth—a framework which can embrace the fact that such movements have become a feature, not only of developing pre-industrial societies, but of apparently stable advanced industrial nations as well. In searching for such a framework, two classical theoretical perspectives might be expected to provide some help. One would be Marxian theory, which, after all, was created in an effort to account for the rise of revolutionary movements in contemporary society. But Marxism, since it emphasizes the role of classes as revolutionary agencies, has a difficult time assimilating student revolutionary action. First, students do not themselves constitute a class. Second, students do occupy class positions, but these are typically privileged ones. Indeed, one fact about the American student movement is that participation in it tends to be associated with high family status and income (Westby and Braungart, 1966; Flacks, 1970), and the same pattern may be found in other countries as well. Thus, a problem for Marxian theory of revolution would be to account for the mass defection of students from their families' class, and for the tendency of privileged youth to identify with the plight of the dispossessed in their society. This is particularly problematical in the advanced industrial societies: here we have a situation in which at the present time organized political and cultural opposition to capitalism appears to be more extensive and militant among students than among workers. There is no straightforward way to derive this fact from the body of Marxian theory.

A second theoretical perspective which one might find useful is that of Parsons. Indeed, one of the few theories about the conditions giving rise to generational conflict is that of Eisenstadt (1956) whose perspective flows directly from Parsons (Cf. Parsons, 1962, for a recent formulation).

This perspective focuses less on the revolutionary thrust of student and youth movements than on their functional character. What is most salient to Parsons and Eisenstadt is the formation of distinctive groups or movements among persons at the same stage in the life-cycle. The appearance of such groupings among youth is seen as a consequence of the differentiation of the family from the occupational structure, resulting in a sharp discontinuity between the values and role-expectations operative within the family and those prevailing in the larger society. As youth move out of the family and experience such discontinuities, major problems of socialization are created by the necessity for them to successfully orient toward occupational roles. Such problems are not manageable within the family, nor within the institutions of formal schooling. What is needed are institutions which can combine some of the features of family life with those of the occupational structure. Youth groups, youth cultures, and youth movements serve this function of aiding the transition to adulthood by combining relations of diffuse solidarity with universalistic values.

This perspective predicts that the sharper the disjunction between family values and those in the larger society, the more distinctive and oppositional will be the youth culture. In particular, one would expect that students in societies undergoing a rapid breakdown of traditional authority, and in which new bases of legitimation had not yet been established, would most acutely experience problems of achieving adult status and would be most likely to form autonomous, oppositional movements. By the same token, young people in the advanced, stable, industrial, democratic societies, although experiencing marked discontinuity between familial and occupational roles, would not experience the same intense cultural dislocation found in developing countries. For, although familial and occupational roles are disjunctive in advanced industrial countries, families in these societies tend to be congruent in their values and expectations with other institutions. Thus the industrialized societies would exhibit distinctive youth cultures, but these implicitly support other socializing agencies in identity formation and orientation toward adulthood. In short, the Parsons-Eisenstadt perspective leads us to expect student movements in societies where traditional authority is disintegrating under the impact of industrialization, Western ideas, and modernizing trends, and where families continue to adhere to traditional culture. Depicting industrial societies as ones in which both parental and political authority support modernity and change, this perspective leads us to expect a distinctive youth culture, but not an "alienated" oppositional, revolutionary one in societies like our own (Eisenstadt, 1956; Parsons, 1962).

As I have suggested, this perspective was a viable one—until this decade. Now each passing year makes it less and less easy to assume the stability of the developed western societies, less and less safe to adopt the view that the U.S. represents some culmination point in cultural development, or that there is a fundamental congruence among socializing, political and economic institutions and the values which prevail within them in our society.

A comparative perspective on student movements and generational revolt leads us to seek a theoretical framework which transcends the Marxian view of the sources of revolutionary impulse in capitalist society, and the Parsonian view that such impulses are not characteristic of advanced industrial society. If such a framework existed it would undoubtedly constitute a synthesis of Eisenstadt's insight that student movements are a symptom of cultural disintegration and the Marxian insight that capitalism and its culture are themselves unstable and capable of being negated.

II

If recent events lead us to discard the view that student movements are characteristic only of societies in which traditional culture and authority are breaking down, we nevertheless ought to be able to specify why such movements have been endemic under such conditions. The Parsons-Eisenstadt hypothesis provides us with at least a partial answer: the university student in an agrarian society is someone who is compelled to abandon the values with which he was raised, who is exposed to a set of new cultural influences, but who is becoming an adult in an historical period in which the new values have not been clarified, new roles have not been created, new authority has not been established or legitimated. The student movement, with its diffuse, fraternal interpersonal life, its identification with the masses of the people, its disdain for privilege and authority—combined with a commitment to rationalism, democracy, nationalism and other "modern" values —enables them to develop the political skills and motives which may be necessary to challenge the established elites, enables them to undergo the personal transition which is an aspect of the historical transition through which the whole society is going.

In addition to this hypothesis, which locates the sources of "strain" in the cultural and psychological consequences of modernization, there are additional and equally powerful factors at work in such societies which make such movements extremely likely. (A summary of such factors appears in Lipset, 1968.)

There is, for example, the widely remarked fact that typically in developing countries there is an "overproduction" of educated youth—the available jobs for university graduates often are not commensurate with the training or aspirations they have as a result of their educational attainment. Prospective or actual unemployment, and the frustration of aspiration, is presumably a politicizing experience for many educated youth in such societies.

Another politicizing and radicalizing feature of these societies is the backwardness and authoritarianism of political authority. Political authority in these societies plays a paradoxical role for students; on the one hand, it sponsors the formation and expansion of a university system in order to promote technical progress, while simultaneously it resists the political, social, and cultural transformations which such progress requires. In this situation, students inevitably come into conflict with the state and other established elite institutions. The more intransigent the established elites are with respect to nationalist, democratic, and modernizing aspirations, the more likely it is that the student movement becomes the breeding ground for a "counter-elite" and the spearhead of revolutionary politics (Ben-David and Collins, 1967).

Still another factor likely to generate discontent is the quality of life in the universities of these societies. Living and working conditions are likely to be extremely impoverished. The schools are likely to be overflowing; the quality of instruction and facilities for study are likely to be totally inadequate; and material poverty among students is likely to be substantial.

If cultural disintegration, overproduction of the educated, reactionary regimes, and university conditions generate discontent leading to politicization and radicalism, additional factors promote the emergence and growth of autonomous student movements in developing nations. For example, the autonomous character of student movements in these countries is facilitated by the absence of other oppositional forces. To the extent that peasants, workers and other strata are poorly organized or passive or suppressed, students, with their high degree of interaction and their sophistication may become the only group in a society capable of initiating oppositional activity. Moreover, students may have a degree of freedom for political action which is not available to other opposition forces. This freedom may in part be due to the fact that many student activists are the offspring of elite or upper status families, in part because of the recognition of the fact that students are indispensable to the future of the society, in part because of an established tradition of university autonomy which makes it illegitimate for police power to invade the campus. Given the relative leniency toward students and the ambivalence of authorities toward them, instances of repressive action taken against students are likely to be especially discrediting to the regime. Thus, the weakness of other oppositional forces, the wide opportunities for intensive interaction available to students, the large numbers of students likely to be concentrated in particular locales, and the special freedom for political expression which they are likely to have all combine to foster the growth of a student movement as an independent oppositional movement.

The conditions we have been describing may be regarded as the "classic" pattern presaging the emergence of students as a revolutionary force. Put another way, these conditions help us understand why student oppositional movements have been a regular feature of developing societies.

III

Our analysis has suggested that the classical student movement is a symptom of marked cultural incoherence, of political stagnation, and of severe problems of identity for educated youth in the face of the social and technological changes associated with the process of "modernization." Because this analysis emphasizes that student movements are an aspect of the modernization process, it appears to be quite inadequate for accounting for the rise of student movements in societies like our own, which are not agrarian, which are not dominated by traditional culture and authority, which are not struggling to achieve national identity and independence, where democratic, rationalistic and egalitarian values prevail, where families orient their offspring toward active achievement in a technological society, where the freedom to organize political opposition is available and used. At least at first glance one would be led to believe that the advanced industrial capitalist societies of the West would provide the least hospitable soil for a revolt of educated youth.

Yet a student movement has grown up over the past decade in American society. Over these years, it has become increasingly radicalized, and indeed now includes an avowedly revolutionary wing. Like the classical movements, it contains a strong component of generational revolt—that is, of implicit and explicit hostility to the authority of older generations, and an emphasis on the moral superiority of the young as such and on their capacity to be an agency of social transformation. Like the classical movements, the student movements of the West are intensely anti-authoritarian, egalitarian, and populist. They also resemble the classical type in being completely independent of other, "adult" political groups.

Are there any ways to comprehend the appearance of such a movement in American society that will account for its comparability with classical student movements?

The most parsimonious hypothesis, perhaps, would focus on possible similarities between the immediate situation of the student in the advanced industrial societies and in the developing countries. For example, it seems plausible that the rapid expansion of higher education and the great influx of young people to the universities has led to a devolution in the quality of educational institutions and of student life in the U.S. and Western Europe. It is also plausible that the rapid growth in the numbers of educated youth has produced the same kind of sectional unemployment of the educated which is present in the developing nations.

There may be considerable validity to these hypotheses; indeed, much of the commentary on the French student revolt has emphasized these factors as crucial ones. But it is much harder to see how they can be applied to the American case. For instance, data on the distribution of student protest on

American campuses quite clearly show that the student movement had its origins at the highest quality state universities and prestigious private universities and colleges, that the movement continues to have its widest following on such campuses, and that it has only recently spread to schools of lower prestige and quality (Peterson, 1966; 1968). There is, in short, a negative correlation between the quality of an institution and the proportion of its student body which is activist, and between the selectivity of an institution and the radicalism of its student body.

It is equally hard to make a case that the student movement in the U.S. originates in overproduction of educated youth. In the first place, there is no dearth of opportunity for college graduates. Still, one might hypothesize that students who are attracted to the movement experience "relative deprivation"—for example, they may be students who cannot hold their own in academic competition. However, the data on student protesters indicate otherwise; there is, in fact, a tendency for activists to have above average academic records in high school and college, and most of the several studies on student protesters indicate they include a disproportionate under-representation of students with poor academic records (Flacks, 1967; 1970). Student protesters come from families with high income and occupational status; they tend to be most prevalent at the top schools; they have above average aptitude for academic work, and perform at above average levels. If there is an overproduction of educated youth in this society at this time, it is hard to see how this would affect the structure of opportunities available to the academic elite from which activists tend to be recruited.

It seems clear that any effort to explain the rise of a student movement in the U.S. must take account of the fact that the movement originated among highly advantaged students, that it did not begin as a revolt against the university, and that its active core contains many students whose aptitudes, interests, values, and origins suggest a strong orientation to intellectual and academic life.

Indeed, one of the most striking findings about American activists has to do with their intellectualism. I refer here not only to the variety of studies which find activists exhibiting intellectual interests and achievements superior to those of the student body as a whole. More persuasive and more sociologically relevant are findings concerning the socioeconomic backgrounds of participants in protest activity. These findings may be briefly summarized as follows: activists are disproportionately the sons and daughters of highly educated parents; in a large proportion of cases, their parents have advanced graduate and professional degrees; a very high percentage of activists' mothers are college graduates; the parents tend to be in occupations for which higher education is a central prerequisite: professions, education, social service, public service, the arts; both businessmen and blue and white collar workers tend to be underrepresented among the parents of activists; family interests—as they are expressed in recreation, or in dinner-table conversation, or in formal interviews—tend to be intellectual and "cultural" and relatively highbrow; these are families in which books were read, discussed, and taken seriously, in which family outings involved museums and concert-halls rather than ball-parks and movies, etc. They were families in which "values" were taken seriously—conventional religion and morality were treated with considerable skepticism, while at the same time strong emphasis was placed on leading a principled, socially useful, morally consistent life. They were, finally, families in which education was regarded with considerable reverence and valued for its own sake, rather than in utilitarian terms.

In short, the student movement originated among those young people who came out of what might be called the "intellectual" or "humanist" subculture of the middle class. In the last two years, it has become considerably more heterogeneous, but it was created almost exclusively by offspring of that particular stratum. (A more detailed review of these findings appears in Flacks, 1970.)

At first glance, it would seem that nothing could be more incomparable than the situation of these middle-class American youth and the situation of educated youth in underdeveloped countries. The former, as we have said, can look forward to an array of high status occupational opportunities. Their lives as students are well-subsidized, comfortable, and intellectually rich. Their parents are highly "modern" people, playing central cultural roles, well-informed about and sympathetic with the latest cultural developments. All of this is especially true in comparison with the position of educated youth in developing countries, whose futures are extremely uncertain, whose lives as students are likely to be meager and oppressive, whose families are likely to be locked into traditional ways and attitudes and stand as positive hindrances to the emancipation of their children.

These contrasts are striking, but they may be quite superficial. What I want to do is to restate some of the major factors which we have seen to be central in accounting for the appearance of classical student movements— and try to determine whether comparable factors are at work in American society, especially in relation to the situation of students who come out of the educated middle class.

1. We have said, after Eisenstadt, that a central determinant of the appearance of youth and student movements is sharp discontinuity between values embodied in the family and those emerging in other institutional contexts. From this perspective, as we have suggested, the student movement serves as a "secondary institution"—a way of re-establishing family-like solidarity to ease the achievement of independent adult identities and role-orientations. For youth in developing countries, discontinuity arises because of the fundamental conflict between the traditional orientation of the family and the modernizing orientations encountered in the university and the cosmopolitan community associated with it.

This kind of discontinuity could not be one experienced by the offspring of the educated middle class in America—if anything, students from this stratum are likely to experience less disjunction between familial and university values than any other groups of students. But there are grounds for feeling that humanist youth in America do experience a kind of discontinuity between family and larger society that may have comparable implications for the establishment of identity.

Our studies (cf. Flacks, 1967) of the parents of student activists show that these parents differ from others in the middle class in the following respects:

First, as mentioned, there is a strong commitment to intellectuality and "culture" and a considerable disdain for mass culture and mass leisure. Their children were expected to be intellectually aware and serious, artistically creative or at least appreciative, serious about education and self-development.

Second, these parents were unusual in their political awareness and their political liberalism. Although they were not necessarily politically active, they tended to stress to their children the necessity for social responsibility and service, and active citizenship, and encouraged their children to support racial equality, civil liberties, and other liberal political goals. In this respect, these families were likely to see themselves, correctly, as different from the vast majority of politically passive or conservative families in their community.

Third, these parents were overtly skeptical about conventional middle-class values, life-styles, and religious orientations. Most of these parents were explicitly secular; those who were actively religious tended to belong to particularly liberal religious denominations or to have a strong social gospel kind of religious commitment. Many of these parents were articulate critics of conventional middle-class mores—by which, in particular, they had in mind sexual repressiveness, materialism, status-striving, and strict methods of rearing children. Many were quite explicit in hoping that their children would be more successful than they had been in leading self-fulfilling, socially responsible lives rather than participating in the "rat race," the "suburban way of life," the "commercial world."

Finally, these parents tended to express these values implicitly through the structure of the family and the styles of child rearing which they adopted. These were parents who encouraged "self-expressive" and "independent" behavior in their children, who interacted with each other and with their children in relatively "democratic" ways, who refused to impose conventional stereotypes of masculine and feminine conduct on their children (e.g., they tended to foster aesthetic and intellectual interests in their boys and assertive behavior on the part of their girls). It was not that these parents were unusually "permissive" or over-indulgent—for instance, their very explicit expectations about intellectuality and social responsibility indicate that they did not adopt a "laissez-faire" attitude toward their children. But they rather consciously organized family life to support anti-authoritarian and self-assertive impulses on the part of their children and rather clearly instructed them in attitudes favoring skepticism toward authority, egalitarianism and personal autonomy (Flacks, 1967, 1970; Keniston, 1968b).

Now what happens when these intellectual, anti-authoritarian, socially conscious, somewhat unconventional children move on to school and street and peer group? I think it is clear that they are likely to experience a considerable discontinuity between the values they encounter in these settings and the values with which they were raised. They are likely to find authority in school to be petty, arbitrary, repressive. They are likely to feel considerable isolation from the conventional culture of their peers. They are likely to be particularly sensitive to the hypocrisies, rigidities, and injustices of particular institutions and of the society as a whole as they experience it.

Most American youth experience some dislocation as they move from their families into the larger society, if for no other reason than that the rapidity of social change prevents any family from adequately preparing its offspring for the world as it actually is developing, and because proper, moral behavior for children in the American family is inescapably different from proper, moral behavior in the competitive, impersonal society beyond. The existing primary and secondary institutions—school and youth culture—which Parsons and others have expected to be serviceable in easing the transition to adulthood, have failed to incorporate humanist youth, who were in fact raised to question many of the fundamental premises of these institutions. As more and more such youth have entered upon the scene, they have tended to find each other and to create a kind of counter-culture, much as Black urban youth, similarly unincorporated, have created theirs. This new humanist youth culture embodies norms concerning sex-role behavior, worthwhile activity, and personal style which are quite opposed to those which prevail in conventional adolescent society; it expresses values which seem quite subversive of conventional middle-class aspirations, and an attitude toward adult authority which is quite clearly defiant. The American student movement is an expression of that new youth culture, although by no means the only one.

In a peculiar sense, then, the appearance of a student movement and a rebellious youth culture in American society in recent years supports the Eisenstadt hypothesis that such phenomena are rooted in sharp discontinuities between family values and values in the larger society. It is a peculiar kind of support for that hypothesis because, unlike the classical case, the discontinuities we refer to do not have to do with incongruence between a traditional family and a modernizing culture. If anything, the reverse may be the case.

2. As we have suggested, a second major factor contributing to the rise

of classical student movements has been the "overproduction" of educated youth—a factor which appears to be largely absent in the American situation. Nevertheless, there are severe problems for humanist youth with respect to vocation. These problems have to do, not with the scarcity of opportunity, but with the irrelevance of the opportunities which do exist. One of the most characteristic attributes of students in the movement (and an attribute which they share with a large number of apolitical students) is their inability to decide on a career or a vocation. This indecision is less the result of the wide range of choices available, than of the unsatisfactory quality of those choices. What is repellent about the existing opportunities is not their incompatability with the status or financial aspirations of these youth— but that they are incompatible with their ideals. Business careers are rejected outright as acquisitive, self-seeking, and directly linked to that which is defined as most corrupting in American society. Careers in government or conventional politics are regarded as either self-deluding or "selling out." Professional careers—particularly such established professions as law and medicine—are attractive to some, but only if one can become a doctor or lawyer outside of the conventional career lines; otherwise such careers are regarded as just as acquisitive as business. Teachers and social workers are seen as agents of social control; a few are attracted to scholarship or science, but with profound anxiety. To take an ordinary job is to give up any chance for leading a free life. In general, embarking on a career within the established occupational structure is regarded as morally compromising because it leads to complicity with established interests or because it requires abandoning personal autonomy or because it draws one away from full commitment to radicalism or because it signifies acceptance of the norms and standards of bourgeois society or because it means risking corruption because of material comfort and security.

Although some of these attitudes are undoubtedly the result of participation in the movement rather than a determinant of such participation, it is clear that an underlying revulsion with conventional adult roles and established, institutionalized careers predates movement involvement for many students. One reason for believing that it does is the fact that such revulsion is observable among young people who do not become political activists; indeed, a widespread restlessness about becoming committed to conventional careers and life-styles is evident on the American campus. This has been particularly surprising for those of us who remember the decade of the Fifties and the prevailing feeling of that era—namely, that affluence was producing a generation which would be particularly conformist, complacent, status-conscious, and bourgeois.

It now appears that the opposite may be equally true. Although people with high status and material security may typically be motivated to maintain their position, it is also the case that being born into affluence can foster impulses to be experimental, risk-taking, open to immediate experience, unrepressed. For some at least, growing up with economic security in families of secure status can mean a weakening of the normal incentives of the system and can render one relatively immune to the established means of social control, especially if one's parents rather explicitly express skepticism about the moral worth of material success. Post-war affluence in our society then has had the effect of liberating a considerable number of young people from anxieties about social mobility and security, and enabled them to take seriously the quest for other values and experiences. To such youth, established careers and adult roles are bound to be unsatisfying. What is the sense, after all, of binding oneself to a large organization, of submitting to the rituals, routines and disciplines of careerism, of postponing or foregoing a wide range of possible experience—when there is little chance of surpassing one's father, when the major outcome of such efforts is to acquire goods which one has already had one's fill of, when such efforts mean that one must compromise one's most cherished ideals?

In newly industrializing societies, students become revolutionaries, or bohemians, or free intellectuals and artists, because established careers commensurate with their education had not been created. In our society, large numbers of students do the same, not because opportunities for conventional achievement are absent but because they are personally meaningless and morally repugnant. We began with the proposition that a blockage of economic opportunity for the educated is a determinant of student movements. Our comparative analysis leads us to a reformulation of this proposition—any condition which leads to a weakening of motivation for upward mobility increases the likelihood of student rebellion—such conditions can include either blocked opportunity *or* high levels of material security. In short, when numbers of youth find occupational decisions extremely difficult to make, their propensity for collective rebellion is likely to increase.

3. What we have so far been discussing may be described as a kind of cultural crisis—the emergence of a sector of the youth population which finds its fundamental values, aspirations, and character structure in sharp conflict with the values and practices which prevail in the larger society. We have said that, in certain respects, this conflict is similar to that experienced by youth in societies undergoing rapid transition from traditional to "modern" culture; and in both cases, we find these youth responding to their crisis by banding together in movements of opposition to the older generations and attempting to generate what amounts to a counter culture.

In some ways, this kind of crisis is not new in American society. For more than a century, at least, small groups of intellectuals have expressed their revulsion with industrial capitalism, and the commercialism, philistinism, and acquisitiveness they saw as its outcome. By the turn of the century, what had largely been an expression of genteel criticism was supplanted by a more vigorous and intense revolt by some educated youth—expressed through bohemianism and through a variety of political and social reform movements. Indeed, opposition to Victorian morality and business culture has been characteristic of American intellectuals in this century (Hofstadter, 1966); and the emergence of large numbers of humanist youth out of relatively intellectual families is an indication of the impact this opposition has had on the society. What was once the protest of tiny pockets of intellectuals and artists has become a mass phenomenon, in part because the ideas of these earlier critics and reformers were taken up in the universities and became part of the world-view of many members of the educated middle class. These ideas influenced not only sentiments regarding commercialism, material success and intellectuality, they also had a direct bearing on the treatment of women and the raising of children, since an important element of anti-bourgeois thinking had to do with the emancipation of women and the liberation of the child from repressive and stultifying disciplines.

What is new in this decade is, first of all, the degree to which this cultural alienation has become a mass phenomenon—an extensive, rooted subculture on the campus and in major cities, with a wide and steadily growing following. Equally important, the present movement is new in the degree to which it has expressed itself through political opposition—an opposition which has become increasingly revolutionary, in the sense that it has increasingly come to reject the legitimacy of established authority and of the political system itself.

As we have previously pointed out, political rebellion by students in other countries has largely been a response to authoritarian, reactionary regimes—regimes which were incapable of or unwilling to adapt to pressures for modernization, and which tended to meet such pressures by attempting to repress them. Thus, classical student movements tend to arise out of the cultural crisis created by the processes of modernization, and tend to go into active political opposition when the political system stands against those processes.

It is perhaps hard for American social scientists to understand why American students should undergo a similar reaction to the American political system. After all, many of them have spent years demonstrating that the system was pluralist, democratic, egalitarian, and highly flexible; thus, while it may be rational for Russian, Chinese, or Latin-American students to have become revolutionary in the face of tsars, war-lords, and dictators, it is, for them, irrational for students in the U.S. and other Western countries to adopt revolutionary stances against liberal, democratic regimes. (For one example cf. Glazer, 1968.)

To understand why the cultural alienation of intellectual youth in America has become politicized and radicalized requires an historical analysis—the details of which are beyond the scope of this paper. Without attempting such an analysis we can, I think, at least point to some of the most relevant factors.

The first point would be that culturally alienated intellectuals in America have not historically been revolutionary. They have, instead, either been anti-political or have placed their hopes in a variety of progressive, reform movements. In part they have been sustained by the view that the national political system, whatever its flaws, had progressive potential because of its democratic character. They have also been sustained by comparisons between the American system and the rest of the world.

During the New Deal and World War II period, a kind of culmination was reached in the formulation of an ideological perspective for the educated class in America. At the heart of this perspective was the view that inequality, injustice, and business culture could be controlled and offset by effective political and social action through the Federal government. The rise of labor as a political force, the passage of social legislation, and the subsidization of reform by the government would create the conditions for a just and humane society. Not incidentally, the expansion of the public sector would also create vast new vocational opportunities for educated people with humanitarian concerns—in education, in social service, in public health, mental health, child care, public planning, and all the rest. Thus the creation of the welfare state and an American version of social democracy was crucial for the expanded intelligentsia, not only because it provided a solution to the social ills that contributed to their alienation, but also because it offered a way to realize themselves vocationally outside of the business economy and in terms of their values. It is perhaps important to mention that it was in this ideological milieu that the parents of the present generation reached maturity.

In the past twenty years, however, two things have been happening simultaneously: on the one hand, the ranks of the educated middle class have greatly expanded, due in considerable degree to government support of higher education and of public sector types of occupations which required advanced education; on the other hand, the social benefits anticipated from this development have not been forthcoming—that is, liberal politics have not eradicated gross social inequality, have not improved the quality of public life, and perhaps above all have not created a pacific, internationalist global posture on the part of the American government. Instead, the educated middle-class person is likely to see his society as increasingly chaotic and deteriorating, to feel that enormous waste of material and human resources is taking place, and to believe that his nation is not a liberalizing force internationally, but perhaps the reverse.

The offspring of this stratum, as they began to throng the nation's universities in the early sixties, entered political involvement at just the point where their parents had begun to experience disillusionment with progressive ideology. But the early phase of the student movement tended to continue traditional middle-class faith in the democratic process. The New Left, in its beginnings, rejected all received ideology; for fairly obvious reasons, it found neither social democracy, nor Marxism-Leninism, nor liberalism at all adequate foundations for renewing radical politics. Indeed, in an early age, many New Leftists would not have attempted to create a youth-based radicalism at all; they would instead have found their way into one or another established radical or reform movement. It is important to realize that the exhaustion of existing ideologies in post-war Europe and America meant that young people with radical impulses had to start afresh. The starting point in the U.S. was to take democratic ideals seriously; to try to make the system work, by participating in and catalyzing grass-roots protest against glaring injustice—particularly against segregation and the threat of nuclear holocaust. Such an outlook included a fairly explicit expectation that the creation of protest and ferment from below would provide an impetus for major change at the top—on the part of the federal government (in behalf of the constitutional rights of Negroes, for example) and on the part of established agencies of reform such as the churches, the universities, the labor movement. Until about 1964, this political model seemed to be working to a considerable extent—civil rights laws were passed, the Kennedy Administration was moving toward détente with the Soviet Union, a war on poverty was declared, and a spirit of social renovation seemed to be taking hold in the society. In this situation, the SDS and other student radicals retained a considerable willingness to operate within the conventional political system; it is well to remember for example that in the election campaign of 1964, SDS adopted the slogan, "Part of the Way with LBJ."

The escalation of the war in Vietnam marked a turning point for radical students—it began a process of progressive disillusionment with the political system, a process which, for many, has culminated in a total rejection of its legitimacy. I cannot here recount in any adequate way the series of events which contributed to this process; but it is clear that the war itself was crucial to it, as was the use of the draft to prosecute that war and to "channel" young men educationally and occupationally, as was the failure of the war on poverty (a failure directly experienced by many young activists as they tried to work in poverty areas), as was the transformation of the black movement from a struggle for integration to a far more radical struggle for "liberation" and economic equality, as was the revelation that many universities actively contributed to the war effort and military research, as was the increasing use of the police to suppress protest demonstrations in the streets and on the campuses, as was the failure of the political parties to recognize their liberal, doveish constituencies. In short, for young people who identified with the cause of racial equality, who despised war and militarism, and who had hoped to construct lives based on humane, intellectual, and democratic ideals, by 1968 American society did seem largely reactionary, authoritarian, and repressive. (A more detailed review of this history appears in Skolnick, 1969: 87–105.)

This perception is heightened and reinforced by other, more fundamental beliefs. For example, it is very difficult to accept the amount of squalor, inequality, and misery in this society if one is aware of the fact that the society has the material resources to guarantee a decent private and public life to the whole population. It is very difficult to accept war and the arms race and the expansion of militarism when one is convinced that these institutions have the capacity to destroy the human race. And, finally, it is very difficult to maintain a calm long-run perspective, if one believes that the society has the capacity—in its technology, in its large-scale organizational structure, and in the character structure of millions of its members—to obliterate personal autonomy, individuality, and free expression. Many radical students, in other words, have a profound pessimism about the chances for democracy, personal freedom and peace (for an empirical demonstration of this pessimism, cf. Westby and Braungart, 1970); this pessimism, however, leads toward activism rather than withdrawal because many are convinced that the probable future is not a necessary one. The events of the past four or five years have overwhelmingly confirmed their sense of the main social drift, but what has sustained the impulse to act has been the rapid growth of resistance among many in their generation.

Briefly, then, our argument to this point has been something like the following: the expansion of higher education in our society has produced a social stratum which tends to rear its children with values and character structures which are at some variance with the dominant culture. Affluence and secure status further weaken the potency of conventional incentives and undermine motivations for upward mobility. The outcome of these processes is a new social type or subculture among American youth—humanist youth. Such youth are especially sensitized to injustice and authoritarianism, are repelled by acquisitive, militaristic, and nationalistic values, and strive for a vocational situation in which autonomy and self-expression can be maximized. They have been politicized and radicalized by their experiences in relation to the racial and international crises, and by the failure of established agencies of renewal and reform, including the universities, to alleviate these crises. They also sense the possibility that opportunities for autonomy and individuality may be drying up in advanced technological societies. One of the reasons that their political expression has taken generational form is that older ideologies of opposition to capitalism and authoritarianism have failed in practice.

We have also been saying that, although it is clear that the situation of these youth is enormously different from the situation of educated youth in underdeveloped countries, there are important analogies between the two. Both groups of youth confront the problem of discontinuity between family tradition and the values of the larger society. Both confront major problems of vocation and adult identity. Both confront political systems which are stagnated and repressive, and find few resources and allies external to themselves as they attempt to change that system.

There is a final issue in the comparative analysis of student movements that I want to raise. In our discussion of the classical movements, we suggested that the appearance of such movements was a clear sign that processes of fundamental social and cultural change were at work, and that these movements were not simply the result of certain pressures operating on a particular group of young people in a society but more importantly were indications that traditional, agrarian society was being transformed by processes of industrialization and modernization. It is clearly important to ask whether the appearance of student movements in advanced industrial societies are similarly signs that a new social and cultural era is struggling to emerge.

There are those who believe that the current crop of student revolutionaries is not the vanguard of a new social order, but rather, in the words of Daniel Bell, "the guttering last gasps of a romanticism soured by rancor and impotence" (Bell, 1968). In this view, student unrest in industrial societies is regarded as analogous to the protests of the first waves of industrial workers who resisted their uprooting by the machine. Now, it is argued, high-status intellectually and artistically inclined youth resist their incorporation into large-scale organizations—an incorporation which, nevertheless, is as inevitable as was the imposition of the factory on the rural lower classes.

Such a view does implicitly recognize that a major social transformation may be in the making. What I find objectionable in it is the implication that the new radicalism of the young is irrelevant to the nature of that transformation.

An alternative view would emphasize the possibility that large scale social, political, and cultural changes are occurring, that these are reflected in the social origins and focal concerns of student rebels, and that the existence of student rebellion may be a determining feature of this process of change.

First, at the cultural level, the student movement and the new alienated youth culture appear to reflect the erosion, if not the collapse, of what might be called the culture of capitalism—that cluster of values which Max Weber labelled the "Protestant Ethic"—a value system which was appropriate for the development of capitalism and the entrepreneurial spirit but which has lost its vitality under the impact of the bureaucratic organization of the economy, the decline of entrepreneurships, and the spread of affluence. The erosion of this culture is reflected in the transformation of family structure and child-rearing practices, in the changing relations between the sexes, in the replacement of thrift with consumership as a virtue. As Schumpeter (1950) predicted many years ago, bourgeois culture could not survive the abundance it would generate. Thus, the cultural crisis experienced very sharply and personally by humanist youth really impinges on the whole society. It is a crisis because no coherent value system has emerged to replace what has deteriorated; but it is hard not to believe that the anti-authoritarian, experimental, unrepressed, and "romantic" style of the youth revolt does in fact represent the beginnings of the effort to create a workable new culture, rather than the "last gasps" of the old. Such a view gains support when one observes the degree to which the youth revolt has affected popular culture and attracted the interest, if not the total involvement, of large numbers of young people in this country and abroad.

A second major social change which underlies the student movement is the rise of mass higher education. If the student movement is any indication of the possible effects of higher education, then one might have the following expectations about the coming period. First, the number of people in the middle class with critical attitudes toward the dominant culture will rapidly rise. In my view, critical feelings about capitalist culture—particularly negative attitudes toward symbols and ideology which support competitive striving, acquisitiveness, narrow nationalism, and repressive moral codes— are enhanced by exposure to higher education. Such feelings are further reinforced by entrance into occupations which are structurally not bound into the private, corporate economy—for example, occupations associated with education, social service, social planning, and other intellectual or human service work. These occupations embody values which tend to be critical of the culture and of the going system and tend to have an ethic which emphasizes collective welfare rather than private gain. It is important to recognize that the current student activists were born into the social stratum defined by these occupations, and many students with activist sympathies end up in these occupations. Data collected by Lubell (1968) show a general tendency for students oriented toward such occupations to move toward the left, politically. In a certain sense, then, the student movement may be seen as an outgrowth of a new level of occupational differentiation, i.e., the development of a distinct stratum organized around these occupations. This stratum is one of the most rapidly growing occupational sectors, and its political impact can already be seen, not only on the campus, but in such developments as the "new politics" movement during the recent elections. I am not arguing that this "new middle class" of intellectuals, professionals, upper white-collar workers, technical workers, public employees, etc., is politically homogeneous, or class-conscious, or radical. Indeed, it contains many antagonisms, and its participants are hardly ready for massive collective action, much less the barricades. But it does seem to me that the student movement, with its opposition to nationalism and militarism, its identification with egalitarian ideals, and particularly its opposition to bureaucratic and rigid authority in the university represents a militant version of the kinds of attitudes which are increasingly likely to prevail in the stratum to which I am referring. It seems particularly likely that the spread of mass higher education will mean increasing pressure against bureaucratic forms of authority and for "participatory democracy" within the institutions in which the newly educated work. The political trajectory of the educated class will, in large measure, be a function of the responsiveness of the political and economic system to their deinternational policies, more personal autonomy and participation in decision-making, and a more authentic and humane cultural and public life. More Vietnams, more racial turmoil, more squalor in the cities, more political stagnation, more debasement of popular culture—in short, more of the status quo is likely to increase the availability of members of this stratum for radical politics.

One may continue at great length to enumerate other cultural and social changes which seem to be implied by the appearance of a student movement in our society. For example, it clearly signifies a process of change in the position of youth in the society—a change which involves protest against the subordination of youth to rigid and arbitrary forms of authority in the school system and in the general legal system, and which also may involve an extension of youth as a stage of life beyond adolescence (Keniston, 1968a). The student movement may also signify a general decline in the legitimacy of military authority and nationalist ideology—a decline associated with rising education levels, with changing character structure, and with the impact of mass communications.

My point in mentioning all of these potential cultural and social transformations is not to stake a claim as a prophet, but rather to urge that we take seriously the possibility that the appearance of student movements in advanced industrial societies really does signify that a new social and cultural stage is in the process of formation. A comparative perspective leads us to that hypothesis, because the classical student movements were, as we have suggested, just such signs. If we were to take the student movement sense, then we would, I believe, be less likely to assume the stability of our social and political order and the cultural system sustaining it, less likely to dismiss campus unrest as a momentary perturbation or a romantic last gasp, less likely to focus on particular tactics and bizarre outcroppings of the youth revolt. Instead, we would open up the intellectual possibility that our kind of society can undergo major transformation, that it can generate, as Marx anticipated, its own "internal contradictions" and "negations," and that the future need not be like the present only more so.

References

Altbach, P.
  1967   "Students and politics." Pp. 175–187 in Seymour Martin Lipset (ed.), Student Politics. New York: Basic Books.
Bell, Daniel
  1968   "Columbia and the new left." The Public Interest. (Fall): 61–101.

Ben-David, J., and R. Collins
1967 "A comparative study of academic freedom and student politics." Pp. 148–195 in S. M. Lipset (ed.), Student Politics. New York: Basic Books.
Eisenstadt, S. N.
1956 From Generation to Generation. Glencoe: The Free Press.
Flacks, R.
1967 "The liberated generation: An exploration of the roots of student protest." Journal of Social Issues 23 (July): 52–75.
1970 "Who protests: The social bases of the student movement." Pp. 134–157 in J. Foster and D. Long (ed.), Protest! Student Activism in America. New York: William Morrow and Company.
Glazer, N.
1968 "Student power at Berkeley." The Public Interest. (Fall): 61–101.
Hofstadter, R.
1966 Anti-intellectualism in American Life. New York: Vintage.
Keniston, K.
1968a "Youth as a stage of life." New Haven: Yale University (mimeo).
1968b Young Radicals. New York: Harcourt, Brace and World.
Lipset, S. M.
1968 "Students and politics in comparative perspective." Daedalus 91: 97–123.
Lubell, S.
1968 "That 'generation gap'." The Public Interest. (Fall): 52–60.
Parsons, T.
1962 "Youth in the context of American society." Daedalus 91: 97–123.
Peterson, Richard F.
1966 The Scope of Organized Student Protest in 1964–65. Princeton: Educational Testing Service.
1968 The Scope of Organized Student Protest in 1967–1968. Princeton: Educational Testing Service.
Schumpeter, J.
1950 Capitalism, Socialism and Democracy. New York: Harper and Bros.
Skolnick, Jerome
1969 The Politics of Protest. New York: Simon and Schuster.
Westby, D. and R. G. Braungart
1966 "Class and politics in the family backgrounds of student political activists." American Sociological Review 31 (October): 690–692.
1970 "Activists and the history of the future." Pp. 154–183 in J. Foster and D. Long (ed.), Protest! Student Activism in America. New York: William Morrow and Company.

Student Rebellion as Ritual [1]

Robert Endleman

Human beings need to live by myths and illusions, and need some kind of ritual expression of the agonies and ambiguities of their life experience. New complexes of such myth and ritual—i.e. religious movements—appear at particular points in history. Under changed conditions, an old complex of myth and ritual decays. It fails to meet people's psychological needs, fails to give coherent meaning to their existence, fails to provide resonant forms of collective symbolic action, and fails to show exemplars of a healthy state of the soul. It is during these periods of history that new religious movements arise.

This is such a time.

In the socially and culturally chaotic conditions of the late twentieth century, a multitude of new religio-expressive movements are coming into being. Many wear a secular guise; one is "New Left" radicalism in the Western industrialized nations. This paper is devoted to the major ritual invention of this movement—the campus rebellion—and its associated mythology.

The development of a religious movement follows certain characteristic processes. Many similarly situated individuals experience a roughly similar state of malaise. They have similar diffuse and imperfectly articulated anxieties, confusions, and aggressions, which cannot be expressed through established social rituals. These feelings relate in an unclear way to changes occurring in the contemporary surrounding culture, social structure, or technological or ecological milieu. Some individuals begin to set forth *ideas* that begin to crystallize their hitherto unarticulated feelings. They or others also begin to improvise new forms of *action,* largely symbolic in form, and some of these "catch on"—i.e. they resonate well with some of the prevailing, unexpressed feelings. These improvisations are added to, refined, elaborated, and developed, as more individuals with similar underlying conflicts and anxieties join in. From improvisations they move to increasingly stylized and repetitive patterns of symbolic action. This is done less by conscious design than by a kind of unconscious collective dynamic. Correspondingly, the set of associated ideas becomes increasingly developed and stylized, and increasingly remote from critical judgment and reality-testing—

[1] The themes sketched in this paper are developed in fuller detail in a forthcoming book-length study, *The Ritual of Student Rebellion.*

i.e. they become a *mythology*. The pattern of stylized, repetitive, and largely symbolic action that emerges—although it may not be recognized as such—constitutes essentially a body of *ritual*. Although its practice may also have tangible, practical consequences, it functions primarily as a gratification of expressive needs. These needs in turn are given a focus and a name, a set of controlling images, by the emerging mythology. Virtuosos of symbolic action appear—the innovators and organizers of *ritual*—as well as virtuosos of ideas—the articulators and systematizers of *myth*. These may be the same or different individuals.

In this process, similarity among individuals is transformed into communality, and a social aggregate becomes a communal group. The sharing of ritual and mythology cements these bonds, and the group then develops a commitment and a kind of expressive "vested interest" in preserving and disseminating the myth and the ritual.

The patterns just described appear to fit rather closely to what emerged in the "New Left" activism in the 1960s, with its development of a distinctive mythology (in the form of a secular ideology) and a major form of ritual invention, the campus revolt. This is not to deny that there were any rational or empirically realistic elements in the mythology or rational instrumental-political elements in the campus confrontations. Of course there were some of both, as there are likely to be in any religious movement. But the focus here is on the mythic and ritual elements.

Malaise

The psychological grounding of a religious movement is a commonly experienced *malaise* [2] among large numbers of similarly situated individuals. In this case they are university students in modern Western industrialized nations.[3] Not all university students, of course, were involved in this movement. The "activists" were only a small part of that substantial minority (estimated at about 40 per cent—*Fortune*, 1969, p. 9) who did *not* see the university as a preparation for a specific career. Perhaps only about a fifth of the activists appear to be potential active recruits into the ritual drama of

---

[2] I use this deliberately vague word, since no more precise term—such as *frustration, deprivation, apathy*—adequately conveys the range of feelings and vaguely apprehended reactions to the world that pervade the atmosphere to which we are referring. The specific psychodynamic constellation may be highly variable from one individual to another, as may the phenomenology of the experience. *Malaise* expresses a common denominator of all of these, a feeling that "the world is out of whack."

[3] Data drawn on here are mostly from North America; accounts from Western Europe show broad similarities. Cases in less industrialized nations seem to vary somewhat in background characteristics: cf. Feuer, 1969, and Ross, 1969, for India specifically.

confrontation, although in any particular event, the number of participants (at any level) may run as high as half of the student population. (Cf. Auger et al., 1969, Glazer, 1969, Seligman, 1969.) Specifically, the students who are most susceptible to participation tend to be academically brighter students from upper-middle to upper-class backgrounds, with fathers who are more frequently in the professions, and mothers who have careers, often in some humanitarian-service field, and with both parents being more highly educated than average. (Braungart, 1969a, Flacks, 1967, Keniston, 1967, 1968, Lipset, 1968, Somers, 1965, Watts and Whittaker, 1966.) The parents of the activist students are likely to be nonreligious, Jewish, or liberal Protestant, and very disproportionately, these students profess *no* religious affiliation themselves (Auger et al., 1969, Braungart, 1969a, Flacks, 1967, Lipset, 1968, Watts and Whittaker, 1966.) The parents are typically liberal, left-liberal, or radical in their political orientation. The parents of student activists are also likely to be permissive and egalitarian in their child-rearing styles, antiauthoritarian, respect the child's autonomy, and encouraging of his individuation and the development of a questioning attitude toward the world. Activist students are more likely than their colleagues to be enrolled in particular noncareer-oriented studies that are largely concentrated in the humanities and the "softer" social sciences. (Auger et al., 1969, Braungart, 1969, 1969a, Flacks, 1967, Keniston, 1968, Somers, 1965; and from France: Ellul, 1968.) The proportion of females among the activists may vary from about one-third to one-half, depending upon the level of participation, with fewer females being involved at the more extreme levels or in leadership positions. (Auger et al., 1969, Braungart, 1969a, Watts and Whittaker, 1966; and deductions from Avorn et al., 1969, Rader, 1969, Lipset and Wolin, 1965, and much other literature on the New Left.) [4]

What emerges is a portrait of a highly verbal, articulate, and sensitive minority of noncareerist "vanguard youth" from advantaged, socially aware, cosmopolitan backgrounds, largely deracinated from traditional Judeo-Christian religion, and products of, and participants in, the more "advanced" cultural trends of a sophisticated advanced-industrial world. For them, traditional religion has essentially decayed or is already dead: Judeo-Christian myths been eroded by the rationalism of a scientific-technical-industrial civilization. These students also show an ambivalent relationship to the official secular mythologies of their nation-state: adherence to its universalistic ideals combined with a great distrust of its specific institutional

---

[4] Since the various studies differ widely in their criteria for inclusion as *activist,* and many do not clearly distinguish between fully committed leader and strong supporters and peripheral followers, or between a revolutionary and a reform orientation; since some refer only to "big events" such as Columbia 1968, whereas others refer to a variety of universities, all of these generalizations are necessarily rough and approximate, presenting a synthetic composite picture where different studies are basically in agreement, at least in direction, if not precise proportions.

arrangements and the specific personnel in power. They are highly sensitive to the obvious gaps between official ideals and actual social conditions, especially on the issues of freedom and equality.[5] Their socialization has also given them a generalized suspiciousness toward all forms of authority. Their parents have displayed at least verbal concern with the issues of freedom, equality, and social justice, and have encouraged their children in taking a critical stance toward received and conventional opinion, as well as toward authority in general. These youngsters are also thus more likely to gravitate to these more culturally cosmopolitan universities that emphasize openness and relativism. A consequence of this is an intensification of feeling on the part of these youth, of a lack of fixity or certainty about anything, and a general quality of shapelessness to their lives.

Their stage in the life cycle, and the special amorphousness of their status of college student, also intensify their malaise, ambiguities, and anxieties. The extreme prolongation of sociological adolescence (or, more precisely, subadult status) has been noted by many scholars. (Cf. Berger, 1969; Keniston, 1968; Erikson, 1963; Goodman, 1960.) This is experienced especially by bright youngsters who have many years of college and post-graduate study ahead of them. For them the status of student is primarily negative: *not* a child or an adolescent; *not* an adult; *not* currently subject to the draft; *not* a gainfully employed worker. This feeling is further intensified for thoughtful and questing students who cannot at this stage decide what to do with their lives and will not commit themselves to any definite career that their talents could easily open up for them. Furthermore, the very ideals of a "liberal education" as propagated notably by a humanistic faculty intensify their anticareerist orientation, and thus contribute to the limbo feeling of shapelessness and lack of direction in their lives.

An entire complex of social and cultural changes, attendant upon advanced industrialism, combined with the especially conflict-ridden state of the whole social structure have combined to erase almost all points of fixity and certainty for youth in general, for college youth especially, and for these specific college youth in particular. It is thus hardly surprising that "alienation" [6] emerged as the chief ideological slogan for expressing the particular quality of shapelessness in the lives of these students.

---

[5] Youth is probably *generally* more sensitive to discrepancies of this kind, than are older people, as Kingsley Davis, 1940, set forth in a classic sociological formulation. Universally, Davis argued, in the nature of the life cycle, youths are more likely to take seriously and literally the ideal moral values of the society, than are the middle-aged, and especially so in a society in a state of rapid social change. Still this does not necessarily apply to all youths. It applies especially to the segment of youth we are concerned with here, for the reasons discussed.

[6] Significantly, a word of *religious* reference, historically, though the proximate sources for these students are secular, in Marxian and neo-Marxian literature.

The Crystalization of Secular
Myths and Rituals

New-Left activism, along with its complex of myth and ritual—neither explicitly recognized as such—the illusion of secular rationality had to be maintained—emerged in the 1960s as one kind of response to this widely felt malaise. All the constituent elements of this movement have their historical roots and antecedents, but the amalgam or configuration appeared (especially to the communicants) as something new bursting upon the world. The mythology and the ritual (in the participants' language, the theory and the praxis) are complexly interdependent: the mythology partially determines the aspects of the ritual; the ritual confirms and also modifies the mythology. For analytic purposes, they are presented separately here and in a schematic form that exaggerates the uniformity and coherence they showed in reality.

THE MYTHOLOGY

The basic elements of the mythology of this movement run roughly as follows:

Man is by nature good, with an inherent potential for beneficence, communality, and cooperation with his fellow men. Alas, however, he has become malformed and alienated by a corrupt society over which certain evil forces hold tenacious sway. These forces do so by brute power (through porcine agents, and an array of powerful, magical, destructive devices) and through intricate manipulation. The rulers of this society are vastly rich and determined to maintain their wealth and power. They enslave the powerless, and manipulatively co-opt their lackeys by providing them with a modest level of comfort and the illusion of prestige. By terror and military might they exert an imperialistic control over the poorer peoples of the world, both inside and outside their borders, and they ruthlessly suppress any efforts of the powerless to rise up and liberate themselves.

Within, the powerless are kept in a state of perpetual misery, as an ever-ready resource for the senseless production machine, and for the armies sent to fight overseas wars of suppression. The less destitute are kept enslaved by manipulation, tranquilized by useless gadgets, contrivances, and entertainments, routinized into mindless bureaucratic discipline, and brainwashed into illusions of freedom. The rulers keep their monopoly of power by their control over the military, the technological instruments of destruction (instant Doomsday at their fingertips), and over the ostensible, supposedly popularly elected "government" of the country. Most important, the rulers control the priests of the society, the putative wise men inhabiting comfortable retreats called universities. These priests, deceiving people into believing that they are defenders of freedom and independent spirit, are in fact agents of the same evil ruling powers. The priests provide their crafts for the techno-magics of the rulers to brainwash the innocent with their theological justifications of the existing order, and train the cadres of future technicians and lackeys for the ruling powers while they ruthlessly suppress their junior confreres who support real freedom for the young. This monastic or priestly order should be free, as it claims to be; it should be the vanguard of liberation. Among the masses of trainees under its tutelage are to be found eccentrics and malcontents who see through (or can learn to see through) the lies of the system—young people who by some circumstance have not been thoroughly brainwashed. They, along with their allies from the younger priests and mandarins, must and can bring together the masses of potential allies, drawn inevitably primarily from among the young. For only the young have not as yet thoroughly sold out to the ruling powers, and in them beats loudest the throb of man's innate potential for good and for liberation. The monasteries ("universities")—microcosms of the whole society—must and will be the vanguard of the liberation, which will begin with the overthrow of the corrupt power structure within the monasteries themselves and then spread to the entire society. The day of liberation is at hand! [7]

SIGNIFICANCE OF THE MYTHOLOGY

It is evident that this mythology can work to counter the malaise of the concerned and activist students. It provides a measure of certainty and meaningfulness to a world that otherwise abounds in confusions and contradictions. It does so in an acceptable, manifestly secular form, without reference to discredited or decayed transcendental allusions. It appeals to idealism rather than to crass self-interest. At the same time it promises egoistic gratifications in the notion of student power (meaning radical-student-power.) It provides a sweeping "understanding" of the past and the agonizing present, and promises a redemptive future. It counters the shapelessness of the late-adolescent and student roles by elevating youth (and specifically this kind of youth) to a central and redemptive role as the vanguard of a new, liberated society. It also presents an extreme simplification of the dramatis personae of the world into sharply etched heroes, villains, and dupes, focusing the intense moralism of late-adolescence and youth.

---

[7] Distilled from representative statements of "New Left" positions. Cf. Long, 1969, Luce, 1968, SDS, 1964; the subjects of Keniston, 1968; the many New Left position papers reprinted in Wallerstein and Starr, 1971; see also the dissection of the illusions and absence of reality testing in the Harvard New Left's beliefs in 1968–1969, in Kelman, 1970, where the "dreamworld" (mythology in the present paper) is documented in detail.

The Ritual

The central ritual is the full-scale campus rebellion. Its form is an apparently improvised ritual drama whose basic script is written by the dissident students, with the antagonists and subsidiary protagonists being coerced or manipulated or swept along by events into taking their appropriately heroic, villainous, or buffoonish roles, to fulfill what became, by the end of the 1960s, an essentially stylized and standardized drama. In its basic process-structure it follows four main stages: The Great Moral Issue, Confrontation, Climax, and Aftermath, the last being followed by a confused period of transition back to the first stage.

1. *The Great Moral Issue.* The powers-that-be commit some act that becomes the Great Moral Issue. They try to bar an outside speaker or they invite a "war-mongering" chemical company to recruit on campus or they try to discipline participants of an earlier protest or they "fire" a popular teacher. Many kinds of action may provide the spark. The fire of militant protest is ignited: the act is seen as the very embodiment of Evil; it must be protested and combatted. The ritual drama as morality play is set in motion. Initial Protest: an orderly public meeting, letters, broadsides, calls to action, peaceful picketing. Administrators respond with silence or "evasion." Protest escalates, adopts more obtrusive (still nonviolent and noncoercive) tactics: Awaken the campus. Push more and more students and faculty to take sides. Polarization begins. Increasingly lurid portrayals of the enemy's villainy and the victims' and protesters' moral purity are presented. Then: *The Incident* occurs—some misguided or ill-timed reaction by the administrators. This provokes a larger action by the activists, at first largely improvised, but leading quickly to stage two.

2. *Confrontation.* A massive disruption of a public event, the seizure of a building, a hostage taken: the Great Confrontation is on. Once taken, the step becomes a Point of No Return, quickly gathering masses of supporters and sympathizers. Civil disobedience escalates to distinctly illegal acts. The motley collectivity welds into a community of righteous taboo-violators. Numbers and emotional charge submerge (for a time) divergences among the participants. The élan of "liberation" of buildings generates an atmosphere of *Carnival* in a great exaltation of generational solidarity. The privatized self dissolves in communal ritual; for many it is happening for the first time in their lives. They discover the Group, the Movement, the Collectivity, submerging the tyranny of individual autonomy. They celebrate the abrogation of conventional constraint and traditional taboos. Chants and slogans, newly minted, fill the air. A great moral community is achieved.

The authorities, torn by conflicting feelings and advice, play their role. They hesitate and vacillate. The ritual rebels hold fast, progressively incapacitating more of the university. The Confrontation becomes more purposive and stiffly spined. The initial demands expand from three, to five, to ten, or more. Further grievances and dissatisfactions are discovered. Complete Amnesty for all the protesters (now in the hundreds) becomes a critical issue. The conflict escalates, involving and polarizing a constantly increasing part of the students and faculty, the administration, alumni, trustees, and, vicariously, an ever-widening public outside. The media make the event into a major public ritual. Some liberal faculty members attempt a negotiating or mediating role—in vain. A few faculty members align themselves as "heroes," siding openly with the dissidents. Many others are openly opposed, assuming "villain" roles alongside the administration, demanding strong counteraction. However, most faculty members are torn, partly sympathetic with the goals and ideals of the "radicals" but dismayed at the coercive and illegal tactics employed by them, and fearful of an imminent apocalypse of violent brutality. Their indecision marks them for roles as classic "fools." But progressively the indecisive faculty members become polarized to one side or the other, swept by the emotional drama of the events. Interminable meetings and caucuses take place on all sides. On the students' side, polarization has also proceeded apace. A portion of the students, declaring themselves a "rational majority," line up against the dissidents and try to sabotage the occupation: arguments, scuffles, and minor violence occur. More students join to support the dissidents' cause, and more and more find it impossible to maintain a neutral position. Attempted negotiations fail. Virtuosos of "praxis," hard-line radicals, emerge as the leadership among the building-occupiers, intent on their nonnegotiable demands. In response, the administration stiffens, and faculty "mediators" find themselves traduced by both sides. As tensions mount, some new provocative Incident finally determines that the administration has no other recourse but to call in the public authorities—the police. Thus arrives:

3. *Climax: The "Bust."* This is the high point toward which the whole ritual drama has been building. The Moral Community of the protesters, ignited by the initial Carnival, and sustained, enlarged, and deepened by the extraordinary common experience of days of occupation, cooperation, meetings, and especially the emotional charge of collective taboo-violation and the communal facing of physical danger—reaches its apotheosis in the actual arrival of the police and their violence. The bust, awaited for days and nights in an exhilarating shudder of terror-filled anticipation, becomes Reality. Many feel they would not have missed it for the world. The police more than fulfill the demonstrators' expectations in their violence against rebels and bystanders alike. All the while, the remaining "liberators" scream, shout, and chant, great choruses of ritual incantations against the cops— just the sacred-taboo obscenities most likely to spur the irrational frenzy of the foe. Calculational errors by the administration (e.g., grossly underassessing the number of building-occupiers) force a hasty revision of police

procedure. Disciplinary control over the cops by their own authorities breaks down. Left free to improvise, the cops unleash waves of irrational fury, and thus perform perfectly the role assigned to them by the radicals in the ritual drama: the "fascist pigs" of radical fantasy materialized into full bloody reality.

4. *Aftermath: Horror: Radicalization.* Physically defeated, the radicals emerge as moral victors. Horror engulfs the campus and much of the on-looking world. Martyrdom wins hundreds of converts to the radicals' faith. "They were right: this *is* a brutal fascistic police-state." "No more straddling fences: indifference does mean collusion. We must fight the system." A general strike is called, with vast support from this newly enlarged community of the faithful plus thousands of erstwhile neutrals who have by now moved to the "left." If it is late in the old ritual calendar (April or May), the whole institution may be in effect shut down for the rest of the monastic year.

Interlude. Later, moderates, not radicals, undertake "reforms" of the university. It is a slow and tortuous process. Outcomes of complex compromises and conciliations, the reforms are undramatic and not far-reaching. The radicals then cast about for new "issues" to start the ritual cycle over again. For most of the active participants, the aftermath dissipates the religious exaltation of community achieved during the Confrontation. Rituals of renewal are needed. The emergent elect of the movement hope to provide it, and try.[8]

These are the basic patterns of the ritual drama of student revolt. As with any nascent religious movement, the patterns are far from fully standardized at this point, allowing considerable improvisation and innovation in each specific performance of the rite. Some innovations become incorporated into future enactments of the ritual drama—"what we have learned from Berkeley (or Columbia, or Harvard, etc.)."

SIGNIFICANCE OF THE RITUAL

The significance of the ritual in relation to the preceding malaise of the major hero protagonists can be analyzed in three main contexts: the sacralization of aggression; the utilization of sacred-taboo language; and the emergence of communality.

[8] This schematic picture is based upon personal observations plus the documentary evidence available on the major campus rebellions of the 1960s. The best documented are the Berkeley disruptions of 1964–1965, and the Columbia crisis of 1968. Major sources for Berkeley are: Draper, 1965, Feuer, 1969, ch. 9, and Lipset and Wolin, 1965; for Columbia: Avorn *et al.,* 1969, Cox Commission Report, 1968, and the participant-observer memoirs of Kunen, 1969, and Rader, 1969. On the Harvard 1969 confrontation, see Kelman, 1970. In addition, news journals and general intellectual journals have all carried voluminous (and variably reliable) coverage and commentary on the campus disorders, which I make no attempt to cite systematically here. Other scholarly studies of specific aspects of the disorders, or on student radicals specifically, are cited at relevant points elsewhere in this paper.

Sacralization of Aggression. A major function, and hence appeal, of the ritual to the student "heroes" of its drama is to provide avenues of release for aggression derived from the varied frustrations and deprivations that contribute to the generalized malaise. With nondeliberate ingenuity, the ritual releases this aggression in such a way as to give it sanctity and righteousness. With the intense moralism of the righteous cause, the student heroes—especially the virtuosos—become immune to any sense of moral dilemma about their contribution to the violent denouement of the drama. The whole struggle is portrayed in absolute hues of blackest Evil and whitest Purity, in the familiar pattern of religious fanaticism. Clearly moral dilemmas are involved in the decision facing the administration, of whether or when to call in the police, and in any attempt to assign relative weights of moral responsibility as between student provocateurs and administrative decision-makers. But for the student participants in the ritual, and especially their leaders, no such moral dilemmas are even recognized. The extreme position is: we are right; therefore calling the police is entirely their moral responsibility. The resulting actual horrors and brutalities of the police bust "confirm" this view, since it is "they" and not "we" who are manifestly guilty of violence.

New Left mythology until late 1969 insisted on the nonviolent purity of its student heroes.[9] In that context, aggression must be expressed in other than overtly violent ways. It is expressed overtly in response to physical violence initiated by other students—there it is excused on the basis of "unavoidable provocation" by others, but still treated with some ambiguity, neither outright condemnation nor approval. Thus it retains the myth of New Left nonviolence. Verbal aggression, however, abounds. This is not considered as "violence" by the rebel heroes, neither is the major coercive use of force, which is the central action of the rebels: seizure of buildings, hostages, files, or the calculatedly outrageous stances toward the authorities. This kind of aggression is moralized and sacralized by rationale deriving from the mythology: this is the "only way to force the oppressors to change things, since all standard channels for dissent have proved to be fruitless." Or, the occupation of buildings is not wrong, since the "campus belongs to the students in the first place—this is *our* university."

Still, a major direction of the students' aggression is against themselves, through the indirect method of maneuvering the authorities into having "no choice" but to call in the police. Here we find a parallel to the method of

[9] The analysis of aggression patterns here refers to situations that prevailed in most campus rebellions until the end of the 1960s. After that there was escalation of manifest violence by the student protesters themselves. Abandonment of the nonviolent ethos by portions of the Left styling themselves "revolutionaries" (rather than "radicals") split off of some of these elements from a campus base and direction of their terroristic acts to outside the campus, as in the urban guerrilla tactics of the Weathermen faction of SDS. To preserve the historical context, I have left the text here (largely written in 1969) unrevised.

directing aggression against oneself through the agency of outside forces, found in such phenomena as the Mohave Indian "witch" who, in effect, commits suicide by progressively provoking his fellow-tribesmen to kill him.[10] Here it may rarely go to the point of getting student rebels killed (it finally did at Kent State and Jackson State in 1970), but the dynamics are similar, and no doubt the more extreme "radicals" welcome such martyrs.

The provocation of police brutality is a deliberate, conscious tactic (and in that sense rational-instrumental) on the part of the more dedicated true believers among radical leaders: "We'll force them to reveal their fascistic brutality and oppressiveness." This does not preclude, even for these leaders, that provocation has nonrational unconscious roots as well. For the followers, the provocation of the police is rarely a deliberate, conscious tactic, but appears as a regrettable consequence of the choices the antagonists make. Here, to be provocative probably feeds unconscious masochistic needs. How do we know? One may look at the emotional intensity concentrated on the anticipation of the "bust." Psychodynamically, the bust appears as the high point, the climax toward which the whole ritual drama is directed; if it were not, the more moderate elements among the building-occupiers would be better able to counteract the apocalyptic direction in which the intransigence of the "leadership" is clearly pointed. Instead, basically, the followers passively accept that direction. One may therefore presume that it meets some unconscious needs. In turn, the fulfillment of what must be basically a masochistic fantasy, by the actual brutality of the police, releases the verbal aggression of outraged invective, and intensified moral righteousness in the ritual participants, now clearly cast as innocent victims. The mythology is vindicated: we have felt that brutality of the "system" on our own heads and bodies.

Collective excitement of mass activity enables the individuals here to carry out activities of provocative, aggressive, and outrageous content and style that most would find themselves incapable of doing as separate individuals. But it is not only the collective sanction but the *moralizing* and *sacralizing* of these aggression-releases that makes them possible. That the means employed are coercive and infringe upon the rights of others with an equal claim as "members of the university community" is brushed aside in the waves of moral righteousness and indignation at the opposition.[11]

The ritual thus provides a focus and a complex channeling of aggression, and a moral and sacred mystique for its expression.

Sacred-Taboo Language. The language of ritual is stylized, dramatically hyperbolic, arcane, full of sacred-taboo words and expressions. This is also true of the language of confrontation ritual, which is also replete with the

[10] Compare Devereux, 1961.
[11] Other psychodynamic connections of these processes are developed in Endleman, 1970, and in a forthcoming larger study, *The Ritual of Student Rebellion.*

sacred-taboo, in the form of what the conventional society calls obscenities. "Bullshit!" "Motherfucker!" become sacramental invocations, which depend for their effect not so much on their denotative meaning, as on their connotative and contextual aura. In the Confrontation, the use of these words becomes a defiant badge of rebellion, used for their shock effect upon the older generation, and especially the genteel academics.[12] Much of this speech is clearly aggressive in intent.

Although at the manifest level, the obscenities are used connotatively and metaphorically, one can look at their denotative representations to find some of the latent content of the ritual of confrontation. "Motherfucker" reveals the obsession with the Oedipal situation. And "faggots, cocksuckers, and asslickers" reflect the struggle with the demons of failed masculinity. In effect, the rebels are saying, not we, but they (cops, administrators, the enemy) are guilty of Oedipal and homosexual crimes. And the ritualized chanting of these epithets at the police is precisely the kind of provocation— much more than any physical resistance—that drives the police to irrational fury, vented as brutality upon the rebels. "Sticks and stones can break our bones, but names can never hurt us," runs the children's rhyme. But deep down the rebels know this is false. Raised in families valuing verbal facility and the substitution of words for physical violence, they intuitively know the magical emotive power of language, and are here using it to the hilt, not all consciously, of course. The projection of Oedipal and homosexual guilt upon the enemy—especially the cops—suggests some of the deeper resonances of the rebellion.[13]

The Development of Community. A major function of ritual is to create bonds of communal solidarity by collectively shared symbolic action. This is clearly evident in the campus rebellion. Communal experience of ordeal marks the experience as consensualized ritual and provides the setting for cognitively structuring the whole event along the "correct" rhetorical lines, i.e., in terms of the mythology. The communal element here is salient enough to be consciously recognized as the high point of the whole experience, by great numbers of the participants. Avorn and his (Columbia University newspaper) *Spectator* associates devote a whole chapter to the emergent life-style of the "communes" within the "liberated" buildings of Columbia, entitling it (without any evidence of intended irony) "The Liberated Life." (Avorn et al., 1969, Chap. 6.)

> The takeover of the buildings had begun as a political tactic designed to bring about the goal of social reconstruction. It quickly evolved into the realization, on a small scale, of that very goal. The process of personal liberation was founded on a common existential credential—all

[12] Cf. Mark Rudd's "Bullshit" speech to the Columbia faculty (Avorn et al., 1969, p. 140).
[13] For further development of these themes, see Endleman, "Oedipal Elements . . .," *op. cit.*

the students in the buildings had placed their careers at Columbia in some jeopardy by joining the protest; a common tactic—confrontation; a common enemy—the administration; and a common set of immediate goals—the six demands. In addition, in the day-to-day conduct of the demonstrations, each student could feel that he was in direct touch with the sources of power and decision-making within the strike apparatus. This was accomplished through participatory democracy, a central element of SDS ideology. . . . Students could, within the strike context, *make the decisions that affected their lives.* [Italics in original] . . . Once the old social and intellectual patterns were shattered by the demonstrators, students were eager to create their own life-designs. The academic world would be resurrected later in the "liberation classes." But now the first order of business was to restore people's working and living relationships to a condition of humanity.

The communal cohesiveness in the student-controlled buildings began soon after each takeover. The students who occupied Low, for example, had developed considerable *esprit de bâtiment* as early as Wednesday evening. [i.e., within 12–14 hours after the occupation] . . . The spirit of the students in Low was partially derived from the distinction that the quarters they occupied were the *sanctum sanctorum* of Columbia University. [President] Kirk's offices had *de facto* been off limits for students of the University, except under extraordinary circumstances.

—Avorn et al., 1969, pp. 117, 118, 119

Here we see the dependence of communal solidarity upon the collective violation of taboo, further illustrated in the special élan of the students in appropriating the president's office, snooping for evidence of the remote god's personal life-style, as well as invading of his personal files. This was rationalized as a political act for the purpose of uncovering evidence of "secret collusive deals" with other "branches of the power structure"— military, governmental, and industrial.

The life-style developed in the occupied buildings was a mixture of carnival spirit, proliferation of busy committees, marathon ideological and tactical bull-sessions, and expressive and sexual liberation. Sexual segregation of toilets was abolished and privacy was almost totally abandoned. Nearly all of the restrictions and compartmentalizations of ordinary middle-class life were joyously overthrown in an ecstasy of generational and rebellious solidarity. Many of the participants were convinced that this was in fact "the revolution." [14]

Specifically ritual elements are recognized by the student-journalists documenting the Columbia events:

The occupants of the "liberated" buildings were not without their own traditions and sacraments. One night late in the occupation, the Pageant

[14] The acceptance of such illusion by bright students ordinarily committed to standards of rationality is an indication of the religio-expressive quality of the experience, sufficiently strong that even the *Spectator* journalists, whose book generally shows a remarkable degree of objectivity, are partially taken in by the illusions, as indicated in the preceding quotation.

Players, a group of street actors, came into Fayerweather Hall to perform "guerrilla theater" for the student strikers. A makeshift stage was put up in a large room, and the actors set their scene with a few painted cardboard props: a castle in a kingdom "very far from here." The story line was simple: the poor people of the kingdom were getting out of control, so the king and queen provided them with welfare, medicare and moldy bread, and sent them off to war. But once they were given guns, the people turned full circle and aimed at the king. The king resigned [*sic*], and the people stormed the castle and knocked it down. The room was packed with almost all of the three hundred students who were living in Fayerweather, and with the defeat of the monarchy they all began chanting, cheering and dancing wildly over the castle ruins. An effigy of Grayson Kirk was thrown into the middle of the room, and the strikers tore it to shreds as makeshift drums beat out a thundering rhythm. The students—many of them dizzily waving glowing candles—formed one long chain which snaked around the darkened room as the drums became louder and the tempo faster. [Followed by a description of the wedding performed on the spot, with the minister concluding, "I now pronounce you children of the new age."]

—Avorn et al., 1969, pp. 129–130.[15]

The impact of this communal solidarity upon an individual participant is poignantly shown in Dotson Rader's personal memoir of the Columbia uprising (Rader, 1969). Finding himself temporarily outside the building he had been co-occupying with other demonstrators for nearly a week, and hearing about the impending "bust," Rader frantically tried to get back into the building—in vain. He was deeply upset not to be in on the grand climax of the confrontation, not to be inside where he "belonged" with his comrades in the struggle. Prevented from entering the building, he managed, however, to join a group of students and faculty in the futile chain trying to block police entrance to the building. (Rader, 1969, pp. 131 ff.)

Thus, the ritual of the campus rebellion works to develop or intensify solidarity among the student participants. When brought to its "proper" climax of the police raid and its ensuing brutality, it can bring a major part of the student population of a campus into a great emotional wave of generational community. Erstwhile partial sympathizers are "radicalized," and former indifferents and "fence-sitters" are moved at least somewhat "leftward." Not to at least sympathize with and identify with one's age- and status-peers who have been subjected to so brutal an "oppression" comes to be felt as a kind of generational treachery. Thus, for the moment at least, the ritual functions to promote horizontal integration among large

[15] Where the *Spectator* journalists single out this guerrilla-theater incident as a specifically ritual element in the Columbia rebellion, I would carry the matter further and argue that the "rebellion" in its entirety partakes of this ritual and sacramental quality; "guerrilla-theater" as a genre makes a point of trying to break down the lines of distinction between theatrical experience and the "real world." This distinction appears to have broken down for the rebels in relation to the whole process of the rebellion.

numbers of previously fragmented or isolated individuals or groups. This reduces the "alienation" of privatized and encapsulated lives, while at the same time intensifying collective "alienation" from legitimate authorities and structures.

It may also, momentarily, promote some degree of vertical integration— i.e. integration between the generations, to the extent that the bust brings portions of the faculty into sympathy with the rebels, or provokes guilt-laden efforts on their part to be more responsive to the students' needs and demands in the future. However, any resulting alliances between (part of) the faculty and the rebel students against the common enemy (the discredited administration) are likely to be fragile because of discrepancies of "commitment" to the ongoing university, and of generational perspective. Rather the major integrative force exerted is horizontal, i.e., generational.

There are built-in difficulties, however, for this kind of ritual development as an emergent device for dealing with the manifold "religious" needs of the young. The drama is excessively dependent upon progressive escalation of the level of conflict in successive enactments. Such escalation then runs the risk of losing a portion of the converts as its irrationalist penchant toward violence by the students themselves and the suicidal potential of provoking armed agents of authority become increasingly manifest. The continuity of the ritual is also threatened by the transiency of any specific cohort of student participants: many of this year's "leaders" graduate, drop out, or are expelled: then what?

RELATION OF THE RITUAL TO THE UNDERLYING MALAISE

The ritual of student rebellion expresses and partially answers much of the malaise of its student protagonists. In place of the shapelessness or negative quality of the student status, the ritual places the students in a central and apparently decisive position in the ambiguous cultural complex known as the university. It works a symbolic status transformation of the students involved, providing them not with "instant adulthood" but with the illusion of instant power and centrality on a national, even international stage. In this respect, as in the importance of shared ordeal as a condition for the communality (at least momentarily) achieved, it shows some analogies to initiation ceremonies, especially those for males, found in tribal societies.[16] Against the limbo state of delay and the indefinitely prolonged "preparation for real life," the ritual of rebellion dramatically asserts the primacy of NOW! Against the passivity of the imbiber of learning, it provides ACTION that is designed to have an actual impact on the condition of one's life, and of the surrounding world. Against the split of intellectuality from "actual participation in the real life of the world," it asserts a fusion of "theory" and "praxis" in the way the ritual enacts and provokes a

[16] This aspect is developed in Endleman, *Ritual* . . . (forthcoming), Chap. XI. Compare Endleman, 1967, Chap. 4, for a general discussion of such ceremonies and their manifold meanings; cf. also Whiting et al., 1958, Young, 1965, Bettelheim, 1954.

confirmation of the associated mythology. Against isolation and interpersonal fragmentation, the ritual provides a highly emotionalized communality of sacralized taboo-violation, collective danger, and moralized
collective aggression against a visible and identifiable enemy. For many a
participant, it is the first time in his life, he feels really alive. The ritual also
provides a sacralized release for a variety of rages and discontents and
achieves all these results in the guise of a rational secular action that gives
the illusion of actually doing something concrete to combat the injustices
and oppressions of the world.

It is an essential condition of this ritual that it be the creation of the
young themselves. The same conditions that foster the development of a
broader complex of youth culture, with assured subsistence and comfort,
ample leisure, and freedom from "adult responsibilities," also facilitate the
development, by a portion of these youths, of their rituals and ceremonials.
Old faiths and practices decayed and the older generation discredited for
the "mess they have made of the world," or "their failure to effectuate the
ideals they profess," the young feel they must take things into their own
hands. And what could be more fitting for the sophisticated children of the
television age than to stage their rituals as exciting morality drama before
an audience of millions? Their skill in thus utilizing the mass media is un-
deniable; at last they are being *taken seriously,* not only coercing the older-
generation antagonists into playing roles assigned them by the young, but
compelling the attention of a vast audience "out there in the real world."

Still, as enactment of fantasy, this is ritual. The "revolution" brought into
being in the "communes" of "liberated" buildings is an illusion. The
mythological "oppression" of students must be provoked into reality by the
ritual of rebellion itself. The moral absolutism of the central protagonists
obfuscates the complex realities of the actual world in which they live. The
"power" attained by the rebels during the ritual revolt—a huge university
ground to a halt—proves to be temporary and illusory. The objective
impact on the larger "power structure" of the society is either negligible or
is in a direction opposite to the announced intentions of the rebel leaders.
Thus a frenzied need is generated to renew the ritual in intensified and
escalated forms.

The secular guise and the lack of clear transcendental reference points
vitiate the beliefs and practices as mythology and ritual. At the same time
the irrationalist and illusionary elements vitiate the instrumental politics
that the rebellion pretends to be.

Epilogue, Late 1971

Most of the foregoing was written in late 1969. Since that time—especially
after the Kent State and Jackson State events of May 1970—student revolts

along the pattern of the late 1960s have abated. (Still, the extent to which this and other turbulence of the 1960s caught social scientists off guard should make us cautious of making any prediction that the rebellions are now a thing of the past.) If the analysis in terms of ritual has any cogency, then we should now have to say that it was an *aborted* ritual that failed because of the instability of its escalationary and illusionary drives, and the inherent conflict between its illusions and the attempt at a secular appeal. But since there is no evidence that the *needs* for ritual and mythology among the young have in any way abated, one can expect the young to turn in still other directions, perhaps with even more irrationalist content and style.

References

Auger, Camilla, Allen Barton, and Raymond Maurice
    1969   "The Nature of the Student Movement and Radical Proposals for Change at Columbia University." Paper presented at meetings of the American Sociological Association.

Avorn, Jerry, and associates (staff of Columbia U., *Spectator*)
    1969   *Up Against the Ivy Wall: A History of the Columbia Crisis.* New York: Atheneum.

Berger, Bennett
    1969   "The New Stage of American Man: Almost Endless Adolescence." *New York Times Magazine,* Nov. 2, 1969, pp. 32–33, 131–136.

Bettelheim, Bruno
    1954   *Symbolic Wounds: Puberty Rites and the Envious Male.* New York: The Free Press.

Braungart, Richard G.
    1969   "Family Status, Socialization and Student Politics: A Multivariate Analysis." Paper presented at meetings of the American Sociological Association.
    1969a *Family Status, Socialization and Student Politics: A Multivariate Analysis.* Ph.D. Dissertation in Sociology, Pennsylvania State University.

Cox Commission
    1968   *Crisis at Columbia.* New York: Random House (Vintage).

Davis, Kingsley
    1940   "The Sociology of Parent-Youth Conflict." *American Sociological Review.* Vol. 5, pp. 523–535. (Also in Bobbs-Merrill Reprint, S-67.)

Devereux, George
    1961   Mohave Ethnopsychiatry and Suicide. *Bureau of American Ethnology. Bulletin, 175.* Washington, D.C.

Draper, Hal
    1965   *Berkeley: The New Student Revolt.* New York: Grove.

Ellul, Jacques
    1968   "The Psychology of a Rebellion. May–June, 1968." *Interplay.* Vol. 2, No. 5, pp. 23–27.

Endleman, Robert
    1967   *Personality and Social Life*. New York: Random House.
    1970   "Oedipal Elements in Student Rebellions." *Psychoanalytic Review*. Vol. 57, No. 3, pp. 442–471.
Erikson, Erik H. (ed.)
    1963   *Youth: Change and Challenge*. New York: Basic Books.
Feuer, Lewis
    1969   *The Conflict of Generations*. New York: Basic Books.
Flacks, Richard
    1967   "The Liberated Generation: Exploration of the Roots of Student Protest." *J. of Social Issues*. Vol. 23, No. 3, pp. 52–75.
Fortune (Magazine editors)
    1969   *Youth in Turmoil*. New York: Time-Life Books.
Glazer, Nathan
    1969   "The Jewish Role in Student Activism." In *Fortune, 1969, op. cit.* pp. 94–107.
Goodman, Paul
    1969   "The New Reformation." *New York Times Magazine*, Sept. 15, 1969. pp. 32–33, 142–155.
Kelman, Steven
    1970   *Push Comes to Shove*. Boston: Houghton Mifflin.
Keniston, Kenneth
    1967   "Sources of Student Dissent." *J. Soc. Issues*. Vol. 23, No. 3, pp. 108–137.
    1968   *Young Radicals*. New York: Harcourt, Brace & World.
Kunen, James S.
    1969   *The Strawberry Statement*. New York: Random House.
Lipset, S. M.
    1968   "The Activists: A Profile." *The Public Interest*, No. 13, pp. 39–51.
Lipset, S. M., and S. S. Wolin (eds.)
    1965   *The Berkeley Student Revolt*. Garden City: Doubleday (Anchor).
Long, Patricia (ed.)
    1969   *The New Left: A Collection of Essays*. Boston: Porter Sargent.
Luce, Phillip A.
    1966   *The New Left*. New York: David McKay.
Lyonns, Glen
    1965   "The Police Car Demonstration (Berkeley): A Survey of Participants." In Lipset and Wolin, 1965, *op. cit.*, pp. 519–529.
Rader, Dotson
    1969   *I Ain't Marchin' Anymore*. New York: David McKay.
Ross, Aileen D.
    1969   *Student Unrest in India*. Montreal: McGill-Queens University Press.
Seligman, Daniel
    1969   "A Special Kind of Rebellion." In *Fortune, 1969, op. cit.*, pp. 13–30.
Somers, Robert H.
    1965   "Mainsprings of the Rebellion: A Survey of Berkeley Students in November, 1964." In Lipset and Wolin, 1965, *op. cit.*, pp. 530–558.

Students for a Democratic Society
  1964   *The Port Huron Statement*. New York: S.D.S.
Wallerstein, Immanuel, and Paul Starr (eds.)
  1971   *The University Crisis Reader*. New York: Random House, 2 vols.
Watts, William, and David Whittaker
  1966   "Free Speech Advocates at Berkeley." *Journal of Applied Behavioral Science*. Vol. 2, No. 1, pp. 41–68.
Whiting, John W. M., et al.
  1958   "The Function of Male Initiation Ceremonies at Puberty." In E. Maccoby, T. Newcomb, and E. Hartley (eds.). *Readings in Social Psychology*. New York: Holt, Rinehart and Winston, 1958. Variously reprinted, e.g. in Endleman, 1967, pp. 294–309.
Young, Frank W.
  1965   *Initiation Ceremonies*. Indianapolis: Bobbs-Merrill.

Section VI

Youth
and Drugs

INTRODUCTION

This final section deals with the most widely discussed and, at times, the most disturbing aspect of modern youth behavior. Whenever youthful idealism and its potential for creating a better, more civil, and humanistic society are debated, skeptical minds, however otherwise hopeful they may be, point to the widespread patterns of drug use among modern day youth and suggest that Utopia will surely not emerge in the next generation. Within the politics of drug use, few of the larger public, namely the older generation, can be convinced by spiritual, mystical, hedonistic, or existential rationales that widespread drug use is useful, uplifting, or necessary for individual and social well-being. And although this may be perceived by the young as the hypocritical attitudinizing of their elders, since drug use is prolix in postyouth age groups as well, adults remain dismayed and troubled by the dramatic increase in the magnitude and variety of drugs ingested by the young during the last decade.

In fact, the likelihood of becoming a drug user, occasional, habitual, dependent, or addicted, is highly correlated with youth. With the exception of the unusual circumstances of accidental medicational habituation and the occupational addiction of a small percentage of physicians and nurses, most drug use begins during the time of youth. Drugs, then, tend to be a potential problem of youth and later, as they grow older, may become a problem of their adulthood.

Although patterns of drug use have begun to shift, the kinds of drugs used and, thus, the types of use patterns effected, are largely a function of the social class and the age of the user. For example, the use of heroin and marijuana was previously the domain of the lower class; heroin use is still largely confined to the lower class with only slight diffusion to the middle classes, whereas marijuana has emerged as the favored, most widespread used drug in the middle classes. Synthetic hallucinogens, such as LSD, are mainly a middle-class drug; amphetamines, barbiturates, and tranquilizers also tend to be middle-class drugs. As youth become older, their drug patterns also change. Glue-sniffing is the drug of the very young (median age twelve), marijuana use begins a little later, whereas hard narcotics, hallucinogens, amphetamines, tranquilizers, barbiturates, and alcohol all tend to begin during late youth, and drugs taken in combinations also begin later in youth.

Whether drug use begins as a result of specific interactional conflicts (Alexander) or larger, complex societal forces (Winick and Gioscia), patterns of drug use evolve primarily within various subcultural contexts and social groups. Drug use is rarely an individualized act; much of the support, encouragement, and defense against legal authority and sanction is played out among users in mutual interaction and assistance to one another (Mayer and Von Hoffman). And a large part of the drug experience

418

not only rests on the physiopharmacological quality of different drugs, but also depends considerably on the definitions, expectations, and "guidance" one receives from fellow drug users.[1]

Indeed, the widespread use of drugs has not only turned our attention to the dynamics of drug use and its determinants but has also made it necessary to weigh the impact of this process on social institutions and social change in future generations. Thus, moral disapproval has been tempered by a lessening of legal sanctions. As drug use is conceived more as a disease and less as a form of criminality, we also become aware of the criminalistic by-products of overpowering dependency and addiction. In sociopolitical terms, this may eventually augur a new, perhaps revolutionary, set of innovations in the legal status and treatment approaches to the drug user, particularly since many personal and social tragedies begin and end in youth.

[1] See: Howard Becker, *Outsiders* (New York: The Free Press, 1963). Esp. Chap. 3, "Becoming a Marijuana User," for an extensive discussion of this process.

Alcohol and Adolescent Rebellion *

C. Norman Alexander, Jr.

Deviant Responses
to Cultural Proscriptions

When people find psychologically gratifying behaviors that have poten-tially disruptive consequences for the social system, norms must arise to regulate activities in the area. If absolutely negative sanctions effectively eliminate widespread incidence of these behaviors, then total proscription is an efficient and simple means of maintaining social control. However, when a sizeable proportion of the population is motivated and able to deviate from the norm, then strict prohibitions may actually increase the disruption that results from these behaviors. For to "condemn and forbid" both prevents the emergence of more realistic means of achieving normative *regulations* of behaviors and, also, explicitly identifies the kinds of behaviors that can function to express rebellion against or rejection of social authority.

Societies encounter this dilemma in many areas of human behavior, but the normative regulation and social control of the use of alcoholic beverages provide a particularly striking example. In the Jewish culture norms regulate and ritualize the use of alcohol. By contrast, among Mormons, moral norms of total abstinence from alcohol preclude the societal regulation of drinking patterns, if any Mormons drink. The possible consequences of these norma-tive differences are well illustrated by contrasting the drinking patterns in the two cultural groups.

Among Jews alcohol serves a ritual function; its use is normatively regu-lated, integrated into the social life of the community, and associated with activities which emphasize the social solidarity of the group. While most Jews use alcohol, problem-drinking is rare.

Among Mormons, where drinking is strongly condemned by moral sanc-tions, the use of alcohol is not merely a matter of individual deviance, but a threat to the maintenance of group values. The Mormon who drinks does so in a normative milieu that defines his behavior as deviant and casts him

From C. Norman Alexander, Jr., "Alcohol and Adolescent Rebellion," from *Social Forces,* The University of North Carolina Press (Vol. 45, No. 4, June 1967), pp. 542–550. Reprinted by permission of the publisher.

* This analysis was conducted under a grant to the author from the Division of Alcohol Problems and General Welfare, General Board of Christian Social Concerns of the Methodist Church. I am indebted to Ernest Q. Campbell (principal investigator, National Institute of Mental Health Grant M-4302) for the use of these data and to the Institute for Research in Social Science, University of North Carolina for provision of facilities for the analysis.

in the role of the "horrible example." Abstinence norms both preclude the integration of drinking activities with other social behaviors in the community [1] and define the drinker role in terms of the very behaviors that are most conducive to individual and social disorganization.[2] It is not surprising to find that Mormons, while less likely to use alcohol, have an extremely high rate of problem-drinking.

This interpretation implies that the relevant differences between Jews and Mormons are due to the differential normative integration of drinking behaviors within the patterned social life of the two groups and to the differences in the role defined for drinkers. If an individual in an abstinent environment begins to drink, unfortunate consequences are likely to ensue— because he is engaging in normatively unregulated, deviant behaviors oriented toward a role-image defined in terms of socially disapproved and personally dysfunctional behaviors.

Bales [3] has suggested another possibility, one which links the dysfunctional consequences of drinking to the factors responsible for the initiation and continuance of the behavior in an abstinent environment. He has reasoned that abstinence norms may actually encourage the use of alcohol as a means of symbolic aggression against social authority.

> The breaking of the taboo becomes an ideal way of expressing dissent and aggression, especially where the original solidarity of the group is weak and aggression is strong. Thus total prohibition sometimes overshoots the mark and encourages the very thing it is designed to prevent. This situation is frequently found among individual alcoholics whose parents were firm teetotalers and absolutely forbade their sons to drink.[4]

This hypothesis views much abstinence-oriented drinking behavior as a form of rebellion against society and those who symbolize the authority of the normative order. The dysfunctional consequences of such drinking (as seen among Mormons, for example) could be attributed to its *anti*normative and *anti*social character rather than to the *non*normative nature of the social situation. Those who are frustrated by their social situation and who are provided no socially sanctioned outlets to relieve this frustration may well develop hostility toward the social order. If they drink, they may do so precisely because drinking serves both to relieve their tensions and to symbolize their aggression against society.

[1] Robert Straus and Selden D. Bacon, *Drinking in College* (New Haven: Yale University Press, 1953).
[2] Jerome H. Skolnick, "Religious Affiliation and Drinking Behavior," in Richard L. Simpson and Ida Harper Simpson (eds.), *Social Organization and Behavior* (New York: John Wiley & Sons, 1964), pp. 432–439.
[3] Robert F. Bales, "Cultural Differences in Rates of Alcoholism," in Raymond G. McCarthy (ed.), *Drinking and Intoxication* (Glencoe, Illinois: The Free Press, 1959), pp. 263–277.
[4] *Ibid.*, p. 268.

Unfortunately, this fascinating hypothesis, like so many other interesting hypotheses phrased at a total-societal level, is all but impossible to test empirically. More confidence in the "rebellious drinking" hypothesis would result if these behaviors could be linked explicitly to a general, social psychological theory and if, within a relatively homogeneous cultural setting, individuals could be located in social situations that roughly parallel the differences thought to be relevant between the Jewish and Mormon cultures. This paper attempts to accomplish this by exploring the rebellious use of alcohol by adolescent males in communities where abstinence norms are prevalent. The basic relationship to be considered is the adolescents' affective relationships to their fathers. First, the substantive and theoretical aspects of the situation will be discussed; then relevant data will be presented.

Adolescent Rebellion and Defiant Drinking

Drinking may represent an expression of hostility toward the normative authority of the total society; and, similarly, it may provide a means for expressing aggression against an individual who symbolizes that authority. This seems particularly likely to occur in the case of an adolescent and his parents, for the adolescent's parents—and, especially, his father—are to him the primary representatives of social authority. They are the immediate sources of reinforcement for normatively regulated behaviors and serve as the foci of his strivings for independence.

During the period of adolescence many children appear to aggress directly or indirectly against the authority of parents. While this takes many forms and usually concerns matters of privileges, proprieties, and tastes, perhaps the majority of disputes arouse more emotion than their importance would seem to justify. Even though the adolescent's hostility may be temporal, the behavioral and orientational patterns that he forms during this period may well persist beyond the conditions of their origins. Probably, most of these are unimportant. However, if orientations toward the use of alcohol are established in connection with rebellion against parental authority or with deliberate intent to defy parental proscriptions, the future consequence may be quite serious.

If rejection of parental authority includes the deliberate defiance of parentally supported abstinence norms, then the adolescent's current and future drinking patterns are likely to be affected by orientations toward alcohol as a symbol of rebelliousness and personal independence. Drinking may become a behavior that is symbolic of defiance of authority; it may become an expression of rejection of the normative demands of the social order and of those who enforce them.

Origins of the antinormative orientations toward alcohol that Bales hypothesizes may well lie in such adolescent-parent relationships. Whatever the origin, however, the antinormative orientations toward authority that constitute the essential factor in the Bales hypothesis may profitably be examined in the context of adolescent orientations toward the father as the major authority-figure in the social environment. By concentrating on individuals who symbolize the normative authority of society, rather than on the total moral order itself, we can formulate hypotheses that can be tested empirically with data on a relatively homogeneous cultural group.

These hypotheses can be derived from the social psychological theory of balance.[5] The theory postulates relationships among "person's" affective orientations toward an "other" and their co-orientation toward an important object of common relevance. It is hypothesized that "person's" positive affect toward "other" is directly related to their agreement in attitudes toward the relevant object of co-orientation. If we take "person" to be an adolescent male, his father can serve as "other" and his drinking behavior as an object of common relevance. We may then examine the implications of balance expectations for this particular situation.

Assuming that the attitude of the adolescent's father toward his use of alcohol is prior to and independent of his behaviors, we may formulate several expectations about the relationship between the adolescent's drinking and his affect toward his father. If the father adopts a permissive attitude toward the use of alcohol, we expect the adolescent to be likely to drink to the extent that he is positively attracted toward his father; correspondingly, the adolescent drinker should be more likely than the abstainer to have positive affect toward a permissive parent. If the father adopts a negative or abstinent attitude toward his son's use of alcohol, then the likelihood of the adolescent's drinking should relate inversely to his attraction toward his father; also an abstainer should be more positively attracted to an abstinent father than a drinker.

The crucial concern of present interest involves the temporal sequence in which changes of behavior and changes in affect occur when the father has an abstinent attitude toward his son's use of alcohol. We want to know whether drinking behavior is initiated as a consequence of negative affect toward the father or whether negative affect results from the disparity between the father's attitude and his son's independently adopted drinking behaviors. In the former instance we might view the adolescent as beginning to drink for reasons essentially unrelated to parental opposition—for example, because his peers pressured him to drink. In the latter, the adolescent could be seen as beginning to drink precisely because of the opposition of a parent whose authority he rejects.

Now it is obvious that there are many reasons why an adolescent might begin to drink, and data of psychoanalytic depth would be necessary to

5 Fritz Heider, *The Psychology of Interpersonal Relations* (New York: John Wiley & Sons, 1958).

support any claim that a particular individual began to drink in order to rebel against parental authority. Nevertheless, it is possible to compare adolescents' drinking behaviors in conditions under which they are differentially likely to be related to affective orientations toward the father. We shall assume that adolescent drinking is more likely to be related to rejection of an abstinent father if peer support for drinking is lacking.[6] In other words, (1) when his best friend drinks, the drinking of an adolescent is likely to be due to this peer influence rather than to his orientations toward parental authority; but (2) when his best friend abstains, this increases the probability that his drinking is related to rejection of an abstinent father. This assumption is reasonable; and, while it provides only a crude index to assess the differential relevance of abstinent parental norms, we shall find that it serves adequately to differentiate between drinkers so classified.

Drinking Behaviors and Attitudes Toward Alcohol

If an adolescent drinks as a consequence of rebellion against parents, his drinking patterns should show all of the "unhealthy" aspects that one would expect to be associated with rebellious, antinormative behaviors, behaviors which relate to problem-drinking in later life. It is anticipated that, when drinking is most likely to be relevant to abstinent parental expectations, adolescent drinkers exhibit potential problem-drinking patterns if they reject their father. Specifically, rejection of parents should be associated with frequent drinking, extreme effects experienced from drinking, and emphasis on psychological benefits rather than social factors as reasons for drinking.

Data were gathered from 1,410 males in 30 high schools in the spring of their senior year.[7] All of the schools were located in the Eastern and Piedmont sections of North Carolina, an area in which the dominant religious

[6] The importance of peer influence on adolescent drinking behaviors in an abstinent environment is shown in C. Norman Alexander, Jr., "Consensus and Mutual Attraction in Natural Cliques: A Study of Adolescent Drinkers," *American Journal of Sociology,* 69 (January 1964), pp. 395–403; and C. Norman Alexander, Jr. and Ernest Q. Campbell, "Peer Influences on Adolescent Drinking Behaviors," *Quarterly Journal of Studies on Alcohol* (in press).

[7] These data were gathered as part of a larger study, "Normative Controls and the Social Use of Alcohol," National Institute of Mental Health Grant M-4302, Ernest Q. Campbell, principal investigator. Questionnaires were given to 5,115 seniors of both sexes in 62 high schools selected to be representative of those in the Eastern and Piedmont sections of North Carolina. The sample in this paper includes only males in the 30 high schools that met the following criteria: (1) more than 15 males responded; (2) more than 95 percent of the males gave their names; (3) more than 90 percent of the males completed the questionnaire; (4) more than one-third of the males planned to go to college. The fourth criterion resulted in the elimination of only one school which would otherwise not have been eliminated. The criterion was included because there are certain data (in the larger study) available only for those adolescents who reported plans to attend college.

groups support moral norms of total abstinence from alcohol. The independent variables of primary interest, together with their operational definitions are: (1) Parental attitudes toward the adolescent's use of alcohol: When will parents give their permission for the adolescent to drink? [8] (2) Attraction-rejection of father: "How close is your relationship to your father?" [9] (3) Peer influence on drinking: Does the adolescent's best friend (his first-named choice on a "realistic" sociometric question asking for actual associations) drink or abstain—as defined by the friend's answer to the question: "Do you now (since the beginning of this school year) drink alcoholic beverages in any form?"

First, we are interested in whether or not the adolescent drinks as a function of his relationship to his father. Balance theory leads to the hypothesis that the proportion who drink will vary *directly* with positive attraction to parents who are permissive and *inversely* with positive attraction to parents who are negative toward the adolescent's use of alcohol. Table 1

TABLE 1. Percent of Adolescents Who Drink—By Parental Permissiveness and Closeness to Father

	Parental Permissiveness	
Closeness to Father	Permissive	Nonpermissive
Closer than average	59.3	29.7
	(27)	(381)
As close as average	44.8	31.9
	(29)	(517)
Less close than average	60.9	39.6
	(23)	(338)
$d_{xy} =$	.00	—.09

presents the data relevant to this hypothesis. When fathers are opposed to the adolescent's use of alcohol, the incidence of drinking is inversely related

[8] The actual question asked is: "Parents sometimes tell their children that when a certain time comes they can then decide things for themselves. On *drinking alcohol,* which of the following represents the way your parents feel about it—" Permissive: I can drink if I want to while I am in high school. Non-Permissive: I can drink if I want to when I graduate from high school . . . when I am 18 . . . when I am 21 . . . after I set up a home of my own. They'd never give their permission for me to use alcohol. Only parents who would presently permit the use of alcohol are classified as permissive, since granting permission to drink only after the attainment of a certain age-related status might well encourage the adolescent to view drinking as an independence-seeking activity. Since the number of cases in these categories is too small to permit separate analysis, it was decided to equate the concepts of independence-seeking and the more genuinely rebellious defiance of absolute parental prohibitions.
[9] The father of these adolescent males was the parental figure selected because the father is the primary authority figure in the family, and at least the titular head of the family insofar as disciplinary measures are concerned.

to the closeness of the adolescent to his father $d_{xy} = - .09$).[10] When the father is permissive, there is no linear relationship between attraction to him and drinking ($d_{xy} = .00$). This is contrary to expectations, but its interpretation must be somewhat equivocal, since "permissiveness" indicates only that parents do not oppose their son's drinking—i.e., a neutral rather than a positive attitude.

The small number of cases who have permissive fathers does not permit further analysis to determine the reasons for lack of confirmation of the hypothesis; and we are unable to introduce controls on the drinking behaviors of peers. Since this is a crucial variable in the analysis, we are forced to drop cases with permissive fathers and to consider in the following analyses only the behaviors of those whose fathers oppose their drinking.

To the extent that adolescents are negatively attracted to their abstinent fathers, they should legitimate the use of alcohol by their age-peers. This relationship should exist whether or not they drink, but it should increase in strength to the extent that parental factors are relevant. Thus, for both drinkers and abstainers the relationship between negative attraction to father and legitimation of drinking should be stronger when peer support for drinking is lacking.

Table 2 presents the percent legitimating drinking behaviors—by close-

TABLE 2. Percent of Adolescents Who Legitimate Drinking—By Closeness to Abstinent Father, Drinking Behavior, and Peer Support

	Drinkers		Abstainers	
	Best Friend		Best Friend	
Closeness to Father	Drinks	Abstains	Drinks	Abstains
Closer than average	32.8	25.6	19.0	6.7
	(61)	(39)	(63)	(163)
As close as average	32.6	38.7	16.0	9.8
	(89)	(62)	(75)	(235)
Less close than average ..	40.0	42.5	13.3	13.8
	(70)	(40)	(45)	(130)
$d_{xy} =$	+.07	+.15	−.09	+.16

ness to father, drinking behavior, and peer support.[11] Our prediction about the relative strengths of the relationships is confirmed: the relationships between closeness to father and legitimation of drinking are strongest in the

[10] Robert H. Somers, "A New Asymmetric Measure of Association for Ordinal Variables," *American Sociological Review,* 27 (December 1962), pp. 799–811.
[11] An adolescent is said to legitimate drinking behavior if he responded, "Yes, it's all right," to the question: "So far as moderate drinking by other people your age is concerned, do you think this is all right if they want to do it?"

absence of peer support (d_{xy} values of $+ .15$ and $+ .16$ compared to $+ .07$ and $—.09$). The direction of the association is positive, as predicted, in only three of the four columns, a curious reversal occurring when the best friend of an adolescent abstainer drinks. The percent legitimating drinking actually increases with increases in attraction to an abstinent father—a finding contrary to the basic expectation that legitimation of drinking will vary inversely with attraction to one who supports abstinence norms. Before proceeding with the major analysis, then, some explanation for this unanticipated reversal must be sought.

In attempting to account for these data, it was reasoned that adolescents who are negative toward an abstinent father and who experience peer pressure to drink are more likely to use alcohol—unless they have some additional reasons for abstaining (such as religious commitments or internalized, negative attitudes toward alcohol use). To the extent that they continue to abstain despite pressures from peers to drink and rejection of support for abstinence from parents, then their own attitudes should constitute the source of resistance to drinking. If this line of reasoning is correct, the negative association between closeness to an abstinent father and legitimation of drinking should decrease in strength (and become positive) with increasing pressures to drink from the abstainer's peers.

This possibility was examined by an additional control on *perceived* peer pressures to drink—each nondrinker being classified by whether he reported being urged or teased to drink by his friends. Table 3 presents the percent

TABLE 3. Percent of Abstainers Legitimating Drinking—By Closeness to Abstinent Father, Peer Support, and Experienced Pressures to Drink

Closeness to Father	Best Friend Drinks		Best Friend Abstains	
	Pressure	No Pressure	Pressure	No Pressure
	(41)	(22)	(94)	(69)
Closer than average	19.5	18.2	9.6	2.9
As close as average	17.8	13.3	9.6	10.1
	(45)	(30)	(136)	(99)
Less close than average ..	9.4	23.1	12.8	15.9
	(32)	(13)	(86)	(44)
$d_{xy} =$	−.15	+.03	+.06	+.31

of nondrinkers legitimating drinking—by closeness to his abstinent father, peer behavior, and experienced pressures to drink. These data support the rationale to account for the unexpected reversal of the relationship between attraction to an abstinent father and legitimating of drinking. When the abstainer does not report experiencing pressures to drink and his best friend abstains, the association between closeness to an abstinent father and legitimation of drinking is strongly negative. It remains negative, though weak, when pressures are reported and the best friend abstains and, also, when the best friend drinks and no pressures are experienced. But, when the abstainer reports pressures to drink and his best friend drinks, the relationship is positive. If we may presume that these reported pressures originate with the best friend, they should be immediate and intense. In this situation in order to continue to abstain the adolescent would require strong, negative attitudes toward alcohol to the extent that he rejected parental support for his abstinence.

Drinking Patterns

Let us turn now to consideration of drinking patterns and their relationship to negative affect toward the father. The present analysis suggests that *anti*normative rebellious drinking is directly associated with negative attitudes toward the father only if the adolescent drinks without incentives to drink from his best friend. When his drinking cannot be explained in terms of his best friend's influence, then it is assumed that affect toward father is likely to be relevant to the adolescent's use of alcohol. The drinking patterns to be examined are frequency of use, effects experienced, and reasons given for using alcohol.

First, however, we shall attempt to establish a more direct connection between the behaviors of drinkers and the rejection of abstinent fathers. Ideally, we would wish for data in which the adolescent insightfully recognized and reported drinking behavior as a function of rebellion against parental norms. In lieu of such data, the plausibility of the antinormative interpretation of drinking behaviors is supported by responses to the question: "Have you ever deliberately done something you weren't supposed to do as a way of getting even with your parents?" Though it does not specifically mention drinking, the question is precisely in the spirit of the "rebellious drinking" hypothesis and, importantly, it immediately followed the series of direct questions about drinking. Thus, it is reasonable to assume that the issue of alcohol use and its possible connection to rebelliousness was quite salient when respondents encountered this question.

Hence, among those who drink without peer support, we expect that there will be a strong relationship between rejection of father and the frequency with which they report spiteful disobedience as a means of "getting even" with parents. Table 4 presents the percent of drinkers who report frequent wrongdoing as one means of getting back at parents—by closeness to father and peer support. The data show that, when peer support for drinking behaviors is absent, there is a striking, inverse relationship between closeness to father and the reported frequency of spiteful disobedience ($d_{xy} = .32$). If the drinkers have peer support, the relationship is relatively weak ($d_{xy} = .05$).

TABLE 4. Percent of Drinkers Who Deliberately Defy
Parental Authority—By Closeness to Abstinent
Father and Peer Support

| | Best Friend | |
Closeness to Father	Drinks	Abstains
Closer than average	32.8	12.8
	(61)	(39)
As close as average	21.6	21.0
	(88)	(62)
Less close than average	37.1	42.5
	(70)	(40)
$d_{xy} =$	+.05	+.32

In order to use this measure as an independent variable in the following
analyses, cell frequencies make it necessary to combine cases who report
being average and above average in closeness to father. Since our major
interest centers in those who indicate some degree of rejection of father, this
is not especially serious. Thus, we may proceed to examine the relevant
behaviors and attitudes of drinkers as they differ by closeness to abstinent
fathers, support from peers for drinking, and the frequency with which
parents are spitefully disobeyed.

Table 5 presents the percent of drinkers who have used alcohol at least

TABLE 5. Percent of Drinkers Who Drank Last Month—By Closeness to
Abstinent Father, Peer Support, and Deliberate Defiance
of Parental Authority

	Best Friend			
	Drinks		Abstains	
	Deliberately Disobeys		Deliberately Disobeys	
Closeness to Father	Frequently	Infrequently	Frequently	Infrequently
At least average	61.5	67.9	38.9	51.8
	(39)	(109)	(18)	(83)
Less close than average	61.5	75.0	76.5	78.3
	(26)	(44)	(17)	(23)
$Q =$	.00	+.17	+.67	+.54

once in the month preceding the date of their responses to the questionnaires. When they are close to their fathers, drinkers lacking peer support
are less likely to use alcohol frequently than are drinkers whose best friends

drink; but, when the father is rejected, drinkers lacking peer support are more likely to use alcohol frequently. The relative strengths of the relationships between frequency of use and rejection of father are shown by the values of Yule's Q. As expected, when deliberately disobedient behavior is common among drinkers without peer support, the inverse relationship between closeness to father and frequent drinking is stronger.

Table 6 examines the percent of drinkers who have experienced at least

TABLE 6. Percent of Drinkers Experiencing Some Effects from Drinking—By Closeness to Abstinent Father, Peer Support, and Deliberate Defiance of Parental Authority

	Best Friend			
	Drinks		Abstains	
	Deliberately Disobeys		Deliberately Disobeys	
Closeness to Father	Frequently	Infrequently	Frequently	Infrequently
At least average	82.1	78.2	77.8	69.9
	(39)	(110)	(18)	(83)
Less close than average	80.8	77.3	82.4	78.3
	(26)	(44)	(17)	(23)
$Q =$	—.04	—.03	+.14	+.22

some effects ("I felt 'high' or 'gay' ") from their use of alcohol. Though differences are too slight to be very important, it is interesting to note that drinkers who reject and frequently disobey their abstinent fathers and who lack peer support are those most likely to have experienced effects from their use of alcohol. Positive relationships between effects of drinking and rejection of father exist only for drinkers without peer support, but differences between nonsupported drinkers reporting frequent and infrequent acts of spiteful disobedience are not in the expected direction. However, since "some" effect from drinking is hardly an indication of problem-drinking as a future-potential, we shall examine the percent among those reporting effects who have been drunk or passed out as a result of alcohol use.

Table 7 presents the percent of affected drinkers who have become drunk or passed out. It is clearly evident from this table that nonsupported drinkers who reject abstinent fathers and frequently disobey "to get even" with them are most likely to experience extreme effects from their use of alcohol. An association of $Q = + .64$ exists between the rejection of father and the likelihood of experiencing extreme effects for frequent disobeyers without peer support for drinking. Finally, we shall examine the reasons

TABLE 7. Percent of Affected Drinkers Who Have Become Drunk or
Passed Out—By Closeness to Abstinent Father, Peer Support,
and Deliberate Defiance of Parental Authority

	Best Friend			
	Drinks		Abstains	
	Deliberately Disobeys		Deliberately Disobeys	
Closeness to Father	Frequently	Infrequently	Frequently	Infrequently
At least average	31.3	20.9	14.3	10.4
	(32)	(86)	(14)	(58)
Less close than average	19.0	26.7	42.8	11.1
	(21)	(34)	(14)	(18)
Q = ...	—.32	+.10	+.64	+.04

given for drinking,[12] contrasting psychological benefits (i.e., drinking when
unhappy, bored, or troubled; in order not to be shy) with social reasons
(i.e., it's the thing to do; to be with the crowd). Table 8 presents these

TABLE 8. Percent Giving Social or Psychological Reasons for Drinking—
By Closeness to Abstinent Father, Peer Support, and
Deliberate Defiance of Parental Authority

	Best Friend			
	Drinks		Abstains	
	Deliberately Disobeys		Deliberately Disobeys	
Closeness to Father	Frequently	Infrequently	Frequently	Infrequently
Social reasons:				
At least average	26.3	24.0	22.3	36.3
	(38)	(104)	(17)	(80)
Less close than average	34.6	27.3	13.3	34.8
	(26)	(44)	(15)	(23)
Q = ...	+.19	+.08	—.33	—.03
Psychological reasons:				
At least average	42.1	31.7	41.2	32.5
Less close than average	50.0	34.1	66.7	34.8
Q = ...	+.16	+.05	+.48	+.05

[12] The question asked: "Check the *one best reason* why you drink: To be with the
crowd; I like the taste; When I'm unhappy, bored, or troubled; Because it's served at
home; In order not to be shy; It's the thing to do."

data. Frequently disobedient drinkers who reject abstinent fathers and lack peer support are least likely to drink for social reasons and most likely to drink for the psychological benefits provided by alcohol. Furthermore, the relationships between rejection of father and reasons for drinking are strongest among frequent disobeyers whose best friends abstain.

Summary

It has been shown that the likelihood of drinking and of legitimating the use of alcohol (in opposition to parental expectations) is inversely related to the closeness of the adolescent to an abstinent father. Furthermore, among drinkers who lack peer support for alcohol use, rejection of father is associated with frequent disobedience of parental authority in order to "get even" with them. And, when positive peer influence to drink is lacking, the rejection of parental authority (negative affect and frequent disobedience) is associated with frequent drinking, excessive drinking leading to extreme intoxication, and drinking for psychological rather than social reasons—all of these early drinking patterns being common in histories of problem-drinkers. In anticipating these results it was reasoned that drinking, when not due to positive pressures to drink, is a negative response, an expression of rebellion against the paternal authority figure.

The present data support Bales' hypothesis that drinking in a normative setting of abstinence is largely antinormative. Drinking in this type of social situation tends to become rebellious behavior when drinkers lack social support. Thus the high rates of problem-drinking and alcoholism among religious and cultural groups who promulgate abstinence norms may well be due to similar, socially aggressive drinking patterns. Other observers have examined differential rates of alcoholism, interpreting abstinence-oriented drinking behaviors as nonnormative (lacking social regulation), pronormative (adoption of the "horrible example" role-model), and antinormative (rebellious). This analysis has specified the "rebellion" hypothesis in terms of a more general social psychological theory and has subjected it to test in a relatively homogeneous cultural milieu in the context of father-son relationships. Hence, it has been possible to demonstrate that *anti*normative aspects of drinking are important in abstinence-oriented social situations and that this is certainly a significant factor in the high incidence of problem behaviors among those who drink in these social environments.

Some Reasons for the Increase in Drug Dependence Among Middle-Class Youths

Charles Winick

The last decade has witnessed a growing realization that an increasing number of middle-class youths have become drug dependent. In the last several years, many communities have reported substantial numbers of middle-class young people, some of them pre-adolescent, who were dependent on heroin. The "dope fiend" mythology is so potent that the realization of the possibility of heroin use among the young led to an extraordinary, almost national response; partly dismay, partly disbelief, partly denial, partly "what did we do wrong," and partly "what can we do about it?"

In reality, there was no real upsurge in heroin use nor in the use by middle-class young people of any psychoactive chemical substance. The 1960s represented the decade in which there was a greater awareness of drug dependence, but the prevalence of drug dependence in the 1960s itself represented the continuation of a trend that had begun shortly after the end of World War II in 1945.

The best available information on the incidence of drug abuse is that there are today between 16 and 17 million young drug dependents. Drug dependence appears to be increasing steadily each year. A wide range of substances is available, each of which appears to have some relationship to a particular age group. Thus, glue sniffing peaks from eleven to thirteen, marijuana use is common from fourteen to eighteen, amphetamine use is most common from seventeen to nineteen, and barbiturates and LSD tend to be used by young adults in their 20's.

We do not know how much drug dependence there is beyond the age of young adulthood because we have no valid large-scale information about the incidence of drug abuse outside of institutional settings such as schools, colleges, and the military, where there is regular contact with large numbers of young people.

The thesis of this paper is that there has been a slow to steady increase of drug dependence of many different kinds since 1945, and that this increase reflects a variety of developments in American social life. Awareness of these developments can help us to understand why so many American young people are dependent on psychoactive drugs without recourse to psychological or personality variables.

Original article, hitherto unpublished. First publication, in this volume, by permission of the author.

Ten significant changes in American social life are suggested as important contributors to the increase in the incidence and prevalence of drug dependence of middle-class youths for the last generation.

1. *Affluence.* The period beginning in 1945 represents the largest continuous period of general prosperity that this country has ever experienced. The few recessions that occurred have not seriously impaired the economy's forward movement. Such prosperity creates a subtle but important climate in which many middle-class youths feel that, not only are they unlikely ever to starve, but they are willing to "take a chance" on trying an illegal substance. Such youngsters feel that they will have a second and even a third chance if they get into difficulties as a result of their drug use.

2. *Changing Sex Roles.* The women's liberation movement is only the most recent and widely publicized example of the substantial changes in sex roles that have occurred during the last quarter century. One of the attractions of psychoactive drugs to a substantial proportion of their users is their degenderized nature. As one teen-age girl said, "Drugs are neither masculine or feminine."

Because psychoactive drugs may, in the view of a number of psychoanalysts, provide an "alimentary orgasm," they may offer a special attraction to youths who are overwhelmed and anxious about conventional genital sexuality. Drug use could be a "copping out" of sex-role expectations.

There has been a tremendous acceleration of the age at which young people, even preadolescents, are being bombarded with sexual stimuli, which may overload their sensibilities and be threatening and anxiety-provoking. On the other hand, by the time of adolescence, the concepts of masculinity and femininity are likely to be very blurred. What is and what is not masculine and/or feminine can no longer be identified very easily, in dress, leisure preferences, and in many other aspects of daily decision making. For a good many teen-agers, drugs have provided a convenient series of activities and interests that are degenderized.

3. *Need for Rituals.* Among the activities related to psychoactive drug use are many that are ritualistic and involve a shared secret language. Consider the techniques of drug buying and taking; in an America where rites of passage are so few, the ritual aspects of the drug scene could be very compelling. Freshmen and seniors, who are in role situations most in need of the support provided by group rituals, are overrepresented among drug-dependent youths.

4. *Vietnam.* Drug use among middle-class youths peaked in the mid and late 1960s, during our major involvement in Southeast Asia. Many young men, facing the possibility of being sent to Vietnam, felt that the conventional "deferred gratification pattern" was meaningless for them and were willing to experiment with the attractions of mood modifying substances.

5. *Rock Music.* Many early rock performers and writers, including

musical giants such as Bob Dylan and the Beatles, celebrated the psyche-delic effects of music, and the synergistic effects of listening to music while on drugs. Although Dylan and the Beatles, along with other performers, have since disavowed their earlier writings, those writings were influential in helping to influence and extend attitudes in favor of drug use by the young.

6. *Television.* Television became a national phenomenon in the early 1950s. The average elementary school student today watches television for three hours daily. A substantial part of those hours is devoted to watching commercials, which contain many messages about the variety of chemical products available for coping with everything from "nerves" to "housetosis." Such exposure could help to create an atmosphere of expectation about "better living through chemistry."

7. *Nonrationality.* Perhaps because rational thinking as applied to na-tional and international affairs has led to such a series of disasters, many middle-class youths have become pessimistic about the merit of rationality. They have sought out the immanent and experiential, stressed the sensibility over the intellect, and otherwise pursued authenticity. Drugs are widely believed to provide a shortcut to the dimension of the nonrational and to the "wisdom of the East," which is often related to drug use. As young people have explored new life styles that question conventional values such as rationality and order, they have sought out drug experiences.

8. *Competition.* Our society is younger than ever, with a median age of twenty-seven. One implication of this reality is that today in this country there are more young people at every age than ever before. Wherever a young person turns, he sees many others competing with him for the same goals, such as school placement or grades or job training opportunities. One way of dealing with this competition is to "drop out" of it by drug use.

9. *Reward for Illness.* Many middle-class teen-agers were brought up in homes in which there was almost a reward for being ill. Their parents over-medicated them, as young children, and helped to make them relatively comfortable about the illness role. As a result, they are favorably conditioned to self-medication and are good potential consumers of psychoactive sub-stances.

10. *Risk-Taking Behavior.* Our society offers the middle-class youth very little in the way of legitimate forms of risk-taking behavior. For some middle-class youths, drugs represent a special attraction *because* they in-volve so many risks: health, the possibility of arrest, and other potential hazards. Part of personality development involves the constructive assump-tion of challenges and tackling new situations. Where a society provides few opportunities for facing challenges and taking risks, some young people will enter the social system of the drug user.

We are suggesting that these ten reasons contribute substantially to the epidemic of drug dependence among middle-class youths today. If this is so, conventional "drug education" programs will be of little effect because they are only concerned with symptoms rather than the underlying causes. Three of these reasons have already begun to be less operative—affluence is turning to recession and price and wage fixing, the war in Vietnam is "winding down," some rock musicians such as Donovan and Sonny and Cher have written antidrug songs. And if some of the other dimensions cited become less operative, we may see the beginning of a decline in the incidence and prevalence of psychoactive drug dependence among middle-class youths.

Faust in the Hashbury

Milton Mayer

A doctoral dissertation by a University of California sociologist reveals that every hippie in the Haight-Ashbury district of San Francisco has now been interviewed 12.32 times by University of California sociologists, whose uniform conclusion is that a Flower Child—you grow 'em, we throw 'em— is a white American with dirty feet who thinks that love is wonderful. And an exhaustive investigation by a team of Stanford psychologists discloses that last summer's influx of 250,000 teeny-boppers (or cub hippies) failed to materialize because word had reached them that all of the previously available pads in the Hashbury were now occupied by priests in plain clothes assigned by their bishops to outreach, empathize, and identify.

The hippies are this season's a-go-go conversation piece. They have the cheapest come-on yet, requiring for its raw materials nothing but the totems and taboos of primitive American society. In such a society you have only to do what comes unnaturally on a twenty-four-hour show-and-tell basis, and you have it mesmerized.

Like the hippies, I was an attention-getting device in my childhood, but I do not recall that I got the attention after I'd cut my second teeth. When I was "high," my old man told me to get out and come back when I could behave myself, and when I was "down" he told me to get out and come back when I could be sociable. Ma dropped me in the suds every night and got my farina down me; Pa honed his razor-strap on me pretty regularly; but they had their own little lives to "lead," Pa on the streetcar with his paper-box samples and Ma over the washtub in the basement. Pretty soon I'd grow up —or I wouldn't—and be off their backs and they could settle down to a little serious cribbage.

From Milton Mayer, "The Young: Their Cause and Cure II: Faust in the Hashbury," from *The Progressive* (The Progressive, Inc., Vol. 31, No. 10, October 1967), pp. 29–33. Reprinted by permission of the publisher.

My kids, in contrast, have their second teeth into me. *Mea culpa.* Instead of beating them lightly and sending them to the salt mines to earn their own dime for the movie, I bought their sulks and their pets, celebrated their birthdays instead of the saints' and the martyrs', and took them on bum trips so that they could have the advantages of the Profligate Society. But I wouldn't let them out of my arms. In desperation they had to jump for it and land on their heads in the Hashbury, the great post-adolescent temper tantrum.

Their only motivation, and it isn't a bad one, all things considered, is to be what I'm not and to drive me wild. Listen to Mr. John J. Thompson, the twenty-two-year-old tyke credited with the Dirty Word outbreak in Berkeley: "I was trying to arouse adults"—your hippie is the World's Oldest Teenager—"to the fact that a four-letter-word like "kill" is respectable and mine isn't." Why use a five-letter-word like "louse" to indict a loused-up society when a four will do?

By subjecting my analyst to rigorous examination I have been able to recall, dimly, that when I was an adolescent (at seventeen, not twenty-two) I was red-hot to "find myself" by means of experimentation. (I never did.) Ma and Pa said that what I was doing was looking for trouble. They weren't; they'd found it. Me too, now. Now I deplore all experimentation.

The difference between my kids—it's yours I'm talking about, not mine— and me is that I accepted my parents' values while mine reject mine. Of course I violated the values; I was just as reprobate as my kids are. The difference is not in the violation; it's in the rejection.

The hippie rejection is a spectacular discontinuum in an age whose hallmark is discontinuity in practice and continuity in pretense. The Wild Flower Children are on a berserk search for the orthodoxy we pulled out from under them and the humanity we surrendered when we surrendered the liberal arts for the straitjacket of specialization.

Nothing visible defines a hippie except (in the male) the six inches of hair that have us all shook up. (The female is only slovenly.) There are a few thousand of them strolling the country's Hashburys, and a few of them on every campus (where their coevals admire them). And more than a few million marching to their anti-success anti-music. In the Hashburys they are dropouts by choice; the bright ones, not the future Marines and used-car salesmen. They are nearly all hopheads, but a majority of them hit it weekends (as we do the bottle), a minority evenings, and only a hard-case few full time. These last (in Haight-Ashbury) favor a joint called the Drog Store, where they spook the Flower Children, who don't like what they see in the Drog Store mirror.

There are communes in Berkeley, but the hippies are outside the University of California protest movement (or "syndrome"; you can't get into Berkeley without saying "syndrome"). The Berkeley syndrome is orthodox rebellion against orthodox repression. Hippies are not orthodox rebels. They're runaways. They couldn't care less—which means (if you know your

Buber) that they couldn't love at all, because the opposite of love is indifference, not hate. They are irresponsible.

The responsible citizens who spawned them, and whose responsibility consists of Supporting Our President, Our Local Police Force, and Our Boys in Vietnam, hope that they will come back and settle down on the burning fuse under the wall-to-wall carpet. They won't. They have enrolled, for a season, or for all seasons, in the College of Soft Knocks to study their own (and one another's) navels. When the navel shrivels for want of sustenance, they go back more resentful than ever to hook the innocents they left behind them. I have never met an ex-hippie, only some who have had to land to refuel.

Almost none of them has dropped *off* his parents' backs. Remittance children, playing with poverty and driving Mom and Dad up the wall by getting pasty on a diet of pasta. "My little one"—age twenty-two—"isn't taking care of himself."

You bet he isn't. The free Hashbury clinic in San Francisco, making "contact," like the padres, had just under ten thousand visits June 9–September 5. Its unpaid doctors were amazed, not at the incidence of gonorrhea (up fourfold in five years) but at the prevalence of caries and malnutrition and the universal susceptibility to upper respiratory infections. If the Flowers bloom until they're sixty they won't smell as good as they do now—not even to each other. But they're betting on not having to live to be sixty.

Don't ask them where they're going: "We live where we are." But Mom and Dad live there with them, on *their* backs (as our ancestors live on ours). What we are drives them to the Hashbury, and when they get there, there we are in mournful spirit "bringing them down." Alas, no pleasure without pain: The dreadful truism, as it drives us to drink, drives them to drug, and when they sober up their devils are waiting for them; and so on to the next trip to Nirvana by way of Nepenthe. And the intervals between trips, as the pain abates the pleasure, grow shorter in the Hashbury as they do everywhere else. To live on pleasure is to live off capital.

Sensuality, with its by-products, is all there is to hippieism. There isn't a trace of asceticism or self-denial in it. But happiness is an abiding state of the soul, not a jolt to the central nervous system. Sensuality's pay-off ends when the trip ends, when the money ends, when the law begins, when the VD gets you, when you have to feed both the chick *and* the child, when the draft board calls.

Until then it's a ball.

A costume ball; but whoever wore a costume except to be seen in it? You preen in your pad and hit the street. So even before it ends it operates on appearances, psychedelic or just plain carnival. Like all mummery, it is based on antithesis. No "straight," no "groovy." The symbiosis (ah, there, Berkeley) has us living off each other. We sorrowful clowns wear our paint, they theirs.

Are they having a good time at the ball? Because if they are, what would you, even I, even Faust, not give to be invited? The intrepid sociologist gets himself an invite. After the "trip," usually on marijuana, he remembers that the conversation was brilliant and the good feeling pervasive. (The dry-ball at the cocktail party found the din unbearable, the conversation witless, and the feeling antagonistic.) "You have no idea what it"—or, I suppose, suicide—"can do for you until you've tried it. You can't *understand*."

With *son-et-lumière,* who doesn't see through a bar glass brightly? But color and noise, as they approach excess, maximize pleasure to the point of pain. Eyes and ears hurt. The characteristic hippie expression is joyless, his decibel panic a painful retort to the sonic boom and the Musak and the mis-sile. A good time? Their powers atrophying, they're as deadly as Dean Rusk, suffering solemnly even when they're jumping to the tom-toms in their jungle.

LSD's effects are "unpredictable," and the Mafia, up from L.A. and Vegas to "service" the neighborhood, adulterate it with cocaine and heroin to expedite the addiction. The straight world's scary analysis scares the part-timers off it. But the full-timers are no more to be scared than their parents by the "unpredictable" effects of booze. Marijuana (or Mary Jane) is *physiologically* non-addictive—but your gone junkie usually began on it. By virtue of its being forbidden (one to ten years in most states) the hippies have sown its seeds across the country; sampling puts its campus use at ten to fifteen per cent of the college students.

Legalize it and its use will *not* decrease (any more than whiskey's) if it assuages an unbearable pain. There is no way to get at the junk but to get at the pain. We and our ambitions "for them" have made our kids' lives unbearable. I don't suppose that we are going to change our lives—*comme nous, le deluge*—and without changing our lives we cannot make life bear-able for our kids.

"All empirical investigations indicate that alcohol constitutes a far greater social danger than marijuana." The sick physician goes on to rebut the hippie campaign for the legalization of marijuana by reciting the horrors of alcohol. Does the sick physician conclude that alcohol ought to be illegal-ized? Not on your life. The sick physician needs a drink, the sick salesman a bottle, the sick Senator a case.

"You have your poison," says the hippie, "and I have mine, and mine is cheaper and quicker." But booze is defensible by the species' addiction to it: The drink and the drinker exercise a mutual control. The sauce is a sub-sidiary—however absolutely necessary—of a life lived sober. The drinker (unless he's shot) does not use drink as life itself and does not, therefore, have to develop a compensatory illusion about life. When he sobers up he knows that it was his bladder, not his brain, that was expanded.

Like booze, dope releases the cultural inhibitions, but, like booze, it in-duces a euphoria that is antiaphrodisiac. A team of seven hundred Columbia sexologists (on a Ford Foundation grant) found that there is less fornication (and masturbation) in the Hashbury than there is on Nob Hill (or at Columbia); and a team of one nonsociologist (on a *Progressive* grant) found that the male hippie, already in rebellion against anthropoid American virility, grows ever more sinuous as the female grows more strident and aggressive. What draws the chick from Peoria is the bed-hop, and what sends her from bed to unsatisfied bed is the dream of being happily unmarried. She winds up emasculating the male; the modern Delilah leaves him his hair. Hippie homosexual experimentation likewise has a platonic patina; the genuine fag (whose capital is San Francisco) cruises the Hashbury disappointed.

No wonder the hippies never laugh sober; nor would we if we had their sweet candor. A municipal judge, continuing a case against a hippie, said to the defendant, "The next time you come in here, take those stupid beads off," and the hippie replied, "I will if you'll take that stupid necktie off." Their candor has produced the only humor to be found nowadays on the American scene, in the form of the two-bit buttons that have made American Button Consolidated rich. (Even the slogans now come out of the gag factories. But it was the hippies, who have quit wearing the buttons, who gave the racket its saturnine spur.)

"JESUS SAVES GREEN STAMPS," "I AM A HUMAN BEING—DO NOT FOLD, SPINDLE, OR MUTILATE," "THE GOVERNOR OF ALABAMA IS A MOTHER," "SUPPORT MENTAL HEALTH OR I'LL KILL YOU," "WEAR PINK UNDERWEAR AND AVOID THE DRAFT," "SMOKING IS SAFER THAN BREATHING," "GOD IS A TEENY-BOPPER," "KILL A COMMIE FOR CHRIST," "ANASTASIA, HITLER, JUDGE CRATER, STALIN, AMELIA EARHART, TROTSKY, DRACULA, AND GOD ARE ALIVE AND WELL IN TRANSYLVANIA," "DON'T MASTURBATE— FORNICATE," "DRAFT BEER—NOT STUDENTS," "HELP STAMP OUT THINKING,"—this is social commentary, as savage as Swift's and a lot more cryptic.

Hippieism is seductive to the whole rising generation except for the Young Americans for Goldwater, and all addicts (of anything) are pushers; the teeny gets a free drag on a reefer. Its variants are world-wide, and the "existentialists" of Paris, the mods and the rockers of London, and Moscow's guitar-playing "hoodlums" are at least as old as the domestic variety. Alienation is inheriting the earth, and there is no more communication between the young and the old than there was between Marx's bourgeois and his proletariat. There is only exploitation. Haight Street is "shamelessly" panhandled from end to end and the mendicant Diggers feed their kind from the back door of the supermarkets. In the Profligate Society it's a gas.

They won't work; but to say that they're lazy is wrong: nobody's *that* lazy. They will sleep the clock half-way around and arise only to resume their languid tomfoolery. What they are is paralyzed. They want so badly not to work that they can't. In the straight world the "American ethic" of work has given way to work for a Tiffany tiara. The pursuit of the tiara gets you a coronary. Why let Khrushchev *or* your wife bury you? Why see Naples and die? What's Naples got that Mary Jane hasn't?

They animate each other in a desultory way. As you go panting past them on your way to get an extension of the mortgage or a prescription filled for your (or their) cough, you catch snatches of their patter: "Pure molecular energy . . . beyond Maya . . . selective expansion . . . inner participation . . . self-realized reality . . . opens you to God . . . the *thing*ness of the thing . . . *That's* IT, man . . ." But your presence, even in passing, is a "roadblock." If you pause, as you pass, they're paralyzed, like toddlers conspiring to steal the jam.

The trouble with the paralyzed life is that man does not live by day-old bread alone. The grass and the acid cost money. The cars cost money (Hippies "don't feel like walking"). Rent, VD, bail bond, Pills, boots (fifty bucks for a groovy pair) cost money, and the money has to come, one way or another, from that good old Togetherness chump, your old "pal," Dad. The consequence is the demimonde life of deception. In order to get what it takes, you have to promise the old folks whatever they want and "do your thing" on the sneak. The art of the independent hippie is the wiliness of the dependent.

One of the Founding Fathers of hippiedom told me that not one "kid"— they're all "kids" to one another—has been drafted from the Hashbury in the three years he's been there. How do they beat it? Not by splitting the scene for Canada, but by faking addiction, "psych," or "homo." "The easiest way is to show up and put on a freakout. Just scream or go glassy. There's nothing they can do. It's *too* much."

They're not above whimpering: The duplicity is imposed upon them by the straight world with its idiocies. And they are idiocies, the draft law among them. But courage to stand up to them is outside the Hashbury lexicon. The truest-blue hippie would rather switch than fight. He's a pacifist; see? Besides, "A fellow's got to live."

And not just live, but live creatively. Their creations are created when they're high, "out of the psychedelic experience." They paint and they tootle and they strum; none of them writes, unlike the beatniks of not-so-old. Here's a sympathetic art critic's try at one of their art shows: "Robert Comings is the house psychedelic painter, in the form of diamond-shaped canvases with a base of prismatic radii and microscopic cell-shapes shooting out from a God's eye, and an overlay of gynecological anatomy, plus a hair bird and what looks like a snake." Dali did it better, and sober.

If you have to be high to create it, you have to be high to dig it. You're not, and they are. "What's he doing?" I asked, of a male writhing in front of a group. "He," I was told, "is *with* it. He gets *to* them. It's so—so—." "It's so what?" "So—so—*immediate*."

In a world whose thermonuclear creation consumes all its others, non-creation may have something to be said for it. The Void may have been a nicer place to visit than the Gracious Monterey Peninsula of California, which ten thousand hippies invaded last summer for an acid-rock festival. The gracious boobs were scared silly. They hired a million extra coppers and actually hid the National Guard in the Armory. By the time the festival was half over the coppers had been canned and the Guard disbanded under cover of night; and when it was over the Monterey police chief testified that there never had been so orderly a gathering.

One way to have the straights on is to keep them off balance. The sugar-cube set even cleaned up their litter before they left Monterey. The Hell's Angels saga is even more marvelous: Nobody, but nobody, has been able to make contact with the demonic Angels on their stolen "bikes," but the hippies got to them (with acid) and now they're the Hashbury bodyguard. At Monterey they had their own watchful encampment on the hill above the festival, to protect their friends from the bewildered fuzz; and when an Angel was killed in San Francisco, the Grateful Dead played a "big music" memorial concert. Or: When the San Francisco Health Department raided the Hashbury, its inspectors came back with the disheartening report that ninety per cent of the violations they found were in domiciles occupied by the same family for ten years or more. There are a thousand ways to bug the straights.

The hippies don't go to Mississippi. They don't go to Hunters Point (which is San Francisco's Watts). (Every Negro seventh-grader in San Francisco's integrated Roosevelt Junior High, in an essay, "My Thoughts on the Hippies," said, "They're dirty.") They don't go to the demonstrations or the sit-downs or to Vietnam or to Head Start or Hind Most or the Peace Corps. They don't, in their argot, "go to the opera." They go where it's beautiful, man, beautiful.

"They don't care." Oh, but they do; they care for Careless Love. But what they love is themselves and their pleasuring, so their love doesn't mean much more than an alley cat's. A little more, perhaps; the chant itself is enchanting. But they're hung up on the theological error of angelism: they cannot face the hard-rock reality of conflict, in others or in themselves. But it's there—they wouldn't be hippies if they weren't indignant—and their passive hostility comes smiling through. It proceeds by provocation. They turn up their *Hare Krishna* until it brings the cops. They glide down to Market and Mission Streets, where their regalia gets them beaten up by sailors; one way or another they get themselves stoned. Their acute consciousness that they're bugging the straights approaches paranoia. ("They hate the hippies.")

Love is the fruit of agony, never ripened, never ready; not wanting, but willing, the good of the other. Up and down Haight Street the listless Lovers go, their ankle-bells tinkling to notify some shepherd-to-be that they're there. They hold their warm kittens to them; happiness is a warm kitten, and a cuddle a commune. A commune not of Lovers but of fun-Lovers, like Palm Beach, the Tuileries, and the Winter Palace. Outside the commune are the ashes of their fathers and the temples of their gods. Outside are Hunters Point and Vietnam. Outside is man killing and being killed and killing himself; death is the straights' bag. Their jewelry includes all kinds of icon, but never, ever, a representation of the Passion.

But Christianity without the Cross is not the invention of the hippies. It is the invention of the Church Triumphant, perverting grace to gratification and reason to the reasonable. The hippies have turned upon grace and reason, taking the perversion for the pure. Buddhist non-attachment "interests" them, and they carry those old Buddhists, Kirkegaard and Hesse, around with them. But they don't read; unlike the Buddha, they have no attention span sober. So they smoke their wild oats, sow their poppyseeds, spin their bright cobwebs, and grunt their starved vernacular. (As children of fifteen they had two adjectives, "neat" and "keen"; as adolescents of twenty-five they are down to one, "groovy.")

They will tell you that theirs is a religious movement, a kind of Immobilize for Christ. Uninvolvement—can't you see Christ uninvolved, man? —is its watchword. Until you find yourself you cannot be involved. Involvement conceals existence. Becoming stunts being, and what the straights take for being is nothing but becoming. Be by letting your consciousness expand and letting go of compunction. Leave the sordid "static" of tribulation and despair behind you. Find yourself.

The straights wag their hard heads: Life finds you, Hunters Point finds you, Vietnam finds you, the landlord finds you, the electric light company finds you, the draft board finds you, the VD finds you. Monday morning finds you.

There's no Monday morning in the Hashbury. Monday morning is the Lost Weekday.

I have known a few of these transfiguration pushers fairly intimately. After two or three years of acid-rock they are just about what they were two or three years ago, or ten or fifteen, when they came bouncing into the house hollering, "School's out!" A little less bouncy. A lot less responsive. And an awful lot less considerate of the everyday "straight" amenities (like taking one of their flowers to an aged lady). The quick-change artists— Look, Mom, no crucible—have yet to produce the quick change. The psychedelic color has yet to produce the blinding flash of the road to Damascus.

They're giving us a bad time, when what we want, and all we want, is a good one. But what we want is no more attainable than what they want. What we have done is reproduce our kind, with pinwheels. We ought to be thankful for the privilege they afford us of seeing ourselves in caricature. We ought to be afraid that they'll pass.

Maybe they will. We have the money, and with the money we have them by the long hairs. We pay the Jefferson Airplane $5,000 for a concert and the Grateful Dead $10,000 for a recording; and then we sit back and wait for Old Corrosion to take effect. Some "groups" fall apart; others start talking about getting out of the "phony" Hashbury and moving to the Russian River up north, or to Santa Fe, or New York. Somebody wants more than somebody else, somebody else a Red Mustang or a groovier pair of boots. They get high on *our* poison, too: Last summer's non-hippie looting spree on Fifth Avenue had as its objective a shop that sells $56 alpaca sweaters. "If you've got one," said one of the non-hippies, "you fly, you really know what's happening."

We keep telling ourselves that they won't endure. Maybe they won't. They're bucking all the odds—not only Old Corrosion. There is no such thing as free love, no hedonism on the cheap, no going up without coming down, no getting more out of life (or less out of death) than there's in it, no chemical compound to retard human spoilage, and not even an unsure cure for the mortal affliction of Adam. The right answer is Yes to the question, "Is this all there is to it?"

That doesn't mean that they won't spread. Their "let it happen" is the token of their flexibility. They have brains and feeling and guts enough to have tried to make some sort of break. But as long as we go on over-reacting to them, we'll keep them fixed in their follies: "The hippies," says one "liberal" columnist, "are a distasteful and meaningless collection of misfits . . . totally dependent upon dope for their philosophy, their religion, and their escape." As sticks and stones won't break their bones, so names will never hurt them. Nor will banalities like, "Pot is the car key Dad wouldn't give him." Dad *did* give him the car key, so pot must be something else. Pot is Dad, to whose bag the hippies are a reaction, not a revolution.

How can they help doing more good than harm? All they have to do is do what Dad won't do and refuse to do what he does; what he does does more harm than good, and what he won't do would do more good than harm. The CBS man concluded his Big Report on hippies with, "Granted the short-comings of our society. Nevertheless—." Oh, grant the shortcomings of our society quick, and get on to the nevertheless. Tell us all about the horrors of LSD; we already know more than we want to know about the horrors of LBJ. No credit to the hippies, then. All credit to us. We are, in reverse, the measure of all their things.

If they blow up, or drift off, we'll be exactly as happy as we are the day after the tanks shoot down the riots in Newark and Detroit. We won't have to hear about *them* any more. But what caused them—you and I—will still be there. We are better do-it-yourself technicians than the Romans: We are our own barbarians. If the Flower Children wilt, they will be succeeded by something much less presentable, much less entertaining, and much more expensive. Their bacchanalia will have been a charming interlude.

We Are the People Our Parents Warned Us Against

Nicholas von Hoffman

At the beginning of the Summer of Love there was a pleasantness about the Haight. The ratio of frightening people to nice ones was favorable, and the nice ones, like Al Rinker and George Darling, were doing low-keyed, relaxed things. They'd opened what they called the Switchboard, which was more like a telephonic bulletin board. You could call there any hour of the day and night to leave a message or get one; the Switchboard would also supply you with the best and newest rumors, and sometimes it was able to steer you toward a crash pad or even a free lawyer. Late at night, if you didn't feel up to the madmen in the House of Do-Nuts, you could go over to the Switchboard, sit in the kitchen, and listen to Al discuss acid. He was an amateur acid scientist and he loved to discuss his findings:

"Two years ago I had a friend who took acid and he kept taking more acid, forty or fifty trips. I had the idea if you took a lot of acid in a short period of time it would deteriorate your personality, so I began to study this thing. I pre- and post-tested people on acid, not in a clinical situation but in the Haight-Ashbury. Then I checked out my first twenty-five cases. I was really surprised. I found there was a *positive* change equivalent to about three years of effective therapy. But I got another impression from my data. My impression is that people who have taken thirty or forty trips and never had a bummer aren't in as good shape as those who have. I also believe that no person who has really let go can avoid having a bummer. The person who's had a few good trips and thinks he's learned something is deluding himself. He only has it on a conceptual, not an experiential, level. He may be the type who thinks, as a result of his acid, he's living like a saint, and then, bang! he gets a glimpse of himself . . . I know of one case—a professor at San Francisco State—who had four or five good trips, then he took one and went through hell. He got a look at all the evil inside himself. They had to bring him down with thorazine after six hours.[1] His trip was the worst trip ever recorded. He saw the male and female personification of

[1] This is one of a number of preparations that will bring you down if you're bad-tripping, but the lore of the dope world is against it. It's felt that a chemically induced come-down is like premature termination of pregnancy. You get an unpleasant, residual effect for a while. The favored method is "talking" people down. For some dope, like STP, there is no known antidote. About the best they can do for you, if you're having a bummer on it, is shoot you full of tranquilizers and wait till the stuff wears off.

evil in himself. He called the one Prince and the other Becky. After the trip, he always had a fear he'd see them whenever the phone rang or somebody knocked on the door. Finally, he made a simple act of faith, that it would be all right even if he met them, and that seemed to work. Actually, what he was getting was an acid recurrence—sometimes they call it a flash. Now I believe an acid recurrence is the spirit trying to work through an incomplete trip.

"It's a very complicated subject and it keeps changing. For example, when they first had acid in the Haight-Ashbury, some people singled themselves out by having religious experiences. Do you know, there was one guy at 1090 Page who actually had a throne and people were waiting on him just like he was—you know. But now lots of people have religious experiences. Enough people have taken acid and had them so they're not impressed by your religious trip anymore. I know a commune where they all picked up and moved out, all but two meth freaks, because this one guy would sit there with that religious smile on his face all day, but he'd never do the dishes."

The Switchboard people were hipped on the notion that they were the best interpreters of the Haight to the straight world, so they sailed out on evangelizing missions. George and his girl, Joan, in the company of several others, were invited to talk to a Montgomery Street businessmen's group. "As the word goes," said George, who would never have made a public speaker, "we're there in the Haight trying to do our thing. We were doing it too, until people were told by *Time* and *Life* the housing was free. Now there're hoards of them walking around being pinched by the police. Perhaps if we can get them housing, they'll be able to do their thing."

"In other words, they're a bunch of freeloaders," said one of the men in the luncheon audience.

"Well, some of them who come to our community are amazing," said one of George's colleagues. "I've seen them drive in and park their $7,000 Mercedes-Benz sports cars, change their expensive clothes and put on rags, and then go sit on the curb on Haight Street and panhandle."

"Another thing, why do they get so dirty?"

"We don't know about that. I'm clean. I take baths all the time," George told them. "See, we're not here to talk about the kids who come to smoke a little dope and go home. We're trying to build a community with stores and institutions. You should be in favor of that."

"Yeah?" said one guy, who wasn't exactly agreeing, "What I want to know is at what age do you change from being a hippy into being a bum?"

His fellows thought that was pretty funny. George replied, "Maybe the guy sitting next to you is a hippy." They thought that was funnier. The message wasn't getting across. George and his friends put their heads together to discuss inviting these obtuse men out to the community. They couldn't agree, and at length one of them said to the businessmen, "If you have any sons and daughters who escape and drop out, you'd better be thankful that there are people like us in the Haight-Ashbury who aren't like that Mission Street crowd, who destroy everybody with needles and VD."

At that point the toastmaster said, "I think we should commend them for the way they conducted themselves here." Some applause followed.

WE ARE THE PEOPLE OUR PARENTS WARNED US AGAINST
—Graffito, coffeehouse wall, Summer 1967

Every day the scene got a little heavier, a little crazier. Pot was getting harder to find. There was plenty of acid, but you can only take acid every other day or so; more often than that and you won't get off. The body builds an absolute tolerance to it very rapidly. More alcohol, more speed, and more freaky people appeared on the streets. Like Chancellor. Chancellor was a white boy whose curly, uncut hair made him look like a fuzzy-wuzzy. His real name was unknown. He was called Chancellor because of the discarded, orange-red doorman's coat he wore. On the coat were stitched the words, "Hotel Chancellor." Chancellor didn't walk; he rotated in order to achieve locomotion. He would gyrate in unexpected directions, sometimes whirling out into the traffic. As he did this, he emitted a buzzing-humming noise, and when going at top speed he would bounce off automobile fenders like an incredible, haired-over, distended top.

Papa Al was spending more and more time in the neighborhood, getting there a little earlier, leaving a little later. "There are no undercover agents from the narcotics squad in the Haight as of yesterday. The last one had his cover blown. It will be a month before another group can come in. It's getting to be a very heavy scene," he said one afternoon, while taking a private walk in the park, which he did occasionally. "But don't think about it. Just do your thing, whatever's right."

He began spending more time at the Free Clinic. Next, he unaccountably was being called the clinic's "senior supervisor." It changed the tone of the place, because Papa Al's street commandos and dealers followed him. Kurt Feibusch and Shalom objected to their hanging out, but they were always coming in and looking for him: Big Tiny, Hutch, Apache, Cowboy, Iron Man, White Preacher, Spider, the lot of them. They had an unsettling effect on White Rabbit, who seemed to be riding out his identity crisis quietly while doing voluntary chores of an unclassifiable nature for the clinic.

White Rabbit liked to say things that would blow your mind: "I can turn on radios by feeling waves through the back of my neck. I just recently put a clamp on it because I was going around turning on people's radios and TV sets, and it was beginning to bug them." After he'd say something like that, he'd twinkle at you, twitch the end of his long nose, and be disappointed if you changed the subject. His Princeton father and his Vassar mother combined to make a well-to-do, upstate New York family, where White Rabbit, the oldest of four children, grew up in the better private boarding schools until he reached an age (twenty) when he could say, "Even before I was accepted at Berkeley, I was having psychological problems which I couldn't straighten out with the psychiatrist at prep school. I had a nervous breakdown two weeks before school ended."

On the whole, White Rabbit's childhood must have been quietly pleasant. One of his earliest memories is of an electric Santa Claus bowing mechanically from the living room fireplace. His father, he remembered, slapped him once, but it was never traumatic; usually he was sent to his room or had his allowance cut or couldn't watch TV. He had diagnosed himself: "I have a sexual identity problem. Many people have it but they repress it. Everybody has almost equal parts maleness and femaleness, but they don't know it. Acid helps to break down these barriers. After acid, I was able to think about it and talk about it."

Papa Al took one look at White Rabbit and came to a different understanding. "Hippies like fuzzy rabbit here were lost before they ever came to the Haight," Papa Al said. "To them acid is instant psychiatry, a way to find out where your head's at . . . Of course, it's on their neck, where it's always been, but White Rabbit doesn't know that. He's a typical product of a permissive society, so he's suffering from what most of them are suffering from, a massive Peter Pan complex. There's a tremendous amount of regression among these kids, like this large rodent here next to me with the white fur. Look at them up on Hippy Hill every day, smoking pot, flying kites, and blowing soap bubbles. Regression."

Papa Al could talk that way when he wanted to. He was supposed to have a master's degree in psychology; he was also supposed to be an ex–social worker who'd gotten rich in the stock market. It was true that almost every afternoon he bought a paper and said, "I want to see how I'm doing," as he turned to the final market quotations.

It changed day to day with White Rabbit. Sometimes he used the scene as a backdrop for costumes. Then he appeared to be capitalizing on the social weightlessness of the Haight, the strange place where you could assume any role you chose, make up any kind of personal history you wanted. At other times, White Rabbit had no personality of his own; what he had was derived from the scene; the backdrop, the set made him into a person. On those days he was especially susceptible to Papa Al's group. He'd appear and ask, "Know where I can hide out?"

"Why do you want to hide out, White Rabbit?"

"There's a contract let out on me!"

"You mean somebody wants to kill you?"

"That's right, there's one, maybe two contracts out on me. I've gotta hide out for a while. I may have to split the scene completely."

"White Rabbit, you're bragging. You've never done anything important enough to merit somebody murdering you, or even short-sheeting your bed."

"It isn't anything I've done."

"I'm sure of that."

"No, this is serious. It's something I've heard. I was with a chick and she took me to this house where there were some very heavy cats, and they said some things in front of me . . . Well, if it ever got out—I can't tell you any more, except it concerns a lot of important people, like Papa Al."

"White Rabbit, can you get the DT's from acid?"

"They didn't realize this chick had brought me, and, oh, wow! I wish she hadn't!"

Other days he'd come on square-shouldered and talk out of the side of his mouth: "Goin' over to the islands."

"Yeah?" you were supposed to answer, just as tough as he. "Some action over there?"

"I might tell ya, but ya can't come. Let ya in on it, 'cause you've been righteous. Only reporter around here that writes the truth."

"How would you know? You've never read a word I've written, not even a post card."

"We know. Doncha think we check you guys out? We have a line on everybody who stays around here for more than two days, but you can't write about this. There's a bunch of us going over to the islands to make a hit on Useless."

"Useless? What's Useless done now?"

"Nothing, but he pulled an $11,000 burn, and we're not going to let him get away with that."

"Look, Walter Mitty White Rabbit, Useless didn't burn you. You've never even met Useless."

"He burnt my friends."

Each day grass got tighter and the scene got freakier. Dr. Smith, the director of the clinic, kept on an even keel, saying the same things to the reporters. They'd come around of an evening and catch him in the room in the clinic that had FCREW YOU painted on the wall above the filing cabinet:

> I was three-fourths of my way to a Ph.D. when the Haight-Ashbury struck. There was a void created and somebody had to respond. There still is a void in many ways because this society doesn't treat drug abuse as a health problem but as a police problem. . . . The Haight-Ashbury has tremendous energy. It's broken with the past, but it hasn't found a new way yet, so it symbolizes what I call a "generation at risk." . . . My biggest criticism of the straight community is that they don't try to understand why the kids do it, and it's not just a few kids. Do you know that in the month of July we treated over two thousand of them?

As the grass shortage continued, the doctor's talk became less visionary and more stridently concerned:

> "I still think of this as a movement, but the rebellion is crumbling at the edges. They're hung up on drugs, too many of them; they're not moving on to something else. I am appalled at the number of teeni-boppers who've taken LSD three hundred and four hundred times. They stay stoned all the time. What are we going to do with them? Drag them back by the hair? They think they know better. . . . I don't know, I don't know, I guess you could go down Haight Street tonight and arrest half the boys as draft dodgers. . . . It's getting frightening. One day the Hell's Angels stormed in here, demanding to know if we'd called the police. I don't know what they might have done if we had. . . . We don't tell the police anything but what the law says a doctor has to; a rumor got around that we were reporting to the fuzz, and I was worried for a while. I thought everybody might just decide we were all a big come-down, but the underground papers helped us. They put out the word that we were cool. . . . I've never seen such paranoia.

The clinic kitchen was run by John. When he was sober, he tried hard to give the place a certain institutional class. He wasn't a snob; he was a forty-six-year-old Irishman from New York, and that meant he was always braced, waiting for some mark of condescension. His tactic was to strike first. "These children's English! . . . It's such a pleasure to talk to some-one who can speak the language correctly, who knows how to make his meaning clear. A hippy—this I do believe is the real definition of a hippy—well, a hippy is a person who persists in committing grammatical mistakes even after he's been corrected. I thank God I went to Cathedral College, but then I had the benefit of a classical education. I studied for the priesthood but I realized in time that my vocation wasn't celibate. I thank God for that or I would never have married Shirley. We'd been married fourteen years when she died of a massive stroke. I took up the bottle the day Shirley died . . . could you contribute, well, let's say $10, or call it a loan until tomorrow? . . . some sisters and priests are coming for lunch, and, as usual, this establishment is bereft of funds . . . The religious want to see our work and I think we should offer them some food. I have a very nice luncheon menu."

"John, if I give you this will you drink up tomorrow's lunch? I can't afford to make two contributions."

"Oh, gracious no. You know, it's such a pleasure talking to you. Your English—you do speak exceptionally well. I wish you'd known Shirley. She had a doctorate—in English. I never drank until the day she died. You know, I've sat in Park Avenue apartments where there were bigger hippies than there are here. I've never cared for that kind of life. I could have done it if I'd wanted, but I didn't. I've made a success in two business careers. Oh yes, I was an assistant buyer at Macy's. I left Macy's when they told me they were going to promote me to buyer but they had to 'sell' me upstairs first. I didn't have the Harvard or the Yale background, you see. They were going to sell me upstairs. I told them they needn't bother. After fourteen years of working in their store, I didn't care to be sold upstairs, so I went home after fourteen years and I told my wife I had quit. I'm square, buddy boy. That's what I did. Then I went into the printing business and I was very successful, but one day I told my partner, 'Here, you can have it,' and I walked out to come to San Francisco. I can go back any time I want. I don't have to be here. These children think they're revolutionaries! I've known Dorothy Day. We had Peter Maurin speak at Our Lady of Lourdes Holy Name Society. They were revolutionaries. I know. I was with the *Catholic Worker*. Oh, these children aren't doing anything I don't know about. I studied for the priesthood. Oh, don't tell me. *Introibo ad altare Dei. Ad Deum qui laetificat juventutem meam* . . . Don't tell me."

John made an excellent hash, a hunky, meaty hash with crusty potatoes. It gave the clinic a solid, institutional continuity. Then one day he was gone. Nobody ever explained why anybody was gone from the clinic. They became nonpeople, and the staff looked as though you'd done something in bad taste if you mentioned them. John was replaced by George, who was less critical and had the enthusiasm of a coolie, always running and offering to get things; but he couldn't cook.

It got freakier. The room with the FCREW YOU on the wall was the theater for strange dialogues and dramas in which the characters would push their way in, say their lines, and leave.

Freak Night in the Fcrew You Room

WHITE RABBIT: Aldous Huxley died high on acid . . . died high and happy, just tripped out of life into death.

SHRINK: Yes, but have you ever thought of the possibilities of chromosomal damage? You kids never think of the side effects. You can't play fast and loose with nature. It makes you pay.

WHITE RABBIT: He was dying of cancer.

SHRINK: Why are you so angry with me?

WALLY *(an aging fag):* I tell you, Teddybear, I used to hate the hippies. I hated the hippies. I hated the hippies 'cause I am what you call an entrepreneur. I buy and sell property. But now I work twenty-four hours a day for them. Before, when I'd see these people on the street corner, I'd say that it was abominable. They were doing nothing. Oh, but I changed. I dropped acid. Then I saw them panhandling an' I saw that they give to each other.

TEDDYBEAR: You can't o-d on acid. I took four white Owsleys on the Fourth of July. *(exit* SHRINK; WHITE RABBIT *stands in front of the filing cabinet and eats potato chips)*

WALLY: When I take acid, I know why I like the hippies. I'm a homosexual. I'm a persecuted minority too. So now, every night, I take off the business suit; I put on the beads; I'm a happy, hippy homo.

TEDDYBEAR: We're the most hated minority in America. We have no rights. We're lower than the spades and the spics. Our hippy women are raped, and we go to the police station and they don't even write it down.

SPEED FREAK (*entering as he holds a bleeding hand*): I need somebody to fix this.

SHALOM: The only doctor we got right now is a shrink, and this shrink won't bandage people. Says he's forgotten how. You got to come back tomorrow or go to a hospital.

SPEED FREAK: If a fuckin' psychiatrist comes in here I'm gonna kill 'im. (*plucks at his tufty beard*)

SHALOM: I know what kind of a trip you're on. I know your trip.

SPEED FREAK: I know yours too.

SHALOM: You can leave. I tried to talk to you reasonably.

WALLY: Well, I tell you honestly, Teddybear, the hippies run down property values.

SPEED FREAK: I thought this was a place ya come for help.

SHALOM: Don't put your bum trip on me.

SPEED FREAK (*exiting*): I won't be back.

WHITE RABBIT: Speed freak.

SHALOM: Speed freak.

TEDDYBEAR: We don't run down values. We build values. People copy from us—styles, music, everything.

WALLY: You do, you do, Teddybear. I can tell you. By day I'm establishment. The savings and loan associations have drawn a line against you. That means you drop property values. I wouldn't rent to you. Maybe that means I'm hypocritical.

WHITE RABBIT: I'm on librium. Very low high. (*re-enter* SHRINK, *followed by* PLEADING GIRL, *followed by* PAPA AL *and* BIG TINY, *who are doing their own thing*)

PLEADING GIRL: Aren't you going to help my friend? She's old. She must be nearly fifty an' she's bum-tripping bad.

SHRINK: She's been bum-tripping for thirty years.

PLEADING GIRL: It's the universe that's been on a bad trip.

SHRINK: I'm sorry. I shouldn't have said that.

BIG TINY: I want the Angels so bad, I don't want anything fuckin' else, Papa Al.

WHITE RABBIT: Talk about bad trips! Kelly's back from Fresno. He looks awful. Been on a series of death-ego trips. Wow!

SHRINK: Why the hell are you bothering me if you don't want me to take . . . for a forty-eight-year-old woman with multiple cuts and abrasions, malnutrition, and occasional hallucinations.

PLEADING GIRL: Where're you going to send her? I'll take care of her. What she needs is macrobiotic food and serenity.

SHRINK: Why the hell are you bothering me if you don't want me to take care of your friend?

PLEADING GIRL: There's a lot of shit happening around this city.

SHRINK: Agreed.

WHITE RABBIT: You're feeling the tug of the tribal imperative, doctor, and you're resisting. Flow with it.

SHRINK: White Rabbit, will you—oh, never mind. I've been here too long tonight.

PLEADING GIRL: I almost died last Sunday of sensitivity . . . and a few mind poisoners, doctor. I'm going.

SHRINK: In peace, in peace. *(exit* SHRINK *and girl, who is almost knocked over by* COWBOY *entering)*

COWBOY: Papa Al, Papa Al, I gotta talk to you. I need your thirty-eight. I gotta have it now.

PAPA AL: Well, well, well, if it isn't Cowboy.

BIG TINY: I'm talkin' to Papa Al.

PAPA AL: Cowboy's upset. He's having his monthlies . . . Tsk, tsk, you missed the most interesting part of the evening, Cowboy. A nine-year-old boy was up here earlier freaking out on acid. Maybe you sold it to him. It was quite interesting. The kid's tongue was hanging out of his mouth and he couldn't get it back in . . . hung over his teeth dripping spit.

COWBOY: There's too many fuckin' people around here.

PAPA AL: Well, you split, Cowboy. Big Tiny and me are doing our thing and we don't need you.

COWBOY: Papa Al, I gotta have a gun. I gotta have a gun fast.

PAPA AL: Cowboy, you can't make it as a biker, you can't make it as a dealer, you can't make it as a hippy, you can't make it as a human being.

COWBOY: Don't call me "Cowboy." That's not my name.

BIG TINY: Me an' Al are talking.

COWBOY: Gee, wow! I'm stoned. I'm behind everything, grass, acid, STP, speed, alcohol. I'm behind everything. Stoned outta my brain. Papa Al, I gotta have a gun.

BIG TINY: Me an' Papa Al are talkin'.

COWBOY: *Me* an' Papa Al are talkin'.

BIG TINY: Don't hassle me, Cowboy. You're comin' down on me.

PAPA AL: Okay, son, you got what you wanted. You're the center of attention.

COWBOY: I'm not your son.

PAPA AL: Okay, Cowboy, then.

BIG TINY: Papa Al, if he don't get outta here, I'm gonna cold-cock him.

COWBOY: My name's Mike an' there're too many fuckin' people around here. *(exit* COWBOY*)*

VOICE FROM DOWN THE HALL: Panic button! Panic button! I'm pushing the panic button! There's a boy in here who's all sliced up. The Angels or the spades got 'im. He can't talk. Who wants to drive him to the hospital?

COWBOY *(sticking his head back in for an instant):* It was the syndicate. An' they're going to get me too, Papa Al, 'cause you won't give me your gun.

BIG TINY: I'll cold-cock the son of a bitch.

PAPA AL: So Tiny, you want to be an Angel, do you? Well, well, well, an' all the time. I thought you were the only 315-pound woman's hairdresser in the world. But, seriously, son, if you want to be an Angel, you better watch yourself. You keep jumping in on their fights, you're going to be in trouble. You're not going about it right.

BIG TINY: I'm always helping 'em. I always jump in on their side. St. Louis said I could go on the next run if I can get a bike, but Papa Al, where am I going to get a bike?

PAPA AL: You be careful, Tiny. You could get stomped, you know.

WHITE RABBIT: Fcrew you all. *(titters at himself and trips out making a silent, laughing face)*

PAPA AL: Whatever's right.

Groovin' on Time: Fragments of a Sociology of the Psychedelic Experience

Victor Gioscia

Introduction

The task of this paper is to focus the sociological imagination on data derived from participant observation of the psychedelic scene. What is attempted is an examination of the processes in society which help to account for the emergence of what many call a drug subculture. It will be argued that the consumption of LSD and related substances is an epiphenomenon, i.e., "symptomatic" of deeper changes occurring in contemporary post-industrial society. The hypothesis uniting the pages that follow is that psychedelics are primitive psychochemical machines by which a new generation seeks to master a range of new societal forces. Thus, the new drug tech-

Victor, Gioscia, "Groovin' on Time: Fragments of a Sociology of the Psychedelic Experience," from *Psychedelic Drugs*, Hicks/Fink, eds. (New York: Grune & Stratton, Inc., 1969), pp. 167–176. Reprinted by permission of the publisher and author.

nology is produced by, hence does not by itself produce, a new kind of societal agony.

Prolegomenon on Method

Participant observation is a form of scientific experience which escapes the trap of fragmented overspecialization because it necessarily confronts the full plenum and contextual variety of its chosen subject. It enables the observer to experience the interconnections which controlled experimentation often defines as out of the way. It reduces the social distance between subjective and objective data, by defining the observer as less unlike his subjects than laboratory research defines him. It makes it possible for the observer to observe his own experience as well as the experiences of his subjects, creating an empathy which facilitates candid disclosure while reducing the potential of paranoid reaction in the observational field. These and other qualities of the technique of participant observation make it a particularly useful method for one who chooses to focus his attention on the contemporary drug scene.

But participant observation is not without traps of its own. Vivid description is open to the charge of over-identification. Empathy may be construed as loss of objectivity. Generalization becomes more difficult as the number and range of particulars increases. Coöptation and one-dimensionalization becomes increasingly possible to the extent that the observer penetrates the universe of inquiry. Further, the drug scene creates the danger of arrest for felonious complicity as one more closely observes the behavior in question.

Nevertheless, it may be argued that participant observation is the method of choice when the universe to be observed is not yet sufficiently defined to warrant the use of those sampling techniques which lend themselves to more precise and exact statistical quantification. In the absence of a census of drug-related behaviors, participant observation yields up an array of data which make it a valuable method, its shortcomings notwithstanding. The knowledge that it is the method preferred by those observed adds to the value of its adoption. The fact that it provides ethnographic concreteness is no less a value in its favor.

One spells out these criteria in order to confront the criticism, increasingly met, that scientific exactitude is especially needful in the matter of societal problems, an arena laden with values, biases, and political choices. Agreed. One should confront as well, the critique which holds that we should aspire to no more exactitude than is genuinely possible, and that, if indeed, it is the experience surrounding psychedelic substances on which we focus our inquiry, then we should seek no more exactitude than such experiences warrant. This is especially the case when we focus sociological attention on the cultural, social and personal sources and outcomes of the psychedelic experience, as in the paragraphs that follow.

History as Inquiry

Being there (Dasein), Heidegger tells us, engenders a feeling of having been thrown (*geworfenheit*) as if one suddenly awakens to find himself having been deposited in a strange oppressive place, charged with the task of figuring out not so much "who threw me here" as "now what?" One feels simultaneously lost and impelled, driven and trapped. These were the emotions characterizing the heroin addicts we observed in a study completed a few years ago, and these were the emotions characterizing the participant observer.[1] In those days, heroin was the medication of choice to which many adolescents looked for the anaesthetic revelation of their desires. We hypothesized that these young people sought from heroin a temporary relief from the falterings of an imperfect civilization which inflicted upon them the impossible task of seeking a forbidden deliverance from their lower class plight. The situation was relatively uncomplicated—one drug, one class, even one principal ethnicity, making it possible to generalize from the particular turmoil of these adolescents to the plight of similar adolescents elsewhere.

Quickly thereafter, a much younger population, no higher in class but quite different in ethnicity, seized on the inhalation of glue fumes and similar substances for the relief of their special turmoil. This forced a modification of prior hypotheses, not solely with regard to age and ethnicity, but also with regard to the range and scope of substance choice.[2] But one could still adhere to the view that drug misuse was the predilection of a relatively small number of young "deviants" in our society without risking professional scorn although it was becoming increasingly clear that the "problem" was becoming increasingly serious.

Then, as everyone knows, LSD use spread among the middle-class youth of the nation as a fire through a field of hay, spreading with it an array of substances (marijuana, mescalin, peyote, psilocybin, DMT, *et al.*) across ages, classes, ethnicities, cities, and subcultures. The situation came more and more to resemble the well-stocked bar of the average American home, such that specific drugs for specific experiences at specific times and places became the rule, rather than the exception. The drug scene,[3] like that of its parents', produced connoisseurs conversant with a variety of drugs which induced desired experiences under chosen circumstances, with degrees of social appropriateness shaded as finely as the gradations of the Japanese bow. The "problem," it was agreed, had reached epidemiological proportions. It was occasionally noted, *en passant,* that the new drugs had been available and in use by a small number of cognoscenti for twenty years, and

that some had been in use for literally thousands of years. The question
arose, why are so many young people now using so many drugs. Parallels
drawn to the use of alcohol, sleeping pills, stimulants, tranquillizers, ciga-
rettes, aspirin and a veritable horde of socially sanctioned analgesics were
deemed not to the point. This was "different."

It was not difficult to assemble "data" from magazines and newspaper accounts supporting the view that a stratification of drug taste was in evidence.
Lower class youth preferred "body" drugs (largely heroin and other mor-
phine derivatives); upper-lower youth were beginning to favor "speed"
(methamphetamine and other stimulants); the initial sample of LSD users
seemed to be dropouts from a middle-class life style; their parents were
astonished to find the young were not enjoying life to the hilt and were, in
fact, specifically critical of its alleged crass materialism, i.e., spiritual
vacuum. Their out of hand rejection of affluence was especially shocking to
those by whom this affluence was newly won, i.e., the nouveau bourgeois.

And, some noted, "this" was also international.[4] Like the jet set chron-
icled in the mass media, youth in many world cities were equally conversant,
although differentially supplied, with the whole panoply of drugs that so
concerned their elders. To make matters worse, it emerged that the therapy
industry to which parents had been accustomed to turn for the relief of their
offsprings' alleged symptoms, was increasingly regarded with suspicion,
distrust, and not occasionally, outright disdain by young drug users. This
was partly because parents assumed that drug use was *ipso facto* pathogno-
monic of emotional disorder, and partly because legislatures decreed that
drug use was *ipso facto* criminal. In short, the young were told that a major
norm of their subculture was either sick or wrong, although no one could
dispute their right to a subculture without vitiating his right to his own. Intellectuals murmured "double bind"; youth growled "hypocrisy."

Into this breach bravely rode the ill-starred "Hippies," whose philosophy
was abhorred by the very media which extolled and subsequently expropri-
ated their aesthetic. Settling into Haight-Ashbury in California and the East
Village in New York, hippies pronounced, as the Spenglerian Beats of the
fifties had pronounced before them, the imminent demise of Western civilization. Unlike the Beats, however, the hippies set about systematically replacing those institutions of straight society which, they charged, had brutally
alienated them from the joys of their own lives.

In July of 1967, at the Dialectics of Liberation conference convened in
London by R. D. Laing, Allen Ginsberg described the new generation, variously called hippies, flower children, the love generation, the now generation,
and subsequently freemen, as having a whole set of subcultural institutions
of their own. For social workers, there were the diggers; for politicians,
provos, for police, Hell's Angels and other Bikers; religion consisted of an
amalgam of Tibetan, Egyptian, Hindu, Zen and astrological speculation, all
facing in a deliberately mystical direction, drugs and sexual rituals serving

as sacraments. For charismatic leaders, there were Leary, Kesey, and others. Language was reinvented, as was music. Philosophy, art, morality, justice, truth and beauty; each received a psychedelic rebirth and transfiguration. Extensive media coverage of these events turned most Americans, whether they liked it or no, into observers of the psychedelic drug scene in varying amounts and degrees of participation. If one wished now to observe, with some aspiration of scientific method, one had to abandon hypotheses restricted as to age, drug, or locale, for the "problem" was manifestly societal in incidence and prevalence, if not yet demonstrable in origin. We set ourselves the task of examining those societal processes which might help to answer the query heard now in virtually all quarters—why indeed were so many young people using so many drugs in so many ways?

Sociogenesis

B. F. Skinner could not have devised a more negative stimulus for the young people in the East Village who regularly use psychedelic drugs than the word Bellevue, a hospital on the fringe of the community which they regard somewhat less positively than a medieval dungeon replete with chambers of torture. The establishment it is said to represent found itself hoist by its own petard when its propaganda convinced an already irate citizenry that LSD turned sweet-faced youngsters into psychotic monsters, dangerous criminals, irrepressible rapists, and habitual thieves. The public turned around and demanded for its safety that these same either be incarcerated or therapized and preferably both. Though the young avoided both with nimble and embarrassing alacrity, they were aware and made no secret among themselves that living in voluntary poverty and using drugs whose street-calibrated dosages bore little if any relation to actual content, created psychological, medical and sociological problems which might benefit from the ministrations of psychotherapists, physicians and community craftsmen, if only a "hip" variety of these could be found. A number of helping institutions soon decided that, ideological differences notwithstanding, there were more young people with more "unmet needs" than history had witnessed in a long time, and that ameliorative intervention could no longer be deliberated. Mountains of bureaucracy shuddered, and hippy projects were founded, the most famous being Dr. Smith's clinic in Haight-Ashbury. A less famous semi-counterpart, called the Village Project * attempts to care for some of the psychosocial ailments of the local young "residents." One may there "rap" (talk) with groups of young people on topics of their selection. One of their favorite topics is the subject of this writing—Why drugs? Their astonishing wisdom as sociologists both simplifies and com-

* Sponsored by Jewish Family Service of New York.

plicates my task, since sociologists, like their therapeutic colleagues, seek to understand, not simply accept, the manifest content of behavior even, perhaps especially, the behavior called understanding.

Rap session participants at the Village Project are uniformly agreed that "dope" is central but not causal, i.e., a necessary but not sufficient explanation of their life-style: They feel that getting high, getting stoned, tripping, (via LSD, STP, Mescalin, marijuana, or any other desired combination) is like opening a door to other voices and other rooms. But, after you've opened the door, it's up to you to keep walking and actually *do* the trip during which, if you're up to it, you will meet all manner of new turned-on experiences which are very much your own solutions to your very individual plight. Dropping out of alienated societal roles is said to be a prerequisite to real tripping, since the ego-trips of which society is said to consist become visible as cul de sacs and blind alleys, to which a return is unthinkable. A new freedom, the right of phantasy as self-exploration, is ordinarily proclaimed *prior* to tripping, and only subsequently reinforced by good trips. Bum trips are said to be due to fear of letting go or to contaminated drugs, not to the substances themselves. Up tight people are to be avoided during trips since their fear and their violence are said to be as contagious as they are dangerous.

It is claimed that two convergent trends in society are principally responsible for the drop-out phenomenon, to which the added enticement of tripping is secondary. These trends are: (1) *Automation:* the attainment of an incredibly high level of affluence and abundance in post-industrial computerized society, it is said, renders the work-for-a-living (Calvinist) ethos a superfluous relic of the first industrial revolution. Since supermarkets, restaurants and other food merchants have far more than necessary, simply asking for the remainder provides enough to live on. This makes it possible to afford the leisure time needed to engage in self-exploration via tripping, sexual variety, residential mobility and so forth. Parents who covertly send checks they can easily afford to send, now that junior has left home, are not rare. In short, now that automation has replaced work, it is said, play has assumed its rightfully central role, and, if you know how, acid (LSD) is a powerful yet pleasant toy. (2) *Cybernation:* contemporary society has the power to communicate vast amounts of information almost instantly. Just as the first generation of mass media (linear print and film) fostered mass consumption through mass advertising at the behest of mass production, so now the second generation of media (electronics—audio and video tape, computerized pattern recognition) have created an era of global communication where nothing is foreign, nothing remote. In McLuhanesque terms, the content of the electric media is the former mechanical media, just as the content of the trip is yesterday's psychology. Once, a psychoanalytic foray was bedrock—now, all such forays become the ingredients of emergent psychic forms—called trips.

It will be perceived that electricity is common to both of the societal trends the Villagers put forward as explanations of psychedelia. This supports the view that if Hoffman hadn't invented acid it would have been necessary to do so since acid renders the organism capable of enjoying the information overloads which have become characteristic of our electrified society. The analogy runs like this—as water is to fish, so acid is to the children of the age of electric communication. In the wake of such massive societal forces, it follows that new social forms must emerge to handle, as a trip handles for the individual, the information impact on social organization. Hence, the retribalization process McLuhan has described is said to be the accommodation youth culture has made to its electric environment. The commune (be it urban or rural, an insignificant distinction in an era of global information) is a natural social response to the age of electronic sociogenesis.

The convergence, then, of automation and cybernation is offered by East Villagers as the explanation for the existence of psychedelic drugs. These drugs, they say, are simply the psychochemical responses to of an electric society in which automated energy is cybernetically processed.

Just as there are said to be two fundamental societal processes at the root of psychedelic culture, so there are two "sick" institutions which protagonists of psychedelic experience diagnose as particularly in need of replacement, i.e., war and education. Wars, it is said, are fought for the preservation of territoriality which no longer matters in an age of planetary communication by people who have not yet learned that all violence is self-destructive exactly to the extent to which it is efficient. Wars which require the young to fight for the very values of the old they have rejected are thus said to be doubly unjust in that they enrole pacifists in aggression, and simultaneously, pit young brothers in an emergent planetary culture against each other. Hence, the young reject what they regard as a forced choice between suicide and fratricide. Besides, it is added, the trip experience is as delicate and fragile as it is lovely, to which even subtle psychological violence is abhorrent and disgusting not to mention physical brutality. It is said that trips teach the futility of violence, wars included.

Schools, which claim to teach the heritages of their societies, are rejected no less vehemently for making that very claim. The young who proclaim the appropriateness of their electric sensibilities argue that a school system which attempts to foster industrial values is engaged in a process of mechanical propaganda no less insidious than any other form of brainwashing. It is said that schools and, especially, multiversities are information factories designed to process young people into readiness for alienated roles in the military-industrial complex from whom the young are already in full flight. Some even argue that universities are worse than battlefields since they are the training grounds for them without acknowledging that that is their nature. Universities are said thus to add hypocrisy to their irrelevance to the electric age.

Attending to these themes over and over again, the participant observer gradually shucks off his surprise that "heads" engage so earnestly and so solemnly in "raps" on art and media in the same breath as they rap about war and education. Their earnest solemnity is distributed equally over these topics because they are, in their view, struggling for the very existence of the only culture that gives meaning to their daily experience. They are literally fighting for their lives.

Every culture selects from the range of human potentials, and moulds the organisms that are its raw stuff in its own image. And every culture, by its agreement that some values and behaviors are central, defines other values and behaviors as peripheral, less central, "deviant." This is no less true of the participants in the Village Project so that, in what follows, the inference that each and every one of these young people is singlehandedly responsible for the birth pangs of a new civilization should not be drawn. For every sane "head" we confront, there are two lost or mad ones. Yet the point lies deeper—for if, as it seems, there is a new culture aborning, then for many the birth process is extremely painful if not injurious. But not, we emphasize, for all.

Once this is understood, one also understands why the young will gladly ignore a serious upper respiratory infection gained from a shared pipe or a piece of glass in a bare foot acquired on a stroll together. They are felt as red badges of courageous solidarity incurred in a collective struggle, in a revolution they say, with nothing less than culture itself at stake.

Understanding Understanding Media

The reader will recall that we have set ourselves the task of understanding why the psychedelic culture understands itself the way it does. He will recall that our inquiry regards the electric metaphor as the manifest content which itself requires explanation. In the language of my discipline, stated explanations are regarded as ideologies, themselves requiring explanation. Sociologists refer to this specialty as the sociology of knowledge, a field heavily indebted to such giants as Marx, Mannheim, and Marcuse for their elaboration of the view that men's situations determine their thoughts far more than their thoughts determine their situations. Thus armed, we turn our attentions to the social process which has elevated the electric metaphor into a believed mythology.

It was Marx, correcting Hegel, who first revealed what now is regarded as a commonplace, although at first it seemed esoteric and arcane. In the dialectical view, when men reflect on their situation, they diagnose the injustices of their condition, and then seek to change it. They attempt to change the world as they find it into the world they want it to be by their work. When by their work they do transform their situation and then again reflect on it they, like God in Genesis, see that the world they have made is good or, at least, more just than it was. This process of work changing reflection and reflection leading to further work is described as the dialectical relation between substructure and its ideological superstructure. Thus the industrial revolution, itself a new mode of changing the world, transformed the preindustrial Calvinist ideology of thrift into the post-industrial Veblenist ideology of progress, i.e., conspicuous consumption. Before it, the devil made work for idle hands; after it, the popular view was that all work and no play makes Jack a dull boy. Mobility supplanted class struggle as inevitably as the machine replaced the bicep.

It remained for Marcuse to show that societies' efforts to generate demand even beyond the greedy dreams of conspicuous consumers required them to foster what he called "surplus repression," [5] i.e., to get people to believe that it was more important to repress instinctual eroticism than to develop it, because it was more important to consume for society than to transcend and alter society. Subsequently, Marcuse revealed that post-industrial society employs its media to establish an ideology hostile to transcendence itself, such that citizens are bidden to remain one-dimensional men.[6] Those who attempt to rise above the one dimension society permits by creating works of two dimensions (the prototype is the consciously alienated artist who depicts the new dimension in all its transcendent glory) will find their works reduced to one dimensionality through mass-media mechanisms. Such work will be mass produced and mass marketed and thus made ordinary and routine, if not tawdry and banal. A case in point was noted—the appropriation of psychedelic art forms by the "plastic" advertising industry. One could also add long hair, acid rock, "hip" jargon and "freaky" clothes.

The relevance of these theories to our inquiry is the following: Marx envisioned a process that took one hundred years to have its full impact, and, within that time, Marcuse saw processes take their toll in less than a generation. *The New York Times* of November 4, 1968, contains a column, in the business section on the third and fourth generation of computers, which have all come about within a decade.* If we regard computers in general as the new technological means of production and information configurations as the new ideological products of that process, we may calculate that societies now change ten times faster than their original depictions by Marx' pen. If we count each generation of computers separately, we confront a society which can change the structural base of its ideology four times *within a decade.* If ideologies are formed by reflection on the world we make by our labors, it follows that we are living in an era of such rapid change that those accustomed to it will regard even a five-year-old ideology as hopelessly irrelevant, since it no longer describes the world one confronts.

---

* First generation, vacuum tubes; second, transistors; third, integrated (printed) circuits; fourth—holographs.

The extremity of this situation may be directly observed in what sociologists call intergenerational stratification, i.e., the generation gap. In a society which changes so rapidly the very process of socialization, in which parents attempt to acculturate their infants, is doomed since the contents of that socialization will be obsolescent even before the process is over even if most of it, as the psychoanalysts tell us, is accomplished in the first five years. Such a pace of change makes obsolete the very possibility of teaching an ideology which explains the world situation to those in a dissimilar world. When the world changes four times in a decade, it had better invent a way of comprehending itself that changes as fast as experience does. And that, I argue, is exactly what psychedelics are—a psychochemical technology which no longer bothers with the simple enumeration of the *content* of processes, but focuses the inner eye on the *exponents* of such processes. That, I submit, is the inner meaning of the term *tripping,* which is focusing on the rates of change of a changing experience not simply on the changing world itself.

Bitter conflicts are thus generated between those who trip and those who do not know what tripping is, who hurl the epithet *hedonism* as if that, finally, was that. Other epithets are employed, ranging all the way from subversion to seduction. Subcultural confrontations no less acrimonious than "race riots" are not rare, and little documentation is needed to remind us that, but for one rare summer of flower power, relations between police and the psychedelic community have not always been cordial. The point, of course, is this—tripping stratifies the forms of consciousness, giving rise to behaviors which uninitiates must regard as strange and unfamiliar, if not as weird, sick, or demented. The public media reveal that this new sort of consciousness *is* the issue. Is it sick, we are asked? Can it possibly be healthy?

The science media are uniformly in agreement that psychedelics alter the time sense of experience. Just as computers can process billions of bits (binary digits) of information per second, so when high, can one seem to experience hours and even years in a few minutes. That is the meaning of the word "high," which describes in spatial terms an experience in which one seems to be able to scan vast horizons from above, encompassing thousands of bits of experience as astronauts take in thousands of miles in a glance.

But do not be misled by the spatial metaphor, nor by the electric one, for a more important property of the expanded time phenomenon is the following. When you expand time, you give yourself the ability to pay full emotional attention to events which in "real" clock time would have sped by too rapidly for your empathy to catch hold. This accounts for the observation frequently made that a true "head" will "play" with an unknown object while one more hurried than he will simply not have the time to spend on it. This property of the psychedelic experience also helps us account for the alleged aphrodisiacal properties of LSD and related substances, since, when it is not hurried, when one can give one's full emotional appreciation to each caress, sexual enjoyment, any enjoyment, for that matter, is materially enhanced.

I have alluded to but two of the time changing properties of the trip—the ability to appreciate changes in rates of change, and the ability to dwell on detail. If they seem contradictory, perhaps a bit of clarification is in order, for we have not yet touched bottom.

It lies in the very nature of generalization that, once made, it clarifies particulars. We are all familiar with the experience of uncertainty when perceiving a vaguely familiar object at a distance. As we draw nearer and its outlines become sharper, we exclaim—ah yes, it's one of those. It is just so in the case before us—with a slight variation. For acid, I believe, is only the first of many engines soon to be constructed, which engenders the ability to generalize and classify not objects, but *times*. Thus, the ability to dwell on *rates* of change brings with it the ability to more exquisitely dwell on instances of change.

You see where the argument leads. Just as the automated second industrial revolution generalized the first by dealing with the informational exponents of energy processing rather than simply with energy constellations (objects) *seriatim;* so the psychedelic second chemical revolution generalized the first anaesthetic one by dealing with the temporal exponents of getting high rather than simply getting smashed (drunk) time after time.

That is why the process of generalization, which we poor mortals attribute to the power of our intelligences, is a far more naturalistic process than we often perceive. Generalization, it begins to emerge, is that natural process whereby instances transcend their classes of events. Just as galaxies generate stars which expand the limits of galaxies, as men make worlds which outmode their world views, so now we are witnessing one of the most far-reaching revolutions ever to come from human effort. We are beginning to pass beyond (*depasser, aufheben*) the era of human history which, impelled by the scarcity of objects, clung to the dream that the endless production of objects would set us free. Now that the young can directly experience a world in which cybernetic automation makes scarcity an obsolete concept, they begin to inhabit another whole realm, the dimension of time, which Einstein brought to earth after his Promethean intellectual trip.

If I seem wholly supportive of the values of the young psychedelists, let me not be misunderstood. Our task here is to analyze the sociological currents on which psychedelia floats, not to examine in detail the pathologies of its incumbents. It is one thing to examine the social forces which drive a movement. It is another to focus on the plight of those so driven. Entirely another matter is the question of action—what shall we do to treat those damaged by misuse of psychedelic substances? These are tasks for another writing.

Conclusion

I hold, then, the view that our culture has so accelerated the pace of societal change that the simple serial encountering of one experience after another has become obsolete for its young, who are trying to dwell exponentially, i.e., to generalize, on what we elders can only manage arithmetically. They are not only as comfortable in the realm of time as we are in the realm of space, but they have the sense of adventure and discovery about time which many of us have about space. While we build rockets to take us to the stars, they build a culture which will take them into temporal regions of mind which we will fail to comprehend with only spatial models.

In my view, this adventure, and its corollary misadventures, is absolutely central to what we are about as a species. The young seek nothing less than the next step in the evolution of human consciousness, the transcendence of spatial, linear, one-dimensional consciousness.

It is clear that this is no small undertaking—that the risks are terrible, that the likelihood of tragic mistakes is high, that there will be fatalities and large numbers of casualties. I fervently wish that they were unnecessary and aim my work to prevent as many as possible, and to assist in the healing of those we fail to prevent. For it is true that most of those embarked on this adventure are as blind to its dangers as they are unaware of them, so that they are often foolish and often injured.

And yet there are some who know, who hear the music of the spheres, who accept the deeper challenge to carry history forward. These will be found, on close examination, when they have removed some of the outmoded ideological baggage we force them to carry, to be engaged in founding a new form of temporal consciousness, "groovin' on time."

References

1. Gioscia, Victor J.: "Adolescence, Addiction, and Achrony," in R. Endleman, Personality and Social Life. New York, Random House, 1967.
2. ———: "Glue Sniffing: Exploratory Hypotheses on the Psychosocial Dynamics of Respiratory Introjection," in proceedings of a conference on Inhalation of Glue Fumes and Other Substance Abuse Practices Among Adolescents, Office of Juvenile Delinquency and Youth Development, U.S. Dept. of Health, Education and Welfare, Washington, D.C., 1967.
3. ———: "Psychological and Sociological Proneness to Drug Use in Young People," paper presented to Amherst College Symposium on the Drug Scene, Amherst, 1967.
4. ———: "LSD Subcultures: Acidoxy Versus Orthodoxy," Amer. J. Orthopsychiat. 39: 13 (April 1969).
5. Marcuse, H.: Eros and Civilization, Boston: Beacon Press, 1955.
6. ———: One Dimensional Man, London, Tavistock Publications 1967.

INDEX